Medieval Mercenaries

VOLUME I

The Great Companies

For Ann

Medieval Mercenaries

Kenneth Fowler

VOLUME I
The Great Companies

BLACKWELL
Publishers

Copyright © K. A. Fowler 2001

The right of K. A. Fowler to be identified as author of this work has been asserted in accordance with the Copyright, Designs and Patents Act 1988.

First published 2001

2 4 6 8 10 9 7 5 3 1

Blackwell Publishers Ltd
108 Cowley Road
Oxford OX4 1JF
UK

Blackwell Publishers Inc.
350 Main Street
Malden, Massachusetts 02148
USA

All rights reserved. Except for the quotation of short passages for the purposes of criticism and review, no part of this publication may be reproduced, stored in a retrieval system, or transmitted, in any form or by any means, electronic, mechanical, photocopying, recording or otherwise, without the prior permission of the publisher.

Except in the United States of America, this book is sold subject to the condition that it shall not, by way of trade or otherwise, be lent, resold, hired out, or otherwise circulated without the publisher's prior consent in any form of binding or cover other than that in which it is published and without a similar condition including this condition being imposed on the subsequent purchaser.

British Library Cataloguing in Publication Data
A CIP catalogue record for this book is available from the British Library

Library of Congress Cataloging-in-Publication Data
Fowler, Kenneth Alan.
  Medieval mercenaries / Kenneth Fowler.
    p. cm.
Includes bibliographical references and index.
  ISBN 0-631-15886-3 (alk. paper)
  1. Mercenary troops—Europe—History—To 1500. 2. Military history, Medieval. 3. Military art and science—Europe—History—Medieval, 500-1500. I. Title.
  D128.F68 2001
  355.3′54′09409023—dc21

00-009323

Typeset in 10/12 pt Sabon
by SetSystems Ltd, Saffron Walden, Essex
Printed in Great Britain by Biddles Ltd,
www.biddles.co.uk

This book is printed on acid-free paper.

Contents

	List of Maps and Plans	vii
	Preface	ix
	Abbreviations	xiii
1	Dramatis Personae	1
2	An Elusive Peace	24
3	From Brignais to Launac	44
4	Seguin de Badefol in Auvergne	75
5	The Navarrese Imbroglio	86
6	Crusading Projects	118
7	Castles in Spain	155
8	The Prince's Intervention	191
9	The Return North	223
10	A Provençal Interlude and a Sicilian Marriage	240
11	The Sardinian Proposals and the Drama of Montiel	259
12	Pontvallain	283
	Glossary	303
	Note on Money	306
	Appendix A Documents	309
	Appendix B Tables of Captains	323

CONTENTS

Appendix C   The Numerical Strength of the Great Companies   329

Appendix D   Forces Recruited by the Duke of Anjou in 1369   333

Appendix E   The Death of Sir Robert Birkhead in 1368 and
the Supposed Death of Sir Robert Cheyney at Olivet   336

Sources and Bibliography   338

Index   357

Maps and Plans

1	The provinces of France and the principality of Aquitaine	*facing* 1
2	Principal places occupied by the Companies in Burgundy, the Saône and Rhône valleys and the surrounding territories, 1361–5	29
3	The lands of the houses of Armagnac and Foix-Béarn at the time of the battle of Launac, 1362	60
4	The Normandy front and the Navarrese counter-offensive, August–October 1364	97
5	The Archpriest's 'Crusade', June–August 1365	134
6	The Iberian kingdoms in the fourteenth century	156
7	The invasion of Castile by the Companies, January–May 1366	178
8	The Black Prince's intervention in Spain, February–September 1367	209
9	The return of the Companies into northern France, October 1367–February 1369	229
10	The invasion of Provence, March–September 1368	244
11	Sardinia in the fourteenth century	260
12	The *chevauchée* of Sir Robert Knowles and the battle of Pontvallain, July–December 1370	291

Genealogical Table

The Succession to the Duchy of Burgundy, 1361   89

Preface

Warfare was a fundamental element in the development of medieval societies, and with the emergence of paid armies in the later Middle Ages, based on contractual arrangements rather than on tenurial obligation or communal service, the use of mercenary forces to attain political goals had a profound impact on the development of European states. Rulers engaged in ambitious policies in pursuit of personal wealth and territorial aggrandizement, setting examples which others sought to emulate or were forced to follow. Wars became more protracted. With the emergence of a professional soldiery dependent for their livelihood on pay and other profits of war, the cessation of hostilities could spell ruin or at the very least the prospect of unemployment. In times of truce garrison forces had to be maintained, but at a reduced level. With the conclusion of peace whole armies were disbanded and soldiers of all ranks demobilized. Those unable to find employ elsewhere joined up with others to form independent companies making war on their own account. They were the scourge of western Europe before the emergence of standing armies in the fifteenth century.

Medieval Mercenaries tells the story of some of the more famous and notorious among them, whose activities spanned the second half of the fourteenth century in much of western Europe. This volume deals with the Great Companies, formed on the conclusion of peace between England and France in 1360, which were active in the French kingdom, in Spain and in the western territories of the Empire until the renewal of the Anglo-French war in 1369. I have been particularly concerned to establish their numerical strength and personnel, to distinguish them from other companies operating during the period, and to assess their importance in other wars during that decade, both in France and in the Iberian Peninsula. Little can be gleaned about their rank and file, but some attempt has been made to establish the social and geographical origins of their captains, and to follow the fortunes of a number of military entrepreneurs who commanded them, most notably the Breton knight Bertrand du Guesclin and Sir Hugh Calveley from Cheshire. I have also thought it appropriate to survey the defensive and other measures taken by the pope and secular princes to contain the companies and to limit the damage which they caused. The enormous demands which the *routiers* placed upon royal finances and those of local communities have also been underlined. The second volume will be primarily concerned with the activities of the English, Breton and Gascon mercenaries active in Italy in the years 1361–94, and particular attention will be given to the career of Sir John Hawkwood. I shall also give some consideration to those companies, for the most part Gascon, who continued their operations in France after 1370, and in particular to those who came to occupy castles and fortresses in the central and eastern provinces of the kingdom in the late 1370s and 1380s, a large number of whom were recruited for service in Italy in 1391.

The impact of warfare on the political, economic and social structures of the later Middle Ages is not easily disentangled from other causes of disequilibrium and change. That it was a significant contributing factor in many of the developments which occurred cannot reasonably be doubted, but in the process of change it is hard to single out what resulted from the activities of independent mercenary companies as opposed to other military forces. Certainly, they were a major problem for European rulers, whether kings, princes or republics, who tried to eliminate them, but were frequently forced to take them into their employ. Such attempts as were made to contain them fostered developments in diplomatic and intelligence arrangements, particularly in Italy. Their employ and the defensive and other measures which had to be taken against them when they were operating on their own account contributed to the ever-increasing fiscal burden placed upon government. This in turn accelerated the development of taxation and military and political structures which ultimately reinforced central authority. The road which led to these solutions sharpened contemporary attitudes to consent and to notions of freedom, liberty and tyranny in the new polities which emerged. Differences in approach acquired an ideological dimension. The regional variations in the incidence of war and the redistribution of wealth which it occasioned, impoverishing some sections of the community while enriching others, contributed to a shift in the economic and social structures of western Europe. These developments were certainly not restricted to the fourteenth century, but the period marked an essential turning point in the evolution of European states. I hope to be able to give some consideration to these questions in a subsequent volume.

Medieval Mercenaries has been a long time in the making, and as the project has grown many of my colleagues have wondered whether it would ever come to fruition as, amid many other distractions, I have sometimes wondered myself. During its long gestation I have incurred many debts, not least to the various bodies who have provided funding for the research upon which it is based: the Travel and Research Committee of the University of Edinburgh, the British Academy and the Leverhulme Trust. The staff of the many libraries and archival repositories I have worked in have given unfailing and courteous help and support. In particular, I would like to mention Jacques Bousquet, director of the Archives départementales de l'Aveyron at Rodez at the time of my first forays into the French departmental and communal archives in pursuit of the companies, whose many kindnesses went far beyond the call of duty, including an unforgettable journey to visit some of the *routier* fortresses beyond the mountains of Aubrac to the north of Espalion. He also introduced me to Louis d'Alauzier, whose knowledge of their activities around Cahors was profound. In the old royal premises of the Archivo de la Corona d'Aragón in Barcelona, where I first met Peter Russell, both he and the then librarian, Dolores Mateu Ibars, helped me to find my way through the immense riches of that repository. In Pamplona, José Ramón Castro, sometime director of the Archivo general de Navarra in Pamplona and editor of a large part of the *Catálogo* of the documents of its Sección de Comptos, aided my researches in the immense wealth of that collection, and Béatrice Leroy, whom I first met whilst subsequently working there, has done me many kindnesses. In Edinburgh University Library, Jill Evans, Head of Inter-Library Loans, has been unfailingly helpful in tracking down books and articles which I would have otherwise found difficult to consult.

Among the many friends who have helped me over the years in our conversations and in other ways frequently unknown to them, I should mention, in addition to my colleagues in Edinburgh, Philippe Contamine, whom I first met at a conference held at Vernon in Normandy in 1964 to commemorate the sixth centenary of the battle of Cocherel, and Christopher Allmand, whom I have known for almost as long. The Société des historiens médiévistes de l'enseignment supérieur public has made me feel one of their number, and has given me the privilege of contributing papers at several of their annual reunions. Among the historians concerned with later medieval Spain whom I have met at various conferences there, I should mention in particular Adeline Rucquoi, Denis Menjot, Luis Díaz Martin, Emilio Mitre Fernández, Hilario Casado Alonso and Jon Andoni Fernández de Larrea Rojas, all of whom have assisted me in one way or another. In Paris as previously in Kiel, Werner Paravicini has been helpful and encouraging. One other person I would single out for special mention is Marie-Madeleine Gauthier, whose death in 1998 robbed many of a loyal friend and a true medievalist. To our many conversations I owe much more than a simple acknowledgement here can begin to convey.

PREFACE

All historians working on medieval French history are aware of the immense debt they owe to the accumulated French historical scholarship of more than a century, and the historiography of the companies provides no exception. The studies of the activities of the companies in different regions of France, such as those of Guigue, Boudet, Finot, Vernier, Petit and Monicat, biographies of captains by Chérest, Molinier and Luce, and the works of countless local historians have exploited much of the available documentation and added immensely to our knowledge. Among wider studies which give attention to the companies, the works of Simeon Luce, Le Père Henri Denifle and Roland Delachenal stand out. In the chapters of this volume what I owe to them will be immediately obvious. The footnotes to Luce's edition of Froissart's *Chroniques* are in themselves a monument to his immense erudition, and I have judged it appropriate to make clear what I owe to him, as opposed to Froissart, in my citations of that work. If, as the painter George Devlin once remarked to me, 'you cannot paint the Seine at Vétheuil without Monet looking over your shoulder', no more can you recount the events of the reign of *le sage roi* Charles V without being aware of the presence of Delachenal. Only occasionally have I parted company with him in his interpretation of the events which he relates. These differences are mainly of emphasis, save in the case of episodes where documentation of which he was unaware has subsequently come to light.

Lastly, but not least, my thanks go to my wife Ann, who has had to live with the mercenaries, and has listened patiently to many drafts of this volume, corrected proofs and given me constant support and invaluable encouragement over many years.

Abbreviations

AC	Archives communales/municipales (France)
ACA	Archivo de la Corona de Aragón (Barcelona)
AD	Archives départmentales (France)
AGN	Archivo general de Navarra (Pamplona)
AGN	Catálogo del Archivo General de Navarra
AHG	Archives historiques de la Gironde
AHP	Archives historiques du Poitou
AHR	Archives historiques de Rouergue
AHSA	Archives historiques de la Saintonge et de l'Aunay
AM	Annales du Midi
AN	Archives nationales (Paris)
AS	Archivio di Stato (Italy)
BEC	Bibliothèque de l'École des Chartes
BIHR	Bulletin of the Institute of Historical Research
BL	British Library (London)
BN	Bibliothèque nationale (Paris)
BPH	Bulletin philologique et historique du Comité des Travaux Historiques et Scientifiques
BPR	Register of Edward, the Black Prince
CCR	Calendar of Close Rolls
CDI	Collection de documents inédits relatifs à l'histoire de France
CDM	Colección de documentos para la historia del reino de Murcia
CIPM	Calendar of Inquisitions Post Mortem
CPR	Calendar of Patent Rolls
EHR	English Historical Review
EUL	Edinburgh University Library
HGL	Devic, C. and Vaissete, J., *Histoire générale de Languedoc*
JGR	John of Gaunt's Register
JJ	Chancery Registers
MA	Le moyen age

ABBREVIATIONS

MR	Maestro Racional
PJ	Pièces justificatives
PO	Pièces originales
PRO	Public Record Office (London)
RH	*Revue historique*
RHS	Royal Historical Society
RO	Record Office
RP	*Rotuli Parliamentorum*
RS	*Rolls Series*
SHF	Société de l'histoire de France
SHMESP	Société des historiens médiévistes de l'énseignement supérieur public

Published sources (section B of the bibliography) are cited in the notes by abbreviated title or by author/editor and abbreviated title. Secondary works (section C of the bibliography) are cited by author alone, followed by date of publication where more than one work by the author is listed.

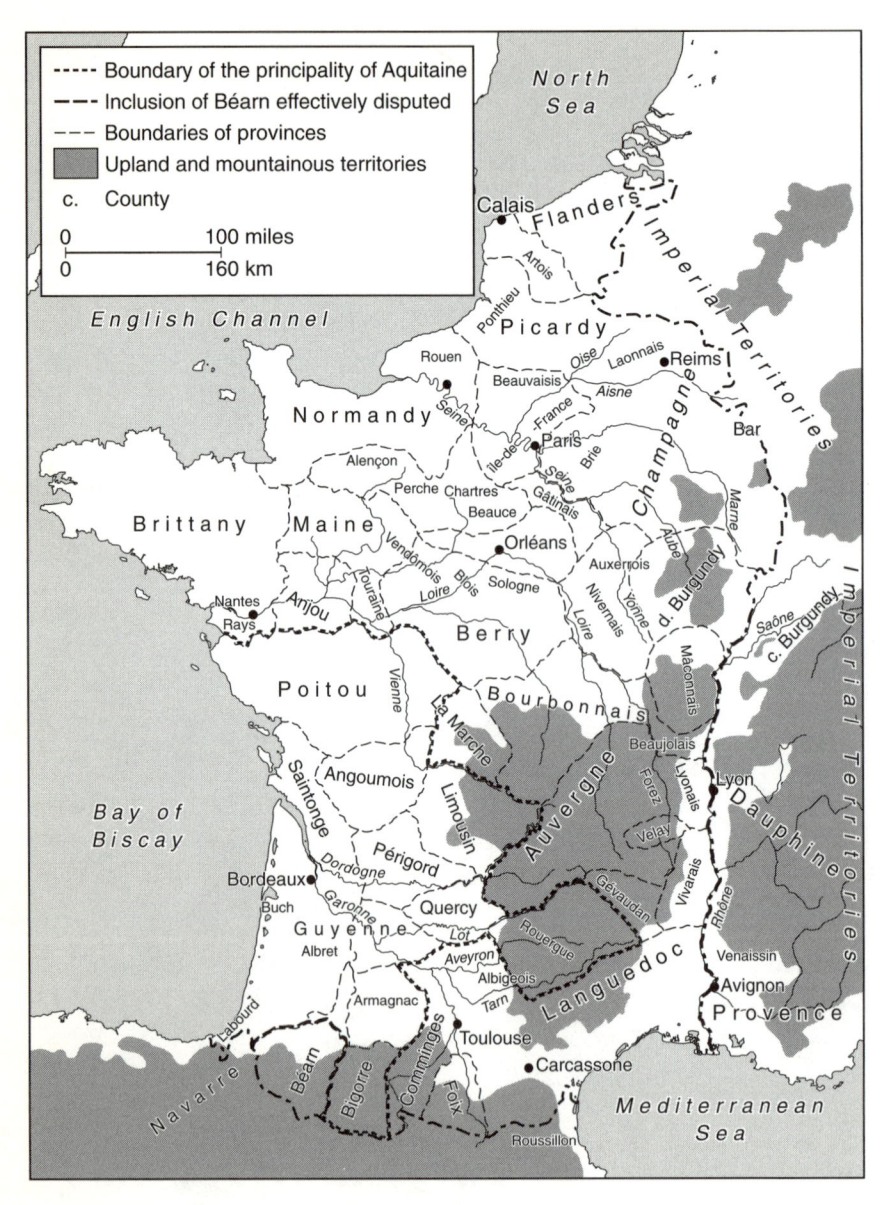

1 *The provinces of France and the principality of Aquitaine*

1

Dramatis Personae

The chapters of this volume tell the story of a group of military companies, composed of contingents (known as *routes*) of professional soldiers, who came together in the decade following the conclusion of peace between England and France in 1360 to make war on their own account, or in the pay of whatever prince or lord would hire them. In terms of the laws of war, as they were understood in the fourteenth century, only when they were fighting for a lord 'with just title' were their activities considered to be legal; when they fought for themselves, their conduct was seen as criminal, and in some cases traitorous, treasonable and even heretical. In some of the chronicles and biographies of the time their exploits were given a chivalric gloss and, whether fighting in the service of princes or on their own account, their actions were frequently veiled in deeds of heroism and romance. While for some of their leaders this imagery represented part of the reality of their lives – the desire to better themselves in wealth and social standing – violence, greed and the desire for sexual gratification lurked not far below the surface, most evidently among the rank and file. Some of the more flagrant deeds in which the companies were involved, especially in the country towns and villages they passed through or were billeted in, if committed today, would hopefully be subjected to scrutiny by an international war crimes tribunal. While we must put their actions into their historical context, there can be no doubt that they outraged many contemporaries. In the second half of the fourteenth century the companies constituted one of the major problems facing those responsible for government and the rule of law in western Europe, and churchmen in particular spoke out against their actions. The emperor, kings and princes sought to employ them in other lands. The popes devised several measures to deal with them, employing a whole range of spiritual and temporal sanctions, launching crusades against them, and offering indulgences to those who took up arms to bring about their destruction. But the existence of the companies and their way of life were rooted in the political, military and economic structures of the time, and such efforts as were made to deal with them met with limited success.[1]

Of all the *routes* operating in France after 1360, the most notorious called themselves, and were called by others, 'the Great Company'. The name itself was not new. It had been employed by the Italian-born Roger of Flor, once a Knight Templar, of German parentage on his father's side, for the company of Catalans who fought under him in Byzantium in the early years of the fourteenth century, and it was used in Italy for the companies of the Swabian knight Werner of Urslingen in the 1340s and of Montreal d'Albarano, a Provençal knight, who had for a time been a Hospitaller and whom the Italians called Fra Moriale.[2] In 1357–8 a company of troops operating in Provence under a relapsed cleric from Périgord, the sometime archpriest of Vélines, Arnaud de Cervole, was referred to by Pope Innocent VI as a *magna societas armigerorum*, and by the treasurer of Dauphiné, through which territory they passed, as *la grant compaignie*.[3] The soldier-chronicler Sir Thomas Gray of Heton, writing about some of the independent bands of English who had assembled in Burgundy, Brie and Champagne in the following year, tells us that one of them, which took the city of Châlons-sur-Marne by night escalade, called itself the Great Company, but adds that it was disbanded on the arrival of Edward III's army in the vicinity.[4] However, in the months which followed the conclusion of the Anglo-French peace, the name was widely adopted by the companies who assembled together from the disbanded armies, and they succeded in establishing themselves on a more permanent footing.

'At the time', wrote the author of the *Grandes Chroniques* of France, speaking of events in November 1360, 'there were great numbers of English and others in Brie and Champagne, who ravaged all the countryside, killing and ransoming men, and doing all the evil they could, of whom some called themselves the Great Company.'[5] Froissart also spoke of these assemblies of men in Burgundy and Champagne, some contingents of which may have called themselves, or have been called by others, 'the Latecomers' (*les Tards-Venus*), because they were operating in provinces already stripped.[6] 'Those sons of Belial and men of iniquity', wrote the

---

1 For chivalric chronicles and biographies, see, for example, Froissart's *Chronicles*, especially his account of the Bascot de Mauléon's military career, supposedly told by the Bascot himself, which has been conveniently edited by Diverres in Froissart, *Voyage en Béarn*, pp. 88–103; Chandos Herald, *Vie*; Cuvelier, *Chronique*. Some of the wider issues are treated in Fowler, 1967, ch. 4, and 1971, Introduction, and by Allmand 1971. For a recent survey of the relations of the military with the civilian population, and the attitude of contemporaries, see Wright, 1998.
2 Trease, pp. 32, 36; Schäfer, i, p. 81ff; Villani, *Istorie*, pp. 229–30.
3 Denifle, ii, pp. 209, and 188–9 for Cervole's early life; cf. Delachenal, i, p. 311, n. 3.
4 *Scalacronica*, pp. 148–9.
5 *Chron. Jean II et Charles V*, i, pp. 327–8.
6 Froissart, *Chroniques*, vi, pp. 61, 257.

Carmelite friar, Jean de Venette, 'warriors from various lands who assailed other men with no right and no reason other than their own passions, iniquity and hope of gain, and yet were called the Great Company'.[7] Having witnessed the consequences of the pillaging and destruction of the soldiery in the Beauvaisis, including the burning of the village of Venette near Compiègne, where he was born, his feelings are understandable. A more detached assessment was given by Henry Knighton, who, writing in the peace of Leicester Abbey, had this to say in an account of the escapades of an Anglo-German company commanded by Albert Sterz, which was operating in the count of Savoy's lands in the Canavese towards the end of the following year:

At this time was organized a certain company of strong men called the Company of Fortune (*Societas fortunae*), which some called the Great Company. It was composed of men from different parts, who, now that there was peace between the two kingdoms, had no means of livelihood other than through their own efforts. They were bold and warlike fellows, experienced and strenuous, who congregated together from different nations, and who lived by war, since in time of peace they had nothing.[8]

This company, which came to be known as 'the White Company', was only one of a larger body of companies operating in the Lower Rhône valley in the winter of 1360–1, which had been recruited for service with the marquis of Montferrat, who was then at war with the Visconti in Milan, and which was returning to re-infest Avignon.[9]

Not all of the independent companies operating in France in the decade after 1360 in fact belonged to the Great Companies. Both Froissart and Matteo Villani distinguished between them and the Anglo-Navarrese companies, the first of which were formed following the arrest of Charles of Navarre in 1356, and other companies which came into being after the collapse of royal authority following the capture of King John at the battle of Poitiers. Most notable among the latter were the bands brought together by Arnaud de Cervole, who first came into prominence with their invasion of Provence in 1357–8, and the companies operating under two captains from Cheshire, Robert Knowles and Hugh Calveley, whose forces penetrated from Brittany and the Loire provinces into the Auxerrois, Nivernais

---

7 Venette, *Chronicle*, p. 93.
8 Knighton, *Chronicon*, ii, pp. 114–15. The action he then refers to was clearly the attack on the town of Lanzo in the Canavese (see below, ch. 3, p. 45 and n. 5).
9 Ibid., p. 145. For the name 'the White Company', *Alba Comitiva*, see Walsingham, *Hist. Angl.*, i, pp. 295–6; *Chron. Angl.*, p. 50. It was not then commanded by Englishmen, as Walsingham states, but by the German mercenary Albert Sterz. However, the English appear to have predominated among the subordinate officers (see below, p. 45 and n. 5). The composition of Sterz's companies will be reviewed in *Medieval Mercenaries II*.

3

and Auvergne in 1357–9. The Hainaulter Eustache d'Auberchicourt was particularly active in Champagne and Brie, sending out raiding parties from his bases in the upper Seine valley to Troyes, Provins, Château-Thierry and Châlons-sur-Marne. Other companies conducted raids in the lands situated between the rivers Seine and Loire, of which those under the leadership of a bandit called Ruffin were the most notorious.[10] None of these belonged to the Great Companies, which were formed at a later juncture. When recounting the general demobilization which followed the Anglo-French peace, Froissart made a clear distinction between those forces who returned home, those who continued to make war 'under cover of, and in the name of the king of Navarre', and those who chose to continue to make war on their own account.[11] It was this latter group who came to form the Great Companies, and they continued to be distinguished in the records from the Navarrese, the Bretons, the men of the Archpriest and other groupings in the years after 1360.[12] Villani records the activities of no fewer than five different companies operating in the Midi between late 1360 and the spring of 1362, all of which congregated for a while in the lower Rhône valley and in Provence.

The first of these, which assembled in Champagne and descended on Pont-Saint-Esprit above Avignon, formed the nucleus of the Great Companies, of which some contingents were recruited for service with the marquis of Montferrat. Others who joined up with them were drawn from another large group, possibly as many as 6,000 cavalry (*barbute*), which he refers to as the 'White Company' (*la Compagna Bianca*), almost certainly prematurely, and which was evidently the same as the company referred to by Knighton. It too assembled in Champagne and the surrounding territories, and likewise descended into Provence by way of the Lyon and the Rhône valley. Another company, Anglo-Navarrese and Gascon in composition, formed from among the partisans of Jean V, count of Harcourt, who had been executed by the king of France in 1356, and which was then operating in Languedoc, also made for the lower Rhône,

---

10 Froissart, *Chroniques*, v, pp. 93–5; Villani, *Istorie*, xiv, cols. 456–7, 533–4 and *passim*. See Delachenal, i, pp. 308–12, 335, 369; and especially ii, ch. i, pp. 21–45. The list of fortresses occupied by the Anglo-Navarrese companies in 1356–64 (Luce, *Du Guesclin*, pp. 459–509) gives some idea of the scale of their activities.
11 Froissart, *Chroniques*, vi, pp. 60–1, on which see the apposite comments of Contamine, 1975, pp. 372–3.
12 Burgundian financial documents invariably distinguish between operations conducted by English, Gascon, Breton and other *routes* (e.g., AD, Côte d'Or, B 6,557, cited Finot, p. 75 n. 5). In June 1362 the keeper of the castle of Saint-Seine was instructed to maintain strict guard of his castle because of *la Grant Compaignie des Anglois et ... les Bretons qui estoient au pays*. Messengers were sent to the governor of Burgundy to inform him of the movements of *la grant compaignie des Ynglois et des gens de l'Archiprestre* (AD, Côte d'Or, B 5617, cited Finot, p. 71 n. 5). The Bretons generally kept apart from the Great Companies (see appendix B, table 3).

where some of its contingents were likewise recruited by the pope for service with the marquis of Montferrat. In the early months of 1362, another company, which had been operating for some three years in Gascony, where it had been engaged in the more or less constant warfare which was being conducted there between the great seignorial houses of Foix and Armagnac, left the south-west, where there was a shortage of food and a serious outbreak of the plague, and it too made for the territories around Avignon. Here it joined up with a Spanish company under the exiled Enrique of Trastámara (*la Compagna Spagnuolo*), which in the previous year had been engaged against the Great Companies in Upper Languedoc and the Auvergne.[13]

The 'Great Companies' were thus new formations, bringing together various elements of the different units demobilized after the conclusion of peace. The name was given to them when they joined together for combined operations, and after 1365 when they were being recruited for service, and were subsequently serving in Spain.[14] It was also adopted by the companies themselves.[15] As a group, they were made up of separate *routes* drawn from different regions and countries, each retaining its individual identity under an acknowledged captain. Mainly Gascon and English, some were drawn together under captains of their own choosing, like the Englishmen John Amory, John Cresswell and Robert Birkhead. Others were brought together under powerful captains like Seguin de Badefol from Périgord and the Gascon Bertucat d'Albret. Still others were assembled by captains from Germany and the Low Countries, notably Albert Sterz, Winrich von Fischenich (alias Ourri l'Alemant), Folekin Volemer, Johann Hazenorgue and Frank Hennequin.[16] But although powerful captains like Badefol and d'Albret might secure hegemony over a large number of them, giving subordinate commands to others whom they appointed their lieutenants, there was no single overall organization, and

---

13 Villani, *Istorie*, xiv, cols. 566, 624, 642–3, 647, 648, 651–2, 674.
14 The Navarrese registers of accounts sometimes refer to *la Grant compaynna* or *la Grant compaingne* (e.g., AGN, Comptos, regs. 113, fo. 45r, 118, fo. 126r; 120, fo. 65v), but more frequently to *las Grans compaynnas*, *las Grandes compaynnas* (e.g., ibid., reg. 118, fos. 139v, 181r; 121, fos. 100r, 111r, 172v). Aragonese chancery documents are more varied in their terminology: *las grans companyas*, *las grandes companyes de França*, as well as *las companyes de França*, *grans companyas d'alamanya e de França*, *grandes companyes françesas e stranyas*, etc. (e.g., ACA, Cancilleria, reg. 1386, fos. 185v–6v; 1388, fos. 26r–v, 42r–v, 80v–81r; 1390, fos. 16r, 22v).
15 See, for instance, the acquittances given to the receiver-general of Brittany in 1368 by twenty-seven persons describing themselves as *cappitaines et chevetaennes des genz des routes des englaes des granz compaignes* (AD, Loire-Atlantique, E 119/12, 13; see also BN, nouv. acq. franç., 5216, no.12. For the captains in question, see appendix B, table 1).
16 *Scalacronica*, pp. 170, 172, and see appendix B, table 1. For the identification of Ourri l'Alemant, see Paravicini, i, pp. 166–7.

they acknowledged no single leader. They were, as the English chroniclers described them, *gens sine capite, gens aciphalica*.[17]

The numerical strength of the companies depended upon the number of *routes* brought together for a particular operation and upon the size of each contingent. The Bascot de Mauléon, in his famous interview with Froissart at Orthez, put the total number of men who assembled after the conclusion of peace at Brétigny in 1360 at 12,000, of whom 3,000 to 4,000 were 'really fine soldiers, as able and adroit in war as any man could be; in planning a battle and seizing the advantage, scaling and looting towns and castles, as expert and experienced as you could wish'.[18] That their numbers were substantial is evident from the major engagements in which they were involved, at Brignais in 1362, when they defeated a French royal army, and in 1367, when they made up a substantial part of the prince's forces which were victorious at Nájera. In a letter to the *bailli* of Chalon of 20 September 1363, the governor of Berry and Auvergne estimated the strength of the companies who congregated around Brioude in Auvergne during the week after its capture (of which Seguin de Badefol, Johann Hazenorgue, Bertuquin, Heliés or Elias Machin, alias Petit Meschin, Menaud de Villers, alias Espiote, and Vaire de Cap were among the captains) at 2,000 lances, not counting the mounted archers and infantry, which totalled a further 1,000 cavalry.[19] The total strength of companies serving in Castile with du Guesclin in 1366, and with the Black Prince at the time of his intervention in the following year, was probably around 3,000 men-at-arms.[20] According to Froissart, on the renewal of war between England and France in 1369, the companies who joined the armies of the protagonists amounted to some 4,500 combatants.[21] This is an entirely plausible figure, given that it is certain that not all of the companies operating in France in the 1360s accompanied du Guesclin, and subsequently the prince, to Spain.

Of some 166 captains known to have commanded companies operating in and from France during the decade after 1360, ninety-one are referred to as captains of one or other of the Great Companies. Of the remaining seventy-five, forty-five had Breton captains, most of whom had close ties with Bertrand du Guesclin and served with him in Spain in the years 1366–70. Some of the other thirty were Anglo-Navarrese companies, and

17   Walsingham, *Hist. Angl.*, i, p. 284; see Delachenal, ii, p. 315 n. 6.
18   Froissart, *Chroniques*, xii, p. 98.
19   Kervyn de Lettenhove in Froissart, *Oeuvres*, xx, p. 234, from the original letter from the archives of the Chambre des Comptes in Dijon. The letter is published *in extenso* by Petit, x, pp. 55, from a copy in the collection de Bourgogne, xxvi, fo. 118r, where the latter figure is given, evidently erroneously, as 10,000 cavalry.
20   For the strength of the companies at Brignais and in Spain, see below, pp. 48–9, 169, 197–8 and appendix C.
21   Froissart, *Chroniques*, vii, p. 336.

some may have belonged to the Great Companies, although no contemporary source specifically states that they were.[22] In addition to these, in the late 1370s and 1380s there were some thirty captains, mostly Gascon, controlling fortresses in the Massif-Central and its foothills, for the most part in Auvergne, Velay, Rouergue, Périgord and Quercy. Their fortunes will be considered later.[23] Our concern here is primarily with the ninety-one captains whose companies are known to have formed part of the Great Companies. Of these by far the largest group (thirty-six) came from England and twenty-seven (possibly twenty-nine) from the principality of Aquitaine, excluding Béarn. Of the latter group at least nineteen, possibly twenty-one, came from Gascony (including Labourd), four from Périgord, two from Quercy, and one each from Poitou and Limousin. Five came from Béarn and one from the Pyrenean foothills, one from Normandy, and possibly one from the Toulousain. Eight came from outside the French kingdom: five from Germany, two from Provence (Étienne Anger, alias Ferragut, and Louis Roubaud, from Nice), and one from Scotland (Hagre, the Scot). The remaining ten cannot be placed. These statistics are revealing. Of those captains who came from the kingdom of France, the overwhelming majority were from the south-west, and few or none from other French provinces – from Picardy, Normandy, the Île-de-France, Poitou, Berry, Champagne and elsewhere. It is perhaps also significant that of the ten English captains whose origins can be traced, eight came from the northern counties, from Lancashire, Cheshire, Yorkshire and Northumberland, and it was Cheshire that produced the two most eminent of their leaders in France during the 1360s, albeit not themselves captains of the companies: Sir Hugh Calveley and Sir Robert Knowles.

The geographical spread, and what we know of the activities of the Great Companies, also lend support to the views of Charles V and his councillors, conveyed to the pope in 1364 and again in his justification for renewing the war with England in 1369, that the Great Companies favoured the interests of Edward III and the Black Prince, who had employed them in France contrary to the terms of the peace.[24] So also had King Charles of Navarre up to the peace he concluded with France in the early summer of 1365. But in all of the retainers which involved the performance of homage in return for fief-rents, concluded between the Navarrese king and those captains of the Great Companies who came from England and Gascony, the captains reserved their primary allegiance to Edward III and the prince.[25] When Charles was seeking support to pursue his military plans in France in February 1365, a Navarrese spy in the

22 See appendix B, tables 1–3.
23 See *Medieval Mercenaries II*.
24 Secousse, *Recueil*, pp. 206–8; Froissart, *Oeuvres*, vii, p. 422.
25 For these retainers, see below, pp. 175–6.

prince's chancery in Bordeaux listed the names of fifteen captains of the Great Companies over whom the prince could be expected to exercise his authority, five of whom had already been brought into the pay of Charles of Navarre.[26] In the autumn of that year, when a large number of companies were concentrated near the frontiers of Savoy for their supposed employ on a crusade, the prince wrote to their captains instructing them to desist from inflicting damage on the lands and subjects of the count.[27] Less than two years later he was able to recruit a substantial number of them – some twenty-five companies, perhaps some 3,000 troops in all – for his intervention in Spain. In January 1367, unable to move against Castile because of the stand taken by Charles of Navarre, who controlled the Pyrenean passes, he assigned thirteen companies to the Mallorcan Pretender, who was to have employed them to invade Aragonese territory through Roussillon.[28]

Consideration of the first of the two other groups of companies active in the 1360s – the thirty captains of whom some at least were probably associated with the Great Companies – does not significantly alter the geographical balance of recruitment and its implications. Ten, possibly twelve of the captains came from England and the principality of Aquitaine, two from the Pyrenean lordships of Béarn and Comminges, one from Burgundy, and probably eight from outside the French kingdom. The origins of the other seven are not known. The position of the Breton companies was more significant. They played an important – albeit frequently destructive – rôle in the defence of the duchy of Burgundy against attacks from both the Great Companies and Navarrese partisans operating from the county of Burgundy in the early 1360s and, more significantly, under the command of du Guesclin, in implementing French policy in Castile in the last three years of the decade. They were an important resource – well-trained men, experienced in the profession of arms – on whom he could call when serving Charles V in Normandy in 1364 and in the war with England, following his return from Spain and his elevation to the office of constable of France in 1370.[29]

It is not possible to gain a detailed picture of the internal organization of the companies operating in France and Spain, largely because of the absence

---

26 AD, Pyrénées-Atlantiques, E 520; appendix A, document 3.
27 AS, Turin, Corti stranieri, i, no. 4, published by Cordey, p. 330, PJ no. 33 (letters dated Angoulême, 4 November 1365, addressed to 'touz capitains et autres genz de compaignie').
28 See below, p. 202.
29 See appendix B, tables 2–3. In the early summer of 1364 du Guesclin sent from Normandy Briand de Lannion and Guillaume de Quélen to bring him 'les compaignies Bretons estans ou duchie de Bourgoingne', of which the main group were in garrison at Pontaillier (AD, Côte-d'Or, B 1416, fo. 64v, cited by Chérest, 264 n. 2). This was probably for the campaign to mop up Navarrese fortresses in Normandy after the battle of Cocherel (see Delachenal, iii, p. 52 n. 3).

of letters of retainer, contracts of service and retinue lists for men who fought primarily for their own profit, and who were irregularly in the service of a prince or some other lord. A certain amount of documentation survives concerning the *routes* of a number of captains retained in French service in 1368–9, although it is doubtful if any of this relates to units which formed part of the Great Companies.[30] In addition some information has survived concerning the composition of the English *routes* of the Great Companies in 1368, and in particular that commanded by the Englishman Robert Birkhead, who died towards the end of that year.[31] Nevertheless, it is reasonable to conclude that the organization of most of the independent companies was not essentially different from that prevailing in the royal armies in which many of the captains had served before 1360 and, more importantly, from those of their number who went on to Italy in 1361, and for whom contracts of service and other documentation are much more abundant.[32] In the English and possibly some Gascon companies the well-established practice of combining men-at-arms and mounted archers and dismounting to fight was maintained, and the progressive introduction of professional pillagers in each *route* is also evident.[33] A command structure existed within the larger companies, with their constables, secretaries and treasurers.[34] The most successful captains, like Seguin de Badefol and Bertucat d'Albret, who

---

30 For the documentation in question, see Contamine, 1975, pp. 387–96 and PJ nos. i–v, to which may be added the muster and order for payment of Hervé de Kerlouet (Gimont, 21 December 1368) in BN, PO 1603, doss. 36,916 (de Karaleu), nos. 2, 3.
31 AD, Loire-Atlantique, E 119/12, 13; BN, nouv. acq. franç., 5216, nos. 10–12. See appendix B, table 1, and key 11 thereto. Frequently referred to as Briquet, his real name is made evident in a treaty concluded with a number of captains of the Great Companies sometime before 30 December 1368, in which it is rendered as Birkhed and Bircked, as well as Briqued (Samaran, 1951, p. 642).
32 This will be reviewed in *Medieval Mercenaries II*, pending publication of which, see Fowler, 1998, pp. 136–7, 139, 141–2.
33 See the payments made to the companies recruited for service in Navarre in 1378–9, where the number of *pillarts* in the companies of Bertucat d'Albret, the bastard of Armagnac, Gaillard d'Aspremont, bastard of Orta, Monnot de Plassan or Plassac, Pierre de Galard, and others who were to have been retained (Gaillard de la Motte, Bernardet d'Albret, Pierre de Montaut, Poco de Lantar, Jean de Lomagne) were in nearly every case equal to or slightly more than the number of men-at-arms (AGN, Comptos, reg. 161, fos. 104r–20v; see Fernández, pp. 115–16, appendix xiii).
34 See the important agreement concluded at Rivarolo Canavese on 22 November 1361 between the marquis of Montferrat and the *magne societatis Anglicorum et Alamanorum*, of which Albert Sterz was captain and which names twelve constables, of whom we may note, in addition to Andrew Belmont and John Hawkwood, William Folifet or Folifait, possibly related to Thomas Folifet, one of the captains of the English *routes* of the Great Companies in 1368 (on whom, see below, pp. 19 and *passim*), and William Quatreton, who was named in a *condotta* concluded between Sterz and Florence in July 1364 (Fowler, 1998, p. 139). For constables, secretaries, treasurers and other clerks of castles controlled by the companies in France in the 1380s and 1390s, see, for example, AD, Aveyron, C 1338, fo. 62r; 1339, fos 23v, 24v; *Reg. Saint-Flour*, pp. 78, 152, 158 and n. 3, 160, 273 n. 3. Jannekin Hoderington was clearly acting in a secretarial capacity for the English *routes* of the Great Companies in 1368 (AD, Loire-Atlantique, E 119/12, 13).

on Seguin's death in 1365 took over many of the fortresses formerly controlled by him, employed other captains as their lieutenants and were able to gain an ascendancy over extensive territory by putting them in charge of towns and fortresses and taking a share of their profits. Arnaud-Amanieu, lord of Albret, although never a captain of the Great Companies, kept a tight grip on the activities of other members of his family in the 1360s, when much of the Auvergne came under their control, and that of Seguin de Badefol. In the 1370s Bertucat d'Albret and Bernard de la Salle secured Figeac and other towns and fortresses in Quercy, from which they exercised an ascendancy not only in that province, but over a much wider expanse of territory, conducting raids and taking fortresses in Gévaudan and the Auvergne, and roaming as far afield as the Rhône valley and to the Mediterranean coast of Languedoc. In the 1380s and early 1390s Bertucat's nephew and designated heir, Ramonet de Sort, also from Gascony, consolidated his power base in the upland territories of the Massif-Central, taking over the command of most of Bertucat's lieutenants, captains like Noli Barbe, who had served under the command of Robert Cheyney in 1375, Bernard Doat, the *bourcs* of Albret and Garlanx and the *bourc* Camus.[35]

The name *bourc*, a word used in southern France for a bastard son, often of a noble family, occurs frequently among members of the companies, and the number of bastards in their ranks is significant.[36] Of ten who were captains of the companies (see tables 1 and 2), the *bourc* de Breteuil, the *bourc* Camus and the bastard of Savoy (alias Perrin Boias or Bouvetault) were among the more notorious. All three were executed in 1369. Other features that are noteworthy are membership of the same family,[37] and occasional examples of brotherhood in arms – for instance between Calveley and Knowles, Calveley and Matthew Gournay, Louis Roubaud and Limousin – which reinforced these and other lines of

---

35 The evidence for these lieutenancies is abundant. Raymond Bernard de la Roque, alias Sandos, and another captain known as Sobrossa were acting in that capacity for Bertucat d'Albret in the 1360s (Boudet, 1895, p. 12, and 1900, p. 145). John Cresswell was lieutenant of John Amory in 1363 (*HGL*, x, cols. 1302–3, preuves, no. 496). For Bertucat's officers and the succession of Raymonet de Sort, see *Medieval Mercenaries II*; *Reg. Saint-Flour*, p. 309, and Alauzier, 'Comptes consulaires', pp. 98–103. Ramonet de Sort came from a family based in the Landes, at Sort-en-Chalosse, some four miles to the south-east of Dax, but which also held property in Rouergue (*Reg. Saint-Flour*, p. 309 n. 1). Noli Barbe was one of his principal lieutenants, holding seven castles in his name in Quercy in 1383–5 (ibid., pp. 310–11). The careers of these captains and the places they controlled will be reviewed in *Medieval Mercenaries II*.
36 E.g., Bertucat d'Albret, the *bourc* Camus, the *bourcs* of Breteuil, Lesparre and Périgord and the bastard of Savoie in table 1, the *bourcs* of Armagnac, Aussain, Campagne and Monsac in table 2, and of des Isles in table 3. For the incidence and importance of bastardy among noble families of the Bordelais see Boutruche, pp. 169–70, 177, 293–4 and 294 n. 1, 356, 379 and n. 8.
37 The Albrets, Badefols, Browns, Cresswells, Feltons, de la Salles and Worsleys in table 1; the Chauffours in table 2; the Budes, Kerlouets, Maunys and Saint-Pols in table 3.

solidarity.[38] Other characteristics are the use of surnames denoting geographical origins, and of abbreviated names and pseudonyms making identification difficult.[39]

The latter two features may be indicative of the humble origins of some of the captains. Early on in their careers Limousin (Arnaud de Solier) and Petit Meschin are said to have been valets, and according to Jean le Bel, Frank Hennequin, from Cologne, had begun life as 'a poor German boy'.[40] Whilst we must be wary of the capacity of some chroniclers to denigrate the names of certain of the more unscrupulous and irascible *routiers*, and of men who rose rapidly from ordinary enough backgrounds, the evidence of the low social status among them, and of some of their leaders, is not lacking.[41] Froissart's account of the rise and fall of Sir Robert Salle, who was a victim of his former peasant brethren in the Great Revolt in 1381, is substantiated by documentary evidence. In 1335 a bondman of the village of Salle in Norfolk, he got himself recruited by the commissioners of array for service in Brittany in the 1340s, and by 1373 he had done sufficiently well for himself in the army to be made captain of the fortress of Marck in the Pas-de-Calais, by which time he had been knighted.[42] The freebooter John Jouel, who became renowned for his exploits in Normandy between 1357 and 1364, had been a bondman at the abbey of Abbotsbury on the Dorsetshire coast above Weymouth before setting out on his military

---

38 For the probability of brotherhood in arms between Calveley and Knowles, see the entry of C. L. Kingsford on Knowles in the *DNB*, xxxi, p. 281; for that between Calveley and Gournay, see the indenture between du Guesclin and Calveley (*Et comebien que le dit moss' Hues aet fete compaingne au moss' Matheu de Gornay, la quelle est dou consantemont dou dit moss' Bertran*) in Fowler, 1991b and 1992, document i, and appendix A (7) below; for that between Louis Roubaud and Limousin, Froissart, *Chroniques*, xii, pp. 110–15. Calveley probably also became a brother-in-arms of du Guesclin in 1366 (Fowler, 1991b, pp. 253–4 and PJ no. i). For the relationship, see Keen, 1962, pp. 1–17.
39 Some, but by no means all of these, have been identified. See appendix B, tables 1–2.
40 For Limousin and Petit Meschin, see Froissart, *Chroniques*, vi, p. xxi n. 3, and xii, pp. 111–12; for Hennequin, see ibid., v, p. liii n. 2, and vi, p. xxi n. 5; Jean le Bel, *Chronique*, ii, pp. 278, 284.
41 Walsingham, *Hist. Angl.*, i, p. 286, says Robert Knowles was 'a poor and humble valet' who became 'a great leader of soldiers, possessed of regal riches'. Jean le Bel, *Chronique*, ii, p. 251, curiously says that he was a German and that he had been a tailor, before becoming a brigand and amassing a fortune for himself. He was in fact the son of a burgess of yeoman stock from Tushingham in Malpas parish, Cheshire (see Bennett, p. 182 and n. 96, and the entry on him by M. Jones in the *New DNB*). For Matteo Villani (*Istorie*, col. 679), Petit Meschin was a 'huomo Alvernazzo e de niente, e per sua prodezza e maestrìa di guerra montade in grande stato'. He also recounts (*Istorie*, col. 566) the activities of one Giana della Guglia (John of the Needle), who has sometimes been confused with Hawkwood, who was said to have in his youth been apprenticed to a London hosier (*Westminster Chronicle*, p. 520). The tradition that he was apprenticed to a London tailor was long accepted in England, and stated as a fact by Fuller (see Temple-Leader and Marcotti, pp. 7–9).
42 For the details, see Fowler, 1971, pp. 10, 25 nn. 35–6.

career, the exact circumstances of which elude us.[43] Sir John Stokes, who was captain of Saint-Sauveur-le-Vicômte in the 1360s, had started his military career as an archer, and the less well-known William Hugate, who was serving with the English *routes* of the Great Companies in 1368, had been a valet to the archbishop of York in 1346, before enrolling for service in Brittany.[44] The names of many other captains suggest modest origins, relegating them to oblivion.

However, whilst there is thus clear evidence for the lowly beginnings of some of the captains of the companies, there can be no doubt that the more important among them, both in France and England, were those who had chivalrous backgrounds or pretensions. Some of them were themselves knights. Others were knighted during the course of their military careers in France and Spain, seeking entry into the *petite-noblesse*, in England the gentry, through the practice of arms. By carefully reinvesting the profits of war in military equipment, even archers and infantry could rise through the ranks. War was a lottery, and although the stakes were dangerously high, they were still worth the gamble.

This was also true of many noble families, men used to exercising the profession of arms, whose fortunes had, for more than a generation, been closely linked with those of the royal protagonists. For them, the conclusion of peace in 1360 presented financial as well as occupational problems. Among the captains from Gascony and Périgord, the most important were from well-established families. Seguin de Badefol, described by Froissart as 'the chief and sovereign master of the companies', was the son of a powerful Périgordian lord, Seguin de Gontaut, lord of Badefol and Lalinde in the Dordogne valley, which for long had been, and in the 1370s was again to be, frontier territory between lands in French or English control.[45] Bérard and Bertucat d'Albret were both scions of the powerful house of Albret, of which Arnaud-Amanieu had been lord of the senior branch since the death of his father, Bernard-Ezii II, in 1359, and of whom Bérard was a legitimate and Bertucat an illegitimate brother. The family's power base was in the Landes, in the territory situated between the rivers Adour and

---

43 *CPR, 1340–43*, pp. 283–4. Jouel is said to have been present at the battle of Poitiers, was captain of a company serving in Normandy either independently or under Philip of Navarre after 1357, and was one of the captains whom Charles of Navarre had brought into Paris in 1358. In October 1363 he secured control of the keep of Rolleboise, which dominated the bend in the Seine below Mantes, but he was wounded in battle at Cocherel in the following year, and died a few days later at Pont de l'Arche (Froissart, *Chroniques*, v, p. 93; *Chron. premiers Valois*, pp. 49, 62, 81, 89, 95,129, 147–8; *Chron. norm.*, pp. 164, 172 n. 5; *Chron. Lescot*, pp. 135, 165, 169, 172; Venette, *Chronicle*, p. 122; *Chronographia*, ii, p. 307).

44 For Stokes, see PRO, C 76/ 20, m. 32, and for his captaincy at Saint-Sauveur, see Izarn, *Compte*, pp. 301–2; Delisle, PJ nos. 96–8, 103–4, 106. Robert and Hugh Stokes, who were also serving with him there, were evidently related (Izarn, pp. 225, 301; Delisle, PJ no. 105). For Hugate, see *Foedera*, III, i, p. 98; AD, Loire-Atlantique, E 119/13.

45 Froissart, *Oeuvres*, xviii, p. 395; xx, p. 232. For his family, see below, p. 75.

Garonne, and extended into the Bordelais through a string of important lordships, including Sainte-Bazeille, some four miles downstream from Marmande, of which Bérard was lord. These possessions put them into an uneasy relationship – pacific or hostile – with the great seignorial houses of Foix and Armagnac, which in part depended upon wider political allegiances to the English or French monarchy, of which the fluctuations during the period under review had important consequences.

Before the death in 1379 of Bérard III d'Albret, who descended from a younger branch of the family, the lands which he inherited from two of his uncles made him the most powerful lord in the Bordelais, and a significant portion of this patrimony came into the control of captains responsible to Bertucat d'Albret following Bérard III's defection to the French in 1377. Up until 1368, when Arnaud-Amanieu and Bérard went over to Charles V, they gave their allegiance to Edward III and the Black Prince. In the absence of conflicts nearer home they spent much of the 1360s extending or renewing their fortunes, and in the case of Bertucat seeking one, in military exploits far away from the family patrimony. The rôle of these three men, and in particular of Bertucat, on Froissart's testimony 'a great captain of men-at-arms and *routes*', consequently had wider ramifications, as did that of other captains of the companies who came from the south-west, many from families who had a long tradition of serving in the English or French armies.[46] Some of these were clients of the Albrets, like Lamit, who was one of Arnaud-Amanieu's esquires, and Barradeco, who came from the town of Saint-Pierre on the frontier of Albret territory on the outskirts of Bayonne.[47] He was also a client of Charles of Navarre in 1364–6.

Another prominent mercenary from the south-west was the *bourc* de Lesparre, the bastard son of a member of the Gascon family of that name, and probably the half-brother of Florimund, lord Lesparre, whose lands were situated on the west bank of the Gironde estuary in the Médoc. A collateral branch of the same family held the lordships of Labarde, Listrac, Cussac and Montignac, also in Médoc, together with lands further down the Garonne, at Bouglon, Thouars-sur-Gironde and Madaillan in the Agenais. The family's territorial interests were thus not dissimilar from the Albrets'. Florimund was staunchly loyal to the English cause; but with the renewal of the war the *bourc*, like Bertucat, wavered. After initially rallying to the English, as the duke of Anjou's forces advanced up the Garonne valley in 1370, along with the lord of Labarde he switched sides, but was back in the Black Prince's service in 1372.[48] Gérard Chabot, a young man

---

46 Boutruche, lib. ii, cap. xi, and *passim*; Froissart, Oeuvres, x, p. 79.
47 *AGN, Comptos*, vi, nos. 743, 745 (Lamit). For Berradeco, see ibid., v, nos. 401, 440 and *passim*, vi, 92, 365, 631 and *passim*.
48 Luce in Froissart, *Chroniques*, vi, p. xxii n. 2; Boutruche, p. 169; Froissart, Oeuvres, vii, p. 326, 338, viii, pp. 3, 32, and Lettenhove's index, xx, pp. 99–100.

in his early twenties, not himself a captain of the companies, but who led a contingent of them on the Black Prince's expedition in 1367, was lord of Rays, in that part of Brittany which lay to the south of the Loire. Froissart tells us that he went at his own expense, hoping to renew his fortunes after having paid a hefty ransom since being taken prisoner at the battle of Auray.[49] Also prominent among the leaders of the companies, Gourderon de Raymont, lord of Aubeterre-sur-Dronne in Saintonge, at the time situated in the county of Périgord, and 'reputed among men exercising arms to be a great captain, upright and courageous', played an important rôle as a military entrepreneur, recruiting among the Anglo-Gascon companies for the intervention in Castile in 1365.[50]

Among the captains who came from the Pyrenean foothills, two men were closely associated with the count of Foix: Guyonnet de Pau, an *escuiers d'onneur* of the count, 'a really skilled man-at-arms', and another esquire, Menaud de Villers, called Espiote after the place of Espiute, to the south of Orthez, near Sauveterre-en-Béarn, with which he was evidently associated and where he may have been born.[51] In 1364 he was also in the service of Charles of Navarre, did homage to him, in return for fiefs-rents, and along with Petit Meschin, Berradeco and another Gascon esquire called Bertuquin, he was recruited for service in his wars in France.[52] Among other Béarnese captains we may perhaps also include the Bascot de Mauléon, the first historian of the Great Companies, possibly a figure of Froissart's imagination, created to tell the story himself.[53] Garciot du Castel, already a knight in 1362, probably came from Bigorre. During his visit to the south of France in 1388, Froissart tells us that when travelling from Carcassonne to the court of Gaston Fébus in Orthez he was escorted for part of the journey by Sir Espan de Lyon, himself from Béarn, who during the course of a conversation while they were riding together on the road to Lourdes reminisced about 'Sir Garciot du Castel, a very wise man and a valiant knight, from the country around here *(de ce pays ici)* and a good Frenchman'.[54] Garciot played a prominent rôle among the captains

---

49 Froissart, vii, pp. 7, 262. Cf. Chandos Herald, *Vie*, cols. 2261–2, 3244–8. On him see Blanchard, pp. 18–24.
50 The quotation is from a legal case which came before the French *parlement* in 1391 concerning the payments made to him for the campaign (Molinier, PJ xci, p. 325). See Luce in Froissart, *Chroniques*, vi, p. lxxxi n. 3; Delachenal, iii, p. 288 and n. 1.
51 Froissart, *Oeuvres*, viii, pp. 195, 316; AGN, *Comptos*, v, no. 186 and *passim*; Desplat, p. 34. For their careers, see the index to Froissart, *Oeuvres*, xxi, p. 163, and xxii, p. 324, under 'Pans'.
52 Fowler, 1988, p. 28, and for Espiote's homage and fealty, and the fief-rents, AGN, *Comptos*, v, nos. 186, 209, 215.
53 Remarkably, I have found no record of his existence in archival sources. See my forthcoming article, 'Froissart's Bascot de Mauléon'.
54 Mirot, in Froissart, *Chroniques*, xii, p. xv n. 9, misinterprets this passage (pp. 36–7), and believed him to come from Béarn. Luce, in ibid., vii, p. lxvii n. 2, had already noted its true

of the Great Companies, in particular in recruiting from their number for an intended expedition to Spain in 1362. Taken prisoner by a soldier in the army of the count of Foix whilst serving on the Armagnac side at the battle of Launac (5 December 1362), he joined the companies who accompanied du Guesclin to Spain in 1366, and was one of the first of their captains recruited by Louis of Anjou on the renewal of the war in 1369.[55] In the summer of 1372 he was rewarded, somewhat tardily, for coming into French obedience with the lordship of Gontaut in the Agenais. Steward of the duke's household by September of that year, captain and governor of a string of towns in the Garonne valley between Agen and La Réole, he was retained with a company of 120 men-at-arms.[56]

Another Gascon captain, Bernard de la Salle, came from a noble family in the diocese of Agen. Early on in his career he demonstrated a capacity for military feats of extraordinary audacity, in particular in taking towns by escalade, a skill at which the Gascons seem to have been particularly adept. A legend soon grew up about 'this strong and subtle scaler of walls', as Froissart called him, who took the castle of Clermont-en-Beauvaisis in November 1359 'climbing like a cat', a feat he was reputed to have repeated at La Charité-sur-Loire, an important base and staging post for the companies, taken by night escalade four years later, and which was carried out again at Figeac in Quercy, taken with Bertucat d'Albret in October 1371. All three enterprises, it may be noted, took place in the late autumn. In 1375 he was recruited by Pope Gregory XI for service, first in the Comtat Venaissin and then in Italy, where his career as a *condottieri* was in many respects not dissimilar from that of Sir John Hawkwood, whom he pre-deceased by three years. In 1391 he was killed in an ambush in the foothills of the Alps when he and the count of Armagnac were conducting a large number of companies from France to serve the rival employers in the war between Florence and Milan.[57]

None of the English captains of the Great Companies came from established families like the Albrets and the Gontauts, but among their number several names stand out. Most, but not all, were men on the make.

---

meaning. Lettenhove, in Froissart, *Oeuvres*, xx, p. 549, ingeniously made him a Breton, a view thoroughly demolished by both French editors of the *Chroniques* (vi, p. xxiii n. 3; vii, p. lxvii n. 2; xii, p. xv n. 9). The details of his career are recounted below, pp. 38–9 and *passim*. He is referred to as 'Messire' in the treaty of Clermont of 23 July 1362 (Hay du Châtelet, preuves, p. 313).
55 See below, pp. 284, 334.
56 Luce in Froissart, *Oeuvres*, vii, p. c n. 4; BN, PO 612, doss. 14,399 (du Castel), no. 5; cf. Delachenal, iv, p. 442 n. 3.
57 For his career, see Durrieu, pp. 75–7 and 107–70, and for his origins, ibid., p. 110. For his skill at escalades, see Froissart, *Chroniques*, v, pp. 134, 350–1, and for that of the Gascons in general, Gabotto, p. 23 n. 1; cf. Delachenal, ii, p. 132 n. 1. For the places taken in France, see below, pp. 18, 93 301. For Figeac and his career in Italy, see *Medieval Mercenaries II*.

Sir John Amory († 1364), in words reputed to have been spoken by the Bascot de Mauléon, 'the greatest captain that we had', probably came from Cheshire and may have been related to Roger Amory, who accompanied the Black Prince to Aquitaine in 1355.[58] Sir John's centre of operations in the early 1360s lay in Rouergue and the Albigeois. He was already a knight at the beginning of 1363, but his *compagnon* and sometime lieutenant, John Cresswell, probably from Cresswell on the Northumberland coast above Morpeth, and who was retained by the prince around 1368, seems never to have been knighted. Nor was Edmund Cresswell, possibly a younger brother. John Cresswell was prominent among the English captains of the companies throughout the 1360s, and both men were captains of the English *routes* in 1368, and served in the royal army after the renewal of war in the following year. Active in the campaigns in Poitou and Saintonge in 1371-4, John was twice taken prisoner during these years, the second time during the siege of Lusignan, of which he was captain. He died shortly afterwards.[59] It was his son, also called John, who established the family's position in Northumberland, securing extensive lands in the vicinity of Cresswell in lieu of eight years' arrears of his father's retaining fee.[60]

Nothing is known about the background of Sir Robert Birkhead, along with Cresswell one of the founder captains of the English *routes* of the companies, and in 1367-8 their *souverain capitaine*.[61] The two men were closely associated throughout their military careers in France, down to Birkhead's death sometime before the end of 1368. They were both involved in operations in the Rhône valley above Avignon in the winter of 1360-1, took part in the battle of Brignais (6 April 1362), and were among the *routes* assembled by Louis of Navarre to prosecute war in eastern France after the battle of Cocherel in 1364. After accompanying Bertrand du Guesclin to Spain in 1365-6, they were among the contingents of Sir Hugh Calveley's forces which spearheaded the initial attack on Castile, when they were both retained by Charles of Navarre, in return for annual fief-rents of 200 *livres tournois*. Recalled to Aquitaine by the Black Prince, they both served in his campaign in Castile and were present at the battle of Nájera (3 April 1367). It was at the outset of this expedition that Birkhead was knighted by Sir John Chandos, along with two other captains of the companies, Aimery de Rochechouart and Gaillard de la Motte.

58 Froissart, *Chroniques*, xii, p. 101; *BPR*, iii, p. 249; Hewitt, p. 196. For his career, see below, pp. 39, 56, 64, 66, 69-71, 73.
59 For his career, see below, pp. 39, 56, 64 and *passim*. In 1378 Edmund Cresswell joined Sir John Neville in the siege of Mortagne-sur-Gironde (*Foedera*, iv, p. 131).
60 *CPR, 1385-9*, p. 287.
61 Froissart, *Oeuvres*, vi, p. 328, 331. See Luce in Froissart, *Chroniques*, vi, p. xxii n. 8, citing AN, JJ 104, no. 164, for the description of him as *souverain capitaine*.

Following the prince's return to Aquitaine, the two captains were among the companies who conducted a destructive campaign northwards by way of eastern France as far as Champagne, before turning south and west to arrive in Lower Normandy, Anjou and Maine in the summer of 1368. It was towards the end of that year, after the siege of Louviers and the capture of Vire and Château-Gontier, that Birkhead met his death, probably in an engagement outside the fortified abbey of Olivet in the Orléanais.[62]

Two other men among the captains of the 'English' *routes* of the Great Companies in late 1368 were in fact from the continent. One of them, Folekin Volemer, alias Folcquin l'Alemant, had been involved in the capture of Vire with Hodgkin Russell and Thomelin Bell in the summer of that year.[63] The other, Lopez de Saint-Julien, came from a seignorial family established in the frontier territories of Labourd, in southern Gascony, adjacent to the Navarrese lands of Ultrapuertos, to the north of the Pyrenees.[64] Captain for Charles of Navarre at Saint-Sever in Normandy in 1364, taken prisoner by du Guesclin at Cocherel and handed over to Charles V, he continued in Navarrese employ after the renewal of the war in 1369, and was retained as one of the Navarrese king's ushers-at-arms in 1370.[65] During the summer of 1378 he was captain of Pamplona, and he appears still to have been alive in 1392, when he was among the many Gascons whom Richard II instructed to see that the truce prolonged at Leulinghen was observed.[66] Both men probably joined the English *routes* in Normandy, during the summer of 1368.

Only a handful of the captains of the companies were themselves knights: two of the ten who were party to the treaty of Clermont in 1362, three of the fifteen who appeared in the Navarrese spy letter of 1365, and four (if we include Birkhead) of the twenty-six captains of the English *routes* of the Great Companies quartered on the frontier with Brittany in

---

62 See Lettenhove's index to Froissart, *Oeuvres*, xx, pp. 461–2, under Briquet, and xxi, pp. 66–7, under Cresswell. Full references are given in the ensuing chapters. For Birkhead's death, see appendix E.
63 Fréville, pp. 274, 278.
64 Lopez de Saint-Julien, of the seignorial house of Sault, was lord of *las salas* de Saint-Julien and of Sault de Labourd by January 1375 (*AGN, Comptos*, ix, nos. 674, 696, 830). He was captain of the castle of Mortain in November 1369 (Izarn, *Compte*, p. 125). For his retention and service in Normandy in 1369–70, see ibid., pp. 125, 260–1, 284, 286, 288. For another member of the family, see Zabolo Zabalegui, p. 296 n. 1318.
65 Honoré-Duvergé, 1964, p. 104; Luce, *Du Guesclin*, pp. 451–2; Cuvelier, *Chronique*, ii, p. 392, PJ no. A iv. For his retention and service in Normandy in 1369–70, see Izarn, *Compte*, pp. 125, 260–1, 284, 286, 288. He was captain of the castle of Mortain in November 1369 (Izarn, *Compte*, p. 125).
66 *AGN, Comptos*, xi, nos. 341, 610, 643, 786, and see also nos. 113, 375, 476, 504, 933; EUL, MS 183, fo. 79r (Lopez, sire de Saint-Julien) for the truce. Lopez de Saint-Julien, esquire, possibly his son, was in receipt of moneys and rent from Charles of Navarre in 1387–8 (*AGN, Comptos*, xvi, nos. 792, 802, 1545–6; xvii, no. 111).

1368.⁶⁷ Of the latter, Cheyney, who possessed a number of manors in Kent, was possibly the oldest. He appears to have gone to France on Edward III's great expedition of 1345–7, and subsequently to have abjured the realm on account of a murder and prison-breaking at Canterbury.⁶⁸ In the company of another Kentish man, Thomas Fogg, he was active among the Anglo-Navarrese bands operating in Normandy after 1357. From 1364 to 1368 Cheyney's career followed much the same pattern as that of Birkhead and Cresswell.⁶⁹ The Bascot de Mauléon was almost certainly wrong in recounting that he was killed, along with Birkhead, in the battle of Olivet.⁷⁰ After the renewal of the war Cheyney took part in the siege of Compeyre in Rouergue in June 1369, and three years later we find him with Bernard de la Salle and Bertucat d'Albret, who were occupying the town of Figeac in Quercy.⁷¹ Sir Geoffrey Worsley came from Lancashire, and was retained by John of Gaunt in 1381. The first reference we have to him dates from 1364, when he secured letters of protection to go to Brittany in the company of Walter Huet, a distinguished soldier who had served there for some time. In 1368 he was among the *routes* who took Château-Gontier, doing much damage in the Cotentin and raiding as far as Cherbourg, possibly intending to take the place, and coming away with a rich haul of prisoners. Several members of the same family appear to have served with him: notably Robert, also among the English *routes* of the companies, who was likewise subsequently retained by Gaunt, and who was committed to the Tower of London at the end of Richard II's reign; William, killed in action at Chizé in Poitou (21 March 1373); and possibly also John.⁷²

Very little is known about Sir Robert Mitton and many of the other captains serving with him in 1368. Seven years earlier he had been in charge of an English company which was operating on its own account in

---

67   Appendix B, table 1, key 11 and the sources there cited.
68   *Foedera*, III, i, p. 48; *CPR, 1358–61*, p. 524. He secured a pardon for the murder on 14 March 1361. For his manors in Kent and on the Isle of Sheppey, see Kervyn in Froissart, *Oeuvres*, xx, p. 562. He was taken prisoner whilst captain of le Neubourg in 1357 (*Chron. norm.*, pp. 121–2). For his association with Fogg (on whom see Fowler, 1969, pp. 184, 280 n. 50), who was captain of Auvilliers in 1357 and 1359, see *Chron. normande*, pp. 121, 150.
69   See Lettenhove's index to Froissart, *Oeuvres*, xx, p. 562, under Cheyne, Cheney.
70   See appendix E.
71   For Compeyre, see *Docs. Millau*, p. 161, no. 332; for Figeac see below, p. 295n. He may have been back in England in February 1374, when a certain Robert Cheyne was pardoned for outlawry at the suit of Walter Huet touching a plea of debt of £10 (*CPR, 1370–74*, p. 405). Froissart, *Oeuvres*, xii, pp. 221–2, also refers to a Sir Robert Cheyney who was freebooting with Sir Richard Elmham in the Auvergne and Limousin in 1387.
72   *Foedera*, III, ii, pp. 731; Delisle, *Fragments*, pp. 8, 18; *JGR*, II, i, nos. 38, 580. See Froissart, *Oeuvres*, xxiii (index refs.) p. 296, and below, pp. 235, 294, 300. For Robert Worsley, see *JGR*, II, i, p. 11 and DL 29/738/12096 m. 3; *CCR, 1385–9*, p. 298; *1396–9*, pp. 348, 353. For Huet, see Jones, 1970, references in index.

the frontier territories of Anjou and Maine, and which was defeated by the French at Champgeneteux. In 1370 he was in Normandy with other English *routes* under Geoffrey Walton, Henry Brown and William Hilton, who were extracting payments from the Navarrese to desist from inflicting damage in the *vicomtés* of Carentan and Valognes. Following the renewal of the war he was captain of Moissac, and subsequently of Chizé during the siege by the French.[73] William Bardolf was one of the many captains who refused to lay down arms on the conclusion of peace in 1360. A colourful character, at the end of that year he was captain of Saint-Thorette, near Vierzon, in Berry, from where he continued to extract *patis*, which he claimed to be outstanding to him.[74] Like Richard Holm, from Beverley in Yorkshire, who left for France after killing a man in Coventry in 1359, his past remains a mystery, and nothing is known about either man before they appear among the captains of the companies in 1368. Holm was on active service in Poitou on the renewal of the war, one of the captains holding Saint-Sévère for John Devereux in 1372, before being taken prisoner, along with Cresswell and David Holgrave, in the engagement at Chizé in 1373. By the spring of 1376 he was back in England with some of his companions-in-arms – including Matthew Redman and John Shakell – who together formed an armed confederacy in Lincolnshire, where they perpetrated deeds little different from those they were used to committing in France, perhaps settling old scores from their time there. Fortunately, Holm did not stay long in the kingdom. In September 1380 (by which time he was one of Richard II's esquires) he was appointed captain of the castle of Oye outside Calais, and two years later was transferred to the captaincy of Hammes, which was granted to him for life, and which he held until 1397, when he was pensioned off with a life annuity of 100 marks.[75]

Many of the captains of the English companies who had come north in 1368 were young men, and the greater part of their careers lay in the future. Thomelin Bell, Hodgkin Russell, Roger Hilton, William Botiller, Thomas Folifait (alias Filefort, Folifet), William Shelton and, from those serving under them, Willicot Tee were all among the companies who had

---

73 *Chron norm.*, pp. 158, 328–9; Izarn, *Compte*, p. 303; Froissart, *Oeuvres*, xxii, p. 247 (see index refs); and for the identification of 'Montsach' as Moissac, Luce in Froissart, *Chroniques*, vii, p. lxviii n. 2.
74 AD, Pyrénées-Atlantiques, E 38. On him, see Fowler, 1971b, pp. 192–3.
75 Beverley: *Foedera*, III, i, p. 122; CCR, *1385–9*, p. 566. Killing: CPR, *1358–61*, p. 280. Poitou: Froissart, *Oeuvres*, viii, pp. 154, 156, 234. Confederacy: CPR, *1374–77*, pp. 317–18. Oye: *Foedera*, iv, p. 98; PRO, E 101/68/9, no. 216 (indenture renewing custody for a year from 27 November 1381). Hammes: *Foedera*, iv, p. 147 (appointed 2 June 1382); *CPR, 1396–9*, p. 85 (granted for life, 1 April 1385); see also *CPR, 1391–6*, p. 668. Pension: CPR, *1399–1401*, p. 69. The Bascot de Mauléon's account of his death at Saint-Sévère in 1372 (Froissart, *Chroniques*, xii, p. xxxv, 106) is evidently erroneous.

arrived in Normandy by August of that year. Botiller was among those recruited by du Guesclin for service in Spain in 1366, and was retained by Charles of Navarre during the invasion of Castile in March of that year. He may have been related to John Botiller of Marton, who was involved in a confederacy in Lancashire in the 1370s, or to the John Botiller of Warrington who had been retained by Gaunt by 1371.[76] The companies led by Bell and Russell, along with those of Cresswell and Volemer, were primarily responsible for the capture of Vire.[77] John Norbury, from Cheshire, was serving under John Neville in Gascony, where he was captain of Libourne in 1377–8, and one of the marshals of the army during John Neville's lieutenancy of the duchy. Thereafter serving in Brittany, where he was lieutenant to the captain of Brest in the 1380s and 1390s, he greatly exploited that office for his own profit, to the extent, it was believed, of a capital sum of 18,000 francs and an annual income of 8,000. Through these and other profits he was able to purchase extensive lands in England and advance himself socially. Retained as one of Henry IV's esquires, he was among the king's closest friends and councillors during the early years of his reign, and rapidly advanced to the treasurership.[78]

Jannekin Nowell may have been a member of his company in 1368, and the two men were evidently closely associated. The son of Lawrence Nowell, from Clitheroe in Lancashire, he was serving in the garrison of Saint-Sauveur in 1375. Two years later he was at the siege of Mortagne-sur-Gironde with Norbury, and served with an Anglo-Gascon force in the defence of Navarre in 1378–9. Retained by Sir Hugh Hastings in May 1380, even in fourteenth-century terms he was a man of criminal and violent character. The circumstances which lay behind an order which was put out for his arrest and appearance before the king and council at Westminster in 1360 elude us; but in the 1380s and 90s he secured pardons for felonies and trespasses (save treason, rape and larceny), for murder and debt. He served with Sir John Stanley in Ireland in 1386 and again in 1400, and by the latter date had also been retained as one of Henry IV's esquires.

---

76 *AGN, Comptos*, vi, nos. 152, 167, 263; *JGR*, I, i, no. 8, II, i, p. 8; Walker, p. 166 and appendix i, p. 265.
77 Izarn, *Compte*, p. 346; Fréville, pp. 273, 277; see below, p. 233. The youth of some of them is perhaps also conveyed by their names: Thomelin, Hochekin, Willicot. Following the renewal of the war Russell, like Thomas Cheyney, was serving in Rouergue with the seneschal Thomas Wetenhale (*Docs. Millau*, nos. 332, 354, 356; Rouquette, p. 198). Shelton (Cheteltun, Chelleton) was a hostage for the garrison of Saint-Sauveur in 1375 (Delisle, *Saint-Sauveur*, PJ no. 167). For Folifait, see below, pp. 129, 135, 234, 294. On the move north, see the apposite comments of Froissart, *Oeuvres*, vii, pp. 325–6.
78 Guyenne: PRO, E 101/181/1, no. 18; C 61/90 m. 1 (request to him and the constable of Bordeaux to muster all the men-at-arms). See also *Foedera*, iv, p. 131, and *CCR, 1381–5*, p. 84. Brittany: Fowler, 1964, pp. 68 n. 98, 70. For his retention by Henry IV, land purchases and subsequent career, see Barber, 1953, pp. 66–76, and Bennett, pp. 188–9.

He was still alive in 1415, when a further order was put out for his arrest and appearance before the court of chancery.[79]

David Holgrave, likewise probably only briefly a captain in the companies, was closely associated with John Cresswell senior. He came from Cheshire. The French chronicler Cabaret d'Orville remarked that he was a huge and proud man, who always had with him two swords, one attached to his belt and the other to the pommel of his saddle. He evidently rose through service with the Black Prince, and remained in France with Cresswell up until 1373. After the elder John's death their families continued to be associated in Northumberland following his marriage to Elena, the daughter and heiress of Sir Robert Bertram of Bothal, which brought him considerable interests in that county, as well as in London and Calais.[80]

Not all of the captains of the companies and their familes were as successful in improving their wealth and standing as Norbury, Cresswell and Holgrave, but the opportunities were there, as for other soldiers serving in the wars on the continent. The careers of Calveley and Knowles, of Arnaud de Cervole, du Guesclin and some of the Bretons in his service, amply demonstrate this. Military service could enhance a man's fortunes, not only through ransoms and booty, the profits of protection rackets and other financial exactions, known as *patis* and *suffertes*, and through lands and annuities either seized in war or granted to them, but also through the esteem and increased social connections which successful soldiering might bring them. Through marriage to a wealthy heiress or dowager, and the rewards that could be secured from royal, princely and other employers, they were sometimes able to acquire substantial properties and titles. But the reverse of all of this was also true, and the evidence suggests that among the captains of the Great Companies, most met with ill fortune. There were long periods when they were not in any lord's pay, and the danger that they might be taken prisoner and ransomed themselves was always present. To the risks of falling victim to the plague, which were present for all sections of society in the fourteenth century, must be added those which arose from other diseases more prevalent in camp, the risks of death in battle, from the wounds sustained in martial conflict, and of execution for conducting illegal warfare. Of the ninety-one captains of the Great Companies, eight are known to have died in battle, one was poisoned and nine were executed. To the latter number should doubtless be added

---

79 Delisle, *Saint-Sauveur*, PJ no. 167. Mortagne: *Foedera*, iv, p. 130. Navarre: *AGN, Comptos*, xii, nos. 635, 694, 700. Indenture with Hastings: Norfolk RO, MR 314 242 x 5. Origins, family, character, Ireland, king's esquire: *CCR, 1360–4*, p. 131, *1381–5*, p. 427; *CPR, 1381–5*, p. 212, *1385–9*, p. 126, *1396–9*, p. 398, *1399–1401*, pp. 181, 248, *1413–16*, pp. 158, 346. See Bennett, p. 44 n. 14.
80 Cheshire origins: Bennett, p. 167. Cabaret: *Chron. Loys de Bourbon*, p. 85. For his subsequent career, see below, pp. 70n, 294, 297–300.

some of another eleven of the captains of other companies who were also executed (listed in table 2), some of whom were closely associated with the Great Companies. Of this second group, three Englishmen – Thomas Morville, John Vieleston and Robert Scott – who had made war in the king of Navarre's name, were all executed.[81]

The low social standing and dubious background of many of these men inevitably meant that the leadership passed to the most experienced among them: Amory, Cresswell and Birkhead. But in harnessing their undoubted military potential in the wars in France and Spain, Edward III and the Black Prince relied upon captains who, in the 1360s, were more amenable to their directives, but who from their earlier careers in France could command their loyalties. The most important among them were the Cheshire knights, Sir Hugh Calveley and Sir Robert Knowles, who had long experience of the wars in France, particularly in Brittany and the surrounding territories, which had given them an ascendancy over many of the soldiers who came to form the companies. A similar function was performed by a knight from Hainault, Sir Eustache d'Auberchicourt, who, through his marriage to a niece of the queen and his influence with the Anglo-Navarrese companies in Normandy, both was well connected and enjoyed an ascendancy among these forces. None of the three was ever a captain of the companies, but the rôle they played among them – not only in the service of monarchs and princes, but also out of self-interest and personal aggrandizement – was a crucial factor in the decade after 1360. Their story, especially that of Calveley, is integral to the history of the Great Companies, just as that of Hawkwood is to the group of Englishmen around him who followed Albert Sterz to Italy. A similar rôle may be assigned to Bertrand du Guesclin and Arnaud de Cervole among the Breton and other companies whose allegiance they came to command; agents of Charles V and his son, Louis of Anjou, but also having much in common with the men over whom they exercised their ascendancy. They acted as the principal intermediaries between the Crown and the companies, especially when recruiting them to further royal and princely policies. Only the Gascons, as was their way, were relatively impervious to outside control, and among the Great Companies of the 1360s Seguin de Badefol

---

81 For the statistics, see appendix B, tables 1 and 2. The sources for most of those who died in battle or as a result of wounds sustained in battle, or who were executed, may conveniently be found in the list given in Contamine, 1975, p. 383 n. 1. Cresswell and Cheyney should be deleted (see above, pp. 16–18, below, pp. 295–9, and appendix E). The *bourc* Camus, and possibly also of Caupenne, should be added to those executed (Froissart, *Oeuvres*, vii, p. 422; *Chron. normande*, p. 193). Amory was taken outside Sancerre. For a brief biography of Munde Bataillier, Contamine, 1975, p. 380 n. 1. On Guiot du Pin, see Luce in Froissart, *Chroniques*, vi, p. xxi n. 1.

and Bertucat d'Albret stand out for the power they exercised among them, and their independence, just as Ramonet de Sort and Aimerigot Marchès were to do in the 1380s. The story which follows is as much about them as it is about the Great Companies. They were all mercenaries.

2

An Elusive Peace

Although the problems posed by independent military companies operating on their own account were already evident early on in the war in France, particularly in Brittany and on the frontiers of Gascony, where garrison forces proved difficult to control, and from the demobilization which followed the truce of Bordeaux, it is generally agreed that the formation of the Great Companies dates from the conclusion of peace at the end of the Reims campaign, which wound up the first stage of the Hundred Years War.[1] The territorial clauses of the treaty then concluded at Brétigny on 8 May 1360 provided for the transfer to Edward III of considerable territories, many of which involved the evacuation of towns, castles and fortresses held by forces in French allegiance.[2] In the south-west of France, in addition to what Edward held in Guyenne and Gascony prior to the commencement of the war, he was to have Poitou, Saintonge, Agenais, Périgord, Limousin, Quercy, Bigorre, Gaure, Angoumois and Rouergue. In northern France, in addition to Calais, the surrounding fortresses and the county of Guines, which he already largely controlled, he was to have the town of Montreuil and the county of Ponthieu (save what had been alienated by his ancestors). All this was to be completed by 29 September 1361, and was to be facilitated by a truce concluded for the intervening period.[3] For his part, Edward was to evacuate, at his own cost, all the fortresses taken by his subjects, allies and adherents elsewhere in France, notably in Touraine, Anjou, Maine, Berry, Auvergne, Burgundy, Champagne, Picardy and Normandy, save in Brittany, where the succession to the duchy by the rival contenders still had to be resolved. During the period of truce no further towns, castles or fortresses were to be taken by either side, and all robberies and pillaging were to cease, save that the captains in

---

1 Denifle, ii, p. 376ff; Delachenal, ii, p. 315.
2 For the text of the treaty, see *Foedera*, III, i, p. 487ff.
3 Ibid., III, i, p. 486.

English allegiance could continue to levy ransoms from the territories surrounding their fortresses at the rates then operative (supposedly for the upkeep of the fortifications and to pay for victuals), but they were not to augment them.

When the treaty was ratified at Calais on 24 October 1360, the evacuations to be carried out by Edward were spelled out in detail. These were to be concluded by 2 February 1361, within a month of which date King John was to hand over some of the specified territories ceded to Edward, failing which certain named hostages were to be surrendered in Calais. Edward was to evacuate all places in Champagne and Brie, the Nivernais, Auxerrois, Burgundy, Orléanais and Gâtinais, of which eighteen were named, on the completion of which the county of Ponthieu would be handed over to him. In the Île-de-France, Perche, the Chartrain and the Drouais, four places were enumerated. On their delivery, the county of Montfort was to be surrendered to John de Montfort, the English candidate in the Breton succession dispute. Twenty-four fortresses in Berry and Bourbonnais, fourteen in Touraine and all the fortresses held in the Auvergne, the Mâconnais and Lyonnais were to be handed over, contingent upon which John would surrender Angoulême and the Angoumois. The town of Saintes and Saintonge would be handed over following the evacuation of all fortresses in Normandy, Anjou and Maine, of which twenty-seven were enumerated.[4]

The prospect was hardly one which appealed to the garrison forces, many of whom, in the absence of pay or to supplement it, had made a living out of collecting ransom money from the countryside surrounding the fortresses which they occupied. Some determined to hang on, others to sell out for sizeable payments, known as *rachats*, and to continue their conquests and pillaging. Within a week of the conclusion of the preliminary treaty at Brétigny, on 13 May the earl of Warwick decided to evacuate nine fortresses around Paris for 12,000 gold francs, to be paid by 24 June, and gave up all claims for arrears of ransoms.[5] His action was unusually swift. Others waited to see how matters proceeded, holding out for as much as they could extract. Violations of the truce were so frequent that they threatened to jeopardize the peace itself. In July 1360, Edward appointed Stephen de Cosington, marshal of the Black Prince, to conduct the constable and two marshals of France and three others, to deliberate with Bartholomew Burghersh and other English conservators of the truce on how best to deal with the situation.[6]

Negotiating with the captains of fortresses could be a long-drawn-out

4   Ibid., III, i, p. 535ff.
5   AN, Xla 20, fos. 218v–9r; see Luce, *Du Guesclin*, pp. 543–5, PJ, no. xx.
6   *Foedera*, III, i, p. 504.

business. In one instance alone, a company of Bretons under the command of the Basquin de Poncet, which occupied Véretz near Tours and continually harassed and damaged the inhabitants of that town, involved Cosington and his French colleagues in several weeks of negotiations before they could get an agreement with the captain. This provided that his troops would stop pillaging and allow merchants to bring provisions into the town. Prisoners were to be exchanged without ransom, save a payment to the Basquin (who in future was not to enter the town with more than ten unarmed men) of 1,500 gold *moutons*.[7] The evacuation of Véretz was not finally negotiated until the following February, and involved a heavy payment by the inhabitants of Tours. By then the Basquin had secured another fortress at La Roche-Posay, which he was still holding on to a year later.[8] The volume of violations was such that in August 1360 another group of English commissioners was appointed to deal with infringements.[9] Then, on 30 September, Thomas Holland, earl of Kent, was appointed lieutenant and captain-general in France and Normandy, with power to assemble and lead an army against the malefactors.[10]

When the peace came to be ratified at Calais in October, new measures were taken by Edward III to implement the evacuation of 'all castles and fortresses occupied and detained by reason of war, and taken contrary to the last truce by our subjects or others in our name'. These were to be implemented by twelve commissioners, working in six circuits, and proceeding 'personally or by deputy, from castle to castle or other fortress occupied by our subjects or others in our name', who were to enter them, deliver them to commissioners appointed by the king of France, and punish all rebels and contrariants on pain of banishment. The men appointed to do this were drawn from among the principal holders of castles and fortresses in the regions in question, with a vested interest in holding on to what they could.[11] It is hardly surprising that in nine out of ten cases they,

---

7 *Reg. comptes Tours*, i, p. 177, no. 948 and n. 1; p. 179, no. 959 and n. 1.
8 La Roche-Posay, Vienne. A sum of 2,900 écus had to be raised to pay him off, 2,060 from the burgesses and inhabitants of the town and 840 from the ecclesiastics (ibid., p. 229, no. 1181, n. 1, and Chaplais, 'Some Documents', p. 4).
9 Notably Richard de Stafford, Miles de Stapleton, Nigel Loring, and two Gascon lords, Amanieu d'Albret, lord of Langoiran, and Amanieu de Pommiers (*Foedera*, III, i, p. 507). Albret's main work appears to have been in Berry, where he attempted to carry out the evacuation of Brouillamenon and Sainte-Thorette, on the banks of the river Cher near Bourges, which had been taken since the truce, the first by a Gascon called Morilhon, and the second by an English captain, William Bardolf (AD, Pyrénées-Atlantiques, E 38; see Fowler, 1971b, pp. 191–3). Loring seems to have spent some time negotiating in Paris, and to have been involved in the evacuation of fortresses taken by English troops in Burgundy (Vernier, p. 225 n. 1).
10 *Foedera*, III, i, pp. 509–10.
11 Ibid., III, i, p. 546ff. William Grandson and Nicholas Tamworth were to deliver the fortresses in Champagne and Brie, the Auxerrois and Burgundy, Orléanais and Gâtinais; Thomas Fogg and Thomas Cann in the Île-de-France, Perche, Chartrain and Drouais; the lord

and the captains brought under their jurisdiction, refused to surrender their fortresses before they had been paid substantial sums to depart, in addition to all ransoms outstanding from the surrounding countryside. Between October 1360 and March 1362, the evacuation of some fifty fortresses in northern France alone involved payments amounting to some 1,431 kg of gold (i.e. 150,400 *écus* of King John, 110,600 *moutons*, 49,000 *royaux* and 15,000 florins).[12] No arrangements were made for dealing with disbanded troops. In a few places the garrisons were taken on by the French, but for the most part they were left to re-form under captains of their own choosing. It was these men, finding themselves put out of employ by the execution of the peace treaty, who formed the basis of the Great Companies.[13]

The duchy of Burgundy was the first part of France to be evacuated by the English and their allies. There, a treaty had been concluded at Guillon with Duke Philip de Rouvres on 10 March 1360 whereby, for a ransom payment of 200,000 gold *moutons*, Edward III agreed to hand over the fortress of Flavigny and, implicitly, the whole of Burgundy.[14] In July William Grandson, lord of Saint-Croix, and Nicholas Tamworth were employed in evacuating fortresses held by the English and Navarrese companies, many of which had arrived in Burgundy since the conclusion of the treaty of Brétigny in May and before its ratification in Calais in the following October.[15] An unusually large assembly of men in the plains of Champagne, who called themselves the Great Company (*la grant compaigne, magna societas*), were already menacing the duchy at the beginning

---

of Pommiers, Bérard and Arnaud d'Albret in Bourbonnais and Berry, in the Auvergne and Touraine, Mâconnais and Lyonnais; Amaury de Fossat and Élie de Pommiers in Périgord, Quercy and Agenais; the captal de Buch and the lord of Montferrand in Normandy, Anjou and Maine; Thomas Holland, earl of Kent in Normandy, Anjou, Maine and throughout France. The commissions were notified to all captains, castellans, constables, keepers of fortresses and other fortified places and all other subjects in the king's obedience.

12   Chaplais, 'Some Documents', pp. 42–5. See Fowler, 1992, p. 218 n. 3, for the calculation of the weight of gold coins.
13   'Le roy d'Engleterre devoit faire vuidier les forteresces à ses despens, et néanmois pluseurs Englois descoururent sur le royaume de France en pluseurs routes. Et estoient d'iceux qui desdites forteresces estoient partis et se tenoient par manière de compaignie. Et pluseurs s'en alèrent en Bretagne à Jehan de Montfort. Et s'en assembla une grant route qui s'en ala vers Avignon, et prisrent le pont Saint-Esperit, etc.' (BN, Suppl. franç., no. 530, fo. 79v; unpublished chronicle cited by Paulin Paris in his edition of the *Grandes Chroniques*, vi, p. 221, n. 1). Cf. Froissart, *Chroniques*, vi, pp. 59–61, 256–7.
14   *Foedera*, III, i, p. 473; see Delachenal, ii, pp. 168–72. The principal documentation relating to the treaty is preserved in AC, Côte d'Or, B 11922–5, to which should be added PRO, E 30/102, 104, 123, 182, 184, 186, 1425, 1496, and the documentation relating to payments and other matters recorded in E 43/361, 598; E 101/28/29; E 404/6/37, nos. 14, 41, 86; E 404/6/40, no. 64; E 404/509/61. As late as 1377 the entire episode led to an action in the Paris *parlement* between the countess of Flanders and the three estates of the duchy of Burgundy over obligations entered into in respect of the ransom (AN, Xla 27, fos. 231-2, no. 39). This and other documentation is utilized in a forthcoming article on the treaty.
15   Chérest, pp. 128–9, 129 nn. 1 and 2.

of August, when a scouting party was intercepted in the environs of Montréal-en-Auxois.[16] During the course of that month Grandson and Tamworth concluded an agreement with this Great Company, which, in return for the payment of protection money, agreed to cross the province as speedily as possible on its route south.[17] These were early indications of the flood that was to come following the ratification of the treaty of Brétigny in October. As the work of evacuation of fortresses controlled by the English and the delivery of territories to Edward III progressed, the number of companies was swollen to make them, when they operated together, a professional military force, under tried captains, of considerable size and potential. The first contingents were assembling in Champagne and Brie at the beginning of November,[18] and had moved into the Midi before the end of the year. During the night of 28–9 December, one of them, apparently English and Gascon in composition, seized the town of Pont-Saint-Esprit, situated on the west bank of the river Rhône some twenty-five miles upstream from Avignon.[19]

Considering its strategic importance Pont-Saint-Esprit was not particularly well defended, and it is clear that the town was not fully enclosed by walls.[20] Whilst the river Rhône offered some protection from the east, the 'new' ramparts, constructed in 1231, which enveloped the earlier defences on all sides, were in a bad state of repair. An inspection carried out by an officer of the seneschalsy in 1358 had revealed numerous deficiencies, and although further extensions and improvements to the fortifications had commenced (notably a new curtain wall with towers), they remained incomplete for lack of funds, and had to be supplemented by a wooden palisade on the outer side of a moat or ditch. The main defensive structure remained the central tower or castle, constructed in 1202. The bridge, completed between 1305 and 1309, which gave access to the imperial territories on the east bank of the Rhône, was protected at each end by a crenellated tower. Responsibility for the defence of the walls and the bridge rested with a citizen militia, whose arms and armour were prescribed in the municipal ordinances. Shortly before the arrival of the companies they had been reinforced by a small garrison under the command of a Luccese

16 Ibid., pp. 129–31.
17 Ibid., pp. 132–3, and PJ no. xii bis.
18 'Et lors [*beginning of November 1360*] avoit grant foison d'Anglois et autres es pays de Brie et Champaigne qui gastoient tout le pays, tuoient et raençonnoient genz et faisoient du pis qu'il povoient, dont aucuns se appelloient la Grant Compaignie. Les quels, après ce que ilz orent sceu que le dit roy de France estoit delivré de sa prison, se partirent du dit pays de Brie et s'en alerent en Champaigne, là où ilz tenoient pluseurs forteresses' (*Chron. Jean II*, i, pp. 327–8).
19 Froissart, *Chroniques*, vi, pp. 71–2; ix, p. 156; *Thalamus parvus*, p. 357. See below, nn. 21–3 and pp. 35–7, for the arrangements concluded for its evacuation by the 'Great Company'.
20 For what follows, see Bruguier-Roure, pp. 98, 102–7.

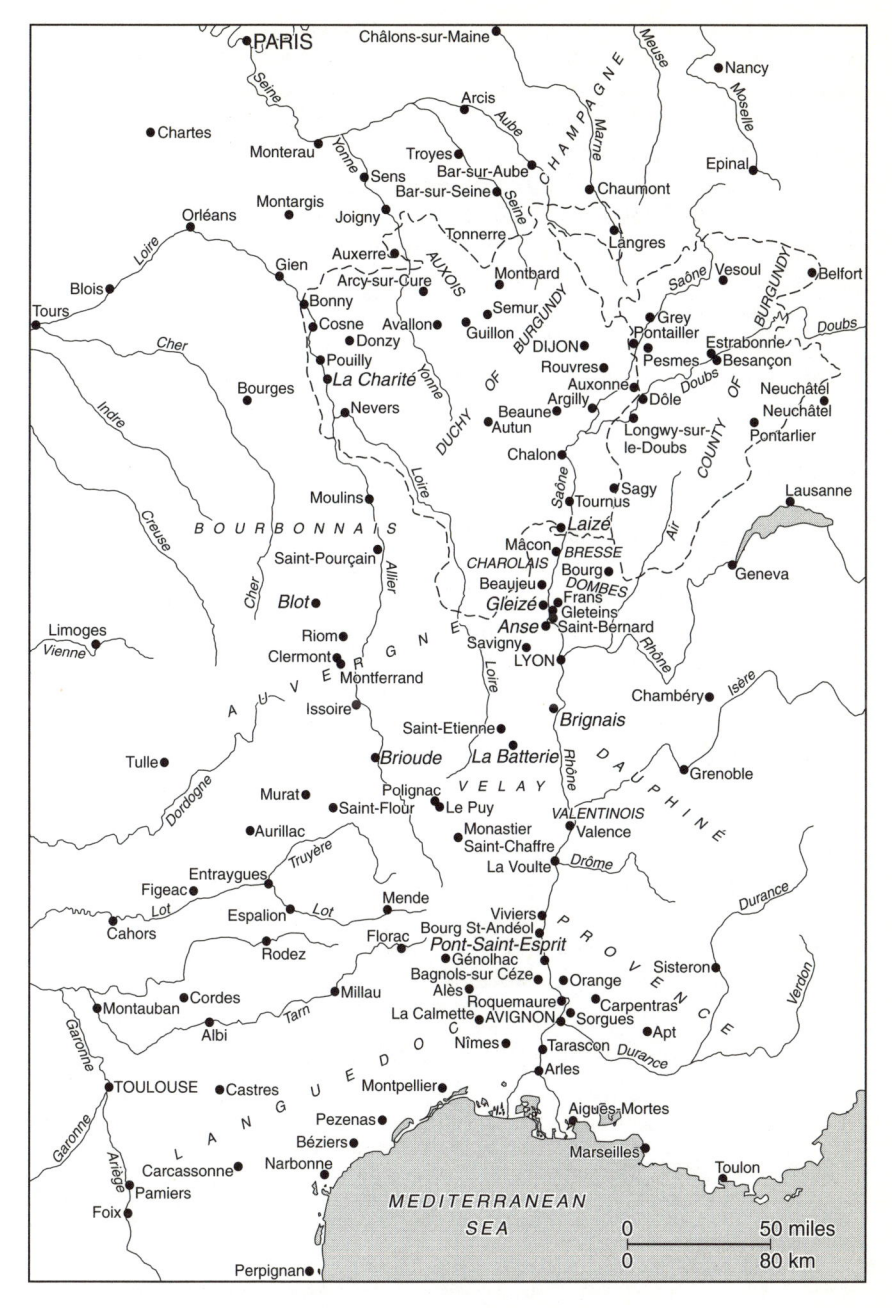

2 *Principal places occupied by the Companies in Burgundy, the Saône and Rhône valleys and the surrounding territories, 1361–5*

soldier, a sergeant-at-arms of the king of France, who held the office of provost or *viguier*. To add to these defences, on the west bank lookout posts were in place on the summits of the neighbouring hills, from which signals from the surrounding peaks could be relayed should the enemy approach from that direction and attempt to cross the rivers Ardèche and Cèze, or seek cover in the neighbouring woods and scrubland, which provided an ideal terrain for conducting ambushes. A bell in the castle tower could be rung to sound the alarm. If resistance proved futile, three gates which gave access to the river would facilitate escape to the marshland on the east bank.

There are inevitably significant discrepancies in the chroniclers' accounts of the occupation of Pont-Saint-Esprit, and it is possible that the assault was carried out by more than one *route* of the companies, although there is no clear-cut indication of the names of the commanders who were in charge of the operation. The *Thalamus parvus* of Montpellier simply says the town was taken by 'a company of English and renegade Frenchmen',[21] which might allow for the apparent contradiction in Froissart's different accounts of the action. In one of these, written long after the event, he attributes it to Munde Bataillier, Guiot du Pin, Lamit and Petit Meschin.[22] In another, dealing primarily with events in Italy in 1379, but which may have been written before the previous account, he recounts the early years of the career of John Hawkwood in France and recalls the part played by Hawkwood and Bernard de Sorgues, who 'assisted' in the action.[23] Nor can we be sure from which side of the town the attack came, for although there is general agreement that the main company or companies responsible for the initial onslaught had arrived from Champagne by way of Burgundy and Lyonnais, it is clear that some contingents were conducting raids to the south of Pont-Saint-Esprit on the west bank of the Rhône before the attack took place. On 27 December they were in the neighbourhood of Roquemaure, less than nine miles up-stream from Avignon; the same day they burned and pillaged Chusclan, about the same distance further north,

---

21 'Item, aquel an meteys an LX, la nuog dels Innocens, fo pres lo luoc de Sant Esperit sus lo Roze per une companha dAnglezes e de fals Franceses' (*Thalamus parvus*, p. 357).

22 'à ce que j'ai depuis oy recorder, Bataillier, Guiot dou Pin, Lamit et Petit Meschin chevaucièrent et leurs routes une nuit toute nuit bien quinze liewes et vinrent sus le point dou jour à la ditte ville dou Pont Saint Esperit, et l'eschiellèrent et le prisent' (Froissart, *Chroniques*, vi, pp. 71–2; my italics). The author of the *Thalamus parvus*, p. 358, places Petit Meschin in the army assembled by the constable of France which entered Montpellier on 13 April 1361, but was well aware of his rôle as a captain of the companies in subsequent references (ibid., pp. 361, 382, 384).

23 'et fu Haccoude uns [des chiefs] par especial avoecques Briquet et Carsuelle, par qui la bataille de Brinai fu faite, et *aida* à prendre le pont de Saint Esperit avoecq Bernart de Sorges' (ibid., ix, p. 156; editor's brackets, my italics). I cannot understand why Henneman, ii, p. 154, makes Seguin de Badefol one of the two captains who took Pont-Saint-Esprit along with Hawkwood.

near Bagnols-sur-Cèze; on the 28th they took the village of Codolet, which lay between the two.[24]

It is possible that these actions were carried out by the companies which took Pont-Saint-Esprit. Both Froissart and Matteo Villani inform us that the assault was carried out by an advance party after a forced march through the night, and both writers indicate that it took the inhabitants unprepared.[25] According to Froissart the attack took place at daybreak and the town was taken by escalade, a view not at odds with the fate of the commander in charge of the defence, Jean Souvain, seneschal of Beaucaire, who fell off a wooden platform projecting from the ramparts and broke his leg.[26] According to Villani, the companies, having found their passage down the Rhône valley blocked at Lyon, feigned an attack on one district of that town, which preoccupied the defenders, while the companies sent a detachment of 1,000 lances (*barbute*) through the mountains of *Ricodano* unopposed. The route in question, which brought them early the following morning into the plain to the west of the Rhône, within striking distance of Pont-Saint-Esprit, was the old Roman road through Forez and Velay, which descended into the Rhône valley by way of Génolhac, Alès and La Calmette, to the north of Nîmes.[27] If they left this route at Alès, the journey to Pont-Saint-Esprit was less than forty miles by way of Bagnols-sur-Cèze, slightly more if they first made for Roquemaure.

According to Villani the detachment of the companies responsible for the action, after their long journey through the night, halted for a while in the Rhône valley to refresh themselves, lighting fires to get warm, seeking provender for their horses and victuals for themselves, before making for Pont-Saint-Esprit. This may account for the raids on the 27th and 28th, and it may have been at this juncture that Hawkwood teamed up with Bernard de Sorgues. The proximity of Sorgues to the scene of action, less than seven miles to the north of Avignon and just across the river from Roquemaure, suggests that this may well have been the case. Villani tells us that the inhabitants did not put up any resistance, and that the Luccese castellan was taken prisoner, released, but then arrested in Avignon by order of the pope, fanning suspicions that he had surrendered the castle without a struggle. Some of the inhabitants sought refuge in the church, which had been fortified, and where they took their most valuable pos-

---

24   Denifle, ii, p. 388.
25   'Tr'al giorno e la notte appresso l'alpe (della Ricodana) passarano, che di mala via furono oltre a miglia quaranta, e alla dimane si trovarono nel piano, presso a Santo Spirito in sul Rodano' (Villani, *Istorie*, lib. x, cap. xxvii). See n. 22 above for Froissart's account.
26   *Thalamus parvus*, p. 357.
27   Bruguier-Roure, p. 114. See also Monicat, p. 19, citing Camille Jullian, *Histoire de la Gaule* (Paris, 1921), p. 542 n. 4.

sessions, hoping for the arrival of a relieving force.[28] Under the terms of an arrangement which they made with the companies, after six days they agreed to pay a ransom of 6,000 florins to spare their goods and their lives. Villani adds that, although the money was paid, the agreement was not respected by the companies, who robbed their victims and detained some of the young women 'in the service of the company'. Unlike Froissart, he does not say that some of the men were killed and the women raped, but these incidents were commonplace.

The strategic importance of Pont-Saint-Esprit, which commanded one of only four bridges over the Rhône, soon became evident to the companies.[29] Control of the fortress, town and bridge gave them access to territories on either side of the river, and facilitated access to the environs of Avignon by the left bank and Villeneuve by the right bank. It enabled them to ransom merchants and travellers, who included the large numbers of lay and ecclesiastical dignitaries and others conducting business at the papal curia, and to intercept convoys of food and other merchandise passing down the Rhône valley.[30] During the ensuing months, as the number of companies operating in the area was swollen to mega-proportions, Avignon was blockaded, and its supply lines to the north cut off.

While this became evident as the weeks passed by, it is unlikely that the companies had any predetermined plan to besiege Avignon, or even to blockade the city. Their immediate objective, which determined the timing of their operation, was to seize the money collected in the seneschalsies of Toulouse, Carcassonne and Nîmes for the payment of the first instalment of King John's ransom. They were evidently aware that this was to have been transported to Paris under armed escort by the seneschal of Beaucaire, Jean Souvain, who had arrived in Pont-Saint-Esprit on the night of the 27th or the morning of 28th December. The companies may have been tracking him, but were not aware that he was not then in possession of the money, which had been entrusted at Nîmes to two commissioners appointed by the treasurer of France, Pierre Scatisse, to be handed over to him at Pont-Saint-Esprit. The commissioners in question, Master Jean de Lunel and Jean Gilles, were running a day behind schedule, and only

---

28   Villani's account is here substantiated by an inquiry which Louis of Anjou, as lieutenant in Aquitaine, subsequently ordered to be made concerning the theft of the goods which one of the inhabitants had taken into the church (Bruguier-Roure, p. 115 n. 3).
29   For the strategic significance of Pont-Saint-Esprit, see Labande, 1901, pp. 83–4, and Brugier-Roure, pp. 96–8, 116.
30   Villani was particularly well informed on this point: 'e il Ponte afforzarono in forma, che le navi, che venieno di Borgogna a Vignone con vittuaglia non potieno passare. Onde la Corte sostenne grave carestia' (*Istorie*, lib. x, cap. xxvii), and again: 'E l'una che si nomava la Compagna Bianca, venne appresso a Vignone a trenta miglia, e teneva mercato d'havere danari dal Papa, e di levare quella di Santo Spirito, che per cagione, ch'havea il Rodano di sopra in sua Signoria, gravava la Corte, non lasciando uscire la vittuaglia di Borgogna' (ibid., lib. x, cap. xxxiv).

arrived in Avignon on 26 December with their pack-horses and leather sacks containing some 46.4 kg of gold coins (5,200 *moutons*, 2,500 *vieux royaux*, 2,100 *vieux écus* and 1,400 *nouveaux royaux*). On hearing of the capture of Pont-Saint-Esprit, they returned to Nîmes, where the money remained until the following March.[31] The element of surprise, so necessary to the success of the enterprise, had not been lacking, although Pope Innocent VI had been well aware of the danger posed to Avignon and its environs since the invasion of Provence by Arnaud de Cervole in 1358. The great ramparts and ditches of the city and of Pont-de-Sorgues, although by no means complete, had been under construction for over a year, and for more than a week before the capture of Pont-Saint-Esprit the movements of the companies had been carefully reconnoitred. On 18 December the pope had even instructed his chamberlain to release 500 florins to Scatisse for the payment of certain reinforcements being sent to that town.

The first instalment of King John's ransom may have eluded the companies, but the occupation of Pont-Saint-Esprit acted as a magnet in attracting further contingents to the area. During the early months of 1361 the bulk of the companies formed as a result of the general demobilization, and of the evacuation of further fortresses following the confirmation of peace at Calais, made their way into the lower Rhône basin and the region around Avignon.[32] Those which had assembled in Champagne and Burgundy made their way south through the Mâconnais and Lyonnais on staggered dates and by different routes. At the beginning of January, the first contingents were observed proceeding along the west bank of the Saône, avoiding the French garrison at Bagé-le-Châtel, situated on the east bank. The duke of Burgundy and the lord of Beaujeu seem to have been taking some measures to resist them, assembling their forces at Belleville, to the south of Mâcon. From Lyon, messengers were sent to the fortified town of Anse and other places up-stream from Lyon, enjoining them to enforce the watch, bring all food within their walls, and provide men for the army then being assembled. By the middle of the month these first contingents had arrived in Lyonnais and the second were approaching Beaujolais. A month later, the third and largest were near Mâcon, although the rearguard did not leave the vicinity until the middle of March. Like the advance party sent ahead of them, most of these troops avoided a confrontation in the Saône and Rhône valleys, and passed to the west of Lyon, some by way of the fortified town of Saint-Symphorien-sur-Coisne, and further south and west by the fortified church of Estivarelles, in the confines of Forez and Auvergne. Arriving in the Midi, some detachments made for

---

31 The story, told by Froissart, is substantiated from documentary evidence by Luce in *Chroniques*, vi, pp. xxx–xxxi and xxxi n. 1, pp. 71–2.
32 See above, pp. 2–5. For what follows, see Guigue, pp. 49–55.

Pont-Saint-Esprit, whilst others spread out in the three southern seneschalsies.

Innocent VI had not been inactive in his efforts to repulse the companies. Blockaded in Avignon with the Sacred College, he first summoned the companies to depart, then excommunicated them and finally, during the first days of January, launched a full-scale crusade against them, promising the same indulgences to the crusaders as those going on the expeditions to the Holy Land, and appointing the Cardinal Bishop of Ostia captain-general of the Crusade:[33]

Arise therefore, faithful of Christ and devoted sons of the Roman church and apostolic see. . . . Put on those arms both health-giving and glorious . . . as the lord inspires each of you, either fighting in your own persons, or sending others to forward the affair in your own place, or contributing money according to your means, so that each receives his fair share of this benediction and grace, and by carrying out God's business, each exchanges a short spell of earthly labour for heavenly rewards.[34]

The same day he wrote to the bishop-elect of Valence, requesting him to keep him informed of the movements of the 'Great Company', on 9 January to the Hospitaller Juan Fernández de Heredia, instructing him to come to the defence of the Comtat Venaissin, and on the 10th to the duke of Burgundy, the governor of the Dauphiné and others, requesting them to stop other companies from crossing their territories, and informing them of the crusade which he had launched.[35] Between 17th and 26th further letters were despatched to the king of France, the emperor Charles IV, the king of Aragon, the doge of Genoa, and many French dukes, counts and other nobles and towns requesting troops for the forthcoming campaign. Another was sent to Robert de Fiennes, constable of France, who was about to arrive with a force under his command and that of one of the marshals of France, Arnoul d'Audrehem. On 26 January he sent a safe-conduct to the seneschal of Charles of Blois in the *vicomté* of Limoges to bring reinforcements. On 8 February he enrolled a contingent of forces in the service of the Church, and during the course of that month despatched further letters to lay and ecclesiastical lords whose jurisdiction encompassed territories in or adjacent to the Rhône valley – the count of Savoy, the count of Valentinois, the archbishops of Lyon and Vienne, the bishop of Viviers and the bishop-elect of Valence – requesting them to obstruct the passage of

---

33   Guigue, p. 56; Labande, 1901, p. 146; Bruguier-Roure, pp. 116–17. For the bull launching the crusade, see Denifle, ii, p. 395 and n. 2.
34   Housley, 1982, pp. 262–3, quoting from a letter to the people of Embrun.
35   For this and the remainder of the paragraph, see Luce in Froissart, *Chroniques*, vi, p. xxxii nn. 1 and 2; Guigue, p. 56; Labande, 1901, p. 147.

'brigands' who were advancing from all parts of France to join those already at Pont-Saint-Esprit.

During the course of January and February the crusaders assembled at Carpentras, on the east bank of the Rhône, under the supreme command of the cardinal archbishop of Ostia, Pierre Bertrand de Colombier.[36] The forces assembled at Bagnols, on the west bank, were commanded by the constable of France, who had recently been appointed the king's lieutenant in Languedoc, and by Marshal Audrehem. The three estates of the seneschalsy of Beaucaire, meeting in Nîmes, had agreed to an *impôt* to raise troops, and the nobles of Velay, Vivarais and Gévaudan also brought contingents to Bagnols. The king of Aragon sent 600 men-at-arms and 1,000 infantry to join the crusading forces, and the archbishop of Lyon had promised a further 200 men-at-arms. These, and probably other forces, together laid siege to Pont-Saint-Esprit. Those under the cardinal conducted their operations from the east bank, where they scored a success in an initial encounter at Mondragon. The French royal forces conducted their operations from the west bank, where Audrehem, who arrived from Montpellier, had recently dislodged some of the companies from Massilargues, situated to the east of Montpellier, on the road to Nîmes. However, neither the papal nor the French royal forces appear to have wished to risk an engagement with the companies if it could be avoided, and money was lacking in both camps to pay the troops. According to Froissart, the pope expected the crusaders to serve without pay.[37] Disgruntled, some returned home, others went to fight in Italy, and some even deserted to the companies. By mid-February it was clear that the siege was making little progress,[38] and both the pope and the officers of the king of France decided to treat with the companies. Divisions within the command structure may have contributed to this decision, but the decisive factor may well have been the plague, which was raging in the Midi and claiming victims with a fearful intensity in Avignon and up the Rhône valley.[39]

There was no single treaty for the evacuation of Pont-Saint-Esprit, which was the subject not of one but of several agreements negotiated independently with different contingents of the companies by the main interested

---

36 For what follows, see Labande, 1901, pp. 147–8; Guigue, p. 56; Bruguier-Roure, pp. 117–18.
37 Froissart, *Chroniques*, vi, p. 74.
38 'Al modo delle guerre de'Prelati la boce fu grande, e la difesa fu piccola' . . . (Villani, lib. x, cap. xxvii).
39 'Per simile nel Reame di Francia nella Proenza trafisse ogni maniera di gente. Vignone corrupe in forma, che non vi campava persona. Morironvi nove Cardinali, e più di settanta [*another MS says* settecento] Prelati, e gran Clerici, e popolo innumerabile' (ibid., lib. x, cap. xlvi). The population of la Voulte-sur-Rhône (Ardèche, arr. Privas) was virtually wiped out (Luce, in Froissart, *Chroniques*, vi, p. xxxiii n. 3).

parties, the texts of none of which appear to have survived.[40] One or more of these, concluded by the pope, provided for some of the companies, mostly English and German, to be recruited by the marquis of Montferrat for service in his war with the Visconti of Milan. According to Villani, who was well informed on the matter, these agreements together cost Innocent more than 100,000 florins, of which 30,000 were paid directly to the companies occupying Pont-Saint-Esprit, and the remainder to the marquis to recruit troops from their number.[41] For his part, Froissart says that, in addition to substantial wages for their prospective service in Lombardy, the companies received 60,000 florins from the marquis for their departure from Pont-Saint-Esprit, of which Hawkwood had for his part 10,000 for himself and his *route*.[42] On 13 February Innocent had appointed Juan Fernández de Heredia and two others to treat with a certain *Waltero*, possibly the Scottish knight Sir Walter Leslie, described as a captain of the Great Company, and with John Hawkwood and Richard Musard, alias 'the Black Squire', his marshal and constable respectively,[43] and subsequently certain moneys were made over to Heredia by the pope's treasurer for payment directly to the marquis.[44] In return for these payments and absolution for their crimes, the companies agreed to quit the Comtat Venaissin and Provence, and on 21 April Innocent requested letters of safe-conduct for the passage of the marquis and his forces through Provence.[45]

Another agreement, for the territories to the west of the Rhône, and in particular the seneschalsy of Beaucaire, was concluded sometime before 22 April by Fiennes and Audrehem, on the one hand, and a number of other companies, mostly Gascon, on the other. Once again, the departure of the companies was purchased, on this occasion for service in Aragon, where a war with the neighbouring kingdom of Castile had been proceeding for some five years. A first payment of the necessary money was advanced by the king's treasurer in Languedoc, and the whole was to have been recovered from a *taille* to be approved by the estates of the seneschalsy of Beaucaire; but these arrangements were overtaken by events elsewhere. On 13 May Aragon and Castile concluded peace at Terrer, and the companies

40 The best account of the evacuation is to be found in Labande, 1901, pp. 148–51; see the principal document here utilized (ibid., pp. 152–64).
41 *Istorie*, pp. 651–2.
42 Froissart, *Chroniques*, vi, pp. 74–5; ix, p. 156; xii, p. 99.
43 *Thes. anecdot.*, ii, cols. 882–3. Another possible identification of *Waltero* is Walter Hoo, who may have been related to Sir William Hoo, captain of Oye and Hammes in the Pas-de-Calais in the 1380s. See Fowler, 1998, p. 137. The matter will be reviewed in *Medieval Mercenaries II*.
44 On 6 June 1361 the pope issued a letter of acquittance to Heredia for 14,500 gold florins made over in this way (*Thes. anecdot.*, ii, col. 995; see Froissart, *Chroniques*, vi, p. xxxiii, n. 3). This sum may have been the total amount advanced to the marquis, but was more probably an instalment.
45 *Thes. anecdot.*, ii, col. 933; see Labande, 1901, p. 149.

which were proceeding south from Perpignan were stopped on the Aragonese frontier. They consequently continued to ravage Languedoc, in particular the lands around Perpignan and Montpellier.[46] In addition to these agreements another arrangement, contracted in mid-April by the *syndics* of Pont-Saint-Esprit, acting on behalf of the inhabitants of the town, involved a loan of 8,000 florins raised from one Jean Arbalestier, then in residence in Avignon.[47] Yet another arrangement, also for an unknown sum, was concluded with the prince of Orange for the evacuation of his territory, which had been devastated from early in January.[48] Through these and perhaps other arrangements, Pont-Saint-Esprit and the lower Rhône valley were finally evacuated by the companies towards the end of April; but those among their number who did not take the road to Italy or Aragon dispersed themselves thoughout the southern seneschalsies of the kingdom of France, where they joined up with others already operating there, making them a more difficult target for military and diplomatic operations.

Among the companies who did not go to Aragon, that of the Périgordian captain, Seguin de Badefol, was probably the largest. In April he was operating to the west of Montpellier, where he took and ransomed Aniane, burned part of the barriers of the neighbouring town of Gignac and then moved further south and west to Pomerols, Florensac and other places around Agde. From there he proceeded north and east beside the network of *étangs* and other waters that mark this area of the coast to Frontignan, which was taken by force at sunrise on 13 April, although not without considerable losses among Seguin's forces. They held this town for three weeks, using it as a base for conducting raiding parties into the surrounding countryside, one of which even penetrated the outer defences of Montpellier, where a number of citizens were abducted from the church of Saint-Côme. An army assembled by the constable and marshal of France, which arrived in Montpellier and was joined by a citizen militia under the town banner, then prepared to meet the company at Frontignan. Hearing of their intentions, Seguin moved his forces northwards, pursued by the royal army, into the Cevennes around Le Vigan; but an attempt to force them to a battle near Ganges was forbidden by the constable, who was not prepared

---

46 Molinier, pp. 90–4; Labande, 1901, pp. 149–50; *Thalamus parvus*, pp. 357–8; *HGL*, x, cols. 1488–9. Henneman, ii, p. 158, rejects the view that there was any treaty for the companies who evacuated Pont-Saint-Esprit to be sent to 'Spain'; but the evidence is quite clear from a letter of remission dated Villeneuve-lès-Avignon, December 1362 (AN, JJ 93, no. 82, published by Molinier, p. 98 n. 1). For the peace of Terrer, named after the place where the negotiations took place and the agreement was concluded, see García y Lopez, i, pp. 231–2; Delachenal, iii, p. 257 and n. 5. The terms were approved by the king of Castile at Deza on 13 May, and by the king of Aragon at Calatayud on the 14th.
47 This arrangement is only known to us because the loan in question was the subject of subsequent litigation, which dragged on into the next century. For the details, see Bruguier-Roure, p. 118 and n. 5.
48 Labande, 1901, p. 148, n. 5, citing Arch. com. Orange, BB1, fo. 75.

to risk an engagement.[49] Seguin was still in this region at the end of July, menacing the neighbourhood around Millau, where the plague was then at its worst. On 4 July a solemn procession was held in the town for the victims of war and plague. The *consul-boursier*, Bertrand Guibert, noted the deaths of five of his colleagues during the course of the year, and in a register containing the terms of a contract for work on the town walls another scribe wrote 'everything is dead, everyone is dead' *(tot es mort, totz son mortz)*.[50]

The constable's efforts to re-establish peace in Languedoc proved fruitless. In June and July, Castilian and other troops under the king of Castile's bastard half-brother, Enrique of Trastámara, threatened to re-enter France across the Aragonese frontier,[51] and in August Seguin returned into Bas Languedoc, where a new wave of companies was arriving from the provinces still being evacuated further north. One of the largest of these was that of the Gascon Bérard d'Albret, who had previously been operating in the Bourbonnais, and who arrived before Montpellier on 2 August. Having breached the barriers outside the town walls, Bérard took up quarters in the church of the Friars Minor, his troops burning and destroying buildings in the *faubourgs* and conducting ambushes there during the space of four days. They then moved off to the Narbonnais, where they were joined by the Seguin's forces, which had been operating in the Albigeois, and other companies, including those of the lord of Castelnau in Quercy and Garciot du Castel. From here the combined army invaded Roussillon, where they remained for twelve days. Short of victuals, they then turned back north and west, riding some forty miles through the night up the Aude valley to arrive in the Carcassès and Toulousain, sacking a string of towns between Carcassonne and Castelnaudry, including Montolieu, Villepinte and Saint-Papoul, but avoiding the fortresses, which were too well defended. Once again, the companies had to be bought off. By a treaty concluded on 23 September the four captains placed themselves under oath not to do any further damage in the seneschalsies of Toulouse, Carcassonne and Beaucaire, and they undertook to get their companies to swear to abide by its terms.[52] This agreement provisionally liberated the three seneschalsies from further depredations. In the Albigeois, the bishop

---

49 For these details see the *Thalamus parvus*, pp. 357–8; Molinier, pp. 92–3; Ménard, ii, pp. 223–4; Maubourguet, 1938, pp. 215–16.
50 *Docs. Millau*, pp. 118–19 no. 241 and p. 119 n. 2. For other ravages of the plague, which raged for six to seven months in 1361, see *HGL*, ix, p. 276.
51 Molinier, p. 93 and n. 5, listing payments which appear in the accounts of the treasurer of Carcassonne for officials inspecting defences and conducting musters of garrisons on the frontier with Aragon. For what follows see *Thalamus parvus*, pp. 358–9.
52 *Arch. Montpellier*, i, p. 76, no. 750. Delachenal, ii, p. 318, wrongly believed this to be dated 23 November. The agreement was concluded by the lords of Carman and Villemur, for the three seneschalsies, and the four captains, of whom Seguin de Badefol is the first named.

of Albi had to pay 3,000 florins to get them out of his diocese. Some respite was also purchased in Rouergue, where Garciot, on quitting the Toulousain, had occupied Bournac before the end of October, and where he for a time joined forces with a company under Bertucat d'Albret, who occupied Monastier. At the beginning of November they agreed to evacuate their forces from the province for a further 5,200 florins, to be raised by the Estates, but another company, under the Englishman John Amory, who occupied the strategically well-placed town of Espalion, refused to sell out.[53]

Such attempts as were made to purchase the evacuation of the companies from the Midi were inevitably short-lived. The subsidies approved for the evacuation of Pont-Saint-Esprit by both the Estates of the Comtat Venaissin and those of the seneschalsy of Beaucaire had proved difficult to recover, and did not address the continuing problem.[54] At the end of June and the beginning of July, to the ravages of the plague and those added by the activities of the Gascon companies, a further menace was occasioned by the forces under Enrique of Trastámara, which threatened to enter the seneschalsy of Carcassonne from Aragon.[55] On 8 July the constable of France had authorized the towns of the seneschalsy of Beaucaire, for a period of six months, to hold assemblies and form leagues against the companies.[56] On 22 September King John had instructed the seneschal of Beaucaire and all other officers and keepers of gates and passages to prevent 'the evildoers of the Great Company' who had 'gone to Lombardy and diverse other countries' from returning into the kingdom.[57] Two days earlier the constable had been recalled from Languedoc and Marshal Audrehem, who had left the province in July, was sent back as captain-general.[58] The problem of the companies, which he somehow had to redress, was exacerbated by the formation of new *routes* following the continuing evacuation of fortresses, now mainly from the English garrisons in Aquitaine, as well as the threat posed by those returning from Italy and Aragon.

Until the end of 1360 Thomas Holland, earl of Kent, had been the main person in charge of the evacuation of fortresses in France garrisoned by the

---

53 For the occupation of Espalion in 1361, see *Docs. Millau*, pp. 122–3, no. 248, and Bourgeois, p. 4. In Rouergue, during the course of that year, the companies had appeared in the faubourgs of Millau, attacked Saint-Affrique, Saint-Rome-de-Tarn, Saint-Léons, the Sévérgais and Vabres, which was besieged in September and October, and taken Rebourguil, Mélac, Villeneuve, Savignac and Bar in addition to Bournac and Espalion (ibid, p. 17).
54 Labande, 1901, pp. 150–64.
55 Molinier, pp. 93–4.
56 AD, Hérault, A 5, fos. 128r–9r.
57 Ibid., fos. 132v–3r.
58 Molinier, pp. 94–5.

English and their allies. Following his death, at the end of December 1360, he was succeeded by Sir John Chandos, who, on 20 January 1361, was appointed 'lieutenant and captain general ... and special conservator' of the peace and truce throughout France, with extensive military as well as judicial powers to evacuate all towns and fortresses held by those in Edward III's obedience which were to be retained by the French.[59] The same day a sergeant-at-arms of the king, Thomas Dautre, was ordered to arrest sixteen ships for his passage to France,[60] and on 18 February he disembarked at Saint-Vaast-La-Hougue with a retinue of thirty-nine men-at-arms and sixty mounted archers.[61] During the next five months Chandos was occupied with carrying out the evacuation of the remaining allied fortresses in Normandy, Anjou, Maine, Touraine and parts of Poitou.[62] It was not an easy task, treating with the captains of castles and fortresses, forcibly expelling those who resisted his orders, providing safe-conducts for the French captains assuming command, and dealing with rebels. As soon as he arrived at La Hougue he found it prudent to increase the strength of his retinue with a further thirty men-at-arms and thirty-six mounted archers.[63] Even after he had returned to his castle of Saint-Sauveur-le-Vicômte in the Cotentin at the end of July, not all of the fortresses had been evacuated and the business of dealing with the companies in Aquitaine had still to be tackled.

During the next eight months Chandos was largely occupied in receiving the major part of the lands, towns and castles in Aquitaine ceded to the English under the terms of the peace.[64] On 29 July he set out for Paris with

---

59 *Foedera*, III, i, p. 555. On 5 February he was given a separate commission empowering him to grant letters of pardon (Carte, *Cat. Rolles françois*, ii, p. 81).
60 *Foedera*, III, i, p. 554.
61 Bardonnet, *Procès-verbal*, pp. 260, 263–4.
62 Ibid., pp. 260–1. Little is known of his activities during this period. He appears to have been in the neighbourhood of Bayeux on 5 March and he returned to Saint-Sauveur-le-Vicômte on 20 July. On the 23rd he received 5,986 écus of 6,000 écus arrears of ransoms due from Robin de Ewes, Dakin de Hestonne and Janekin Wolde for the evacuation of the fortresses of Saint-Vaast and Lingèvres; on the 24th a messenger brought him a letter from Edward III, with instructions for a confidential mission to King John; on the 29th he left Saint-Sauveur for the French court (Delisle, pp. 121–2, PJ no. 94). Another document, apparently from this period, lists the names of fourteen persons who acted as pledges for 9,000 *royaux* due to him in respect of some other evacuation in Lower Normandy (BN, Pièces originales, vol. 669, Chandos, no. 2). Robert atte Euse and Dekyno de Heton are described as captains of Saint-Vaast in Bardonnet, *Procès-verbal*, pp. 258–9; so presumably Wolde was captain of Lingèvres.
63 Bardonnet, *Procès-verbal*, p. 260.
64 A commission to this end was issued to him, Richard de Stafford, seneschal of Gascony, Stephen de Cosington, Nigel Loring, Richard de Totesham, Adam Houghton and William Felton (Bardonnet, *Procès-verbal*, pp. 254–5), but there can be no doubt that Chandos was the chief person involved. Stafford was largely responsible for securing possession of Saintonge, and Houghton the Agenais and Bigorre (see Bardonnet, *Procès-verbal*, pp. 167, 173–4. The procès-verbal of the delivery of territories to Houghton has not been published, but is preserved in the PRO, E 30/1277).

Sir Thomas Chandos, Sir Richard Totesham, Sir John Basset, and his secretary Pierre Pigache to secure the necessary documents for the cession by the French of Poitou, Saintonge and Angoumois, but it soon became clear that there were problems. In an audience with King John on 11 August, the French commissioners tried to hold up the cession of some of the territories in the south pending the evacuation of certain fortresses still occupied by the English and their adherents, notably Barfleur and Graffart in Normandy, La Roche d'Iré (held by a German captain, Raudekin l'Alemant) and Port-Joulain (held by Gerard Gos) in Anjou, and Le Plessis Buret (held by Gerard le Bourguignon) in Maine.[65] This was not inconsistent with the terms of the treaty, but would nevertheless have been a setback for the English commissioners in their attempts to carry out their task within the agreed timetable.

After the transfer of territories began, Chandos had to find ways of having recalcitrant captains forcibly removed from the towns and castles ceded to Edward III. In October 1361, these places included Taillebourg and Tonnay-Charente in Saintonge, which were occupied by captains holding them on behalf of the lord of Caupenne and Pierre de Landiras, and Verteuil in Poitou, where one Peyran de Sault was forced to surrender the castle.[66] During the first week in November, when he was in Thouars, he was informed of the capture of the town of Pirmil, near La Flèche, by the redoubtable captain James Plantin, who, together with the companies assembled at Trèves and Acrivant near Saumur, was making war in Anjou. The French refused to continue further with the transfer of territories until he had been north to deal with the matter.[67] In December he had to assemble an army of 1,000 men to resist a number of Breton companies operating in Limousin, who were rumoured to be intending to impede his work. In the following January, the consuls of Gourdon and Cahors insisted that he undertook to deal with companies of English, Gascons and other pillagers who were ravaging that province before they agreed to transfer their allegiance to Edward III. These included the companies of

---

65 Bardonnet, *Procès*, p. 127. For the names of the captains of these fortresses, see Chaplais, 'Some Documents', p. 19. The 'Renequin Lalemant' here referred to was also captain of Le Biard in Maine. He had previously served in Brittany, where he had taken the castles of Blain and Vielle-Cour, which he held between 1359 and 1361 'ex conquestu suo proprio' (PRO, E 101/174/4 and 175/5), where he is called 'Raudekinus Almaund de Alamania'). Chaplais, 'Some Documents', p. 19, n. 18, suggests that for 'Renequin' one might read 'Henekin'. He may possibly be identified with the German mercenary, Frank Hennequin, alias 'Hennequin le Grant Alemant', whom we know to have been garrisoning Carhaix for John de Montfort in 1369. On this personage see above, p. 11, and below, pp. 45n and 284. Gos was also captain of Huillé in Anjou, and of Ségrie, Vaucé and La Plesse in Maine (Chaplais, 'Some Documents', p. 19).
66 Bardonnet, *Procès-verbal*, pp. 170–1.
67 Ibid., pp. 188–9. Pirmil was retaken by assault by the lord of Craon, who swore to hold it for Edward III. For Plantin, see Venette, *Chronicle*, pp. 122, 294, and *Chron. premiers Valois*, p. 81.

Bertucat d'Albret, who held the fortresses of Fenelon, Masclat and Lamothe on the southern bank of the Dordogne above Gourdon, and of Ayme Duthel, who held Costeroste.[68] In March he successfully negotiated the evacuation of Espalion in Rouergue, held by John Amory, who, as we have seen, had refused to sell out to the French seneschal of Rouergue in the previous November, and who was now replaced by a captain who garrisoned it on behalf of the Gascon lord, the seigneur of Caumont.[69] Thus, from the fortresses transferred to the English officers as well as to the French, the displaced troops either moved on elsewhere or joined up with other companies operating on their own account.

The business of evacuating allied fortresses in France also dragged on into 1362, when the English commissioners requested letters of acquittance, acknowledging receipt of the remaining fortresses. Their French counterparts pointed out that they had not all been handed over by 2 February 1361, as envisaged in the peace treaty. Nor had such places as had been returned been evacuated at the expense of Edward III, and without the payment of heavy ransoms, over and above those agreed. Moreover, many more, they argued, remained to be evacuated.[70] The English responded that the prearranged date for delivery had not been met owing to the death of Thomas Holland at the end of December 1360;[71] that the payments demanded by the captains were not new ransoms, but arrears due to the garrisons; that while the king and his council could not believe that certain other fortresses remained to be evacuated, they would be glad to have details of them and of the damages caused by the troops. The French handed over information concerning the sums paid for the fortresses which had been evacuated, and a list of fortresses still held by captains whose allegiance was said to be to Edward III. In February–March 1362 they included La Roche-Posay (held by the Breton captain the Basquin de Poncet), Chanceaux, Le Châtelier, Lusault and Nouans, and in addition other fortresses which had been taken since the conclusion of the peace. Nevertheless the French were prepared to let the English have their acquittance, in return for one for the territories which they had handed over to Edward III. Thus, by the spring of 1362 the work of evacuating fortresses and transferring territories had largely been completed. As a result, many of the disbanded forces either continued their independent

---

68 Bardonnet, *Procès-verbal*, pp. 203–6, and see the 'Requête de la ville de Cahors' in Moisant, *Prince noir*, pp. 197–8, appendice iii.
69 Bardonnet, *Procès-verbal*, p. 235. For the work of Chandos in Quercy and elsewhere in Rouergue in January–February 1362, see Albe, 'Inventaire', nos. 455–61 (Gourdon); BN, Doat 127, fos. 195r–207r (Moissac); 145, fos. 117r–34r (Millau); 146, fos. 250r–51v (Saint-Antonin); 147, fos. 70r–92v (Villefranche de Rouergue).
70 For this and what follows, see Chaplais, 'Some Documents', pp. 10, 12–13, 15, 17–20, 32, 39–40, 42–5, 47.
71 Holland died on 26 or 28 December 1360 (Chaplais, 'Some Documents', p. 15, n. 1).

life-style, or re-formed into independent companies under new captains, many of them with long experience of the business of war.[72] When operating together they were sufficiently large not only to seize well-defended fortresses and towns, but also to take on major engagements in the field. This became evident within a matter of months and it was to be a continuing saga in the coming years.

---

72 As late as 12 January 1363 Edward III commissioned the count of Tancarville, Chandos and William Felton to seize and punish English captains and their men who were pillaging in France (AN, J 641, no. 15).

3

From Brignais to Launac

After the conclusion of the agreements with Seguin de Badefol, Bérard and Bértucat d'Albret, and Garciot du Castel in September and November 1361, which provisionally liberated Languedoc from their depredations, a large number of the companies had turned their attention northwards. At the beginning of January a company under the command of Elías Machin, who had deserted French service, appeared on the borders of Forez and Auvergne, where they took the castle of Viverols and the fortified priory of Estivareilles.[1] By early March a company under a Savoyard captain, Perrin Bouvetault (alias Perrin Boias, alias Perrin de Savoy) had entered the Auvergne and taken Saugues near Le Puy, while other companies approached from the south-west of Lyon, by way of Montbrison. In the middle of that month they joined up with the troops of Boias before the castles of Rive-de-Gier and Brignais, some twenty and eight miles respectively from Lyon, and attacked and gained control of both of them.[2] More serious, some of the companies which had joined the marquis of Montferrat after the evacuation of Pont-Saint-Esprit had been returning into the kingdom of France since the end of that year, probably through Savoy and in the direction of Lyon.[3] They may have included the *routes* led by Sir John Hawkwood, Sir John Cresswell and Sir Robert Birkhead, of Munde Bataillier and the Gascons Naudon de Bageran and the *bourcs* Camus, Breteuil and Lesparre.[4] Hawkwood had been serving in Italy with a company of English and Germans under the command of Albert Sterz, which, along with others, had blockaded the count of Savoy in the town of

---

1 Guigue, p. 59.
2 Ibid., pp. 61–2. Cf. Molinier, p. 98.
3 Knighton, *Chronicon*, p. 115, specifically refers to the companies returning from Lombardy through Savoy but, like Froissart, was confused about the sequence of events. Cf. Denifle, ii, p. 389, who follows his account.
4 Froissart, *Chroniques*, xii, p. 99, names these captains as being among the forces recruited by the marquis of Montferrat. See also ibid., ix, p. 156.

Lanzo in the Canavese in late October and November 1361, and extracted a ransom of 180,000 florins from him.[5] If he did return to France, he soon rejoined Sterz again in Italy, and the subsequent careers of Cresswell, Birkhead and the others were certainly in France.[6] Other companies controlling the upper Loire valley, which had been preying on the rich merchandise passing through Chalon and Saint-Jean-de-Losne on the river Saône since Christmas, proceeded south to Tournus, between Chalon and Mâcon, besieged but failed to take Charlieu and occupied Marcigny-les-Nonnains on the right bank of the Loire, controlling the river crossing at that point.[7]

The threat posed by this concentration of forces soon became apparent. They might attempt to take Lyon and so control the river traffic passing up and down the Rhône and Saône valleys; they might return north into Burgundy or descend *en masse* once again into Languedoc. The French government seems particularly to have feared a second invasion of Burgundy following the partition of the inheritance of the last duke, Philip de Rouvres, and the claims to the duchy advanced by Charles of Navarre.[8] It was French royal policy to prevent this, to contain the companies and force them to battle in the neighbourhood of Lyon before the contingents returning from Italy through Savoy arrived to join forces with them.

The plan involved the creation of two great commands with the primary goal of eliminating the companies in the provinces most affected by their activities. For central and eastern France and the territories bordering the Saône and Rhône valleys, Jean de Melun, count of Tancarville and chamberlain of France, was appointed lieutenant in the duchy of Burgundy, the counties of Champagne and Brie, the bailiwicks of Sens, Mâcon, Lyon and Saint-Pierre-le-Moutier, the duchies of Berry and Auvergne, the counties of Nevers and Forez and the baronies of Donzy and Beaujeu, with the express mission of engaging the companies. It was Tancarville's task to prevent the first columns from returning northwards, while Marshal Audrehem, who

5 For the Lanzo affair, see Fowler, 1998, p. 138. The full story will be recounted in *Medieval Mercenaries II*. In an agreement between the marquis and the 'magne societatis Anglicorum et Alamanorum', of which Sterz was captain, dated at Rivarolo Canavese on 22 November 1361, Hawkwood is the second named among a list of constables, after Andrew Belmont (Cognasso, pp. 158–60, documenti xvii). None of the other captains said by Froissart to have gone to serve with the marquis is here listed. Of the two German captains, Albert Sterz and Winrich von Fischenich (alias Ourri l'Alemant), whom Froissart names among the captains of the companies formed after Brétigny (*Chroniques*, vi, p. 62), we have no evidence that Sterz returned to France and took part in the battle of Brignais.
6 Froissart's account is here much confused by his having inverted the dates of the capture and evacuation of Pont-Saint-Esprit and the battle of Brignais.
7 Guigue, p. 61; Froissart, *Chroniques*, vi, pp. xxiv–xxv and n. 8. These may have included the other companies mentioned earlier by Froissart, namely of Arnaud de Tallebard, Guiot du Pin, Amanieu d'Ortigue, Guyonnet de Pau, and possibly also those of Bernard and Hortingo de la Salle, Frank Hennequin, Hagre le Scot and Bourdeille *(Chroniques*, vi, p. 62).
8 Delachenal, ii, p. 290. See below, pp. 92–3.

was elevated to a lieutenancy in Languedoc and the neighbouring provinces, was to pursue those companies remaining in the Midi. The two armies were to advance towards each other, working in conjunction.[9] Tancarville immediately set about raising the necessary troops. He convoked the *ban* and the *arrière-ban* of the nobility of Burgundy, Champagne, Sénonais, Auxerrois and Nivernais, and attempted to divide the companies by commissioning Arnaud de Cervole to recruit all the mercenaries he could to resist them.[10] On 24 February he ordered these troops to assemble at Autun on 6 March, concentrated his transport and supplies there, and had arrived on the scene to take up his command by 10 March.[11]

Other forces, assembled by Jacques de Bourbon, count of La Marche, were drawn from the nobility of Auvergne, Limousin, Provence, Savoy, Dauphiné, Forez and Beaujolais.[12] Also, in late February, the towns of the three seneschalsies of Languedoc engaged the Spanish forces of Enrique of Trastámara, the half-brother of King Pedro I of Castile. In early March they joined up with the southern army under Audrehem's command, which had arrived to besiege Saugues on 12 March and was attempting to prevent some contingents of the companies from descending into the seneschalsy of Beaucaire.[13] Meanwhile, the forces assembled at Autun proceeded south across the Mâconnais and Beaujolais to arrive on the outskirts of Lyon before the end of the month. Here they laid siege to Brignais and awaited the forces assembled by Jacques de Bourbon.[14] The junction of the two armies was deemed necessary before any engagement with the companies, and following the capitulation of Saugues on 25 March, Audrehem's forces were free to join up with the main army under Tancarville.[15] However, before this took place, on 6 April 1362, a part of the French royal army suffered a crushing defeat at the hands of the companies at Brignais.

There is no satisfactory contemporary account of the battle of Brignais. Both Froissart and the Florentine chronicler Matteo Villani wrote fairly fully about the engagement, but their accounts are confused and on a number of points contradictory.[16] Not surprisingly, historians have differed

---

9   AN, JJ 93, fo. 124v, no. 301 (letters of King John, appointing Tancarville, dated Beaune, 25 January 1362). See Chérest, pp. 159–60; Guigue, p. 60; Delachenal, ii, p. 319.
10 Chérest, pp. 161–2; Delachenal, ii, p. 319.
11 Chérest, pp. 164–5; Guigue, pp. 65–6.
12 Guigue, p. 64, who lists the main nobles who responded to the summons. Cf. Chérest, p. 161.
13 Molinier, pp. 97–9.
14 Chérest, p. 165. Tancarville appears to have arrived in Lyon ahead of the main army. On 22 March he had ladders and movable shelters for the besieging forces sent from Lyon to Brignais, but was obliged to borrow 5,000 florins from the burgesses to pay his troops (Guigue, p. 66).
15 Chérest, p. 165.
16 Froissart, *Chroniques*, vi, pp. xxiv–xxix, 64–9, 259–65; Villani, *Istorie*, lib. x, cap. xcv, cols. 680–2.

widely in their interpretation of events, and there has been much disagreement as to the site of the battle and the disposition of the different forces involved.[17] Another contemporary account, in the *Thalamus parvus* of Montpellier, merits greater attention, but only relates the bare essentials:

In the year 1362, the enemy having taken and occupied the place of Brignais near Lyon, it was besieged by the count of Tancarville, lieutenant of our lord the king, Jacques de Bourbon, count of La Marche, the count of Forez, the lord of Beaujeu and his brothers, the Archpriest of Velines, the *bailli* of Mâcon and many other great lords, until the 6 April. At nones [around 3.00 p.m.], the enemy, who were before Brignais, and the others who had come from Saugues, together fell upon the besiegers in such a way that they defeated them, so that the counts of La Marche and Forez and the *bailli* of Mâcon were wounded and died a few days later from their wounds, and the aforesaid other great lords were taken prisoner.[18]

The little town of Brignais, situated in a plain surrounded by hills at the entrance to the Garon valley, a tributary of the Rhône, in some senses served as an advance post for Lyon from the south-west.[19] In the fourteenth century it was well-enough defended by a castle, a double line of walls surmounted by two towers, a moat, which was filled with water from the Garon, and a third tower or barbican which defended a bridge situated before the castle. As early as 1360 the castle had been taken for a short while by the companies, who used it as a base to menace Lyon. In response to this particular threat the town of Lyon, which lay partly within the kingdom of France and partly in the Empire, had hastily completed its defensive system with a second line of walls, known as *La Retraite*, begun in 1347, on the heights of Saint-Just, which adjoined the walled quarters situated to the north-west of the Saône. The town was consequently better prepared when Brignais was again taken by the companies in March 1362. At the end of January the new fortifications had been inspected by the lieutenant of the *bailli* of Mâcon, and it was doubtless as a result of his report and the deteriorating military situation that measures were taken to improve them. Following the capture of Brignais in March, the town was put on full alert. The *bailli* himself arrived to supervise the defence, the garrison was reinforced with men-at-arms, artillery and artillerers, and the town lanterns were kept burning throughout the night. For his part, the governor of Dauphiné saw that every attention was given to ensure the defence of the crossings (*ports et passages*) along the Rhône and other rivers.

17 The principal secondary accounts, in order of publication, are: Allut (1859), pp. 189–270; Chérest (1879), pp. 166–85; Guigue (1886), pp. 69–78; Mollière (1894), pp. 1–69.
18 *Thalamus parvus*, p. 360.
19 For this and what follows, see Mollière, pp. 17–20, 41; Guigue, pp. 60, 62, 179, 183; 'Compte Louppy', pp. 17–19, no. 62.

There seems to be little doubt that Jacques de Bourbon's immediate objective was to take Brignais, and that his forces were surprised by the companies while the siege was in progress. Villani says that it was the capture of Brignais by Elías Machin that determined King John to launch the expedition, and that the commencement of the siege while the *routier* captain was out raiding in Forez occasioned the companies to engage the royal forces:

In March, the king of France, affronted by the company of Petit Meschin of Auvergne, his fugitive little servant, notwithstanding that he had engaged the Spanish Company [i.e. of Enrique of Trastámara], which had not yet arrived in Burgundy, hastily assembled an army of around 6,000 cavalry, of French, Germans and others then in France, and having given command of it to Jacques de Bourbon, a prince of the blood, he sent him into Bourbonnais with 4,000 sergeants. At this time the company of Petit Meschin had taken one of the king's castles, called Brignais, and having garrisoned it with 300 men from his company, he raided the county of Forez with 3,000 *barbute* and 2,000 *masnadieri*, the major part Italians of his company. Meanwhile, Jacques de Bourbon arrived with his army, camped near Brignais, and believing he would rapidly secure it, besieged the place fearlessly. But, having nothing but contempt for his adversary, he took no proper precautions and was not on his guard. Petit Meschin, who was experienced in matters of war and captain of a well-organized company which was spoiling for a fight, was a day and a half from Brignais. Having been informed of the disorder in the French camp, with the agreement of his company and tempted by the prospect of considerable booty, he hurriedly retraced his steps and, taking a short cut, arrived unexpectedly above the French camp several hours before daybreak and without any let-up attacked them with great noise and clamour. Taken by surprise, and frightened by the terrible cries, the French lost heart and although they ran for their arms to repulse the enemy, the companies already pressed so hard upon them that they gave them no time to arm themselves. An army which included so many barons and valiant knights thus had the misfortune to be routed and put to flight, and many were killed and wounded. Those who were able to mount their horses and don their armour nearly all fell into the hands of that vassal of the king of France, Petit Meschin . . . So great was the value of the ransoms and booty that all the company became rich. Their victory made them so confident and daring that the court of Rome, which had experience of being fleeced by the companies, feared that it would see them arrive at Avignon.[20]

The points of agreement between this account and that of Froissart are few. Like Villani, Froissart placed the command of the French army with Jacques de Bourbon rather than with the count of Tancarville. He also attributed the decision to engage the companies to the capture of Brignais and, implicitly, the raids in Forez, of which Bourbon was governor for his

---

20 Villani, *Istorie*, lib. x, cap. xcv, cols. 680–1.

nephew. But there agreement ends. Villani reveals his penchant for surprise attacks by the companies and insists upon the unpreparedness – the *sprovvedutezza* – of their opponents. For Froissart, this was a set-piece battle with considerable similarities to the battles of Crécy and Poitiers rather than a surprise engagement. There was even time for Bourbon to dub several new knights: his son, Pierre de Bourbon, his nephew, the young count of Forez, and the lords of Villars and Roussillon, who were all made knights-banneret, and the lords of Montélimar and Grôlée from Dauphiné. He gives no particular prominence to Petit Meschin, or to the 'Italians' in his service – presumably men drawn from the companies previously operating in Italy. From his account it would appear that Seguin de Badefol, with 2,000 troops under his immediate command, was in charge of the companies, which he estimated to total between 15,000 and 16,000 combatants. In a later book of his chronicles he gives particular importance to the part played by John Hawkwood, Robert Birkhead and John Cresswell.[21] He implies that some twenty other captains of the Great Companies who came into prominence in the 1360s were present on this occasion, of whom five were certainly party to a subsequent agreement concluded with ten captains of the companies at Clermont in July: Garciot du Castel, the *bourc* de Breteuil, Menaud de Villers, alias Espiote, Elías Machin and an esquire of the count of Foix, Arnaud de Tallebard.[22] According to Villani the two armies were about equally matched, with around 6,000 cavalry in each – a more likely figure than Froissart's 15,000–16,000.

However, Froissart is the only one of the three chroniclers to give some account of the course of the battle and the terrain upon which it was fought, and the most exhaustive study of the battlefield and the country around Brignais appears to bear him out.[23] From his account it would appear that the companies divided their forces into two battles, which were placed on high ground above the French camp. The first of these – some 5,000 to 6,000 badly armed troops – took up their position on the slopes of a wooded hill, situated at the foot of the Barolles hills before Brignais, and known as Goyet wood. The second, which contained their most experienced and best-equipped troops under the command of the élite among the captains of the companies – Seguin de Badefol, Petit Meschin, Naudon de Bageran, the *bourc* Camus, Espiote, Munde Bataillier, the *bourc* of Lesparre, Lamit, Guiot du Pin, the *bourc* of Breteuil and several others – were placed behind Goyet wood in the hollows of another area of

21 *Chroniques*, ix, p. 156.
22 The other captains of the companies mentioned in the treaty of Clermont were John Amory, who heads the list, Bérard d'Albret, Bertuquin, Pierre de Montaut and Johann Hazenorgue (see below, p. 56). For Tallebard's origins see Desplat, p. 34, and Lettenhove in Froissart, *Oeuvres*, xxiii, p. 179.
23 Mollière, especially pp. 30–64.

high ground known as Mont-Rond. Allowing the French scouts to observe their advance-guard at close hand, the intention of the companies was evidently to mislead the enemy into underestimating the opposition they would face and so encourage them to launch an attack, as at Crécy and Poitiers, without being sufficiently informed about the disposition of the companies. This was carried out by Arnaud de Cervole, who had command of the French advance-guard, which was made up of 1,500 combatants, and apparently against his advice.[24]

For their part, the companies assembled their forces in a semi-circular formation on the slopes of Goyet wood and the neighbouring heights, which gave them an excellent view of the positions the French had taken up in the plain of Basses-Barolles and Mont-Rond. The French assaulted the companies on the Goyet slopes, but both the advance-guard under the Archpriest and the main battle commanded by Jacques de Bourbon were repulsed with heavy losses to the royal forces. From their elevated positions the companies were able to hurl stones at their assailants, dinting their basinets and either killing or wounding some of them. At this critical juncture the second, more professional battle of the companies, until then concealed, after skirting the hill of Goyet surprised the right flank of the French lines, wielding newly cut makeshift lances of around six feet in length, and attacked them so vigorously that they were put to flight.

When we piece together the essentials of this account with those of Villani and the *Thalamus parvus*, and take into consideration the features of the landscape around Brignais, a plausible sequence of events can be reconstructed. On leaving Lyon the forces commanded by Jacques de Bourbon arrived outside Brignais before the end of March (probably around the 22nd and by the road which in the fourteenth century passed by the bridge of Baunan), and set up camp before the town at the south-western end of the plain of Basses-Barolles, a position which they still occupied on the night of 5 April.[25] Informed of the plight of the defenders the companies under Petit Meschin, who had ridden out to plunder, hastened to join up with those which had evacuated Saugues and, having concentrated their forces, approached Brignais, probably from the heights which dominated the plain to the south-east. Under the cover of night they occupied all of the hills which surrounded the plain, thus encircling the

24 Froissart, *Chroniques*, vi, p. 68.
25 The two roads which, in the fourteenth century, led from Lyon to Brignais followed different routes from the existing roads. The first, leaving Lyon by the Saint-Irenée gate, followed the heights of Sainte-Foy, descended to the bridge of Baunan, crossed the little river of Izeron and rejoined the road which then, as today, led from Francheville to Brignais. The second, which left from la Quarantaine, passed by Fortanières, below Sainte-Foy, to the old bridge of Ouillins, and continued from there a little to the right of the present road as far as Saint-Genis-Laval, and proceeded from there to Brignais, at the foot of the Barolles (Mollière, p. 41).

royal army. The greater part of their forces took up position on and behind the hill of Goyet wood, and it was at this point that the battle commenced. During the morning of 6 April, when the French army detected the forward positions taken up by the enemy, they turned their back on Brignais and prepared to attack them. The companies then attacked the flank of the main French battle, whereupon the garrison of Brignais also went onto the offensive and fell on the rear of the French army. Those who tried to escape by the only line of retreat – the road which led to Baunan on the side of the Barolles – were tracked down and slaughtered in the neighbouring plain of Aiguiers.

The battle of Brignais thus had many features in common with that of Poitiers, in which some of the captains of the companies may have served with the Black Prince. It was a set-piece battle on a plain – the plain of Basses-Barolles – as that of Poitiers had been fought on the plain of Maupertuis. On both occasions the French command was divided and their forces imprudent enough to launch an attack on a well-disciplined army holding a strong position. If the rôle of the stone-throwers at Brignais was only a pale imitation of that of the archers at Poitiers, nevertheless the principal reason for the success of the companies in 1362 was the deployment of the major part of their army from behind the hill of Goyet at a critical juncture. The two battles were also alike in the rich haul of prisoners taken by the victors. At Brignais they included: Jean de Melun, count of Tancarville, whose part in the battle remains a mystery, but who was certainly taken prisoner and ransomed; the Archpriest, taken by his compatriot from Périgord, the bastard of Monsac; Jean, count of Saarbrück; the vicômte of Uzès; Robert and Louis de Beaujeu; Jean and Louis de Chalon; Renaud de Forez; the lords of Roussillon, Chalançon and Solière; Guillaume de Melun and Jeannin de Boves, chamberlain and pantler respectively of the Dauphin; Gérard de Thurey, marshal of Burgundy; Jean de Grôlée, *bailli* of Mâcon and seneschal of Lyon; and the best part of a hundred other knights, who included Humbert d'Albon, Pierre Verdet, Barthélemy de la Maldière together with his brother Jean, esquire, and Guillaume de Beausamblant. The total number of dead and wounded is not known, but it must have been large. Among the nobility we may note Jacques de Bourbon, count of La Marche, and his son, Pierre de Bourbon, who sustained several mortal wounds and who, along with other wounded, were taken to Lyon, where they died a few days later; Louis, count of Forez, Jean de Noyers, count of Joigny, the lord of Montmorillon, and perhaps also the lord of Tournon, who all died on the battlefield.[26]

26 The fullest lists of those taken prisoner or who died are to be found in Froissart, *Chroniques*, vi, pp. xxvii–xxviii, 69, 263, 265, and Guigue, pp. 72–6. Froissart was not clear as to whether the lord of Tournon was taken prisoner or killed. According to the *Thalamus parvus*, p. 360, Jean de Grôlée died a few days later from his wounds. Villani, *Istorie*, lib. x,

The body of Louis of Forez was buried in the cathedral of Lyon, in the chapter of Mary Magdalen. Following their deaths in Lyon, those of Jacques de Bourbon and his son were provisionally buried in the convent of the Jacobins. In 1395 they were exhumed and removed to be interred in their final resting place at Vendôme.

In addition to dealing with the casualties of war the citizens of Lyon set about securing money and men-at-arms for their defence. Four separate *tailles* were imposed, which brought in just over 14,285 florins. Marshal Audrehem, who arrived in the town on 9 April, took charge of the defence and posted artillerers and such infantry as were available at the most vulnerable point of the town walls, at Saint-Just. By 22 April he had been joined by some of his men-at-arms. Further troops were recruited by his officers for the defence of the town and a number of scouts were engaged to keep a close watch on the enemy's movements. By the end of April, Lyon was too strongly defended for the companies to risk an attack.[27] During the week that followed the battle both victors and captives were preoccupied with the business of ransoms. The more notable of the prisoners, having negotiated with their captors, were released on parole. Audrehem acted as guarantor of the Archpriest's ransom, which appears to have amounted to at least 100,000 florins, of which King John paid a large part, if not the whole.[28] The count of Tancarville had secured his liberty by 13 April, by which date, with royal approval and the help of Audrehem, he had negotiated an agreement whereby the companies were to leave the realm (evidently in return for a substantial sum of money), and pending the execution of which a truce was concluded with them until 26 May.[29] This arrangement appears to have been only a preliminary to further discussions, and the task of working out the definitive treaty was given to Audrehem. For his part Innocent VI, understandably alarmed by the victory of the companies, charged Cardinal Guy de Boulogne to join his efforts to those of the royal negotiators.[30] In the absence of a supreme commander

---

cap. xcv, col. 681, erroneously states that Marshal Audrehem was taken prisoner, and also adds Brocard de Fénétrange, who he says was a German and captain of 400 *barbute* (he came from Lorraine: Delachenal, ii, p. 41), Amelin des Baux and the count of Cluny to the list. Villani also makes special mention of the fact that the vanquished were allowed to remove the dead and wounded from the battlefield. Guigue confuses Froissart's lists in respect of Renaud de Forez, uncle to the young count Louis, and the lord of Montmorillon, who were killed, not taken, but adds several other names not given by the chronicler, together with much valuable information with regard to the prisoners and their ransoms and those who were killed or wounded.

27 Guigue, pp. 78–80.
28 Luce, in Froissart, *Chroniques*, vi, p. xxvii, n. 3.
29 Letter from Tancarville to the *baillis* of Chalon, Autun and La Montagne, dated 13 April 1362 (BN, coll. Bourgogne, xxi, fo. 4v; see Vernier, p. 232). The truce is also referred to in the accounts of Dimanche de Vitel, receiver-general of the duchy of Burgundy (AD, Côte-d'Or, B 1412, fo. 53r; see Chérest, p. 189 and n. 1).
30 Chérest, p. 189.

of the companies, the main problem which they faced was in getting all of the captains of the different contingents or *routes* of which they were composed to agree to an arrangement. After the battle there were too many of them concentrated in the neighbourhood of Lyon for them to remain there for any length of time, and the majority dispersed fairly speedily. Some detachments made for Vivarais and Forez, others for Burgundy, in particular the territory situated between the rivers Saône and Loire.[31] On 14 April Henri de Bar, governor of Burgundy, instructed the *baillis* of the duchy that 'because of the events at Brignais, and because the enemies are riding out with the intention of entering the duchy of Burgundy', they were to 'bring everything in the open country into the fortresses and destroy all bakehouses, mills and fortresses that cannot be defended'.[32] On 28 April, Tancarville sent Guillaume d'Aigremont from Dijon to La Ferté-sur-Grosne, with its rich abbey, 'to the companies who have arrived there, to find out if they intend to recognize the truce concluded ... until 26 May, and to accompany them out of the duchy'.[33]

The difficulties in Burgundy were compounded by the arrival of numerous Breton companies in addition to the Great Companies. Both Tancarville and the governor of Burgundy did what they could to negotiate their departure. At the end of April the governor sent a Burgundian knight, Jean de Chardoigne, from Dijon, to speak with the Bretons at La Borde-au-Château, near Beaune, and Reulée and Fontaine near Chalon. On 11 May a messenger was sent to the captain of another company called Lyon de Vaulx 'to speak with him about a certain treaty for the evacuation of Burgundy by the Bretons and to bring him to Dijon to speak to the said governor'. De Vaulx, accompanied by an escort of some twenty-four mounted men, duly came to Dijon, where he was lodged for three days at ducal expense whilst he discussed with the governor the conditions of a treaty 'by which he and his other Breton captains are to evacuate Burgundy'. Several other Breton captains agreed to enter Burgundian service. One of them, Henri Spic, was appointed captain of Pontailler-sur-Saône; but this was so unpopular with the inhabitants that they first of all refused him and his Bretons entry and then succeeded in having them removed.[34]

This initial attempt to prevent the companies from carrying out their usual depredations in Burgundy was only partially successful and, after the truce ran out on 28 May, during the course of June and July the duchy was invaded and ravaged from all sides. A *route* from the county of Burgundy under Hughues de Cromary and a pillager called Jean de Bolandoz, alias

---

31 Guigue, pp. 81–3.
32 AD, Côte-d'Or, B 1412, fo. 40r. See Chérest, p. 193, and Vernier, p. 233 n. 4.
33 AD, Côte-d'Or, B 1412, fo. 53r. See Chérest, p. 189, n. 1, and Vernier, p. 234 n. 1.
34 Chérest, pp. 193–4. For the company of Lyon de Vaulx or de Val, see, in addition, Luce, *Du Guesclin*, pp. 339, 594.

Brisbarre, crossed the Saône and ransomed Pontailler, to be followed shortly afterwards by 'the Great Company of the English', 'the Bretons' and 'the men of the Archpriest'. Around the same time several houses were burned by 'the Great Companies' at Saint-Jean-de-Losne, and on 3 July there was a new alert at Pontailler following news of 'the Great Companies and the Bretons who are in the country'. The country around Guillon was raided on several occasions: at Montréal the captain was obliged to increase the number of crossbowmen in his garrison when 'the Great Company' was in the neighbourhood, but the town was taken by a company of Bretons from the Auxerrois. Rumours of treasonable acts were rife, and frequently not unfounded. Even the roads out of Dijon were intercepted by robbers, and the *bailli* of Auxois, who had been summoned there by the governor and his council on 27 June, was obliged to stay on for five days 'because the enemy were in the country, as a result of which he did not dare to travel'.[35]

In Languedoc some protection had been afforded to the three seneschalsies by the employment of the forces of Enrique of Trastámara, the bastard son of Alfonso XI of Castile and half-brother to Pedro I, with whom Enrique contested the Castilian throne. In the summer of 1361 he had been obliged to seek refuge in France following a temporary interruption of hostilities between Pedro I and Peter IV of Aragon (Pere III of Catalonia), mediated by Cardinal Guy de Boulogne in May. In the bitter war between Castile and Aragon, which had been going on since 1356, Enrique had been fighting on the Aragonese side and had become a vassal of Pere. One of the conditions of the peace concluded in May was that Pere would withdraw his protection of Enrique and his brothers Don Tello and Don Sancho, who were to be expelled from Aragon together with other Castilian knights and esquires in their service there.[36] In July they had crossed the Pyrenees and entered France by way of the seneschalsy of Carcassonne, despite the efforts of Pierre de Voissins, lord of Rennes-les-Bains, to prevent their passage through the frontier country of Fenouillèdes.[37] There they may have offered their services to Marshal Audrehem, but until the end of February they were employed, probably on their own account, in Provence.[38] At the end of that month they returned into France and were posted on the frontier of the seneschalsy of Beaucaire and Auvergne, with the

---

35 For the above, see Vernier, pp. 233–5, and Chérest, p. 195.
36 This was the peace of Deza, ratified by Pedro I on 13 May 1361 and by Peter IV on the 14th (Pere III, *Chronicle*, ii, 531, n. 1; Ayala, *Crónica*, i, pp. 511–12). For the general situation, see Russell, p. 3, and Delachenal, iii, pp. 256, 259–60.
37 Ayala, *Crónica*, i, p. 511 and n. 5.
38 The editor of Ayala, *Crónica*, p. 511, n. 5, believed that an agreement was concluded with Audrehem whereby Enrique and his Castilians were to serve against the companies from September. I have found no evidence of their service in Languedoc, whereas there is clear testimony to their involvement in Provence (see above, p. 5, and below, p. 55 n. 39).

special task of preventing the companies then in Auvergne and Burgundy from entering the three seneschalsies of Languedoc, whose inhabitants were to pay for their services at the rate of 10,000 florins a month.[39] During the course of March Audrehem had deployed them before Saugues, which had been taken by Perrin Boias.[40]

After the victory of the companies at Brignais, Trastámara's task became that much more pressing. There was daily fear that the companies would descend into the seneschalsy of Beaucaire. At Nîmes the consuls mounted watch on the walls of the *Tour Magne*, and in expectation of their arrival Trastámara and his Castilain forces arrived there in the middle of May.[41] In anticipation of the expiry of the truce concluded with the companies on 26 May, Audrehem had called a meeting of the estates of the three seneschalsies in Montpellier on the 28th, when he secured a grant of 60,000 gold francs a year to meet the costs of defence.[42] Then, on 3 June, came the first real break in fortune, when Enrique and around 400 Castilians under his command, having returned to the northern frontier, surprised a company some three times their size under the command of the *bourc* de Breteuil and completely defeated it before Montpensier, near Riom in Auvergne, killing some 600 men and taking 200 prisoner.[43]

This may have done something to persuade the companies to resume negotiations for an evacuation agreement along the lines envisaged during the overtures at Lyon in April; but the renewal of the war betwen Aragon and Castile was probably a more important factor, since it would appear that the king of Aragon had once again sought Enrique's assistance.[44] Whilst at Perpignan on 17 June, Peter IV had heard of the arrival of Pedro I and his forces under the walls of Calatayud. According to the Castilian chronicler, Lopez de Ayala, it was at this juncture that the Aragonese king

---

39 *Thalamus parvus*, p. 360; *HGL*, ix, pp. 736–7. Cf. Monicat, p. 22, and Molinier, pp. 97, 99 n. 5. Both Ayala, *Crónica*, i, p. 522, and the *Thalamus parvus*, p. 360, are clear about their service in Provence, and the latter chronicle makes it evident that they returned into France from across the Rhône in February. (Ayala comments: 'É el Rey de Aragon ... non podia allegar compañas; pero avia enviado á la Provenza, do andaban el Conde Don Enrique, Don Tello é Don Sancho sus hermanos, é muchos Caballeros de Castilla con ellos ... e por mantener facian guerra en aquella tierra de Provenza'. The *Thalamus parvus* observes: 'Item, aquel an meteys, a xxii jorns del mes de febrier, los Espanhols passeron lo Rozer de Prohensa en lo reyne de Fransa, e pueys esteron continuamens a las frontieyras de la senescalcia de Belcayre a l'intrar dAlvernhe.'). Henneman, ii, p. 174, misunderstood the latter passage, and believed that Enrique and his Castilians entered France from Aragon in February 1362.
40 Molinier, p. 99 and n. 5.
41 Ménard, preuves, ii, pp. 243, 244 and *passim*; Molinier, p. 106.
42 Molinier, p. 104. The grant was made on the proviso that the *impôts* for John's ransom were dropped.
43 *Thalamus parvus*, pp. 360–1. Molinier, p. 107, attributes the victory to Audrehem, although there is no evidence that he was even present.
44 Delachenal, iii, p. 260.

raised the possibility of an intervention on his behalf by Trastámara and such of the companies as he was able to recruit.[45] In the negotiations which ensued, Enrique offered not only the services of himself and his brothers, together with the Castilian forces then in France, at a cost of 40,000 florins, but also the services of 3,000 lances of the Great Companies for a further 100,000 florins, of which half were to be paid in advance and the remainder within one month. Pere's council did not see how this amount of money could be secured in so short a time, and proposed what they considered to be a more realistic figure of 60,000 florins a month (on the basis of 20 florins per lance) for the remuneration of the Great Companies, although they were worried that the companies contained so many 'rebels' among the number.[46]

During June and July, while the negotiations with Peter IV's council were proceeding, Audrehem and Enrique were holding discussions with the companies at Clermont in Auvergne, which, after a last-minute breakdown had finally been avoided, resulted in a definitive treaty of 23 July.[47] This was concluded with most, but not all, of the captains of the companies who had been operating in southern France, of whom the following are named: John Amory, Garciot du Castel, the *bourc* de Breteuil, Bérard d'Albret, Menaud de Villers, alias Espiote, Bertuquin, Pierre de Montaut, Johann Hazenorgue, Petit Meschin and Arnaud de Tallebard. By its terms the companies undertook to enter Trastámaran service in return for 100,000 gold florins – a sum evidently in addition to that which Enrique had proposed to Pere[48] – to be paid to them before 8 September and within a day's march of the French frontier. They were to swear fealty and homage to their new employer, to leave France for good within six weeks, and never to return except in the eventuality of a recommencement of war between the kings of England and France or between the counts of

---

45 Ayala, *Crónica*, i, pp. 520, 522. See Delachenal, iii, p. 260 n. 3.
46 ACA, Cartas Reales, Pere III, 50/6178, fos. 1r, 2r–v. For the value of the Aragonese florin, see Fowler, 1992, p. 223 n. 25, and see my 'Note on Money', below, p. 307.
47 The text of the treaty, dated Clermont, 23 July 1362, is to be found in AN, P2294, fo. 359 (Mémorial D de la Chambre des Comptes, fo. 49; vidimus de la Chambre des Comptes, Paris, 2 August 1362) and was published by Hay du Châtelet, preuves, pp. 313–15. Chérest, p. 180, believed this to be a defective copy. It was concluded between Audrehem, Enrique, the bishop of Clermont, the count of Boulogne, the sire de Montagu, the sire de la Tour, Robert de Lorris and the governor of Montpellier, on the one hand, and, on the other, 'les capitaines des compaignies estant au royaume de France de par de ça [in Hay du Châtelet "de Paris en çà"] et tous les gens d'armes de leurs compaignies', and is analysed most fully by Molinier, pp. 107–9. Cf. Guigue, p. 86; Cherest, p. 190. Two days earlier, on 21 July, Audrehem had informed the seneschals of Beaucaire, Carcassonne and Toulouse from Clermont that all the companies planned to invade Languedoc, but that he and Trastámara would pursue them. He therefore instructed them to see that all victuals were immediately taken to fortified places (Molinier, p. 107, and PJ no. xxxv).
48 The sum agreed at Clermont was to be raised from the towns of Auvergne, Mâconnais and Languedoc (Henneman, ii, pp. 176–7).

Armagnac and Foix. In leaving the realm they were not to stay more than six days in any one place and not to demand anything of the inhabitants of the places they passed through, save for food for themselves and provender for their horses. In the event of war being renewed in France, Audrehem and Trastámara undertook to lead the companies into Guyenne, if they so requested it. Any ransoms still outstanding to them were to be paid, providing that they put in their claims to Audrehem within ten days. For their past misdemeanours they were to secure a pardon from the king of France, and every effort would be made to secure like pardons for them from the king of England and the pope. As a guarantee of these terms both Audrehem and the contracting captains agreed to hand over hostages to Trastámara, the contracting captains and their hostages swore to abide by the terms of the treaty, and the captains themselves undertook to hand over any of their companions who attempted to violate any of its clauses. In the event of such violation the hostages for the companies were to be handed over to the king of France, but if the king of France broke the treaty, both Trastámara and Audrehem undertook not to take up arms against them. A final clause allowed the companies the right to secure the release of any of their companions held prisoner by the count of Armagnac.

News of the treaty spread rapidly through Languedoc. On 29 July one of Audrehem's esquires, Enguerrand, delivered letters with the news to the consuls of Nîmes, where processions were held, the inhabitants believing themselves delivered from the companies.[49] But the treaty still had to be approved by King John and implemented by the contracting captains. To this end Audrehem and Trastámara went to Paris, where the treaty was ratified on 13 August and supplementary letters drawn up by which Enrique confirmed his undertaking to take the companies who were party to the treaty of Clermont out of the realm, to whom were now added the Archpriest and his men. He also did homage to John and undertook to see that his brother, Sancho, and all the other barons in his service exiled from Castile who were to accompany him, would also do homage to the king and serve him against all who opposed him. In return, John undertook to grant him properties with an annual value of 10,000 *livres*, to be enjoyed during the lifetimes of himself, his wife and eldest son. If he and his companions were unable to accomplish their projects and were obliged to return to France, the king would provide them with the necesary means of existence, in default of which they could 'seek their livelihood wherever they pleased', provided this did not contravene the homage which Enrique had done to the king, and which Don Sancho and the other barons were to do to Audrehem, acting for John, on pain of the annulment of the treaty concluded between them. During the following spring a number of towns

---

49 Ménard, ii, preuves, p. 245; Molinier, p. 109.

and castles to the north-west of Béziers were handed over to Enrique in part realization of his annuity, all the other conditions relating to the treaty having been completed.[50]

Throughout these negotiations, the main persons acting for the companies appear to have been the Pyrenean captain Garciot du Castel and one of his lieutenants, Garciot du Nassi. It was largely as a result of their work, in persuading the principal captains to agree to the terms concluded at Clermont and going to Paris to negotiate acceptable arrangements for their implementation, that the companies had been brought on board, and it was to Castel that the 100,000 gold florins were ultimately paid for distribution to the companies.[51] By the 21 August he was back in the Midi, and lodged in Nîmes at an inn called *Les Deux Pommes*.[52] The town clearly played an important part in the implementation of the treaty, in large measure because of the presence of royal and Trastámaran officers there, and also Enrique's wife. On 2 August the hostages provided by the companies as guarantors of the treaty had been brought to the town under Spanish escort. On the 16th the *bourc* of Breteuil arrived and had a meeting in the church of the Preaching Friars with a number of the consuls of the town and some of the king's officers in Languedoc including, it would seem, the treasurer of France, Pierre Scatisse. Before he left, he was obliged to swear an oath, in the presence of all of these persons and that of the captain of the town, Enrique's treasurer and procurator-general, and the countess of Trastámara that he and his men would in no way damage the citizens of Nîmes, a wise precaution in view of subsequent events.[53]

During Audrehem's absence in Paris the count of Tancarville had been acting as lieutenant in Languedoc, but this appointment was only temporary. On 13 August the marshal's powers were renewed and by the end of that month he and Trastámara were back in the south.[54] For their part, the captains who had agreed to the treaty of Clermont began to implement their part of the bargain. After making their way south by the Rhône valley and the neighbourhood of Villeneuve-les-Avignon, the *Thalamus parvus* of Montpellier recorded the passage through the neighbourhood of that town during the last week of August of all of the captains who had agreed to the treaty save Bérard d'Albret (who probably took a different route from

---

50 AN, J 603, no. 58 (original of the supplementary letters of 13 July); P 2294, fo. 379 (vidimus in Mémorial D of the Chambre de Comptes, fo. 50v); Hay du Châtelet, pp. 315–16; Molinier, pp. 110–12. Russell, p. 3 n. 1, following Paz, *Documentos existentes en los archivos nacionales de Paris*, no. 329, believed Enrique's homage to have taken place a year earlier, on 13 August 1361.
51 Luce in Froissart, *Chroniques*, vi, p. xxiii n. 3.
52 Ménard, preuves, p. 246; Molinier, p. 113.
53 Ménard, p. 238, and preuves, pp. 245–6.
54 For this and what follows see Molinier, pp. 112–15; *Thalamus parvus*, p. 361; Henneman, ii, pp. 176–7.

Gascony) and Arnaud de Tallebard, but including another captain of the companies, Perrin Boias. The lure of gold coins on the frontier had proved irresistible, but they proved difficult to collect at short notice. The money was to be raised through a tax of a florin per hearth in walled towns and a half florin in unwalled towns and country villages, and this was not forthcoming by the appointed date (8 September). The burden of the tax fell on the inhabitants of those regions of France whose population had already been decimated by warfare, famine and two epidemics of the plague, and who were also expected to contribute heavily to the ransom of the king. Moreover the assessments were based on old lists of hearths, many of which no longer existed. Audrehem did everything he could to speed up the payment and keep the treaty intact, but when he and Enrique arrived in Nîmes in early September they found that the payments were seriously behind schedule. On the 10th of that month Audrehem wrote to the royal officers in Languedoc 'if one doesn't make haste the treaty will be broken and the consequences irreparable'. When they moved on to join the companies in mid-September, some of Enrique's Castilian forces stayed behind, living off the countryside and harrying the citizens of Nîmes, who were once again obliged to live in conditions approaching a state of siege.

The point of concentration of the companies was Pamiers in the county of Foix, and it was around this town and that of Mazères that they camped – both within a day's march of the Aragonese frontier and where the 100,000 florins were to be handed over to them. In an effort to ensure the implementation of the treaty Audrehem requested the count of Foix to do all he could to persuade the companies to leave the kingdom, and went personally to Pamiers to entreat them not to turn back north. The difficulty remained in getting the money together. Before his death Innocent VI made a contribution, and some money may have been extorted from the Jews. The consuls of Nîmes were permitted to negotiate a loan of 500 florins to pay their share. Other towns also had difficulties in raising the money, and it proved necessary to divert funds from the tax collected for the king's ransom. It was not until the middle of November that Pierre Scatisse, accompanied by the seneschal of Carcassonne and a bodyguard of sixty men-at-arms, arrived in Pamiers with the money, which was made over to Garciot du Castel in two payments: one of 90,000 florins and the other of 10,000. By then the companies, without employ and tired of waiting, had begun to break up. Some of them – certainly those of the *bourc* de Breteuil and Bertuquin – had already retraced their steps into the seneschalsy of Beaucaire by the end of October, and for them as for others new prospects were in store.[55]

Several factors led to the failure of the companies to leave France. From

---

55 For this paragraph, see Molinier, pp. 115, 118–20, and Henneman, ii, pp. 176–7.

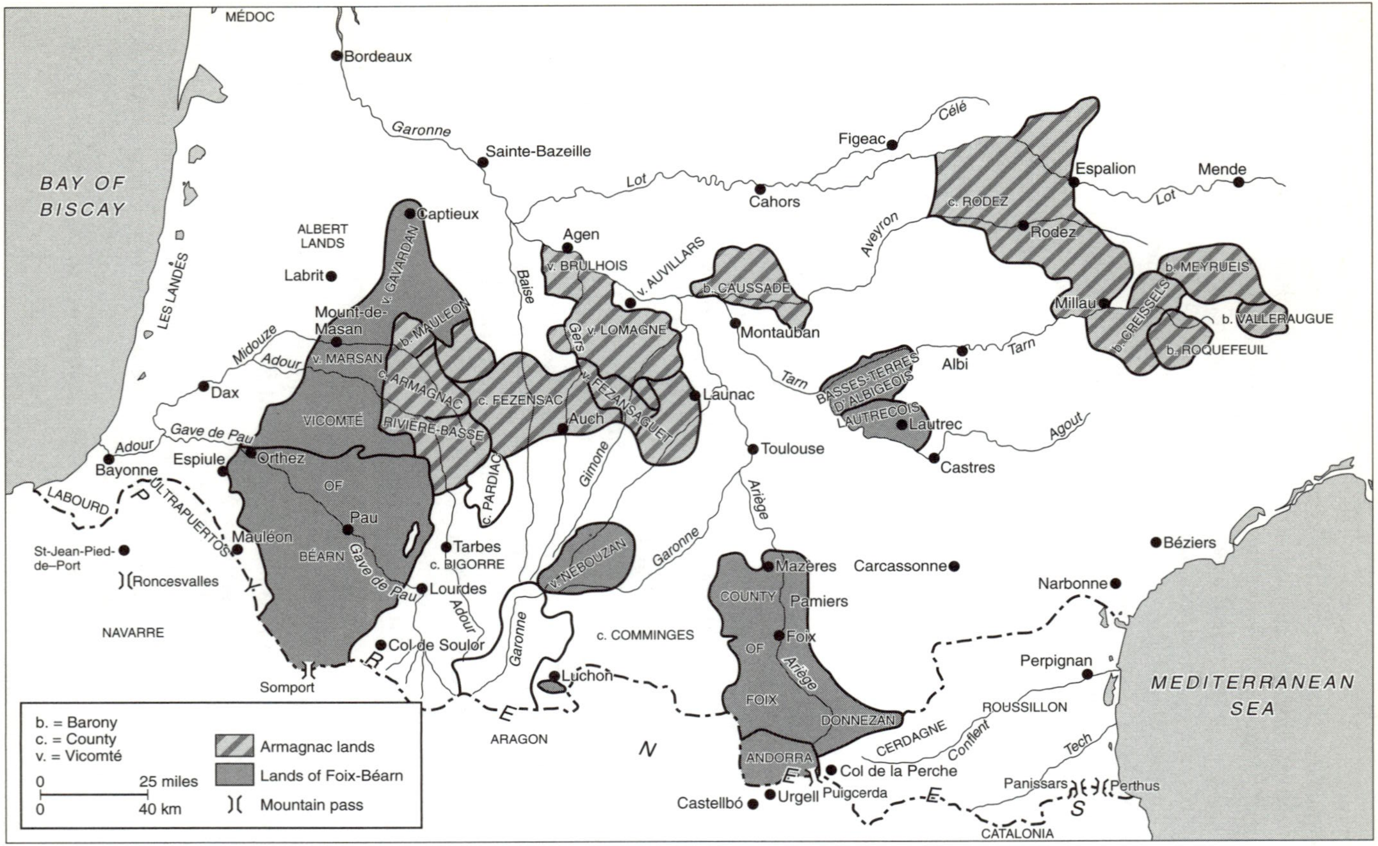

3 The lands of the houses of Armagnac and Foix-Béarn at the time of the battle of Launac, 1362

the outset the timetable envisaged in the treaty was too tight: the six weeks allowed for the collection of the money was insufficient, and the *fouage* imposed to raise it was still being collected in 1365. Secondly, the whole plan presupposed the cooperation of Peter IV of Aragon. Whilst he needed all of the support he could get after Pedro I had renewed hostilities against him in early June 1362, he remained uneasy about the plan to bring the Great Companies into his kingdom. After the fall of Calatayud to the Castilians on 27 August, when all western Aragon seemed likely to fall to the invaders, Pere's need for troops was urgent, but the intervention of Enrique's forces was patently still a long time away and those among Pere's councillors who favoured a peace settlement were daily growing stronger.[56] However, the most important factor was the war which was again imminent between the counts of Foix and Armagnac and for which both sides had begun to recruit forces from among the companies, a possibility which the mercenaries themselves had envisaged and catered for in the treaty of Clermont.

The conflict between the houses of Foix-Béarn and Armagnac was over a century old by 1362. In origin it arose from the disputed succession to Béarn and Bigorre following the betrothal of one of the daughters of Gaston VII of Béarn, Marguerite, who married Géraud V, count of Armagnac. Over the years new grievances had been added to old animosities among the heirs to these powerful families whose territorial holdings were in part contiguous and too closely interwoven for comfort. They were also rivals for the lieutenancy of Languedoc, with its extensive powers and patronage, which was in the gift of the French Crown. The kings of France had intervened to their advantage in sequestrating the county of Bigorre and providing for its administration pending a solution to the dispute, which was constantly deferred. Periodic outbreaks of war were exacerbated by the succession to the county of Comminges, with whose ruling house both parties had complex marriage alliances. Their rivalry divided the seignorial houses of the Midi into opposing factions, and behind it lay much greater ambitions. Control of Bigorre and Comminges would give the count of Foix-Béarn hegemony in the Pyrenees and allow him to consolidate his divided possessions into a unitary state stretching from Foix to Orthez. For his part, the count of Armagnac hoped to achieve a comparable predominance by controlling the central Pyrenees and their northern foothills, together with all the Gascon hill country.[57]

---

56 See Russell, pp. 26–8. A definitive treaty between Enrique and Pere to dethrone Pedro and partition Castile was not concluded until the following year, on 31 March, at Monzón (ibid, p. 28, and Luce in Froissart, *Chroniques*, vi, p. lxxxiv, n. 1).
57 For the origins of the conflict and the early rivalry between the two houses, see Bonal, pp. 272–9, 341–3, and Tucoo-Chala, 1960, p. 81 and n. 1, 1976, p. 20.

Jean I, count of Armagnac, was fifty-one in 1362. In addition to the counties of Armagnac and Rodez, which he had inherited from his father, the family also possessed a string of other adjacent lordships in Guyenne and Gévaudan, and Jean I still pursued his claims to Bigorre. Through his first marriage he had acquired the *vicomtés* of Lomagne and Auvillar, while his second marriage brought in the county of Charolais in Burgundy, which was invested in his son and heir, also called Jean.[58] Down to the treaty of Brétigny in 1360 these territories had placed him firmly in the French camp. As royal lieutenant in Languedoc from 1352 to 1358 his successes in the war in Gascony had made him the principal target of the Black Prince's campaign there.[59] The lieutenancy had also exacerbated the quarrel with the count of Foix, whilst his relations with his successor in that office, Jean, count of Poitiers and subsequently duke of Berry, his son-in-law from 1360, had given him continued influence.[60] But after the peace of Brétigny he became a leading vassal of Edward III in the extensive territories in south-western France which were subsequently erected into the principality of Aquitaine for Edward's son and heir, the Black Prince. A new political orientation in his relations with the kings of France and England was thus not only possible, but essential.[61]

Gaston Fébus, count of Foix and vicomte of Béarn, of whom Froissart gave such a memorable portrait after visiting him in Orthez in 1388,[62] was some twenty years younger than Jean I, and ruler of an important feudal conglomeration made up, in the west, of the *vicomtés* of Béarn, Marsan and Gavardan, which formed part of the duchy of Gascony, and in the east of the county of Foix with its dependencies (Donnezan and the co-seigneury of Andorra), Nébouzan (situated half-way between Béarn and Foix), lower Albigeois and the vicomté of Lautrec. The scattered disposition of these territories placed him in a potentially difficult position, but one which could also be exploited to his own advantage. A vassal of the king of England as duke of Gascony, and subsequently of the Black Prince – although he disputed their suzerainty and claimed that Béarn was sovereign territory, an allodial land – it was nevertheless essential for the inhabitants of the three *vicomtés* that good relations should be maintained with Bordeaux. They needed access to the seaports of that town and Bayonne; their Pyrenean flocks were moved as far afield as the Bordelais and the Libournais for winter pastures; the fortunes of many knightly families depended upon service in the Anglo-Gascon armies, in which they had

---

58 Breuils, pp. 46–8; Bonal, pp. 304–24; Samaran, 1907, pp. 2–21.
59 Breuils., pp. 47–52.
60 Tucoo-Chala, 1960, p. 82. The count of Poitiers married Jean I's daughter Jeanne at Carcassonne on 24 June 1360 (Breuils, p. 68).
61 Breuils, pp. 69–70, seems to ignore this.
62 Froissart, *Chroniques*, xii, pp. 76–9; *Voyage en Béarn*, pp. 66–9.

traditionally fought; the trading interests of others were with England and the Iberian Peninsula rather than with the rest of France. For his eastern territories, by contrast, Fébus was a vassal of the king of France; the inhabitants of these provinces were in the political and economic orbit of Toulouse, the centre of French royal government in the south of France, and this remained as true after the peace of Brétigny as it had been before it.[63]

Given these territorial and political realities, Gaston's policy became evident within a short time of the conclusion of his mother's guardianship of his inheritance in 1345. While complying with the military requirements of his vassalage to the king of France, he avoided open confrontation with the Anglo-Gascon armies and moved towards a policy of neutrality in the Anglo-French conflict. When the Black Prince conducted his great *chevauchée* to Carcassonne in 1355 he avoided involvement – but found time for a friendly encounter with the prince – and his lands escaped pillage while those of Armagnac, as the representative of French royal authority in the south of France, were systematically sacked.[64] Imprisoned in the Châtelet after a journey to Paris in the following spring – in circumstances which remain something of a mystery, but which may have been connected with his refusal to do homage for Béarn and his favourable disposition to Charles of Navarre – in the following year he had taken part in a crusade to Prussia, and on his way back found time to conclude his chivalric rôle in putting down some of the *Jacques* at Meaux. On returning into southern France he found his rival, Jean I, on such good terms with the new lieutenant of Languedoc, Jean, count of Poitiers, that it was not long before war broke out again between the two houses in 1359 and proceeded, with intermittent truces and attempts to negotiate a settlement, until December 1362.[65]

As the conflict deepened, both sides were active in recruiting troops. When the truce ran out at the beginning of January 1362, Jean I concluded alliances with numerous Gascon lords. In addition to Arnaud-Amanieu, lord of Albret, they included Pierre Raymond, count of Comminges; Arnaud-Guilhem, count of Pardiac; Jean d'Armagnac, *vicomte* of Fezensaguet; and Jean de la Barthe, lord of Aure. Among the lesser nobility who pledged their support were the lords of Barbazan, Montaut, Pardailhan, Montesquieu, Verduzan, Bourrouilhan and a host of others.[66] With the assistance of some of the companies Fébus invaded the county of Com-

---

63 Tucoo-Chala, 1960, pp. 36–52, 1976, pp. 11, 37, 45–9, and, for the question of sovereignty, Tucoo-Chala, 1961, pp. 79–88, 136–7.
64 Tucoo-Chala, 1960, p. 70; 1976, p. 27; Hewitt, pp. 45, 64, 77.
65 Tucoo-Chala, 1960, pp. 71, 74–84; 1976, pp. 27–31, 38–9.
66 For Armagnac's forces and the details which follow, see Breuils, pp. 70–1; Tucoo-Chala, 1960, pp. 84–5 and nn. 10, 11.

minges and took Saint-Farjou, but in the event major hostilities were avoided through the mediation of the bishop of Toulouse, who, acting on behalf of Pope Innocent VI, succeeded in patching up a further truce for a period of fourteen months, to be effective from 22 March. It gave both sides a further period to build up support. By September Jean I had taken his alliance-building to the frontiers of Béarn itself. On the 20th of that month, he secured the adherence of Raymond, lord of Lanes in Bigorre, who, in return for a life annuity of 100 *livres* in rent and an immediate sum of 600 gold florins, agreed to serve Armagnac against the count of Foix 'and all his other enemies'. On 9 October Fébus wrote to Jean I, warning him of the disasters that would follow if he persisted in this bellicose stance, but for his own part he was not inactive.

From the beginning of September the companies who had been party to the treaty of Clermont had been pouring into Foix, and by the end of November at the latest Fébus had secured the services of the most important among them: Espiote, Johann Hazenorgue, Bertuquin, Petit Meschin and John Amory.[67] For his part Armagnac had recruited Garciot du Castel, Bérard and Bertucat d'Albret and Pierre de Montaut.[68] The two Albrets and Montaut doubtless opted for service with Armagnac because that was the side taken by senior members of their families; the decision of Castel is less obvious, save that he had been operating with Bertucat d'Albret a year earlier.[69] It is not clear if two other captains mentioned in the treaty of Clermont – the *bourc* de Breteuil and Arnaud de Tallebard – were recruited by either side; but the most experienced captains, and probably the larger part of the companies, were recruited by Gaston Fébus, whose remaining forces were drawn almost entirely from his eastern territories, from the county of Foix and its dependencies.[70] In the event it was Jean I who denounced the truce and sent a defiance to Fébus.[71] For his part, the count of Foix, having established his revictualling base at Cazères-sur-Garonne, moved his forces eastwards to encounter those of Armagnac, who was installed at Launac, a village situated several miles to the north-west of Toulouse, and it was here that a decisive engagement took place on 5 December.[72]

There are several accounts of the battle, although they diverge on various points of detail and the best among them, those of Miguel del Verms and Arnaud Esquerrier, both archivists of the count of Foix, were written some

---

67 Ayala, *Crónica*, i, p. 530. For his engagement of Petit Meschin, who was then established at Mirepoix, to the east of Pamiers, see *HGL*, ix, pp. 740–1, x, pp. 1339–40.
68 The *Thalamus parvus*, p. 362, mentions both Castel and Bérard d'Albret as fighting on Armagnac's side. For the others see below, pp. 66–7.
69 See above, pp. 38–9.
70 Tucoo-Chala, 1960, p. 86.
71 Ibid., p. 85, but the reference given (BN, Doat, 195, fo. 236) is erroneous.
72 Ibid.

considerable time after the events they record.[73] In particular, we have no idea of the size of the opposing armies, although it seems clear that Armagnac's forces were distinctly larger, in that he had assembled an important part of the Gascon nobility, together with their vassals.[74] This heavy cavalry gave Armagnac numerical superiority, but at the expense of manoeuvrability. For unlike Fébus, who had smaller forces, but an important body of archers among them, Armagnac had few if any infantry, either archers or crossbowmen. Both the composition and tactics of the two forces reflected the distinction, already classic, between the French and English armies of the period.

According to Esquerrier the battle took place in the morning and was brief. Jean I opened the attack with a frontal assault which was countered by an encircling movement in which Fébus deployed his archers under cover of a copse; the archers attacked Armagnac's forces in the rear, cutting them down with their arrows and creating disarray among the cavalry, whose horses stampeded under the archers' fire. Armagnac's forces were rapidly routed and, among those who attempted to flee the battlefield, Jean I was himself hunted down by a German knight – possibly one of Hazenorgue's men – who found him hiding 'like a fox' in a neighbouring wood.[75] By midday it was all over. Fébus had achieved an overwhelming victory and secured a rich haul of prisoners. The distinguished biographer of Gaston Fébus has summed up the battle thus:

As it unfolded, the combat recalled the numerous battles which engaged the armies of France and England during the Hundred Years War. Jean I, a perfect example of the nobility in the king's service, already once before having been made prisoner, believed only in the virtue of courage, in the frontal assault in which one could measure one's strength, without artifice, against one's adversary; in brief, he had not learned the lesson of the numerous defeats which the French troops had suffered when faced by their adversaries. Gaston III, on the other hand, had perfectly assimilated the tactical lessons demonstrated on several occasions by the English. While reserving a preponderant rôle for the cavalry, he had accorded a special rôle to the archers who, in the country of Foix, were carefully recruited and trained; he had understood that a simple frontal assault should be completed by an

---

73 Miguel del Verms (Michel du Bernis), *Cronique*, pp. 583–5, and for the account of Esquerrier, *Chroniques romanes*. On Miguel del Verms, see Courteault, pp. 272–300. Two brief, but important accounts are to be found in Ayala, *Crónica*, i, p. 530, and *Scalacronica*, p. 172. Other accounts are to be found in Froissart, *Chroniques*, xii, pp. xiii, 28, and *Thalamus parvus*, p. 362. See Tucoo-Chala, 1960, p. 85, n. 16.
74 Tucoo-Chala, 1960, p. 86. The observations of Miguel del Verms, p. 583, should be noted: 'Et ja sos que lo comte de Foix agues petita gent à esgart del comte d'Armanhac que era en gran nombre, mas la del comte de Foix eran bona gent, habils en armas et à luy fizels, et feriren aspremen contra la batalha del comte d'Armanhac.'
75 According to Miguel del Verms, pp. 583–4, the German knight had been on a pilgrimage to Santiago before the battle. Tucoo-Chala, 1960, p. 87 n. 17, who is ill informed about the rôle of the companies, remarkably suggests he may have been one of Petit Meschin's men.

encircling movement. Moreover, at Meaux, as du Bernis recounts, he had learned that such a movement was effective: thanks to it he had easily crushed the *Jacques*.[76]

There is no mention here of the companies, which included English and Gascon contingents, experienced in these tactics. 'Before Christmastide', wrote Sir Thomas Gray, 'a great battle took place in Gascony between the count of Foix and the count of Armagnac. The count of Foix obtained the victory by the help of many English, a band [*route*] of the Great Company.'[77] The Castilian chronicler, Lopez de Ayala, was more specific:

And the count of Foix had that day five captains of the companies, that is Espiote, Johann Hazenorgue from Germany, Bertuquin, Petit Meschin and Sir John Amory, who were fine men-at-arms and had very good companies. And that day the count of Foix secured great honour and considerable ransoms for the prisoners which amounted, it is said, to 30,000,000 of the money of Castile.[78]

There can be no doubt that Fébus made a fortune out of his prisoners, who included a large part of the Gascon nobility as well as the captains of some of the companies. If the Foix tradition of 900 prisoners is exaggerated, it is nevertheless evident that all of the principal knights in Jean I's army were captured. Besides Jean I himself, these included the count of Comminges, the count of Monlezun and the *vicomte* of Fezensaguet. From the house of Albret, Arnaud-Amanieu, lord of Albret, and his brothers Bérard, lord of Saint-Bazeille, and Géraud; their cousin, Bérard d'Albret, lord of Gironde, Raymond, alias 'Moni', d'Albret of Bazas, and, from the companies, Bértucat d'Albret. To these must be added the lords of Aure, Terride, Le Falga, Lanta, Aspet, Pardiac, Montesquiou, Xaintrailles, Barbazan, Castelbajac, Sensacq, Lomagne, Rivière, Moncaut, Vergonhat, Pontenas, Gunat, La Barrière and Bilsera; and from the companies, in addition to Bértucat, Garciot du Castel and Pierre de Montaut.[79] The figure of 1,000,000 francs which Froissart gives for the ransoms secured by Fébus may be an exaggeration, but it is uncannily close to the sum of 30,000,000 *maravedis* given by Ayala.[80] It has been established from documentary

76 Tucoo-Chala, 1960, p. 87.
77 *Scalacronica*, p. 172.
78 Ayala, *Crónica*, i, p. 530.
79 See the list of prisoners given by Tucoo-Chala, 1960, pp. 87–8, to which should be added the vicomte of Fezensaguet, the lords of Aure and Montesquiou, and 'lo Baroat de la Lega' (BN, Doat, 195, fos. 42r–56v, 69v–81v, 96v–110r). The Albrets are identified in BN, Doat 195, fos. 27r–42r, 89v–96r.
80 The equivalent sums in florins of Florence for the francs would have been 909 florins, and for the *maravedis* 1,200,000 florins at the exchange rate prevailing in 1358, but only 666,666 florins after the debasement of 1369. Allowing for some slippage during the period 1358–62, it is not unreasonable to suggest an equivalent of around 1,000,000 florins at the end of 1362; but it is more likely that Ayala, who wrote up these events much later, was referring to their value after the debasement. See Fowler, 1992, p. 227.

evidence that the ransoms of five of the leading prisoners alone amounted to 465,000 florins, and that the minimum price demanded by Fébus – for a knight, Guilhem de Jaulin – appears to have been 1,500 florins.[81] Bearing in mind the twenty-five other prisoners cited in the list above, a *minimum* total of 600,000 florins (2,124 kg gold) has been suggested, but this estimate may well be on the conservative side.[82] The total haul may well have been larger. The *Religeux de Saint-Denis* spoke of the 'considerable treasures' which Fébus was said to have amassed in the Moncade tower at Orthez, and he reports that the count had the walls of the principal room of the castle covered with great paintings representing the vanquished, a gallery of portraits and military trophies which he showed off to his visitors.[83] At the time of his death Fébus had a fortune equivalent to 700,000 florins in the Moncade tower, a large part of which must have been amassed from the ransoms of prisoners taken at Launac.[84] He justifiably felt that God was with him on that day, even though he proved not to be as scrupulous as he might have been in his subsequent dealings with those who had fought in the battle.[85] In no doubt about the importance of the victory to the fortunes of his house, Fébus started the habit of celebrating its anniversary splendidly, and some twenty-eight years later, when writing up the account of his visit to Orthez, Froissart had occasion to observe:

On the night of Saint Nicholas, in winter, the count ordered solemn feasts to be conducted throughout his lands, as great or greater than those of Easter Day, as I have seen for myself, for I was there on such a day. All the clergy of the town of Orthez and all the people, men, women and children went in procession to the castle to find the count, who left the castle barefoot with the clergy and the processions, and proceeded to the church of Saint Nicolas, where they chanted a psalm from the Psalter of David, which goes as follows: *Benedictus Dominus, Deus meus, qui docet manus meas ad prelium et digitos meos ad bellum*.[86]

How much did the companies in Foix's service profit from the victory? The evidence suggests that at least some of them were defrauded. Shortly after the battle Fébus took the first measures to protect the enormous capital his prisoners represented. While appearing magnanimous, allowing them to choose between Mazères and Pamiers as their places of imprisonment, and to hunt from sunrise until sunset around their residences, he

---

81 See Tucoo-Chala, 1960, pp. 90–1, where the figures are totalled incorrectly.
82 Ibid., p. 91, and see his conservative calculations for the other prisoners in nn. 35, 36.
83 *Chronique*, i, p. 721; cf. Tucoo-Chala, 1960, p. 90.
84 Tucoo-Chala, 1960, p. 92.
85 See below, pp. 67–9.
86 Froissart, *Chroniques*, xii, pp. 94–5; cf. Froissart, *Voyage*, pp. xi and 87. The psalm in question is Psalm cxliv, verse i.

obliged them in enormous fines for any attempted flight and arranged immediate supervision of the counts of Armagnac and Comminges, who were compelled to stand security for the other prisoners taken at Launac and to undertake to remain prisoner in the towns to which they were assigned until 6 April.[87] Not only did Fébus fix the levels of the ransoms himself, he refused to honour the contemporary conventions regarding the immediate release of prisoners, once their ransoms had been agreed, and the division of the spoils of war, even among his lieutenants.[88] It was doubtless this which persuaded some of the companies who had supported the count of Foix to join the Armagnac camp within a very short period of the battle.

Negotiations for a peace between the two counts began immediately after the engagement and continued throughout the winter. The new pope, Urban V, who had succeeded Innocent VI in September, intervened forcefully to secure an agreement, sending the bishop of Cambrai to bring the two parties into accord, expressing his concern about their plight in letters to the vanquished, and writing to Fébus urging him to be generous to his prisoners, in imitation of 'the lion, the king of animals, who understands how to spare his victims'. Two separate problems required resolution: the territorial basis of a general settlement and the immediate business of the ransoms. It is quite clear that the discussions were long and difficult, and that it was only at the end of several months that Fébus accepted the appointment of a single representative for the entire Armagnac party to discuss the terms of a settlement. Thereafter, an agreement was soon reached and a treaty ratified at Foix on 14 April. This effectively confirmed the *status quo ante*, Armagnac renouncing all pretensions to the Foix-Bearn succession and definitively recognizing the possession by Fébus of the territories of Marsan and Gavardan with its annexe Captieux. For his part, the count of Foix confirmed his rival in possession of the Brulhois and the country of Rivière-Basse. But if Febus was generous on the territorial aspects of the negotiations, he remained intransigent on the terms of the ransoms, which he fixed unilaterally. While he may have bowed to the pope's requests in releasing several prisoners, it was only against heavy guarantees; many remained in his control for at least two years, until the end of 1364. One of the consequences of this intransigence was that the

---

87 These terms and obligations were the subject of seven contracts: Bérard d'Albret, his brother Géraud and their cousin Bérard each obliged themselves to pay 200,000 gold florins; Jean d'Armagnac, *vicomte* of Fezensaguet, and Jean de la Barte, lord of Aure, 100,000 florins each; the lords of Pardiac and Montesquiou, 50,000 florins each; Garciot du Castel and Pierre de Montaut, donzels, 60,000 each; Bértucat and Raymond d'Albret, 50,000 florins each; 'lo Baroat de la Lega', 10,000 florins (BN, Doat, 195, fos. 26r–110r, and fos.110r–15r for the contracts with the counts of Armagnac and Comminges).
88 Tucoo-Chala, 1960, p. 89.

captors, including the captains of the companies who had fought for him, were threatened with substantial loss.[89]

During the interval which elapsed between the battle and the conclusion of peace Jean I's son, Jean d'Armagnac, took over the defence of his father's lands and clearly intended to bring such pressure to bear on the negotiations as he was able to. He also had in mind a further campaign against Gaston Fébus, and in order to achieve this he clearly needed the support of the companies. Two of the first captains with whom he chose to deal were John Amory and his lieutenant John Cresswell. Both were experienced soldiers, and both of them may have served with the Black Prince in Aquitaine during his great expedition of 1355–7 and remained in the south-west of France after the prince's return to England.

Amory's base of operations between the winter of 1358 and the spring of 1363 had been in Rouergue. In December 1358 he was in command of a sizeable company menacing the country around Saint-Antonin in Rouergue and Gaillac in the Albigeois, and during the following year he had taken Cordes-Tolosanes near Castelsarrasin, to the west of Montauban. In the winter of 1360–1 he may have been with those companies around Pont-Saint-Esprit who subsequently remained in France when Hawkwood and others went off to join the marquis of Montferrat in Italy, as recounted by the Bascot de Mauléon, but later that year he took the town of Espalion in Rouergue, which he surrendered to Chandos in March 1362, and then only against substantial indemnities. He next secured two other places in Rouergue: Bournac, which had previously been held by Garciot du Castel, but subsequently surrendered, and Combret, both situated to the south-west of Saint-Affrique, near Millau. Whether or not he had taken part in the battle of Brignais, he headed the list of captains of the companies who were party to the treaty of Clermont, and was subsequently recruited by Gaston Fébus. He had played a leading rôle in the battle of Launac, on which day Bernard II, lord of Terride, was among his prisoners. In the early part of 1363 he was very much in evidence around Saint-Antonin and Montauban, and during the first two months of that year, from his base at Combret in Rouergue, he was conducting operations in Armagnac territory along the Aveyron valley between Bruniquel and Laguépie and several other places around Saint-Antonin. His evident military ability and knowledge of the country made his employment invaluable to Armagnac.[90]

---

89 For this paragraph see ibid., pp. 88–90 and nn. 23 and 25; Breuils, p. 73 and n. 4.
90 For his activities in Rouergue and Albigeois, see *Docs. Millau*, nos. 248–9; *Comptes Saint-Antonin*, pp. 31, 51–3 (where his capture of Terride is noted); *HGL*, p. 756 n. 1; Bourgeois, p. 4; Galabert, pp. 167, 169. Sumption, ii, p. 485, confuses this Combret with another castle of the same name near Marcillac (see Salch, pp. 351, 837, 1002). The place was besieged by the militia of Millau in the spring of 1363 and not surrendered by Amory

Cresswell probably came from Northumberland and was retained for life by the prince sometime before 1368. Although Froissart places him among the founding captains of the Great Companies and says that he was present at the taking of Pont-Saint-Esprit, then went with Hawkwood to Italy and was present at Brignais, he seems to have played a subordinate rôle as one of Amory's lieutenants up until 1364. Thereafter, he had a distinguished career ahead of him.[91]

On 27 February 1363, at Cassagnes-Royaux in Rouergue, Jean d'Armagnac concluded a fifteen-day truce with Amory's lieutenant, Cresswell, whereby both parties agreed to desist from all military activity against one another, and Cresswell undertook to see that the troops in Amory's company in no way damaged Jean d'Armagnac, his brother, their men and their lands, save to secure necessary victuals. During its course, or shortly after its conclusion, both Amory and Cresswell concluded an agreement with the lord of Terride (who had been taken prisoner by Amory), Raymond Arnaud of Preissac, otherwise known as the Soudich of Preissac and La Trau, and Menou de Castelpers, acting for Jean d'Armagnac, whereby they agreed to serve Jean, together with their companies, until Easter (2 April) for the sum of 5,000 gold florins. If during this period they or any of their men were in the service of others, or were not employed in war by Armagnac, they were to make up for the missing days after Easter. If they took any fortresses whilst in Jean's service, they were to hold them for him and in his name; if they wished to sell or ransom any of them, then Jean was to have the first option on them at the upset price, or less. If Jean conducted a *chévauchée* against his enemies before 2 April, and the agreement terminated during its course, then they were to be obliged to serve him for a further six to eight days whilst he returned to his lands

---

until 16 June 1363, when it was finally handed over to the newly appointed English seneschal of Rouergue. For the Bascot's observations, see Froissart, *Chroniques*, xii, pp. 99, 101.

91 There were several families of Cresswell in the fourteenth century. The John Cresswell with whom we are here concerned probably came from Cresswell in Northumberland, and although he was clearly not the John Cresswell named in *Controversy*, ed. Nicolas, i, pp. 128–9; ii, pp. 328–9, he may have come from a collateral branch of that family. It is probable that he was the John de Cresswell, senior, whom the prince retained sometime before 1368, and whose son, also called John, received a grant from Richard II in 1386, in lieu of eight years' unpaid arrears of his father's retaining fee, of extensive lands in the vicinity of Cresswell in Northumberland, notably around Bamburgh, Wooler and Morpeth (see *CPR, 1385–9*, p. 287). He is unlikely to have been the John Creswey of Burnham who was granted letters of protection to go to Aquitaine in the prince's retinue (*Foedera*, III, i, pp. 325; Hewitt, p. 201; Froissart, *Oeuvres*, xxi, p. 66), but may have been the John de Cressewell to whom the prince granted property in the forest of Macclesfield in Cheshire on 14 September 1358 (*BPR*, iii, pp. 316–17). In his subsequent career in France he was closely associated with David Holgrave, who through marriage came to be associated with the castle and manor of Bothal, also in Northumberland (*CPR, 1377–81*, pp. 1–2). Holgrave had interests in Shropshire, where another branch of the Cresswell family also lived (see Burke's *Landed Gentry*).

beyond the Garonne. Concerning those of the prisoners taken by Foix's forces at Launac who had broken their faith, in the case of those from the lands of the count of Armagnac, Jean would see that justice was done *selon droit d'armes*, and in the case of those from the county of Comminges and the lands of the lord of Albret, he would also, to the best of his ability, see that similar justice was done to the aggrieved parties. As concerned a sum which Amory and Cresswell claimed was still due to them for the evacuation of the town of Espalion (which had been taken by Amory in 1361, but surrendered against payment in March 1362), they agreed to abide by the arbitration of four persons, chosen two by either side. Two further clauses concluded the agreement. The first provided that if Fébus were to be taken by them in battle or otherwise, or by any of their companions, then he was to be handed over to Jean for a sum already agreed. The remaining and final clause provided that Amory, Cresswell and their companions could, for a period of eight to ten days from the making of the agreement, serve wherever they pleased, providing that it was not with Jean d'Armagnac's enemies and providing that at the end of that period they came into Jean's service and gave up whatever other service they might have entered into.[92]

In the ensuing months, southern France enjoyed no relief from the depredations of the mercenaries and the taxation they occasioned. To the devastation of the troops were added the costs of paying forces to resist them and, when these failed, of paying the *routiers* off. In the Armagnac lands the sums required to pay the enormous ransoms of the count and other noble prisoners were added to these costs. After Launac, some of the companies released from service with Foix joined Armagnac, some returned to base further north, others joined forces with those which had not been recruited in that war, sometimes fighting on their own account and living off the country, at other times seeking employment in local quarrels which were particularly rife in the Albigeois. Among the latter, a number of bands were recruited in a war being waged between the bishop of Albi and his neighbour, the lord of Lescure, which involved other lords of the region and occasioned a great deal of destruction. After surrendering Combret in the middle of June, Amory's company joined forces with those of Seguin de Badefol, in the service of the *vicomte* of Montclar, who was at war with the lord of Saint-Urcisse, in operations which involved two sieges of the latter's castle and much destruction of the countryside to the east of Montauban during the course of July. The Albigeois was so devastated by these and other conflicts that later that year Marshal Audrehem felt obliged

---

92 Truce: *HGL*, x, pp. 1302–3. Treaty with Armagnac: BN, Doat, 194, fos. 269r–71r (see appendix A, no. 1). Of the 5,000 florins, 3,500 were to be paid immediately, and a copy of the acquittance for these has survived (ibid., fos. 317r–v; see appendix A, no. 2). Neither document bears any date.

to exempt it from the taxes being levied in Languedoc.[93] Seguin appears to have returned to the province in early May, to recover some of the moneys still outstanding to him under the agreement negotiated with the three seneschalsies in September 1361. He was accompanied by Johann Hazenorgue, Bertuquin, Petit Meschin, Espiote and Berradeco de Saint-Pierre and their companies. Together, they took the opportunity, whilst in the Toulousain, to extract a further sum of 50,000 florins, of which 40,000 were to be paid by Toulouse, in return for their agreement to desist from further activities.[94] The towns of Lower Languedoc were more resilient. At Montpellier the consuls called together an enlarged meeting of the council on 4 July, to decide whether they should follow the example of Toulouse and put up a resistance. They unanimously decided to fight.[95]

The situation was much the same elsewhere. After the collapse of the projected expedition to Aragon, Enrique of Trastámara's forces, which were established in the seneschalsies of Beaucaire and Carcassonne, when they were not engaged by Audrehem frequently turned to rioting. Like the Great Companies before them, the Castilians still awaited the money which they were due under the terms of the treaty of Clermont, the final payment of the full 53,000 florins of which remained outstanding to Enrique until the end of April 1363. It was only then that they quit the region.[96] Among the companies foraging around Montpellier at the beginning of March of that year, on the 6th one of them, commanded by a Provençal captain, Louis Roubaud of Nice, seized the ambassadors of the king of Aragon, who were coming to treat with Audrehem concerning the forces under Trastámara, and carried them off to his base at Nébian, near Clermont l'Hérault, in the mountains to the south of Lodève. They were followed by Amory's forces, who three days later were in the neighbourhood of

---

93 Denifle, ii, pp. 435–7; Boudet, 1895, p. 10; *HGL*, p. 765 n. 3. For Seguin's movements in July, see *Comptes Saint-Antonin*, p. 59.
94 The agreement and the names of the contracting captains are given in AC, Montpellier, BB 4, fo. 4v, where the amount to be paid by Toulouse is given as 40,000 gold florins. Audrehem imposed a subsidy of 50,000 florins to pay for their departure (AC, Toulouse, CC 1847, fo. 7v: 'Item, anno domini Mccclxiij, die xix Juih, sunt soluti per dominos de capitulo Tholose seu eorum thesaurarium Stephano de Montemediano, thesaurario predicto, de dicto subsidio L milia francorum auri imposito per dominum Audenanum pro tradendo domino Seguino de Badafollo, uni capitaneo magnarum societatum, de quibus hanc tilletam cujus tenor est: Sapian totz . . . los cals au baylat a mossenhor Segui de Badafol, i dels capitanis de las grans companhas, per la financa a lu promesa', etc.) For further payments by Toulouse, see ibid., CC 1848, fo. 21r (p. 20) and *passim*. The negotiations with Seguin appear to have taken place at Montauban in May, and in July Toulouse sent two delegates to Caraman, in Lauragais, to the south-east of Toulouse, where they paid him and Hugonet de Saint-Amans 2,385 French florins (ibid., CC 687, fos. 74v, 126r).
95 AC, Montpellier, BB 4, fo. 4v. The council agreed unanimously *quod fiat guerre*. See *Arch. Montpellier*, xiii, pp. 77–8, nos. 737–8.
96 *HGL*, x, pp. 1224, 1226–7, 1231, 1233, 1241, 1248; BN, coll. Languedoc, 159, fos. 105–7; Molinier, pp. 121–2.

Montpellier, perhaps in search of the same prey, before proceeding in the direction of Nîmes.[97]

Whilst Languedoc continued to suffer from the companies based there, the momentum of their activities was shifting north. At the beginning of November 1362 Perrin Boias, who like Seguin de Badefol had been involved in neither the treaty of Clermont, nor the war between Armagnac and Foix, seized le Monastier-Saint-Chaffre (now le Monastier-sur-Gazeille), a fortified Benedictine abbey on the road south from Le Puy, at the beginning of November 1362. The place had been taken once before by the Scot Walter Leslie and a person calling himself 'the Master of the Ships' during the descent of the companies on Pont-Saint-Esprit in 1361, before the two of them went off to Italy with other companies in the service of the marquis of Montferrat. From Monastier, Boias pillaged and ransomed Velay and its neighbouring provinces, conducting raids deep into Languedoc. He was not removed until the following March, and only then after a seven-week siege conducted by troops hired by the seneschal of Beaucaire, supported by further forces under the *vicomte* of Polignac and the local nobility. The garrison forces were cut to pieces, save Boias, who escaped through a disused passage. Shortly afterwards one of Bertucat d'Albret's lieutenants, Sobrossa (Fabrossa, Fabrousse), in charge of a company of some 1,000 cavalry whilst his superior was still imprisoned, took and burned Florac, to the north-east of Millau.[98] After their operations in the Albigeois, Seguin de Badefol and John Amory had also moved north, in their case to Auvergne. By the late summer of 1363 only a few contingents of the Great Companies remained in Bas Languedoc: those of Louis Roubaud and of Bertuquin, who had been party to the treaty of Clermont.

On 28 July, Roubaud took the castle of Lignan, less than five miles to the north-west of Béziers, and sometime before the end of October was joined there by Bertuquin. Béziers itself felt threatened and its defences were known to be inadequate. An inspection carried out in the previous year had found the walls and ditches in a bad state and the gates not properly protected. The operations of the companies who used it as a base

---

97 For Roubaud, see Molinier, p. 127 and nn. 2–4, who corrects the account in the *Thalamus parvus*, p. 362, repeated elsewhere, that the ambassadors were from the king of Castile and on their way to see the pope and others in Avignon. For Amory, see Ménard, ii, p. 251, and preuves, p. 252.
98 For the two occupations of Monastier, and Boias, see Monicat, pp. 19, 21 (where Boias is identified), 22–6 and *passim*; Molinier, pp. 139–40; *Preuves Polignac*, ii, pp. 31–2, no. 230; *Spicilegium Brivatense*, p. 390, no. 139; Ménard, ii, preuves, pp. 250–2, 283–4, where Monastier is said to have been taken by 'societates Galterii, dicti Lestoc [i.e. le Scot] et cujusdam se dicentis magistrum navium, et quasdam alias societates per illas partes trancitum facientes, et ultimo per Petrum Boias'. It was also around the time of the first seizure of Monastier (i.e. December 1360) that Seguin de Badefol took Châteauneuf in Velay (Monicat, p. 20). For Leslie and the 'master of the ships' see *Medieval Mercenaries II*. For Florac, see Ménard, ii, preuves, p. 253, and Boudet, 1895, p. 12.

extended along the Mediterranean coast from the Rhône basin to the Pyrenees, as well as to the inland towns of the region. On one of his raids Bertuquin, with a small troop of eighty lances, even succeeded in penetrating the walls of Montpellier, where he abducted a number of the citizens, including two members of the consulate, and made off with a large number of cattle. Lignan was not evacuated until the beginning of November. It cost Béziers 10,000 florins to pay Roubaud off, on top of another 10,000 for the forces raised to remove him. He then made for Auvergne, where he joined up with the companies established there. The remaining contingents, including one led by Bertuquin, were among the *magna et maledicta societas* which a few days later, on 11 November, took Peyriac in Minervois, to the north-east of Carcassonne. The place was only retaken after several sieges in mid-June 1364, when all of the companies holding the place were massacred, except seven nobles. Bertuquin, who had been liaising with Seguin de Badefol's forces in Auvergne since the previous September, and who had recently been recruited by Charles of Navarre to serve with other contingents of the companies in Burgundy, was among them.[99]

At the end of 1363, as the companies began to regroup beyond the marches of Languedoc, the inhabitants of the three seneschalsies, with Audrehem's support and perhaps under his direction, formed a league against the companies, the main purpose of which seems to have been to prevent them from returning into their territories. As on so many other occasions their actions only transferred the problem elsewhere, this time to the French provinces bordering the upper Rhône and the Saône valleys, and Burgundy. Nevertheless, Urban V, alarmed for the security of Avignon, re-engaged Juan Fernandez de Hérédia as captain-general of the Comtat Venaissin for a further period and put together an alliance, to be funded by himself, the counts of Forcalquier, Valentinois and Savoy, the governor of Dauphiné, the seneschal of Provence and the bishop of Valence. In the event, the companies did not cross the Rhône into Provence and the Comtat Venaissin, and the threat from troops returning from Lombardy proved less real than the alarmists had predicted.[100] The real momentum had shifted further north, to Auvergne and the surrounding provinces, where the companies were regrouping, some under new captains, among whom the most successful and notorious was Seguin de Badefol.

---

99 Lignan: *Thalamus parvus*, pp. 363, 364, 366; HGL, ix, pp. 760–1, 763–4; *Arch. Montpellier*, xiii, nos. 737–8. According to Ménard, ii, preuves, p. 254, Lignan was taken by a *routier* called 'Spincta', but Mascaro, *Libre*, pp. 55, 56, also attributes the action to Roubaud. For Peyriac, see Denifle, ii, pp. 438–40 and 440 n. 1; Prou, pp. 116–17. Bertuquin and his company were among those which had entered Auvergne following the capture of Brioude by Badefol at the beginning of September 1363 (BN, coll. Bourgogne, xxvi, fo. 114r; Petit, x, p. 55). For his recruitment and death, see *AGN, Comptos*, v, nos. 297–9, 330, 374.
100 Denifle, ii, pp. 441–2; Prou, pp. 32–5, 104–5, 106, 110; Housley, 1982, pp. 263–4.

4

Seguin de Badefol in Auvergne

Among the captains who had not been party to the treaty of Clermont, Seguin de Badefol was to emerge as the principal leader – the sovereign captain – of the Great Companies in the late summer of 1363. One of the four legitimate sons of a powerful Périgordian lord, Seguin de Gontaut, lord of Badefol and Lalinde, he took his name from the castle of Badefol, situated on the south bank of the Dordogne some sixteen miles east of Bergerac, where he was born, probably shortly after 1330. This was frontier territory, long disputed between the English and French. Seguin had doubtless gained his earliest military experience there, and he may have served under the Black Prince and participated in the battle of Poitiers. Whatever the case, he had already turned to fighting on his own account by 1357, and in the months which followed the confirmation of the peace of Brétigny he had gained notoriety as the captain of one of the companies which descended on Pont-Saint-Esprit, following the evacuation of which he had turned to making war in Languedoc as captain of a company known as *La Margot*.[1]

Following the treaty concluded in September 1361, which had provisionally liberated Languedoc from the depredations of his company, he may have joined forces with other bands of mercenaries operating further north, in particular in Auvergne and Velay; but the records are singularly silent about his movements in the period which elapsed between this treaty and his reappearance in Languedoc in the early summer of 1363. If he took

---

1 The best account of Seguin's life is to be found in Maubourguet, 1938, which corrects some of the errors in the earlier, but still useful works by Chanson and Labroue, 1891, pp. 111–61. For his activities in the Lot valley in 1357, see *Comptes Rodez*, I, i, p. 459 n. 2; Lacoste, iii, p. 161; Lehoux, i, p. 108. Froissart, *Chroniques*, vi, pp. 62, 72, 266–7, places him in a prominent position from the moment the Great Companies were formed in Champagne and Burgundy, and says that the companies operating around Pont-Saint-Esprit made him their 'chapitainne souverain'. His chronology of events at this juncture was faulty, and in retelling the story in the account of the Bascot de Mauléon in book 3, Seguin enjoyed no special notoriety before the late summer of 1363 (*Chroniques*, xii, pp. 99–100).

part in the battle of Brignais, he was certainly not party to the treaty of Clermont, and there is no evidence to suggest that he took the road to Pamiers or that he was present at Launac. Perhaps, in view of his previous experiences, he mistrusted Enrique of Trastámara's entire Iberian plans. Nevertheless, it seems unlikely that he went into semi-retirement in his native Périgord.[2] Within weeks of the agreement at Clermont, at the beginning of August 1362, the company under his command was operating with that of Petit Meschin on the west bank of the Rhône. Anxious to know if they intended to cross to the east bank, the *syndics* of Carpentras sent scouts to monitor their movements between Pont-Saint-Esprit and Avignon.[3] But in 1363, after his operations in the Albigeois and Toulousain, he pushed north into Gévaudan where on 19 August his brother Tonnet, sometimes known as Gaston, together with Bérard d'Albret, had taken the castle of Balsièges, on the river Lot some five miles south of Mende, but evacuated it against payment on 3 September.[4]

The Albrets had been active in the Auvergne since 1357, when both Arnaud-Amanieu and his bastard cousin Bertucat had occupied the fortress of Sermur. The interests of the family in Auvergne were recognized by the Black Prince, who had included Arnaud-Amanieu and his younger brother Bérard among the four conservators appointed for the region in the truce of Bordeaux. In the confirmation of the treaty of Brétigny at Calais in October 1360, Edward III had likewise included them among the commissioners for the evacuation of fortresses there.[5] It is doubtful that they had fully complied with their mandate. In March 1363 one of Bertucat d'Albret's lieutenants, Sobrosso, had raided across the limestone plateau known as *la Causse* with a thousand cavalry and attacked and burned the little town of Florac before moving on to Mende and raiding the surrounding countryside.[6] Bertucat's forces had pushed further north and taken the castle of Montbrun, to the south of Saint-Flour, from which, together with another of his lieutenants, Raymond Bernard de la Roque, also called Sandos, he harassed the town as he had previously done from Caylus in the Carladais. The place was only recovered in June after a fierce battle beneath its walls conducted by the inhabitants of Saint-Flour, in which some 400–500 of the citizen militia were killed. Bertucat was taken prisoner and the inhabitants, with the support of the *vicomte* of Polignac, intended that he should be put to death; but he was released on ransom as a result of the intervention of the *vicomte* of Murat, who

---

2   Sumption, ii, pp. 473, 486.
3   André-Michel, 1913, p. 345.
4   André, p. xxvi; Maubourguet, 1938, p. 294.
5   *Foedera*, III, i, pp. 350, 546; Lehoux, i, p. 98, n. 4.
6   Ménard, ii, preuves, p. 253; André, p. xxvi; Maubourguet, 1938, p. 293.

was also in conflict with the town and with whom Bertucat had concluded a pact.[7]

By comparison with what was to follow these were minor affairs; but the concentration of companies in the Massif-Central took on a new significance with Seguin's capture, during the night of 13 September 1363, of the the little town of Brioude in Auvergne, which belonged to the rich chapter of Saint Julien. Although the town was enclosed, it was not well defended, and Seguin and his men had little difficulty in taking it, scaling the walls at a point where a number of adjoining buildings had not been demolished, systematically looting the place and ransoming a large part of the population. News of the capture of Brioude spread rapidly, and the town acted as a magnet for other contingents of the Great Companies. For the best part of the next ten months it became the principal base for their operations, acting as Pont-Saint-Esprit had done almost three years earlier.

The shock created by the fall of Brioude is evident in a letter which the governor of Auvergne wrote to the *bailli* of Chalon from Riom a week after its fall. While he exaggerated in describing the town as 'the strongest, finest and richest in all Auvergne', he was certainly right in referring to its capture as 'une très grand mal aventure'. It had been taken, he says, by escalade and treason, and the news would astound the whole of Auvergne, indeed the whole of France. The letter also contained important information on the personnel and strength of the companies, and their perceived intentions. After Seguin and several other captains had taken the place many other companies had arrived, commanded by Johann Hazenorgue, Bertuquin, Petit Meschin, Espiote and a captain called Vaire du Cap, among others. The governor believed that when they assembled together their numbers amounted to some 10,000 cavalry, that is some 2,000 lances of men-at-arms, archers and sergeants. He had heard from others who had spoken to them that they planned to head for Burgundy, where they would be glad, they said, to serve Philip, duke of Touraine (who was then having to deal with incursions into the duchy from the county of Burgundy). But if he did not wish to employ them they would join 'whoever else can use them'. He indicated that measures were being taken to recover the town: Jean d'Armagnac had already arrived with a substantial force, and an assembly of the three estates had been called at Montferrand, 'because it is necessary to recover the said town by peace [that is by a negotiated settlement, involving payment] or war, or else the whole country will be lost'. He therefore advised the *bailli* to instruct the inhabitants of Burgundy to bring all the victuals they could into defended places, and he would

---

7 Boudet, 1895, pp. 11–12, and 1893, pp. 341–2; cf. Maubourguet, 1938, pp. 293–4. Both authors also attribute the operations conducted by Seguin de Badefol and John Amory in June 1363 (see above, p. 71) to this region, having confused Saint-Urcisse in Albigeois with Saint-Urcize to the north of Espalion, across the mountains of Aubrac.

prolong the discussions of the assembly which he had called in order to give time for the grapes to be harvested.[8] The governor's estimate of the strength of the companies was in all probability realistic, and to those he identified others can be added, notably the brigade of Louis Roubaud and some contingents of Enrique of Trastámara's Castilian forces, and probably also those of Arnaud de Tallebard, and the Poitevin captain, Guiot du Pin, who took up service in Burgundy along with two Gascon lords recruited by the ducal council: the Soudich de la Trau and Amanieu de Pommiers.[9]

From the outset the companies used Brioude as a base of operations from which to conduct raids in Auvergne, Velay, Forez, Lyonnais and as far afield as Bourbonnais and Dombes. But Auverge and Velay bore the brunt of the attacks as their forces swept up to Clermont, Montferrand and Riom in the north and Le Puy in the south, and conducted raids in the immediate vicinity of Brioude. Roads were blocked and travellers and their goods seized and ransomed. Unwalled towns and villages were burned and pillaged; larger centres saw their suburbs devastated. The lands of Béraud II, count of Clermont and dauphin of Auvergne, one of the hostages for the treaty of Brétigny, were particularly hard hit. So too were a number of places in Velay, which owed Seguin *patis* from the time of his operations there in 1361, and had consequently been excluded from the treaty made with the southern seneschalsies in September of that year. His revenge was swift and devastating. The fate of Le Puy was not atypical. Here, the houses and other buildings in the suburbs were destroyed and the inhabitants taken prisoner, ransomed and obliged to find food, clothes and shoes for the assailants, who threatened to uproot their vines if they did not comply. The town had no alternative but to pay them off. Audrehem's response was speedy, but measured. He first instructed the *bailli* of Velay to constrain the inhabitants of certain towns, mostly around Le Puy, to take refuge in their nearest fortresses; but then felt obliged to authorize the inhabitants to treat with Seguin and his *tirannida societate*, instructing the *bailli* to constrain all sections of the community to contribute to a special tax to pay him off. It was hardly realistic. The province had been so devastated by the continuous attentions of the companies that the money could not be raised speedily, and the period assigned for its collection had to be prolonged. The story was much the same elsewhere. During the

---

8 For the capture of Brioude, see *Thalamus parvus*, p. 363; Luce in Froissart, *Chroniques*, vi, p. xxxiv n. 1. The governor's letter was published by Petit, x, pp. 55–6, after BN, coll. Bourgogne, xxvi, fo. 114r. For the original see Kervyn in Froissart, *Oeuvres*, xx, p. 234, and for a partial translation, Fowler, 1991a, p. 72. For the access by way of the buildings adjoining the walls, see *Arch. Montpellier*, xiii, pp. 74–5, and Monicat, p. 27 n. 1. For the looting and ransoms, Luce, in Froissart, *Chroniques*, vi, p. xxxiv n. 1, and Moisant, pp. 267–8.

9 Petit, x, p. 57 and nn. 1–2, pp. 72–3; *Itin. Phil. le Hardi*, p. 459; Chérest, p. 235; Luce, in Froissart, *Chroniques*, vi, p. xx, n. 4. Roubaut: *Preuves Polignac*, ii, pp. 41–2. Castilians: Lehoux, i, p. 184. Du Pin's origins: *Rec. doc. Poitou*, 3, in *AHP*, xvii, pp. 328–30.

period of its occupation Brioude became a major centre of exchange as a result of the immense booty brought there: convoys of cattle, money and objects of all kinds, a large part of which the companies had to dispose of. The agglomeration of food attracted the attention of bands of brigands and outlaws known as the *Tuchins*, whose behaviour was little different from that of the companies. Warfare between local lords, frequently in league with the one or the other, also contributed to the devastation, causing further dislocation and revolt. In November a company of Bretons recruited by the Archpriest, which ostensibly came to the assistance of the province, made war on their own account to the north of Clermont. The two provinces succumbed to a state of virtual civil war.[10]

Having sacked Auvergne and Velay, Seguin and his associated captains turned their attentions to the territories lying further east, to Forez and Lyonnais, whose capital he had long had in his sights. Montbrison, including its hospital, was pillaged, as was the neighbourhood of Roanne, on the frontier with Beaujolais. During the course of October he occupied the Benedictine abbey of Savigny, only twelve miles to the west of Lyon and, as on so many other occasions, had to be bought off by the inhabitants of that region. The share of Lyon was 2,400 florins. The worst fears of the governor of Auvergne then began to materialize. After passing several days at Savigny, Seguin's forces crossed the Saône above Lyon, entering Burgundy by the province of Dombes. From Montluel the castellan sent information on their movements to Simon de Saint-Amour, the ducal official in charge of the inspection of fortifications in Bresse. On 24 October they menaced Bourg-en-Bresse, where Simon had called a council of war. There Séguin called a halt, possibly because the arrival of a Gascon force under the Soudich de La Trau and Amanieu de Pommiers persuaded him not to proceed further, as has been suggested; but it seems more likely that the incursion was never intended to be more than a reconnaissance raid for operations in the Saône valley, which he was not to carry out until almost exactly a year later. Other raids were conducted by the companies of the captains who had joined Seguin at Brioude. Whilst Bertuquin had returned into Lower Languedoc to liaise with Louis Roubaud, Johann Hazenorgue pushed on north of Clermont, penetrated the Bourbonnais and, proceeding north of Vichy, threatened to take Saint-Pourçain-sur-Sioule by escalade.[11] The operations of the companies may have taken them further south, into

---

10 Lehoux, i, pp. 183–6; Ledos, pp. 43–4; Monicat, pp. 20–1, 26–9, 216–17, PJ no. x; Luce, in Froissart, *Chroniques*, vi, pp. xxxiv–xxxv; Labroue, 1891, p. 77; 'Inv. du Puy', pp. 687–8; Ménard, ii, preuves, p. 275; *Preuves Polignac*, ii, pp. 33–5, no. 232; Molinier, pp. 139–40; Boudet, 1895, pp. 13–17.
11 Montbrison: Luce in Froissart, *Chroniques*, vi, p. xxxiv n. 7. Roanne and Savigny: Guigue, pp. 95–6, 222, PJ no. iv. Bresse and Dombes: Perroud, p. 272, citing AD, Côte-d'Or, B 7115, B 8550; Saint-Pourçain: AD, Allier, 4E 258: CC 1, fo. 159v.

Rouergue, Gévaudan and the plains of Languedoc, and south-east into the Rhône valley to the marches of the papal state; but the evidence for this is shaky and we cannot be sure that the raids in question were carried out from Brioude, or at this particular juncture.[12] Bertucat d'Albret, who was in Gévaudan at the end of November 1363, was rumoured to be threatening to descend into the seneschalsy of Beaucaire, but we have no evidence to suggest that he had arrived there from Auvergne. By the following spring he had transferred his attentions to the duchy of Burgundy.[13]

Brioude remained in the hands of the companies until the end of June 1364, when it was finally evacuated along with the fortress of Varennes, near Le Puy, following a treaty concluded at Montferrand on 4 April. This was negotiated between John, duke of Berry and Auvergne, John, count of Auvergne and Boulogne, Béraud II, dauphin of Auvergne, and representatives of the Estates of Auvergne, on the one hand, and by Seguin, Bérard and Bertucat d'Albret, and other captains and companies occupying Brioude and Varennes on the other part. Significantly, it was mediated by Arnaud-Amanieu, lord of Albret.[14]

The main provision was that, in return for 40,000 gold florins and 1,000 silver marks, the companies would evacuate the mountains of Auvergne, Velay and the lands of the dauphin of Auvergne situated in Gévaudan, and surrender all claims and desist from all hostilities there in the future, except in the event of the king of England, his sons and officers, the count of Armagnac or the lord of Albret waging a 'just war' there.

A substantial part of the treaty concerned debts: (i) All sums outstanding to the companies from the inhabitants, including the expenses connected with them, were anulled, save certain sums which Seguin claimed to be outstanding from the lord of Cousant, in particular in respect of the *vicomté* of Villemur; these were to be resolved by the lords of Albret and Mussidan or their deputies. (ii) Seguin also undertook to see that the country was released from all demands which the lord of Châteauneuf-de-Randon, near Mende, might make on them. (iii) Bertrand II de la Tour was to be released from a *pati* demanded from him and the inhabitants of his lands.

Provision was made for a number of special situations and possible eventualities: (i) Inhabitants of the provinces referred to in the treaty, while travelling in France, Guyenne and elsewhere to raise the moneys stipulated

---

12 *Docs. Millau*, p. 141, no. 283; *Comptes Louppy*, p. 52; Urban V, *Lettres*, no. 1522; see Sumption, ii, p. 488.
13 Ménard, ii, preuves, p. 281; Lehoux, i, p. 184; Guigue, p. 98.
14 The treaty has been published twice by Chassaing: 'Traité', pp. 163–73; *Spicilegium*, pp. 361–8, no. 134. It was possibly concluded following a military setback for the companies near Montferrand; the evacuation took place on 23 June (*Spicilegium*, p. 372, no. 136, and 389; see Monicat, pp. 32, 39).

in the treaty, or travelling in the course of trade, were not to be impeded, neither were their goods to be arrested. (ii) The town of Brioude, its relics and *trésor* were to remain in the possession of the chapter and canons of Saint-Julien, who had the lordship of the town; but if difficulties arose between the canons and the companies, the town was to be surrendered to the duke of Berry or his representatives. (iii) Prisoners taken by the captains and their companies during the negotiation of the treaty were to be released.

Other clauses concerned the payment of the 40,000 florins: (i) These were to be made to the lord of Albret at Clermont or Montferrand in three instalments: 15,000 on the evacuation of Brioude, Varennes and the other fortresses held by the companies of the contracting captains, 12,500 at Christmas and 12,500 at All Saints (i.e. 1 November) 1365. (ii) The additional 1,000 marks were also to be paid at Christmas, a third by the chapter and inhabitants of Brioude and the remaining two-thirds by the provinces to be evacuated.

Certain arrangements were stipulated concerning the timing and manner of the evacuation: (i) All towns, fortresses and other places were to be evacuated within eight days of the first payment, pending which the companies were to desist from all hostilities, including the seizure of persons, animals or goods, except a reasonable amount of food for their sustenance; all infringements of this provision were to be reported to the lord of Albret and his deputies, and deducted from the sums due. (ii) After the first payment had been made and the towns and fortresses evacuated, three named castles (belonging to the duke, the count and the dauphin respectively) were to be surrendered as surety for payment of the remaining 25,000 florins to the lord of Albret, who could appoint whomever he chose for their custody, and who was to return them to their owners (the duke, the count and the dauphin) on the completion of the payments, in default of which they were to surrender hostages; but in the event of the stipulated payments not being made by the due dates the companies were not to resume hostilities. (iii) If the contracting provinces were invaded by other companies so that they could not raise the money by the agreed dates, the terms of payment were to be prolonged for as long as they were thereby impeded.

Four clauses attempted to secure the compliance of the contracting companies: (i) In the event of any of their members contravening the treaty, the contracting captains undertook to make war on them, together with and at the expense of the duke and the men of the contracting provinces. (ii) For the better accomplishment of the treaty, twenty captains chosen by the governors of the affected provinces, including in their number the contracting captains, Gandon de Mons and Tonnet de Badefol, were to swear under oath that they would in no way allow the treaty to be infringed. (iii) If any of them contradicted it they would be forever held as false, bad and traitorous by all courts of all lords and would be punished as such. (iv) In the event of dispute or non-compliance the contracting captains and companies submitted themselves to the jurisdiction of the papal court, to that of the kings of France and England, the duke of Berry and Auvergne, the lord of Albret and all other secular and ecclesiatical judges whom these rulers and the country chose. All of this was to be drawn up into a public instrument.

For the greater surety of these terms: (i) The contracting captains and the other captains from among the twenty mentioned above appended their seals and, in the absence of Seguin, the lord of Mussidan promised on his behalf to abide by its terms. (ii) The lords of Albret, Mussidan and Curton undertook to get the captains and the companies to abide by them. (iii) The lords of Albret and Curton promised to join the duke of Berry and the men of the contracting provinces in pursuing defaulters, unless they were impeded from doing this because they were otherwise occupied with their own wars or those of their allies and rightful lords. (iv) The governors, in the duke's name, undertook to try and secure for the captains and companies of the town of Brioude both papal absolution and pardons from the king of France and the duke of Berry.

The negotiators of the treaty with the companies were unrealistic if they believed that the provinces in question could be evacuated in this manner. In the ensuing months the problem of raising the necessary finance in lands devastated by the enemy became all too obvious. As on so many other occasions, the money for the *vuidement* proved difficult to raise and the delays envisaged for payment by instalment did not facilitate matters. The companies were well aware that if they left the upland territories of the Massif-Central they were likely to meet stiff opposition, since defensive measures had been put afoot in both Burgundy and Languedoc. Although Brioude was evacuated before the end of June, a large number of companies did not quit the provinces specified in the treaty. Seguin took the precaution of leaving some detachments in the vicinity of Brioude to ensure the receipt of the stipulated moneys. One of these, under Nicholas Dagworth, occupied the castle of Saint-Cirques, on the river Allier to the south of the town. As late as early October 1364 Bertucat was blocking the road between Montferrand and Riom.[15]

The first instalment of the 40,000 florins was to have been paid to the contracting captains on the completion of the evacuation of the fortresses which they held. Despite Marshal Audrehem's instructions to the *bailli* of Velay of the previous October, to levy a tax for the purpose of paying off the *routiers*, little seems to have been accomplished, and it is likely that the

15   Dagworth and Bertucat: *Spicilegium*, p. 394; Boudet, 1895, p. 17; Lehoux, i, p. 186.

necessary money for the first payment was not available in some if not all of the provinces to be evacuated. This certainly seems to have been the case in Velay, but Seguin evidently believed that further military pressure had to be applied, either to secure the residue of *patis* still outstanding to him from 1361, or to speed up the collection of the moneys due under the terms of the treaty, or both. To this end he assembled a large army around Saint-Paulien, some nine miles to the north of Le Puy, with the apparent intention of besieging the town. Most of his forces were drawn from contingents of the companies which had previously been operating in Auvergne and Forez; but he had also brought siege engines, artillery and other equipment down from Brioude, and was rumoured to be awaiting further reinforcements. On 28 August, he sent Louis Roubaud with an advance party to set fire to the surrounding villages and besiege Saint-Vidal, and Polignac, to the immediate north-west of the town. The lord of Saint-Vidal resisted the assault, calling on the assistance of another *routier* captain, Arnaud du Solier, alias 'le Limousin', who attacked Roubaud's rear-guard with some success. Roubaud's forces then moved on to besiege Polignac, but were driven off to continue their pillaging and killing in the surrounding villages. According to a Hospitaller who had been taken prisoner by the companies, but subsequently escaped, Seguin's intentions were to remain before Le Puy for eight or ten days, either to besiege the town or to sack the neighbourhood, destroying the vines and burning the mills. He would then divide his forces, and descend on Lunel, to the north of Montpellier, where he would confront Audrehem. All of this information was contained in a letter of 30 August which the consuls of Le Puy wrote to their counterparts in Nîmes, requesting them to pass on its contents to the king's officers in Languedoc and the consuls of Montpellier. The ink was hardly dry when the *bourc* de Breteuil appeared outside the walls with an estimated 2,000 cavalry, to be joined by Roubaud. The two established their camps in the immediate neighbourhood of Le Puy, awaiting the arrival of Seguin. The inhabitants of Le Puy put up an heroic resistance, with their crossbowmen, espringals and other war machines, but lacked outside support, money and victuals. 'We do not know what will become of us' *(Que faren ne que no, non saben ren)*, they concluded.[16]

The letter met with an appropriate response. The king's commissioners hastened to call together representatives of the towns of the seneschalsy of Beaucaire in Nîmes and secured a grant of enough money to support 1,450 troops for one month. Hoping to avoid a battle, Audrehem tried to speed up the collection of money to pay the companies, but encountering

---

16 The letter is published in Molinier, pp. 312–14, PJ no. lxxxvii, and *Preuves Polignac*, ii, pp. 41–2, no. 237; cf. Monicat, pp. 32–4. The consuls estimated Seguin's forces to be made up of 4,000 to 5,000 good combatants, including pillagers, in all some 10,000 to 11,000 horse. He awaited a further 200 lances.

resistance because of an exemption which he had previously granted to the abbey of Saint-Chaffre, which increased the contribution of other inhabitants of Velay, on 15 September he revoked the exemption and required all the inhabitants to contribute to buying Seguin off. He then revoked the permission previously granted to the towns of Beaucaire to raise troops to resist the companies in Gévaudan, possibly because he judged it imprudent – and it is noteworthy that Cardinal Guy de Boulogne and Juan Fernandez de Hérédia advised him on this matter – or because the immediate danger had subsided. Instead, he called a meeting of the estates of Languedoc for 6 November, to deliberate on the measures to be taken to combat the companies.[17]

The details of how this affair ended are by no means clear; but Seguin evidently abandoned his plans to descend into Lower Languedoc and was finally bought off.[18] Further pressure was then applied in Auvergne. Returning into that province at the beginning of October, his forces blocked the main roads and threatened Clermont, Montferrand and Riom. While Seguin took up quarters at Beaumont, to the immediate south of Clermont, Bertucat d'Albret threatened Montferrand from his base at Pont-du-Château, to the north-east, and Arnaud-Amanieu d'Albret, who had mediated the evacuation treaty, took the castle of Blot to the north-west of Riom. Paradoxically these operations, which were clearly intended to speed up the payment of the evacuation money, hardly facilitated its collection. At the beginning of October the consuls of Montferrand found it impossible to attend a meeting of the Estates convoked at Riom, owing to the presence of some of Bertucat's forces at Marsat, to the immediate south-west of Riom. Pont-du-Château was strategically more important. Situated on the north bank of the Allier some eight miles from Clermont and slightly more from Riom, the town had been briefly occupied by Robert Knowles some five years earlier. It commanded the bridge over that river on the road to Lyon, controlled communications between Auvergne and Forez and, most important of all, gave access to the lands lying to the east: to the Loire, Rhône and Saône valleys.[19] It was in this direction that Seguin planned his next attack.

The French authorities endeavoured to keep each other informed about the intentions of the companies. When Seguin had left Velay for Forez and Auvergne, marshal Audrehem had also proceeded north by way of Forez and Lyon to Chalon during the course of October, and doubtless briefed the city, the ducal council in Burgundy and the duke of Anjou (who was about to replace him as lieutenant in Languedoc) about the movements

17   Molinier, pp. 165–6; Dognon, p. 609; Henneman, p. 191.
18   'Inv. du Puy', pp. 687–8; Monicat, p. 35.
19   Lehoux, i, pp. 181, 186 and nn. 3 and 4, 187 and n. 1, 189; Boudet, 1895, pp. 17–18; Bouchard, p. 250 n. 3.

and intentions of the companies as he perceived them.[20] On 22 October Jacques de Vienne, lord of Longvy and captain-general and lieutenant for the king and the duke of Burgundy in the Lyonnais, wrote to the *bailli* of that province that he had seen letters sent to the duchess of Berry, countess of Auvergne, containing news that 'messire Seguin de Badefol, is in Auvergne with a large body of men whose number is increasing daily, and who are doing a great deal of damage there; and it is certainly their intention to come soon into Burgundy'. He therefore instructed the *bailli* to see that all victuals and other things that might assist Seguin's forces should be brought inside fortified places and urged that a tax imposed to raise troops should be collected as quickly as possible.[21] The duchess of Berry's informant had got it wrong. Seguin's prey in fact lay elsewhere. Ten days later, on 1 November, he carried out his next major coup with the capture, after a surprise attack, of the town of Anse to the north of Lyon. Before turning to this episode it is necessary to examine the course of events in Burgundy, where the companies had been causing serious disruption for some time.

20   Molinier, p. 167, n. 2, p. 316, PJ no. xc.
21   BN, coll. Bourgogne, xxvi, fo. 114.

5

The Navarrese Imbroglio

During the years 1363 to 1365 the activities of the companies were increasingly connected with the ambitions of Charles of Navarre in France, and in particular in regard to his interests in Burgundy, where the young duke, Philip de Rouvres, had died in November 1361. Charles was twenty-nine years old at the time. 'A small man with a lively spirit and a penetrating eye, he had a pleasing and natural eloquence. His astonishing shrewdness and affable manner, which distinguished him among the princes, won him the support of men of substance as well as of the common people', was how one chronicler, not exactly disposed in his favour, subsequently described him.[1] Cunning, ambitious and utterly unscrupulous, he had spent nearly all of his young manhood in France, determined to avenge several grievances which he held against the Valois monarchy. These ultimately derived from the exclusion of his mother, the daughter of King Louis X of France and I of Navarre, from the succession to the French throne on Louis's death in 1328, and from certain lands and pensions which she had been awarded in place of the county of Champagne, which she had been obliged to surrender to secure the kingdom of Navarre. The compensation for Champagne had been several times renegotiated, and shortly before his mother's death in 1349 had been reduced to a few scattered lordships given in exchange for the county of Angoulême and an annual pension, which was largely in arrears. Charles's inheritance was thus greatly diminished. King John had tried to win him over with a grant of the lieutenancy of Languedoc in 1351 and the hand of his daughter, Joan, in marriage the following year. At the same time he pronounced Charles, although still a minor, to be of age. But John's apparent astuteness was undermined by the favour which he showed to another ambitious man at court, Charles of Spain, great-grandson of Louis IX, of the de la Cerda line, whom he had appointed constable of France and granted the county

---

1   *Chron. Rélig. Saint-Denis*, i, p. 468.

of Anglouléme shortly after his succession to the throne in 1350.[2]

Charles of Navarre's resentment of this favourite and the award of Angoulême to him finally drove the Navarrese king to arrange the ambush and murder of Charles of Spain at l'Aigle in Normandy in January of 1354, and to get in touch with the duke of Lancaster, seeking military assistance to meet the inevitable consequences. He may well have been serious in his intention to secure English troops, but by raising the spectre of their intervention on his behalf, he was able to put pressure on John to conclude an advantageous settlement of the differences between them. Although John forgave the murder, and awarded Charles considerable territories intended to meet his grievances, a feud had begun between the two men which was never really laid to rest during John's reign. Showing a serious lack of judgement, John awarded Charles the compensatory lands in Lower Normandy. In addition to the county of Beaumont-le-Roger, Breteuil and Conches, they included the viscounty of Pont-Audemer and a large part of the Cotentin peninsula. Together with the county of Évreux, which Charles had inherited from his father, these territories had substantially increased his income and, more importantly, gave him a powerful base in northern France, near Paris, which allowed easy access from England. After Charles had again colluded with Lancaster, once more threatening to facilitate the entry of English troops into Normandy, in April 1356 John had him arrested in Rouen, and began the process of recovering the lands and castles in Navarrese control. Following the English landings in Normandy in June of that year, Charles's younger brother, Philip, had concluded an alliance with Edward III at Clarendon on 4 September, and on 19 September King John was taken prisoner at Poitiers.[3] The combination of these different factors facilitated the prosecution of hostilities by Anglo-Navarrese forces during John's captivity in England.

The war was initially conducted between Philip and the dauphin Charles, who was responsible for the government of the realm during the captivity of his father, first as the king's lieutenant and then as regent. In the ensuing years English and Navarrese garrisons were established in a large number of towns and fortresses, not only in Lower Normandy and the Loire provinces, but further north and east, into Picardy, Beauvaisis and the Île-de-France.[4] In November 1357, Charles of Navarre had escaped his imprisonment and had entered Paris, where discontent against the

---

2 Delachenal, i, pp. 74–82, and for the Champagne settlement, see Viard, pp. 268, 270–3.
3 Delachenal, i, pp. 82–93, 106–9, 140–72; Fowler, 1969, pp. 122–9, 139–44, 147–53.
4 See the list of some 457 fortresses occupied by Anglo-Navarrese companies between 1356 and 1364 in Luce, pp. 459–509. Some of these were in fact occupied by the Great Companies.

government of the dauphin was daily increasing, and secured considerable support among the populace and Charles's councillors. The dauphin had little alternative but to accept an accommodation with Charles of Navarre, which included the return of all the lands, castles, towns and fortresses taken since his arrest, but the relations between the two men remained strained. Following the outbreak of a revolution in Paris, Charles was made captain of the city by the revolutionary leaders, and the war with the dauphin had continued until a settlement was concluded between the two men at Pontoise on 21 August 1359. When the Anglo-French peace was confirmed at Calais in 1360, a separate reconciliation with King John was mediated by Edward III, under the terms of which Charles recovered all of the lands and castles which had been taken from him during the course of the war. At a meeting with John in December, Charles undertook to abide by this peace and swore to be a 'good and loyal son and subject' of the French king. But the evacuation of fortresses occupied by Anglo-Navarrese companies presented essentially the same problems as did the submission of others, which were to be returned to the French under the terms of the treaty of Brétigny. The war against them continued throughout the remainder of John's reign, and was effectively reopened between the old protagonists at an official level following John's decisions in regard to the Burgundian succession, which provided Charles of Navarre with a new grievance to add to the old animosities.[5]

The prevailing political and military situation in Burgundy was complex. After the death of Duke Eudes IV in 1349, the duchy was in the hands of an infant, Philip of Rouvres, who had succeeded his grandfather, his own father having died at the siege of Aiguillon in Gascony in 1346. In 1350 his mother, Joan, countess of Boulogne and Auvergne, had remarried to John, later to become king of France. Philip was only fifteen when the king, on returning to France from his captivity in England, by an act dated 20 October 1360, gave him possession of his inheritance as if he had reached his majority, although its government thereafter remained in the control of his mother, the queen. In the following July he was married to Margaret of Flanders, the daughter of Louis de Male, count of Flanders, Nevers and Rethel, but four months later, on 21 November 1361, he was killed in a riding accident, as his father had been before him.[6] Philip's inheritance had then been partitioned between a number of rival claimants. On his mother's side his great uncle, Jean de Boulogne, had secured the counties of Boulogne and Auvergne. The remainder was divided between two claimants. Philip's great aunt Margaret of France, widow of the old count of Flanders, Louis

---

5 The best account of these events is still that of Delachenal, i, pp. 265–6, 323–7, 367–70, 417ff; ii, pp. 1–20, 119–32, 257–9, 265, 313, 352–62.
6 Chérest, pp. 101–2.

The Succession to the Duchy of Burgundy, 1361

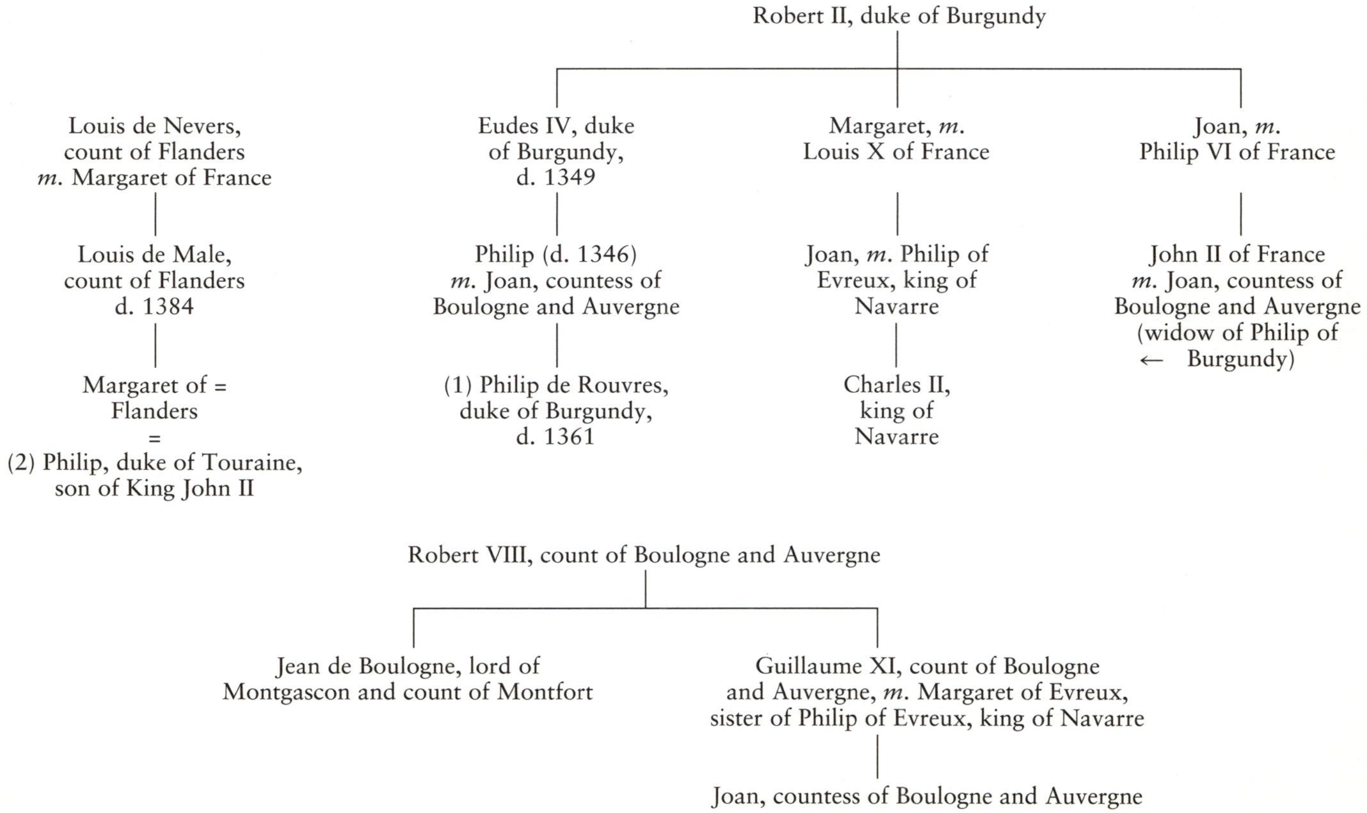

Robert II, duke of Burgundy
- Eudes IV, duke of Burgundy, d. 1349
  - Philip (d. 1346) *m.* Joan, countess of Boulogne and Auvergne
    - (1) Philip de Rouvres, duke of Burgundy, d. 1361
- Margaret, *m.* Louis X of France
  - Joan, *m.* Philip of Evreux, king of Navarre
    - Charles II, king of Navarre
- Joan, *m.* Philip VI of France
  - John II of France *m.* Joan, countess of Boulogne and Auvergne (widow of Philip of ← Burgundy)

Louis de Nevers, count of Flanders *m.* Margaret of France
- Louis de Male, count of Flanders d. 1384
  - Margaret of Flanders
    =
    (2) Philip, duke of Touraine, son of King John II

Robert VIII, count of Boulogne and Auvergne
- Jean de Boulogne, lord of Montgascon and count of Montfort
- Guillaume XI, count of Boulogne and Auvergne, *m.* Margaret of Evreux, sister of Philip of Evreux, king of Navarre
  - Joan, countess of Boulogne and Auvergne

de Nevers (d. 1346), and sister-in-law of Philip's grandfather, Eudes IV, secured the territories which had belonged to her mother, namely the counties of Burgundy and Artois, together with a number of castellanies and *prévôtés* in Champagne and Brie, known as the *terre de Champagne*. The other beneficiary was King John of France, who, as cousin of Philip de Rouvres' father, secured the duchy of Burgundy.

This settlement had created discontent on two fronts. On the one hand, it was disliked by the nobility of the county of Burgundy, which lay within imperial territory. They had never been happy about the acquisition of the county by Eudes IV, who had succeeded his mother-in-law there in 1330, and in the years after 1350 their discontent had been exacerbated by King John's guardianship of the young Philip de Rouvres. The other aggrieved party was Charles of Navarre, whose mother, like King John, was also a cousin of Philip's father, and who nursed added grievances over the disposal of the *terre de Champagne*, since he had never openly renounced his claims to Champagne and Brie, despite the numerous settlements of alternative lands and rents which had been made in lieu of them.[7] Moreover, the death of Philip de Rouvres had released onto the European marriage market his twelve-year-old widow, Margaret of Flanders, heiress to the counties of Flanders, Nevers and Rethel and now, through her grandmother, Margaret, also heiress to the counties of Burgundy and Artois. As early as February 1362, Edward III had begun negotiations for her marriage to his son Edmund Langley, earl of Cambridge, and Margaret's father was favourable to their union.[8] Had it come about, it would have greatly altered the balance of power in western Europe, and the acquisition of the county of Burgundy, where Edward had already been at work promoting his interests, would have provided a base for operations in eastern France.

For his part, Charles of Navarre had greatly resented the Burgundian succession settlement, believing that his claims were greater than those of King John, but through his mother, which French custom did not admit in the case of collaterals, and which Roman law limited to the first degree of kinship, namely between nephews. King John was, his councillors argued, Philip de Rouvres' closest relative 'as first cousin of his father and on the side from which the inheritance of the duchy derived'. Charles's lawyers, on the other hand, argued that in the matter of representation the custom of Burgundy made no distinction between different orders of succession. A century later, the official redaction of that custom would have borne them out. In the event, the succession had been settled on political grounds. Charles had not only been left out of the partition of the inheritance of

---

[7] Delachenal, ii, pp. 287–91, iii, pp. 27–8; Chérest, pp. 101–2, 108.
[8] Vaughan, p. 4.

Philip de Rouvres, but did not even get the castellanies and *prévôtés* which constituted the *terre de Champagne*. Frustrated in what he regarded as his legitimate rights, he ignored the declarations which he had made at the time of the peace of Pontoise in the summer of 1359 (to the effect that he would order his forces to abandon the castles which they had taken in the years which followed the battle of Poitiers), and the assurances given to John II when the two kings had met at Saint-Denis in December 1360. He now determined to secure by force of arms what he regarded as legitimately his.[9]

The annexation of the duchy of Burgundy by John II also aroused concern in the county of Burgundy, where the nobility had not welcomed the king's attentions in their affairs during the minority of Philip de Rouvres. Even Eudes IV, in attempting to build up his authority in the county, had met with singular opposition from some of the leading families – the Chalons, Montfaucons, Neufchâtels, Faucogneys – who were closely interrelated and had important political and family connections elsewhere in the Empire: in the imperial territory of Bresse, the county of Neufchâtel in present-day Switzerland, and in the marches of Lorraine and Upper Alsace, as well as in the kingdom of France. Already before the death of Philip of Rouvres, Edward III had exploited these differences, perhaps hoping to gain a foothold in eastern France as he had previously done in Flanders and Brittany. He had subsidized the discontented with pensions and other money payments, as well as a number of families in the neighbouring province of Bresse. Some of these, like Jean de Chalon-Arlay, whose French possessions were concentrated in Auxois and Nivernais, had returned into French allegiance and were pardoned for their confederations, but others remained intractable. After King John's capture at Poitiers, they had made no secret of their allegiances. The lords of Faucogney and Neufchâtel were included on the English side in the truce of Bordeaux in 1357, but Neufchâtel and the lord of Rigny, near Gray, were also in the pay of Charles of Navarre.[10]

Jean de Neufchâtel, son of Louis, count of Neufchâtel, and of Jeanne de Montfaucon, was connected on his mother's side with all of the leading families of the county of Burgundy, especially through his grandfather, Henri de Montfaucon, count of Montbéliard, and he himself had added to these alliances by his marriage to Jeanne de Faucogney. Sometime before 1358 – we cannot be sure precisely when – he had gone into Navarrese service, and in March of that year he had secured from Charles of Navarre, then in control of Paris, a safe-conduct to travel throughout France for two

---

9 Delachenal, ii, pp. 287–91.
10 Chérest, pp. 109–14. Bresse: *Inventaire-sommaire, Côte-d'Or*, ii, p. 109 (B 4392). Truce: *Foedera*, i, p. 348. For Neufchâtel's supporters, see Finot, p. 82.

months, together with his friend and companion, Henry of Longvy, lord of Rahon, and thirty mounted persons in their entourage.[11] Their purpose, like that of other English and Navarrese partisans, had been to conduct espionage activities on the frontiers of the duchy of Burgundy and to join up with the companies then occupying Champagne in attacks upon it. During the course of that summer, in conjunction with two disaffected natives of Champagne, Thibaut and Jean de Chauffour, he had conducted a campaign in the northern marches of Burgundy, doing a great deal of damage in the neighbourhood of Chaumont and Langres, from where he made continual incursions into the duchy. On one of these the two brothers, with the assistance of the company of Guillaume Pot (alias Guillemin Pot, Guillampot), took the strongly fortified castle of Montsaugeon.[12] He also contributed forces to the defence of the castle of Beaufort in Champagne, which was of the inheritance of the duke of Lancaster and occupied by an Anglo-Navarrese garrison under Peter Audley.[13] In the following year, in operations conducted with Girard de Mairey, marshal of Navarre, he took the castle of Brion-sur-Ource, which assured their entry into the duchy by the *bailliage* of Châtillon, and on 2 July completely defeated a small force which had been brought up to resist them. Three weeks later, in a treaty concluded for its evacuation, the names of a number of English captains were listed as conducting operations under the Navarrese umbrella, including Robert Knowles, who was installed at the castle of Regennes, his lieutenant John Waldboef, and William Starkey, who had established himself at Ligny-le-Châtel.[14] At the end of that year he joined Edward III before Reims, and along with another noble from the county of Burgundy, William Grandson, lord of Saint-Croix, he guided Edward's army through the passes which gave access to the heart of Burgundy, and was instrumental in negotiating the treaty of Guillon with him.[15]

From the moment of his acquisition of the duchy John had thus faced opposition from three quarters: from the nobility of the county, from Charles of Navarre, and from the English and Navarrese companies whose operations into the duchy had intensified after Edward III's campaign there in 1359–60. John had acted quickly to forestall any immediate trouble. Within nine days of Philip de Rouvres' death he appointed the count of

11   The compiler of the *Grandes Chroniques*, vi, pp. 96–7 (*Chron. Jean II*, i, pp. 160–1), recites the text of the safe-conduct.
12   Chérest, pp. 117, 119; Froissart, *Chroniques*, v, pp. 135–6, 352, and Luce in ibid., p. xliii n. 10.
13   Chérest, pp. 117–18; Froissart, *Chroniques*, v, p. 135 and, for Lancastrian claims thereto, see Fowler, 1969, index, sub Beaufort.
14   Chérest pp. 118–20; Petit, ix, pp. 160–1; cf. Delachenal, ii, pp. 167–8. For the treaty (AD, Côte-d'Or, B 11935, no. 1) see Chérest, pp. 393–5, PJ no. xii.
15   Froissart, *Chroniques*, v, p. 401; PRO E 101/393/11 (Grandson); Chérest, pp. 125–6; Delachenal, ii, p. 164; Fowler, 1969, p. 205 and n. 46.

Tancarville his lieutenant in the duchy and instructed him to take up his charge immediately. He had also secured the services of the Archpriest and, before Christmas, visited the duchy, confirming privileges and granting pensions to the chief officers.[16] Then, in June 1363, he had replaced Tancarville with his son, Philip, duke of Touraine, and on 6 September he had secretly invested him with the duchy.[17]

In the months which followed the occupation of Brioude there was a general alert on the western frontiers of Burgundy, where other *routes* of the Great Companies were making incursions. On 23 October 1363, the ducal council informed the *bailli* of Chalon that some 1,200 men-at-arms, equipped with scaling ladders, were planning to take Tournus or Uchizy, on the west bank of the Saône between Chalon and Mâcon, or some other town which they could use as a bridgehead to cross that river. They instructed him to advise the inhabitants and captains of fortresses on either side of the river to be on their guard by day and night, especially the abbot of Tournus; to inform those possessing boats which could be used to cross the river to prevent them from falling into the hands of the enemy; to evacuate the towns and fortresses in the open country and to order the inhabitants of his *bailliage* to do everything to prevent damage being done to the country.[18] Further west other *routes*, including among their number Robert Knowles, Robert Birkhead and John Cresswell, were menacing the territory between the rivers Loire and Allier, from Moulins in Auvergne to Saint-Pierre-le-Moutier and Saint-Pourçain in the Bourbonnais.[19] These different contingents were probably in liaison with those operating from Brioude, and it was at this time that Saint-Pourçain was threatened by a company commanded by Johann Hazenorgue.[20] At the end of October, one of these *routes*, predominantly English and Gascon in composition and possibly commanded by Bernard and Hortingo de la Salle, crossed the Loire at Marcigny-les-Nonnains and, secluding themselves in woods during the day, proceeded by night until they reached La Charité-sur-Loire, which they took by escalade, shortly after midnight on 29 October.[21]

The town of La Charité, on the east bank of the Loire, was a substantial

16 Chérest, pp. 143–9; Delachenal, ii, pp. 290–1.
17 Delachenal, ii, p. 355; Vaughan, p. 3. The grant was confirmed by Charles V shortly after his succession in June 1364 and the lieutenancy extended to include the dioceses of Lyon, Mâcon, Autun, Chalons and Langres.
18 BN, coll. Bourgogne, xxvi, p. 118; Petit, x, pp. 59–60.
19 Froissart, *Chroniques*, vi, pp. 137–8. Delachenal, *Charles V*, iii, p. 141ff., demonstrates that Louis de Navarre could not have been involved at this stage.
20 See above, p. 79.
21 Only Froissart, in one of the manuscripts of the first book of his *Chroniques*, vi, p. 138, attributes this action to the de la Salles. Luce in ibid., vi, p. lxi n. 2, quotes from a letter of remission of January 1367 where it is said that the town was taken in October by 'Angloiz, Gascons et autres gens de Compaigne'. For the exact date, see Froissart, *Chroniques*, vi, p. 315, and Petit, x, p. 62 n. 2.

place and strategically well situated.[22] It commanded one of the best crossings of that river and the road from Bourges which led into Burgundy by way of Varzy. Dominated by the Cluniac priory and its great romanesque tower, the town was encircled with ramparts which were commanded by nine towers, and access and egress were limited to four well-defended gates. The castle was situated to the north-east of the town, on the side adjoining the river, above the bridge, and commanded both the plateau and the valley. The town was thus an ideal stronghold from which to conduct raiding parties westwards, from the bridge which led over the river, into Berry and the Orleánais, to the east into Burgundy, and to the south into Nivernais. It gave the companies control of the upper Loire valley and was a base from which they were able to threaten the entire western frontier of Burgundy. It could be used as an entrepôt for amassing booty, and was an excellent place of refuge. Its capture was unquestionably a major success for the companies, who held it until the spring of 1365, and a disaster for the surrounding countryside, in particular the duchy of Burgundy.

The count of Nevers had no sovereign rights at La Charité. The jurisdiction of the town rested with the prior, save the right of garrison, which had been claimed by the king of France since the time of Saint-Louis. Aware of the menace which its seizure by the companies posed for the surrounding provinces, during the second week of November Philip of Touraine, now duke of Burgundy, held a conference at Semur-en-Auxois, at which the Archpriest was present, which favoured immediate action against them. However, as the garrison of La Charité was daily reinforced by the companies, further intelligence ruled out any serious consideration of immediate action there, which would entail a long siege. Philip's first priorities were to clear the companies operating from across the western frontiers of the duchy, from Arcy-sur-Cure, to the south-east of Auxerre above Avallon, which was occupied by Gilles Troussevache, and Vésigneux to the south of Avallon. Detachments of the same band also occupied other places in the Auxerrois and around Tonnerre. Troussevache was bought out of Arcy, which was subsequently demolished, whilst Vésigneux was besieged. The menace from La Charité did not seriously present itself until the following February, when Gascon and Breton companies operating out of there pushed into the Avallonais and Auxois, threatened to take Châtillon-sur-Seine, and burned a number of places on the outskirts of Auxerre. The ducal council even believed that Nuits-Saint-Georges, Beaune and Chalon were threatened by their operations, and during the course of that month were constantly sending messengers to different parts of the duchy

22 See the excellent description of La Charité in Bossuat, pp. 31–3.

'for information about the state of the country and about those of La Charité'.[23]

During the second half of 1363 a more serious threat to the duchy of Burgundy was perceived to come from across the Saône, from the county of Burgundy. From August of that year the Chalonnais and Dijonais were at the mercy of bands who took several castles by escalade and ransomed merchants going from Troyes to the fairs of Chalon, necessitating the provision of armed escorts. Towards the end of the year the ducal council was despatching messengers almost daily, informing its officials of enemy troop movements 'from across the Saône', which they believed threatened Pontailler-sur-Saône and Saint-Jean-de-Losne. Hugues de Chalon-Arlay and Jean de Neufchâtel and their forces were rumoured to be intending to cross the Saône in the neighbourhood of Mâcon, and to enter the duchy at points which they had already reconnoitred and prepared. Sporadic incursions began at the end of December 1363 when a contingent from the county secured the Saône crossing at Apremont, below Gray, taking a number of places west of the river, notably the castles of Dampierre and Montot. Neufchâtel and the lord of Rigney pushed further up the Saône and along the Vingeanne valley, which took them to the outskirts of Langres, before returning into the neighbourhood of Vesoul.[24]

The ducal council clearly feared a full-scale invasion of the duchy, and Philip the Bold immediately set about recruiting forces to resist them, installing new garrisons and appointing new captains to places under threat. These included the companies of a number of Gascon lords, in addition to those of the Soudich de La Trau, lord of Préchac, and of Amanieu de Pommiers, which had been recruited earlier, namely those of Amanieu's brother, Jean de Pommiers, of Jean d'Armagnac, of Giraud de Montaut of the house of Mussidan and of Guillaume Raimon de Cadillac, lord of Rauzan. A number of other companies, mostly Breton, were also hired from among the Archpriest's forces or through his agency, notably those of Jacques de Pencoédic, Yvon de Lacoué, Ernauton and Jean de Saint-Pol, Jean de Saint-Ryot and Munde Bataillier. The policy was disastrous. Few mercenary companies were prepared to fight against their kinsmen and former companions in arms, and most of the Gascons had fought with the Black Prince at Poitiers.[25] After a short campaign along the Saône frontier, which accomplished very little, but left the western

---

23 Petit, x, pp. 63–7, 76; Chérest, pp. 239–40; Vernier, pp. 249–50.
24 For the above, see Vernier, pp. 252–3; Chérest, pp. 230–1; Petit, x, pp. 67–9; Finot, pp. 84–7.
25 Chérest, p. 234, and for the Gascons at Poitiers, Delachenal, i, pp. 192–3. In 1363 Bataillier had been serving under the Archpriest, who had been engaged by Henri de Joinville, lord of Vaudémont, in his war against the duchy of Bar in 1363 (Contamine, 1975, p. 380 n. 1). For his questionable activities in Burgundian service in the summer of 1364, see Petit, x, pp. 90, 96, 104, 108–9, 114, 120.

approaches of the duchy open to attack from Gascon and Breton companies operating out of La Charité, an accommodation was reached with the countess Margaret of Burgundy in February and Philip demobilized most of his mercenary forces, including the companies of Jean d'Armagnac, Amanieu de Pommiers and Arnaud de Tallebard. Among the Gascons, only the services of the Soudich de La Trau, with a relatively small company of men, were retained. With their pay heavily in arrears, they turned to raiding the country they had been engaged to protect, in search of food and money, burning villages, holding the inhabitants to ransom and extracting payment for safe-conducts. Arnaud de Tallebard even arrested the ducal receiver-general of taxes on the public highway and helped himself to what he claimed was due to him. The garrison of Pontailler, which was composed of Bretons and Gascons under the command of Jean de Saint-Ryot, Yvon de Lacoué and Ernauton de Saint-Pol, refused to depart until they were paid. The situation was much the same elsewhere: the necessary money was not available to pay Philip's erstwhile servitors off. It was not until June 1364, when Bertrand du Guesclin was recruiting forces for service against the Navarrese in Normandy, and sent two of his esquires to Burgundy to engage the Breton companies operating there, that the garrison of Pontailler finally quit. Others remained behind, establishing themselves in the duchy, blocking roads and living off the countryside. A number of contingents of the Great Companies took advantage of the resulting chaos. At the beginning of March, Guillaume Pot and Bertucat d'Albret took La Ferté-sur-Grosne and Saint-Gengoux, on the west bank of the Saône above and below Tournus. In April another company took Romenay, on the other side of the river, south-east of Tournus. In June others penetrated to the north-west of Dijon, taking up quarters at Chaumes and Darcy. By the end of the following month their numbers were estimated to total some 6,000 cavalry under the command of Pierre d'Oignel, Tallebard, Munde Bataillier and Jean de Saint-Pol; they continued to ravage the neighbourhood until the end of October. The situation was not helped by Philip the Bold, who, at the end of June, had taken the feudal contingents of the duchy off to Normandy, where they were employed against the Navarrese.[26]

From May 1362 Charles of Navarre had determined to settle his differences with King John by force of arms, but it was not until the autumn of the following year, after he had concluded an offensive and defensive alliance with the King of Aragon at Uncastillo (25 August 1363), that he was able

---

26 Petit, x, pp. 79–80, 87–90, 130–1; Vernier, pp. 250–1 and 251 n. 3; Chérest, pp. 240 n. 5, 263–4, 264 n. 2, and PJ no. xviii.

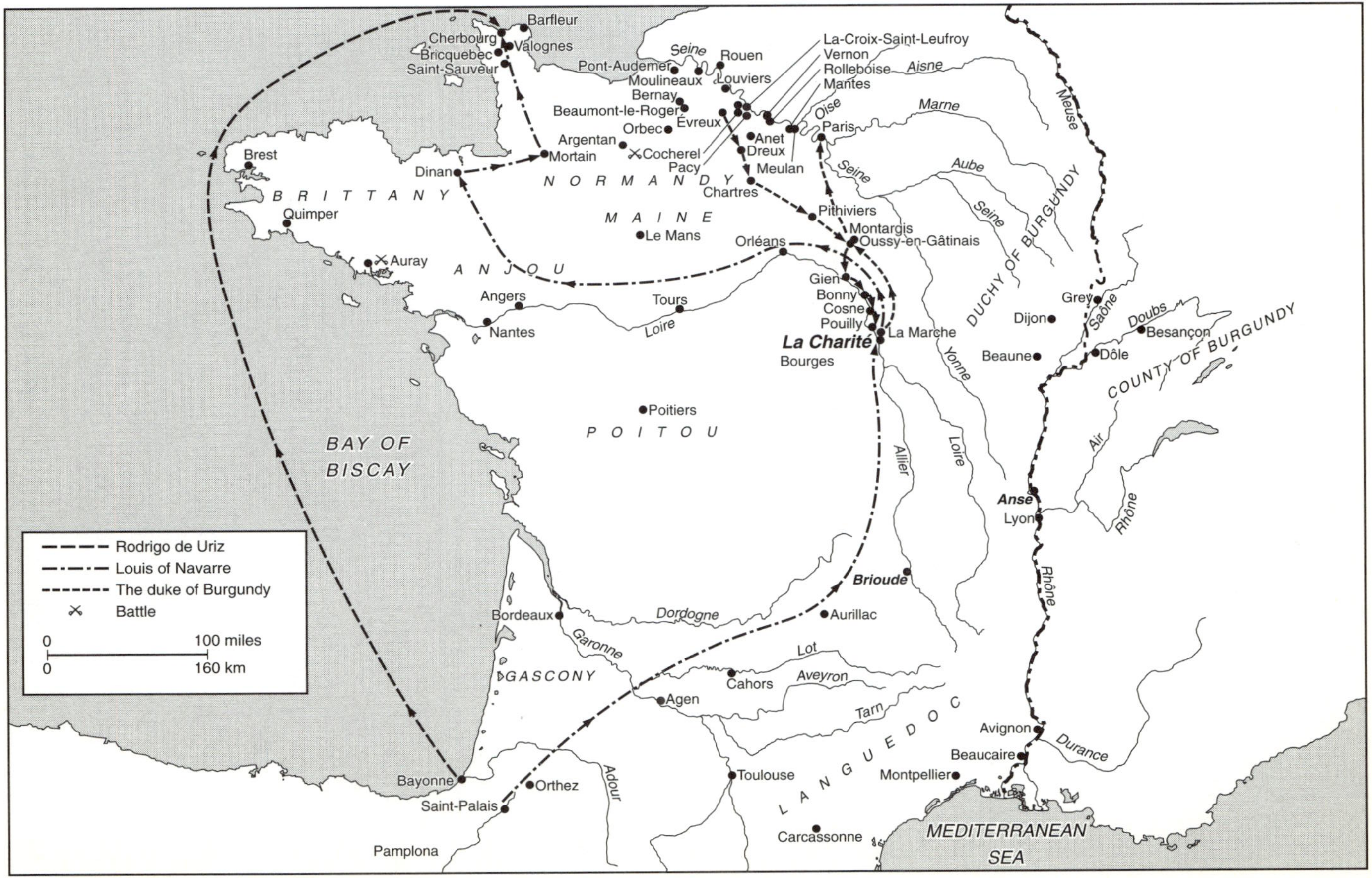

4 *The Normandy front and the Navarrese counter-offensive, August–October 1364*

to pursue his objectives seriously.[27] By the terms of this treaty Charles undertook to support Peter IV of Aragon against Pedro of Castile, after which they were to make war together in France, Charles undertaking to cede the seneschalsies of Beaucaire and Carcassonne to Pere once he had acquired them. The king of Navarre may have received certain subventions from the king of Aragon to this end, and by mid-October was evidently recruiting forces in Spain for an eventual campaign against King John.[28] By the early spring of 1364, plans had clearly been worked out for a two-pronged attack in France. One army was to operate from the west, where the Navarrese garrisons in Normandy were to be reinforced by forces arriving by land and sea from Gascony and Navarre. Another, under his brother Louis, was to be recruited from several contingents of the Great Companies who were to join up with others established in central and eastern France, most notably at La Charité-sur-Loire. With support from his old friends in the county of Burgundy they were to invade the duchy on two fronts.

It is difficult to be sure when the first steps to implement this plan of campaign were taken, but it is likely that the envisaged attack on the duchy of Burgundy followed a progressive consolidation of Charles's relations with a number of the Great Companies, and with Jean de Neufchâtel and other nobles from the county including, from the neighbourhood of Besançon, the lord of Rigney and Jean de Quingey, all of whom had been in receipt of pensions from Charles from an early date.[29] In April 1363 payments were being made from the Navarrese treasury to a number of Neufchâtel's esquires,[30] and it is evident that serious negotiations were in progress by October of that year.[31] It is possible that the capture of La Charité in October 1363 and Neufchâtel's incursions into the duchy at the end of the year were already part of a consolidated plan of action. Whatever the case they wittingly or unwittingly provided some of the building blocks for Charles's plans. These clearly involved a tacit understanding with Edward, the Black Prince, through whose territories the Navarrese forces had to pass. The prince could not be seen to be giving open support to Charles, and the subject of their contacts was veiled in secrecy. Nevertheless, during the course of 1363 several Navarrese embassies were sent to the prince and to Jean de Grailly, captal de Buch, who

27 For this and what follows, see Fowler, 1988, pp. 26–31.
28 *AGN, Comptos*, v, nos. 228, 378; vi, no. 1096. For the treaty, see Delachenal, iii, p. 30 n. 1, and for the subventions Honoré-Duvergé, 1964, p. 100.
29 AD, Jura, E 533 (Neufchâtel and Ringey); BN, Clairambault, 92, p. 7179 (acquittance of Jean de Quingey, 'chevalier du roi de Navarre', 26 September 1362); BN, Clairambault, 80, no. 77. See Finot, pp. 81–2; Honoré-Duvergé, 1964, p. 100.
30 *AGN, Comptos*, iv, nos. 1109, 1117.
31 In October 1363 an esquire of Burgundy who had been sent to Navarre was *enviado en su pais por necesidades del rey* (ibid., iv, no. 1504).

was to have charge of the western army. At the end of December Charles himself travelled to Agen to meet the prince and Sir John Chandos, and it seems likely that Edward gave the final go-ahead at this meeting. The presence of Chandos was important. As constable of Aquitaine he was in charge of the forces of the principality, and as lord of Saint-Sauveur in the Cotentin peninsula he controlled one of the principal fortresses in Charles's lands there. He also maintained contacts with the English and Gascon contingents of the Great Companies.

In the ensuing days the arrangements were probably discussed with the captal, whom the king of Navarre met at Cadillac immediately after his meeting with the prince.[32] Charles also promoted his interests with a number of the prince's household officers: his marshal Guichard d'Angle and his steward Sir Henry Hay were retained for considerable sums in February.[33] Around the same time he was seeking to recruit forces from among the Gascon lords held prisoner by the count of Foix since Launac, and among the captains of the Great Companies with whom Gaston had maintained contact: Espiote, Bertuquin, Johann Hazenorgue and Petit Meschin.[34] Sometime before 10 May, at Orthez in Béarn, Louis of Navarre negotiated an arrangement with them for the employment of their companies.[35] All four had served with the count of Foix at Launac. Espiote had remained in his service in 1363, and the negotiations conducted with them at Orthez had also involved the count.[36] The part played by Espiote was crucial. Following a meeting with Charles at Orthez at the beginning of April, and his homage to the king at Larrasoaña shortly afterwards, he was the first of the captains of the companies to go into Charles's pay.[37] In return for 20,000 florins they were to take part, with their *routes*, in a campaign in France under the command of Louis, who assembled an army

---

32 Honoré-Duvergé, 1964, p. 101; *AGN, Comptos*, iv, nos. 1703, 1708; v, nos. 261, 547, 576. Cf. Sumption, ii, p. 505.
33 AGN, Sección de Comptos, reg. 111, fos. 53r (grant dated 28 February of 800 florins to Guichard and 700 florins to Hay). Honoré-Duvergé, 1964, p. 101, gives the sums of 800 and 200 florins respectively, citing ibid., fo 90r, and dating the grants 6 February.
34 The missions of Peyron de Gavastón to Béarn in January 1364 were almost certainly in this connection (*AGN, Comptos*, v, nos. 31–2; Tucoo-Chala, 1960, p. 97 and n. 50). See Secousse, *Recueil*, p. 206, art. 21.
35 'Item al muyt noble Don Loys, Inffant de Navarra, por fazen sus expensas en yr a Pont d'Ortes a fablar al conte de Foix et a Espiote de ciertos negocios tocantes al seynnor Rey, segunt pareçe por su lettra data x° dia de mayo, anno lxiiii°, ii° escudados veios, cada uno por xviii sueldos, vallen ix^{xx} libras, (AGN, Sección de Comptos, reg. 111, fo. 35r). See also *AGN, Comptos*, v, nos. 297–9, 327, 340, 342; Secousse, *Recueil*, p. 206, art. 23.
36 *AGN, Comptos*, v, nos. 327, 340, 342. On the relations with Foix, see Larroyoz-Zarranz, p. 132.
37 *AGN, Comptos*, v, nos. 186, 209, 215–16, 264, 269. On 26 May he acted as proxy for Hazenorgue's homage (ibid., no. 271). Petit Meschin did his same day (ibid., no. 270), but Bertuquin, who was in Languedoc, was dead by 14 June (ibid., no. 330; see above, p. 74).

of 800 lances and 2,000 infantry in the Pyrenean foothills, in the marches of Bigorre and Navarre around the town of Saint-Palais.[38]

By the time this army was assembled, the original plan of action had been overtaken by events. During the course of March the captal de Buch had proceeded north from the principality of Aquitaine with a small force, largely Gascon in composition, which was intended to reinforce the Navarrese garrisons in Normandy whilst further troops were assembled in Navarre for the forthcoming campaign. By the time he reached his destination at the end of April, French royal forces had conducted a lightning campaign, securing the Seine bridgeheads at Mantes, Meulan and Vernon, as well as the stronghold of Rolleboise, and Vertheuil and Rosny, on the banks of the river. Hastily gathering together at Évreux such forces as he could, the captal had engaged a French army commanded by du Guesclin at Cocherel on 16 May, and was completely defeated, the greater part of his army being either killed or captured, the captal himself being taken prisoner.[39]

There can be no doubt that the Navarrese position in Normandy had been seriously compromised, and the roads to Paris blocked; but in other ways the battle was not immediately decisive. Although Charles V followed up the victory on three different fronts, sending du Guesclin to besiege Valognes and even placing contingents around Évreux, the position of the Anglo-Navarrese remained strong in Lower Normandy and in the Cotentin. They continued to hold Évreux and a number of places which formed a second line of defence along the rivers Eure and Risle: Pacy, Anet, Beaumont-le-Roger and Pont-Audemer; and they reconquered Acquigny, below Louviers, from the French. Most of the territory between the rivers Risle and Touques, bounded to the south by the Charentonne, remained in their hands, with sizeable garrisons at Bernay and Orbec. In addition they held a number of smaller places to the east of Argentan. In the Cotentin, they could be assured of friendly neutrality from the garrison of Saint-Sauveur-le-Vicômte and, most important, they held on to Cherbourg, through whose port Charles could continue to ship in reinforcements and supplies. Cherbourg was itself protected from the south by the fortresses of Brique-

---

38 Berrardeco de Saint-Pierre and Moret de Buch evidently substituted for Hazenorgue and Bertuquin: 'Item, a Menaut de Villers, dicho Espiote, a Moret de Buchg, Hellias Machin, dicho Petit Machin, et Berradeco de Sant Per, capitanes de la grant compaynna, los quoals el seynnor Rey les mando dar por ciertos composiciones at aveniencas factas entr'eill et los dichos capitanes por la yda que fazen en Francia et en Normandia en compaynnia del seynnor Inffant Don Loys de Navarra, segunt pareçe por lettra del dicho seynnor Rey, data xx° dia d'agosto anno lxiiii°, xx^m florines, cada uno por xiii sueldos, vallen xiii^m libras' (AGN, Sección de Comptos, reg. 111, fo. 64r); cf. AGN, Comptos, v, no. 532. Numbers: Petit, x, p. 116. Saint-Palais: AGN, Sección de Comptos, reg. 111, fo. 42v; AGN, Comptos, v, nos. 343, 453.
39 Delachenal, iii, pp. 33–64; Honoré-Duvergé, 1964, pp. 102–5; Larroyoz-Zarranz, pp. 122–8; cf. Sumption, ii, pp. 505–11.

bec, Magneville and Valognes, and had a second line of defence in a number of smaller places which extended southwards from the north-west of the peninsula. After the capture of the captal, the defence of these territories fell to his cousin Pierre de Landiras, acting as lieutenant of the captal until Louis de Navarre was able to take over command.[40]

Undeterred by the crushing defeat at Cocherel, Charles pressed ahead with his plans. The shipment of reinforcements through Cherbourg, already envisaged before Cocherel, became that much more pressing as the French royal forces continued with the reduction of towns and fortresses in Normandy, albeit at a slower pace. The plan was now to draw them off by a pre-emptive strike through central France in the direction of Burgundy, and during the two months following Cocherel preparations were speeded up to give these stratagems effect. At the end of July a small expeditionary force under the command of Rodrigo de Uriz was embarked at Bayonne together with artillery and other supplies bound for Cherbourg.[41] In Normandy, Charles's forces went on the offensive and scored a major success at the begining of August when Pierre de Sault, a Béarnese captain in Navarrese service, took the fortress of Moulineaux on the south bank of the Seine below Rouen.[42] In the Pyrenean foothills Louis of Navarre, who was appointed Charles's lieutenant and captain-general 'in France, Normandy and Burgundy', assembled his army around Saint-Palais during the last fortnight in July, and was joined there briefly by Charles on 4 August.[43] On the 5th he made a grant to the prior and convent of the hospital of Roncesvalles for a chaplain to incant a perpetual mass for his wellbeing during his lifetime and after his death for the salvation of his soul, before setting out on the long trek north on the 6th.[44] From Saint-Palais his forces proceeded through the principality of Aquitaine, making their way by the upper Dordogne to reach the outskirts of Aurillac in the march of Auvergne by 22 August.[45] Marshal Audrehem, who may have expected them to head for French territory by the valley of the Aveyron, assembled an army of

---

40 Delachenal, iii, pp. 124–5; Honoré-Duvergé, 1964, p. 105; Masson d'Autume, p. 11.
41 AGN, Sección de Comptos, reg. 111, fos. 64r, 65r; AGN, Comptos, v, nos. 341, 348, 356, 358–9, 365, 367, 370, 383, 402, 404–5, 409, 413–20, 432, 434–9, 447–51, 463–9, 476, 480, 483. This material is analysed by Larroyoz-Zarranz, pp. 133–8. See also Goyheneche, pp. 110–11.
42 Chron. premiers Valois, pp. 154–5.
43 Louis had been appointed lieutenant in July 1364, and was in Saint Palais by the 22nd of that month (AGN, Comptos, v, nos. 453, 473; Brutails, Documents, pp. 93–4, no. xciii; and for the title Delachenal, iii, p. 31 n. 3). Charles was at Saint-Palais 4–6 August, but at Saint-Jean on 7th and 8th, at Roncesvalles on the 9th and back in Pamplona on the 12th (AGN, Comptos, v, nos. 490–6, 499, 501, 508). Delachenal, iii, p. 141, was mistaken in concluding that Louis took advantage of the treaty of Uncastillo to enter France via Roussillon, although this may have been the original intention.
44 AGN, Comptos, v, nos. 491, 499.
45 BN, coll. Bourgogne, xxvi, fo. 116r; Petit, x, pp. 116–17.

800 lances and 6,000 infantry to block their progress on the frontier, or to pursue them if they made for Auvergne.[46] Louis's forces evidently eluded him and pushed north to La Charité, where they had arrived sometime before 23 September.[47] The French had clearly feared that he would join up with other contingents of the Great Companies occupying fortresses between the rivers Loire and Allier, and had initially concluded that their ultimate destination was the duchy of Burgundy,[48] where Jean de Neufchâtel had reopened hostilities. At the end of June, he conducted a preliminary attack across the Saône with 200 lances and 300 infantry, burning the *faubourgs* of Pontailler and six neighbouring towns before returning to the county where his uncle, the count of Montbéliard, under instructions from the countess Margaret, had been mobilizing a larger army since the 24th of that month. These forces were ordered to recover a number of places on the east bank of the Saône and elsewhere in the county, which had been taken by the companies under Philip's command since December 1363, and their invasion of the duchy was expected around 9 July.[49]

Charles of Navarre's hand can certainly be seen behind these preparations. In early June he had sent the Hospitaller, Brother Juan de San Julián, on a mission to Jean de Neufchâtel, the subject of which is not disclosed, but is evident from the course of events, and from subsequent documentation.[50] Jean de Montagu, lord of Sombernon and governor of Burgundy, attempted to put together an army to resist Montbéliard's forces, calling on such feudal contingents as remained in the duchy to assemble at Dijon, the greater part having been taken off to Normandy by Philip the Bold.[51] Once again the services of the Archpriest had to be called upon, together with the Breton companies of Jean de Saint-Pol and Munde Bataillier, and the Gascons under Amanieu de Pommiers and Jean d'Armagnac, although the ducal council was perplexed as to where the money was to be found to

---

46 'Et nous sommes ez frontières bien viii^c lances et vi^m servants de pié très bien armez ... et est nostre entente, à l'ayde de Dieu, de leur deffendre l'entrée et de les combattre, se ils viennent vers nous, et se ils vont vers vous par le duchié, j'ay intention de les poursieurre' (BN, coll. Bourgogne, xxvi, fo. 117r; Petit, x, pp. 115–16). The letter is dated at 'Martial', 5 August. Petit, p. 115 n. 4, makes this Martial, a commune of Salles-Curan, to the north-west of Millau, but Martiel, to the west of Villefranche-de-Rouergue, is equally possible. It should be noted that both places lay within the principality of Aquitaine.
47 This is evident from a letter written by Philip the Bold to the *bailli* of Auxois when he was near Cosne-sur-Loire, where he arrived on the evening of 23 September (BN, coll. Bourgogne, xxvi, fo. 129r; Petit, x, pp. 122–3; *Itin. Phil. le Hardi*, p. 13). By that date Louis may in fact have been there some time.
48 Petit, x, pp. 92, 116–17, 120–1; Finot, pp. 83–4; see Froissart, *Chroniques*, vi, pp. lxi and n. 1, 137–8.
49 BN, coll. Bourgogne, xxvi, fos. 119r, 125r; Petit, x, pp. 92–5; Chérest, p. 270. For the main contingents under Montbéliard's command, see Finot, p. 82.
50 *AGN, Comptos*, v, nos. 412, 453; AGN, Sección de Comptos, reg. 111, fo. 73v; AD, Jura, E 533; see below, pp. 114–15.
51 Petit, x, pp. 93–4.

pay them.[52] The combined forces, under the command of the governor and the Archpriest, crossed the Saône at Auxonne and proceeded north to Pesmes and Gray, where they sought an engagement with Montbéliard. The count declined it and withdrew his troops to the plain above Villers-Farlay, to the south-east of Dôle. This was doubtless a better place to engage the ducal forces should a battle prove inevitable.

The French intelligence services were on red alert during the summer of 1364. Charles V, who had been kept fully informed about the situation in the duchy through the agency of the *bailli* of Sens, who met with Margaret's councillor, Anseau de Salins, concluded an arrangement with the countess Margaret, which on 25 July resulted in a truce until 21 November, by which time it was hoped that a settlement of outstanding disputes could be reached. Under its terms Philip the Bold was to evacuate his forces from the county, including the companies in his service, to restore to the countess the places taken by them, and to hand over prisoners detained in Dôle. The count of Montbéliard and Jean de Neufchâtel were not obliged to accept a suspension of arms, but pressure was evidently put on them to do so. If they declined, Philip retained the right to resist them and undertook that the countess would be fully indemnified for any damage done in her lands. The arrangement was obviously makeshift and the evacuation arrangements difficult to implement. But from Margaret's point of view it offered the prospect of removing the companies from her territories, and for the French it reduced, if only temporarily, the threat from the county. For his part Neufchâtel refused to be bound by it, but kept a low profile until the following spring.[53]

News of Louis of Navarre's progress northwards had the desired effect of drawing French forces off from Normandy. There were two armies operating there at the beginning of September, one under the command of the duke of Burgundy and Marshal Boucicaut, which had begun to besiege Moulineaux, and another commanded by Mouton de Blainville, which was besieging Évreux. Under Charles V's instructions both sieges were abandoned on 12 September. After joining forces at La Croix-Saint-Leufroy, the combined army under the command of the duke of Burgundy proceeded eastwards by way of Dreux, Chartres, Pithiviers, Corbeilles and Oussoy-en-Gâtinais near Montargis to deal with the new threat. On 20 September Philip reviewed his troops at Oussoy, retaining them for a further month, evidently in expectation of a long siege. The following day he was at Gien-sur-Loire, from where he proceeded along the east bank of the Loire to Bonny, Cosne and Pouilly, to the north of La Charité, and on the 26th he

---

52 BN, coll. Bourgogne, xxvi, fo. 119r; Petit, x, pp. 95–7; Chérest, pp. 269–70; Finot, pp. 82–3.
53 Ibid., pp. 98–100. Truce: AD, Doubs, B 59; Finot, pp. 88–90.

established his quarters at La Marche, some two-and-a-half miles upstream from La Charité and on the same side of the river. By the time they had reached Cosne-sur-Loire on the night of 23 September, after a leisurely enough progress, Louis was already firmly entrenched at La Charité. From a letter to the *bailli* of Auxois, written that day, it is evident that Philip was not clear about Louis' intentions – whether he was heading further into France or would make for the duchy of Burgundy. In either event, the duke indicated that he had an army of 2,500 lances, that their numbers were increasing daily, and that he was ready to engage Louis's forces. The country was so denuded of supplies that his army soon found itself without victuals and sufficient forage for the horses, a large number of which died of starvation. Louis meanwhile refused to budge and had the added advantage that, being in control of the bridge over the Loire, he was able to replenish his supplies from the west bank of the river. After little more than a week, on 2 October, Philip abandoned the place and, returning north by way of Montargis, arrived in Paris on the night of the 7th and remained there for the rest of that month.[54]

The reason for Philip's swift departure from La Charité was in all probability the arrival of news that Charles of Blois, the French candidate in the Breton succession dispute, had suffered a crushing defeat at Auray on 29 September, and that a large number of prisoners had been taken, including du Guesclin, who had joined Charles's army along with other royal forces from Normandy. The battle had significantly depleted the French garrisons in the Cotentin and Lower Normandy, and a substantial number of their captains either were dead or had been taken prisoner. It had also released for service elsewhere some of the English companies who had served in the army of the rival claimant to the duchy, John de Montfort. These may have included contingents sent to Brittany by Louis, either from La Charité or during his march through central France.[55] If Louis's intention had been to invade Burgundy, he soon abandoned it and headed along the northern bank of the Loire through Anjou with his army, making first for Brittany, where he had discussions with Montfort and recruited a number of English companies, before proceeding into Lower Normandy in the middle of October.[56] To the embarrassment of Edward III, the companies included contingents led by the Hainaulter Eustache d'Auberchicourt, Robert Scott and Sir Hugh Calveley. D'Auberchicourt was married to a niece of the queen, and had come to be closely connected with England, but he had also been retained by Charles of Navarre,

---

54 *Chron. normande*, p. 175; *Chron. premiers Valois*, pp. 156–8; *Itin. Phil. le Hardi*, pp. 13–14; *Mandements*, nos. 84, 93, 107, 126. For the muster, see Delachenal, iii, p. 143 n. 1, and for the *bailli's* letter BN, coll. Bourgogne, xxvi, fo. 129; Petit, x, pp. 122–3.
55 *Chron. premiers Valois*, p. 159.
56 *Chron. normande*, p. 178.

accepted fief-rents from him, and already before Cocherel had been appointed guardian of Charles's lands in Normandy, Burgundy and elsewhere in France.[57] With the assistance of these men, in the ensuing two months Louis recovered Valognes and Barfleur from du Guesclin's lieutenants, thereby restoring Navarrese control in the Cotentin peninsula. By mid-December he felt able, and was probably financially obliged, to pay off some of his troops.[58] The companies at La Charité held on until March 1365, when, after several attempts by the count of Sancerre to negotiate its evacuation, they finally agreed to depart for 25,000 gold francs, in return for which, during the space of three years, they were not to take up arms against the king of France for the king of Navarre.[59]

While these events at La Charité, in Brittany and in Normandy had been unfolding, during the summer and early autumn of 1364 a number of *routes* of the Great Companies were creating havoc in Burgundy and the surrounding region. Once again, these included contingents formerly in Burgundian pay. In July, Jean de Saint-Pol, Jean de Pommiers and Munde Bataillier at the head of 1,200 cavalry occupied the duke's castle of Argilly for several days, seizing all the food for themselves and their horses which they could lay their hands on. Saint-Pol and Bataillier further embarrassed the duke by making frequent raids into the territories of the count of Savoy from the ducal castle of Sagy, to the south of Chalon. The same month Guillame Pot, Guiot du Pin, the *bourc* Camus and Bertucat d'Albret threatened to ransom the entire *bailliage* of Chalon unless they were paid off. At the beginning of August some of the companies occupying fortresses in the Autunois and Auxois were rumoured to be intending 'something big'.

The exact nature of this enterprise soon transpired. From their castle of la Vèvre, to the north-west of Autun on the road to Château-Chinon, Pot and du Pin, in league with Arnaud de Tallebard and with the assistance of a number of the inhabitants who acted as spies, attempted to take Autun. However, the city was too well defended and, unable to breach its walls, they had to content themselves with sacking the suburbs. They were then rumoured to be intending to take two places in the Seine valley below Troyes, namely Châtillon and Bar-sur-Seine, and to conduct raids as far as Troyes itself. Jean d'Armagnac, once again in ducal service after securing

---

57 *Foedera*, III, ii, p. 754, and, for Auberchicourt, *AGN, Comptos*, v, nos. 202, 313; AGN, Sección de Comptos, reg. 111, fos. 52v, 56r.
58 *Chron. normande*, p. 178. The first act which testifies to Louis's presence in Normandy is dated Mortain, 21 October 1364 (Luce, in Froissart, *Chroniques*, vi, p. lxvi n. 1). He was at Cherbourg on 31 October, Bricquebec on 2 November, Valognes on 16 November and Avranches on 16 December (ibid.).
59 Froissart, *Chroniques*, vi, p. lxi n. 2, 147; Delachenal, iii, p. 143.

certain guarantees and a fat advance on the arrears of pay outstanding to him, was commissioned to pay them off. A number of castles were then evacuated for finance, including that of Monnay, held by du Pin, for 4,000 florins and La Vèvre for 2,500. The latter was handed over to the Archpriest as security for a loan which he advanced, the ducal council not being able to find the money. On Thursday 19 September Pot and a large number of his men were taken in an engagement outside Dijon. A letter written the same day by the *bailli* of Auxois, Guillaume de Clugny, to the ducal council, relates the circumstances and gives something of their flavour:

Very dear and good friends, on Wednesday Guillemin Pot, who was lodged at Maisières, was passing by Beaune with 120 good lances and at least 100 other combatants, not counting the pillagers. As soon as they had passed we mounted our horses and pursued them until we took four or five of their men-at-arms and some 30 pillagers, who were killed, hung or taken prisoner, the others returning to their quarters. We then continued our journey to Dijon, as was our intention, and this Thursday morning the marshal [Gui de Pontailler, marshal of Burgundy] sent 15 *glaives* to form an ambush on the road they would have to take, but it was discovered and the entire *route* fell upon our men, who fled to Givrey, where they fought for a long time at the barriers, and Jean de Blaisy and two or three of our men were taken. We then left Givrey for Dijon ... and while passing between Rouvres and Dijon we fell upon them ... and with God's help they were defeated and either killed [in the engagement], taken prisoner or put to death. And Guillemin Pot and others of his *route* have been taken prisoner to Dijon.[60]

Mistakenly, Pot was released on certain conditions, which he subsequently violated, returning to his old ways; but Philip the Bold's officers thereafter pursued a more determined policy. At the beginning of October, when du Pin was captured by a Burgundian knight, Philibert Longie, whilst raiding merchants attending the fair at Chalon, he was handed over to the duke's officers for 200 *livres* and executed, his head pilloried in the main square of the town, where it remained on view for eight months before being carried off by one of the companies occupying Anse. A similar fate awaited Gilles Troussevache, captain of Arcy-sur-Cure to the south of Auxerre, who was captured by an esquire of the Avallonais, Guillaume de Railly, purchased for 160 florins of Florence by the governor of the duchy, handed over to the *bailli* of Auxois and executed at Semur.[61] These were only the

---

60 BN, coll. de Bourgogne, xxvi, fo. 129r; Petit, x, pp. 121–3.
61 For the above, see Petit, x, pp. 88, 105, 108–15, 121–3, 128–30; Guigue, p. 110; Charmasse (1898), p. 10ff. For the agreement concluded for the evacuation of la Vèvre, see Plancher, iii, preuves, xix, and Dumay, preuves, x.

first of a growing number of summary executions visited upon some of the captains of the companies during the coming years.[62]

These minor operations paled into insignificance with the appearance in late October of Seguin de Badefol in the lower Saône valley on the frontiers with Bresse, and his capture, probably by escalade, of the town of Anse one night during the first week of November.[63] The town was made up of two parishes, that of Anse, where the old consular tower had been reconstructed as a castle at the beginning of the thirteenth century and was encircled by a crenellated wall protected by numerous towers. The other, of Saint Ronan, was little more than a suburb by the 1360s, but several of its buildings adjoined the walls at numerous points and had given concern to the authorities for some time. The town was not properly garrisoned, and although a small force under the *bailli* of Valbonne was guarding the east bank of the Saône, when Seguin carried out his night attack it was patrolling the river further downstream, between Neuville-sur-Saône and Lyon.[64]

It seems likely that it had for some time been Seguin's intention to establish a centre of operations in the Saône valley, such as La Charité was on the Loire. He had reconnoitred the Seine bridgeheads a year earlier, when he had occupied the abbey of Savigny to the west of Lyon. He may now have aspired to secure Lyon and control the river crossings which gave access to the lands of the count of Savoy across the rivers Saône and Rhône, but it is more likely that he wished to use Anse as a base from which to prey upon Lyon and its rich commercial traffic, in much the same way as the companies had used Pont-Saint-Esprit to blockade Avignon. Already before the end of October his forces had crossed the Saône and appeared outside that part of the city which lay beyond the Lantern gate and was situated between the rivers Saône and Rhône, in imperial territory. Certainly, the inhabitants of the suburbs in that part of the city feared for their safety, but Lyon was well protected. The city's fortifications were largely completed, its artillery was at the ready and the citizen militia had

62 Petit, x, pp. 142, 161–2, 181, 211; Sumption, ii, 530–3. See below, p. 285.
63 The exact date and circumstances of the capture of Anse have not been clearly established. In a letter dated 6 November the captain of Mâcon reported that 'messire Seguin de Batefol, à grant force de gens, est a nuyt entré en la ville d'Anse' (Coll. de Bourgogne, xxvi, fo. 113r; see Petit, x, p. 135). Sumption, ii, p. 521, following Guigue, p. 105, whose account pre-dates the information published by Petit by some twenty-three years, gives the date of 1 November. The date given by Guigue, p. 105, is based on a letter of acquittance given by the consuls of Lyon on 26 June 1367, which includes the terms of the evacuation of Anse, but only states that the town was taken '*circa* festum Omnium Sanctorum' (ibid., 323–8, PJ no. lvii). The *Thalamus parvus*, p. 367, indicates that the town was taken by escalade, and in the early hours of the morning (*egal mattinas*), but wrongly attributes the action to the end of November.
64 Guigue, pp. 105–7, 218–19, 314–15; Perroud, p. 273.

been reinforced by other contingents of men-at-arms and infantry. Two armed ships patrolled the Saône upstream from its juncture with the Rhône, and a great chain – the chain of Pierre-Scize – was in place across the first of these two rivers, at the northern side of the city. To the west of the Saône, in that part of Lyon which lay within the French kingdom, the Trion gate had been walled up and, following a royal order of 23 August, all of the buildings which might compromise the city's defences, in the suburbs of Saint-Iréné and Saint Just, and at Saint-Vincent, had been demolished. The movements of the companies operating in the region had been carefully monitored in all directions by the city authorities. In September, when news of Louis of Navarre's advance had sent shockwaves as far as Lyon, Marshal Audrehem had been informed of the situation, and had made his way there by the beginning of October. His presence may have done something to reassure the city and keep the enemy at bay; but, having been recalled to Paris and replaced as lieutenant-general in Languedoc by the duke of Anjou, he had left Lyon during the course of that month. This proved to be the moment that Seguin decided to seize Anse.[65]

Situated at the confluence of the rivers Saône and Azergue just over fifteen miles north of Lyon, Anse was a place of some importance in the fourteenth century. Like Brioude and La Charité, it was an ecclesiastical town, which, along with other smaller towns in the neighbourhood, belonged to the chapter of the cathedral of Lyon. It commanded both the road and the river between Mâcon and Lyon, as well as the valley of the Azergue at a point where that river could not always be forded. From it the companies could control navigation of the Saône and the considerable river traffic between Burgundy and Lyon. Their first actions included the occupation of Saint-Germain-au-Mont-d'Or, further downstream, and also on the west bank, and the castle of Gleteins almost immediately opposite Anse, on the east bank. Control of Gleteins enabled them to utilize the ports of Saint-Bernard and Frans, a little further upstream, for river crossings. From these places Seguin's spies were also able to secure information for the invasion of Dombes and Bresse, although the value of their findings was frequently diminished by agents of the *bailli* of Bresse, who were active in the business of counter-intelligence, in particular a woman called Ancelise, who was residing in Anse. The town was in more senses than one what Pont-Saint-Esprit had been for Avignon: the companies occupying it could rapidly be beneath the walls of a large town whose riches they coveted, cut communications in the river valley, stop convoys descending it and ransom prisoners. For the best part of a year they were

---

[65] Guigue, pp. 99–105. It is not clear when Audrehem left Lyon, but he appears to have proceeded north to Chalon-sur-Saône during the month of October (Molinier, pp. 167–8).

able to use the town as a base for their operations, preying on the country between Mâcon and Lyon and intercepting communications between the Lyonnais and Beaujolais. With the only ford between Mâcon and Lyon, just upstream at Saint-Bernard, in their control, they were constantly able to menace the province of Dombes on the east bank. The rich traffic between Burgundy and Lyon thus came under Seguin's control. Merchants and others had to secure safe-conducts from him, and the companies operating under him secured so tight a grip in the region that one of the Chalon fairs, the *foire chaude*, habitually held on the 28 August, had to be postponed because neither merchants nor buyers were prepared to take the risk of going there.[66] Trade came to a standstill.

According to the Bascot de Mauléon, recounting his experiences to Froissart in 1388, by the time Seguin controlled Anse the companies also held more than sixty fortresses in the Mâconnais, Forez, Velay and Lower Burgundy.[67] Certainly, the documentation of the period bears ample testimony to the scale of their operations, sometimes commanded by Seguin himself and sometimes by his lieutenants. Anse became the centre of a network of fortresses whose captains co-ordinated their operations over a large part of central and eastern France, raiding north into Autunois and Auxois, and occasioning alarm across the Rhône, in Dauphiné and Valentinois.[68] In December 1364 one of Seguin's principal lieutenants, Louis Roubaud, even raided as far south as Nîmes, ransacking the country between the mouth of the Vidourle, to the east of Montpellier below Lunel, as far as the Gorges du Gardon, to the west of Pont du Gard. At the beginning of the following May, when returning from one of these long-distance raids, possibly also into Lower Languedoc, whilst passing through Velay and Vivarais with a rich booty, he was ambushed in a wooded valley in the mountains some eight miles to the south-east of Saint-Etienne at a place called La Batterie. According to Froissart he had been betrayed by his comrade-in-arms, Limousin, following a dispute over a woman. His entire company was cut to pieces and Louis himself handed over to the lord of La Voute, who sold him on to the duke of Anjou. He was then taken to Villeneuve-lès-Avignon, beheaded and quartered.[69] But above all else it was the unprotected towns and villages of the Lyonnais, of Dombes and Bresse, that suffered from the garrison of Anse, their churches profaned and abbeys sacked.

66 Guigue, pp. 107–9, 117, 332–4, PJ no. lx; Monicat, p. 35; Perroud, pp. 273–4; Chérest, pp. 327 and n. 2, 329.
67 Froissart, *Chroniques*, xii, pp. 99–100.
68 Guigue, pp. 109–11; Petit, x, pp. 145, 152–3, 156, 159. Sumption, ii, p. 521, says that they raided as far south as the papal state and northern Provence, but without citing his authority.
69 *Thalamus parvus*, p. 367; Monicat, pp. 36–40; *HGL*, ix, p. 776; Froissart, *Chroniques*, xii, pp. 110–15.

With the departure of Marshal Audrehem, the city of Lyon had largely been left to its own devices, calling on the help of the governor of Dauphiné to settle the resulting quarrels of its citizenry. The troops assembled by the count of Tancarville and the duke of Burgundy were employed to deal with other companies ostensibly serving Charles of Navarre, who, from the places they held in Normandy, Champagne and Brie, had penetrated the western marches of Burgundy from Auxois. The forces raised by the authorities of Lyon were not strong enough to risk an attack on Anse or Saint Germain and it would have been imprudent to reduce the garrison of the city. There were already insufficient troops to garrison the towns, castles and other properties belonging to the cathedral chapter. Some, like the fortified house of Laye at Saint-Genis-Laval, on the west bank of the Rhône just below Lyon, had to be abandoned, and others destroyed. Some forces had been left behind by Audrehem, but their main purpose seems to have been to gather intelligence concerning the movements of the garrison of Anse and to pursue isolated groups of brigands who could easily be picked off. Lack of adequate financial resources to pay for more troops was the determining factor. The accounts of the receiver of *aides* in the province bear ample testimony to the inability to collect revenues because of the activities of the companies occupying Anse.[70]

Although the earliest direct evidence that Seguin was holding Anse for the king of Navarre comes from a letter of protection issued by him on 5 August 1365, it is clear from other information that, shortly after Cocherel, Charles had recruited his services against the promise of 1,000 *livres* of annual rent to be paid from the revenues of certain places in Navarre.[71] Already in their attacks on Le Puy in August 1364, the companies under his lieutenant Louis Roubaud had adopted 'Navarre' for their battle cry, although this may have been to give their activities a semblance of legality.[72] A more 'important' person recruited by the Navarrese was none other than the mediator of the treaty for the evacuation of Brioude, Arnaud-Amanieu, lord of Albret, who on 26 February 1365 finally confirmed a treaty of alliance with Charles of Navarre, who appointed him his lieutenant in France on the 28th.[73] Under the terms of the treaty Arnaud-

---

70 Guigue, pp. 111–14, 323–80, PJ no. lviii; Chérest, pp. 293–4; Charmasse, 1881, pp. 501–6; *Compte Louppy*, p. 56, no. 120.
71 Guigue, pp. 107–8, publishes the letter of protection. For the 1,000 *livres*, see *Chron. Charles V*, ii, p. 301 (deposition of Jacques le Rue, 1378).
72 Molinier, p. 312, PJ no. lxxxvii; see Secousse, *Recueil*, p. 203, art. 10, and Keen, 1965, p. 116.
73 The treaty was drawn up in duplicate in the Navarrese chancery and was confirmed by Albret on 26 February (*AGN, Comptos*, v, no. 849; Brutails, *Documents*, pp. 100–3, no. ci; see Yangas y Miranda, iii, pp. 106–8). The version in Pau (AD, Pyrénées-Atlantiques, E 40; copy in BN, coll. Doat 195, fos. 283r–289r) has been published, together with the letters appointing Albret as Charles's lieutenant, dated 28 February, by Loirette, 1910, p. 246ff. This includes some significant corrections and additions to the copy published by Brutails from the

Amanieu undertook to serve Charles in his wars in France in return for the restoration of the lands of Mixe (which had been confiscated from his father by Charles's father, and recently granted to the captal of Buch) and the sum of 60,000 Aragonese florins as the price of his services. He agreed to make war against all of Charles's enemies, excepting the duke of Berry, and not to make peace without Charles's agreement. All fortresses taken by him during the anticipated hostilities were to be occupied for Charles and in his name. Half of the 60,000 florins were to be paid to him before 2 February.[74] Of the remaining 30,000 florins, 15,000 were to be paid before 22 July, or by 1 November at the latest, and although no time was set for the payment of the final sum of 15,000, Charles immediately made over to Arnaud-Amanieu, as a pledge, jewels to that value.[75] In addition he took over the debts which the lord of Albret had contracted with the sire de Mussidan and Seguin de Badefol.[76]

The reasons which led Arnaud-Amanieu to conclude an alliance with Charles are not difficult to find, although it is evident from the time he took to confirm the proposals that he had some hesitations about it. Having been taken prisoner by Gaston Fébus at Launac in December 1362, by February 1364 he had made an initial payment of 37,333 florins towards the ransom of himself and his brothers Bérard and Géraud. But whilst this down payment had secured the release of his brothers, until then prisoners at Foix, a further larger sum remained to be found.[77] On 28 February 1365 Charles appointed him his lieutenant and captain-general in Languedoc, Burgundy and elsewhere in France, with the full military and judicial powers pertaining to that office: to prosecute war on his behalf; to protect and defend his lands and subjects; to appoint, dismiss and punish officers, from simple sergeants to castellans and *prévôts*; to appoint new officers and to receive oaths of fealty to the king.[78] On the same day, in Pamplona, Arnaud-Amanieu declared that of 4,000 *libras* rent which he had received by virtue of the treaty of alliance, he had made over 1,500 *libras* each to the lord of Mussidan and Seguin de Badefol, and 500 each

---

Navarrese archives. Loirette also has some important observations on the date of the original proposals.
74   For their payment, see *AGN, Comptos*, v, nos. 875–6.
75   For Albret's acknowledgement of receipt, dated Pamplona, 26 February 1365, see *AGN, Comptos*, v, no. 851.
76   On 28 February Albret acknowledged receipt of 4,000 *libras* of rent due to him by virtue of the treaty of alliance, of which he had made over 1,500 each to Raymond de Montaut, lord of Mussidan, and Seguin de Badefol, and 500 each to Seguin de Mussidan and Tonnet de Badefol, on condition that they became his vassals (*AGN, Comptos*, v, no. 856). The sums awarded to the lord of Mussidan and Seguin de Montaut (i.e. Mussidan) were assigned to them in Normandy, in return for which they did homage to Charles of Navarre, and undertook to serve him against his enemies, especially the king of France (ibid., nos. 902–3).
77   Tucoo-Chala, 1960, p. 90 n. 30; Loirette, 1910, pp. 240–1.
78   AD, Pyrénées-Atlantiques, E 40; BN, coll. Doat, 195, fos. 292r–5r.

to Seguin de Mussidan and Tonnet de Badefol, on condition that they swore fealty to Charles.[79] Tonnet's employment in Navarrese service could have proved critical. In the summer of 1365, when the duke of Burgundy was going to meet the emperor, who was journeying to Avignon through the territory of the count of Savoy, Tonnet planned to ambush the duke, but the stratagem was disclosed and the occasion therefore missed.[80]

It was against this background that the initial overtures for the evacuation of Anse were made in February 1365, when Jean de Talaru and Jacques Coligny, respectively dean and precentor of the cathedral chapter of Lyon, in the name of that church, and Ayard de Villeneuve, in the name of the town, were appointed to negotiate. These preliminary negotiations, which probably took place at Villefranche in Beaujolais, and in which the governor of Dauphiné, acting for the pope, played an important part, were inconclusive, and during their course the precentor was robbed by the companies. It may be that Seguin's demands were too high, or that no proposals were formulated. Cathelin la Ville, who held the neighbouring castle of Saint-Germain-au-Mont-d'Or, negotiated with the chapter for its evacuation for 400 florins, exacted 500 and then refused to depart, on the grounds that he would have to hand the place over to Seguin. Evidently the negotiations had to be conducted by the 'king of the Companies' himself. Urban V was requested to use his good offices, and it was at the papal court in Avignon that negotiations were resumed in March.[81]

Urban had been making efforts to bring about the evacuation of Anse for some time, and had written to Edward III endeavouring to persuade him and the Black Prince to join the king of France in his efforts to expel the companies from France, sending Guy de Pruniers, governor of Montpellier, and subsequently seneschal of Beaucaire, to the prince with this intent.[82] The details of what ensued are known from a letter written by a Navarrese clerk in the prince's chancery, Berthelot Guillaume of Estella, who was also in Charles of Navarre's intelligence service.[83] He reported to his master that the governor arrived in Angoulême on Thursday, 13

---

79 AGN, *Comptos*, v. no. 856.
80 Guigue, pp. 110, 117; Finot, p. 97 and n. 2; Delachenal, iii, pp. 227, 234.
81 Guigue, p. 114. For the part played by the governor, see *Compte Louppy*, pp. 56–7, nos. 120, 121.
82 Prou, p. 47, and PJ, p. 126, no. 1. The governor's name here as elsewhere is given as Guy de Prohins, from the Latin documents in which he appears as Guido de Prohins or Guido de Prohinis. The French form of his surname appears in the *Compte Louppy*, p. 56, no. 121, which is written in French: 'Pour autres despens fais par le dit gouverneur, en sa compaignie messire Guy de Pruniers, gouverneur de Montpellier, commis and ordené par nostre saint père le Pappe pour traictier et accorder avecques messire Seguin de Badefol et le dit gouverneur du Dauphiné, commis a ce faire par le Roy nostre seigneur pour le fait et delivrance de la ville d'Ance, que le dit Segun et ses compaignons tenoient and occuppoient lors.' For Pruniers, see Guigue, p. 133ff.; Delachenal, iii, pp. 236 n. 4, 362.
83 AD, Pyrénées-Atlantiques, E 520, appendix A, document 3.

February, bearing letters patent for the prince and Sir John Chandos from Edward III, obtained at the instance of Charles V of France and by request of the pope. On receiving them, to obey both the orders of Edward III and the request of the pope, the prince gave instructions for letters patent be drawn up in his name, incorporating Edward III's letters, and ordered that they should be sent to no fewer than fifteen captains of the Great Companies. That they concerned the possible mobilization of the companies in Navarrese service is evident from the remainder of Berthelot Guillaume's letter. In addition, the spy reported, the governor handed the prince a number of articles of request, which included one to the following effect: 'Item. Having heard that the lord of Albret is preparing to go against the king of France for the king of Navarre, may it please you to take steps to see that he does not', about which the prince sent similar letters patent to Arnaud-Amanieu.[84] Nevertheless, the spy explained that he understood that neither the prince nor his council intended to compromise Navarrese interests and, in reciting Edward III's letters, the prince had deliberately employed the phrase 'know that we have received from our very dear lord and father, the king of England, his letters *obtained at the instance of the king of France*', in order that the captains would realize that the instigator was the king of France and would therefore disregard the prince's order. Otherwise, the spy believed, only the words 'we have received letters patent from our very dear lord and father containing the form ... etc.' would have been used.

Perhaps the most revealing information contained in the letter is the list of names of the captains of the Great Companies to whom the prince sent his instructions. At the head of the list were four knights: Seguin de Badefol, Jean de Castelnau de Berbeguenes and Bertucat and Bernard d'Albret. These were followed by Billos la Roche, Louis Roubaud, the *bourc* of Breteuil, the *bourc* Camus, le Cozi, Lamit, Espiote, Berradeco de Saint Pierre, Hazenorgue, Petit Meschin and Étienne Anger, alias Ferragut. Before concluding, the spy requested that the information he was divulging should be kept secret. He was only sending it because he was a loyal subject of the king of Navarre and wished to further the king's 'honour'. Moreover, if the lords of the prince's council heard about what he had done, he would be finished, in body and goods, and he added, 'in truth, lord, I would rather lose 500 nobles than incur the indignation of the lords of the council, that is to say the chancellor and others; for being presently employed in the chancery, I have been ordered to stay in the privy seal, and that will take me into everything'. As if to guarantee satisfaction, he

---

84 Arnaud-Amanieu was one of the prince's vassals, having done homage to him in St Andrew's cathedral in Bordeaux on 19 July 1363. The *procès-verbal* of this homage is contained in a notarial instrument in AD, Pyrénées-Atlantiques, E 40.

concluded: 'And I do not want to write about other matters which concern you until I can be certain that you have received these present letters.'

Whether the spy was wrong about the prince's attitude or the pope was taken in by the Black Prince remains a matter for speculation. Certainly, Urban took the prince's orders to the companies at face value, for on 5 April he sent the governor of Montpellier to Charles V with the good news.[85] It may be that Edward III was concerned about the growing Navarrese interest in France, and had been persuaded that a settlement of Charles of Navarre's conflict with the French king was in his own interests. The prince may have taken a different view, possibly having got wind of the duke of Anjou's plans for a Franco-Aragonese alliance, shortly to be discussed in Toulouse, for an arrangement whereby the two would-be allies, with the support of the companies, would proceed to the conquest of Navarre and Gascony after the king of Aragon's dispute with Castile had been resolved.[86]

Certainly, at this juncture the Navarrese interest seemed to be in the ascendant. In Normandy their position, although reduced from what it was before Cocherel, had been consolidated, whilst in central and eastern France the number of fortresses occupied by the companies operating in their name was growing daily. Following the occupation of Baigneux-les-Juifs, some thirty miles to the north-west of Dijon, by a company of English and Gascons in the autumn of 1364, during the night of 22-3 February a Navarrese company took Villaines-les-Prévôtés, just above Semur-en-Auxois. This daring enterprise threatened to bring the companies to the heart of the duchy. Then, on 23 March, whilst Villaines was under siege, Jean de Neufchâtel took the town of Pontailler-sur-Saône, which had for so long been in his sights. The news was conveyed to the *bailli* of Chalon by the duke himself:

Bailli of Chalon, the men of the count of Montbéliard have this Sunday evening taken our town of Pontailler. We therefore order you, without delay, to bring to us at Auxonne as many men-at-arms, archers and crossbowmen as you can find, and carpenters. And also load as many large ships in the river as you can find. And make sure there is no default. Our lord have you in his keeping.[87]

The same day Jacques de Vienne, captain-general of the duchy, was instructed to leave Semur with his men-at-arms and to come as speedily as possible to Dijon. The capture of Pontailler and that of Villaines were

---

85 Prou, p. 47, and PJ, p. 126, no. 1.
86 The letters of accreditation for the Aragonese ambassadors are dated Tortosa, 16 February 1365. Their instructions had been issued on 12 November 1364 (Delachenal, iii, pp. 267-72, and especially p. 270 n. 1). See Russell, pp. 33-4, and below, pp. 126-7.
87 BN, coll. Bourgogne, xxvi, fo. 113r; Petit, x, p. 148.

probably linked. Both places had been taken by companies in Navarrese pay, and it is possible that the action was part of a carefully planned strategy for the invasion of the duchy from east and west. In that event the plan soon fell apart. By a singular stroke of luck, Pontailler was recovered after a surprise attack by one of Philip's councillors, Guillaume de Choiseul, only four days after its capture, and Jean de Neufchâtel and others from among his company were among the prisoners. Handed over to Gui and Guillaume de la Trémouille, who surrendered him to the duke for 8,000 *livres*, Jean de Neufchâtel was finally imprisoned in the dungeons of the keep of Saumur, where he remained, closely guarded, until the autumn of 1369. By the terms of a treaty for his release, concluded with the ducal council on 23 August of that year, he had agreed to renounce all pensions from the kings of England and Navarre, and undertook to serve the king of France in all his wars against them, but this had not come into effect before he died in prison on 10 September, in circumstances about which the documents remain silent.[88]

By that time he was past history. In the early months of 1365 Charles of Navarre, as was his way, had again been playing a double game. His bellicose stance had been intended to put the maximum pressure on Charles V for a settlement of his grievances, and he may have concluded that in his endeavours for a military solution the cards were stacked against him. Whatever the case, at the end of November 1364 he had agreed to send an embassy to Avignon to treat before the pope with the ambassadors of the king of France of the differences between them, and this embassy arrived in Avignon at the end of January 1365. Around the same time the duke of Burgundy sent Girard de Longchamp, *bailli* of Chalon, and Master Thomas de Chapelles, his secretary, 'on secret and important matters touching the honour and profit of the king', first to the pope, and then to the duke of Anjou, who was the chief representative of Charles V's interests in these preliminary discussions at Avignon.[89] On 19 February the king of France appointed the embassy he had promised to send to Avignon for 2 March. On 3 March, whilst protesting against his eviction from the succession to Burgundy 'the which appertains and should appertain to us', Charles of Navarre empowered the lord of Albret to treat with Charles V 'on the subject of the duchy, which has been the cause of so much misfortune'.[90] On 6 March the clauses of a treaty were concluded between the proctors of the two kings. These were ratified by

---

88 For the above, see Charmasse, 1881, pp. 501–6; Petit, x, pp. 130–1, 147–94; *Itin. Phil. le Hardi*, pp. 462, 480. The treaty is preserved in AD, Jura, E 533, and is analysed by Finot, pp. 90–1.
89 Prou, pp. 41–5; cf. Loirette, 1910, p. 239.
90 Loirette, 1910, p. 245 and PJ no. x, from AD, Pyrenées-Atlantiques, E 40; BN, coll. Doat, 195, fos. 296r–7r, published in *Vet. script.*, i, col. 1478.

Charles of Navarre in May and by Charles V in June.[91] They provided a general amnesty for the subjects and partisans of the two sides who had been involved in hostilities since the release of Charles of Navarre in November 1357. Only the one-time bishop of Laon, Robert le Coq, was specifically excluded from this provision.[92]

Territorially, the chief beneficiary was undoubtedly Charles V, who succeeded in evicting Charles of Navarre from everything that was rightfully his in the Seine basin: the towns of Mantes and Meulan, as well as the county of Longueville, which was subsequently granted to Bertrand du Guesclin. By way of compensation Charles of Navarre was to have the 'town and barony of Montpellier', as an enclave in Languedoc, cut off from his hereditary possessions and giving him no military or strategic advantage. As for the fortresses occupied during the war, these were to be restored to their rightful owners. This was no easy task for Charles of Navarre to accomplish, given that his partisans included diverse companies which maintained themselves through *patis* levied on the neighbouring countryside. Moreover, as had been the case after the peace of Brétigny, these levies were to cease, although due arrears could be collected. As recompense for his part in bringing about the treaty, Charles V released the captal de Buch from the ransom he had incurred at Cocherel, whilst the servitors of Charles of Navarre detained in the Châtelet were to be released. Finally, Charles of Navarre's claims in the Burgundian succession dispute were to be submitted to the arbitration of the pope, who was to give his judgement by 1 October 1365. This period could be prolonged; but during the time which then elapsed neither side was to resort to war over outstanding disputes, which were to be resolved by the pope, as sole judge. Urban was also to settle Charles of Navarre's claims to two parcels of rent, together totalling 22,000 *livres*, a sum of 600,000 *écus* and other indemnities. After some difficulties over Montpellier, to which Louis of Anjou believed himself to have a claim, the 'town and barony' were handed over to the captal de Buch, as Navarre's representative, on 17 February 1366, although not without subsequent dispute. The provisions over the Burgundian succession, on the other hand, remained a dead letter in that the period envisaged for the papal sentence was put off until Easter Sunday 1368 and a year later negotiations for a new treaty were opened between the two kings.[93] No arrangement concerning Anse was made in this settlement. The evacuation of the town was not accomplished until Septem-

---

91 Loirette, 1910, p. 245; Prou, p. 45. The best account of the provisions of the treaty is that of Delachenal, iii, pp. 190–3.
92 He had been transferred to the bishopric of Calahorra in 1360 and subsequently died there (Delachenal, iii, p. 190).
93 Delachenal, iii, pp. 194–204.

ber 1365, as part of a much wider arrangement for the removal of the companies from France.[94]

With the settlement of the Breton succession dispute and an apparent end to Navarrese hostilities, with Edward III and the Black Prince seemingly neutralised, from the summer of 1365 there seemed to be a real prospect of peace in France, provided that the companies could be starved of new employers and either persuaded to disband or removed from the kingdom. Shortly after the transfer of Montpellier, Louis of Navarre left Normandy to marry Joan of Sicily, duchess of Durazzo and heiress to the kingdom of Albania. Seizing the chance to be rid of him and his Navarrese partisans, Charles V lent him 50,000 florins to help him recover this distant principality. Louis was to die in Apulia some ten years later and was buried in Naples. Some of his men remained in Greece, where they formed the Navarrese Company, which was involved in the conquest of the Morea and conflict with the Catalan Company, which had been implanted more than fifty years earlier in the duchies of Athens, Neopatras and Thessaly, where they had replaced the Frankish barons of the Champagne dynasty as the dominant force.[95]

---

94 See the next chapter.
95 Delachenal, iii, pp. 204–6; Luce in Froissart, *Chroniques*, vi, lxxviii n. 3.

6

Crusading Projects

The death of Innocent VI in September 1362, and the election of Guillaume de Grimoard, abbot of Saint Victor of Marseilles, to succeed him, brought a very different man to the throne of Saint Peter. Unlike his predecessor, who was advanced in years, of sickly disposition, easily depressed and of a somewhat vacillating character, Urban V was in his early fifties, and had a happy combination of qualities that made him popular. A man of meticulous routine, a scholar, and perhaps the most spiritual of the Avignon popes, he nevertheless conversed amiably with his familiars and servants, and in the evenings liked to stroll along the covered walks of the papal palace and the gardens which he had enlarged. Whilst he had early on in his pontificate demonstrated his dislike of luxury and ostentation, ate frugally and was never able to throw off the monastic habit, he had a friendly disposition and was generous to a fault. He was also a man of action and great builder. Petrarch praised him for his reforming zeal. But above all else it was his determination to restore the papacy to Rome, and his courage and perspicacity in ultimately carrying it out, that marked out his pontificate. In the achievement of this goal he seems to have been genuinely convinced of his ability first of all to contain the companies and then to employ them in the recovery of the Holy Land. When these schemes failed, it was primarily the need to protect Avignon and the Comtat Venaissin from the depredations of the companies that persuaded him to send them on crusading ventures of more doubtful purport.

The attitude adopted by the popes to the companies operating in France and Italy in the second half of the fourteenth century was paradoxical, although founded on well-established precedents.[1] On the one hand the popes issued crusading indulgences to those who fought against the companies, and on the other hand they hoped to recruit the companies in a

---

1 For what follows, see Housley, 1982, pp. 253–80; Denifle, ii, pp. 443–51 and *passim*; Delachenal, iii, p. 244 n. 2.

Christian Holy War, whether in the eastern Mediterranean, the Balkans or the Moorish kingdom of Granada. Whilst the popes felt a heavy responsibility to defend Christians, and especially ecclesiastics and church property, they were also directly affected by their vulnerability to attack in the papal states in Italy and more particularly in the Comtat Venaissin and in Avignon. There, in addition to the destruction inflicted on the neighbouring countryside, the papal court was particularly at risk through its supply lines, and the constant flow of prelates, bankers and courtiers going to and from Avignon who could be seized and ransomed. Avignon had already been threatened in this way in 1357, 1360–1 and 1363, as it was to be again during the course of 1365, in 1366 and in 1375.

Up until 1363 the pope had for the most part restricted his action against the companies to particular instances, which were primarily concerned with their activities in the French Midi and the Alpine regions. In the early years of his pontificate Urban V adopted the defensive measures of his predecessors, for instance the reissue of Innocent VI's bull *Ad reprimendas insolentias* of 1356, which on 31 January he sent to the town and diocese of Grenoble. His own work was contained in three great bulls of more general compass. *Cogit nos*, of 27 February 1364, was the first to preach a crusade against the companies. Its purpose was to provide spiritual back-up for a league concluded against them by the three seneschalsies of Languedoc, and its justification was defensive rather than coercive or punitive:

The wickedness of our age, in which the sons of iniquity have multiplied and, fired by the flames of their own greed, are dishonestly attempting to gorge themselves on the labour of others, and for that reason rage the more cruelly against the innocent peoples, compels us to draw on the resources of the apostolic power to counter their evil strategems and to strive with ever greater energy and effectiveness to organise the defense of these peoples, especially of those whom these wicked men have so far attacked, and are now attacking.[2]

After rehearsing their crimes, it excommunicated the companies, exhorted princes and others to take up arms against them, and granted a plenary indulgence for two years to those who died fighting against them. In July 1364, Urban had responded to a request from the bishop, nobles and commoners of Saint-Flour by granting the diocese these indulgencies for those taking up arms against Seguin de Badefol, and in the following January, when Urban again used this bull against Seguin, appropriate clauses were employed to isolate the companies operating in his name.

The second bull, *Miserabilis nonnullorum* of 27 May 1364, was also intended to isolate the companies. It ordered them, under threat of excom-

---

2 Denifle, ii, p. 445; trans. Housley, 1982, p. 265.

munication, to disband their *routes*, to surrender the places they occupied, and to repair the damage they had done, all within one month. Clerics and laymen were forbidden to join, employ or favour them, to hold any office for them or to carry any of their banners. Excommunication was extended to anybody supplying them with money, food, horses, arms, carts, boats and other provisions and merchandise, or who in any other way counselled or aided them. Culpable towns were to be placed under interdict. Bishops were to report the names of the companions and their accomplices so that action could be taken against them. Nevertheless, as a small concession to the realities of the situation, a few days later supplementary letters provided that prisoners could pay their ransoms, in money or in kind. As in *Cogit nos*, so also in *Miserabilis nonnullorum*, a plenary indulgence was granted to those who died fighting against the companies, although in November 1364 it was found necessary to add that this was only intended for those who died fighting them under a properly delegated authority.

The third bull, *Clamat ad nos* of 5 April 1365, was directed against those who employed and led the companies as well as those who joined and favoured them. It developed the sentence pronounced in previous bulls, in particular *Miserabilis nonullorum*, once again excommunicating the mercenaries and placing their lands under interdict. All towns, villages and individuals who negotiated with them and paid protection money to them were threatened, in the case of communities with the withdrawal of their rights and privileges, and in the case of individuals with the confiscation of their liberties and fiefs. Thereafter, all those found culpable, including their descendants to the third generation, were to be ineligible for public office, and their vassals would be released from their oaths of fealty. In a further bull of 10 February 1368, Urban added another sentence against the companies by denying them church burial and declaring that if any of their members were buried in a church or cemetery, even after receiving absolution, it was to be placed under interdiction until the corpse had been exhumed and removed. Those who received absolution during illness, but recovered their health, were to go to the Holy See to do penance and obtain absolution.[3] In addition to issuing bulls the pope also encouraged the formation of defensive leagues. At the beginning of 1361 a full-scale crusade had been launched by Innocent VI against the companies holding Pont-Saint-Esprit,[4] and the popes had encouraged the formation of leagues, backed up by indulgences, when the terrorizing of the countryside reached its height in 1363–5.

The alternative approach, of recruiting the companies on crusades, also had precedents in the first crusade and, more recently, in the employment

3   Denifle, ii, p. 504.
4   See above, p. 34.

of the Catalan Company after the conclusion of the Sicilian war in 1302.[5] In 1363, with the arrival of King Peter of Cyprus in various courts of western Europe, proposals for a crusade were once again in the air, and on Good Friday of that year Urban V had given the cross to King John, Peter of Cyprus and a large number of French and Cypriot noblemen. A crusading force was to have set sail on 1 March 1365 to fight the Turks in Asia Minor and thereafter regain the Holy Places, but it had been Urban's wish that this crusade would also benefit the West by drawing off the companies. In a letter of 25 May 1363 addressed to the captains and their men in the most flattering terms, he suggested that they were better qualified than others to undertake this great enterprise, because they had been cut off from the profession of arms by circumstances beyond their control. By fighting for the recovery of the Holy Land, he suggested, they could do penance for their crimes against Christians.[6] In the event the proposed crusade foundered with the death in January 1364 of Cardinal Talleyrand of Périgord, the apostolic legate for the Holy War, followed during the ensuing summer by that of King John.[7] But more determined efforts were made with the demobilization which followed the conclusion of the Breton succession dispute and the war with Charles of Navarre. In these, both the pope and the emperor played an important rôle.

In the early summer of 1365, the Emperor Charles IV determined to visit Pope Urban V in Avignon and to demonstrate his authority in the kingdom of Arles by having himself crowned there in the ancient church of Saint-Trophine. The desire to reaffirm imperial authority in his western territories, amid much pomp and display, was probably the principal motive for his visit to the pope; but there were others: the prevailing situation in Italy and the desire of both Urban and Charles for the pope's eventual return to Rome, a projected crusade to the Holy Land, and the need for some concerted action by the princes of the West in order to put an end to the ravages of the companies.[8] In descending the Rhône valley he hoped to demonstrate to his distant vassals that his imperial authority was in no ways diminished. Leaving Prague during Holy Week, he celebrated Easter at Nuremberg, then made his way to Alsace, arriving in Strasbourg on the evening of 23 April. Deliberately avoiding the Saône valley, infested by the companies, he made his way by the Swiss towns of Bâle, Soleure, Berne and Geneva to gain access to the lands of the count of Savoy and the valley of the Isère, arriving in Chambéry on 11 May in a brilliant procession of

---

5 Housley, 1982, pp. 269–71. For the Catalan Company, see Lowe.
6 Denifle, p. 377 n. 2, 444; Delachenal, iii, p. 245 n. 1.
7 Atiya, p. 334.
8 For this and what follows, see Werunsky, iii, pp. 318–25; Delachenal, iii, pp. 210–18.

at least 2,000 cavalry. Count Amadeus VI, 'The Green Count' of Savoy, had by then accompanied him for a week, having awaited the emperor's arrival at the extremity of his lands, in the little town of Morat, a century later to be the scene of a bloody defeat for the last Valois duke of Burgundy, Charles the Bold. On Monday 12 May he did homage to the emperor, receiving in return the coveted but purely honorific title of imperial vicar, not only in his hereditary lands, but also in Piedmont, French Switzerland and those parts of the dioceses of Lyon, Mâcon and Grenoble forming part of the county of Savoy. Following the count's homage, a gala dinner was held in the Great Hall of the castle and, in accordance with the ceremonial laid down in the Golden Bull of 1356, the count and his barons serving the emperor, who was seated beneath a golden canopy, did so on horseback.

From Savoy, Charles IV was escorted across Dauphiné to Arles and Avignon by the governor of Dauphiné, Raoul de Louppy, who had received instructions to accompany him 'bien et honorablement'. At Valence the emperor was met by the pope's ambassadors: Urban's brother, Anglic Grimoard, bishop of Avignon, and Gaucelin de Déaux, bishop of Nîmes. After leaving Orange for Pont-de-Sorgues, the next to greet him were two cardinals, the papal chamberlain, the bishop of Auch and the duke of Anjou, who was accompanied by a large escort of knights and men-at-arms. At Pont-de-Sorgues, where he spent the night in the papal castle, the rest of the college of cardinals awaited him. The following day, 23 May, some six weeks after he had set out from Prague, he entered Avignon with much solemnity. Mounted on his horse and wearing the closed imperial crown, he rode beneath a dais of cloth-of-gold borne by representatives of the most illustrious families of the kingdom of Arles. The count of Savoy walked before him, bearing the imperial sword, and two counts of the Empire bearing the orb and sceptre. A stunning escort followed, made up of at least 800 cavalry, including the imperial chancellor, numerous prelates, several dukes, counts and barons of Germany and Bohemia, and the high dignitaries of the imperial court. The procession advanced until it reached the foot of the steps leading up to the papal palace, at the entrance to which Urban V, surrounded by his cardinals, awaited Charles and, after the singing of the *Te Deum*, invited him to enter with the kiss of peace.

The emperor's visit to Avignon lasted for two-and-a-half weeks, until 9 June. It was a regular summit. It gave the two leaders of Christendom ample time to discuss at their leisure the principal matters of concern to them. These almost certainly included the projected marriage of the king of Hungary's niece and heiress, Elizabeth, to Albert of Hapsburg, the young duke of Austria, which both the pope and the emperor were set against. Charles IV even suggested the duke of Burgundy as a possible match; but the king of France had other plans for his brother, in the person of the heiress of the count of Flanders, Margaret, who might otherwise take her rich inheritance into the English orbit by marriage to Edward III's son, Edmund of Cambridge. For this purpose Charles V sent an embassy to Avignon made up of three of his councillors, the archbishop of Sens, the bishop of Nevers and Guillaume de Dormans, chancellor of Viennois, who were to treat with the pope and emperor of Philip's marriage and 'other matters'.[9] These matters were not specified in a letter written by Charles V to his brother on 2 May announcing his embassy to the pope, but clearly concerned Charles of Navarre's claims to the duchy of Burgundy, which were to be submitted not only to Urban, but also to the emperor,[10] and proposals which had been under discussion for some time for mounting expeditions intended to secure the removal of the companies from France.[11]

Charles IV was particularly anxious to see the pope return to Italy, but this could only be accomplished after the political and military problems prevailing there had been resolved. Since 1353, the popes had been making a determined effort to recoup their lands and revenues in central Italy, and the papal legate, Gil Albornoz, had been forced to employ the companies to this end. In 1360 renewed conflict had broken out with Bernabò Visconti of Milan over the control of Bologna, and when Urban had concluded a peace with Bernabò in the summer of 1364, it had released a large number of mercenary companies who ravaged northern and central Italy. Their depredations were added to those carried out by the companies employed by other Italian powers, the services of some of which were no longer required after the conclusion of the war between Florence and Pisa in the same year.[12] In France, the settlements which had followed the Breton succession dispute and the conflict with Charles of Navarre had the same effect. The problems posed by the companies prevailing in both countries were therefore much the same. The vulnerability of the papal lands in Italy, the Comtat Venaissin and the papal court at Avignon required urgent action. In Italy an attempt was made to form a league to fight against them, but many of the towns expected to subscribe to it, Florence chief among them, were in the habit of employing them, and preferred the use of bribery and conciliation to secure their departure rather than a more general plan of action.[13]

The expedients which were now under discussion were for the employment of the companies in a general 'crusade', both against the Turks and against the Moorish kingdom of Granada. Urban's earlier attempt to

---

9 Prou, p. 48 n. 3; Petit, x, p. 7.
10 BN, MS fr., 26006, no. 165 (letter of Charles of Navarre, Pamplona, 2 May 1365). See Prou, p. 49.
11 See below, pp. 126–7.
12 These matters will be covered in *Medieval Mercenaries II*.
13 Delachenal, iii, pp. 220–1; Partner, pp. 339–65; Housley, 1982, pp. 255–7, 261; 1986, pp. 74–81.

employ them in the service of the king of Cyprus had been rebuffed; but an expedition over land might prove more tempting to them, especially if it could be placed under the command of a leader they could trust. Adrianople, one of the gateways to Christendom, had recently fallen to the Ottoman Turks. Menaced in his capital, the Byzantine emperor, John V Palaeologus, who seemed disposed in favour of some accommodation between the Greek and Roman churches, had addressed a pressing appeal to the princes of the West, and Louis of Hungary, genuinely concerned about the advance of the Turks and the weakness of Byzantium, was intent upon playing a leading rôle in any action that might be forthcoming.[14] The idea of employing the companies against the Turks may have originated with him, and according to Froissart, Louis wrote to the pope, the king of France and the Black Prince on the subject.[15] Whatever action the prince may have taken is not recorded; but Charles V and Philip the Bold appointed Pierre Aimé, bishop of Auxerre, and a Burgundian knight, Eudes de Grancey, to negotiate with Louis, and they conducted at least two missions to Hungary, passing through Germany and Bohemia.[16] The whole matter was clearly discussed by Charles and Urban in Avignon, and on 9 June, the day of the emperor's departure, the pope wrote to Charles V of France, informing him of their plans:

Your majesty knows that our dear son in Christ Jesus, the very Christian prince, Charles, ever august emperor of the Romans, and king of Bohemia, has lately appeared at the Apostolic See. He has informed us of his interest in peace, in the welfare of Christendom in general and of your kingdom in particular, in the expulsion of the infidels, the propogation of the catholic faith, and the deliverance of the Holy Land; and he has revealed to us his secret intentions for the public weal. Our desires being no less ardent than his, we have held several conferences with him, and, in agreement with each other, we have decided that the most urgent matter is the removal of those detestable companies, which are devastating your kingdom and several other parts of Christendom, by either persuading or forcing them to march against the Turks and other infidels. The emperor is convinced that the illustrious King Louis of Hungary, our well-beloved son in God, will furnish throughout his entire kingdom a free and sure passage for these companies. Consequently he offers to provide, at his own expense, the money required to supply them with food and other necessities from the time of their departure from France until their arrival in Hungary, so that they will not need to forage for themselves. He only demands positive assurances of willingness of the king of Hungary. We and the emperor have therefore chosen the noble Arnoul, sire d'Audrehem, your marshal, and have sent him to the king of Hungary, in order to obtain his definite consent and assurances that he will receive the companies. If,

---

14 Delachenal, iii, p. 222; Housley, 1984, p. 201.
15 Froissart, *Chroniques*, vi, p. 184.
16 BN, coll. Bourgogne, xxiv, fo. 70v; Prou, p. 47.

however, he refuses them passage through his country we have directed that they should be carried overseas by the ships of the Venetians or of some other maritime power of Italy, even though this will take longer and be more difficult. To cover the cost of their transportation the emperor generously offers half of the revenues of his Bohemian kingdom for three consecutive years. Finally, we are informing Your Majesty of these details so that, without any delay, you can make arrangements with the companies now in France, so that when Marshal d'Audrehem returns they will be ready to take the road either to Germany or to Italy, depending on whether or not the king of Hungary agrees to receive them.[17]

Charles V and the duke of Burgundy could have wished for little better. The emperor, wanting to help his 'nephews of France', proposed no less than to send off to the East the companies operating in, and, in large measure occupying, the two Burgundies and the Rhône valley. The person it was proposed should take charge of the expedition was the Archpriest, Arnaud de Cervole, who was thought to have sufficient influence over the companies to lead them across Germany and Hungary to the frontiers of the Byzantine Empire. However, by the spring and early summer of 1365 they were too numerous and too dispersed to be employed effectively in a single operation. The conclusion of the war in Brittany and the peace with Charles of Navarre had left many without employ, and these forces helped to swell the numbers of those already operating on their own account in central and eastern France. The plan now envisaged was for the Archpriest to command the companies operating in the two Burgundies and the territories bordering the Rhône valley, whilst those in Normandy, Brittany, Chartrain and the marches with Poitou were to be led across the Pyrenees by du Guesclin, ostensibly to fight against the Moors in the kingdom of Granada. Both Urban and Charles V had clearly been in communication with the Black Prince on this subject through the pope's special envoy, Gui de Pruniers, governor of Montpellier, from as early as February 1365, and during the course of March further discussions were conducted with Edward, whose position on the subject was conveyed by the pope to Charles V at the beginning of April.[18] On 8 May Urban wrote to the prince, to Chandos and to the captal de Buch recommending du Guesclin to them and intimating his plans for the Breton captain to lead the companies out of France against the Infidel. A proposal for Sir Hugh Calveley to join the expedition may have been broached on the occasion of Bertrand's visit to the prince, without revealing its true purpose or even its precise destination.[19] These had been the subject of delicate negotiations

---

17 Urban V, *Lettres secrètes*, pp. 315–16, no. 1822.
18 AD, Pyrénées-Atlantiques, E 520, see appendix A, no. 3; Prou, pp. 47, 126, PJ no. l.
19 Delachenal, iii, pp. 222–3, 283 n. 3, 286–7; Urban V, *Lettres secrètes*, p. 304, nos. 1762–4; Prou, p. 128, no. liii.

which had been taking place in Toulouse and Avignon since the end of the previous year, but which had been several times modified to meet changing political circumstances.

The origins of this scheme are to be found in the complex internal politics of the Iberian kingdoms. In Aragon, the fall of the king's chief minister, Bernat de Cabrera, in July 1364 had brought to the fore among Peter IV's councillors the Francophile minister Francesch de Perellós, who had headed the party opposed to Cabrera's proposals for peace with Castile.[20] During the winter of 1364–5, Perellós had entered into negotiations with Charles V which envisaged Aragonese assistance in the war against Charles of Navarre, in return for which the French would give support to Pere in his war with Pedro of Castile. These negotiations appear to have commenced amid unusually tight security in Paris in November 1364 and to have envisaged the despatch from France of 2,000 cavalry to invade Navarre and assist the Aragonese in their war against Castile.[21] During their course the possibility of a Franco-Aragonese invasion of Guyenne following the conclusion of the war with Castile may also have been broached.[22] The discussions were then continued with Louis of Anjou in Montpellier and Toulouse, after Louis had left Paris for Avignon around the middle of November to take up his commission as Charles V's lieutenant in Languedoc.[23] Passing by way of Lyon, where he had arrived by 4 December, he was accompanied across Dauphiné and thence to Avignon by Raoul de Louppy, and had arrived at the papal curia before the end of the month.[24]

That the main business discussed with the pope concerned Charles of Navarre is evident from the instructions issued to Louis before he left Paris.[25] It is unlikely that Perellós was party to these talks, since Louis arrived in Montpellier on 13 January, together with the pope's brother, the bishop of Avignon, whilst the Aragonese ambassador was on his way to

---

20 Russell, pp. 28–32.
21 ACA, Cancilleria, reg. 1293, fo. 111v–13v (first instructions to Perellós, dated 12 November 1364); see Delachenal, iii, p. 268 n. 4, 269 n. 1; iv, p. 150 n. 2, 151 n. 1.
22 Ibid. ACA, Cancilleria, reg. 1293, fos. 93r–5r (further instructions sent to Perellós and Francesch Roma, then in France; undated, but probably February 1365). Both sets of instructions make clear that Pere was unwilling to consider any alliance against Edward III before the war with Pedro was concluded.
23 *Mandements*, nos. 120, 124; Molinier, p. 315, PJ no. lxxxix. Louis was appointed lieutenant in Languedoc in June 1364 (Delachenal, iii, p. 15 n. 1). He was in Lyon on 4 and 7 December (ibid., iv, p. 25; AM, Montpellier, Grand Chartier, D XIX, wrongly ascribed in the *Inventaire* to 1358).
24 'Compte Louppy', p. 7, no. 35, pp. 32–3, no. 75. He was in Villeneuve d'Avignon on 27 December (*HGL*, x, col. 1334), in Beaucaire on 31 December (Delachenal, iv, p. 25 n. 2) and in Nîmes on 9 January (*HGL*, x, p. 768 n. 6).
25 Secousse, *Recueil*, pp. 200–8. It is clear from articles 24 and 25 of these instructions that they were not issued before October 1364.

the curia.[26] It was probably in Montpellier that the discussions with Perellós were taken a step further, and from there that he went on to Avignon. Certainly, it was from Montpellier, on 23 January, that Louis wrote a letter in his own hand to Peter IV accrediting Perellós, Jean de Beuil and Charles V's confidential secretary, Gontier de Baigneux, with 'certain great and secret matters'.[27] But when Perellós, along with Pere's vice-chancellor, Francesch de Roma, returned to meet the duke in Toulouse in late February, either the French or the Aragonese, or both sides, drew back from their apparent brinkmanship.[28]

In a treaty which was finally concluded in Toulouse on 9 March, the old confederations and alliances between France and Aragon were confirmed, but such additions as were made were directed against Navarre alone. England was specifically excluded by both parties, as also was Castile by the French.[29] Anjou, or 'some other captain' appointed by the king of France, was authorized to pass through Aragonese territory by way of Roussillon in order to invade Navarre, Pere providing 400 men-at-arms for this purpose. For their part, the French would contribute to the defence of the Aragonese frontiers with a force of 500 men under Marshal Audrehem. These new arrangements seem to have been intended primarily to put pressure on the Navarrese, and included the employment of the companies. During the course of April, the first contingents appeared in the lands of Conflent, a lordship situated within the county of Roussillon, whilst ambassadors of Pedro I were seeking support from the republic of Genoa and from Sardinia for an invasion of Cerdagne.[30] In May the arrangements for the invasion of Navarre became redundant, with the ratification by Charles of Navarre of the peace concluded with France.

However, the plan for French intervention in the war between Aragon and Castile had not been dropped. In discussions which Perellós and Roma subsequently held in Avignon before going on to Paris, they were joined by two other Aragonese then at the papal curia. One was Peter IV's uncle, the

---

26 *Thalamus parvus*, p. 368; ACA, Cancilleria, reg. 1204, fo. 34v (letters of 10 January informing the pope of the imminent arrival of Perellós in Avignon); see Delachenal, iii, p. 269 and n. 2.
27 Miret y Sans, 1914, p. 301; cf. Delachenal, iv, p. 149.
28 There has been much speculation as to how far Louis of Anjou was acting under instructions from Paris and how far he was acting on his own initiative (see Delachenal, iii, pp. 269–70, iv, 152–4). Sumption, ii, pp. 526–7, argues that Louis was largely responsible for the proposals to take the war into Aquitaine, but this possibility had evidently been raised in the discussions held in Paris in November. The notes in Delachenal (iii, p. 270, iv, pp. 151–3; cf. p. 149 n. 6), drawn from the two different sets of instructions, are misleading on this point. See Russell, pp. 33–4.
29 Zurita, lib. ix, cap. lviii. The ambassadors on this occasion were, for Peter IV, Perellos, Roma and Juan Fernández de Heredia, and, for Charles V, Anjou and his chancellor Pierre d'Avoyr, Audrehem, and Pierre Scatisse and Jean de l'Hôpital, treasurers of France.
30 Ibid.

Infante En Pere, sometime count of Ribagorza and of Prades, and now a Franciscan. The other, and probably the more important of the two, was Juan Fernández de Heredia, castellan of Amposta, grand prior of Castile and Saint-Gilles, and future Grand Master of the Order of the Hospital.[31] It was probably these two men who resurrected the old idea of employing the companies across the Pyrenees, now to be dressed up as a 'crusade' against the Moorish kingdom of Granada. Both had considerable influence with Peter IV and Urban V. The Infante En Pere, like Urban a saintly man, was inclined to dreams which he interpreted as prophecies and supernatural visions. Once a tutor of the king, he had become a Franciscan when his uncle, Saint-Louis of Toulouse, had appeared to him in a dream. In his chronicle Peter IV directly credited him and Perellós with the success of the negotiations with France, and had called him back from Avignon for a personal conversation at a critical juncture in them.[32] Fernández de Heredia, on the other hand, was a man very much of this world. Already employed by the pope in defence of the Comtat Venaissin several years before the title of captain-general of the Comtat was conferred upon him, he was fully conversant with the problems posed by the companies, and he had been added to the Aragonese ambassadors who treated with the duke of Anjou and subsequently the king of France.[33] The idea of mounting two 'crusades', the one to be led by the Archpriest and the other by du Guesclin, had clearly been formulated by the beginning of May 1365,[34] and is probably to be attributed to these two men. The matter had clearly been discussed with Louis of Anjou and Charles V's ambassadors to the pope during Charles IV's visit to Avignon, and doubtless also with the dukes of Berry and Burgundy whom the emperor met at Arles and Romans when returning from the curia.[35] On 20 June, in response to a request made by Charles V's ambassadors in Avignon, Urban agreed that an appropriate proportion of the proceeds of a tenth to be levied on the French clergy for such period as the king saw fit were to be assigned to the companies who were joining the Archpriest. Those accompanying him were to enjoy a crusading indulgence, and when the details were finalized a papal legate would be appointed to accompany the crusaders.[36]

During the course of the ensuing month the arrangements were evidently concluded, and on 19 July Urban gave instructions for a two-year tenth to be levied on the French church to pay the expenses of the companies going

31 Delachenal, iii, pp. 270–1.
32 Pere III, *Chronicle*, ii, p. 572.
33 Zurita, lib. ix, cap. lviii; ACA, Cancilleria, reg. 1293, fo. 93ff; see Delachenal, iv, p. 150 n. 1.
34 Delachenal, iii, pp. 222–3; Urban V, *Lettres secrètes*, nos. 1762–4; Prou, pp. 126, 128, PJ nos. l and liii.
35 Lehoux, i, pp. 188–9; *Itin. Phil. le Hardi*, p. 21.
36 Urban V, *Lettres secrètes*, no. 1849. See also nos. 1839–42.

'to Turkish parts or to those of other infidels overseas, to fight them on behalf of the Catholic faith'.[37] Not all of the companies were persuaded to embrace the venture, but that some took papal injunctions and the idea of the crusade seriously is evident. Arrangements for the granting of indulgences to specific individuals had already been taken up earlier in 1365, when a papal legate was sent to Mâcon to absolve the Archpriest and his men, who included Thomas Folifait and other Englishmen who had previously been serving with him in Brittany.[38] However, the viability of papal anathemas and incentives was in large measure determined by careful planning and other practical considerations, and these were not always forthcoming.

The 'crusade' assigned to the Archpriest was misconceived and badly handled from its inception. There was no clear timetable for the expedition, which in turn was not co-ordinated with the evacuation of Anse and other fortresses in central and eastern France. Nor do Charles V and the emperor appear to have made any efforts to synchronize their plans. The Archpriest's forces were already on the French frontier by the beginning of June, before the conference at Avignon was concluded. The itinerary of the mercenary forces was not laid down, no provision was made to victual and supply them *en route* and, perhaps most serious of all, the planners lacked any realistic assessment of the problems that were to be encountered in raising the necessary finance to pay for the evacuations, and in persuading the companies to go on 'crusade'. Whether Charles V was concerned to press ahead with the expedition quickly, or the Archpriest had his own agenda, the movement of the companies to the frontiers of the Empire began too speedily, whilst the peace negotiations with Charles of Navarre were still in progress.[39] From Champagne, where they helped themselves to horses, food, money and other goods which they found in the unprotected villages and in the fields and houses along the roads, they entered the duchies of Bar and Lorraine, making first for the lands around Verdun and then for Metz. The captains of some of the contingents are known to us from subsequent documentation. They included the companies of the Devonshire knight Sir Richard Taunton, who had taken part in the battle of Auray, and of the Gascon captains Lamit, the *bourc* de Breteuil, Naudon

---

37   Ibid., nos. 1884–5. See also no. 1994.
38   'Docs. Mâcon', pp. 165–6; cf. Chérest, 309–10. Folifait (alias Filefort, Folifet, Belifort) had taken part in the 'battle of the thirty' in Brittany ('La bataille de Trente', ed. Brush, i, 526), was subsequently with Cresswell and other captains of the companies at Évreux in 1368 (Izarn, *Compte*, p. 346) and was taken prisoner along with Geoffrey Worsley and others at Pontvallain in 1370 (*Chron. normande*, pp. 197, 198, 351). He may have been related to Walter Ferrefort, an English prisoner detained in Saint-Brieuc in Brittany, possibly in 1375 (Northumberland Record Office, National Register of Archives, vol. 8746, no. 4/60). I owe this reference to my colleague, Professor A. E. Goodman.
39   Venette, *Chronicle*, pp. 131, 301 n. 8.

de Bageran, Gaillard de la Motte, and probably also of Espiote, Frère Darrier, the *bourcs* Camus, d'Aussain and de la Roque, Pierre d'Oingnel, Jehannot le Nègre and Bardot de Roussillon.[40] At the outset some contingents were deflected by a local quarrel which had erupted during the previous year between the count of Blamont, on the one hand, and the bishop of Strasbourg, the young count of Salm and several barons of Alsace, on the other. They then joined in a dispute between Pierre de Bar and the town of Metz over certain lands to the north-west of that town.

None of this was unusual. Already in the spring of 1363 the Archpriest had taken part in a war between the count of Vaudémont and the duke of Lorraine.[41] But with the plan to cross Germany on their way to Hungary, there was a real danger that the companies might now extend their operations further into the western territories of the Empire. This possibility had been a real one ever since the invasion of Burgundy following the treaty of Brétigny, when they had menaced the county of Montbéliard, Alsace and some of the Swiss cantons.[42] As early as January 1361 the bishop of Strasbourg, the abbot-prince of Murbach, the lords of Lichtenberg and Ochsenstein, the free town of Strasbourg and an association of ten imperial towns of Alsace had formed a league for six months against 'the company presently in France, normally called the English'.[43] This had several times been renewed at Colmar, when other Alsatian powers and neighbours like the bishop of Bâle, the count of Furstenberg, the lord of Ribeaupierre, the towns of Bâle and Freiburg, among others, had joined the alliance. In January 1365, when the league again came up for renewal, the confederates had assembled at Sélestat, just below Strasbourg, and agreed to raise a considerable force of men-at-arms, archers and infantry. But, unable to assemble sufficient funds speedily, their preparation had scarcely begun before the arrival of the companies, and the confederates were unable to close the passes of the Vosges mountains against them.[44]

The first contingents of the companies had moved east from the valley of the Meuse during the course of June and encamped to the south-west of Metz around the 23rd, before being bought off for a sum of 18,000 florins. They then made their way towards the Vosges, where the invasion of Alsace was expected at the end of the month, and on 4 July descended from the heights of Saverne to appear below the walls of Strasbourg on the following day. Here the Archpriest – 'the knight of the leaping stag', the *ritter Springhirtze*, as a contemporary German chronicler called him –

40 Chérest, pp. 326, 339; Petit, x, pp. 180, 184.
41 Chérest, pp. 221ff., 315 and n. 4; Delachenal, iii, p. 229.
42 For what follows, see Reuss, pp. 283–5, and *Urkundenbuch der Stadt Strassburg*, v, pp. 452, 498, 502, 554.
43 *Urkundenbuch*, v, p. 452.
44 Ibid., v, pp. 498, 502, 554.

found further progress blocked, the Rhine bridgeheads having been demolished. His forces then turned to pillaging the suburbs of the city, progressively occupying the lands of the bishopric, which were also systematically looted. The German chronicler Königshofen, at the time a young man of twenty, gives a graphic description of both the companies and the plight of the local population. The captains wore long tunics made of expensive cloth, tight-fitting trousers and impressive armour, but many of their men were barefoot and sparsely clothed *(barfuss und nackent)*. Some discipline was maintained in the camps, and Königshofen tells us that few villages were burned, save by negligence of the troops billeted in them, and that passports and passwords were needed to travel around. The nobility, in their castles, and burgesses dwelling in the small fortified towns which were numerous in Alsace, were also safe enough, since the companies had no siege equipment with them. But in the small undefended towns and country villages it was a different story. Large numbers of the peasantry were tortured, taken prisoner or impressed as valets and messengers. The better off were robbed of their silver, horses and clothes. Others had to provide the companies with shoes, horse-shoes and nails – objects which the magistrates of Strasbourg had forbidden to be traded to them. Women and girls suffered the usual outrages.[45]

The Archpriest's forces created havoc around Strasbourg for the best part of a month, whilst the emperor made a leisurely progress north. After leaving Avignon on 9 June, Charles IV spent the night of the 13th at Romans, where he was joined by the duke of Burgundy, who had left his castles of Rouvres near Dijon too late to proceed usefully to Avignon, not least because communications in the Saône and Rhône valleys had been made insecure by the the garrison of Anse. A plot having been uncovered for Tonnet de Badefol to ambush him on his way to the curia, the duke had been obliged to delay his departure and make a detour on his way south to Lyon. From Romans, the two men had passed the 14th at the abbey of Saint-Antoine-de-Viennois before going their separate ways on the 15th, Charles proceeding north by way of Grenoble to arrive in Geneva on 19 June. Here part of his company left for Lausanne, while Charles himself, who was accompanied from Avignon by that crusading enthusiast Count Amadeus of Savoy as far as his castle of Romont in the pays de Vaud, proceeded by Fribourg and Berne to Bâle, then down the Rhine to arrive in Strasbourg by boat on the 29th. A few days later he took up residence at the little town of Seltz, some thirty miles to the north of Strasbourg.[46]

45   Königshofen, *Cronik*, i, p. 487; Philippe de Vigneulles, *Chronique*, ii, pp. 51–2; *Urkundenbuch*, v, pp. 525–6; Chérest, pp. 316–19; Reuss, pp. 285–7.
46   Delachenal, iii, pp. 227–9; *Itin. Phil. le Hardi*, p. 21; Reuss, p. 295, and, for the attempted ambush, Guigue, p. 117; Petit, x, p. 159.

The whole of Alsace was then in uproar about the imminent arrival of the companies. No timetable had been set for their arrival on the Rhine and no arrangements made for provisioning them. Charles's imperial subjects, in particular the Rhenish towns, had not been consulted about the Archpriest's crusade, although rumours about it had been circulating since the emperor's brief stop in Strasbourg on his journey south to Avignon on 24 April.[47] This lack of consultation had doubtless been exacerbated by the Archpriest's unexpectedly speedy mobilization of the companies, in part made possible by their prior involvement in Burgundy and Lorraine. Faced with this crisis, Charles summoned the feudal contingents and levies of the elector palatine and the towns of Mainz, Worms and Spire to assemble in the neighbourhood of Seltz by 16 July, and requested Strasbourg to provide the necessary provisions for the army – a difficult task, with the companies encircling their walls and pillaging the suburbs. Nevertheless, by 22 or 23 July the imperial forces were already on the move and were in the neighbourhood of Strasbourg on the 25th, establishing their camp to the west of the city. There they were joined by further forces under the count of Wurtemberg and the margraves of Baden and Nuremberg. A contemporary chronicler estimated their strength at around 24,000 men, not counting contingents from other towns like Trèves and Augsburg, which were still awaited. The strength of the companies, on the other hand, was put at about 40,000.[48]

The emperor's motives in promoting the crusade in the Balkans have been questioned. Did he really believe that the companies could be successfully conducted across the Empire to Hungary? Did he intend that they should be destroyed on their way? Or had he other ulterior designs? It has been suggested that, while concerned to defend the western frontiers of the Empire, he was hostile to the part played by Strasbourg in organizing a league of towns in the upper and middle Rhine and Switzerland, fearing the increased independence it might bring them. According to this interpretation the reaction to the arrival of the companies led him to denounce his involvement and to appear to intend crushing the Archpriest with an imperial army.[49] It seems much more probable that he had totally underestimated the strength of opposition to the crusade in Alsace and the Rhenish towns, and badly miscalculated the impact that the early arrival of an enormous body of undisciplined troops would have in the Rhineland. The lack of any preparations to conduct and feed them while passing through

---

47 Reuss, p. 292.
48 *Urkundenbuch*, v, pp. 533–4; Reuss, p. 295. Strength: *Chron. de Limbourg*, cit. Reuss, p. 295 n. 6, and, for the companies, *Chroniques ou Annales de Saint-Thibaut de Metz*, published by D. Calmet, *Histoire de Lorraine*, ii, p. 170, cit. Chérest, p. 316. Cf. Philippe de Vigneulles, *Chroniques*, ii, p. 51, who gives 60,000 for the latter.
49 Reuss, pp. 294, 302–3.

imperial territory had forced the league headed by Strasbourg to take such action as it was able. In an attempt to stabilize the situation Charles IV assembled his forces, but took no action against the companies encamped in the open villages around Strasbourg, and made no attempt to cut off their line of retreat by the Swiss towns and Upper Alsace. He resisted pressure from the towns of Alsace to mount an attack and kept his lines of communication open with the Archpriest. At the beginning of August the companies fell back, first to Benfeld and Dambach, then to Sélestat, whilst fairly large contingents proceeded in the direction of Bâle. This movement may have been intended to cover their line of retreat to the Belfort Gap, but, having failed to cross the Rhine at Strasbourg, the Archpriest may have hoped to find a crossing at Bâle. The possibility that he might succeed in this enterprise was real enough. The ramparts of the town, damaged by an earthquake in 1356, had not been rebuilt, and reinforcements had to be hurried in from other Swiss cantons. Soleure and Berne sent 1,500 men and a further 3,000 were provided by Zurich, Lucerne, Uri, Schwitz, Unterwalden, Zug and Glaris. By 10 July the count of Montbéliard had arrived in the town, possibly with additional support, and on 22 July a touching letter was sent to Strasbourg, asking for such troops as they could spare.[50]

Finding himself hemmed in to north and south, and with the projected crusade abandoned by the emperor, the Archpriest had no alternative but to beat a hasty retreat. Around 10 August he took the bulk of his forces through the Belfort Gap, fulminating against Charles IV as he went.[51] The countryside through which his forces passed now suffered the full force of his anger and frustration. Villages were burned, churches and convents looted. At the little town of Rouffach, below Colmar, women and children were violated and the population massacred. Philip the Bold, then staying in Paris, having heard that the companies 'had failed to secure passage into Germany to go overseas', instructed his officers in Burgundy to take appropriate measures, namely those of informing the towns of Burgundy to bring into the security of their walls as many of the country population as possible, together with their belongings.[52] As the companies retreated into France, Königshofen tells us 'the emperor, the princes and the towns each returned home'. Already on 9 August Charles IV was in Spire, doubtless giving some thought to the fiasco he left behind him and the bitterness it had caused. 'More damage came to the country', Königshofen continues, 'thanks to the troops of the emperor and those of his allies than came as a result of the enemies.' The destruction of crops, cereals, fruits

50 Ibid., pp. 296–9; Chérest, p. 319.
51 Reuss, p. 298; Chérest, p. 321 n. 1.
52 AD, Côte-d'Or, B 1417, fo. 39v; Chérest, p. 324 n. 1.

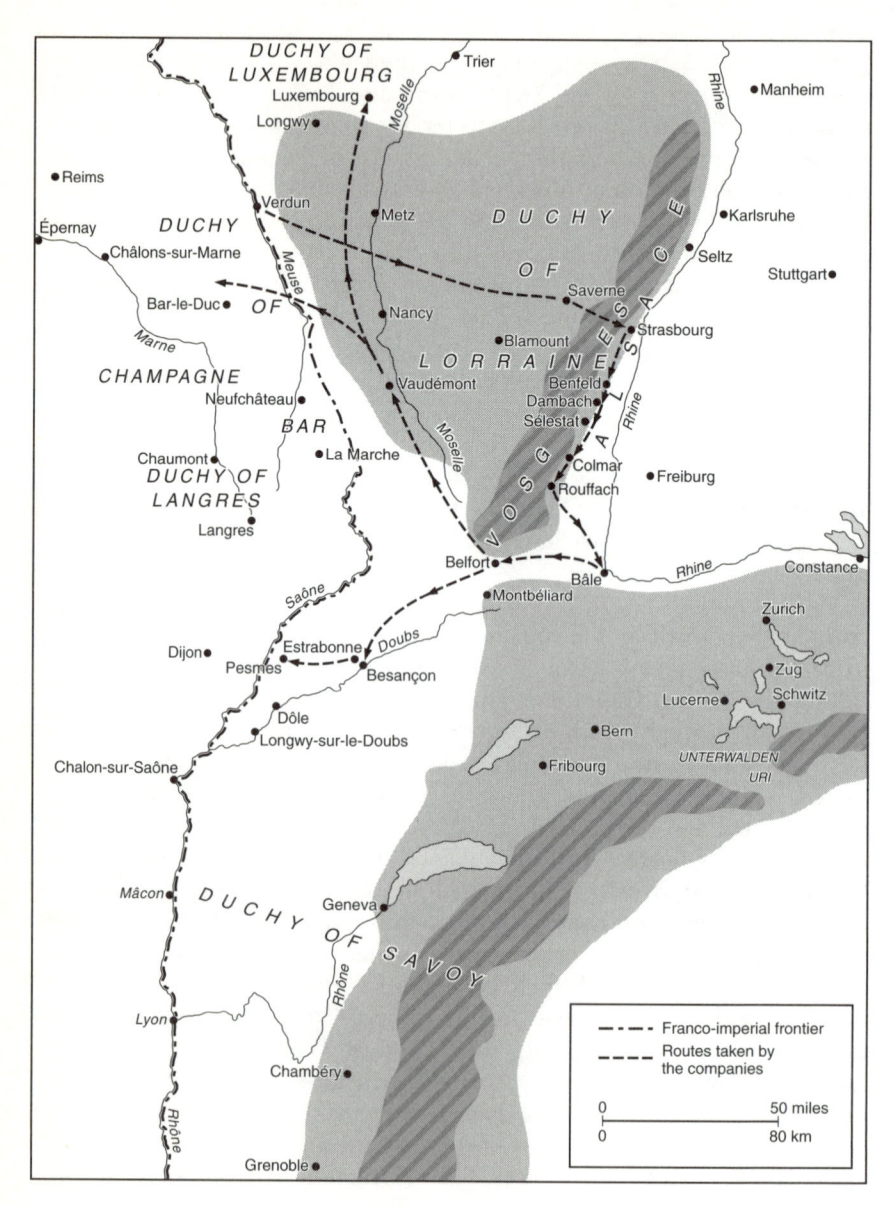

5 *The Archpriest's 'Crusade', June–August 1365*

and vines before the harvest resulted in increased deaths and, according to one account, the effects were felt for some six years.[53]

As the forces placed under the Archpriest returned through the Belfort Gap, the largest part remained in imperial territory between the Rhine and the Meuse, subsequently conducting a second invasion of Alsace. This may have been intentional policy to prevent their re-entering France, but all the evidence suggests that the land crusade against the Turks under the command of the Archpriest had been delayed, but not abandoned. Some meanwhile penetrated as far north as Luxembourg. Some, notably the Bretons, returned into the duchy of Bar. Others headed for the county of Burgundy and took up quarters to the east of the Saône, Sir Richard Taunton at Pesmes and Lamit at Longwy-sur-le-Doubs, and other Gascon contingents at Estrabonne, to the immediate west of Besançon. A few may have penetrated into the duchy of Burgundy, but they were prevented from proceeding further south and west into Champagne, the Mâconnais and the Rhône valley, where the work of evacuating fortresses was still proceeding.[54]

The evacuation of Anse, in particular, had been integral to the plans to send the companies on the crusade against the Turks, but was not completed until the middle of September 1365. As had been the case at Pont-Saint-Esprit and Brioude, the departure of the companies involved a number of interested parties, since the arrangements concerned not only the garrison of Anse, but also those of fortresses controlled by some of Seguin de Badefol's lieutenants in the surrounding territories. Under the terms of the first arrangement, concluded with the duke of Anjou, acting for Charles V, a sum of 4,000 florins was advanced for the evacuation of the companies from the *bailliages* of Mâcon, Saint-Gengoux and Charlieu. The departure of Thomas Folifait and other companies occupying fortresses in the Mâconnais, who joined the Archpriest, probably resulted from this arrangement. In addition, the duke also handed over a further 1,250 florins in the name, but without the knowledge, of the city of Lyon, thereby creating a debt which the citizens subsequently refused to recognize. Another agreement for the evacuation of Beaujolais was concluded with the lord of Beaujeu and financed from a *fouage* imposed on each of the parishes of the province. The total sum involved is not known.

The arrangement for the evacuation of Anse itself followed discussions in the presence of the pope in Avignon between representatives of Seguin de Badefol and those of the cathedral chapter of Saint John of Lyon, who were the legal proprietors. Both parties agreed to the pope's arbitration and to accept his adjudication. Charles V's three ambassadors at the curia

---

53 Königshofen, *Cronik*, p. 489; Reuss, pp. 298, 299 and n. 1.
54 Chérest, pp. 326, 330–2; Petit, x, pp. 184, 189.

– his councillors the archbishop of Sens, the bishop of Nevers and Guillaume de Dormans – represented French royal interests, and the main lines of a treaty had been agreed by 24 June, when the duke of Anjou issued instructions in connection with the financial clauses of the principal agreement.[55] This was embodied in a papal ordinance for 'the evacuation and deliverance of the castle and town of Anse, of the Lyonnais, and of the kingdom of France', the final text of which was concluded during the course of July 1365 after discussions with Charles V's ambassadors and the governor of Montpellier, who had been acting for the pope in this connection since the time of his mission to the Black Prince in February. The main terms were as follows:[56]

1. Seguin and his companions occupying the castle and town of Anse were to deliver them to the dean and chapter of Lyon by 8 August 1365, or before if the first instalment of a total sum of 40,000 small florins (detailed below) was paid before that date. They were to leave the kingdom without making further war there, unless this was 'a just war of their own lords', and were only to make war elsewhere in Christendom if this was likewise 'a just war'. As a guarantee of his good faith, Seguin was to hand over his father and brothers as hostages in Avignon, together with other sureties to be held by the pope until such time as Seguin left France. All of his companions were to swear to abide by these conditions and to issue letters sealed with Seguin's seal and the seals of the most notable members of his company, 'the best and the strongest', before being conducted to the frontier with a royal escort sufficient for this purpose.
2. They were to have absolution for the hostilities they had conducted in France in contravention of papal pronouncements, and Urban also undertook to secure pardons for them from both the king of France and the prince of Wales.
3. In the event of their wishing to join the crusade placed under the command of the Archpriest, the pope would grant them the same absolution as that granted to others going with Seguin, and he would see that they were appropriately received and that they shared in the profits of the expedition.
4. To meet their costs in carrying out these undertakings, and to see that they were properly arrayed and provided for in their departure from the realm, they were to receive 40,000 small florins or 32,000 francs, of which 20,000 florins were to be handed over in Anse against surrender of the hostages, by 8 August 1365 at the latest. The remaining 20,000 florins, or their equivalent, were to paid in Rodez at Christmas

55 AD, Herault, A 5, fos. 286v–8r.
56 Guigue, pp. 120–2; Allut, pp. 157–9.

following, in default of which hostages of sufficient standing and number to guarantee that sum were to be made over to Seguin in Avignon.

5 They were henceforward to desist from taking fortresses, prisoners and goods by way of reprisal or otherwise. They were to refrain from burning places and causing other damage, and were 'to allow good men to harvest their fruit and cultivate their lands as in time of peace'.

Steps had already been taken to raise the money upon which the evacuation depended, and arrangements were now set in train to provide the promised absolution and pardons, to secure the hostages in respect of the initial payment, and to conduct the companies out of France. Of the 40,000 florins specified for the evacuation, 25,000 were to be raised in the Lyonnais and Mâconnais and the remaining 15,000 in the seneschalsies of Beaucaire, Nîmes, Carcassonne and Toulouse.[57] Already before the end of June, Urban V had sent Cardinal Guy de Boulogne to Nîmes to explain to an assembly of the communes of the southern seneschalsies the importance of raising the necessary sums speedily; but the delegates claimed to be unable to commit their constituents, having come without power to bind them on the matter, of which they may have been ignorant before the assembly took place. On 24 June the duke of Anjou, in his capacity as king's lieutenant in Languedoc, instructed the seneschals to see that the representatives of the communes (who were to assemble in Rodez on 1 August in response to a request for 60,000 florins from the duke of Berry and Auvergne, in respect of moneys outstanding to him from the time of his lieutenancy in 1356–60), also came with full powers to approve the 15,000 florins in respect of the evacuation of Anse.[58] The choice of Rodez, in the principality of Aquitaine, for the assembly of the representatives of the communes is probably to be explained by the sums claimed by Berry, which dated from the period prior to the treaty of Brétigny, but it may also be indicative of a wider papal plan of action to secure finance for the evacuation of Anse. The Black Prince had evidently approved the location of the assembly, and it is noteworthy that the communes of Rouergue contributed to the evacuation costs.[59]

In the event it took much longer than both the papacy and royal officials had anticipated to raise the money, and the objections voiced by the town of Montpellier to requests that they contribute two *gros* per hearth, on the basis of 10,100 hearths, to the evacuation of fortresses outside Languedoc are revealing, and probably also reflected the sentiments of other communes. Anse they argued was in French-speaking territory, in *lingua*

---

57 AD, Herault, A 5, fos. 286v–8r; see *HGL*, x, cols. 1343–4.
58 Ibid.
59 AC, Millau, EE 15 (24 June 1365).

gallicana, and when Seguin had hitherto occupied places in Languedoc, Anse had not contributed to their evacuation. Moreover, they argued, in view of other taxes to which they had already contributed, the duke of Anjou had exempted them from contributions to the costs of evacuating Anse, and all other subsidies averaging one *gros* per hearth. Their appeal went before the Paris *parlement* and, whilst it was not rejected out of hand, Montpellier still had to pay 500 florins.[60] In the event, the chapter of Lyon was unable to secure the moneys to meet the initial payment of 20,000 florins before the beginning of September and Anse was not evacuated until the 13th of that month.[61]

As concerned the absolution and the pardons, as early as 16 July Urban wrote to the Black Prince, seeking the pardon he had undertaken to secure:

You have doubtless heard that the noble man, Seguin de Badefol, knight, of the diocese of Sarlat, your subject (although he has for long ceased to fulfil his duties, as captain of a company of men-at-arms, who has taken certain lands in the kingdom of France and there committed numerous depredations, to the grave offence of our very dear son in Christ, Charles, illustrious king of France), has concluded a treaty in the court of Rome with the men of the said king and has undertaken to evacuate the town of Anse in the diocese of Lyon, to cease all attacks against the said king and kingdom, and no longer to fight in these terrible companies, on condition that the king and you pardon him and his accomplices of all offences committed against the said king and kingdom. We, being informed of these intentions and wishing him and his accomplices to put an end to their crimes, confident of the eternal bounty of the king of France and yourself, have given Seguin's envoys assurance that he will obtain your pardon. For this reason, because the king of France's men have promised him this pardon on condition that, for his part, he keeps his promises, and because we shall intercede with the king who will certainly agree to our request, we require your noblesse to grant full remission graciously to Seguin and his accomplices, in so much as they are your subjects, and wish you to draw up letters to this effect and give them to our dear Jean de Sisteron, our messenger, the bearer of these present.[62]

On 21 July Urban sent Dominico de Lucaro to the prince, possibly on the same matter, and on 5 August he issued a safe-conduct for Seguin to go to

---

60 The details are to be found in a judgement of the *parlement*, communicated to the seneschal of Beaucaire on 7 September 1366, of which several copies exist (*Arch. Montpellier*, i, no. 191, copied in AD, Hérault, A 232, Coll. Pacotte, vol. 2, fos 5r–v; BN, MS latin 9175, fos. 96r–7v). See also *Arch. Montpellier*, xiii, nos. 1125, 1208, where one should read Anse for Aussac (*Ancia* not *Aucia*), and ibid., ii *(Documents omis dans l'inventaire du Grand Chartier)*, no. lxxxi, where one should read 1366 for 1376, and note that the quittance for 500 florins (6,000 *gros*) paid by the consuls of Montpellier was for the *rachat* of Anse.
61 Guigue, pp. 123–30.
62 Urban V, *Lettres secrètes*, no. 1880; Prou, pp. 132–3, PJ no. lvii.

Avignon, possibly to receive absolution at his hands.[63] On the same day he wrote to the bishop of Valence requesting him to allow Seguin to cross his lands, under the safe-conduct of the governor of Dauphiné and Guy de Pruniers, acting for the pope, together with a number of his companions whose names would be indicated by the dean of the chapter of Lyon and the governor.[64] At the beginning of August the councillors of Charles V, who had negotiated the evacuation of Anse with Seguin's men, instructed Louppy to secure the hostages to be handed over by Seguin at Lyon. Leaving that town on 6 August, he joined Pruniers at Vienne, and together they went to Lyon and then to Anse to secure the hostages. By the 9th they were back in Valence, apparently without their charges.[65]

At the time of the pope's ordinance for the evacuation of Anse, it was clearly envisaged that the companies under Seguin's command would join the forces which the Archpriest was to lead across imperial territory to Hungary. In early August the three councillors of Charles V instructed the lord of Sombernon, governor of Burgundy, to be at Tournus, on the western frontier of the duchy, along with the *bailli* of Chalon by the evening of 9 August, to conduct Seguin's forces across the duchy to join those of the Archpriest, then in the county of Burgundy. Sombernon was at the time preoccupied with the defence of the eastern frontiers of the duchy from incursions from the companies returning westwards following their check before Strasbourg. On 6 August he requested the *bailli* to deputize for him and instructed the ducal financial officers to provide the necessary funds for the safe-conduct to be provided for Seguin and his companions.[66] In accordance with his instructions the *bailli*, accompanied by a substantial escort to provide the safe-conduct, arrived at Tournus on 9 August, and had just started supper when a messenger arrived with a letter sent from Lyon by the governor of Montpellier, addressed to the governor of Burgundy and members of the ducal council. In view of its apparent urgency, the *bailli* decided to open it, and was astonished to find an order to suspend the entire operation:

Dear lords and great friends, I have heard from the custodian of this town of Lyon, through letters of credence which he has brought to me from the lords of the king's great council, how he has spoken with you and other councillors of my lord of Burgundy on the subject of the evacuation of Anse, of the need to find escorts to conduct them [i.e. the companies occupying the town] safely out of the realm, and how you and the *bailli* of Chalon are to be at Tournus tomorrow or on Saturday

---

63 Prou, p. 55 n. 1 for Lucarro; Urban V, *Lettres secrètes*, no. 1909, for the safe-conduct. Prou, pp. 56–7, doubts if Seguin ever went.
64 Urban V, *Lettres secrètes*, no. 1908; Prou, p. 137, PJ no. lix.
65 'Compte Louppy', arts. 36, 79, 121; Prou, pp. 56–7.
66 BN, coll. Bourgogne, xxvi, fos. 121r–2r; Prou, pp. 55–6.

to provide the aforesaid safe-conduct. Lords, the truth of the matter is that they will not depart unless they all go, and some of them wish to go by way of Auvergne. My lords and I have written to my lord of Berry, requesting him to send a sufficient escort for them, and he has replied that he is held up, and that he is presently on his way to Riom, where he has summoned his council, and that he will at once seek for escorts the persons I have suggested to him, and that as soon as he has time he will send them here, but he has not given me a definite date, since he does not know if he will find them. The bearer of these letters will tell you all you need to know, and you must believe what he says. For this reason, sir, I am not giving you a definite date until I have heard from my lord of Berry, which I am sure will not be long. Wherefore, I urge you, as forcibly as I can, that, for the love of God and the country, you will not depart from where you are, or from the neighbourhood, until I know where I can send for you a certain day, which, with the help of God, will be soon. And in case for any reason you cannot be there, or do not hear from me, then will you please see that your marshal of Burgundy and the *bailli* of Chalon will escort them, and that they will be ready on the day that I write to them. Please inform me of your intentions on this matter by way of the bearer of these letters, and if there is anything I can do, I will gladly do it. God have you in his keeping. Written at Lyon on the Rhône, the 7th day of August. Dear lord, I am sending you a letter which my lord of Anjou is sending to his brother, the lord of Burgundy.

Guy, lord of Phines, governor of Montpellier.[67]

The companies at Anse thus failed to join the Archpriest. On 8 August Sombernon had heard from the duke that some of the contingents returning from Germany, who had taken the fortress of Pesmes and other places the previous evening, had crossed the Saône. Before the end of the month, as we have seen, Longwy-sur-le-Doubs and Estrabonne, near Dôle and Besançon respectively, were also in their hands.

The ducal council multiplied its efforts to defend the duchy. Pesmes and Longwy were too near the eastern frontier of the duchy for comfort. The neighbouring places were speedily inspected and their defences repaired. Reinforcements were sent to Pontailler and Saint-Aubin, and messengers sent in all directions – to Autun and Montcenis, to the captains of castles and other officers in the duchy ordering them to keep watch by day and night.[68] From late August and during the course of September the focus of attention shifted to the western frontier, and the considerable number of letters and messengers mentioned in the ducal accounts, sent every day to lords and captains, to Philip the Bold in Paris and the duke of Anjou in Lyon, bear testimony to the general state of alert in Burgundy.[69] The *foire chaude* of Chalon, which was to have been held on 28 August, was put off until 17 September 'because the companies at Anse have still not departed,

---

67 BN, coll. Bourgogne, xxvi, fo. 121r; Petit, x, pp. 167–8.
68 Petit, x, pp. 169–70, from AD, Côte-d'Or, B 1417, fos. 39ff.
69 Chérest, p. 329; Petit, x, p. 170.

as a result of which neither merchants nor prospective purchasers can come to the said fair'.[70] On 5 September the ducal council received information indicating that 160 men-at-arms and some 200 infantry had left Anse with the intention of taking towns and fortresses in the duchy.[71]

With the evacuation of Anse on the 13th every effort was made to prevent the movement of the companies further north. Some remained in the neighbourhood of Lyon, from where the authorities kept a twenty-four-hour watch, and sent out spies to observe the movements of the departing companies and report any suspicious movements. Forewarned, castellans redoubled their vigilance. For his part, Seguin kept his word, leaving Lyonnais by Saint-Symphorien-le-Châtel, passing by Montbrison in Forez and Brioude in Auvergne with one of the spies, Vialet, still on his tail.[72] After returning to Périgord he made for Navarre with some of his men, in pursuit of lands and money still outstanding to him for his services to the king. In a deposition made some thirteen years later, in 1378, Charles's chamberlain, Jacquet de Rue, explained how, shortly after the battle of Cocherel, the king of Navarre had promised Seguin lands to the value of 1,000 *livres* rent in return for his undertaking to make war against Charles V.[73] Jacquet may have been referring to the moneys which were to have been passed to Seguin by the lord of Albret. Seguin's wish was that these lands should be situated in Navarre – at Falces, Peralta and Lerin – and it was doubtless with this in mind that he journeyed there towards the close of that year. By 13 December he was with Charles at Olite, where he spent Christmas and the New Year with the king, accompanying him to Falces on 12 January.[74] During this prolonged stay, Charles, finding Seguin's demands outrageous, indicated to Jacquet that the old *routier* would have to be eliminated, and enlisted the services of one of his *valets-de-chambre*, Guillemin Petit, to poison him. The deed was accomplished at a dinner held one night in late January or early February in the king's private apartments at Falces, where the valet served Seguin crystallized fruits laced with monkshood, either quince or pears, Jacquet could not remember which. It took six doubtless terrible days before he died. He was buried in the monastery of San Francisco in Pamplona, the king having met the costs of his funeral, as he also met the expenses of some of the men who had accompanied him to Navarre, and who remained there until the following April.[75]

70 AD, Côte-d'Or, B 1417, fo. 6r.
71 AD, Côte-d'Or, B 1417, fo. 40r.
72 Guigue, pp. 130–1.
73 *Chron. Charles V*, ii, pp. 300–1.
74 *AGN, Comptos*, v, no. 1371; AGN, Comptos, reg. 120, fos. 4r–5r; Delachenal, iii, p. 271 n. 1.
75 *AGN, Comptos*, viii, no. 861; AGN, Comptos, regs. 118, fo. 137r; 120, fo. 33r; *Chron. Charles V*, ii, p. 301 and n. 3; for the documentary details see Fowler, 1988, p. 31, n. 21.

What became of others who had occupied Anse and the neighbouring fortresses is less clear. In August 1365 a number of Gascon companies had agreed to surrender the fortresses they still held in Auvergne, and in particular Bertucat d'Albret had surrendered his castle of Blot for an unknown but considerable sum which was financed by a *fouage* of 1 florin per hearth in the mountains of Auvergne.[76] From Auvergne they had gone to swell the large number of companies gathering around Anse, and after its evacuation made for the duchy of Burgundy, with the intention of making war there in late October.[77] An invitation from du Guesclin to Bertucat and Frère Darrier to join the forces which he was leading across the Pyrenees was spurned. Along with other Gascon companies they evidently preferred less distant hunting grounds in the Saône valley.[78]

In the last three months of 1365 the companies quartered to the west of the Saône included, in addition to those of Bertucat and Frère Darrier, those of Espiote, of Pierre d'Oignel, Jehannot le Nègre and Bardot de Roussillon, and of the *bourcs* Camus, d'Aussain and de la Roque.[79] In the county of Burgundy, from the summer of 1365 until January 1366, Sir Richard Taunton and the Gascon companies under Lamit, the *bourc* de Breteuil, Naudon de Bageran and Gaillard de la Motte held on to the fortresses they had occupied to the east of the river. On 10 January these were evacuated for 21,000 florins (of which 5,000 was advanced by the Archpriest against the security of the principal fortresses surrendered), 300 florins in respect of arrears of ransoms outstanding to them, and a further 200 in compensation for a short delay which occurred in realizing the principal sum.[80] Some of these companies had returned with the Archpriest from Alsace, others had moved north following the evacuation of Anse, and some may have been intended to join the expeditionary force assembled by du Guesclin for service in Spain. Their concentration on either side of the Saône threatened the stability not only of that region, but of the territories lying to the south. This caused alarm in Avignon, where an earlier plan to send them to the Balkans by sea from Italy, with which the grand master of the Order of the Hospital, the republic of Genoa and the marquis of Montferrat had been associated, was now resurrected.[81]

In the event it was Amadeus VI, count of Savoy, who assumed the leadership of the expedition. The plan of action was for the Archpriest and his lieutenants – the *bourc* Camus, Bernard Donat and Bertrand de Montprivat – to lead the companies, who assembled at Tournus, in separate

76 Lehoux, i, p. 189 n. 7.
77 Petit, x, pp. 177–8.
78 Ibid., pp. 181–2; Chérest, pp. 335–7.
79 Chérest, pp. 335–9; Petit, x, pp. 177–9.
80 Chérest, pp. 341–3 and PJ no. xx; Petit, x, pp. 183–4.
81 Jorga, p. 272; Galland, pp. 203–4.

groupings down either bank of the Saône valley into Bresse, where they would join Amadeus's army which was destined to embark from Genoa and Venice. About half of the count's army was to be made up of contingents under his hereditary vassals, and the other half was to be drawn from the companies.[82] Although Amadeus was the prime mover in mounting this expedition, Urban certainly gave the venture his blessing, allowing the count to collect the arrears of a tenth of ecclesiastical revenues, initially granted two years earlier to finance a Franco-Cypriot crusade in which Amadeus was to have taken part, but which had been annulled when that expedition failed to materialize. Amadeus was thus able to make use of this facility to raise part of the necessary finance for his expedition from loans until the proceeds of a general subsidy could be collected.[83]

Every precaution was taken by the count as the Archpriest's forces proceeded towards his territories. The defences of all castles and fortified towns were inspected and where necessary hastily repaired. Amadeus gave instructions for all food and other valuables to be brought in from the open countryside. The *bailli* of Bresse, Humbert de Corgenon, ordered a continuous stream of scouts and messengers to different places in order to be sure that he and others were fully appraised of the movements of the companies. On the western frontier around Mâcon, the castellans of Bâgé-le-Châtel and of Pont-de-Veyle took similar action, and in the latter place the seat of government, the *maison du comte*, was moved inside the town from the well-fortified position which it had formerly occupied outside the walls. Further north, on the frontier with Burgundy at Pont-de-Vaux, all the adult population were required to take part in the town watch.[84] Then, on 25 May 1366, the Archpriest was assasinated by some of his men, either at Gleizé, on the outskirts of Villefranche-sur-Saône above Anse, or Laizé, some seven miles north of Mâcon. With his death the plans for them to join Amadeus's expedition collapsed.[85]

While both the Archpriest and Amadeus of Savoy thus failed to remove the companies from eastern France, the third 'crusade', conducted by du Guesclin across the Pyrenees, was better planned, better funded, better led, and certainly a much more attractive prospect for the companies. To be financed to the tune of 300,000 florins, of which the pope and the kings of France and Aragon were each to provide a third,[86] from the outset it had widespread support. Helped on by the settlement of internal disputes in France, Urban had succeeded in galvanizing general approval, even enthu-

---

82 Chérest, pp. 344–51; Guigue, pp. 162–3; Perroud, pp. 278–9.
83 Cox, pp. 204–11; Galland, pp. 200–6.
84 *Inv. sommaire, Côte-d'Or*, iii, B 6792, 7117, 7847, 9173, 9291.
85 Chérest, p. 350; Guigue, pp. 164–6; Cox, p. 210.
86 Pere III, *Chronicle*, ii, p. 572; cf. Delachenal, iii, p. 284 and n. 3.

siasm, for mounting a 'crusade'. Charles of Navarre was anxious to placate him, and his brother, Philip, was about to embark on a new venture which would take the Navarrese companies to Albania. Up until December 1365 even Edward III, getting older, and perhaps moved by a genuine desire for peace in western Europe, had not seen it as a threat to English interests in the Iberian Peninsula, and the Black Prince gave support to the initiatives which were taken to conduct the companies out of France. However, the viability of the crusading projects ultimately depended upon their reception by the companies. Although papal anathemas and absolution clearly encouraged some to take the cross, the expeditions proposed against the Turks were generally not well received. If 'participating in a crusade did possess intrinsic religious and cultural appeal to the mercenaries', as has been suggested,[87] it was clearly more likely to appeal to the captains of the companies if it also offered tangible material rewards. Cuvelier's message in the rhymed life of Bertrand du Guesclin, whilst it certainly poses problems for the historian of events, nevertheless echoes something of the idealism of the times:

> They were all companions of the White Company,
> There was neither knight nor baron in the host
> Who did not bear the white cross as his standard,
> And it was not for nothing that they were called 'the White Company'.[88]

But he also added, in words reputed to have been spoken by Bertrand to the assembled companions:

> As God wishes! whoever wants to believe me,
> I will make you all rich, it won't last long.[89]

The impact of the papal bulls was probably more serious. With the whole range of spiritual and material sanctions pitted against them, a significant number of mercenary captains took the opportunity to secure absolution for their past misdeeds, and clauses to facilitate this were included in the treaties concluded for the evacuation of Pont-Saint-Esprit, at Clermont in 1362 and for the evacuation of Anse. Absolution was also one of the demands of the companies who were to descend on Villeneuve-les-Avignon before the Spanish expedition at the end of 1365.[90] On 31 March of that year, as the Anglo-Navarrese war began to be wound up in the north of France, Urban granted the bishops of Paris, Beauvais and

---

87 Housley, 1982, p. 278.
88 Cuvelier, *Chronique*, i, p. 287, lines 7981–4.
89 Ibid., i, p. 263, lines 7225–6.
90 Delachenal, iii, p. 244; Denifle, ii, p. 486.

Chartres the power to absolve, during a period of six months, all those who wished to return into the bosom of the Church. In May of the following year he stepped up his action against the companies by excommunicating all those who had secured absolution but had gone on to commit further crimes. A further bull of 16 November 1366 specified the penances required of those of the companies who repented. They were to put themselves on oath not to rejoin their comrades, to restore all the property they had taken and to put right the damage which they had caused. Those who could afford it were to visit the Holy Sepulchre in Jerusalem and other places in the Holy Land within the year, and they were to spend as long there as they had been in the companies. They were to take part in any future crusade, and the less well-off were to go to Rome within six months, stay there for a year, visit Saint Peter's and the holy places each week, and then proceed to Santiago de Compostela. In addition, they were to fast on Fridays. Those without any means whatsoever were to submit themselves to the penances ordained by the local archbishop or bishop.[91]

Some particular instances indicate that a number of captains who had conducted illicit warfare in France were moved to reintegrate themselves into society by these measures. Seven years after the sack of Auxerre in 1359, Sir Robert Knowles, 'by remorse of conscience and at the request of Pope Urban V', restored to the inhabitants of Auxerre some 40,000 gold *moutons* which they had been obliged to pay him to escape 'fire, the sword and pillage' at the hands of his men. He also agreed to restore jewels belonging to the abbey of Saint-Germain there, which still remained of the treasure which had been made over to him as a guarantee of this sum.[92] These, and the restoration of a number of places which he and his men had taken in Anjou and Maine, were evidently the conditions upon which, on 29 May 1366, Urban agreed to absolve him, his wife, family and adherents from the excommunications which they had incurred.[93] The case was of particular interest to Urban, who had himself been abbot of Saint-Germain; but it was more than twenty years later that Knowles received a royal licence to go to the papal court 'for the quieting of his conscience, the salvation of his soul, and the fulfilment of his vow'.[94] It may have been on this occasion that he joined Hawkwood and Calveley in the foundation of

---

91 Denifle, ii, pp. 492, 406–8.
92 Lebeuf, iii, pp. 249–51; Denifle, ii, pp. 235–6, 507. For the documentation concerning the jewels in question and their restoration, see Simonnet, pp. 64–8.
93 Prou, pp. 148–50, PJ no. lxix; cf. Denifle, ii. p. 507.
94 *CPR, 1388–92*, p. 94. This was issued on 18 August 1389, only a fortnight before he made his first will (Lambeth, Archbishop Arundel's Register, vol. i, fos. 247v–249r; cf. *Calendar of Wills in the Court of Husting*, ii, pp. 377–8).

an English hospital in Rome, although this foundation is now generally discounted.[95]

Another Englishman, Sir Nicholas Tamworth, one-time captain of Regennes, who had also taken part in the assault on Auxerre, took the cross and went east.[96] Sir John Harleston, who had taken Flavigny in January 1360, was infamous for his exploits. In an inquest into pillaging in Champagne, made in 1375, a witness claimed to have seen him and his companions drinking out of 100 silver chalices stolen from the churches. To atone for his sins he set out on a pilgrimage to Rome, but was taken prisoner in Upper Alsace. He subsequently joined Gui de Pontailler, the future marshal of Burgundy, on a pilgrimage to the church of Our Lady in Nazareth.[97] Although examples such as these are not lacking, it is probable that it was only the more successful of the mercenaries, those who had good reason to safeguard their profits and were concerned about their position and advancement in society, who sought papal absolution. They were the exception rather than the rule.

Crusading, on the other hand, had a wider appeal. In addition to the salvation which it offered, it held out the prospect of tangible material rewards and conformed to a chivalric ideal to which the companies could aspire. The relationship between chivalry and the ambitions of the *routier* captains is problematic, but the career of the Bascot de Mauléon, who fought with the Teutonic Knights as well as at Brignais, Poitiers, Auray and on the Spanish campaigns, recounted in the famous although possibly fictitious interview with Froissart,[98] had many elements in common with that of Chaucer's Gentle Knight, who fought in Prussia, Lithuania, Russia, Granada and Benamarin. As has been remarked, the Bascot 'is a useful reminder of the difficulty of applying any touchstone in order to distinguish the gold from the base metal in chivalry'.[99] Contemporary accounts certainly presented the expedition to Spain as a crusade. According to the *Grandes Chroniques*, du Guesclin recruited the companies on the basis that he was leading a crusade against the Saracens. That is how the chronicler of Montpellier and Cuvelier presented these events, and also Charles V in a document subsequently releasing the Breton captain from all outstanding debts, including '30,000 gold francs which we made to him in three instalments to help him to lead into Granada the men of the companies

---

95   BL, Harl. MS 2111, fo. 100v.
96   Lettenhove in Froissart, *Oeuvres*, xxiii, p. 182. On his career see Chérest, pp. 128–9, 132–4, 135 n. 1, 203 n. 1; Finot, pp. 52, 64; Petit, x, pp. 154, 183.
97   De Fréville, ii, pp. 246 and n. 6; Chérest, 203 n. 1, citing J. Simonnet, *Des institutions et de la vie privée en Bourgogne*, p. 377.
98   I intend to review the evidence for and against the Bascot's career and his supposed interview with the chronicler in a forthcoming article on 'Froissart's Bascot de Mauléon'.
99   Keen, 1976, pp. 32–45, and p. 45 for the quotation; Housley, 1982, p. 279. For an interpretation of Chaucer's knight, see Jones, 1980, chs. 3–4 and *passim*.

who were in our kingdom, whom he conducted there and was for a long time out of our said realm'.[100] Although the war was to begin in Castile, the ultimate destination of the companies was to fight the Moors in Granada.

Others were more sceptical.[101] The war in Castile could also itself be seen as a crusade, as Trastámaran propagandists circulated the most virulent stories about Pedro I, which gained widespread currency: that he was a cruel tyrant, responsible for the most terrible crimes, including the death of his wife, Blanche of Bourbon, the sister of the queen of France; that he was surrounded by Jews, from whom alone he took advice; that he was himself a Jew, who was substituted at birth for the queen's child when she gave birth to a girl; that he persecuted the clergy of Castile; that the pope had publicly excommunicated him in full consistory at Avignon.[102] These and other stories in the same vein were later put about in France by writers like Froissart and Cuvelier, and according to Froissart, after Pedro for the first time lost his throne, they were even current in the Black Prince's entourage in Bordeaux. It would be a work of piety, Froissart suggested, to go and combat a miscreant who was no longer worthy of the royal office and of ruling his kingdom; even the pope had condemned Pedro and supported Enrique, thereby legitimizing his usurpation. Far from being abandoned, the idea of a crusade was reinforced: it would be led against the kings of Granada, of Benamarin and Tlemsen, who were the friends and allies of Pedro; but it would commence in Castile.[103]

Credence is given to these supposed objectives by an indenture drawn up between the two principal leaders of the companies, du Guesclin and Calveley, on the eve of the campaign in Castile.[104] This envisaged their joint conquest of the kingdom of Granada and territories across the Straits in Benamarin, and it was doubtless to accomplish this that Calveley secured a grant from Peter IV of Aragon of 'twenty armed galleys to proceed against the enemies of the faith', and du Guesclin a similar grant of 'diverse large ships and armed galleys paid for six months by the king to go overseas to fight the enemies of the Christian faith'.[105] The indenture

---

100 *Chron. Charles V*, ii, pp. 10–15; *Thalamus parvus*, p. 369; Cuvelier, i, p. 273; *Mandements*, p. 437, no. 851.
101 'loscals ii senhiors dessus nommats [du Guesclin and Calveley] eron capitanis de totas las companhias, loscals anavon encontra lo rei de Castilla e d'acqui en Granada, *segon que dizia*' (*Docs. Millau*, p. 146, no. 293, my italics); see below, p. 151n.
102 Delachenal, iii, pp. 248–9.
103 Froissart, *Chroniques*, vi, pp. 185–7; Cuvelier, i, pp. 240ff., 255–6, 264, lines 6560ff., 6975–7023, 7266–75. Philippe de Mézières, *Songe*, ii, p. 435, was subsequently to propose precisely such a crusading goal for the Iberian kings. For the political situation in North Africa in the fourteenth century, see Atiya, pp. 147, 401.
104 ACA, Cancilleria, reg. 738, fos. 41v–2r; published in Fowler, 1991b and 1992, PJ no. I. See below, p. 170.
105 See below, pp. 170–1.

detailed the division of their conquests, and makes clear du Guesclin's ambitions to carve out a principality for himself in Granada, whilst Calveley, who had already served there, sought to control either side of the Straits of Gibraltar.[106] There was no contradiction to previous crusading practice here: Urban V had made it quite clear that the crusade could offer material as well as spiritual rewards; lands, castles, towns and booty thus gained by the companies, unlike the property gained from the activities against Christians, were legitimate because they were acquired in a just war.[107] As is if to give concrete form to their plans, in a ceremony at Burgos at the end of March 1366, du Guesclin was granted the kingdom of Granada and crowned king by Enrique.[108]

Whatever the motives of the pope, and whatever the ambitions of the captains of the companies, there can be no doubt that the expedition proved extremely popular. For his part Charles V was determined to get the campaign under way as soon as possible, and the companies were initially scheduled to enter Aragon in September. Inevitably, it took rather longer. The first necessity was to secure freedom of action for du Guesclin, who had been taken prisoner by Sir John Chandos at the battle of Auray, but released on parole, by facilitating the completion of the payment of his ransom, which may have amounted to 100,000 florins.[109] From Bertrand's standpoint the arrangements entered into were essentially a business transaction. In August, Charles undertook to advance him 40,000 florins of the total sum against the security of the county of Longueville, which du Guesclin surrendered to him, and advanced a further 30,000 francs towards his costs in evacuating the companies from the fortresses which they occupied in Brittany, Normandy, the Chartrain and elsewhere in the marches with Poitou. In return, by letters dated at his castle of La Roche-Tesson in Lower Normandy on 22 August, Bertrand formally undertook to conduct these companies out of France as soon as possible, and obliged himself to see that in proceeding to the frontier they would only stop to secure necessities for the journey, and would not demand further finance or ransoms from the king or his subjects. On 30 September he renewed

---

106 Calveley already knew Granada from his service there in 1362, when he had commanded a contingent in the army of the king of Castile, who had supported Mohammed V, the deposed Moorish king of Granada, in his war against the usurper, Abu Said (Ayala, *Crónica*, i, p. 517). For possible English ambitions to secure entry into the Mediterranean for their shipping see Lewis, p. 162.
107 Delachenal, iii, p. 245 n. 1.
108 Ibid., p. 281 n. 2; Russell, p. 49 n. 1.
109 Delachenal, iii, p. 282. The documentation (fifteen letters and acquittances) relative to this are to be found in AN, J. 381, no. 13. Some of these have been published by Charrière in Cuvelier, ii, pp. 396–401, PJ nos. vii–xii.

these undertakings in a more solemn act before two papal notaries in Paris.[110]

Du Guesclin was actively recruiting throughout the summer of 1365, together with three other captains who held subordinate commands and were closely associated with him: Calveley, Eustache d'Auberchicourt and Gourderon de Raymont, lord of Aubeterre in Saintonge. Bertrand was to have overall command of the combined forces, but with subordinate commands going to the other three, in particular to Calveley, who was effectively second in command. Not all of the forces they recruited were drawn from the Great Companies. A significant number of those engaged by du Guesclin had served with him in his earlier command as lieutenant between the rivers Seine and Loire, reinforced by others who had been ejected from Brittany by John de Montfort. Among their number, the contingents commanded by Breton captains were in the ascendant: those of Yvon Budes, Auffroy de Guébriant, Yvon Duant, Thibaud du Pont, Alain de la Houssaye, Jean de Kerlouet, Olivier de Mauny and Guillaume Boistel. Others who probably joined him at a later stage included Guillaume de Laval, Alain and Henri de Mauny, Jacques de Pencoédic, Maurice de Tréséguidy, Alain de Beaumont, Yvon de Lacoué, Alain, Raoulet and probably also Jean de Saint-Pol. Calveley was in charge of the English contingents, which were largely drawn from among Montfort's supporters in Brittany and had taken part in the battle of Auray. They included Matthew Gournay, Walter Huet, John Devereux, William Ludlow, William Botiller, Norman Swinford, Robin de Adés and Stephen Cosington, the last probably to maintain liaison with the Black Prince. From the English and Gascon contingents of the companies we may note those of John Cresswell, Robert Birkhead, Robert Scott, Bernard de la Salle, Arnaud du Solier, Renaud de Vigneulles and a lieutenant of the *bourc* de Caupène called Bras de Fer.

There is no corroborating evidence for other contingents listed by Froissart, notably those of Naudon de Bageran, Lamit, Le Petit Meschin, the *bourcs* Camus, Lesparre and Breteuil, Munde Bataillier, Espiote, Amanieu d'Ortigue and Perrot de Savoie. Scott was probably recruited by Auberchicourt, who was accompanied by a number of Hainaulters, but was primarily responsible for raising forces from among the Anglo-Navarrese companies who had been operating in Normandy and the Île-de-France. Some of the Gascon companies were almost certainly recruited by Gourderon de Raymont, who had also fought in Brittany before operating on his own account after Auray. He appears to have subcontracted with du Guesclin to raise a number of companies and certainly acted as their

---

110 Charrière in Cuvelier, ii, p. 393, PJ no. v; *Mandements*, pp. 437–9, no. 851; Delachenal, iii, p. 283–5, 283 n. 5.

paymaster, receiving from du Guesclin payments and letters obligatory for their services at Troyes and Auxerre in early October 1365, and subsequently in Spain.[111]

The point of assembly chosen for the greater part of the combined forces was Perpignan, then situated in the Aragonese territory of Roussillon. In the autumn the different contingents began the long journey there by different routes. Those under Calveley's command proceeded from Brittany by way of the principality of Aquitaine. Those under du Guesclin, who left Paris at the beginning of October, went by way of Troyes and Auxerre, made for the Loire valley at La Charité and Nevers, followed the course of that river and, skirting the duchy of Burgundy, proceeded in the direction of Roanne, where du Guesclin divided his forces. Some contingents then proceeded by the Massif-Central to Saint-Flour and Millau in Rouergue, where they joined up with the bulk of Calveley's forces, which had made their way eastwards across Aquitaine. Others appear to have proceeded by way of Beaujeu into the lower Saône valley above Lyon, and then down the west bank of the Rhône to Pont-Saint-Esprit, where some had arrived by 27 October.[112] The ranks of both armies were swollen as they proceeded south, Calveley's from among the Gascon companies then in Aquitaine, whilst Aubeterre appears to have assembled those operating in Champagne, which joined du Guesclin at Auxerre. Some contingents appear to have made their way directly from Languedoc through the Pyrenean passes that led into upper Aragon and the province of Huesca. It was probably also at Auxerre that other forces joined up with du Guesclin, including those of Adam, alias le Bègue de Villiers, who in the late 1350s had served on the frontiers of Normandy and Brittany in the garrison of Pontorson, of which his brother, Pierre, was captain.[113] Still other contingents which subsequently joined the army included the remnants of those bought out of La Charité, notably the forces under John Cresswell, and of Arnaud de Solier, who had been one of Seguin de Badefol's lieutenants at Anse.[114] Although du Guesclin made overtures to Bertucat d'Albret and Frère Darrier to join him when he arrived before Avignon, these were evidently rejected. He had

---

111 For the above details of the forces recruited by du Guesclin and Calveley, and the documentation substantiating them, see Fowler, 1991b, pp. 245–7. For the Hainaulters serving with Auberchicourt, see Froissart, *Chroniques*, vi, pp. lxxxiii, 188–9, and for Aubeterre see the documentation published by Molinier, pp. 318–28, PJ nos. xciii–xcvi, and Delachenal, iii, p. 288 and nn. 1–3.

112 For the itinerary of the main body of the army under du Guesclin, see Delachenal, iii, pp. 287–94. For the passage of some of his forces by way of Saint-Flour and Millau, and their junction with those under Calveley, on his way to Avignon, see *Docs. Millau*, pp. 145–6, nos. 291–3. News of their arrival at Pont-Saint-Esprit had reached Montpellier by 27 October (*Arch. Montpellier*, xiii, p. 119, BB 8, fo. 12v; see Delachenal, iii, p. 294 n. 1).

113 Delachenal, iii, p. 286 and n. 5. For those proceeding directly to Huesca from Languedoc, see ACA, Cancilleria, reg. 1194, fos. 204v–5r, and below, pp. 165, 167.

114 Froissart, *Chroniques*, xii, pp. 102, 105, 109–10; *Thalamus parvus*, p. 369.

not been charged with recruiting from among the companies then in Burgundy, which, as we have seen, were to have accompanied the Archpriest to the Balkans. If he made any serious efforts to do so, they were certainly not successful.[115]

In the absence of Philip the Bold, who remained in Paris, the governor of Burgundy, Jean de Sombernon, took measures to ensure that the forces assembled by du Guesclin did not enter the duchy, which included the usual precautions of evacuating the population of the open country into walled towns together with their possessions.[116] Bertrand thus steered clear of Burgundy, and it may have been at this juncture that Antoine, lord of Beaujeu, and the young count of La Marche, Jean de Bourbon, were persuaded to join his expedition, the latter, according to Froissart, being moved by a desire to avenge the death of Blanche of Bourbon.[117] But both men doubtless hoped to restore their family fortunes from the profits of his forthcoming campaign. Bourbon's father had been fatally wounded at Brignais, and Beaujeu had been obliged to find substantial sums for the evacuation of Beaujolais. In addition to these forces Charles V had instructed Marshal Audrehem and Pierre, alias le Bègue de Villaines, to join du Guesclin's army, probably in mid-November, when Bertrand arrived in Avignon.[118] They were clearly intended to keep a check on the activities of the forces placed under his command. They certainly needed to do so.

The original plan seems to have been for the main body of the army to proceed directly from Millau to Perpignan by way of Montpellier, while the principal captains made their way to Avignon to secure the pope's financial contribution towards the cost of the expedition, some to secure absolution at his hands.[119] They were joined there by a delegation from the Black Prince's council in Bordeaux, which included Sir John Chandos and the steward of his household, Sir Thomas Percy, doubtless to observe how matters were proceeding.[120] The delay which this occasioned resulted in widespread pillaging. During the course of November the enormous army being assembled – upwards of 10,000 combatants before it was reinforced

---

115 *Itin. Phil. le Hardi*, p. 462; Petit, x, pp. 178–80; cf. Chérest, pp. 338–9; Delachenal, iii, p. 291 and n. 1.
116 Delachenal, iii, p. 289 and n. 1; Petit, x, pp. 175–6.
117 Froissart, *Chroniques*, vi, pp. lxxxii and 188; Delachenal, iii, pp. 285–6.
118 Froissart, *Chroniques*, vi, pp. lxxxii and 188; Pere III, *Chronicle*, p. 573; *Chron. normande*, p. 180; cf. Delachenal, iii, p. 286 and n. 2.
119 Du Guesclin was at Villeneuve from at least 12 to 16 November, but at Montpellier from 29 November to 3 December, when he left for Perpignan (Luce in Froissart, *Chroniques*, vi, p. lxxx n. 3; *Thalamus parvus*, p. 369). Calveley passed through Millau on his way to Avignon, on 22 November, 'e anavon lei [en Castilla, e d'aqui en Granada] al sol del Papa, local anava penre poiamen az'Avinhio' (*Docs. Millau*, p. 146, no. 293).
120 *Docs. Millau*, p. 146, no. 293. The presence of Chandos in Rodez, also on his way to Avignon, is noted in AC, Rodez, bourg CC 127, fo. 9r.

by Aragonese contingents[121] – awaiting pay and further instructions, encamped over a wide stretch of territory in the seneschalsy of Beaucaire, from the lower Rhône valley around Villeneuve-lès-Avignon to Montpellier in the west, where the movements of the different contingents were carefully monitored by the town chronicler.[122] The first *routes* of Bretons under Guillaume d'Acigné, Aufrey de Guébriant and Henri de Dinan encamped in the surrounding villages on 1 November. On the 5th, another company drawn from Brittany and commanded by Robert Birkhead took the fortress of Bellegarde to the south of Nîmes, where they remained for over a month, until 8 December. On 18 November, a Gascon company under Bras de Fer, a lieutenant of the *bourc* de Caupene, took up quarters at Castelnau, now in the northern suburbs of Montpellier, using it as a base to raid as far afield as Rouergue and Pont-Saint-Esprit. They then began rounding up cattle and other livestock, taking prisoners and obliging the consuls to send out an armed force to bring all the grain and flour into the town from the mills in the surrounding countryside.

In the Comtat Venaissin and in Provence, where memories of the invasion of the Archpriest in 1357–8 and of the depredations inflicted on the region during the occupation of Pont-Saint-Esprit were all too recent, the arrival of the companies occasioned widespread panic.[123] News of their approach resulted in a new bout of feverish activity in Avignon and other towns like Carpentras, where the municipal authorities made every effort to improve the defences of the walls, towers and gates, and assembled an enormous artillery to repulse any attack. At Montpellier, where news of the arrival of du Guesclin and his army at Pont-Saint-Esprit reached the consuls on 27 October, all the citizens were required to be on guard in the town and its suburbs by day and night, and arrangements were put afoot for the fortifications to be reinforced. Some of the gates were to be blocked up and others closed. The inhabitants of a number of ecclesiatical establishments were to be evacuated within the walls, and the church of the Carmelites, which lay alongside them, was burned down to prevent the companies gaining access by that quarter. Some discussion took place as to whether refugees from outlying areas, together with their goods, should also be received inside the town. Mills were to be kept working on feast days to ensure that the town was well supplied with flour and bread, and on the approach of the companies the handles were to be removed from those which were operated manually.[124]

121 For the strength of the army, see Fowler, 1988, p. 32, and below, p. 169 and appendix C.
122 *Thalamus parvus*, pp. 369–70.
123 For what follows, see Labande, 1904, pp. 43–59; Delachenal, iii, p. 295; Denifle, ii, pp. 485–7.
124 *Arch. Montpellier*, xiii, p. 119 (BB 8 fo. 12v).

Du Guesclin's undertaking that the companies placed under his command would extract nothing further from the communities they passed through proved impossible to enforce. The greater part of the pope's contribution of 100,000 florins still had to be raised from the proceeds of a double tenth on the French clergy, and Urban was obliged to contract loans from a number of church dignitaries then at the curia before some advances could be made by the apostolic chamber.[125] To make up the shortfall a ransom of 5,000 gold florins was extracted from the Comtat, and Provence had to pay a further 30,000 florins to secure an undertaking from the companies not to cross from the seneschalsy of Beaucaire to the east side of the Rhône. When du Guesclin arrived in Montpellier at the end of the month, a number of rich burgesses were obliged to advance him a further 10,000 francs, effectively a forced loan, before he would depart.[126]

Since the beginning of November Montpellier had seen a constant procession of mercenaries of all nationalities – French, English, Germans, Bretons and Gascons – pass beneath its walls, taking up quarters in the surrounding small towns and villages. As had been envisaged, on their approach the fortifications were reinforced and the gates kept firmly closed. The consuls reluctantly agreed to let a limited number of them approach the palisades and other barriers which had been erected, to purchase necessities for themselves and their horses – bread and other victuals, tunics, belts, tools, horse-shoes, nails, stirrups and spurs. When he arrived before the town, du Guesclin was allowed to enter, with some of his men, and Limousin, who appeared when Bertrand was departing on 3 December.[127] He in turn left on the 5th. Other companies noted by the chronicler as passing by Montpellier on their way to Aragon included those of Robert Scott on the 6th, of the lord of Aubeterre on the 9th, the *vicomte* of Lomagne and Jean de la Roche, a knight from Auvergne, on the 21st, and of Renaud de Vigneulles, Yvon Budes and Thibaud du Pont on 7 January. The only other member of the army, apart from du Guesclin and Limousin, who was permitted to enter Montpellier was the count of La Marche, who arrived on Christmas Eve. By that date the greater part of the companies had crossed into Catalonia.

Alarmed at the impending invasion of his kingdom, in the late autumn of 1365 Pedro I of Castile had sent one of his most trusted councillors, Martín López de Córdoba, master of the Orders of Alcántara and Calatrava, to England with instructions to counter Trastámaran propaganda against him and to request Edward III's assistance under the terms of the

---

125 Prou, pp. 144–5, PJ no. lxiii. It was not until 26 January 1366 that du Guesclin's proctor, P. de Villiers, acknowledged receipt of a remaining sum of 32,000 gold florins still outstanding (Denifle, ii, appendix, pp. 775–7; see Delachenal, iii, p. 298 n. 2, p. 300 n. 2).
126 Molinier, PJ no. xciv, p. 320.
127 *Thalamus parvus*, p. 369.

Anglo-Castilian alliance of 1362. It seems likely that he also had the task of protesting about the English and Gascon companies recruited by Calveley which were to take part in the coming campaign. English policy at this juncture remains obscure, but it seems probable that Edward III and his council in Westminster took a different position from the Black Prince, who had openly given his support to Calveley's involvement in the forthcoming campaign, perhaps still blinded by its crusading purport and influenced by the hostility to Pedro which Froissart claimed was substantial in the prince's entourage. Whatever Edward III's opinions on the matter, he seems to have concluded belatedly that the intervention in the Peninsula was contrary to his interests. On 6 December he issued instructions direct to Sir John Chandos, constable of Aquitaine, and three other persons he believed still to be in the pricipality – Sir Hugh Calveley, Sir William Elmham and Sir Nicholas Dagworth – ordering them to prevent the forces being assembled from entering Spain.[128] It was already too late. At the time the order was issued Calveley's forces were already in the Pyrenean foothills around Perpignan, but, as we shall see, an important rôle was subsequently found for them south of the Pyrenees once the campaign commenced.[129] Only two more *grans companhas* were recorded as passing by Montpellier *en route* for Aragon, one German and the other Gascon, on 18 and 19 February respectively.

Whilst the Spanish expedition certainly removed a large number of the companies across the Pyrenees, it is doubtful that their departure 'proved to be a turning point in the recovery of France', as has been suggested.[130] Quite apart from the evident restriction on the number recruited imposed by financial considerations, Peter IV had himself imposed strict limits on the number of men he was prepared to take. When that quota was met others had to be turned back.[131] The failure of the Archpriest's two proposed crusades against the Turks left dangerous elements of the Great Companies in the Saône valley and in Burgundy.[132] In the summer of 1366 Louis of Anjou twice had to raise forces to deal with English and Gascon companies operating in Languedoc.[133] The relative speed with which events subsequently unfolded in Spain, and the return of the companies who were employed there, meant that the problems posed by the mercenaries were far from over in France.

128 Russell, pp. 37–9; Froissart, *Chroniques*, vi, p. 201; *Foedera*, III, ii, p. 779.
129 See below, p. 177.
130 Sumption, ii, p. 530.
131 Delachenal, iii, p. 319 and n. 1. See below, p. 168.
132 See above, pp. 135, 142, 150.
133 See below, pp. 188–9.

7

Castles in Spain

At the beginning of the fourteenth century, the Iberian Peninsula was made up of five kingdoms of disproportionate sizes and populations. Four – Castile, Portugal, Navarre and the Crown of Aragon (which included Catalonia, Valencia, the Balearics and Roussillon and Cerdagne) – were ruled over by Christian kings; the fifth, the small but rich emirate of Granada, had an Islamic ruler. Castile (including Léon) was by far the largest, with a population of some four to five million, which, although only a third of that of France, was probably at least four times larger than that of Portugal and the whole of the Iberian lands of the Crown of Aragon, which each had approximately one million. Navarre, unable to expand southwards since the eleventh century, had a population of some 100,000 and Granada almost certainly more. The Black Death of 1348 and repeated outbreaks of plague undoubtedly reduced these figures in the second half of the century, especially in Catalonia and Majorca, which formed part of the Crown of Aragon; but it is unlikely that they significantly altered the relative demographic patterns in the different kingdoms.[1]

Castile-Léon, ruled over by Pedro I since 1350, had been at war with Peter IV of Aragon (Pere III of Catalonia) for nine years by 1365. Although sparked off by a minor incident – the capture of two Genoese galleys in the bay of Cadiz by the Aragonese admiral Francesch de Perellós – the conflict had proceeded almost without interruption and, as a result of the different alliances contracted by the protagonists, it had engulfed almost the whole of the Iberian Peninsula. The Castilians had for the most part gained the upper hand and Pedro's financial resources were in a better state than those of Peter IV, depleted by the high costs of putting down rebellions in his Aragonese possessions in the Mediterranean, in particular in Sardinia; but, despite numerous attempts by the papacy to mediate a settlement, no accommodation had been reached by the main warring parties when the

---

1 Pere III, *Chronicle*, Introduction, i, p. 1; see also Hillgarth, *Spanish Kingdoms*, pp. 29–30.

6 *The Iberian kingdoms in the fourteenth century*

project for a 'crusade' had emerged in Avignon in the summer of 1365.[2] With the support of the Great Companies, Pere now hoped to deal the decisive blow to Pedro and, on his removal, Pere's ally, the deposed king's half-brother, Enrique of Trastámara, would replace him on the Castilian throne. The character and ambitions of all three men did much to determine the subsequent course of events, which brought to an end the Aragonese-Castilian war; but the means by which both Pere and Enrique hoped to secure their objectives, and Pedro's ultimate fate, were largely determined by the predominant rôle of the companies in the allied army.

The character of Peter IV is easier to grasp than that of Pedro, through the picture which he left of himself in the official chronicle of his reign, commissioned, reviewed and corrected by him personally, in his speeches to the *Corts* and in his vast correspondence. Throughout his long reign of more than fifty years, from 1336 to 1387, every letter and document that was drawn up in his chancery, including his own voluminous correspondence, were copied in the chancery registers which were deposited in the royal archives, which he had formally reorganized in 1346, and which bear testimony to his immense political and diplomatic activity. In addition, he ordered collections to be made of his speeches, which he wrote himself. Although the self-revelation to be found in these involved much propaganda, Pere being determined to be seen as he wanted, careful analysis of them provides invaluable insights into his mind and springs of action, and the evidence they present can be checked out from other sources, not least from his own chancery registers.[3]

Peter IV had ruled the Aragonese dominions for almost thirty years in 1365. Then aged forty-six, the main traits of his character were evident enough. Although of limited physical strength and not a soldier by temperament, he was brave in the face of peril and took his duties as a military leader seriously. As he had told the *Corts* of Monzón two years earlier, 'although God has not made us great in stature, we have as great will and heart as any knight in the world, to live or die to defend our crown and kingdom'.[4] His love of pomp and ceremony and concern for rank and dignity earned him the name 'the Ceremonious', but he was also referred to as *del punal* or *del punyalet* because of the dagger which he always carried with him and with which he was said to have cut to pieces the privileges of the *Unión* of Valencia, following a rebellion of his subjects

---

2 For the war between Aragon and Castile up to 1365, see the useful survey by Díaz Martín, 1982, pp. 281–93. For the financial dimension, see Sitges, 226; Gutiérrez de Velasco, 1959, pp. 3–43; *Chron. Jean II et Charles V*, ii, p. 13.
3 For different assessments of the king's character, see Pere III, *Chronicle*, Introduction, i, pp. 90–109; Gubern, in *Epistolari de Pere III*, i, pp. 23–40; Abdal i Vinyals, pp. xcvi–ci and *passim*; Delachenal, iii, pp. 253–6; Russell, pp. 22–4.
4 Pere III, *Chronicle*, i, p. 93.

there. He was also, on his own testimony, sometimes called *Cruel*, but the name did not gain widespread currency and, above all, it did not stick. These characteristics were early evident. As a young man of twenty in 1339 he was able to humiliate his brother-in-law, Jaume of Majorca, who came to do him homage, by keeping him standing following Jaume's request for a cushion on which to sit. After much deliberation, he finally accorded him one 'not of the larger size', although, he tells us, he had had larger and finer ones made for the occasion.[5] As a distinguished Spanish historian observed, at this point 'Pere's personality seems to us defined'.[6] However, the documentation also provides evidence for more serious charges which weigh heavily upon his reputation: the death of his brother Jaume, count of Urgell (d. 1347), who had supported the *Unión* of Valencia; the assassination of his half-brother Ferran (d. 1363); the trial and condemnation of his chief councillor, Bernat de Cabrera (d. 1364), who was made the scapegoat for all the disasters which the Castilian war had brought upon his country. Even if the moving force for some of these actions rested with others – the princes and other councillors or, in the case of Cabrera, the queen, who was the main person behind his execution – nevertheless the ultimate responsibility rested with the king.

The harsh and suspicious sides of Pere's character may have derived from the circumstances of his upbringing, far away from his father's court, and a strong element of cunning and artifice were evident in him from an early age. It was not for nothing that he boasted, in the Prologue to his *Chronicle*, of his own 'prudence', 'subtlety' and 'wisdom', and he was apparently confident that his readers would admire his skill in deception.[7] He was a stickler for legal precedents and he had no scruples about using the law to secure his political goals. However, some of his acts not only were ingenious, but reveal a sadistic train of mind and the actions of a torturer. When the leaders of the rebels in the *Unión* of Valencia were captured, some of them were forced to drink the molten metal of the bell they had rung to call their co-citizens to seditious assemblies, and subsequently Pere described the punishment as 'a just thing' which they 'deserved', and almost boasted about its ingenuity.[8] A pitiless gaoler, in 1358 he incarcerated his own nephew, Jaume 'IV', pretender to the annexed kingdom of Majorca, and his prisoner since Jaume III's death in 1349, in an iron cage, and described in meticulous detail all the refinements and necessary measures to prevent his escape.[9] Held thus for four years, by a

5   Ibid., i, cap. ii, para. 34.
6   Soldevila, in *Les Quatre Grans Cròniques*, p. 1176 n. 4, cited by Hillgarth, in Pere III, *Chronicle*, i, p. 96.
7   Pere III, *Chronicle*, i, Prologue, para. 5.
8   Ibid., ii, cap. iv, para. 60.
9   ACA, Cancilleria, reg. 1159, fo. 158v; 1161, fo. 2r-v.

bitter irony Jaume escaped his detainer with the help of an accomplice. His subsequent career, his employment of the companies in an attempt to recover his inheritance and his death in Soria, in which Pere pretended to have had a hand, will be narrated later.[10]

In his behaviour, as in his correspondence and diplomacy, Pere showed himself a match for Charles on Navarre in his duplicity, and he could emulate his Castilian protagonist's sadistic cruelty. But although he was occasionally subject to outbursts of violence, his decisions were seldom dictated by rage, but were for the most part taken after deliberation with his councillors, and for what appeared to be sound political reasons. Unlike Pedro, he was esteemed by his subjects and was not insensitive to their interests, which in part explains his popularity and the touching demonstrations of loyalty bestowed upon him. In the precautions which he was to take to protect the civilian population from the worst depredations of the companies, he showed a much greater concern for their welfare than other rulers of his day, even though he was unable to prevent incidents occurring. Ceremonious he certainly was, but his love of pomp and ceremony went beyond mere etiquette and diplomatic protocol. It derived from his sense of rank and dignity, and his own position, as he saw it, not only as one of the 'great lords of the world', but also as God's vice-regent.[11] Well read, a poet in his own right, an orator and an impassioned student of history and chivalry, had Froissart ever met him he could justly have said of him, as of the count of Foix, with whom Pere had many traits in common, that 'he admired everything that was fine and noble' in history as in life. He was also something of a linguist, speaking and writing Aragonese as well as his native Catalan, which came to be his favourite language for composition, but he had also been brought up with a knowledge of Latin too, and could write in French and in his own hand. His interest in history, and his own place in it, were notable not only in his writings, but also in the paintings, tombs and statues he commissioned and whose execution he even supervised, especially but not only at the Cistercian monastery of Poblet, which became a family mausoleum embodying the continuity of the dynasty, and in the royal palace in Barcelona.

'A figure of flesh and blood; sarcastic and affable, astute and imprudent, proud and easy of manner, avaricious and ostentatious',[12] he was all of these things; but it would be hard to improve upon the assessment of the sixteenth-century historian of the Crown of Aragon, Géronimo Zurita, who was generally hostile to him: 'As this prince was feeble and delicate in his body, his spirit was all the more daring; he was of an incredible

10 *Medieval Mercenaries II*. Pending publication, see also Fowler, 1988, pp. 41–4.
11 *Chronicle*, i, Introduction, pp. 88–9 and Prologue; ii, cap. 5, para. 29.
12 Gubern, in *Epistolari de Pere III*, i, p. 40, cit. and trans. Hillgarth, in Pere III, *Chronicle*, i, p. 108 n. 334.

promptitude and ardour and of great vigour for any enterprise; he was extraordinarily ambitious and haughty and very ceremonious in royal authority and pre-eminence.'[13] Pere could reasonably boast that 'there is no Christian king who has three better cities than we have, that is to say Zaragoza, Valencia and Barcelona',[14] and perhaps his principal achievement, during the course of a long and turbulent reign, was that he managed to keep his inheritance intact and succeeded in rebuilding the unity of the kingdom, which its division by Jaume III had compromised.

By comparison with Peter IV it is difficult to gain a true impression of the character of Pedro I of Castile, so blackened was it by the propaganda of his enemies during his own lifetime, but particularly after his death, earning him the sobriquet *the Cruel*. The long exile of Enrique of Trastámara and many of his supporters, not only in Aragon, but also in France, occasioned much opportunity for disseminating defamatory stories about Pedro, which were taken up by chroniclers and others who had no means of checking their veracity. As a result he had a bad press, not only in Spain, but in a large part of Europe. In Castile, the chronicler Pedro López de Ayala, who wrote the 'official history' of Pedro's reign, having changed his allegiance from the legitimist cause to the Trastámaran regime that was to overthrow Pedro, had to justify his own action as well as Enrique's usurpation. His use of ballads sung in the camps of the Castilian exiles fighting on Pere's side in the war with Castile and of other anti-Petrine propaganda gave a strong bias to his work. Nor can Ayala's account, which is inevitably partisan, be controlled by documentary evidence of the kind available for Aragon. The absence of a central archival repository and the differences in personality between Pere and Pedro – the latter seemingly unconcerned about recording his view of affairs for posterity – leave us largely dependent upon Ayala's record of events, which can be controlled to a much lesser degree by the comparatively limited number of royal orders and other communications, especially newsletters, sent to the different city authorities during the course of his reign. Moreover, it was deliberate policy on the part of the Trastámaran dynasty that replaced him to destroy as much as possible of the archival material which might provide a more impartial view of events.[15]

Pedro's modern apologists, in rejecting Ayala's testimony, have focused

---

13 Zurita, iv, p. 713 (lib. x, cap. 39, lines 122–7), cit. and trans. Hillgarth, in Pere III, *Chronicle*, i, p. 3.
14 Pere III, *Chronicle*, i, cap. iv, para. 57.
15 For different assessments of Pedro's character, see Suárez Fernández, 1966, pp. 3–7; Gimeno Casalduero; Delachenal, iii, pp. 251–3; Russell, pp. 16–22; Mérimée; Sitges, 1910, caps ii and v, *passim*. For Ayala and the ballads, see Suárez Fernández, 1962 and Entwistle, 1930, pp. 306–26; 1951, pp. 157–60. For the lacunae in the records, see the valuable observations of Russell, pp. 17–18, 18 n. 1, and for their survival for Murcia, *Documentos de Pedro I*.

their attention upon the extenuating circumstances which help to explain the conduct of a king who had an unfortunate childhood and was thereafter the victim of repeated acts of treason and perjury. After his birth in 1334 his father, Alfonso XI, had increasingly abandoned him and his mother for Doña Leonor de Guzmán, a young widow from an illustrious family in Seville, who bore him ten bastard children, of whom eight were still alive in 1350. All of them were magnificently apanaged. The eldest, Don Enrique, who was born in 1333, was a year older than his half-brother, Pedro, and had been endowed at an early age with the princely domain of Trastámara, with the title of count. His twin brother, Don Fadrique, when hardly ten years old had become Grand Master of the Order of Santiago. These favours, and the precedence which Alfonso evidently gave to his bastard sons, early aroused feelings of jealousy and hatred in Pedro, who, after reaching his majority in 1352, was surrounded by a turbulent and greedy nobility, organized into two groups, that of the Trastámaras and that of the Infantes of Aragon. To begin with, they courted the favour and support of Pedro's chief minister, Don Juan Alfonso de Albuquerque; but after 1355 they were increasingly frustrated in their ambitions as Pedro sought to impose his personal rule, independent of the different factions at court.[16] These circumstances alone had taught him to mistrust others and they had exacerbated his naturally fiery temperament. In many respects he was not unlike his father, not only in his personal life and habits, but also in his capacity for cruelty and vengeance, and his lack of scruples about going back on his promises.

For all of these psychological and other explanations, it is difficult to avoid the conclusion that Pedro was not an attractive personality, and that he was fundamentally unstable. He was remorseless in his treatment of those who betrayed him and frequently treacherous in his actions. The bloody executions, the odious and futile murders – like those of Don Juan and Don Pedro, the youngest sons of Doña Leonor, who were put to death in 1350 in revenge for the rout of the Castilian army at Araviana, and those of the archbishop and dean of the Chapter of Santiago, who were massacred in their cathedral at a point in Pedro's fortunes when he could ill afford to lose any of his few friends – were not invented by his enemies. It has been pointed out that in acts of treachery he was no worse than Peter IV of Aragon, and that he did not match his uncle Pedro of Portugal in refined brutality; but other matters compounded to establish his cruel reputation. While he probably did not order the execution of his wife, Blanche of Bourbon, sister of the queen of France, who died in mysterious circumstances in 1361, he had treated her atrociously from the beginning, and the charge helped to blacken his name. Even when she had first

16 Gimeno Casalduero, pp. 71–81.

travelled to Castile for their nuptials he had kept her waiting in Valladolid for several months before journeying north to solemnize their marriage. Immediately after his wedding he had abandoned her for his first mistress, Doña Maria de Padilla, to whom he later asserted he had already been secretly married, a story which may well be true.[17] Many of Pedro's subjects believed that Blanche, exiled in Tordesillas on the Duoro, held in close captivity and subjected to solitary confinement during the last years of her life, had been murdered at Medina Sidonia at his instigation. His treatment of her, as much as his easy association with Muslims and Jews, which nowadays would be to his credit, did more than anything to set Urban V against him. As the Black Prince was to discover to his cost, he did not share the chivalric culture of France and England, to which Peter IV of Aragon certainly subscribed. Although there is nothing to suggest that he was lacking in Catholic piety, his preference for Andalusia and the still substantially Moorish city of Seville aroused suspicions as to his true preferences and were an easy target for his enemies. At the very least he had been influenced by the different life of the frontier. How far these prejudices contributed to the unpopularity which he encountered among his subjects in other parts of his kingdom, many of whom had anti-Semitic leanings, can probably not now be determined; but the mounting opposition which he encountered cannot be attributed solely to his conflict with the magnates and changing political circumstances. His distrust of everyone led even his closest friends and servants to disobey and ultimately desert him, and the accusations of tyranny, which his enemies cleverly exploited, finally removed any scruples they may have had.

The position of Pedro's surviving bastard brothers had changed dramatically after Alfonso's death in 1350 and the pre-eminence secured in the councils of the young king by Albuquerque. Doña Leonor was shut up in the Alcazar in Seville and then in the castle of Carmona, where she was treated as a state prisoner before being murdered in the following year. Her eldest son, Enrique, having been secretly married to Doña Juana de Villena, thereby uniting his interests with those of the powerful house of Luna and arousing the hostility of the queen mother and Albuquerque, had not awaited the vengeance of his enemies. A small but well-built young man,[18] then only seventeen, before his mother's removal to Carmona he had fled the length of Spain, accompanied only by two faithful caballeros, Pero Carrillo and Men Rodríguez de Sanabria, all three of them wearing leather masks and enduring many hardships before they reached the relative safety of Asturias. It was to be the first of many forced marches in a turbulent

17 Sitges, 1910, pp. 388–92.
18 According to Ayala, *Crónica*, ii, p. 38, Enrique was 'pequeño de cuerpo, pero bien fecho, é blanco é rubio, é de buen seso, é de grande esfuerzo, é franco, é virtuoso, é muy buen rescebidor é honorador de las gentes'.

career, which had schooled Enrique in the harsh realities of politics and the military life that gave him a remarkable knowledge of men and affairs. Exiled on more than one occasion to France, where he had been himself employed as a mercenary among mercenaries, this remarkably resourceful man had become adept at picking his way through some of the more remote Pyrenean passes, either to escape an enemy or to carry out a surprise attack. His early years had thus equipped him well for the struggle that lay ahead. Not only had he learned much about war and military tactics, but in the early 1360s he had also come to know and do battle with some of the more important captains of the companies. Enrique was not a complex person and had spent almost sixteen years of his life dominated by one ambition, to oust his half-brother from his throne. Nothing and nobody would deflect him from this remarkable singleness of purpose. To achieve it he was unscrupulous with both his friends and allies, and neither honour, kinship nor the welfare of his future subjects were allowed to stand in his way. In the winter of 1365 his long-cherished plans to return to Castile with his fellow exiles and an army of mercenaries had finally come to fruition after what must have seemed, even to him, an immensely long haul.

The first indication of the recruitment of the Great Companies in the war against Castile had been made to the Catalan *Corts* assembled in Barcelona in July 1365. The proceedings had been conducted amid a great deal of secrecy, the deputies having been required on oath not to divulge what they had heard. The campaign against Pedro I had been fixed for September, but a number of considerations, primarily but not entirely financial, resulted in its being delayed for three months. At the meeting of the *Corts*, Peter IV had revealed the full nature of the negotiations which had taken place in France and at Avignon. He explained to the *procuradors* that they must raise the money to pay the companies and that an initial payment of 300,000 gold florins, to which the king of France, the pope and he himself were each to contribute a third, had already been agreed. The news had caused considerable disquiet among the deputies, for whom the thought of raising 100,000 florins on top of the subsidies for the war, which they had already approved at Tortosa at the beginning of the year, was a daunting prospect. Moreover, they objected to the whole idea of bringing the companies into Aragon, for their reputation was legion. Queen Elionor, who presided at a later session in the absence of Pere, who was preoccupied with the siege of Murviedro, pointed out that they would be coming whatever the *Corts* might decide and, if they were not paid, they would live off the country. They might even be employed by Pedro against Aragon, and since the contingents which would be arriving were numerically greater than the entire Castilian army, it would be better to comply.

Faced with these arguments the *Corts* eventually gave way, but not until the beginning of December, by which time they saw that they had no real alternative.[19]

Pere had meanwhile returned to Barcelona by 1 November 1365, a few days after the surrender of Murviedro. Having prorogued the *Corts* until 25 November, he anxiously awaited the arrival of the companies. He had already been in touch with du Guesclin before leaving Murviedro, and within a few days of his arrival in Barcelona he was in direct correspondence with him and Calveley, and a number of envoys were passing to and fro between them. The most important of these was Foucaut d'Archaic, one of Bertrand's companions, a knight of Saintonge of some reputation and now a subject of the Black Prince. Foucaut's mission was twofold: to confirm and settle the details of the undertakings made for the king by Juan Fernández de Heredia and Francesch de Perellós and to confer with Enrique of Trastámara concerning his part in the forthcoming campaign. This business did not take long and he almost immediately returned to Avignon bearing letters from Pere for du Guesclin, Calveley, Marshal Audrehem, Heredia and the pope.[20]

Peter IV was particularly concerned to secure Urban's sanction for the services of Heredia in Aragon. The most important matter to be settled with du Guesclin concerned the arrangements that were to be made for the payment of the companies. In the original plan the 200,000 florins to be advanced by Charles V and the pope were intended to secure their departure from France and the Comtat Venaissin. Pere's contribution of the remaining 100,000 was to be used for service against Pedro of Castile.[21] For some reason or other – possibly because du Guesclin had recruited more companies than had been originally planned – Pere was now expected to provide 120,000 florins, to be paid half in Perpignan and half in Zaragoza.[22] At the beginning of November du Guesclin had demanded that this entire sum should be paid at Perpignan, and Perellós had given way. In the event, the original plan of 60,000 had to be adhered to.[23] Of the first instalment, 50,000 florins was despatched to Perpignan from the king's treasury and the remaining 10,000 was to be raised by loans from certain persons in Perpignan and Roussillon.[24]

Pere's preparations had been elaborate, for he was well aware of the reputation for pillage, as well as the military renown, of the men with

19 Delachenal, iii, pp. 273–8; Russell, pp. 35–6.
20 Delachenal, iii, pp. 303–6.
21 Pere III, *Chronicle*, ii, cap. vi, para. 57.
22 Delachenal, iii, p. 307 n. 1.
23 ACA, Cancilleria, reg. 1387, fos. 156v–7r, 162r–3r, 164v–5r, 191r.
24 ACA, Cancilleria, reg. 1387, fos. 157v–8v (Pere's letters of 26 November 1365 to the consuls of Perpignan, the governor of Roussillon and the bishop of Gerona to this effect. The loans were to be repayable within four months).

whom he was dealing. On 12 November he had written to the governor of Roussillon and Cerdagne giving precise instructions concerning the reception of the companies.[25] He knew that outrages were bound to occur. What he hoped to achieve was to limit the opportunities for pillage, to exercise some control over the number of mercenaries entering the kingdom and, once they had arrived, to see that they were paid, fed and lodged. The governor was to see that all men, women, children, beasts and other food and goods were moved into fortresses and walled towns, and these instructions were repeated in countless letters to other officials and communities in the regions likely to be affected.[26] The mercenaries were only to be allowed into the kingdom in companies or *routes*, each under the command of an authorized captain to whom an Aragonese knight and a porter were to be assigned as guides.[27] No fewer than 200 Aragonese knights were required for this purpose, and it is clear that they were intended to escort the companies encamped around Perpignan and Salses (some nine miles to the north of Perpignan), across Roussillon and into Catalonia by the col de Panissars, first to Barcelona and from there to the general assembly point at Zaragoza.[28] In view of their large numbers, and to facilitate provisioning, their entry into the kingdom was to be staggered, only two companies being allowed to enter each day, one before lunch and another between lunch and dinner.[29] Other companies – evidently under Enrique of Trastámara – were to make their way directly to Zaragoza by way of Huesca, and similar instructions were issued with regard to them.[30]

After crossing the frontier the main body of the army was to proceed to Barcelona according to a predetermined itinerary, halting only at specified places. The defences of the towns and fortresses along their route were to be improved. The population of the suburbs and surounding villages, together with their belongings, were to be evacuated within their walls. The castellan of Laroque in Roussillon was ordered to do this from undefended places from up to three or four leagues around. At Tarragona, the archbishop and the city authorities were instructed to appoint three

---

25 ACA, Cancilleria, reg. 1387, fos. 150v–53r.
26 Ibid., fos. 153v, 156r–v, 159v–60r, 161r–v, 169v–72v.
27 'Item, ordonets e facats ... que les dites companyes sien departides per caps, e que a cascun cap de les dites companyes assignats i cavaller e i porter, d'aquelles que y seran ordanats, qu'els facen tenir lur cami dret fins al coll de Paniçars e apres fin a Barchinona' (instructions to the governor of Roussillon and Cerdagne, 12 November 1365; ACA, Cancilleria, reg. 1387, fo. 151v). See also the instructions to Bernat de Sos of 15 November (*Chron. Jean II et Charles V*, iii, pp. 108–10, PJ no. xiv).
28 ACA, reg. 1387, fos. 159r–v (instructions dated 24 November 1365). See also the instructions cited in the previous note and a letter of 16 February 1366 which provided for late arrivals (reg. 1213, fo. 16v).
29 Ibid., Cancilleria, reg. 1387, fo. 151v. See also Delachenal, iii, p. 309 and n. 1.
30 Ibid., reg. 1194, fos. 204v–5r (1 December 1365); cf. the notes in Delachenal, iii, pp. 308, 310, 312.

persons for each quarter of the town to make the necessary arrangements. Buildings constructed outside the walls, which inhibited effective defence or might facilitate surprise attack, were to be razed. Others were to be used as overnight lodgings for the companies, converted into hostels, and the necessary beds and bedding made available. Food, clothing and other provisions for the troops and their horses were to be brought into the fortified places from within a radius of up to four leagues and made available for purchase by the companies, outside the town walls, at reasonable and fixed prices. On no account were the companies to have cause for complaint. Since they were coming to support the Crown of Aragon, Pere insisted that they should be well treated; but he had no illusions about their likely behaviour, pointing out that they were ruthless men who would take such things as they wanted without paying anything for them if they cost too much, and who would commit the worst excesses possible if they were not well provisioned, at reasonable prices. It was therefore essential to have a ready supply of everything they were likely to need: food, wood for fires, shoes and other necessities for the troops; straw, hay, oats, shoes and other requirements for their horses. Particular attention was to be paid to provisioning Salses, since the major part of the companies were going to enter Aragonese territory there. In this way it was hoped that it would be possible to contain the worst excesses, but at the price of abandoning the open countryside, isolated villages and undefended towns to the depredations of the soldiery. Pere noted in his chronicle that, even when limited by these measures, the pillage was revolting. Not only had the inhabitants of undefended places to be evacuated, but rich monasteries like that of Santa-Cruz were advised to put their precious objects into safe-keeping. One point upon which the king insisted throughout his instructions and correspondence was that the progress of the companies across Aragonese territory should be carried out as speedily as possible. As soon as their concentration was completed they were to be moved without delay to the Castilian frontier. He had taken every precaution suggested by experience of the companies north of the Pyrenees, probably on the advice of Heredia, for the part played by the Hospitaller Guillem de Guimerà in making all the necessary arrangements is noteworthy.[31]

31 For the above arrangements, see Pere's instructions of 30 October to the bishop and *viguier* of Gerona (*Chron. Charles V*, iii, appendix, pp. 103–8, PJ no. xiii), and Delachenal, iii, pp. 309–13 and the notes there cited. To these should be added the important instructions to the governor of Roussillon and Cerdagne of 12 November (ACA, Cancilleria, reg. 1387, fos. 150v–3r), and others issued in the second half of November and early December to Doña Cecilia, countess of Urgell and viscountess of Ager (ibid., fos. 154r–5r), and to the Hospitaller, Guillem de Guimerà, commander of the houses of Tortosa and Grañera, who was to make arrangements there and help with those at Cervera and Lérida (ibid., fos. 160v, 164r, 169v–70v). For Laroque and Tarragona, see ibid., fos. 159v–60r, 161r–v. For Pere's reflections on the pillage, see Pere III, *Chronicle*, ii, cap. vi, para. 60, and García y López, i, p. 321 n. 2.

By the middle of December a large part of the companies had arrived in Roussillon, where they were well enough behaved, but it was important to keep them moving if they were not to do extensive damage.[32] Du Guesclin, who had left Perpignan by 5 December, crossed the Pyrenees with the bulk of the army by the col de Panissars and arrived in Barcelona with the principal leaders shortly after Christmas.[33] In spite of the rigours of the season, others seem to have made their way through the county of Foix and Cerdagne to arrive in Catalonia by the col de la Perche and Puigcerda. They subsequently joined up with the larger forces proceeding from Barcelona to Zaragoza at Lérida, which commanded the exits of the Pyrenean valleys into the Aragonese plain. From Lérida they made for Zaragoza, where the definitive concentration took place, and where they were joined by those companies coming straight from Languedoc to Huesca.[34]

The arrival of the companies occasioned much satisfaction to Peter IV. A 'providential' assistance had been sent to him which, while it did not permit him to close his eyes to the excesses of the mercenaries, would enable him to secure a final victory in his nine-year struggle with Castile.[35] Not only was he strong enough to recover the places which he had lost one by one to Pedro, but he could 'disinherit' his hated enemy, drive him into a corner, and implement the vengeance of which he was later to boast.[36] On New Year's Day 1366 he held an official feast in the great hall of the royal palace in Barcelona, to which the leading captains of the companies were invited, and for which preparations had been going on throughout December. The king presided at the table of honour with, on his right, du Guesclin, and on his left, one of his uncles, the Infante Ramon Berenguer. Next came Marshal Audrehem and Calveley, and the 'Green Knight', Louis de Chalon, was seated at the end of the table. Other tables were placed in the great hall and the adjoining rooms, where the mercenary captains and other guests were treated most courteously, the same respect being paid to them in their hostels and lodgings.[37] The companies themselves were billeted in the neighbourhood of Barcelona, in the district of Vallés (the

---

32 Delachenal, iii, p. 313 and n. 3.
33 Pere III, *Chronicle*, ii, cap. vi, paras. 57–8, and the clarification in Delachenal, iii, p. 314 n. 1. For the crossing by the col de Panissars (situated to the immediate west of the col de Perthus), see above, n. 27.
34 Zurita, iv, p. 538 (lib. ix, cap. lxii, lines 36–61), and Delachenal, iii, p. 314 n. 2, for an interpretation of this obscure passage.
35 Delachenal, iii, p. 315 n. 1. On 30 December 1365 Pere wrote to Perellós, the viscount of Castellbó, du Guesclin and others requesting them to take measures to end the excesses of the companies (ACA, Cancilleria, reg. 1387, fo. 189v). Nevertheless, despite an outrage that occurred at Granollers, on 2 January following he instructed the *batle* of that town that nobody was to take up arms against the perpetrators, in view of the serious repercussions that would ensue (ibid., fo. 190r).
36 Pagès, pp. 235–7; Delachenal, iii, p. 315.
37 Pere III, *Chronicle*, ii, p. 573; Delachenal, iii, pp. 315–16, 316 nn. 1, 3.

area around Granollers) and different places in the valley of Llobregat. They generally behaved badly. The inhabitants of both San Cugat del Vallés and Granollers were pillaged and molested, and Pere had to write to du Guesclin and others firmly about these and other outrages.[38]

Du Guesclin and the companies left for Zaragoza on 5 January to prepare for the coming campaign. Before he left Barcelona he received either a part or the whole of the second instalment of the 120,000 florins he was to be paid for himself and his men.[39] Whatever the case, it was by no means the final settlement of accounts. More companies continued to arrive from France, and an all-out effort had to be made to prevent those who were not officially recruited from entering Aragonese territory. Pere instructed all of the provincial governors of his kingdom only to allow in those companies engaged by du Guesclin, and whose names appeared on an official list, which he had also sent to them.[40] The need to attend to these latecomers, and above all to prevent the disorders which might ensue if they were not paid, obliged du Guesclin to return to Barcelona almost as soon as he had left the city. Here, in the lower chamber of the royal palace, Pere sought to bind him more closely in his service. On 9 January he granted him the castles and towns of Borja and Magallón, which were situated on the Aragonese frontier in the province of Zaragoza, and were at the time in Castilian hands. Together, they were erected into the new county of Borja, a title which Bertrand henceforth bore. Since the revenues attached to them were not large, Pere added the two rich valleys of Elda and Novelda in the kingdom of Valencia, which had previously belonged to his brother, Don Fernand, who had died in tragic circumstances some years earlier. The grant was sealed with a golden bull, and the witnesses to the act of homage which accompanied it included the king's two brothers, the Infantes Pere and Ramón Berenger, the count of La Marche, Marshal Audrehem and Calveley. Du Guesclin thus became a baron of Aragon and, whilst reserving the fealty he owed to the king of France and others, he now had a vested interest in the war with Pedro and Pere's fortunes.[41]

The progress of the companies from Barcelona to Lérida and Zaragoza, which may have begun before 9 January, continued from that date, although not without hitches occasioned by money and the behaviour of the troops. Pere, who followed them on 21 January, had got no further

---

38 Delachenal, iii, p. 317 and nn. 3–4; for Granollers, see above, n. 35.
39 Delachenal, iii, p. 318 and nn. 2–3.
40 Ibid., pp. 318–19, 319 n. 1. The companies continued to arrive in Aragon until February. On the 3rd of that month, those still to come (according to a list provided by Pere) were commanded by Narri de Pedran, Brémond de Laval, Jean de Saint-Pol, Geoffroi de Kerimel and Thibaud du Pont. Pere subsequently instructed the viscount de Castellbó to garrison and hold the strategic points of Roussillon, and in April he refused Enrique's request for further reinforcements from Languedoc (Miret y Sans, 1905, pp. 83–5).
41 Delachenal, iii, pp. 319–21.

than Tarragona before he was visited by du Guesclin and the principal captains of the companies, who demanded and received 20,000 florins for payment to their forces. More serious was news which the king received from Tamarite de Litera in the province of Huesca in Upper Aragon, from where Enrique of Trastámara was refusing to proceed unless he received 70,000 florins, which he claimed were due to him and his men for the three months to the end of January and as an advance for the first half of February. Pere considered this demand altogether unjustified, since in his view they had not performed any service which warranted payment. Du Guesclin and other captains were ready to commence the campaign against Pedro 'with the count of Trastámara or without him', but Pere was more circumspect. Lacking the immediate funds, he authorized Enrique to raise the sum demanded from the disposal of some of the lands which he had hitherto granted him in the kingdom of Aragon.[42] It was hardly an immediate solution to Enrique's predicament, and it may well have occasioned one of the worst excesses of the campaign. On 2 February some of his mercenaries sacked the little episcopal town of Barbastro, close by Tamarite, and set fire to the principal church. Some two hundred inhabitants who had taken refuge there were burned to death.[43] Tighter control was probably exercised over the troops in the main body of the army, but, as the companies advanced from Barcelona to Lérida, Pino de Ebro was sacked and a large part of the population put to flight. Conflicts between the troops and the civilian population certainly took place elsewhere, although they have left little trace.[44]

By mid-February most of Pere's forces, commanded by du Guesclin, were assembled in Zaragoza. They may have amounted to some 10,000–12,000 mounted men-at-arms, for the most part experienced soldiers. Perhaps as many as half of their number, and almost certainly not fewer than 3,000, were drawn from the companies, of which 1,000 men were under Calveley's immediate command. The remainder of the army was made up of Aragonese companies, and perhaps also the contingents brought along by the French lords who accompanied du Guesclin.[45] So large a force of foreign cavalry had not been seen in the Peninsula since the battle of Ubeda against the Moors of Andalusia in 1234.[46] What especially struck the Spaniards was the sight of the armour which the mercenaries wore. Ayala, in particular, commented on their basinets, plate armour and weapons, which were made of hardened and highly polished steel, 'white armour' as opposed to the burnished armour, doublets and sun helmets

42 Ibid., iii, pp. 323–5, 323 n. 4, 325 n. 1 for the quotation; see Fowler, 1992, p. 229.
43 Zurita, iv, p. 539 (lib. ix, cap. lxii, lines 83–90).
44 Delachenal, iii, pp. 325–6, and Mérimée, ii, pp. 377–8, appendix K, for Pino.
45 Fowler, 1988, pp. 32–3; 1991b, p. 247. See appendix C.
46 Zurita, iv, p. 539 (lib. ix, cap. lxii, lines 68–74).

normally seen in Castile, which, he added, earned them the name *la gente blanca*. He also tells us that it was around this time that the word lance was coming into fashion to describe a mounted man-at-arms and a page.[47]

During the second half of February, whilst the forces were encamped around Zaragoza, an arrangement for the division of the spoils of war was concluded between du Guesclin and Calveley, and a number of grants made to them by the king of Aragon, which shed much light on the ambitions of both men. In an agreement concluded between them, drawn up on 16 February in the English diplomatic form of an indenture, the two captains agreed to join forces in a common company *(compagnie, societate)* during the forthcoming campaign in Castile and Granada. Under its terms they undertook to share all of their profits of war, together with all grants and conquests (among which were included Pere's grants to Bertrand of 9 January), du Guesclin reserving three quarters to himself and a quarter being assigned to Calveley. The only exception to this division was the kingdom of Granada, over which Enrique of Trastámara had already made certain undertakings to Bertrand, and which, if conquered, was to be retained by du Guesclin, with the exception of the fortified places of the Moorish king of Benamarin to the north of the Straits of Gibraltar, which were to be assigned to Calveley. Du Guesclin also agreed that Calveley and his men were to enjoy the same wages as those in his own *routes*, according to their rank, and to settle his accounts with Sir Hugh as and when requested. In the event of Edward III, any of his sons, or Sir John Chandos entering the war in the Peninsula, Calveley and those under his command were to be free to join them, and they could also return to England or elsewhere if recalled for good reasons. It was understood that Sir Hugh's prior agreement to join forces with Sir Matthew Gournay was in no way prejudicial to the terms of the indenture, but Calveley was not to join up with any other company whilst it remained in force.[48]

Du Guesclin had already secured from Enrique of Trastámara a grant of whatever territories he might conquer in Granada and, in view of subsequent events, perhaps the entire kingdom; but it was Pere who was to accord the two captains some of the means by which they might realize their ambitions. Du Guesclin was to have two large ships and an armed galley, paid for by the king for six months, 'to go overseas to fight the enemies of the Christian faith', commencing in May 1367 or, in the event of Bertrand not being able to use them then, in May 1368. For his part Calveley was granted the service of twenty armed galleys 'to fight the enemies of the faith' for a period of four months from Easter 1367. These

---

47 Ayala, *Crónica*, i, p. 537 n. 2.
48 ACA, Cancilleria, reg. 738, fos. 41v–2r; published in appendix I of Fowler, 1991b, pp. 254–5; 1992, p. 242.

were to be made available to him upon request, within forty days of Easter; but in the event of Pere not concluding a peace or truce with Pedro within a month of that date, the number of galleys was to be reduced to ten and the period of service reduced to two months. To encourage Sir Hugh in his endeavours, and perhaps as well to give him something of the standing recently accorded to du Guesclin, Pere also granted him a life pension of 2,000 gold florins and the rank of a baron of Aragon, the annuity in question being assigned to him from among the castles then under Castilian occupation in the kingdom of Valencia. Sir Hugh thus became a vassal of the Aragonese king, reserving only his allegiance to the king of England and his obligations to du Guesclin. A similar annuity was granted to his comrade-in-arms, Sir Matthew Gournay.[49]

With the conclusion of these arrangements, du Guesclin and his principal captains were ready to commence the campaign, but only after they secured an advance on the wages of their men and not merely a settlement of arrears. Presented with this condition, and the continuing threat to his lands and subjects posed by the presence of the companies, Pere had once again to resort to contracting loans, this time with the archbishop of Zaragoza and other nobles then in that city. At the same time he instructed his treasurer and other financial officers to do everything in their power to speed up the collection and delivery to him of the necessary revenues.[50]

Peter IV had not been idle in his diplomatic preparations, and an essential element in his plans for the invasion of Castile had been to secure the neutrality of Navarre and Portugal. Since his previous undertakings at Uncastillo and Almudevar, Charles of Navarre had concluded an alliance with Pedro of Castile against France and Aragon in which the Black Prince had been named as mediator in any dispute which might arise between them. But since the summer of 1365, Charles had been at peace with the king of France and Pere had sought to exploit the changed situation. Some twenty days before the arrival of the companies in Barcelona, on 11 December 1365 he conveyed to Charles's marshal, Juan Remírez de Arellano, the text of a proposed treaty with Navarre by the terms of which both sides would undertake not to take up arms against the other or cause any damage to their territories. Pere would provide a monthly pension of 1,000 florins to Charles's eldest son for as long as he wished it, in return for which he was to do homage to him. For a payment of 30,000 florins Charles was to provide a force of 600 mounted men to join the forces

---

[49] For the grants to du Guesclin and Calveley, see Fowler, 1991b, p. 251; 1992, pp. 232–3. For that made to Gournay, see ACA, Cancilleria, reg. 1214, fo. 34r. A similar grant to Sir William Elmham appears not to have been made until after the prince's intervention in the following year (ACA, Cancilleria, reg. 1220, fo. 71v; see Gutiérrez de Velasco, 1951, p. 308).
[50] Delachenal, iii, pp. 329–30, 329 n. 1, 330 n. 1; Molinier, PJ no. xciv, p. 320.

under the counts of Denia and Trastámara in the coming attack on Castile. Once the war commenced neither side was to make peace without the consent of the other and, as a guarantee of their agreement, each party was to surrender to the other five places, with their castles, situated on the frontier between the two kingdoms to the east and west of the rio Aragón, to be held as security for a period of five years.[51] Since the proposed agreement was likely to prove unpopular to some of the men in Charles's entourage, and might even result in retaliatory action by Pedro or the Black Prince, elaborate arrangements were made by Pere to keep it secret, even from officials in his own chancery. This may have been intended to lull Pedro into believing that his northern frontier was secure and that the allied attack was likely to be made against Castilian garrisons in western Aragon rather than across Navarrese territory in the Tudela salient,[52] but it is equally likely that Charles's exposure to hostile retaliation alone warranted the secrecy.

Charles was clearly uneasy about the proposals and well aware that the threat posed to his territories by the impending invasion, spearheaded as it was by the companies enrolled by du Guesclin and Enrique, was likely to be even greater than that posed by Pedro and the Black Prince. He did not trust the king of Aragon any more than Pere trusted him, and their suspicions were heightened by their experience of the devious and tortuous diplomacy of the Iberian Peninsula, which both of them had long practised. His concerns about various aspects of the proposed treaty were conveyed to Pere, who, in a subsequent version which Charles seems never to have received, formally undertook to see that the companies did no damage in Navarre. During the first week of January this guarantee was sought by Charles's envoy, Juan Testador, who was sent on a mission to Aragon to clarify a number of points with Pere, and who also held discussions with several captains of Great Companies, some of whom he evidently succeeded in persuading to consider switching their services to his master.[53]

Throughout January and February Charles did not commit himself, but kept up the discussions whilst preparing for every eventuality. On 27 February, just as the campaign against Castile was about to open, a final set of proposals, drawn up in the archepiscopal palace in Zaragoza between Pere's representatives, Juan Remírez, and Pere's cousin, the count of Denia, acting for Enrique of Trastámara, were entrusted to the count, who was to take them to Tudela for Charles's confirmation.[54] Several of the clauses

51 The main clauses of the treaty are given by Miret y Sans, 1905, pp. 77–80.
52 Russell, p. 43.
53 Miret y Sans, 1905, p. 79, and, for Testador's mission to the companies, *AGN, Comptos*, vi, no. 107.
54 The final proposals are contained in ACA, Cancilleria, reg. 1214, fos. 34v–5r. For the procuration to the count of Denia to 'tractar, fazer et firmar' the proposals with Charles, also

were highly favourable to the Navarrese king and were doubtless intended to assuage his worst fears. If Pedro made war on Navarre following the invasion of Castile, Pere and his allies would come to Charles's assistance. Neither he nor Enrique would conclude a peace or truce with Pedro which did not include him, and Pere envisaged continuing amicable relations between their two countries when the war with Castile was over. To avoid any possible dissensions between them in the future, Charles was to be allowed to retain the deserted towns of Reyal and Santa Eulalia, near Zaragoza, although they were not to be repopulated or refortified, and Pere would pay him 50,000 florins for the return of a number of castles and towns around Huesca and Salvatierra, which had been taken by Charles's forces in previous hostilities between their two countries. But the proposals also contained a clause prohibiting anybody in Navarre, including the companies in his service, from supporting Pedro, and binding him to close the Navarrese passes to any foreign troops who might attempt to cross his kingdom on their way to aid Pedro.[55] Charles's fears were thus twofold, and fully justified by subsequent events. To confirm the treaty as it stood would clearly arouse Pedro's hostility and perhaps also that of the Black Prince. On the other hand, he was also uneasy about the intentions of the companies operating from Aragon and appears to have suspected that they might intend to traverse Navarre in the opening stages of the invasion. In an effort to ensure that his territories were not invaded from either side, he had spent January and February putting the defences of his kingdom in order and mobilizing his forces on both his northern and southern frontiers. In addition, he had engaged the services of the lord of Albret and some of the Gascon companies under his command, as well as those of Eustache d'Auberchicourt, Johann Hazenorgue and John Devereux. His efforts to recruit other captains of the companies at the critical moment of the invasion of Castile were also to prove fruitful.[56]

---

dated 27 February (and not 8 March, as stated by Delachenal, iii, p. 332 and n. 3), see ibid., fos. 35v–6r. On the 26th Pere invited Charles to meet Enrique and the count at Tudela for this purpose (ibid., fo. 28v). Russell, pp. 43–4, suggests that they arrived at the head of an army rather than at the head of a diplomatic mission, but there was adequate time for the treaty to be confirmed by Charles before the main body of the army arrived on 8 March.

55 'Item, quel dicto Rey de Navarra deva jurer e prometer que no consintra que nigun homme de su Regno de alguna valor vaya en servicio del Rey de Castiella, ni consintra que negunas gentes estranyas entren o passen por su Regno a servicio del dicto Rey de Castiella, ante lo destorbara et vedara leyalmente por todo su poder' (ACA, Cancilleria, reg. 1214, fo. 35v).

56 Albret was present in the Navarrese court 1–15 February and 1–26 March, Auberchicourt from 3 February to 19 March, Hazenorgue on 2 February, and Devereux on 4 March (AGN, Comptos, reg. 120, fos. 27v, 41v, 47r–52r and *passim*; AGN, Comptos, vi, nos. 121, 125, 151, 161, 171, 175–7, 203). Devereux was retained by Charles with an annuity of 600 gold florins sometime before 18 February (AGN, Comptos, vi, no. 263; cf. no. 124). He was subsequently retained for life by the Black Prince with an annuity of 200 marks 'for his service

To begin with, the defence measures were primarily, though not exclusively, aimed at preventing any contingents of the Great Companies who might be intending to serve with either Pedro or Enrique from penetrating the Roncesvalles pass.[57] On 8 January 1366 Charles ordered the necessary steps to be taken to provision Saint-Jean de-Pied-de-Port as well as those places most threatened in the *merindads* of the mountains, Sangüesa, La Ribera and Estella. On the 13th the castellan of Saint-Jean was instructed to strengthen the defences of that town, and on the 28th both he and the castellan of Valcarlos were ordered not to allow any of the companies or any foreigners to enter the mountain pass of which they were the guardians. On the same day other instructions were given for defensive measures at Olite, Sangüesa, Cáseda and Tudela, where the inhabitants of the suburbs were brought into the town walls with their belongings, and which were to be well guarded day and night, no foreigners or suspicious persons being allowed to enter. Captains were appointed there and at Corella, Valtierra and Rada in the Tudela salient, and the king's vassals were convoked to be at Olite with their feudal contingents by 2 February at the latest, because the king 'had heard for certain that the men of the Great Company are now near the frontier of Navarre'.

During the month of February the activity was frenzied.[58] The defensive measures then carried out were concentrated on the Castilian and Aragonese frontiers. Along the frontier with Castile, which to the north-west of the Tudela salient ran along the northern bank of the Ebro between Castelón and Calahorra, Cadreita and San Adrian were to be fortified, the walls of Milagro improved, and crossbows and other artillery placed in the castle of Peralta. Despite their protests, the not inconsiderable Jewish and Moorish segment of the population were to contribute towards the defence of Valtierra, and the inhabitants of unwalled towns in the area were ordered to take refuge with their belongings in Caparroso or Peralta and the castle of Cadreita. On the southern frontier with Aragon, which north of the Tudela salient ran to the east of the rio Aragón from Caparroso to its junction with the rio Irati, captains were appointed to Murillo, Santacara, Cáseda and Lumbier, and the inhabitants of the undefended places in this area were instructed to take refuge in San-Martin-de-Unx and Lumbier. Similar measures were taken elsewhere in the kingdom. Estella was to be fortified and a captain was appointed to take charge of the town. To the

---

to him in his journey to Spain, and his wars in Guienne' (*CPR, 1377–81*, p. 17). For those recruited later, see below, pp. 175–6.

57 For what follows, see Brutails, *Documents*, nos. cxxix, cxxxiv–cxxxix. To begin with, the measures were to be taken 'por causa de las grandes compaynas qui vienen en Espayna', and then, from 28 January, because 'nos avemos ovido nuevas ciertas que las gentes de la grand compayna son ya cerca de nuestra frontera de Navarra'.

58 For what follows, see Brutails, *Documents*, nos. cxliii, cxlv, clv, and pp. 135 n. 1, 309–10.

immediate west of Estella the walls of Zuñiga were to be rebuilt so that it could accommodate refugees from the smaller neighbouring communities, and to the south-west those of Aguilar were to be repaired. Captains were also appointed to towns further north, to Echarri-Arañez, west of Pamplona, and in the *merindad* of La Ribera.

Precautions were even taken in Pamplona itself. Although the inhabitants of the *faubourgs* were not to be constrained to take refuge in the *bourg*, the town was to be provisioned and the gates closed from sunset to sunrise, whilst elaborate precautions were taken to see that no foreigners entering or residing there bore arms, hotel keepers being instructed to inform them to that effect. The Jewry was fortified, and even the defences of the gate leading to the priory mill were to be improved. It may be wondered what the poet Geoffrey Chaucer and the three companions travelling through Navarre with him made of it all. Certain passages in the *Canterbury Tales* have the flavour of scenes witnessed by a war correspondent, and it should be noted that the four men were allowed to go wherever they wanted and to converse with anyone they pleased.[59] Other defence measures included the fortification of Monreal, and of Lárraga, to the west of Tafala. Trees were to be felled for the fortification of Olite, and work was commissioned on the tower of Labraza and the castle of Monjardin. Lances and crossbowmen were sent to Peña and, on 22 February, once more concerned about his northern frontier, Charles instructed the castellan of Saint-Jean-Pied-de-Port to allow Eustache d'Auberchicourt to bring up engines and artillery from the Navarrese side for the defence of that town.

D'Auberchicourt may have been one of the captains whom Testador had persuaded to return into Navarrese service, of which he had ample previous experience; but it is more likely that he had proceeded directly to Navarre from Gascony, possibly with Chaucer in his company.[60] In the summer of 1364 he had done homage to Charles, promising to serve him in peace and war, especially the war then being waged against Charles V in France, reserving only his obligations to Edward III, who in November of that year had ordered him, along with Calveley and Robert Scott, to discontinue fighting in France in Charles's name, and to disband his company.[61] By the spring of 1365 he had been appointed guardian of Charles's lands in

---

[59] By letters dated at Olite on 22 February, Charles issued a safe-conduct, to last until 24 May following, to 'Geffroy de Chauserre, escuier englois, en sa compaignie trois compaignons avec leurs varlez, chevaux et bens quelconques, troussez ou a trousser, en males ou dehors, pour aler, venir, demourer, se remuer, converser et retorner partout ou il luy playra, par touz noz villes, forteresses, pors, passages et destroiz, tant de jour que de nuit' (Honoré-Duvergé, 1955, p. 13, who corrects the reading by Brutails, *Documents*, no. clv).
[60] Honoré-Duvergé, 1955, p. 11.
[61] Brutails, *Documents*, no. xcii, and *AGN*, *Comptos*, v, no. 313, for the homage; *Foedera*, III, ii, p. 754, for Edward's orders.

Normandy, Burgundy and elsewhere in France;[62] but after the peace concluded with Charles V was ratified in the summer of that year he was the leader of one of the contingents which enrolled with du Guesclin for service in Castile and Granada. During the last week of January 1366, when the allied forces were concentrating around Zaragoza, he once more switched his services to Charles of Navarre by two agreements concluded in Pamplona, which evidently promised him greater rewards. The first of these was a settlement for past services amounting to 65,000 gold francs, of which 36,000 were handed over to him immediately. The second was an undertaking to serve Charles against all his enemies, save Edward III and the Black Prince, in return for an annuity of 1,000 *livres tournois*.[63] D'Auberchicourt, who had close ties with Edward III and the Black Prince, was almost certainly the main person who, along with Testador, was responsible for bringing a number of captains of the Great Companies and some of the prince's men into Navarrese pay when the campaign opened with an incursion into Navarrese territory by the forces under Calveley's command.[64] These included William Ludlow, John Cresswell, Robert Birkhead, William Botiller, Norman Swinford and Robert d'Ares, who, along with Devereux, were each retained with annual fief-rents of 200 *livres tournois* in return for their homage.[65] On 6 April one of the prince's bachelors, Stephen de Cosington, who had long been in the prince's service and appointed to be in attendance on the prince's person at the battle of Poitiers, also did homage to Charles, who retained his services with an annuity of 1,000 florins.[66] In addition to these men Charles enjoyed the support of Johann Hazenorgue, whom he had taken into his service in the summer of 1364.[67]

62   Lettenhove in Froissart, *Oeuvres*, xx, p. 198; *AGN, Comptos*, v, nos. 202 (wrongly dated 1364), 962, 1193.
63   *AGN, Comptos*, vi, nos. 56–7, dated 23 and 24 January respectively.
64   Brutails, *Documents*, pp. 147–8, no. clxiv; *AGN, Comptos*, vi, no. 171.
65   They were retained to serve 'en toutes les guerres et afaires envers touz et contre touz', excepting Edward III, his sons, and in some cases other named persons (Brutails, *Documents*, pp. 145–6, no. clxi, p. 146 n. 1; *AGN, Comptos*, vi, nos. 150–3, 155–6, 263). It should be noted that Auberchicourt's seal was attached to Ludlow's and Swinford's homages, in the absence of their own. Robin d'Ares or Ades had taken part in the battle of the Thirty in Brittany in 1351, was one of Knowles's lieutenants, and took du Guesclin prisoner at the Pas d'Evran in 1359 ('La bataille', ed. Brush, p. 527; Bridge, pp. 179–80; Luce, pp. 312–13).
66   *AGN, Comptos*, vi, nos. 239, 263; *BPR*, iv, pp. 178–9. He was present in the Navarrese court from 6 April to 28 May (AGN, Comptos, reg. 120, fos. 78r–v, 80v, 82r, 86r, 87r, 109r–10v, 112r, 118v, and the *contrerolle* for April (incorporated between fos. 95v and 100v), m. 1–3).
67   Hazenorgue had become Charles's liege man as early as 26 May 1364 (when he did proxy homage by way of Espiote, his proctor) for 200 *libras Carlines*, and was among the members of the Great Companies recruited by Louis of Navarre for service in France in June (*AGN, Comptos*, v, nos. 271, 297–9; see also Brutails, *Documents*, no. cxcvii, p. 171). He had become Charles's usher-at-arms by June 1365 (*AGN, Comptos*, v, no. 1005; cf. v, nos. 1169, 1208; vi, no. 575). On 27 November of that year he acknowledged receipt of 120 florins for his costs and those of his companions during their stay in Pamplona (Brutails,

Charles thus succeeded in observing an armed neutrality by continuing to court Peter IV's advances until the immediate danger had passed, and by keeping communications open with both the prince and the companies.[68] He was also well aware that Pere's diplomatic plans were not limited to Navarre, and that the Aragonese king wished to complete the encirclement of Castile by including the king of Portugal in a league against Pedro. As the invasion of Castile began, on 4 March Pere sent an embassy to the Portuguese court with proposals intended to secure Dom Pedro's support in the war with Pedro of Castile. Realistically, Pere probably hoped to do no more than to immobilize the Portuguese king while the invasion got under way, in which case he was successful.[69]

The invasion of Castile was launched by the companies under Calveley's command, which formed the vanguard of the allied army. They were sent up the Ebro valley from Zaragoza, swung westwards in the direction of Soria to pick off the towns of Magallón, Borja and Tarazona, and then turned north to enter the Navarrese *merindad* of Tudela. This may have been a feint to cover the left flank of the army advancing up the main road from Zaragoza to Tudela, or occasioned by the need to get the companies moving and avoid conflicts with other contingents of the army. Calveley evidently had a vested interest in securing Borja and Magallón, but neither place put up any resistance, the Master of the Order of Santiago, who was to have defended the frontier with 400 mounted men, having fled into Castile. The town of Tarazona, invested after an encounter in which the Castilians lost a hundred of their men-at-arms, was then used as a base from which raids were conducted into the countryside as far as Agreda, on the road to Soria. The incursion into Navarre was necessitated by strategic considerations: the main road to Burgos passed through Charles's kingdom. But as events proceeded it presented Calveley, perhaps under orders from the Black Prince, with the opportunity to plant some of his forces there for future eventualities.

Meanwhile, the main body of the army under du Guesclin and Enrique had proceeded straight up the Ebro valley into Navarrese territory. On the morning of 8 March du Guesclin appeared before the walls of Tudela, on the right bank of the river, but was refused admission. From their camp at Cascante, a few miles to the south, his forces burned and destroyed the surrounding towns and villages between Tarazona and Tudela, in addition to Cascante itself. All of these places were situated to the south of the Ebro,

---

Documents, no. cxliii, p. 133 n. 1). During the period from April to October 1366 he received several grants for his equipment in addition to his monthly wages (*AGN, Comptos*, vi, nos. 294 and 631).
68   For the contacts between the two courts during February and March, see Brutails, *Documents*, no. cli; AGN, Comptos, reg. 118, fo. 125v; *AGN, Comptos*, vi, no. 169.
69   For the details of these negotiations, see Delachenal, iii, p. 332, and Russell, p. 45.

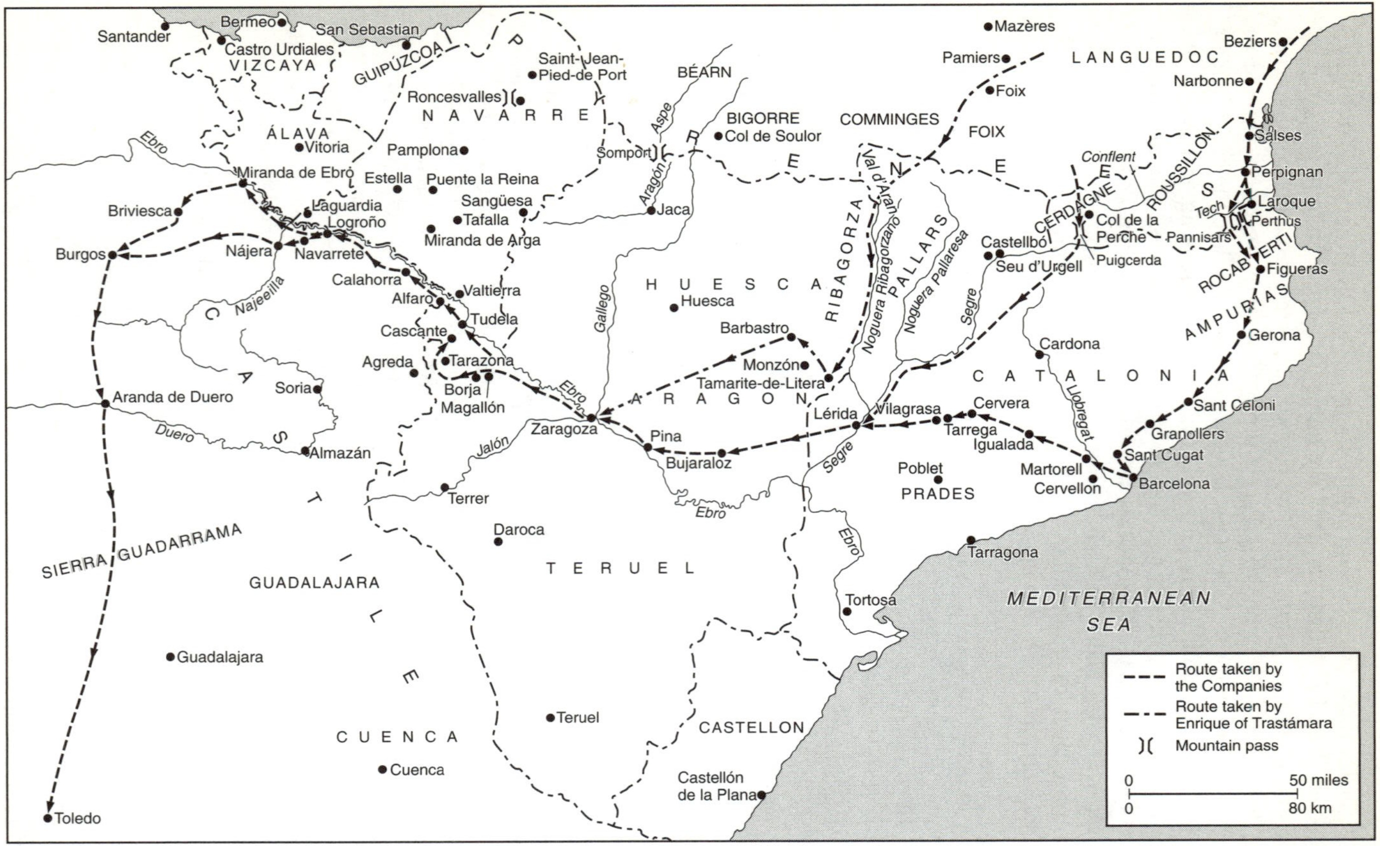

7 *The invasion of Castile by the Companies, January–May 1366*

and Charles abandoned them to their own devices, having made no provision for their defence. Du Guesclin then moved his forces further up the Ebro valley to the fortified Castilian frontier town of Alfaro. From there, hot on the heels of the English vanguard, he proceeded to Calahorra, which, although strongly defended by a garrison commanded by Fernán Sánchez de Tovar, governor of Castile, and the bishop of Burgos, surrendered to Enrique despite the resistance of the citizens, who were prepared to put up a fight.

Already before they entered the town du Guesclin and Calveley, and other captains of the army as well as Trastámaran partisans, had pressed Enrique to assume the Castilian crown and, despite the bastard's feigned protests, on 16 March he was formally proclaimed king in a ceremony which took place in a tent by the Ebro, between Alfaro and Calahorra. His brother, Don Tello, seizing a royal banner, was the first to cry 'Castile for King Enrique', which was taken up by others present. The allies then continued their progress up the Ebro valley in the direction of Logroño, which was too strongly defended to warrant an attack. They therefore swung west to take the unwalled town of Navarrete, followed by that of Briviesca, where the captain, Men Rodríguez de Sanabria, was taken in a skirmish at the barriers by Bernard de la Salle. In less than three weeks from the start of the campaign, Burgos, the ancient capital of Castile, where Pedro had taken up residence earlier in the year, was itself threatened.[70]

Whilst the allied army was being concentrated in Aragon, Pedro had moved north from Seville to Burgos, but believing that the invasion would be launched further south and east, he had left his forces dispersed in the frontier garrisons there. Towards the end of February the lord of Albret and a number of the Gascon lords who were with him in Navarre had visited him in Burgos to offer their support. Albret had indicated to Pedro the serious threat posed by the companies and the desirability of dividing them. The houses of Armagnac and Albret, he explained, were well disposed towards him and they both had clients and vassals among the companies who could be won over for higher pay. The offer was rejected, and Albret returned to Olite in Navarre, where he may have been instrumental, along with Auberchicourt, in bringing some of the companies into Navarrese service.[71] However, the great majority remained in the allied army with Calveley, and their strength and well-known fighting abilities,

---

70 Pere, III, *Chronicle*, i, p. 575; Fernão Lopes, *Crónica*, pp. 206–9; *Chron. Premiers Valois*, p. 167; Miret y Sans, 1905, pp. 81–2; Brutails, *Documents*, no. clxiv; Ayala, *Crónica*, i, p. 538; Delachenal, iii, pp. 330–1, 334–41; Russell, pp. 45–8.
71 Ayala, *Crónica*, i, p. 537; Delachenal, iii, pp. 333–4. Albret returned to Olite on 1 March, in time for supper with the king and Auberchicourt. All three were joined there by John Devereux the following day, and by 'plusieurs chevaliers et autres gens estrangers' on the 4th. On 23 March Charles was at San Vicente, 'et y fut le sire de Labrit et plusieurs chevaliers et escuiers de la grant compaigne' (AGN, Comptos, reg. 120, fo. 65v, and the *contrerolle* for March (incorporated between fos. 121v and 126v), m. 1).

the speed of the allied advance – made possible by avoiding places which might put up serious resistance – and the defection of important officials and captains to Enrique prevented Pedro from regrouping his forces. On 28 March, despite the protestations of the inhabitants, he decided to abandon Burgos after instructing the Castilian garrisons in Aragon to destroy the fortifications and armaments in the towns and castles they were leaving, and to attempt to reassemble in Toledo. He then moved south towards the Guadarrama passes, escorted by a mounted Moorish guard of some six hundred men sent to him by the king of Granada, and with a small entourage of servitors still faithful to him, including, at this stage, Pedro López de Ayala, who subsequently recounted these fateful days in his *Chronicle*.[72]

The companies were then encamped around Burgos, and Enrique of Trastámara was able to enter the town the following day, Palm Sunday, 29 March, and have himself crowned king in the nearby monastery of Las Huelgas. News of it appears to have reached the Aragonese court within the next two days, and its consequences were profound.[73] Defections to the new king were widespread in a large part of northern Castile, although in many places they were brought about under threat of reprisals rather than any new-found loyalty to the Trastámaran cause. The leaders of the army were promptly rewarded with lavish grants of seignorial and crown lands. Most of these were situated in territories still to be conquered, thus adding a powerful incentive to further activity on the part of the beneficiaries. The count of Denia, who led the Aragonese contingent of the allied forces, was granted the lands of Villena with the title of marquis. Immediately following Enrique's coronation at Las Huelgas, the new king had du Guesclin crowned king of Granada, and granted him the county of Trastámara, which was erected into a duchy, and all his possessions in Asturias. Calveley was made count of Carrion in Palencia. Another prominent mercenary, Bernard of Béarn, a bastard son of the count of Foix, was knighted by Enrique and subsequently became one of his councillors and, through his marriage to Isabel de la Cerda, count of Medinacelli. Among the Castilians who benefited from these *mercedes* Enrique's brothers, Don Sancho and Don Tello, were particularly prominent.[74]

Enrique remained in Burgos until at least the end of April, concentrating

---

72 Ayala, *Crónica*, i, pp. 539–40; Fernão Lopes, *Crónica*, pp. 208–11; Delachenal, iii, pp. 341–2; Russell, p. 49.
73 For the date of Enrique's coronation, see Russell, p. 49, correcting Delachenal, iii, p. 281 n. 2, 344 n. 1. The news had reached Barcelona by the end of the month, when Queen Elionor's treasurer sent a messenger to Opol in Roussillon 'a la Reyna de Castella ab lettras que le senyora Reyna li tramatia fient li saber com lo Rey Don Enrich se era coronet en Burgos' (ACA, Real Patrimonio, MR, reg. 488, fo. 67v).
74 Ayala, *Crónica*, i, p. 541; Fernão Lopes, *Crónica*, pp. 210–11; Delachenal, iii, pp. 281 n. 1, 344 n. 1, 346–8; Russell, pp. 49–51.

his forces for the next thrust and awaiting the arrival of his wife and children, whose passage from Roussillon to Castile was facilitated by the king of Aragon with all the honour befitting a reigning queen and her family.[75] Pere was rather less accommodating about Enrique's request to allow the passage of further mercenaries from France, whom Enrique needed to mop up pockets of loyalist resistance in the north and west, and to reinforce those companies already in his service for the final *putsch*. His refusal to issue the necessary safe-conducts for them to cross Aragon, intimated to Enrique in a letter of 30 April, reveals the heavy price his kingdom had been obliged to pay for their initial reception:

In truth, dear king, so great is the damage and destruction which our land has sustained through the passage of the other companies which are already with you, that no-one would believe it. If we now gave passage to any of these people while the corn is in the fields, they would destroy the little that remains and therefore we can in no ways find a means of agreeing to allow the said passage without manifest and irreparable destruction to our land in those parts through which they would have to pass, and so we beg you to excuse us.[76]

By the time the letter was written Enrique's forces were already pushing south, and by 5 May had occupied Toledo, Pedro having abandoned that town for Seville. Although Toledo had excellent natural defences, the town gates were opened to them by a party favourable to the new king, and the Master of the Order of Santiago, Garcia Alvárez de Toledo, whom Pedro had appointed captain, was unable to resist the ground-swell. As at Burgos, the companies were once again paid from the proceeds of loans financed by the Jewish population. Some of these had to be negotiated by the captains, du Guesclin being obliged to Calveley alone, for his wages and those of his men, to the extent of 63,108 gold francs.[77] Enrique remained in Toledo for some fifteen days, during which he received the submission of outlying towns, of which the most notable, specifically mentioned by Ayala, were Avila, Segovia, Talavera, Madrid, Cuenca and Ciudad Real.[78]

The main reason for Pedro's retreat to Seville was probably his inability to put into the field an army capable of resisting the companies and his

---

75 Miret y Sans, 1905, p. 86; Russell, p. 52.
76 ACA, Cancilleria, reg. 1217, fo. 57, cited by Miret y Sans, 1905, pp. 84–5. Similar letters were addressed to du Guesclin and Calveley.
77 Russell, p. 53, gives 11 May as the date of the entry into Seville; Delachenal, iii, p. 349, places it during the first days of May. Du Guesclin's letters obligatory to Calveley for outstanding wages are dated 'in the crypt of Toledo', 5 May 1366 (ACA, Cancilleria, reg. 738, fos. 40v–41r, published by Fowler, 1991b and 1992, appendix II).
78 Ayala, *Crónica*, i, pp. 541–2. According to Cuvelier, *Chronique*, i, lines 9149–79, the bishop of Toledo organized the surrender of the city after Pedro had deserted it with his treasure.

consequent determination not to risk a battle.[79] He may have hoped to secure support from the Moorish king of Granada, Mohammed V, whom he had helped restore to his throne in 1362. This was certainly the view of Ayala, who, in the abbreviated version of his *Chronicle*, specifically attributed the growing disenchantment of the Sevillians towards Pedro to his dealings with the Moorish king. Pedro was doubtless also concerned about his personal fortune, in jewels and precious stones which were held in the city, and the Castilian bullion reserves which were kept in the castle of Almodóvar on the Guadalquivir not far from Córdoba. In addition to these military and financial considerations he must also have given thought to the safety of his three children, his heiress, Doña Beatriz, whom he had been unwilling to surrender to Enrique as security for a peace, and her sisters Doña Constanza and Doña Isabel.[80] From Seville Pedro could also hope to secure support from his uncle, Dom Pedro of Portugal, to whose son and heir, Fernando, Doña Beatriz, although only thirteen, had been betrothed since 1357. He hastily sent her off to the Portuguese court, together with her dowry and other money and jewels, and escorted by two of his loyal servants, having first formally instituted her heir to Castile and Léon in the hope that Dom Pedro would stand by the arrangement. Then, as Enrique's forces began their progress to Seville, he decided to follow Beatriz to Portugal without awaiting news from his uncle. He charged his treasurer, Martin Yañez, to evacuate his treasury from the Almodóvar and to load it, and everything he possessed in Seville, onto a galley destined for Tavira in the neighbouring Algarve, whilst he himself decided to journey overland to Portugal with his two other daughters and as much gold and as many jewels as he could reasonably load onto a number of mules in the train which accompanied him.[81]

Towards the end of May Pedro left Seville in the dark of the Andalusian night and, with the city in an uproar, rode without stopping until daybreak, a conflict having broken out between the Christian, Jewish and Moorish communities of the city, each of which had its separate defences.[82] This

---

79   Russell, p. 53. Fernão Lopes, *Crónica*, pp. 210–11, says Pedro installed garrison forces in Toledo before leaving for Seville. According to Cuvelier, *Chronique*, i, lines 9189–354, on leaving Toledo Pedro made for Cordoba, from where he sought terms with Enrique whereby the latter would retain his conquests to date, but Pedro would remain king during his lifetime. For their part the companies were to receive 100,000 *livres*. However, the securities which Enrique demanded – which included Enrique's eldest daughter and heiress – proved unacceptable.
80   Ayala, *Crónica*, i, p. 542 n. 4; Russell, pp. 53–4; Delachenal iii, pp. 350–1.
81   Ayala, *Crónica*, i, p. 542; Fernão Lopes, *Crónica*, pp. 212–13. Cuvelier, *Chronique*, i, lines 9630–7, mentions, in particular, a gold table which later came into the possession of the Black Prince. See Delachenal, iii, pp. 350–1; Russell, p. 54.
82   Cuvelier, *Chronique*, i, lines 9391–6, seems to suggest they had separate walls. The author of the *Chronique normande*, pp. 180–1, states that the different quarters were protected by barriers and chains suspended across the roads.

appears to have been occasioned by a plot to open one of the gates to Enrique's forces, in either the Jewish or the Christian quarter, and it was exacerbated by Pedro's discovery of it and his precipitate action in executing a number of burgesses whom he mistrusted.[83] Even as he was about to depart a mob, greedy for treasure, proceeded to attack the *alcázar*, his favourite residence, before his very eyes. Pedro, meanwhile, was everywhere pursued by misfortune. As he was leaving Seville some of the men conducting the baggage train turned back with part of his treasure, whilst others came out of the city to rob him of a part of it. Before he reached Portuguese soil he heard that the admiral of Castile, Egidio Boccanegra, who was then in Seville, had defected to Enrique and had seized the galley loaded with treasure whilst Yañez was navigating down the Guadalquivir.

Pedro's arrival in Portugal was not welcomed by Dom Pedro, who found him a considerable political embarrassment. Chivalric etiquette obliged the Portuguese king to treat his nephew courteously and to offer refuge to the infantas; but to offer sanctuary to their father was tantamount to inviting the companies to invade his kingdom. Although his daughters were received and housed in the palace where the Portuguese king was residing, Pedro was obliged to halt his journey at Coruche, some twenty miles south of Santarem, while the Portuguese royal council debated what was to be done. The councillors were divided, but concluded that neither the king nor his son should receive Pedro, that the king could not support Pedro against Enrique, and that Fernando should not proceed with the proposed marriage. The most that Pedro could secure from his uncle was an escort of two Portuguese knights and their retinues to provide him with a safe-conduct to the Galician frontier near Chaves. Even then, he had to pay heavily for their services *en route* as they feared or feigned to fear for their lives in proceeding further. But by the beginning of June he was safely across the Spanish border at Monterrey, to the south-west of Orense, where he set up his headquarters and awaited the arrival of one of his staunchest supporters among the Castilian magnate families, the governor or *adelantado mayor* of Galicia and Asturias, Fernando de Castro, who had kept the province loyal to him and suppressed any inclinations the Galician *fidalgos* may have had to support the Trastámaran rebellion.[84]

At Monterrey Pedro held a council of war and wrote to the towns of Zamora, Soria and Logroño, which had remained loyal to him, as well as to the Black Prince and Charles of Navarre, informing them of his situation in Galicia. He had only 200 mounted men with him, but was informed that he could raise another 500 and 2,000 infantry in the province. He

---

83 Cuvelier, *Chronique*, i, lines 9355–645.
84 Ayala, *Crónica*, i, pp. 542–3; Fernão Lopes, *Crónica*, pp. 214–25; Russell, pp. 54–5; Delachenal, iii, pp. 351–3.

understood that the way was open for him to proceed to Zamora and Logroño, since Enrique and all the companies were in Seville. Some three weeks passed whilst he awaited news and considered the different options put to him by his councillors, who were divided on the next steps to take. His military advisers, in particular Fernando de Castro and Martin López de Córdoba, favoured assembling the loyalist forces in Galicia on the Navarrese frontier, where he could negotiate with Charles of Navarre and the Black Prince without being accused of abandoning his realm. Other councillors, and possibly Pedro himself, felt that it would be more prudent for him to leave Galicia by sea for Gascony. The timely arrival of Gérard de Tartas, lord of Poyanne near Dax, and another knight sent with him by the Black Prince from Gascony, assuring the king that the prince would welcome him in his principality and would assemble an army to help him to regain his throne, tipped the balance in favour of the sea route.[85] After rewarding Fernando de Castro for his faithful services with the counties of Trastámara, Lemos and Sarriá, which belonged to Enrique, he left Castro in charge in Galicia, appointing him commander of all of his military forces in Castile.

Pedro then left La Coruña for Gascony in a fleet of some two dozen merchant ships escorted by a single galley. His immediate entourage travelled in a large carrack and included, apart from the king, his three daughters and some of his closest personal retainers, Martín López de Córdoba and the keeper of his secret seal, Mateos Fernández de Cacéres. He also had with him numerous jewels and precious stones of a considerable value. After sailing along the Cantabrian coast, the royal party halted for a while at San Sebastian, from where the king communicated with the authorities in Bayonne, before they finally arrived in that port in a fleet of three ships and a galley on 1 August. A few days later the Black Prince arrived in Bordeaux to meet the king at Capbreton, a tiny port situated some eleven miles north of Bayonne, where the lord of Poyanne had a number of houses and vineyards. Shortly afterwards discussions were opened between the prince and Pedro in Bayonne in a series of conferences to which Charles of Navarre was also party, and which subsequently included John of Gaunt, the lords of Gascony, and a delegation from Peter IV of Aragon, who, despite his alliance with Enrique, was too deeply concerned about their outcome not to be represented, at least officially.[86]

---

85 Ayala, *Crónica*, i, pp. 543–5; Fernão Lopes, *Crónica*, pp. 224–7; Russell, pp. 56–7, who reads Lord Poynings for Ayala's Señor de Poyana; but there can be no doubt that the chronicler refers to Gérard de Tartas, seigneur de Poyanne in Les Landes.
86 Ayala, *Crónica*, i, pp. 545, 548–9; Fernão Lopes, *Crónica*, pp. 226–7; Luce, in Froissart, *Chroniques*, viii, p. xxvii n. 1; Delachenal, iii, pp. 366–7; Russell, pp. 57–9, who, following

Enrique had heard the news of Pedro's departure from Seville, of the seizure of the royal treasure by Admiral Boccanegra, and of Pedro's flight to Portugal and thence to Galicia, whilst on his way to that city from Toledo. According to Ayala he was received with enthusiasm and every honour both there and, on his way there, in Córdoba. Other writers claimed that Seville was delivered to Enrique by treachery and internal discord. These conflicts may have eased the task of the assailants, who mounted separate attacks on the different quarters, and it is noteworthy that the companies under Calveley's command were the first to breach the walls, apparently of the Jewish quarter, spurring the forces led by du Guesclin to follow suit. The sheer size of Enrique's forces by this stage made the entry into the city a day-long affair.[87] Enrique's stay in Seville was prolonged – perhaps until the beginning of September. His immediate concern was to receive the submission of his southern territories, to make appointments to offices and provide for the defence and government of the lands under his control and recognizing his authority. He concluded a treaty of friendship with the king of Portugal, and did everything in his power to arrange an accommodation between him and the king of Aragon. Notwithstanding du Guesclin's coronation as king of Granada and the arrangements between Bertrand and Calveley for the conquest of that kingdom, to protect his southern flank he also arranged a truce with Mohammed V. He then felt strong enough to disband the greater part of his forces, who were a drain on his finances and were inflicting considerable damage in his lands. They were paid off from the bullion – said to have amounted to thirty-six hundredweight of gold, in addition to numerous jewels, seized from the galley which had been entrusted to Martín Yañez – not only for what they were owed to date, but also to finance their repatriation to France. Only du Guesclin's Breton companies and the English and Gascon companies under Calveley, amounting in all to between 1,000 and 1,500 lances, were retained by Enrique.[88] Others returned to France of their own volition, hoping to secure more lucrative employ with the Black Prince, who had recalled them.[89] Already in July a considerable number were returning across the Pyrenees, and Enrique may have dis-

---

Froissart rather than Ayala, wrongly places the meeting between Pedro and the prince, as well as the subsequent conferences, in Bordeaux.
87 Ayala, *Crónica*, i, p. 545, who is closely followed here, as elsewhere, by Fernão Lopes, *Crónica*, pp. 228–9; Delachenal, iii, pp. 353–4; Berville, i, pp. 407–11; see Bridge, p. 133.
88 Ayala, *Crónica*, i, pp. 545–6; Fernão Lopes, *Crónica*, pp. 214–15, 228–31; Delachenal, iii, pp. 354–5. Du Guesclin's letter obligatory to Calveley for 26,257 florins for the wages of Sir Hugh and his men, and of John, or Janequin, Clerk and his men, was made out before Seville on 3 July 1366 (ACA, Cancilleria, reg. 738, fo. 41r, published by Fowler, (1991b and 1992, appendix III). Clerk was a Yorkshireman in Calveley's service in 1366 and thereafter frequently acted as du Guesclin's proctor and nuncio (see Fowler, 1992, p. 230 n. 4).
89 Luce, Froissart, *Chroniques*, vi, p. 211; Delachenal, iii, p. 354.

banded or released some of these companies too hastily, perhaps believing that he was then safely in possession of his kingdom. A secret mission of Matthew Gournay to Lisbon, which revealed Pedro's latest whereabouts and intentions, only took place after Enrique had disbanded the major part of his forces.[90] Having drawn off the allied army into the deep south, Pedro was now in a position to regroup in the north, and planned a counter-offensive with the help of the Black Prince and Charles of Navarre. Enrique's four months' sojourn in Seville was mistaken. It could have proved, and very nearly did prove, his undoing.

From late June, Peter IV of Aragon at least was aware that an intervention by the prince was a real possibility. In a letter written in Zaragoza to the municipal authorities of Valencia on the 26th of that month he contradicted their view that further taxes for the war against Pedro had been rendered unnecessary by Enrique's victories:

And we do not see that there can be such great peace as you say as long as Don Pedro, who used to be king of Castile, remains alive; because, for certain he does not cease to negotiate and to make alliances with the kings of England, Navarre and Portugal and with the prince of Wales, and we know for certain that the said prince is assembling a great number of companies and should be ready with all his power at Bordeaux by the middle of July.[91]

Three days later he informed the governor of Aragon, Jordan Pérez Durries, that a large army assembled by the prince intended to invade Castile, and instructed him to organize the defence of all places on the frontier and to see that no food was left in places which could not be held.[92]

Renewed requests from Enrique for reinforcements may have been occasioned by these new developments. Certainly they caused Pere to have second thoughts about his earlier decision not to allow reinforcements to reach Enrique through Aragonese territory. Up until the middle of June he had taken every precaution to see that further French, English, German and Breton companies congregating in southern France and threatening to enter his lands did not cross into Aragon. On 13 May he instructed Guillaume de Guimerà to see that the frontier garrisons were well manned and munitioned, and that the local population and their belongings were brought into places that could be defended. In view of the activity of German and French companies around Montpellier in early June he had ordered the despatch of a hundred mounted men into Catalonia to deal with any incursions there. These were to be based in Lérida. Other frontier violations were expected through the valley of Aspe and the Somport Pass,

90 Cuvelier, *Chronique*, i, lines 9876–10270.
91 Miret y Sans, 1905, p. 87.
92 ACA, Cancilleria, reg. 1388, fos. 36v–7r.

the col de Soulor and other Pyrenean passes to the north of Jaca. To deal with these, on 15 June he instructed the governor of Aragon to make special provision for the defence of Huesca, Jaca and other neighbouring towns, as well as of the passes leading into Gascony and Navarre. He was ordered to appoint captains in the cities and towns, and guards in the Pyrenean passes, and was to ensure that any companies who succeeded in crossing the frontier were unable to find food for themselves and their horses. However, by the beginning of July a large number of the companies which had been employed by Enrique were returning to France, and it was known that some of them were being recruited for service by the Black Prince and Charles of Navarre. Most of these were expected to return by way of the province of Huesca and Tarragona, although Pere hoped that some of them might be deflected to return by way of Navarre. On 5 July he gave instructions for all food and other necessities to be taken into fortified places. On the 6th he instructed his officers in numerous towns in the two provinces to complete their defensive measures and to have all goods brought within their walls. On 8 August, as they were approaching the Pyrenean frontier, he instructed the viscount of Castellbó, Roger Bernard of Foix, to assign a knight to each of them, with instructions to assist them in every way, provide them with food and generally treat them well, and he appointed two of his own porters, Alforge and Bascano de Portali, to accompany them on the last stages of their journey.[93]

As envisaged by Pere, other companies were returning to Gascony by way of Navarre and the pass of Roncesvalles. The first alerts were sounded as early as 4 August and the first companies crossed the frontier into Navarre on the 13th. Charles's council gave orders for precautions similar to those taken in Aragon and Catalonia. Women, beasts, victuals and other goods were ordered to be brought into fortified places at Sangüesa, San Adrian and the *merindad* of Ribera, in spite of which much damage was done, not least to the inhabitants of Roncesvalles itself, as the companies continued their return throughout August and September. In an effort to ease the situation Charles hosted Auberchicourt and 'the captains of the Great Companies' at a dinner in Estella on 1 September, but it is doubtful if his intervention had much influence on the behaviour of the troops.[94]

Amidst all of this activity Pere's attitude changed towards those companies who he believed would join du Guesclin and be firmly in his control. On 22 June, Pierre de Wissant, a nephew of Marshal Audrehem and chamberlain to Louis of Anjou, was allowed to pass through Aragon with

---

93 For the above, see ACA, Cancilleria, reg. 1388, fos. 15r–v, 26r–7r, 30r–v, 42r–3v, 45r, 48r–v, 54v–5v. Roger Bernard IV of Foix succeeded his father as *vescomte* in 1350 and died in 1381 (Miret y Sans, 1900, pp. 242, 265).
94 AGN, Comptos, reg. 118, fos. 126r–7v; reg. 120, fo. 170r (*contrerolle* for September 1366). See Delachenal, iii, p. 358 nn. 2–5, and Honoré-Duvergé, 1955, p. 12 n. 3.

a company under his command. At the end of July a number of Breton companies under the command of du Guesclin's cousin, Olivier de Mauny, Guillaume Boistel and another captain called Spincta were finally given permission to proceed through Aragon, but only after agreeing to abide by certain conditions laid down by Pere, following almost two months' delay during which they had done a great deal of damage around Montpellier, which had finally been ceded to Charles of Navarre. They then followed the companies led by Anjou's chamberlain by way of Agde to Roussillon, but the precautions taken to ensure their good behaviour were elaborate in the extreme. In the provisions concluded with Mauny and the other two captains on 30 July, it was laid down that their companies were to cross Aragonese territory in three *routes*, proceeding at two-day intervals when the captain of Roussillon or his deputies so determined. Each of the captains was to hand over three members of his company to the governor of Roussillon, for onward transmission to Pere as security against any damages their companies might do in Aragonese lands. The captains were to undertake that they would pay for their victuals, save grain and hay, which would be provided by the inhabitants of the places they passed through. In the case of Mauny, the hostages named were his brother and two cousins. In addition, the captains were to do homage and fealty to Pere or the captain of Roussillon on his behalf; they were to be bound on oath to do no damage when travelling, not only through Aragon, but through the whole of Spain; they were to take the same route as that previously taken by du Guesclin, and on returning from Spain they were to leave Aragonese territory within a month of entering it, again with an undertaking to do no damage. However, if any member of their companies wished to return to France in advance of the others, for personal or any other reasons, they could pass through Aragonese territory unmolested. On 31 July, Pere ordered all of his officers to allow the passage of these three companies, and on 8 August he instructed the viscount of Castellbó and the captain of Roussillon to provide a safe-conduct for them.[95]

In the event, Mauny did not cross into Aragon until a later date, but was employed by the duke of Anjou to intercept a number of the Great Companies which were making their way to Gascony to join the forces being assembled by the Black Prince for his intervention in Spain. Under the command of Bertucat d'Albret and Frère Darrier, they included Garciot du Castel, the *bourc* Camus and a newly emerging mercenary leader, Rocamadour, among their number. All of these captains appear to have remained in France during du Guesclin's expedition to Spain. In an initial

---

95 Miret y Sans, 1905, pp. 88–9. Olivier de Mauny, lord of Lesnen near Saint-Malo, had stayed in Normandy as captain of Carentan for du Guesclin when Bertrand left for Aragon in 1365. He only arrived in Languedoc with Boistel in the summer of 1366. For their activities around Montpellier on 1 June, see *Thalamus parvus*, p. 372.

engagement which took place on 13 August at Montech, situated in French territory on the eastern frontier of the principality of Aquitaine, twelve miles upsteam from the confluence of the Tarn and Garonne to the southwest of Montauban, Mauny succeded in routing a detachment of the companies, who suffered significant losses. Around a hundred of their number were killed and another eighty taken prisoner along with some 500 horses. The remainder fled the battlefield, but regrouped with the main body on the following day, making a combined force of more than 1,000 combatants under Albret's command. Anjou's forces, under the command of the seneschal of Toulouse, Guy d'Azay, pursued them to the neighbouring town of Villedieu, between Montauban and Castelsarrasin, and the two armies drew up battle lines beside a nearby wood. Six pennons of the companies advanced on the French, crying 'Guyenne, Saint George', but had little impact until a contingent of Gascons in the rearguard of the seneschal's forces, who came from the principality of Aquitaine and claimed to be either allied to or bound by feudal ties to some of the companions on the other side, made a decisive attack on the French rear-guard. A large number of prisoners were taken, including the seneschals of Toulouse and Beaucaire, Arnaud d'Espagne, and the viscounts of Narbonne and Caraman, and from among the companies fighting with the French, the bastard of Béarn.[96]

Some ten years later Anjou was to claim that the day had cost him more than 3,000,000 francs, doubtless in ransoms, but that he had risked the enterprise to counter the Black Prince's moves to restore Pedro to the Castilian throne.[97] The circumstances were an embarrassment for the prince in that the companies claimed to have conducted their operations in French territory in his name and by his express command, which, if true, was in direct contravention of the peace of Brétigny. It was an embarrassing diplomatic incident for Edward III, to whom an official complaint was made by Charles V. Edward was obliged to instruct the prince to withdraw the companies from French territory, punish the malefactors, have the prisoners they had taken released, return any ransom money which had been made over to the captors, and ensure that no further damage was done in Charles's lands.[98]

It is unlikely that the companies had in fact been acting under the prince's orders; but the prince had for some time been actively engaged in

---

96 *Thalamus parvus*, p. 372; *Chron. Charles V*, ii, pp. 111–12; *Foedera*, III, ii, p. 808. See Delachenal, iii, pp. 358–64, who rejects the account given by Froissart, *Chroniques*, vi, pp. 214–16, 218–28, according to whom the encounter took place with a substantial body of the Great Companies returning from Castile by way of Aragon and the county of Foix, which were commanded by Sir Robert Cheyney and Bertucat d'Albret.
97 BN, MS. français, no. 3884, fo. 14r–v.
98 *Foedera*, III, ii, p. 808.

both diplomatic and military preparations for the invasion of Castile, which included recruiting the services of the companies, and Anjou had done everything he could to frustrate his plans. Moreover, Olivier de Mauny and his Breton companies, possibly under Anjou's or du Guesclin's aegis, had not only destroyed property and made a military demonstration around the Navarrese lordship of Montpellier in early June, but had also mounted the initial attack on one of the companies at Montech. While the old rivalries and animosities seemed to have evaporated between professional soldiers engaged south of the Pyrenees, they were easily rekindled in southern France, where the ambitions of two royal princes, with quite different agendas, already foreshadowed a more serious conflict to come.

8

The Prince's Intervention

The failure of the Black Prince to prevent the Franco-Aragonese intervention in Castile and to come to the support of Pedro I before the Castilian kingdom fell to Enrique of Trastámara has attracted much criticism of the prince's conduct of affairs, not least in that the usurper's success owed not a little to the English and Gascon companies which had formed part of du Guesclin's forces; but it is difficult to see what else he could have done in the circumstances.[1] The widespread circulation of Trastámaran propaganda concerning Pedro's tyrannical and unchristian behaviour, and the fact that du Guesclin's intervention had been presented as a crusade, which secured papal support and blessing, had attracted an international response, and in the initial stages both Edward III and the prince had lent their support to it. Charles V could not be shown to have intervened directly in Iberian affairs to secure French interests in the Peninsula, even if the ultimate effect of the allied intervention was to reinforce his position there. Consequently, it was not evident that Edward III or the prince should make overt moves to prevent the intervention before it became clear that their interests might be compromised. However, it would be wrong to suggest that either the king or the prince remained entirely inactive. Edward III's instructions of 6 December 1365, that neither his subjects nor those of the prince should engage in du Guesclin's campaign, although issued somewhat tardily, were not entirely unheeded.[2] A substantial number of English and Gascon companies then operating in France, who subsequently joined the prince, had not accompanied du Guesclin, and the exact rôle of the companies under Calveley's command and the position of those who had accepted fief-rents from Charles of Navarre at the beginning of the allied campaign were, to say the least, ambivalent. When du Guesclin's forces were proceed-

---

1   For some of these criticisms, see Russell, pp. 39–40, 46 and *passim*.
2   Some of the companies who had initially joined du Guesclin, having received payment in Perpignan on 24 December 1365, had then returned into France (AN, K 49, no. 5, fo. 8v; see Luce in Froissart, *Chroniques*, vi, p. lxxxiii n. 6).

ing south in November 1365 the prince had sent some of the more prominent of his household officers to Avignon, presumably to keep an eye on events, in particular to observe the actions of those of his subjects who had been recruited in the principality. He may also have contributed towards bringing about Navarrese neutrality by allowing or even encouraging some of his own officers, as well as a number of captains of the companies, to enter Navarrese service at the beginning of the campaign.[3] Calveley, Auberchicourt, Gournay and Elmham all had close ties with him, and he had kept in close contact with Charles of Navarre throughout du Guesclin's military manoeuvres.[4] Serious consideration had been given to the next steps to be taken, in both London and Bordeaux, long before Pedro's arrival in Bayonne. As early as 8 June orders were given in England to arrest ships for the transport of troops to Gascony, and on 30 July for archers to be arrayed and sent out to the principality.[5] By the time the prince entered into negotiations with Pedro he was probably acting under clear instructions from Westminster, and his action was based on practical politics rather more than on the chivalrous precepts attributed to him by some of his contemporaries.[6] Moreover, the initial discussions in Bayonne were evidently the subject of a prearranged timetable on the part of the three principal negotiators: the prince, Pedro and Charles of Navarre.

The prince's undertaking to help Pedro to regain his throne had been made before the Castilian king left Galicia, and it was based on the Anglo–Castilian alliance of 1362. By the terms of this treaty it was understood that any support which Edward III and the prince might give to Pedro would be financed by the Castilian treasury. The Aragonese–Trastámaran alliance, on the other hand, made the cooperation of Charles of Navarre essential, since he controlled the remaining western Pyrenean passes and the natural route for any invasion from Gascony lay through his kingdom. Both Pedro and Charles were well aware of this, and sometime after his flight from Seville, Pedro had sent his physician, Master Paul Gabriel, to explain his predicament to Charles, who had promptly sent him on to Bordeaux in the company of Sir Stephen de Cosington to elicit the prince's intentions. The prince appears not to have responded immediately to the business entrusted by Charles to Cosington and Gabriel. Before the end of

3 See above, p. 176.
4 On 13 February 1366 Charles issued a safe-conduct to the prince's squire, John Maynard, 'venido en nuestro regno por algunos negocios del dicho princep' (Brutails, *Documents*, no. cli), and in March and April he sent his sergeant-at-arms, Sancho López de Uriz, and John Stokes on missions to the prince and Chandos (AGN, Comptos, reg. 118, fos. 55v, 125v; *AGN, Comptos*, vi, nos. 169, 315, 318). Stokes was captain and lieutenant of Saint-Sauveur for Chandos (Delisle, PJ nos. 96–8, 103–4), and did homage and fealty to Charles on 14 April (*AGN, Comptos*, vi, nos. 289, 294; see Brutails, *Documents*, no. cxcvii, p. 171).
5 *Foedera*, III, ii, pp. 791, 797.
6 Barber, p. 189.

June the Navarrese king found it necessary to send his sergeant-at-arms, Sancho Lopéz de Uriz, to Gascony to find out what was happening.[7] Charles was then officially invited to join in the projected discussions at Bayonne, and he left for Gascony during the first week in July, proceeding by way of Saint-Jean-Pied-de-Port (where he welcomed home his queen, who was returning from a journey in France with their three-month-old son) and Dax, to join the prince in Bordeaux during the last week in July. At this juncture the king and the prince discussed their respective positions, and doubtless how they were to proceed with Pedro. When Edward left Bordeaux to welcome the exiled Castilian king at Capbreton, Charles may well have travelled most of the way with him, but then proceeded further south to Labastide-Clairence (which, although only fifteen miles to the south-east of Bayonne, lay within his own territories of Ultrapuertos), before finally joining the prince and Pedro in their negotiations in Bordeaux during the second week in August.[8]

A good deal of preliminary work had consequently already been done by the prince and Charles before the discussions with Pedro were opened in Bayonne. Although Charles probably took little persuading to agree to the prince's proposals – for he was not naturally inclined to support Enrique, who was backed by the French king, and owed his throne to du Guesclin, who in turn had put paid to Charles's ambitions in France at Cocherel – he was nevertheless determined to extract the highest price possible, in both lands and money, if he was to agree to allow both the prince's and Pedro's forces to enter Castile through his kingdom. In some senses he was in a strong negotiating position, not only because of the strategic disposition of his lands, but also because he was able to point to the substantial territorial advantages Enrique had undertaken to make to him in April. Moreover he had kept in close contact with Peter IV of Aragon, du Guesclin and Enrique, as well with the prince, right through

---

7 AGN, Comptos, reg. 118, fo. 125v. This was probably subsequent to a mission entrusted to Berradeco de Saint Pierre, who on 11 June was also paid for a journey which he had made to the prince in Bordeaux on Charles's behalf (*AGN, Comptos*, vi, no. 408; cf. no. 401). See Delachenal, iii, p. 367 n. 3; Russell, pp. 59–60.
8 Charles's letters were dated at Saint-Jean-Pied-de-Port on 10 July, at Dax on 18 July and at Bordeaux on 24 and 28 July (*AGN, Comptos*, vi, nos. 474–5, 485, 489, 493). For the queen's movements, see AGN, reg. 120, fos. 160v–3r. The prince's letters were dated at Bordeaux on 26 and 28 July (*AHG*, xvi, no. cix; *Mandements*, p. 160, n. 1). Charles acknowledged receipt of 1,000 gold francs from Chandos in Bordeaux on 24 July and 6,000 'fortz' of gold from the prince, also in Bordeaux, on 28 July (*AGN, Comptos*, vi, nos. 489, 493). His letters were dated at Labastide-Clairence on 8 August, but at Bayonne on 14 August; by 20 August he was once more at Saint-Jean, on his way back to Navarre (ibid., vi, nos. 501–2, 504–5). Sometime before 17 August it was reported in Orthez that Charles, Pedro and the prince had already gone to Bayonne to formalize their mutual undertakings (Russell, p. 62).

until the usurper's entry into Seville.⁹ Doubtless he realized that Enrique was unlikely to stand by these earlier undertakings now that he had established himself on the Castilian throne, and was aware that the prince might try to force a passage through his lands or, alternatively, proceed through Guipúzcoa and Álava, which was a dangerous proposition, but one which was perfectly feasible.¹⁰ These factors probably persuaded him, as they subsequently persuaded Peter IV, to review his position and throw in his lot with the prince and Pedro.

The undertakings made at Bayonne were not formally drawn up and ratified until 23 September, when they were embodied in a number of documents sealed in Libourne.¹¹ Charles was on his way back to Navarre by 20 August, and the prince returned to Bordeaux around the same time. He was followed by Pedro, whose entrance to the city was made the occasion of much ostentatious ceremony, and who was lodged with the prince and princess in the abbey of Saint-André. On 5 September Charles appointed his ambassadors to formalize and ratify the league concluded at Bayonne, and the prince and Pedro subsequently issued procurations to their ambassadors. Much detailed work had evidently been done since the initial discussions, and it is quite clear from the final agreements and undertakings that neither the prince nor Charles put a great deal of trust in Pedro.

The principal document is almost entirely concerned with the conditions of Charles's involvement in the coming campaign and the benefits he was to receive for his collaboration. In return for his support against Enrique, and in particular transit rights for the allied forces through Navarre, Charles revealed his ambitions to recover the ancient lands of the kingdom – to include all Basque-speaking Spaniards – which Sancho the Great had temporarily brought together more than three-and-a-half centuries earlier. The territories which he was to secure from Pedro, and which were to be transferred to him with full sovereignty, included the whole of Guipúzcoa, together with San Sebastian and the other ports of that province, the province of Álava, including the city of Vitoria, and a line of fortified towns along the south bank of the Ebro, which included Logroño, Fitero, Calahorra and Alfaro. The possession of other localities, notably the town of Trevino, including Nájera, Haro and Briones, also to the south of the Ebro, and Labastida to the north of that river, all of which Charles claimed had belonged to Navarre as well in ancient times, was to be submitted to the arbitration of the Black Prince. To avoid the possibility that such

---

9   Russell, p. 60 and nn. 2, 3. For other envoys sent to Enrique between April and June, see *AGN, Comptos*, vi, nos. 309, 326, 351, 359, 401.
10   See Delachenal, iii, pp. 368–9, who, however, seems to have thought of a disembarkation n Vizcaya as an alternative.
11   *Foedera*, III, ii, pp. 799–807.

extensive cessions of territory might discredit Pedro in the eyes of his subjects and so undermine his cause, it was agreed that during the opening stages of the campaign, any Navarrese forces which might take possession of any of these places should nominally hold them in Pedro's name. Nevertheless, Pedro bound himself to issue letters patent confirming this change of sovereignty before he left Gascony and, in addition, he was to give an undertaking that he would make it public as soon as he recovered Burgos.[12]

In addition to these territorial concessions both Pedro and the prince agreed that since the campaign against Enrique was likely to incur greater risks, expense and damage for the king of Navarre than it would incur for them, Charles was to receive an indemnity of 100,000 florins, of which the prince would advance 20,000 immediately and Pedro would subsequently settle the whole within a period of eighteen months. For his part, Charles was to contribute 1,000 cavalry and 1,000 infantry towards the coming campaign, at a cost of 36,000 florins a month, of which the prince would meet the first month's payment and, following the arrival of the allies in Logroño, Pedro would pay the remainder from the Castilian treasury for the duration of the campaign. It was also agreed that any prisoners taken by the allies or their men were to belong to their captors, and that the division of their ransoms and other spoils of war was to follow the precedents already established in France. Only those prisoners adjudged traitors by Pedro, together with Enrique's brothers, Tello and Sancho and their wives and children, were excepted; in the event of their capture they were to be handed over to the prince.

The territorial cessions extracted by the prince in return for his support were contained in a separate charter and subsidiary documents. They consisted of the neighbouring Basque county of Vizcaya, together with the ports of Bermeo, Bilbao and Lequeito, and the lordship of Castro Urdiales.[13] In another agreement Pedro undertook to reimburse him, within a period of two years, the sum of 550,000 Florentine florins for the anticipated wages of the troops for a period of six months, from 10 January 1367, for which it was thought the campaign would last. Of this sum

---

12 The entire document, entitled *Articuli conventionum inter Petrum regem Castellae, Carolum regem Navarrae, et Edwardum principem Walliae*, includes the procurations of the ambassadors, and was published in *Foedera*, III, ii, pp. 800–2. For Pedro's undertaking to implement his grant to Charles, and the instructions to his officers in the territories in question, see *AGN, Comptos*, vi, nos. 551–2. Pedro's and the prince's letters of procuration are dated Libourne, 23 September 1366.
13 The charter is published in *Foedera*, III, ii, p. 802ff. For Pedro's intimation of the grant to the inhabitants of the territories ceded and the warrant to Chandos and others to put the prince in possession thereof, see ibid., pp. 804–5. For his promise to perform the covenants in the grant and his undertaking to compel rebels to accept the transfer of sovereignty, see ibid., p. 805.

250,000 florins were to cover the wages of the contingents raised by the prince and the remaining 300,000 were to finance the troops raised by the Gascon lords. Pedro also undertook to meet the wages and bonuses (*regards*) paid over and above these figures (providing these were substantiated by the accounts to be kept by the prince's treasurers), as well as the costs of maintaining the forces prior to 10 January 1367, when the campaign was scheduled to commence. In the interim, the prince would cover all the costs of the army out of his own resources, but against subsequent reimbursement by Pedro, who was to hand over his three daughters as security against repayment. In addition, Pedro also obliged himself to the prince in the sum of 56,000 florins which Edward had advanced to Charles of Navarre on his behalf, and which were to be repaid before 24 June 1367.[14] In the event, the total cost to 10 April 1367, including the wages of the companies, amounted to 1,659,000 florins. The ultimate bill for the campaign was to come to a staggering 2,720,000 florins – nearly 10,000 kg of gold – a sum not far short of the ransom of King John of France following his capture at Poitiers.[15]

Two further documents, sealed in Saint-Emilion on 27 September 1366, completed these agreements.[16] In one the prince informed Charles that Pedro's three daughters and other hostages named at Libourne as securities to the agreements had been duly surrendered by Pedro into his custody. In the other he promised to see that his troops abstained from all pillage when proceeding through Navarre, and that they would not take any castle, town, village or other place, and would not construct fortresses there. A final document to which Pedro appended his seal gave the prince's intervention a thinly veiled crusading context. In it he granted Edward III, the prince and their successors the right of fighting in the first battle against the Moors of Granada, or, if this should prove impossible, of having their banners carried there.[17] It is unlikely that the prince sought in this way to compete with the aura attached to du Guesclin's recruitment of the White Company a year earlier. His propaganda was concentrated upon more secular considerations: the need to avenge the overthrow of a legitimate and consecrated king by a bastard brother and usurper, and the danger to legitimate rulers throughout Christendom if Enrique was not removed and the rightful monarch restored. For the captains of the companies the tangible benefits offered by the prince's intervention – of employ, pay and ransoms – were not essentially different from those offered to them by the Breton leader, even if the prospect of castles and broad estates seemed not

14 *Foedera*, III, ii, pp. 799–800.
15 Pedro's undertakings are contained in *Foedera*, III, ii, pp. 805–6. For his indebtedness to April 1367 and the ultimate bill, see Fowler, 1992, p. 230.
16 AGN, *Comptos*, vi, nos. 558–9.
17 *Foedera*, III, i, p. 807.

to be immediately within their grasp. As Peter IV of Aragon observed, it was natural for soldiers to offer their services to whoever was prepared to pay them.

Edward, the Black Prince, was thirty-five years old in 1366, a man of powerful physique, generous to a fault with money and favour, and with a loyal and close-knit group of men in his entourage. Early on in his career he had gained a reputation for personal courage, and since his victory at Poitiers and the capture of King John of France his reputation was already legendary. After returning from Bayonne to Bordeaux in early August 1366, he gave orders for the mobilization of his forces, although according to reports reaching Barcelona, in June, it would appear that the Gascon garrisons had already been informed that their services were likely to be needed in the Peninsula. Before the end of July it had been agreed that the prince should assume responsibility for the coming campaign himself, but that his brother, John of Gaunt, would be sent out from England to join him with reinforcements, particularly of archers.[18] In Aquitaine the garrisons of the principality were alerted for service in the Peninsula by the seneschals, and the constable, Sir John Chandos, set about recruiting those *routes* of the Great Companies which had not accompanied du Guesclin to Spain.[19]

It is difficult to assess the numerical strength of the prince's army. Reports reaching the French court from spies operating in Bordeaux and Bayonne, which claimed that it was larger than any previous army which Edward III or his son had commanded in France, were certainly exaggerated.[20] So too were the numbers reported by the chroniclers.[21] On the basis of the financial calculations made at Libourne in September 1366 (both of the monthly costs of the forces to be raised by the prince and of the remuneration offered by him for the contingents which were to be provided by Charles of Navarre), the total strength of his forces and those of the Gascon lords who were to accompany him may have been slightly in excess of 3,500 lances. It is not clear whether these included 400 men-at-arms and 800 archers brought out from England by John of Gaunt, and whether or not these archers formed part of a total of 1,600, whose recruitment had been ordered by Westminster on 30 July. If we add to these totals the cavalry and infantry which Charles of Navarre had undertaken to provide, and the handful of supporters who had joined Pedro in Gascony, we arrive at a maximum figure of around 8,500 combatants, but the total may have

---

18   Russell, pp. 62–3, 62 n. 1
19   Chandos Herald, *Vie*, lines 1965–74.
20   Miret y Sans, 1914, p. 84.
21   Chandos Herald, *Vie*, lines 2309, 2350, gives 10,000 for the vanguard and 20,000 for the main battle. Ayala's estimate (*Crónica*, i, p. 553) of 10,000 men-at-arms and 10,000 archers is probably nearer the mark, but still greatly inflated.

been nearer 6,000. It seems likely that the contingents provided by the Great Companies, which amounted to some twenty-five pennons or *routes* (some 3,000 combatants in all), formed between a third and half of the total.[22]

We are on rather more certain ground when dealing with the composition of the prince's army, and in particular the forces drawn from the Great Companies, thanks to the eye-witness account of the prince's intervention attributed to the herald of Sir John Chandos. Chandos had considerable experience of the captains of the Great Companies from his involvement with them both as constable of Aquitaine and as lord of Saint-Sauveur-le-Vicomte in the Cotentin in Normandy. He himself is reported to have recruited fourteen pennons. These included the companies of six Gascon captains (Bertucat d'Albret, Lamit, the *bourc* de Breteuil, the *bourc* Camus, Naudon de Bageran, Gaillard de la Motte), Garciot du Castel, probably from Bigorre, and the Englishman, Sir Richard Taunton, all of whom had remained in France during the campaign conducted by du Guesclin in Spain in 1366. Chandos may have been responsible too for recruiting the companies led by John Sandes and his companion John Alain, and possibly those of John Shakell and Robert Hawley, who had also been in Spain in 1366, when they were in receipt of money from Charles of Navarre. According to Froissart, he had made a *rendez-vous* with them in the mountains after securing the permission of Gaston Fébus for them to traverse his lands, Peter IV having denied them access to the Pyrenean passes from Aragon and Catalonia.[23] In addition to these, the prince recruited some of the companies returning from Spain in two groups. First were those of the Hainaulter Eustache d'Auberchicourt, and the *routes* of John Devereux, John Cresswell, Robert Birkhead and William Botiller, who had joined the 1366 expedition, but who had also been retained by Charles of Navarre at the opening of that campaign, when they invaded the Tudela salient. Second were those of the lord of Aubeterre, Bernard de la Salle and the Welsh company of Owain Lawgoch, all of whom had remained in the company of Enrique of Trastámara until the summer. The remaining companies recruited by the prince were placed under the command of Aimery de Rochechouart, the lord of Rays, Robert Cheyney, William Felton, and either Thomas or John Peverell.[24]

In the final military dispositions which the prince made for the invasion of Castile, the greater part of these companies were placed in the vanguard of the army under John of Gaunt, and they fought under the banner of Sir

---

22   See Fowler, 1988, p. 36 and n. 1, and below, appendix C.
23   Chandos Herald, *Vie*, lines 2278–9; Froissart, *Chroniques*, vi, pp. 214–16. See Tucoo-Chala, 1960, p. 100, where the reference to Froissart is not only wrong, but positively misleading.
24   For the documentation upon which this paragraph is based, see Fowler, 1988, pp. 36–8.

John Chandos. Other contingents of the vanguard were led by Sir Thomas Ufford, Sir Hugh Hastings, the earl of Warwick's younger son, William Beauchamp, John Neville, lord of Raby, and the two marshals of the army, Sir Stephen de Cosington and Sir Guichard d'Angle.[25] The main battle, which was commanded by the prince, included, in addition to Pedro, Louis, viscount of Rochechouart in Limousin, Louis de Harcourt, viscount of Châtellerault, and Guillaume l'Archevêque, lord of Parthenay, both from Poitou, most of the Gascon lords and a sizeable number of seneschals of the different provinces of the principality with their contingents.[26] The only companies in this battle were those attached to Auberchicourt. To provide for every eventuality, the prince placed the *routes* of Bertucat d'Albret, the *bourc* de Breteuil, the *bourc* Camus, Naudon de Bageran, Bernard de la Salle and Lamit in the rearguard, along with the contingents led by three other Gascon lords – the count of Armagnac, Berard d'Albret, the lord of Mussidan – and the Mallorcan Pretender.[27] The lord of Albret and the captal de Buch followed on shortly afterwards with 400 men-at-arms.[28]

The prince concentrated his forces to the south of Dax, in the Basque country and les landes d'Estibeaux, between Dax and Orthez, while most of the Great Companies were encamped in the Pyrenean valleys leading into Navarre, where they were obliged to spend the best part of two months before the army was able to proceed into Spain.[29] The prince left

---

25 Chandos Herald, *Vie*, lines 2243–90. Froissart, *Chroniques*, vii, pp. 7–8, omits Ufford and, from among the companies, Sandes, Alein, Shakell, Hawley and Devereux, the last only being listed in the manuscript of Chandos Herald published by Tyson, line 2281. Froissart renders William Felton as *Guillaume de Cliceton*, but his rendering of Cheyney as *Ceni* is preferable to Chandos Herald's *Camyn*.
26 Chandos Herald, *Vie*, lines 2315–47, who also adds Roger de la Warre and John Lord Bourchier to those whom Froissart places in the rear-guard (see following note). Froissart's list (*Chroniques*, vii, pp. 8–9) is much longer. Although he omits the seneschals of Poitou, Angoumois and Périgord, named by the Herald alongside those of Aquitaine, Saintonge, Quercy and Bigorre, he adds the seneschals of La Rochelle, Limousin, Rouergue and Agenais, the sires of Pons, Puyanne, Tonnay-Bouton, Argenton and Pierre-Buffière, Louis de Merval, Raymond de Mareuil and, among the English, Richard Punchardon, Nigel Loring, Thomas de Wettenhale, Thomas Banaster and the Welshman Gregory or Desgarry Seys. He also adds William Felton, who was probably the same as the Guillaume de Cliceton he places in the vanguard.
27 Chandos Herald, *Vie*, lines 2361–79. Froissart, *Chroniques*, vii, p. 9, adds the counts of Périgord and Comminges, the *vicomte* of Caraman, the lords of Caumont, Lesparre, Rauzan, Condom and Labarde, the Soudich de Lestrade, the lord of Puycornet, messires Aimeri de Tastes, Bertrand de Terride and, from among the companies, Bernard de la Salle's brother, Hortingo. He also adds the sire de Clisson, the three Pommiers brothers (Jean, Élias and Amanieu), Sir Robert Knowles and messire Petiton de Curton, whom the Herald places in the main battle, and the lord of Albret and the captal de Buch, whom the Herald, lines 2387–92, says followed shortly after. Finally, Froissart adds the lord of Albret's nephew Bérard or Bernard, lord of Gironde, to his list of those in the rear-guard.
28 Chandos Herald, *Vie*, lines 2387–92.
29 Chandos Herald, *Vie*, lines 2031–48; see Delachenal, iii, p. 384; Tucoo-Chala, 1960, p. 100 n. 63.

Bordeaux with some of the Gascon contingents on 10 January – the day set at Libourne for the commencement of the campaign – but it was not until the middle of the following month that he was able to cross the Pyrenees by the Roncesvalles pass with the main body of his army, whilst other contingents appear to have proceeded by the Cantabrian coast, from Bayonne to San Sebastian.[30] The delay and the itineraries were determined by two principal factors: the ambivalent position taken by Charles of Navarre and the late arrival of John of Gaunt and the men-at-arms and archers accompanying him from England.

Whilst the prince was making his preparations in Gascony, to the south of the Pyrenees both Peter IV and Enrique had been taking the necessary steps to deal with the threat posed by his impending intervention. Pere's response to the league concluded at Bayonne had been to set about negotiating a triple alliance between himself, Louis of Anjou and Enrique.[31] In view of the treaties concluded with Edward III and Charles of Navarre, Charles V could not be directly involved himself, but during the course of August 1366, the necessary steps had been taken which led to the conclusion of a treaty, sealed by Louis of Anjou on 29 September – within a week of the agreements concluded at Libourne – by the terms of which, with Charles V's assent, they were to join forces to 'disinherit' Charles of Navarre and then proceed to the recovery of the territories ceded to Edward III at Brétigny, notably in Aquitaine. Since Pere was to open hostilities, it was he who would determine when the appropriate moment had arrived to activate the alliance, a prospect he contemplated with some trepidation, knowing that it would lead to a general resumption of hostilities, but which seemed increasingly inevitable towards the close of 1366, when the Black Prince concentrated his forces for the invasion of Castile. For his part, Enrique of Trastámara, after returning north from Seville in the late summer,[32] attempted to prevent some of the English and Gascon companies who had been serving with du Guesclin, and were either intending to or suspected of being intending to join the prince, from returning into the principality. Roads were blocked and ambushes laid to intercept them; even the services of the peasantry were engaged to prevent their return.[33] However, Enrique's immediate concern was to attempt to smash the opposition of the forces under Fernando de Castro, which had remained loyal to Pedro and were particularly strong in Galicia. Castro had taken up a defensive position behind the walls of Lugo, and Enrique, unable to take

---

30 For the date of the prince's departure from Bordeaux, see Froissart, *Chroniques*, vii, p. 2, and Delachenal, iii, p. 384. For the Cantabrian route, see Leroy, p. 140, and cf. Delachenal, iii, pp. 368–9.
31 For what follows, see Miret y Sans, 1905, pp. 89–113, and Delachenal, iii, pp. 374–9.
32 He had arrived in Léon by 13 September (Delachenal, iii, p. 354 n. 4).
33 Chandos Herald, *Vie*, lines 1996–2008; cf. Froissart, *Chroniques*, vi, pp. xc-xci.

the place, was obliged to make terms with him in November. This gave Castro a breathing space which allowed him to recover most of the places which had been occupied by Trastámara's forces.[34] Meanwhile, Enrique took up winter quarters in Burgos, where he called a meeting of the *Cortes* to raise the necessary finances to resist the prince. Here, he had cause for some optimism, since, in spite of the triple alliance concluded between the prince, Pedro and Charles of Navarre at Bayonne, and the formal undertakings entered into at Libourne, Charles's position was by no means clear-cut.

Primarily concerned for the security of his lands, the king of Navarre would have preferred to remain neutral in the conflict which lay ahead, as he had done during the invasion of Castile in the previous spring. This was now a difficult position to sustain, with the prince's forces being assembled to the north of his kingdom and their evident need to traverse it in order to secure their political and military objectives. To grant that facility to them was, on the other hand, to invite retaliation from their enemies, and Charles may have got wind of the plans hatched between Pere and Louis of Anjou to dispossess him of his kingdom, the implementation of which continued to be under discussion between Enrique's representatives and those of the king of France.[35] Faced with this impossible dilemna, in mid-October he refused Pedro permission to send reinforcements to join the loyalist garrisons in Logroño and other places in the Ebro valley.[36] Then, towards the close of 1366 or at the very beginnning of January 1367, when the prince's army was preparing to move, he had a secret meeting with Enrique at the Castilian frontier town of Santa Cruz de Campezo, and agreed to close the Pyrenean passes to the Anglo-Gascon forces and to assist Enrique to resist any attempt the prince might make to force a passage through Navarre. Clearly, a great deal of pressure had been brought to bear in the conclusion of this arrangement, primarily by du Guesclin and the archbishop of Zaragoza, Lope Fernández de Luna, a leader of the pro-French and pro-Trastámaran party in Aragon. Although Charles was to have Logroño (then in the hands of Pedro's supporters) and 60,000 Castilian *doblas*, these were infinitely less than the territories offered to him by Pedro and the prince under the terms concluded at Libourne. His agreement to them can only be explained by his wish to maintain neutrality at any price.[37]

---

34 Ayala, *Crónica*, i, pp. 546–7; cf. Russell, pp. 73–4.
35 Miret y Sans, 1905, pp. 108–9; Delachenal, iii, p. 392 n. 5. See below, p. 240.
36 *Colección de documentos, Aragon*, xxxii, p. 12; Ayala, *Crónica*, i, p. 550; cf. Russell, p. 75.
37 Ayala, *Crónica*, i, pp. 550–1, 550 n. 1; Delachenal, iii, pp. 331–2; Russell, p. 76. Both du Guesclin and the lord of Aubeterre were in receipt of moneys from Charles *por el dono et retinida que tiene del seynor rey* (AGN, Comptos, reg. 118, fo. 139v; cf. *AGN, Comptos*, vi, nos. 278, 626).

THE PRINCE'S INTERVENTION

For his part, Enrique seems to have believed that, with the Roncesvalles pass closed to the prince's forces, the immediate danger had passed. After returning from Santa Cruz to Burgos, he proceeded to Haro, where he disbanded the remaining mercenary forces still in his service, including those of du Guesclin, who, on 2 January 1367, also at Haro, released Calveley from service with him, allowing him to go 'wherever he pleased'.[38] Almost immediately, Calveley proceeded into Navarre, where, within the next fortnight, he occupied Miranda de Arga and Puente la Reina, to the south-west of Pamplona, by force of arms.[39] Sir Hugh may or may not at this juncture have been acting under the prince's instructions,[40] but Charles evidently took notice. In the middle of January Sir William Elmham, who had accompanied Calveley on the campaign in Castile, was paid by Charles for bringing the companies under their command into Navarre.[41] According to Chandos Herald it was Charles who communicated the news of Calveley's action to Edward, and he suggests that it had the immediate effect of negating the agreements concluded with Enrique at Santa Cruz and of restoring the *status quo ante*.[42] The occupation of Miranda de Arga and Puente la Reina was thus primarily intended to secure the kingdom against a Trastámaran offensive from the west, and only indirectly to facilitate the prince's entry across the Pyrenees.

Following the arrangements made at Santa Cruz, Peter IV had also concluded that there was no longer any immediate danger of an intervention in the Peninsula by the prince; but a new alarm was sounded from another quarter. Pere communicated this to the lieutenant of the governor of Roussillon, Arnau de Orcau, in a letter written in Barcelona on 25 January 1367:

an esquire of the count of Foix has come to us and has recounted among other things that, because the peace which the king of Navarre has concluded with the king of Castile, Don Enrique, has made it impossible for the prince of Wales to enter Spain, he has decided not to enter, and consequently the Infante of Mallorca has hired from the companies who were with the prince, thirteen captains, making 1,600 lances, with which he intends to enter Roussillon, and that the cousin of a person called John Guiter (who is with the Infante) is in Roussillon, where he is negotiating, or has already negotiated, that when the Infante arrives all the said land will rise with him, and for certain the said esquire has told us many things in

---

38   Ayala, *Crónica*, i, p. 551, and for du Guesclin's letters releasing Calveley, Fowler, 1991b and 1992, appendix iv.
39   Chandos Herald, *Vie*, lines 2195–8; Ayala, *Crónica*, i, p. 551; *AGN, Comptos*, lii, no. 827; AGN, Comptos, reg. 134, fos. 337–45.
40   This has generally been assumed (Delachenal, iii, p. 383; Russell, p. 78), but in the light of subsequent events rather than from any hard evidence.
41   *AGN, Comptos*, vi, nos. 781, 786.
42   Chandos Herald, *Vie*, lines 2199–206.

secret which we have found to be true; nevertheless, we do not believe what he tells us about the Infante and the said land [of Roussillon].[43]

Peter IV obviously suspected that the real purpose of the squire's mission was to deflect his attention from the Navarrese to the Roussillon frontier, thus allowing the Black Prince to proceed to his main goal with the minimum resistance. The veracity or otherwise of the squire's report was nevertheless an open question, given the count of Foix's policy of non-alignment.[44] Primarily concerned with the integrity of his sovereignty in Béarn, on 26 August 1366 he had written to Pere informing him of the prince's preparations and encouraging him to take some action before they had proceeded so far as to become irreversible.[45] On the other hand, on 19 October he had reported to Pere that the prince had arranged to meet him at Dax to reaffirm their friendship.[46] He had subsequently allowed some of the companies returning from Spain, who had been denied access to the Pyrenean passes from Aragon, to cross his lands in order to enter the prince's service. He had visited the prince and John of Gaunt when the Anglo-Gascon army was being concentrated around Dax, but only provided a small contingent of men-at-arms to take part in the prince's invasion, and he did not participate himself.[47] His attempts to secure immunity – a *suffrensa* or *patis* – for his lands were, on the other hand, without avail.[48]

Nevertheless, until mid-February Pere still feared an invasion of Roussillon by the Mallorcan Pretender. Before the end of January he authorized the count of Urgell, who was at Zaragoza, to conclude an agreement with du Guesclin, who was then on his way back to Languedoc with 1,000 lances, whereby Bertrand and his companies would enter his service, not on the Navarrese frontier, but either in Catalonia, where Bernat de Cabrera's son, the count of Osona, who had also joined the prince's forces, threatened to raise a rebellion in the *vizcondado* of Cabrera, or in Sardinia, where a rebellion led by the *jutge* or judge of Arborea was daily growing stronger.[49]

These anxieties do much to explain Pere's reluctance to allow the companies returning to France from Castile to go by Catalonia. Du Guesclin's

---

43 Miret y Sans, 1905, p. 106.
44 For what follows, despite the profusion of inaccurate references, see Tucoo-Chala, 1960, pp. 374–9, and the references cited below.
45 ACA, Cancilleria, reg. 1077, fo. 95v.
46 *Colección de documents, Aragon*, xxxiii, pp. 11–12.
47 Froissart, *Chroniques*, vii, pp. 2–3.
48 ACA, Cartas reales diplomáticas: Pedro el Ceremonioso, box 52, no. 6318.
49 Miret y Sans, 1905, pp. 104–7, 110–12; cf. Delachenal, iii, p. 378 n. 3, who follows Zurita, iv, p. 549 (lib. ix, cap. lxv, lines 5–12). For the reception of Cabrera's son by the prince and Pedro, see Russell, p. 58 n. 2, and pp. 62–3.

appearance on the frontiers of Aragon seemed particularly menacing, since the demobilization by Enrique of the companies under his command had left him without immediate employ, but with considerable claims still outstanding from the time of his previous engagement by the Aragonese king. Moreover, Bertrand was still obliged to Calveley in considerable sums, some of which were due for payment by Easter of that year at the latest. In a letter written in Tarragona on 9 February, Pere explained to the captain of Lérida that he shortly expected du Guesclin to pass by that town with his companies, and instructed him to provision the surrounding fortresses.[50] It was at Lérida, towards the end of that month, having heard that the prince's forces had entered Navarre, that the two men met to settle their differences and concert their plans. The results of their deliberations were drawn up in a document dated there on 27 February and sealed with their respective seals.[51] In return for du Guesclin's surrendering all claims which he had on Pere, save the grant of Borja and Magallón, which he was to keep with his title of count, Pere agreed to pay him 40,000 Aragonese florins, 5,000 right away in Lérida or Zaragoza, 20,000 by 10 April in Barcelona and the remaining 15,000 in July, also in Barcelona.[52] In addition, the king acknowledged du Guesclin's claims on the ships and galleys previously granted 'to go overseas to fight the enemies of the Christian faith', provided the voyage was taken up by May 1368. In return, Bertrand agreed that if he did take it up, he would commence in Sardinia, at his own expense for fifteen days, and if, at the request of the king or his lieutenant there, he decided to stay longer, Pere agreed he was to have all the lands he was able to conquer from the *jutge* of Arborea and other enemies of the king, save only the lands which belonged to the king or his servants there, and excepting also the towns of Oristano and Bosa.

In view of the news from Navarre, Pere could hardly have expected du Guesclin to take up his Sardinian proposals immediately, and Bertrand's main concern was clearly to extract as much as he could from the Aragonese king. The following day Pere ordered payment of the initial 5,000 florins from the revenues assigned to Enrique's queen in Zaragoza, and at the same time he ordered his treasurer to pay what was due to Marshal Audrehem of 2,000 florins' annual rent he had previously granted

---

50   Miret y Sans, 1905, p. 109.
51   ACA, Cancilleria, reg. 1347, fos. 155r–6r (appendix, A, no. 4). See Zurita, iv, p. 556 (lib. ix, cap. lxviii, lines 1–27).
52   Du Guesclin surrendered all claims deriving from past grants and arrangements, including those arising from the marriage of his brother (? Olivier), for the damages he had suffered in Castile, in respect of all rents, victuals and the 'fet de Bretanya', the valleys of Elda and Novelda, and all other lands granted or promised to him by the king.

to him.[53] The promptness of his action was doubtless occasioned by the news of the prince's arrival in the Peninsula, which he had received on 20 February. On that day, in a letter to his son and heir, the duke of Gerona, he wrote despondently that, with the Black Prince and Pedro already in Navarre and the count of Osona on the frontiers of Catalonia, he now saw no possibility of avoiding war.[54] As late as 9 March he still believed an attack on Navarre to be imminent and expressed his opinion to his son that they would have to defend their honour in the field, because, he added, 'it is better to die well than to live in disgrace'.[55] During the second week in February, at a meeting which the prince had held with Pedro and Charles of Navarre at Peyrehorade near Dax, all three parties undertook to renew the undertakings made at Libourne, and Charles had finally agreed to open the Navarrese passes to the allied forces.[56]

On Monday, 15 February 1367, the vanguard of the army, having been ordered to proceed to Saint-Jean-Pied-de-Port, entered the famous defile which led to Roncesvalles and finally began its long climb – some fifteen miles and to a height of nearly 4,000 feet at the col de Bentarté – to cross the Pyrenees by the route made legendary by Charlemagne and his paladins. The prince, Pedro, and probably also Charles of Navarre followed them with the main battle on the 20th, succeeded shortly afterwards by the rearguard.[57] By 23 February the major part of the forces which had accompanied the prince had encamped around the Navarrese capital of Pamplona. Charles's enforced cooperation had finally proved decisive, but the journey had nevertheless not been an easy one, accomplished as it was during winter snows and hailstorms.[58] The narrow mountain track made a difficult ascent for the large body of troops and horses, accompanied by many of the carts and much of the baggage required by the army.[59] After a long and frustrating wait in the Pyrenean foothills, the temptation to pillage, both on the journey and around Pamplona, proved irresistible. Despite Charles's instructions to his officers to see that the necessary

---

53   Miret y Sans, 1905, p. 111. The payment of 200 of the 2,000 florins due to Audrehem was made to his major-domo, Messire Jean d'Agamatxc, on 28 February, and a further 3,600 florins to du Guesclin's proctor, Janequin Clerk, in May, by which time Bertrand had been taken prisoner at Nájera and had transferred the residue of the 40,000-florin debt to the Black Prince towards the payment of his ransom (ACA, Real Patrimonio, MR, reg. 353, fos. 92r, 125r, 161r).
54   Miret y Sans, 1905, pp. 109–10. See also Gutiérrez de Velasco, 1951a, p. 225.
55   Miret y Sans, 1905, pp. 109–10; Russell, p. 85.
56   Chandos Herald, *Vie*, lines 2202–23. The date of the meeting can be deduced from a subsequent passage, lines 2224–33.
57   Chandos Herald, *Vie*, line 2295 (read Monday 15 February for Monday 14th); Ayala, *Crónica*, p. 551 n. 2; Delachenal, iii, p. 387 and n. 1, p. 388 n. 3.
58   Chandos Herald, *Vie*, lines 2304–6.
59   Ibid., lines 2296–303.

provisions were made available to the army, the troops either paid too little for what was provided or took what they wanted by force of arms.[60] The passage of the troops across Navarre brought judicial proceedings to a standstill between mid-December 1366 and mid-May 1367, and only one hearing subsequently took place in the latter year.[61] Several places in the *merindad* of Pamplona subsequently had to be excused the payment of taxes because of the destruction caused by the companies, which coincided with the bad weather of a particularly nasty spring.[62] Nevertheless, the measures taken by Charles to restrict disorder, and possibly also the injunctions of the prince, prevented a repetition of the worst excesses.[63] On the northern side of the Pyrenees, in the *merindad* of Ultrapuertos, the gates of Uhart-Cize (situated on the river Nive across from Saint-Jean-Pied-de-Port, and giving access to the road to Roncesvalles) had been specially fortified, whilst within Navarre the companies were only allowed to move around in groups of not more than twenty, and they were obliged to surrender their arms when entering the towns during the night and could only retrieve them when leaving the following morning.[64]

After concentrating his forces at Pamplona, the prince's first objective was the city of Burgos, the capital of Old Castile. This involved crossing the river Ebro at the least dangerous point. There were two obvious routes, the one by Puente la Reina, controlled by Calveley, the other by Logroño, which had remained loyal to Pedro. The prince took neither. Instead, he proceeded with his army in a more difficult and westerly direction through the mountains of Álava, by Vitoria and Miranda de Ebro. There were several reasons for this. To begin with, Enrique, who had heard of the arrival of the allied forces in Navarre whilst holding a session of the Cortes in Burgos, had suspended its proceedings on 24 February to establish his military headquarters at Santo Domingo de la Calzada, which lay across the direct route from Logroño to Burgos, and summoned his army to assemble in the neighbouring forest of Bañares, which would afford it some protection from the windy and wet weather then prevailing on the Castilian *meseta*. The prince had been made aware of these movements by a reconnaissance force of some 200 lances and 300 archers which he had sent out from Pamplona under the seneschal of Aquitaine, Sir Thomas Felton, and which included Sir Robert Knowles and his men among its number. They had advanced down the pilgrim route through Estella and Logroño, from where Felton had reported back to base before advancing as far as the Trastámaran outposts on the Nájera and Santo

60 Leroy, p. 140; Froissart, *Chroniques*, vii, pp. 9–10.
61 *AGN, Comptos*, lii, nos. 795, 797 and 800.
62 Ibid., lii, no. 805.
63 *AGN, Comptos*, vi, nos. 609, 728, 737, 773, 995; vii, no. 978.
64 Leroy, pp. 139–40.

Domingo roads, where further information on the enemy's dispositions, secured from Castilian prisoners taken in a skirmish, was communicated to the prince. Felton's force had then encamped some seven miles to the west of Logroño, near Navarrete, from where they were able to keep the movements of the Trastámaran forces under reasonable if somewhat distant observation.[65]

Felton's reconnaissance force may well have been intended to persuade Enrique that the prince intended to cross the Ebro at Logroño with the main body of his army, which, together with the valuable information sent on to him about Enrique's movements, would have allowed Edward's forces to outflank him. But there were other reasons for proceeding by way of Vitoria: the prince's mistrust of Charles of Navarre, specifically referred to by Chandos Herald, and his consequent concern to keep his communications open with Aquitaine by taking a westerly route to the south of the Cantabrian coast, where some of his forces may have been proceeding from Gascony with part of the baggage train.[66] Certainly, such suspicions as he had of the king of Navarre's intentions were well founded. Either after accompanying the prince and Pedro to Pamplona, or after receiving them there, Charles left the Navarrese capital at the end of February to go first to Olite and Estella, and then to Peralta and Tudela, where he received du Guesclin's cousin, Olivier de Mauny, whom Bertrand had appointed his captain in the neighbouring castle of Borja, which lay in Aragonese territory.[67] The king and Mauny, evidently with du Guesclin's connivance, arranged Charles's 'capture' whilst he was out hunting. The incident took place on 11 March and resulted in the king's temporary detention in the castle of Borja. The purpose of the charade – recognized for what it was, both within the Peninsula and abroad – was to provide the Navarrese king with an excuse not to join the prince and Pedro in their campaign in Castile.[68] The plan may have originated during the secret meeting at Santa Cruz at the beginning of January.[69] If this was the case it raises many

---

65 Chandos Herald, *Vie*, lines 2450–77, 2525–62; Froissart, *Chroniques*, vii, pp. 12–13, 15–18.
66 Chandos Herald, *Vie*, lines 2478–503; Leroy, p. 140.
67 Charles's letters were dated at Pamplona on 25 February, Olite on 1 and 2 March, Estella on 4 March, and Tudela on 8, 10, 11 and 12 March (*AGN, Comptos*, vi, nos. 817–18, 820–1, 823, 825–9). Mauny was with him at Peralta on 5 March and at Tudela on 6 and 10 March (AGN, Comptos, reg. 123; see Delachenal, iii, p. 388 n. 6).
68 Ayala, *Crónica*, i, p. 550; *Chron. Charles V*, ii, pp. 29–30. The best modern account is that of Delachenal, iii, pp. 388–91. Cf. Russell, p. 91. Charles rewarded du Guesclin for his part in the affair with a grant of the castle of Gavray in Normandy (Brutails, *Documents*, p. 167 and n. 8). Chandos Herald, *Vie*, lines 2478–503, appears to have taken the incident at face value, although suggesting that the prince may have had some doubts. Walsingham, *Hist. Anglicana*, i, p. 304, believed Charles was taken by treason.
69 This is suggested by Ayala, *Crónica*, i, p. 550, and an entry in the registers of the Navarrese Camera de Comptos (AGN, Comptos, reg. 121, fo. 89r, recited by Delachenal, iii, p. 389 n. 4).

questions as to the precise nature of the agreements reached there, and of Charles's true intentions.

During the last week in February, shortly before Charles left Pamplona, the prince decided to leave Navarre by a westerly route. Given the season and the country he was to take his army through, it was a serious strategic error. His itinerary on leaving Pamplona can be established reasonably accurately from the two principal accounts of the campaign, as seen from the English side, given in Chandos Herald's life of the prince, and a Lancastrian tract written by Walter of Peterborough.[70] Proceeding northwest in the direction of Irurzún, the army entered the passes which led from Navarre into the sparsely populated and rugged country of Álava, where they soon encountered difficulty in securing sufficient provisions for themselves and their horses. The prince may at this juncture have been intending to push further into Guipúzcoa to join forces with those proceeding from Bayonne, but if that was the case he soon turned south-west to arrive before Salvatierra, a small fortified town some thirteen miles to the east of Vitoria, where the junction may have taken place, and where the garrison opened the gates after an initial show of resistance in which Sir Richard Burley was wounded.[71] Exhausted and short of provisions, the army was obliged to halt here for six days before they could advance on Vitoria. They consequently lost any element of surprise and any advantage they might have gained from their flanking movement.

On hearing the news of the prince's advance into Álava, Enrique decamped from Bañares and, having crossed the Ebro, proceeded north in the direction of Vitoria, halting to the south-west of that town at Añastro.[72] After informing the prince of these movements, Felton and his reconnaissance force proceeded through the mountains ahead of the Trastámaran army, halting at Ariñez, a small town situated in a plain some four miles to the south-west of Vitoria, on the main road to Miranda de Ebro, and almost equidistant from the Álavese capital and Añastro.[73] The prince then

---

70 Chandos Herald, *Vie*, lines 2502ff., and Walter of Peterborough, in *Political Poems*, i, p. 109ff. For secondary accounts, see Russell, pp. 87–107; Barber, 1978, pp. 197–206; Sumption, ii, pp. 549–57.

71 Both Francisque-Michel and Pope and Lodge, in their editions of Chandos Herald, lines 2502ff., identify *Sarris* with Arruiz, situated on the road running north from Irurzún to Tolosa and San Sebastian. It is not easy, if apparently more logical, to accept the conclusion of Russell, p. 88 n. 1, that Arruazu or Aranaz on the Pamplona–Vitoria road are more likely identifications. According to Chandos Herald the garrison of Salvatierra made no difficulty about raising Pedro's standard and opening the gates to him. Walter of Peterborough, on the other hand, maintains that the garrison initially gave the army a hostile reception, in which Burley was wounded, before they decided to give way (*Political Poems*, i, p. 109).

72 Ayala, *Crónica*, i, pp. 551–2. Chandos Herald, *Vie*, lines 2673–6, and Froissart, *Chroniques*, vii, pp. 20, 271, state that du Guesclin only joined Enrique's army at a later stage, after it had moved towards Vitoria.

73 Chandos Herald, *Vie*, lines 2543–62.

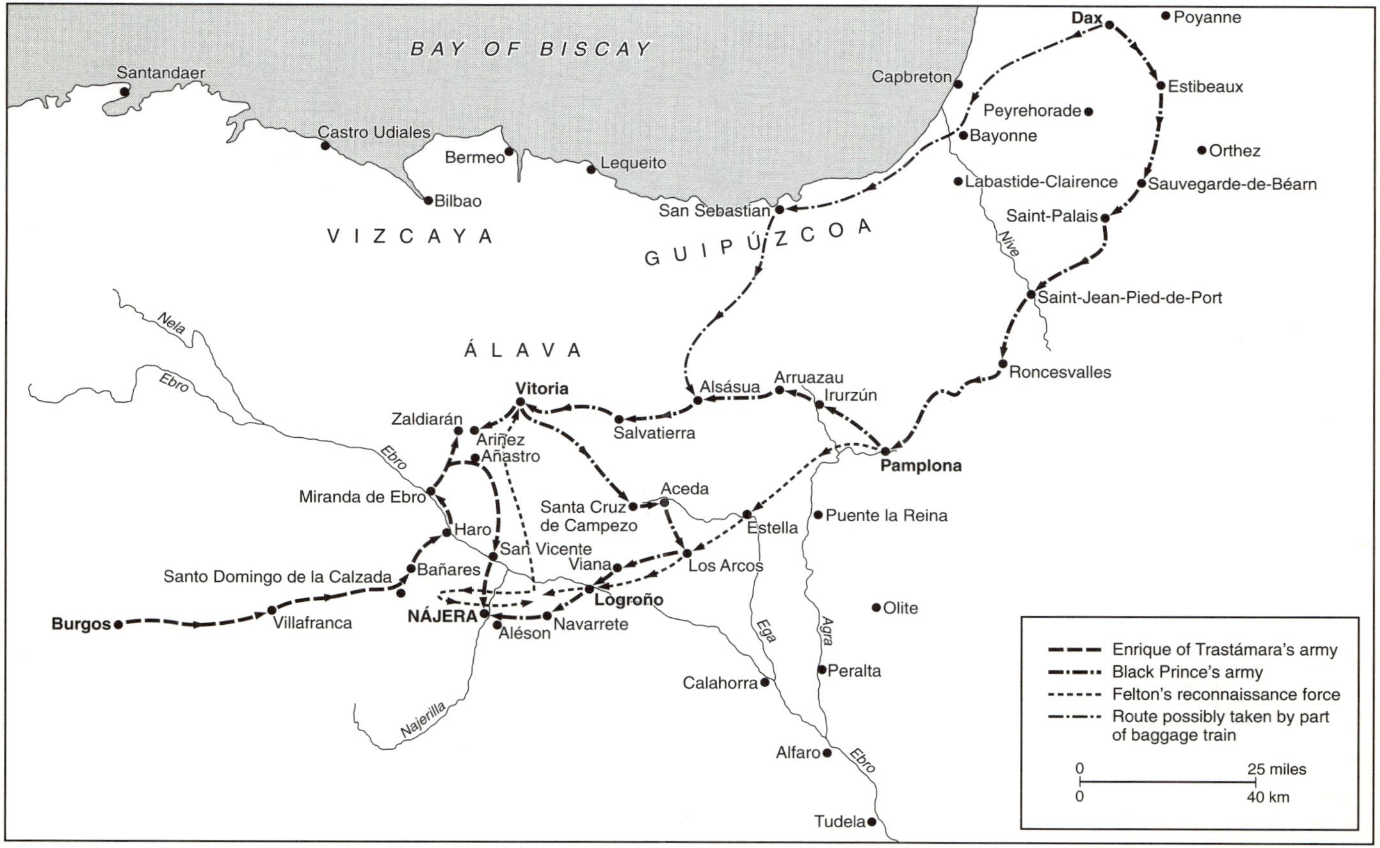

8 *The Black Prince's intervention in Spain, February–September 1367*

resumed his march towards Vitoria, which opened its gates to Pedro but was unable to provide sufficient food and lodgings for the allied army, which was obliged to disperse itself in the surrounding villages and farmhouses. Proceeding beside the Rio Zadorra in the direction of Miranda de Ebro, he found the road blocked by Enrique's forces and took up a position in the plain before Ariñez.[74]

At this juncture both sides appear to have arrayed their forces in expectation of a battle, the prince knighting some 200 of his men as well as Pedro. Enrique's army was still not fully assembled and then – possibly after the arrival later that day of French and Aragonese reinforcements under du Guesclin – a conflict of opinion between Enrique's Castilian advisers and those of his French allies as to the strategy to be adopted led to a change of plan.[75] Both du Guesclin and Audrehem, who had long experience of English military tactics, advised against measuring their strength against that of the enemy, which now included a large number of *routes* of the Great Companies to whom Enrique owed much of his success in the previous year. Their view was supported by a letter which Enrique had received from the king of France whilst he was at Bañares, urging the usurper not to risk a pitched battle with the prince at any price, but 'to make war on him in another guise', Charles V possibly recalling the tactics employed during Edward III's last campaign in France in 1359–60.[76] Audrehem in particular recommended holding the passes leading from the mountains of Álava to the Castilian *meseta*, with the intention of forcing the prince's army to withdraw from Castilian territory for lack of supplies.[77] According to Ayala, Enrique was reluctant to take their advice. Nevertheless, instead of proceeding into the plain of Vitoria to engage the prince's army in battle, as Edward had expected, he took up quarters in the castle of Zaldiarán, a military stronghold which dominated the exit from the mountains at a point where the road from Vitoria descends into the narrow gorge of the river Zadorra, from where it was possible to survey the prince's movements and intercept foraging parties sent out from his army.[78]

Edward's response was to instruct his troops to return to their lodgings and take up their positions again the following day.[79] That night Enrique drew up plans for two attacks on the English and Gascon encampments. The first of these took place in the early hours of the following morning, when a substantial force, commanded by Enrique's brother Don Tello,

---

74 Russell, p. 89; cf. *Political Poems*, p. 109.
75 Ayala, *Crónica*, i, pp. 552–3.
76 Ayala, *Crónica*, i, p. 553.
77 Chandos Herald, lines 2841–60.
78 Ayala, *Crónica*, i, p. 553; cf. Chandos Herald, *Vie*, lines 2631–2 and *passim*.
79 Chandos Herald, *Vie*, lines 2587–645.

conducted a surprise attack on the companies under Calveley's command, killing many of his men in their beds and inflicting severe losses on their horses and baggage. Some of them pressed so far that they found themselves in the encampment of the vanguard, but the commotion had roused Gaunt, who rallied his troops and was ready to ward off any further onslaught. They were then joined by some of the prince's forces, and others under Chandos, and the raiders were quickly driven off. After returning to base, a detachment of Tello's men then attacked the companies under Felton's command, which had taken up their quarters at Ariñez. They were too far away from the main encampments for the prince to risk dividing his army further by sending out a relieving force. But although considerably outnumbered, Felton's forces were established in a strong position on a hillock, where it was impossible to charge them. They were consequently able to put up a brave fight against the Castilians, and were holding their own against Tello's forces until a detachment of the French under Audrehem dismounted and attacked them on foot from another direction. After a fierce resistance they were finally overwhelmed. Felton himself was taken prisoner, along with several of his subordinate captains, including the Welshman Gregory or Desgarry Seys, Sir Richard Taunton and Robert Mitton, from among the companies. His brother, William Felton, was among those killed in the action.[80]

For a second day running the prince's army resumed its positions in the plain before Vitoria, drawn up for battle, with their banners displayed, and waiting for Enrique's forces to descend from their vantage point and attack them. They still made no move, but the prince ordered his forces to retain their positions throughout the night, despite the fact that many of the troops had not eaten, had no protection from the wind and rain, and continued to be subjected to skirmishes inflicted by the Castilian light cavalry, or *jinetes*. Their morale was already low when, the following morning, Edward ordered them to retreat through the mountains and attempt to take the route through Logroño which he had initially rejected.[81] Once again, this took them through barren country, and the difficulties and hardships endured by the troops are made evident by Walter of Peterborough, who himself passed a cold, uncomfortable night, sleeping in a copse. Others fared worse, having little or no footwear and being further burdened by the loss of numerous pack animals, which either died or were so weak that they had to be abandoned.[82] Eventually, Edward reached the Ebro valley by way of Viana, crossing that river unopposed, to enter Logroño on 31 March or 1 April, his army camping in the orchards and olive groves

---

80 Ayala, *Crónica*, i, pp. 553-4; Chandos Herald, *Vie*, lines 2681-826.
81 Chandos Herald, *Vie*, lines 2861-93.
82 *Political Poems*, p. 112.

outside the town.[83] Well informed about the prince's movements, Enrique hastened south to cross the Ebro between San Vicente de la Sonsierra and Briones. He then took up position at Nájera, which commanded the only bridge by which the prince could hope to cross the Najerilla, a tributary of the Ebro which was swollen by the heavy spring rains.[84]

From Logroño the prince replied to a challenge issued to him over a month earlier, from Santo Domingo de la Calzada on 28 February, at which point he was in Pamplona. Expressing his surprise at Edward's arrival in Spain, Enrique had invited him to state the location at which he intended to enter Castile, so that he could meet him to do battle there.[85] The prince had chosen not to take up Enrique's challenge at this juncture, but in a letter, probably written on 1 April and addressed to the 'count of Trastámara', he invited the usurper to surrender the throne and offered his services as a mediator between the count and Pedro. This letter was clearly intended to enrage Enrique, who, in a final communication despatched from Nájera, probably later the same day, addressed his adversary as 'You, Edward, Prince of Wales, who call yourself eldest son of the king of England and prince of Aquitaine' and accused him of being much attached to his own vainglory. He continued by accepting the prince's challenge and proposing that two or three knights from both sides should choose a suitable battlefield, which would offer no advantage to either, and issuing a safe-conduct for the English knights and their retinues for this purpose. Walter of Peterborough reports that the prince and his advisers regarded the latter proposal as a delaying tactic and, possibly recalling the intervention of Cardinal Talleyrand of Périgord before the engagement at Poitiers in 1356, replied somewhat curtly and did not take up the offer.[86]

During the course of Friday 2 April, the prince's forces advanced down the road to Navarrete, a small walled town situated on a hill and dominated by the only fortress between Logroño and Nájera, which Felton's reconnaissance force had used as their headquarters during the previous month. It was from here that the prince's scouts reported that Enrique had abandoned the strong position which his army had previously held on the left bank of the Najerilla at Nájera, and had taken up another position and

83 Ibid., pp. 112–13; Chandos Herald, *Vie*, lines 2884–98; Ayala, *Crónica*, i, p. 554 n. 6.
84 Chandos Herald, *Vie*, lines 2899–906.
85 Different versions of the correspondence exchanged between the prince and Enrique are given by Ayala, *Crónica*, i, pp. 555–6, 555 n. 2; Chandos Herald, *Vie*, lines 2403–49; Froissart, *Chroniques*, vii, pp. 29–30, 276–7; and Delachenal, iii, pp. 554–7, PJ nos. ix–xi, from BL, Cotton Caligula D III, no. 141. Delachenal, iii, p. 394ff., considered the Cotton letters to be genuine copies of the originals and Ayala's versions to be forgeries. However, the letters given by Ayala are to be found in the earliest manuscripts of his works and probably represent his recollections of what the originals contained. In reality, their content is not significantly different from those to be found in the Cotton manuscript (see Russell, p. 94 n. 2). The ensuing review and the quotations are based on the Cotton versions.
86 *Political Poems*, p. 113, and for the cardinal's intervention at Poitiers, Barber, p. 137.

arrayed his troops on gently sloping ground on the right bank of the Najerilla, with that river to their back. This was a determined move on Enrique's part, but one which suited his own temperament. By remaining at Nájera he might have blocked the prince's progress to Burgos, and through the continued use of guerilla tactics frustrated Edward's plans. But such an approach, in Enrique's view, would only have postponed the decisive engagement, which he seems to have regarded as both inevitable and desirable. Low morale and disaffection among his own forces may also have contributed to his decision.

Whatever was uppermost in Enrique's mind, on the evening of 2 April both armies prepared for battle the following day. Enrique had evidently expected the prince's forces to proceed down the main road from Navarrete to Nájera, and his troops had consequently taken up a position across that road, on the far bank of a stream – the Yalde – in the neighbourhood of Alesón, but with their backs to the Najerilla. At this point about ten miles separated his forward positions from the main body of the prince's army. However, the prince and his advisers had already decided against a frontal attack and did not fall into the enemy trap. Under cover of darkness, in the early hours of the morning of Saturday, 3 April, Edward's army decamped from Navarrete and, leaving the Nájera road to their left, proceeded behind a ridge which rises to the north of that road to a height of some 2,694 feet, to appear on the enemy's left flank at daybreak. Although Enrique had sent out scouts, they had failed to observe the prince's movements, and the arrival of his army from the north-east took them by surprise. As the English and Gascon men-at-arms and archers dismounted in the early morning light, the van of Enrique's forces, under the command of du Guesclin, had to be hastily manoeuvred into a new and less favourable position facing the approaching army.[87]

Whether through necessity or by design, Enrique had placed his most experienced troops in the vanguard and, in the event, they were the only part of his forces to engage the prince's army seriously. They included, in addition to the companies under du Guesclin, those of Audrehem and Le Bègue de Villaines, as well as the contingents led by Enrique's brother, Don Sancho, and the *corps d'élite* of Castile, the Knights of the Sash, whose banner was carried by Ayala.[88] As they took up their battle positions they all dismounted, which suggests that they were preparing for a defensive action; but they were supported by two mounted contingents on their wings. One of these was placed under Don Tello, on the left, and the other

---

87 Russell, pp. 96 and n. 1, 99–101; Barber, p. 199.
88 Ayala, *Crónica*, i, p. 557; cf. p. 552. The disposition of some of these forces is confirmed by Chandos Herald, *Vie*, lines 3316–21, 3401–10. Both Russell, pp. 97–8, and Barber, 1978, pp. 199–200, base their account on Ayala's description of the disposition of Enrique's forces at Añastro (*Crónica*, i, pp. 552–3).

under the count of Denia, on the right. The main body of the army was Castilian, under Enrique's immediate command, but it also included a number of Aragonese contingents.

The battle dispositions of the prince's forces mainly corresponded to the formation they had taken up on leaving Gascony. The largest part of the Great Companies were placed in the vanguard, under the command of John of Gaunt and Sir John Chandos, and they fought under Chandos's banner, which was ceremoniously unfurled by the prince and handed to him, so that he fought as a banneret, leading his own company of men for the first time.[89] Lancaster still had with him, in addition to his personal retinue, the contingents led by Ufford, Hastings and William Beauchamp. The two marshals, Cosington and Guichard d'Angle, remained in this part of the army, as well as Devereux and Birkhead, the latter being among those who were knighted. The main body of the army, under the prince's immediate command, included the contingents led by his personal retainers and others recruited by the seneschals, which contained most of the troops drawn from the Gascon garrisons. It also included the Castilian troops under Pedro's immediate command, their numbers now swollen by those loyalist forces who had joined him since his arrival in Spain, and, as the battle commenced, they were in turn joined by deserters from Enrique's army. In addition, the Navarrese contingents under Martín Enríques de la Carra, and some of the Gascons under the captal de Buch and the lord of Albret, were on the right of the prince's battle, with the contingents of Percy, Clisson, Sir Thomas Felton and Sir Walter Huet on his left. Both of these battles were dismounted. Only the rearguard, under the Mallorcan Pretender, which included the companies led by Calveley, Bérard and Bertucat d'Albret, as well as the contingents raised by the count of Armagnac and the lord of Severac, remained mounted, in the same way as the cavalry reserve at Poitiers.

The low morale which overcame Enrique's army just as battle was about to be joined was demonstrated by the defection to Pedro of a detachment of light cavalry or *jinetes* which had been sent out to harass the English advance, and this desertion from the usurper's forces was shortly followed by that of some of the Castilian levies. The engagement then began, with the English van advancing on foot, carrying shortened lances to attack du Guesclin's forces, under heavy covering fire from the English archers. When Bertrand's troops advanced to meet them, the fighting became a hand-to-

---

89 The following account of the disposition of the prince's forces is based on Chandos Herald, *Vie*, lines 3225–353. Russell, pp. 96–7, gives a somewhat different version, based on Ayala's account of their previous dispositions at Añastro (*Crónica*, i, pp. 552–3). Their dispositions at Nájera, as given by Ayala (ibid., p. 557), differ only slightly from those given by Chandos Herald, who makes specific reference to the companies in line 3248, and to Chandos's position as a banneret in lines 3121–56.

hand struggle, in which Chandos himself came near to death as he was forced to the ground before killing his opponent, the Castilian knight Martín Fernández. Some fierce fighting followed amid cries of 'Guyenne, Saint George!' and 'Castile, Santiago!', and for a while the English and Gascons had the worst of it. The prince then moved in the main battle of his army, instructing the centre to support Lancaster whilst the two wings were ordered to attack the mounted troops under Don Tello and the count of Denia. Tello's lightly armoured forces, subjected to the firepower of the English archers, fled the field before they could be engaged, and the count of Denia's men, similarly bombarded, soon followed their example, although the count himself was taken prisoner whilst fighting with the vanguard. Du Guesclin's forces were thus overwhelmed and soon surrounded by those of the prince. Although Enrique made several attempts to bring in the main body of the army to support them, they were constantly repulsed by the massed firepower of the English archers stationed on the wings. As the battle clearly turned against the usurper's forces, many of them were put to flight, only to be pursued by the cavalry of the prince's rear-guard, who hunted them down whilst they were attempting to escape across the single bridge over the Najerilla, which gave access to Nájera, where some important prisoners were taken in humiliating circumstances. The Grand Master of the Order of Calatrava was found hiding in a cellar. The Master of the Order of Santiago and the Prior of the Order of Saint John were captured whilst attempting to take refuge behind a high wall. Enrique himself fought bravely and, if we may believe Fernán Álvarez de Albornoz, whose father helped the usurper's family to escape, he had to be 'forcibly dragged from the battle by his own men'.[90] In the hour of victory, it was Pedro's greatest misfortune that his adversary was not killed or taken prisoner, for it ultimately sealed his own fate.

Several factors contributed to Enrique's defeat. The prince's advance from Navarrete by an unexpected route had clearly taken his forces by surprise. Made up of different nationalities with different fighting traditions, Enrique's forces were not drawn up in an efficient, closely co-ordinated, fighting formation. With their most effective units concentrated in the centre of the vanguard, the normal tactical relationship with the wings and main body of the army could not readily be brought into play. Once the battle commenced, the massed ranks of English archers were able to wreak havoc among the Castilian cavalry and prevented the weaker and badly co-ordinated units of the main battle from fulfilling their traditional rôle. The uncertain loyalty of Enrique's troops ultimately proved decisive. A large part of the army appears to have deserted the Trastámaran cause before and during the battle. Only the vanguard of Enrique's army seriously

---

90 Russell, 1959, p. 326.

engaged the enemy, and in the absence of effective support from the main battle, they were outnumbered, overwhelmed, and most of their leaders either killed or captured.

Following the battle, the prince took up his quarters in the tents where the usurper had spent the previous night, and he remained there throughout the following day, Sunday 4 April, while the prisoners were either paraded or listed and a search made for the more notable among the dead, not least for Enrique himself. On Monday the prince wrote to his wife, who was residing in Bordeaux:

Dearest and truest sweetheart and beloved companion, as to news, it will please you to know that before the second day of April we were encamped in the fields near Navarrete, and there we had news that the Bastard of Spain was encamped with all his army some two leagues from us on the river at Nájera. The next day, very early in the morning, we decamped to draw towards him, and sent out our scouts ahead of us to discover the Bastard's situation, who reported to us that he had taken up his position and arrayed his troops in a good place to await us. Having put ourselves in battle order to combat him, by the grace of God we did so well that the Bastard and all his men were defeated, thanks be to our Lord, and between five and six thousand of his combatants were killed and many were taken prisoner, not all of whose names are known to us at present, but who included, among others, the Bastard's brother Don Sancho, the count of Denia, Bertrand du Guesclin, Marshal Audrehem, Don Juan Ramírez, Jean de Neuville, 'le conte Craundenn', Le Bègue de Villaines, Señor Carrillo, the Master of Santiago, the Master of Saint John, and several other castellans whose names we do not know, up to two thousand noble prisoners; but as for the Bastard himself, we are not at present clear if he has been taken, is dead or has escaped. After the said battle we spent the night in the Bastard's lodgings, and in his tents, where we were more comfortable than we had been for four or five days before, and we stayed there all the following day. On Monday, that is today, when these letters are being written, we have departed and taken the road to Burgos, and so we shall complete our journey successfully, with God's help. You will be glad to know, dearest companion, our brother Lancaster and all the nobles of our army are in good health, thank God, except only Sir John Ferrers, who did much fighting.[91]

There can be no doubt that both the number of prisoners and that of the casualties were extremely high. In addition to the eleven prisoners named by the prince, the names of a further fifty-four persons are recorded. Of these sixty-five, four were French knights, fifteen were Knights of the Sash, and nine were Aragonese magnates. Four of the other prisoners were subsequently executed by Pedro. Of nine among the dead, whose names

---

[91] The original letter has been published several times, by Déprez, pp. 37–59; Prince, pp. 415–18; and Galbraith in *The Anonimalle Chronicle*, p. 171. Alternative translations are to be found in Venette, *Chronicle*, pp. 308–9, and Barber, 1978, pp. 202–3.

have been recorded, four knights of the Sash were among those who died on the field of battle, and four among the other prisoners were subsequently executed by Pedro.[92] Enrique escaped to Illueca, near Calatayud, in Aragon, where a reply to a letter he had sent to Peter IV, and a small escort to assure his security, awaited him. The usurper had proposed, with the debris of his army and with Aragonese support, notably of the garrison of Calatayud, to set up a centre of resistance to the allied invasion around Soria. In addition, he would establish a further base in Seville and secure the loan of an Aragonese galley to get him there. Peter IV, already anxious to establish his neutrality, was not enthusiastic. While he was prepared to allow other fugitives to pass through his lands, it was on the strict understanding that they did not remain there. It did not take long for Enrique to conclude that his best course of action was to seek refuge once more across the Pyrenees. Taking the route which led to the col de Canfranc and Somport, he made his way into the lands of the count of Foix, who received him courteously but with some embarrassment at Orthez before hastening him on to Languedoc. There, the duke of Anjou offered him both exile and assistance, placing the castle of Pierrepertuse, on the frontiers of Roussillon, in the seneschalsy of Carcassonne, at his disposal. From this new base, with the tacit understanding of Charles V, he was subsequently to menace the frontiers of Aquitaine, with the intention of hastening the Black Prince's departure from Spain.[93]

Meanwhile, on 5 April, the prince had accompanied Pedro to Burgos, but did not enter the city until two days after the king, having taken up residence with his entourage in the royal monastery of Las Huelgas, situated some two miles outside the city walls. John of Gaunt was lodged in the Dominican convent of San Pablo, also *extra muros*, but the vast majority of the army, including the companies, were encamped in the surrounding countryside for up to five leagues around.[94] The immediate business to be settled by the erstwhile allies concerned the implementation of the financial and territorial clauses of the agreements concluded at Libourne. It was clear from the outset that there would be difficulties over both. The prince badly needed to recover the considerable outlay the expedition had involved him in. In addition to the significant financial advances which he had already made to the captains of the army, he owed

---

92 These figures are based on the names recorded in Ayala, *Crónica*, pp. 557–8; *Chronica Reading et Anonymi Cantuariensis*, pp. 183–4, 225–7; *Anonimalle Chronicle*, pp. 54–5; Fernán Alvárez de Albornoz, *Memorias*, in Moisant, appendix iii, pp. 277–8 (see Russell, 1959); Gutiérrez de Velasco, 1951a, pp. 279–94. According to Ayala a total of 400 men-at-arms among Enrique's forces were killed. The English chronicles follow the prince's letter in giving 2,000 prisoners and 5,000–6,000 dead. See my forthcoming article on 'The Prisoners at Nájera'.
93 Miret y Sans, 1905, pp. 113–15; Delachenal, iii, pp. 419–26.
94 Ayala, *Crónica*, i, p. 563.

them even larger sums for outstanding wages, which were being further augmented for each day his army remained in Castile. In the circumstances he had no alternative but to squeeze as much out of his ally as he could get. Pedro, on the other hand, was simply not in a position to meet his debts until he had once more established his authority in the kingdom, called together the *Cortes* and imposed and collected the necessary taxes. However, he made matters worse by haggling over the amounts owed to the prince, claiming that he had been obliged to part with a considerable amount of his jewels and treasure at knock-down prices when he was in Gascony, and that this needed to be taken into account in the prince's calculations. He also refused to surrender to the prince twenty Castilian castles as a guarantee of settlement.[95] It took the best part of a month before the final figure was agreed, which, as we have seen, amounted to 2,720,000 gold florins – almost three and a half times the sum envisaged at Libourne, and nine times the sum for which du Guesclin had agreed to lead the companies into Spain a year earlier.[96]

The extent of the prince's mistrust of Pedro was demonstrated by the agreements whereby the Castilian king renewed both his financial and territorial undertakings in a ceremony in Burgos Cathedral on 2 May. The prince insisted, for his own security whilst he was in the city, that a company of English men-at-arms and archers was to occupy one of the gate-towers, that 1,000 men-at-arms and a company of archers were to be placed in the Plaza Mayor, that he and John of Gaunt, although unarmed, should be accompanied by 500 men-at-arms on foot, and that the leading captains of his army would be among their number to witness the king's promises. In a further undertaking, made at Las Huelgas on 6 May, Pedro admitted liability for his recently assessed debts, and undertook to pay half of the sum in question within four months and the remaining half at Bayonne by Easter 1368. The prince's forces were to stay on in Castile pending payment of the first instalment, and a further charge would be made for their services if this was not forthcoming. In addition, Pedro's three daughters were to remain as hostages in Gascony pending settlement of the entire debt.[97] Pedro left for Toledo almost immediately thereafter, and the prince's forces moved to Valladolid in expectation of finding better accommodation and supplies.

For his part the king appears to have made a genuine effort to raise at least part of the money he owed to the prince, through loans, taxation and contributions from local communities. The extreme urgency of the situation is made evident in surviving letters to the different municipalities of the

---

95   Ibid., i, pp. 563–6.
96   Fowler, 1992, p. 230.
97   Ayala, *Crónica*, i, p. 563. For Pedro's undertakings see *Foedera*, III, ii, p. 825 and PRO, E 30/1085.

kingdom. In one written in Toledo on 20 May, Pedro outlined the extent of his indebtedness to the prince to the municipal authorities in the bishopric of Cartagena. He explained that he had neither treasure nor any other funds with which to meet the sum in question, 'and for this reason the companies of the said prince are going through my kingdom doing damage in my lands, as you know, because I cannot pay them the wages due to them, and the costs and damage are increasing daily'. He had therefore no alternative, he explained, but to reimpose the hated sales tax known as the *alcabala*, and to insist that they should continue to pay him those other subsidies which they had granted to Enrique, and provide an advance payment on the sums due up to the end of the year.[98] In another letter of 9 June to García Fernández de Villodre, who had been among the witnesses to the Libourne agreements, he expressed his thanks to his old friend for securing a loan from the *concejo* of Cuenca, urging him to secure other contributions from the Jewish community and the cathedral chapter there, as well as from the towns and villages of that region, since he needed the money 'to give to these companies, so that I can send them away from my land'.[99] On 20 July he imposed a tax of one *maravedi* for every twenty *maravedis* of assessed wealth of all the inhabitants and residents of the kingdom, explaining that he was honour bound to meet his debts, and that he could not expect the companies to depart unless they were paid what was due to them.[100]

As the months passed the companies grew increasingly restive, and the damage already evident in May increased. Although the prince had forbidden his troops to take towns or castles, shortage of victuals drove them to do so. Edward himself was also culpable, taking Amosco and then, from his base camp at Madrigal de las Atlas Torres, besieging Medina del Campo in order to force the inhabitants to provide him with the necessary supplies.[101] But the worst offenders were the Great Companies, some of whose captains doubtless contrasted the treatment they received from Pedro with Enrique's generosity following his coronation a year earlier.[102] According to Ayala some of them even got in touch with the usurper, advising him not to return to Castile until the prince had gone back to Aquitaine, with an evident eye on future employ with him.[103] Others had a different agenda, being more interested in an accommodation with Aragon,

---

98 *Documentos de Pedro I*, no. 160.
99 Cited by Russell, p. 110, n. 1, from *Documentos escogidos del archivo de la casa de Alba*, p. 580.
100 *Documentos de Pedro I*, pp. 215–16, no. 164.
101 Chandos Herald, *Vie*, lines 3644–76.
102 Ibid., lines 3669–73.
103 Ayala, *Crónica*, i, p. 575.

at the expense of both Pedro and Enrique, which they believed would bring them greater rewards.

Peter IV had heard the news of the prince's victory at Nájera within four days of the battle, and throughout the month of April he anticipated an attack on his lands. Not only had his initial suport for Enrique made possible the latter's usurpation, but an embarrassingly large number of Aragonese magnates had taken up arms against the prince, including his cousin and his *mayordomo*, who had been taken prisoner at Nájera. His position had been further compromised by the usurper's initial flight into Aragonese territory and the subsequent arrival of Enrique's wife, Doña Juana. An immediate attack by Lancaster and the Mallorcan Pretender was expected, and Pere's natural response was to seek military support for the defence of his lands from the duke of Anjou.[104] But before the end of the month, the prince sent to the Aragonese court the two men in his service with the greatest personal interest in an accommodation with Pere: Sir Hugh Calveley and Sir William Elmham. They were to inquire whether the Aragonese king was prepared to contemplate a truce with Pedro and withdraw his support of Enrique. In the negotiations which ensued it is impossible not to detect the influence of these two soldiers of fortune, in particular that of Calveley. Both were handsomely rewarded for their services in jewels and cash, and they also used the opportunity to secure moneys outstanding to them by Enrique from Aragonese Crown debts to the exiled Trastámaran usurper.[105] The discussions which they initiated

---

104 Russell, pp. 114–15.
105 A good deal of secrecy surrounds the exact timing of the mission, but it appears that Calveley, Gournay and Elmham were already at the Aragonese court by 2 May, although Gournay had left by the 6th (Gutiérrez de Velasco, 1951a, p. 242 and n. 18). By letters dated at Zaragoza on 5 May 1367, Pere ordered the payment of rent outstanding to the three knights in respect of grants made to them in the previous year, and on the same day he also granted Calveley and Elmham the price of a mule each (ACA, Real Patrimonio, MR, reg. 353, fos. 99r, 174r). Gournay had already left Zaragoza, and Calveley was receiving money on his behalf (ibid., fo. 125v). He may have returned to the prince with Ramón de Peguera and Jaume Dezfar, who, during the course of May, each received 1,000 *sueldos* for expenses in going as messengers to the prince, as well as a further 2,200 *sueldos* 'per algunes coses secretes que fay en regne de Castella ab princep de Gales' (ibid., fos. 121v–2r). Dezfar lost a mule on this mission worth 300 *sueldos* (ACA, Cancilleria, reg. 1344, fo. 133r). On 18 May, also by letters dated at Zaragoza, Pere instructed his Maestro Racional to allow his treasurer 100,000 *sueldos iaccenses* for diverse payments to be made to diverse persons, including payments which were made to Calveley and Elmham in June, 'con vengnere al seynor Rey per ambaxadors del princep de Gales', as well as part payments of the 40,000 florins due to du Guesclin for the settlement made with him in February (ACA, Real Patrimonio, MR, reg. 353, fo. 161r; for the payments due to du Guesclin, see above, p. 204, and below, pp. 251–2). On 23 May Pere again wrote from Zaragoza to Francesch de Perellós, who was then in Toulouse, that Calveley had arrived in his court that day to treat of peace with Pedro 'e volem que sapiats que per aquest tractu havem a fer alscuns dons a diverses et grans personas ... per joyes et altres coses que avem a dar haurem necessaria gran quantitat de moneda'. He therefore instructed Perellós to secure 10,000 florins of a sum of 100,000 still outstanding to him from Charles V (ACA, Cancilleria, reg. 1344, fos. 118r–v).

resulted in a truce between Aragon, on the one hand, and the prince and Pedro on the other, concluded on 14 August and to last until 9 April 1368. More important was the acceptance in principle of the English proposals that, during its course, Pere and the prince were to make a joint demand to Pedro for the settlement of their claims, failing which the prince would make war on Pedro, hopefully with the support of Charles of Navarre, Pere, and possibly also the king of Portugal. The ultimate goal of this projected alliance was the conquest and partition of Castile between the four allies and the elimination of both Pedro and Enrique. The proposals were to be taken a step further at a meeting scheduled for mid-October.[106] For his part in the entire negotiations, two days before the conclusion of these agreements, Calveley secured a grant of the town of Elda and the castle and town of Mola in the kingdom of Valencia, in realization of the grant of 2,000 florins' annual rent made to him by Pere in February 1366.[107]

Meanwhile, in mid-July the prince had moved his forces east from Madrigal to the Aragonese frontier around Soria, where he was able to add some pressure to the negotiations between his envoys and those of Pere, which took place in the frontier town of Ariza, between Almazán and Ateca.[108] Two factors gave some urgency to the deliberations. On the one hand, the prince had received letters from Pedro to the effect that he could not raise the money to pay his debts before the prince removed his troops from Castile and, on the other, he had heard that Enrique was organizing hostile incursions into the principality of Aquitaine.[109] The move may also have been occasioned by the condition of his army, which had remained short of supplies throughout the summer and which was already debilitated by dysentery and probably also malaria.[110] If that was the case it produced no improvement. As soon as the negotiations with Aragon were concluded

---

See also another letter of Pere on the same subject to his treasurers and councillors, which is dated 11 May (ibid., fo. 106r). For previous correspondence with Perellós and claims by Calveley and Elmham on Aragonese debts to Enrique, see Gutiérrez de Velasco, 1951a, pp. 241–2.
106 For these negotiations, see Gutiérrez de Velasco, 1951a, pp. 240–61; Russell, pp. 116–25.
107 The grant is dated 12 August 1367 (ACA, Cancilleria, reg. 1345, fos. 94v–5r; Real Patrimonio, MR, reg. 645, fos. 154r–5r). By letters dated at Tarazona on 9 August 1367, Calveley appointed Uch, viscount of Cardona, to act as his proctor and do homage for the same in his absence (ACA, Cancilleria, reg. 915, fo. 168v).
108 Chandos Herald, *Vie*, lines 3713–20. The English envoys had their headquarters at Deza, some 25 miles east of Almazán and just inside Castilian territory. The Aragonese were at Moros, to the north of Ateca. One of Pere's councillors, Bertran dez Vall, was paid for going to Zaragoza for fifteen days in June 1367, and from there to 'a vila de Fariza per hauer uistes ab los messagers del princep de Gales sobre alguns tractaments qui son entiel dit senyor et dit princep' for five days (ACA, Real Patrimonio, MR, reg. 353, fo. 164v).
109 Chandos Herald, *Vie*, lines 3677–720.
110 Knighton, *Chronicon*, ii, p. 121; Walsingham, *Chron. Angliae*, p. 60.

in the middle of August, the prince began the withdrawal of his forces through Navarre along the road by which he had proceeded some six months earlier. Charles of Navarre escorted him with every honour as far as Saint-Jean-Pied-de-Port, where they feasted royally.[111] After taking his leave of Charles, the prince then went to Bayonne, where he disbanded his army and, following a stay of five days, proceeded to Bordeaux, where, after much celebration, his troops were to have been paid.[112]

Victorous in the field, and with a rich haul of prisoners and booty, it must have been with mixed feelings that the prince now confronted the realities of the situation and the problems which awaited him in Aquitaine. He was deeply in debt to the Gascon lords and the captains of the companies through the inability of Pedro to pay the sums outstanding to him. His titles to Vizcaya and Castro Urdiales, which he employed in his letters, still had no basis in reality. Already, the frontier territories of his principality, and the lands of some of the men who had accompanied him to Castile, were being subjected to the depredations of his enemies.[113] Moreover, he himself may already have been suffering from the first symptoms of an illness contracted in Castile which ultimately proved fatal. The question he had posed to those he had charged to search the battlefield of Nájera for Enrique's body, 'Is the bastard dead or taken?', and the retort he is said to have given to their negative reply, 'Nothing has been accomplished', had only been reinforced through time and doubtless still echoed on the wind.[114]

---

111 Chandos Herald, *Vie*, lines 3721–40; Delachenal, iii, p. 427 n. 2; Russell, p. 125 n. 3.
112 Chandos Herald, *Vie*, lines 3741–50. The prince had arrived in Bordeaux by 17 September (BN, coll. Doat, vol. 196, fos. 201r–2r).
113 In a letter dated Bordeaux, 17 September 1367, addressed to the seneschal of Rouergue or his lieutenant, the prince explained that, during the absence from Aquitaine of Gui, sire de Severac, who had accompanied him on the Peninsular campaign, the companies had taken and at the time of writing still occupied the castle of Peyrelade near Millau, of which Gui was co-proprietor (BN, coll. Doat, vol. 196, fos. 201r–2r).
114 For the quotation, see Delachenal, iii, pp. 407–8, citing (p. 408 n. 1) an abbreviated version of the *Crónicas de los reyes de Castilla*, composed during the reign of Juan II.

9

The Return North

The prince's return from Castile had largely been occasioned by his need to attend to affairs in Aquitaine, in particular to raise the finances to pay off his army and to deal with the incursions across the eastern frontiers of his principality, which became more than a minor irritant during the course of July. He was doubtless also aware of the growing understanding between Enrique of Trastámara and Louis of Anjou, and the increasingly menacing stance taken by Charles V, who, only too well aware of the threat that would again be posed by the return of the companies from Spain, had not only made elaborate arrangements for the defence of his lands against them, but had also set about recruiting a significant number of them into his service.

The raids into Aquitaine were probably minor enough affairs, but carried out on the properties of some of the prince's vassals whilst they were serving with him in Spain, and with the tacit understanding of both Charles V and Louis of Anjou.[1] Most of them seem to have been targeted on the frontier seneschalsy of Rouergue and were conducted either by Enrique himself or by some of the companies recruited by him. The region around Millau was particularly affected. Here, the bastard mounted a violent assault on Nant, to the south-east of Millau, and menaced Vabres and Saint-Affrique, to the south-west, from his base camp around Camarès and the mountains of Brusque.[2] The attack on Nant was repulsed by the companies of Penni Terretá and the *bourc* of Caupène, who were evidently in the prince's service, but to the immediate north of Millau another company, possibly in Enrique's pay, took the castle of Peyrelade, near Peyreleau, which commanded the entrance to the Gorges du Tarn.[3] Around

---

1 Delachenal, iii, p. 426.
2 Rouquette, pp. 88–92. See Froissart, *Chroniques*, vii, p. xxii n. 1.
3 The castle belonged to Gui, sire de Severac, and had been taken while he accompanied the prince on the Peninsular campaign. See on this subject a letter of the Black Prince to the

the same time Enrique recruited the services of Arnaud du Solier, Geoffroi Richon, Yvon de Lacoué, Silvestre Budes, Alyot de Tallay, Alain de Saint-Pol and four hundred other Bretons with whom he had raided into Bigorre and taken the town of Bagnères.[4] Some of these men were closely associated with du Guesclin, who was still held prisoner after Nájera; but it is possible that others, who had served with the prince in Spain and were subsequently recruited by Charles V to prevent them from operating on their own account in France, were also intended, in due course, to support Enrique's restoration to the Castilian throne.

Charles began to take defensive measures in the summer of 1367, in anticipation of the prince's return to Aquitaine. These demonstrated a clear perception of the probable itinerary of the companies thereafter. During the course of July he convoked a meeting of delegates from several provinces of Languedoil, notably from Auvergne, Berry, Bourbonnais, Nivernais, Burgundy and Champagne, first at Compiègne, and then at Sens and Chartres. Their deliberations resulted in two ordinances, of 19 and 20 July, which not only confirmed previous defensive ordinances promulgated by King John, but provided for new measures to be taken, not only in the provinces perceived to be chiefly threatened, but throughout the realm. Their main thrust was defensive, and they were directed against the companies proposing to return into the kingdom. Any military engagement with them was, if at all possible, to be avoided and every effort made to prevent them from taking fortified places, or places which could be fortified, even if the price to be paid was the abandonment of the open countryside, the *plat pays*, to their depredations. To achieve this, the fortresses in each *bailliage* were to be inspected by the *bailli* and two knights. Those worth defending were to be repaired and furnished with artillery and victuals. Structures which might compromise them or offer shelter to the enemy were to be torn down. This was to be done at the expense of their owners, and the names of those who refused were to be reported to royal officials. However, any shortfall in meeting the costs would be met by the Crown. All other fortresses were to be demolished. On the approach of any of the companies, the local population, victuals and other supplies were to be removed into walled towns and castles. In the towns the watch was to be reinforced, especially in those places commanding river crossings. No large armed *routes* were to be given entry without first being clearly identified. To prevent arms and armour falling into the wrong hands, a ban was placed on their export from any of the

---

seneschal of Rouergue, dated Bordeaux, 17 September 1367 (BN, coll. Doat, vol. 196, fos. 201r–2r).
4 Froissart, *Chroniques*, vii, p. 56. Ayala, *Crónica*, i, p. 575, refers to the raids made in Aquitaine by Aranaud de Solier, alias le Limousin, Perrin de Savoie and other captains of the companies whilst the prince was in Spain.

bonnes villes, save through accredited agents. To secure the necessary military forces for the defence of the provinces most affected, captains of fortified towns and castles were without delay to certify the number of men available, over and above those required for local defence, for service outside their *pays*. Similarly, governors were to register and forward to the king details of the numbers of available archers and crossbowmen, and all young men were to be obliged to practise archery and crossbow fire.

The troops thus raised were to be paid from the moneys raised from the *aides* imposed for the defence of the realm; but, together with the *aides* imposed for the payment of King John's ransom, they were in part remitted, as well as their arrears – by a half in the countryside and a quarter in walled towns. The tax on salt was also halved. These concessions were probably made in response to practical considerations, and extracted by the delegates in return for their cooperation. Other clauses dealt with the abuses of sergeants and other tax collectors, whose doings were to be investigated and their numbers reduced. Nevertheless, the ordinances indicated that in response to the threat posed by the companies, local magnates were prepared to tolerate a considerable degree of royal intervention, which frequently involved a greater intrusion into property rights than taxation itself.[5]

To contain the anticipated threat further, Charles V hired the services of Jean d'Armagnac to recruit a part of the companies serving in the Iberian Peninsula. Armagnac took part in the deliberations at Sens in July before proceeding to Paris, where he remained until 13 August. On the 10th of that month he sent one of his esquires, Quarelles, to Spain to make contact with a number of the captains of the companies, before himself proceeding into the Midi. Here, in a communication dated 10 September, Quarelles informed him that some contingents had already returned into France by the Roncesvalles pass. A month later Armagnac returned to Paris, where he remained until 11 November, but in the meantime Quarelles had persuaded some of the companies to enter Charles's service. These were clearly to be placed under Armagnac's command, and on 28 October the king also engaged his services against other companies returning into the kingdom. At a cost of 52,000 gold francs, Armagnac was to provide a force of 1,000 *glaives*, each *glaive* made up of two combatants, of which 900 *glaives*, some 1,800 men in all, were to be recruited from 'the Gascon companies', and the remainder from his own lands. This move was clearly meant to break the solidarity of the companies, which was an essential element in their strength.

The captains recruited by Armagnac were to serve him against all

---

5 *Ordonnances*, v, pp. 14–22. See Henneman, ii, pp. 243–6; Vernier, pp. 279–80; Delachenal, iii, p. 443.

enemies 'without excepting companies and companions-at-arms'. Together with their men they were initially to be engaged under Armagnac's command, or that of his subordinate officers, for a period of three months from the date of their first muster, 'each in his *route*' at a total cost of 52,000 francs for the three months in question. Should Charles V require them, Armagnac was to endeavour to persuade them to remain in the king's service thereafter at a cost of 12,000 francs a month. In the event of the king not requiring their services, or of their subsequent discharge, he was to ensure that they would return to the territories in which they were recruited. In the case of those recruited in lands outside those in Charles's obedience, he was to see that they did not return into the kingdom for at least as long as they had been in his service. In the case of those recruited in territories lying within his kingdom and obedience, he was to ensure that they conducted no hostile acts, such as taking towns, castles or fortresses, setting fire to places, ransoming men and seizing beasts; in short that they would do no damage whatsoever. Similarly, during the period in which the captains in question were in royal service, they were neither to take, attempt to take, nor allow to be taken any city, town, castle or fortress by escalade or otherwise, but to defend them to the best of their ability. If they heard of any such attempt they were to inform Armagnac, who was in turn to inform the king's officers. Neither were they to start fires, take prisoners, beasts, victuals or any other profits, and Armagnac was to see that all infractions were amended. Two days earlier, on 26 October, he had been empowered to issue safe-conducts and to grant pardons for past crimes and misdemeanours to those coming into royal service. He was to be permitted to enter fortresses and walled towns when and as he required, and the companies recruited by him were to be allowed to buy victuals at prevailing prices and to take what they needed in the countryside, without doing any damage. Papal sentences of excommunication previously placed upon them were to be lifted. The principal captain acting on behalf of the companies was Bérard d'Albret, who visited Armagnac on 14 November and fixed the date of the general muster for the 30th of that month. Then, for reasons which we can only surmise, Charles V countermanded the arrangements and renounced the services of the companies. Only 100 men retained by Armagnac on 25 October were to be kept on from 18 November 1367 to the end of the following January.[6] By that time the recruitment of the companies had been overtaken by events.

Deprived of this employment and no longer required by the Black Prince, the companies who had returned from Castile did not linger in the principality of Aquitaine. With the prince's encouragement, they sought to

---

6   For the above, see Contamine, 1975, pp. 384–6; La Chauvelays, pp. 57–62; Vernier, pp. 313–16, PJ no. x.

return to some of their favourite haunts in the kingdom of France.[7] They did not proceed by Languedoc, which was too well protected, but skirting the Massif-Central made their way through Limousin.[8] The first detachments appeared in the Bourbonnais in late September, and by the beginning of October others were reported to have camped between the rivers Allier and Loire. Armagnac had observed their movements in the neighbourhood of Marcigny, situated on the Loire some nineteen miles upstream from Roanne. In an effort to prevent their passage of that river the duke of Burgundy despatched some of his officers to Marcigny, and other potential river-crossings, with orders to see that any barges or boats they might utilize to cross the river were sunk. By 4 November the companions commanded by Bernard d'Albret, Naudon de Bageran and the *bourc* Camus were already conducting raids and attempting to take fortresses in the Nivernais, and they persisted in these activities until mid-December. It may have been these same detachments which had been active around Montluçon before returning to base around Le Puy. This information was conveyed by one of Philip the Bold's mounted sergeants, Jean de Sivrey, to the duke of Berry, who in turn informed the *bailli* of Chalon.

The greater part of the companies did not, in fact, leave the principality of Aquitaine, through Basse-Auvergne and Berry, until December. The earlier raids may have been conducted by advance parties intended to spy out the land. Whatever the case, there can be no doubt that the principal objective of the companies was the duchy of Burgundy. Towards the end of January they attempted to enter it from two directions simultaneously – through Morvan and through Charolais. In a letter written from Dijon on 31 January 1368, Philip the Bold informed the bishop of Troyes that they had already crossed the Loire into the county of Nevers some ten days earlier. His intention then was to confront them there and, he continued, 'Yesterday, we received letters from our *bailli* of Autun that a very large number of other men of the companies have crossed the Allier and could cross the Loire after the others. So we shall inquire as to their doings and will certainly let you know what we are able to find out.'[9]

The threat to the southern territories of the duchy, through Charolais, proved more serious, and was carried out by way of Marcigny at the beginning of February. The duke's earlier measures to prevent the crossing of the Loire at that point proved of no avail. The bridge there was not guarded and the river could be forded. But, lacking essential supplies, the companies had to abandon their plan to penetrate into the heart of Burgundy through Mâconnais. Forced to seek other pastures, when they

7 Froissart, *Chroniques*, vii, p. 65; cf. Delachenal, iii, p. 441.
8 Delachenal, iii, pp. 441–2. For what follows, see Vernier, p. 282ff.; Petit, x, pp. 224–6; Delachenal, iii, p. 442ff.
9 Petit, x, pp. 229–30.

arrived in Auxerrois 'the greater part of them had not eaten bread for a long time and were without shoes'.[10]

In fact, Burgundy had been well guarded. In compliance with the royal ordinance promulgated at Sens in July, on 20 September the council had issued detailed instructions for the defence of the duchy. Commissioners were appointed to inspect the fortresses of the province. Those which could be defended were to be repaired and provisioned, and those which could not were to be demolished. Captains were to be appointed and the necessary garrison forces placed in all *bonnes villes* and fortresses, and regularly mustered. In fortresses of which the jurisdiction rested with ecclesiastics or widows, the commissioners were to appoint appropriate persons for their defence. They were also to advise the ducal council on the necessary levels of artillery to be provided. In the towns the watch was to be maintained through the day as well as at night, and it was to be organized by one or two *porters*, who had the responsibility, among other things, of replacing absentees. The commissioners were also to instruct the lords, captains and other keepers of fortresses to implement certain other instructions with regard to the evacuation of the *plat pays*. The inhabitants of undefended homesteads and communities were to take refuge in fortified places with their victuals and other belongings within fifteen days of instructions being issued to that effect. Any victuals left behind were to be brought into the fortresses by their captains, and a third were to be assigned to the duke. To avoid non-compliance, any victuals evacuated by their owners were not to be seized for debt, other than for arrears of annual rents or other justifiable cause. No ransoms or protection money were to be paid to the enemy for households or beasts, and no horses, wine or other necessities were to be sold to them, on pain of death. Evacuees, as well as permanent residents, were to contribute to the maintenance and defence of fortifications – of watchtowers, ditches, dry walls, palisades, barriers and other defences. All of these provisions were to be carried out at the expense of the lords of the fortresses, with contributions from the evacuees, and they were clearly successful in preventing the companies from establishing themselves in any fortress from which they might have dominated the countryside and supplied themselves with victuals during the winter.[11]

Having fallen back on the Auxerrois, the companies halted for a few days at Cravant and Vermenton, where the churches had been converted into fortified refuges by the local population. Here, the companies were able to secure much-needed victuals and other supplies, before they divided

10   *Chron. Charles V*, ii, p. 38. See Delachenal, iii, p. 442.
11   The ducal instructions have been published by Vernier, pp. 310–13, PJ no ix. For their implementation, see Moranvillé, 'Procès-verbal', and *Chron. Charles V*, ii, p. 38.

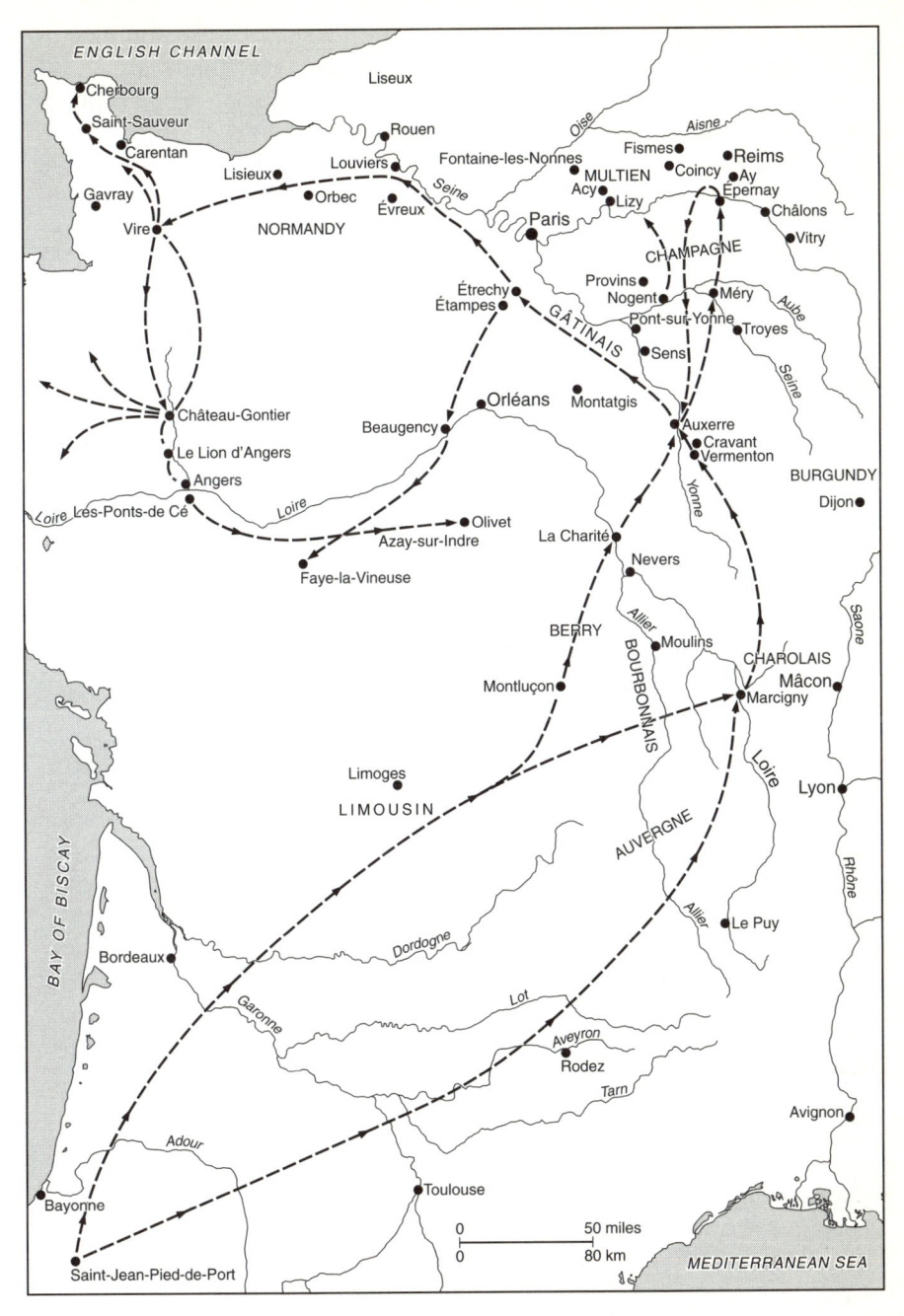

9 *The return of the Companies into northern France,
    October 1367–February 1369*

up into two main groups. One of these, which included some 800 English men-at-arms in a force of several thousand, crossed the Yonne at Cravant and proceeded into Gâtinais. The other band, possibly some 4,000 combatants, with a much larger body of hangers on, proceeded further north, successively crossing the river Seine at Saint-Sulpice and Méry, upstream from Troyes, and then the river Aube, before spreading out into Champagne, where they occupied a number of places around Reims, including Épernay, Fismes and Ay, and Coincy-l'Abbaye near Château-Thierry. At Épernay the inhabitants retreated into the fortified church, which the companies were unable to take by assault and instead proceeded to mine it. The inhabitants then constructed a counter-mine; but in attempting to set fire to the enemy's works they set fire to their own and were forced to retreat into the church tower before agreeing to a ransom of 2,000 gold francs, for which their lives and property were spared. The inhabitants of Ay suffered a similar fate. The fortified monastery into which they retreated was also mined, and they were eventually obliged to surrender for lack of victuals. Meanwhile, the companies who had tried their luck in Gâtinais, but found little booty, returned across the Yonne at Pont-sur-Yonne and then proceeded across the Seine at Nogent to join their comrades at Épernay. They conducted combined operations in the Multien from bases which they established at Lizy and Fontaine-les-Nonnes, near Meaux, and Acy, near Senlis, before turning south in the direction of Châlons-sur-Marne and Vitry-en-Perthois on 12 May.[12]

Although there were substantial garrisons in the walled towns of Sens, Troyes, Châlons, Provins and elsewhere, they did as much damage in the surrounding countryside as did the enemy forces, who continued their usual abuses of arson, murder and rape. The reactions of the native population were predictable. In Auxois, when a group of men-at-arms passed by a procession organized to seek divine intervention against the companies, a neighbour of one of the inhabitants of Pouilly, who was following them, commented that they were under the duke's orders. 'Holy God!', he replied. 'I don't know what men-at-arms they are, for the men of the lord of this county and the men of the companies are all the same, and they would never harm one another.' His words cost him a fine of ten francs. Those of another inhabitant of Auxois, who joked that the duke had brought in the companies to get people to pay their taxes, incurred a similar penalty.[13] On several occasions negotiations were begun to secure the companies' departure from the kingdom, but their demands were excessive – as much as 1,400,000 gold florins according to the compiler of the *Grandes Chroniques*, who seems to have been particularly well

12 *Chron. Charles V*, ii, pp. 39–42.
13 Petit, x, p. 248.

informed about them.¹⁴ It was not until the second week in June that they pushed further south again, to halt at Marigny, about half-way between Nogent-sur-Seine and Troyes, before returning into the Auxerrois, possibly with the intention of making a second attempt to secure a foothold in Burgundy. However, Philip the Bold, who had followed their movements from close quarters – from Sens, Provins and above all Troyes – succeeded in dissuading them from entering his territories. Wisely, he did not venture to attack them, although he could have concentrated his forces for an engagement with them with those of the duke of Berry and the constable of France, who were together defending the frontiers of Champagne.¹⁵ The duke's decision complied with Charles V's instructions to avoid an engagement with the enemy at any cost, although it was hardly approved by the inhabitants of the affected provinces, who evidently took a different view.

Finding Burgundy no easy prey, the companies once again made for the Gâtinais, which they pillaged at their leisure. Crossing the Yonne near Auxerre, they pushed north by way of Châtillon-sur-Loing near Montargis, ransacking and burning towns and villages on their way, until they arrived in the neighbourhood of Étampes, sometime before 4 July. Charles V, fearing that they intended to conduct their operations as far as the suburbs of Paris, and doubtless recalling the stranglehold which the Anglo-Navarrese had secured on the capital less than a decade earlier, summoned reinforcements for the defence of the capital. In the last week of June he had appointed two new marshals to replace Boucicaut, who had died in mysterious circumstances in an engagement with the companies in early March, and Arnoul d'Audrehem, who, feeling his age and obliged to the Black Prince for his capture at Nájera, had resigned his appointment for the less demanding task of *porte-oriflamme*. They were replaced by two younger men, Louis de Sancerre and Mouton de Blainville. In addition, some fifteen days earlier Le Baudrain de la Heuse had been replaced as admiral of France by the Aragonese Francesch de Perellós. These new appointments and the activities of the companies following their return from Spain were an early sign of the coming breach with Edward III.¹⁶

The companies remained to the south of Paris, at Étampes and Étrechy, from 4 to 9 July. During this period a disagreement broke out between the English and Gascon contingents, the causes of which remain obscure, but which may have been occasioned by their different reactions to overtures from Charles V for their departure. The growing disenchantment of some

---

14 *Chron. Charles V*, ii, p. 42.
15 Petit, x, p. 246.
16 *Chron. Charles V*, ii, pp. 43–4. See Delachenal, iii, pp. 447–9.

of the Gascon lords with the prince's rule in Aquitaine may also have contributed to their differences, for many of the Gascon captains of the companies had family and tenurial connections with them. These were doubtless exploited by Charles's agents. The upshot was that the Gascons made for the Orléanais, where they established themselves for the best part of a month on the Loire at Beaugency. It was here that Charles V attempted to negotiate their departure from the realm through the agency of the lord of Albret, then well placed at the French court, having recently become the queen's brother-in-law.[17] The terms of the Gascon captains for an agreement were brought back to Paris by Albret, and their companies meanwhile withdrew south of the Loire into the Sologne, where they awaited a response. Their demands were evidently unacceptable, and in September they withdrew into the Touraine, pursued by a French force to Faye-le-Vineuse, situated to the south of Chinon, near Richelieu, where the pursuit was abandoned.[18] At Faye they were only a short distance from the frontiers of Poitou, where they returned into the principality of Aquitane, some seeking service with the prince for the impending renewal of war between England and France.

The first rumblings of discontent following the imposition of a *fouage* of ten *sous* per hearth on 18 January 1368, imposed to deal with the prince's indebtedness following the Castilian campaign, had by now reached serious proportions. The count of Armagnac alone claimed to be owed some 200,000 gold florins for the wages of himself and his men. He was later to complain that his requests for repayment of this sum had been repeatedly refused, although the prince had settled his accounts with the captains of the companies and several others.[19] The discontented had brought their grievances to the attention of Charles V, who on 30 June had concluded an agreement with the counts of Armagnac and Périgord, and the lord of Albret. The same day he agreed to hear an appeal against the prince which Armagnac had filed on 2 May, two days before Albret's marriage to the queen's sister.[20] On 1 June Charles had granted Albret 4,000 *livres* rent for life and, for a down payment of 10,000 *livres* to be paid from the treasury in Paris, he had engaged his services against the companies and all others, save liege lords to whom he had previously done

---

17 He was married to one of the queen's younger sisters, Marguerite de Bourbon, on 4 May 1368 (Loirette, 1913, p. 324; *Chron. Charles V*, ii, p. 46 n. 1).
18 *Chron. Charles V*, ii, pp. 45, 60–1.
19 See the count's letters to the consuls of Millau, dated Rodez, 22 February [1369], published by Rouquette, p. 186ff., and by Moisant, pp. 211–15, appendix v.
20 For what follows, see *Chron. Charles V*, ii, pp. 45–7, and the important notes on p. 46. The wider issues relating to the *fouage*, the appeals, and both Charles V's and the prince's handling of the situation have been covered in some detail by Delachenal, iv, pp. 53–145. See also Perroy, pp. 91–6.

homage.[21] Since the latter included the Black Prince, the agreement could not be construed as an infringement of the Anglo-French peace; but Albret's appeal against the prince followed shortly afterwards, on 8 September, and on 16 November letters of safeguard were issued to him.[22] Although the count of Périgord did not enter his appeal until 13 April 1369, it was solicited by Charles V as early as the previous November, and the count's brother, Talleyrand, appealed at the end of the month, on 28 November.[23]

These developments were not kept secret and probably determined the actions of the English *routes* of the Great Companies, who may have been acting under orders from the prince. Proceeding from Étampes into Normandy a *route* under Robert Birkhead first attempted to take Louviers, but the town was well defended by a force of some 400 lances under the command of the count of Perche and Marshal Mouton de Blainville.[24] They then proceeded to Vire, which they succeeded in taking in a surprise attack on 2 August 1368, by a ruse which was typical of their tactics. A group of them, estimated to number between forty and sixty, and dressed as townsfolk, entered by one of the gates with their arms concealed under their garments. After killing the gatekeepers at the gate which they had entered, they held it until a more substantial number of their companions arrived. Although the town was not put to fire, it was sacked, and those in the defending force who were unable to take refuge in the castle were killed.[25] The action was conducted by some of the most experienced of the English *routes* of the Great Companies under John Cresswell, Hodgkin Russell, Thomelin Bell and the German captain Folekin Volemer, alias Folcquin l'Alemant.[26] The incident was serious in that it cut the line of defences protecting Normandy south of the Seine and opened the way into the Cotentin Peninsula, to the English garrison at Saint-Sauveur and the Navarrese at Cherbourg.

Although the castle of Vire was not taken, the town was not evacuated

---

21 AD, Pyrénées-Atlantiques, E 42 (original); AN, J 477, no. 2 (*vidimus* under the seal of the *prévôté* de Paris, 27 July 1379); BN, coll. Doat, vol. 196, fos. 271r–3r (seventeenth-century copy of the original). See Loirette, 1913, p. 327.
22 Albret's letters of appeal have been published by Loirette, 1913, pp. 331–3, document I, from the original in AD, Pyrénées-Atlantiques, E 42. A copy of these is to be found in BN, coll. Doat, vol. 196, fos. 287r–90v, which are followed by the letters of safeguard (ibid., fos. 291r–5r). On 16 November Charles informed the three seneschals of Languedoc of the appeals (AD, Hérault, reg. A 1, fos. 144 ff; Loirette, 1913, pp. 336–8, after AD, Pyrénées-Atlantiques, E 42).
23 By letters dated 1 November 1368, Charles V promised the count an annual pension of 40,000 francs if he appealed (BN, coll. Doat, vol. 244, fos. 7r–8r). The offer was renewed on 28 November (see Delachenal, iv, p. 127 n. 4, and pp. 179–81 for further details).
24 *Chron. premiers Valois*, p. 196.
25 Ibid.; *Chron. Charles V*, ii, pp. 44–5; Fréville, iii, p. 275. For the date of the capture, see Izarn, *Compte*, pp. 135–40, and Delachenal, iii, p. 450 n. 1.
26 Fréville, iii, p. 274; Samaran, p. 643.

until 13 September.[27] On hearing the news from the *vicomte* of Bayeux, Mouton de Blainville, who had been among those who had succeeded in resisting the assault on Louviers, replied from nearby Pont-de-l'Arche on 6 August:

Very dear and great friend, we have seen what you have written to us and are deeply grieved by the misfortune that has taken place; but you will be pleased to know that we will deal with the matter as best we can and you will very soon have news from us. Our lord have you in his keeping.[28]

The recovery of Vire took rather longer than he had anticipated and, to confound matters, some fifteen days after its capture a force of 400–500 companions under Cresswell, Birkhead and Folcquin l'Alemant made their way into Anjou and took the town of Château-Gontier by the same strategem which had delivered them Vire.[29]

The control of Vire and Château-Gontier gave the companies two strong bases from which they could pick off smaller places and terrorize the surrounding countryside in Lower Normandy and Anjou. Following the capture of Vire the captal de Buch, as Charles of Navarre's lieutenant in Normandy, feared for the security of both Carentan and Gavray, and had their garrisons reinforced.[30] The insecurity was so great that labourers did not dare to travel from Caen to Bayeux, whilst in the Cotentin Sir John Chandos extracted 15,000 francs in protection money to guarantee the peninsula from attack by the companies between August and Christmas 1368.[31] This arrangement seems primarily to have been intended to cover Charles of Navarre's possessions in the Cotentin and it followed the failure of the captal de Buch to conclude an agreement directly with the companies himself. Sometime before 9 August six of the captains and their men – John Cresswell, Wuilket Tee, William Botiller, Thomas Folifait, William Shelton and Geoffrey Walton – spent two days in discussions with the captal at Évreux.[32] Nothing was concluded on this occasion, and the captal instructed Charles of Navarre's *bailli* in the Cotentin, Guillaume Dourdain, to go from Orbec to Saint-Sauveur with a substantial escort – the companies then being in the neighbourhood of Lisieux – to seek the assistance of Chandos in persuading them to accept the proposals under consider-

---

27 Delisle, p. 147 n. 2; cf. Fréville, iii, p. 278.
28 BN, PO 3,046, document 67,637, Wargnies, no. 18; see Delachenal, iii, p. 450 n. 2.
29 *Chron. Charles V*, ii, p. 45; Samaran, 1951, p. 643.
30 Izarn, *Compte*, pp. 223, 226.
31 Ibid., pp. 35–6; Delisle, pp. 147–8.
32 Izarn, *Compte*, p. 346. The captains here mentioned can be identified from the names supplied from acquittances given to the duke of Brittany on 30 December 1368 and 22 February 1369 (AD, Loire-Atlantique, E 119/12, 13; see below, pp. 236–7, and appendix B, table 1).

ation. In response, Chandos despatched one of his knights, Sir Thomas Simon, from Saint-Sauveur to speak with the captal at Évreux, and it appears that he informed him of the details of the guarantee which Chandos had given to protect the Cotentin from all incursions by the companies up until Christmas.[33] However, when Chandos returned to Aquitaine in November, leaving John Cockayn in charge at Saint-Sauveur, there was justifiable alarm in the Cotentin. Within days the abbot of Cherbourg sent a messenger by way of Évreux to Paris, to speak with the captal and other officers of Charles of Navarre who were then in the capital, to inquire how the security of the Cotentin was to be guaranteed following his departure.[34] The concern was fully justified, since the companies established at Château-Gontier soon entered the peninsula, sacking the countryside and taking both booty and prisoners, with which they made off to their base in Anjou. One *route*, under Geoffrey Worsley, even planned to take Cherbourg, disguised as peasants. Only the keen observation of Philippe Daguenel, who informed the garrison, averted the likely outcome had they not been detected.[35] These operations, conducted in spite of the undertakings given by Chandos in August, provoked an immediate response from the abbot of Cherbourg, who on 18 December sent a strongly worded letter of complaint to Chandos by way of 'Navarre', the *roi des herauts* of Charles of Navarre.[36] Less than a year later, after the war with France had officially resumed, some of the companies still active in Normandy and by then absorbed into the garrison of Saint-Sauveur had taken on the rôle of guaranteeing the security of the Cotentin. For this the Navarrese were paying 12,000 francs a quarter.[37]

Rather less is known about the situation prevailing in Anjou, although it is evident that the activities of the companies there posed a serious threat to the neighbouring duchy of Brittany. Seven years later, in a series of instructions which Louis of Anjou gave to the ambassadors negotiating on his behalf with Enrique II of Castile, the duke claimed that, in retaliation

33 Delisle, p. 148; cf. Izarn, *Compte*, pp. 319, 398.
34 Izarn, *Compte*, p. 319; cf. Masson d'Autume, p. 12. Chandos had left for Aquitaine by 26 November (Delisle, p. 49, and preuves, p. 167).
35 Izarn, *Compte*, p. 100; Delisle, preuves, p. 146. The important rôle of Worsley is indicated in *Fragments d'une chronique*, p. 8. He was among the captains of the companies paid by the duke to keep out of Brittany in December 1368 and February 1369 (AD, Loire-Atlantique, E 119/12, 13; BN, Nouv. acq. franç., 5216, no. 12).
36 Izarn, *Compte*, p. 219; Delisle, preuves, p. 148; cf. *Fragments d'une chronique*, p. 18.
37 From 13 December 1369 to 23 May 1370 it was being paid to John Cockayn, captain of Saint Sauveur, and to Roger (alias Hochequin) Hilton, 'cappitaine dune partie des gens de compaigne', and from 24 June to 29 September 1370 to the new captain, Sir Thomas Caterington, and to William Hilton, Geoffrey Walton, Sir Robert Mitton and Henry Brown, 'cappitaines des gens des compaignes' (Izarn, *Compte*, pp. 36, 303). All of these men were among those to whom the duke of Brittany was paying protection money in 1368–9 (AD, Loire-Atlantique, E 119/12, 13).

for his efforts to thwart the Black Prince's expedition to Castile, the prince had specifically sent the companies into Anjou after their return from Spain and that the damages which they did to his property there ran into several millions.[38] Whatever the nature and extent of these damages, Anjou's claims were serious. The accusation that the prince was behind the activities of the companies following their return from Castile raises important questions about the sequence of events which led to the renewal of the war between England and France. If soundly based, or if the French believed them to be, then the prince, as much as Charles V, must share the responsibility for the recommencement of hostilities. In addition, Charles of Navarre's tortuous diplomacy in the Iberian Peninsula had its repercussions in Normandy, where, before his departure for Castile, Olivier de Mauny had conducted hostilities against Navarrese possessions, and these had been followed by further military operations conducted there by Eustache de la Houssaye and other Bretons, possibly at du Guesclin's behest.[39] The rôle of Chandos is also intriguing. In his capacity as constable of Aquitaine he had recruited a large number of the companies who served under his banner in the prince's expedition to Castile in 1367, and there is every evidence that he had maintained contact with them following their return to France. He had arrived in Saint-Sauveur from the principality in May 1368, had been well received by Charles of Navarre's officers at Cherbourg and elsewhere in the Cotentin, and a mysterious journey which he made into French territory with one of them, Guillaume Bloville, early in that month, appears to have been in connection with the companies.[40]

With the renewal of general hostilities looming, the position taken by Duke John IV of Brittany was likely to be crucial, and the presence of a large number of English *routes* of the Great Companies on the eastern frontiers of his duchy, as well as the English officers still in his service, was perhaps intended to remind him where his future allegiance should lie. Already concerned to maintain a position of neutrality in the coming conflict, the duke concluded a treaty with the companies which involved paying to keep them out of his duchy. The acquittances which their captains gave to him – for 27,500 gold *écus* for the period up to Christmas 1368 and for a similar sum on 2 February following – give a clear idea of the extent of their financial demands, and provide an important indication of their strength and composition at this juncture, including a checklist of the names of their principal captains.[41] Consisting of twenty-six *routes*,

38 BN, MS franç., 3,884, fo. 15, published by Lecoy de la Marche, ii, p. 395; cf. Delachenal, iii, p. 450 n. 5.
39 Izarn, *Compte*, p. 144.
40 Ibid., pp. 343–4, 351.
41 AD, Loire-Atlantique, E 119/12, 13. In addition, there are a number of acquittances given by individual captains during the same period (BN, Nouv. acq. franc., 5216, nos. 10–12).

each under its own captain, the 'English *routes* of the Great Companies', as they called themselves, probably amounted to some 3,000 men-at-arms.[42] A force of this size was clearly in a position to inflict major damage and suggests that the devastation attributed to them by the chroniclers was hardly exaggerated.[43]

The immediate concern of the French authorities was to secure the evacuation of the two principal towns occupied by the companies, either by force of arms or by negotiation. The first steps to recover Vire were taken by Guillaume de Merle, lord of Messei and Charles V's captain-general in Normandy south of the Seine. Lacking sufficient men to recover the town by force, he endeavoured to conclude a treaty with the companies occupying it, hoping that they could be paid off before they took the castle. His intermediary in this affair was a man called Jean Hardi, a prisoner of the companies and probably a burgess of the town. He also acted as an agent of the captain-general in another respect, reporting about the state of the castle and the terms of surrender which the castellan, Raoul d'Auqetonville, was of necessity contemplating. In an effort to contain the activities of the companies, Charles V had already sent the lord of Vigny and Pierre de Villiers, *souverain maistre* of his household, on a mission to Saint-Sauveur to speak with Chandos in July. On returning to Saint-Lô Villiers instructed Guillaume Paesnel, lord of Hambye, to try and reinforce the castle of Vire, and he succeeded in introducing a force of men-at-arms and archers, almost 100 men in all.[44] Villiers then proceeded to Caen, where he held discussions on the terms for the evacuation – the *rachat* – of Vire with Merle, the treasurer of France, the captain and *bailli* of Caen and several others. However, the final arrangement was negotiated by Marshal Blainville, who secured the departure of the companies against payment and the release of six of their number who had been taken by the French.[45]

On the morning of 13 September the two captains of the companies who had remained at Vire (Hodgkin Russell and Thomelin Bell) led off the garrison under their command to join their companions at Château-Gontier, and it was there that three of the prisoners who had been held as a guarantee of their departure were handed over by one of Charles V's sergeants and an English esquire. It was doubtless also after the transfer of their forces from Vire that Russell and another English captain, John Chase, took the neighbouring fortress of Le Lion-d'Angers, which com-

42 See appendix B, table 1.
43 The revenues paid in a number of sergeantries around Vire had to be reduced by a third in the quarter from July to September 1368 because of the activities of the companies there (Izarn, *Compte*, pp. 135–40).
44 Fréville, iii, p. 274–6.
45 Ibid., iii, pp. 276–7. The evacuation treaty was concluded sometime between 27 August and 3 September 1368. The sum of 2,200 gold francs given by Fréville for the *rachat* was almost certainly part payment and not the whole amount.

manded the junction of the rivers Oudon and Mayenne to the north of Angers.[46] The occupation of this and other places in the Loire valley in the year which lay ahead was to have important strategic implications once the Anglo-French war was resumed.

The companies remained at Château-Gontier rather longer than they did at Vire, using the town as a base for operations not only into the immediate locality and the Cotentin, but also south of the Loire. On one of these raids the *routes* of Birkhead and Cresswell were involved in an engagement with a *route* under the command of Amaury, lord of Craon, in which the captain, Mavynet, was captured and ransomed for 3,000 gold francs.[47] Another raid, carried out as far afield as the fortified abbey of Olivet on the river Cher near Romorantin, of which Guillaume de Merle had forewarned the marshals of France, had more serious consequences. Birkhead and Cresswell, together with some 200 combatants, were surprised by a force about half as large again under Louis de Sancerre, Gui de Baveux and the governor of Blois. After an initially indecisive battle, the English were eventually beaten and nearly all killed or drowned in the Cher. Those taken prisoner were put to death, including, it would seem, Birkhead; but Cresswell escaped, to trouble the French until his eventual capture in 1374.[48] Other raids made by the companies in the autumn of 1368 from Azay-sur-Indre, situated to the north of Loches, are probably to be attributed to the Gascon *routes* of the companies who were based there and at Beaugency. The municipal authorities of Tours kept a close eye on their activities: inquiring about the companies at Beaugency in August, informing Louis of Sancerre in Meung-sur-Loire about those in Azay in September, and sending an urgent message to their colleagues at Chinon about the imminent arrival of the companies there towards the end of October. They also made inquiries on 21 October to hear if the English *routes* were at Château-Gontier.[49]

The renewal of the war between France and England was now imminent. Charles V's letters of summons to the Black Prince, prepared on 19 November 1368 and citing him to appear in *parlement* in Paris on 2 May,

---

46 AN, JJ reg. 100, no. 155; see Luce in Froissart, *Chroniques*, vii, p. li, n. 1.
47 Samaran, 1951, pp. 641–4 (letter obligatory of 'mons. Mavynet' to Birkhead and Cresswell). This evidently dates from before 30 December 1368, by which date Birkhead was dead (see below, p. 337). However, although it envisaged the possibility that Château-Gontier might be retaken by the French or evacuated by 'la Grant Companie' before 2 February 1369, it is not a treaty for the evacuation of Château-Gontier, as Samaran appears to have believed. It is in fact an undertaking by Mavynet to surrender himself or hand over the ransom money to the receiver of Bécherel, Hugh Middleton or Milton, in the event of Château-Gontier no longer being in the hands of the companies. For Craon's involvement with the garrison of the place, see below, p. 286.
48 *Chron. premiers Valois*, p. 197; *Chron. normande*, pp. 167, 333. See appendix E.
49 *Reg. comptes Tours*, ii, pp. 29–30, nos. 131, 133, 135–8.

reached the prince early in January 1369.[50] By the end of February, preparations were well advanced in England for the despatch to Aquitaine of a force of 400 men-at-arms and 400 archers under the earls of Pembroke and Cambridge, and they appear to have left Southampton for Saint-Malo at the beginning of March.[51] They were accompanied by a messenger from the king, Robert de Beverley, who was sent on a mission to Château-Gontier, apparently to instruct the captain of the companies there to negotiate its evacuation and either join the garrison forces at Saint-Sauveur-le-Vicomte or accompany the forces under Cambridge and Pembroke to Aquitaine, where they were to be placed under the command of Sir Hugh Calveley, who was recalled from Aragon.[52] An agreement appears to have been reached on an appropriate sum for their departure, which was raised from the proceeds of a special subsidy levied in the diocese of Le Mans and Angers.[53] Within a matter of months the companies had taken up new commands in royal or princely service, either in Normandy or in Aquitaine.

50 Barber, 1978, p. 219.
51 Froissart, *Chroniques*, vii, pp. li, 116. On 16 January 1369, letters of protection were issued to Pembroke, who was going to Aquitaine to join the prince, and letters of attorney were issued to him on 26 February (*Foedera*, III, ii, pp. 857, 862). Protection for forty-three persons going there in the retinue of Cambridge were issued on 23 February (ibid., p. 862).
52 For Beverley's mission, see PRO, E 101/316/1 (Mirot and Déprez, no. cclxxxii). He left England on 5 March, embarked at Southampton, disembarked at the castle of 'Selydow' in Brittany, and proceeded by way of Bécherel to Rennes, Saint-Aubin-des-Landes (near Vitré) and Gravelles to Château-Gontier. Froissart, *Chroniques*, vii, pp. li, 116–18, refers to the recruitment by Cambridge and Pembroke of the companies operating north of the Loire, and adds that, along with the *route* which Calveley brought from Aragon, they were some 2,000 strong. For those *routes* of the companies who made for Saint-Sauveur, see above, p. 235 n. 37. By an act dated 8 September 1369 Amaury de Craon ordered the pursuit of these *routes* who, after leaving Château-Gontier, had penetrated the duchy of Brittany before proceeding to Saint-Sauveur (Froissart, *Chroniques*, vii, p. li, n. 1; cf. Morice, *Mémoires*, i, cols. 1632–4).
53 The exact date and terms of the departure of the companies remain a mystery, although it seems that the final evacuation did not take place until the late summer of 1369. For the subsidy, see Luce in Froissart, *Chroniques*, vii, p. li n. 1. However, it did not bring in sufficient revenues and Guillaume Bequet, receiver-general in the diocese of Le Mans, was even obliged to the companies on account.

10

A Provençal Interlude and a Sicilian Marriage

Among the prisoners taken at Nájera who were brought back to Bordeaux by the Black Prince there were two men whose release had not been determined, namely Bertrand du Guesclin and Marshal Audrehem, whose support for Enrique of Trastámara had resulted in the downfall of King Pedro and precipitated the prince's intervention in Castile. The long delay in resolving their position suggests that there were serious doubts about the advisability of releasing them for as long as Enrique was at large, and that they were being treated as political prisoners. The situation was compounded by the bastard's return to Spain within days of the prince's arrival in Bordeaux, and by the treaty of alliance which he had concluded with Louis of Anjou at Aigues-Mortes on 13 August.[1] While it is unlikely that the prince was conversant with the full details of their agreement, which envisaged an early recommencement of the war with England, his decision to reverse his previous policy over the two prisoners, and to allow them to leave Bordeaux in January 1368, although in keeping with chivalrous conventions, was an act of political folly.[2]

Credence is given, by the accounts of other chroniclers, and by what we know of the prince's character, to Froissart's claim that du Guesclin was released because the Breton taunted the prince that he did not dare give

---

1   The prince was at Saint-Jean-Pied-de-Port on 29 August, but had arrived in Bordeaux by 17 September (see above, p. 222, n. 112). Enrique was at Perpetuse in Roussillon (from where he confirmed the treaty of Aigues-Mortes on 9 September), but at Huesca on 24 September and on Castilian soil, at Calahorra, on 28 September (see Delachenal, iii, pp. 427–9, 437–8).
2   The terms of du Guesclin's release must have been under negotiation before the end of November, since on 7 December Charles V instructed his treasurer, Pierre Scatisse, to pay 30,000 *doblas* to the prince, half within three months of his release and the other half three months later. However, he added, 'Sy ne savons encore se le dit prince asetera la dite obligasion; et sy tost que nous saron, nous le vouz feronz savoir' (Cuvelier, *Chronique*, ii, p. 401, PJ no. xiii; cf. Delachenal, iii, p. 456 n. 4). Bertrand was released from Bordeaux on 17 January 1368 and passed through Montpellier with Audrehem on 7 February (*Thalamus parvus*, p. 382; cf. Delachenal, iii, pp. 456–7).

him his freedom because he, Bertrand, was too great a soldier.³ In Audrehem's case, Ayala recounts that the prince almost had him executed for perjury and treachery, since the marshal, who had previously been taken prisoner at the battle of Poitiers, had been released on condition that he would not bear arms against the prince or Edward III unless war was renewed with France. Moreover, the marshal had not completed the payment of his ransom. According to this story, the case was remitted to twelve knights who accepted Audrehem's explanation that he had not fought in Spain against the prince, who was in charge of the army at Nájera, but against Pedro, in whose pay the prince had campaigned in Castile. The distinction was a subtle one, but according to Ayala, it saved the marshal's skin.⁴ The prince may also have given some consideration to Audrehem's age, and chosen to release him on that account. Some twenty years older than du Guesclin, who was forty-five, Audrehem was no longer in his prime, and the rigours of a long military career were beginning to tell.⁵ Nevertheless, it appears that the marshal was shortly afterwards obliged to return for a further period of doubtless comfortable detention in Bordeaux, pending completion of the payment of an instalment of his ransom.⁶ In releasing both men, and particularly du Guesclin, it is likely that the prince's need for money overruled his political judgement. However, this was not immediately obvious, and an interval was to elapse during which Bertrand and a significant number of the companies under his command were preoccupied with the affairs of Provence.

Du Guesclin had been taken prisoner at Nájera by two English knights, Sir William Berland and Sir Thomas Cheyne, who disposed of their rights in their captive to the Black Prince for £3,000.⁷ Bertrand's ransom was then fixed by the prince at 100,000 *doblas* (around 86,000 Florentine florins) of which 60,000 were to be paid within three months of his release and the remainder three months thereafter. Pending payment, it is probable that he undertook not to bear arms against the prince, and it is certain that he undertook that, in the event of his failure to complete the payment of either instalment, he would return to Bordeaux as the prince's prisoner. It was doubtless to avoid this eventuality that, on Bertrand's request, and that of some of his friends, Charles V agreed to advance 15,000 *doblas* of each instalment. Jeanne de Penthièvre and Gui, sire de Laval, and his wife also obliged themselves on his behalf for undisclosed sums. The first 15,000

---

3 For different accounts of the circumstances of du Guesclin's release, see Froissart, *Chroniques*, vii, pp. 62–4; Ayala, *Crónica*, i, pp. 561–2; Cuvelier, *Chronique*, ii, lines 13,367ff. Delachenal, iii, pp. 451–5, provides and excellent summary.
4 Ayala, *Crónica*, i, pp. 558–9; Molinier, pp. 179–81.
5 Froissart, *Chroniques*, vii, p. 157.
6 Molinier, pp. 181–2.
7 *CPR, 1377–81*, pp. 199, 210.

doblas promised by Charles V was paid to the prince's financial officers in Bordeaux by the receiver-general of taxes in Languedoc on 25 April 1368, and the entire sum of 100,000 *doblas* was evidently paid in full by July of that year.[8]

Bertrand was released from Bordeaux on 17 January, probably along with Audrehem, with whom he made his way to Nîmes in response to an invitation issued to them by Louis of Anjou to join him in a war which he intended to pursue in Provence. The reasons for the duke's intervention have been much debated by historians.[9] It is unlikely that the Emperor Charles IV, on the occasion of his visit to Avignon in 1365, had ceded to the duke his imperial rights in the ancient kingdom of Arles, but it is possible that Louis may have sought them and believed that the emperor would acquiesce.[10] The attitude of the king of France also bears scrutiny. Certainly Charles V followed the policies of his predecessors in wishing to extend French interests piecemeal towards the Alps and the Mediterranean, and it has been pointed out that, having failed to secure the marriage of Queen Joanna of Naples, countess of Provence, to one of the royal princes, he supported the duke's invasion of the county and even provided reinforcements.[11] However, it seems likely that Charles V's main concern at this stage was to rid Languedoc of some of the companies which had returned to France after the Nájera campaign. This also suited Louis of Anjou, whose declared justification for raising subsidies in Languedoc in the spring of 1368 was the need to remove the companies from the three seneschalsies of that province, but there can be little doubt that he intended to employ them for his personal aggrandizement.[12] Ambitious to increase his wealth

---

8   Cuvelier, *Chronique*, ii, pp. 401–7, PJ nos. xiii–xviii. See Fowler, 1992, pp. 230–1.
9   For what follows, see, in particular, Denifle, ii, pp. 509–28, and the documents published on pp. 778–87 thereof; Labande, 1904, pp. 21–39; Bourilly, pp. 161–80; Léonard, 1934, pp. 422–6; Delachenal, iii, pp. 459–63.
10 Delachenal, iii, p. 226; cf. Bourrilly, p. 162.
11 Joanna's second husband, Louis of Taranto, had died in 1362, and she took as her third husband the Mallorcan Pretender, Jaume IV, later that year, on 14 December 1362 (Luce in Froissart, *Chroniques*, vi, p. xcv n. 2). Louis of Anjou was not available, having married Marie de Châtillon, daughter of Charles of Blois, on 9 July 1360 (Delachenal, ii, p. 281 n. 1). For French interest in the Neapolitan succession after the death of Jaume, see Jarry, pp. 4–24.
12 Labande, 1904, p. 22 n. 4; Bourilly, pp. 163–4; Henneman, ii, pp. 202–4. The three seneschalsies agreed to a *fouage* of 1 franc per hearth at meetings in Nîmes and Beaucaire in the spring of 1368. In the preamble to Anjou's letters (dated Beaucaire, 5 April 1368), announcing agreement to the *fouage*, the delegates are said to have been called 'super provisione necessario facienda ut societates gentium armorum patriam discurrentium et dampnificantium et que diutius et magnis temporibus in dictis partibus remanserant regnum Francie et specialiter dictas partes occitanas desererent et penitus evacuarent ulterius seu a modo minime reversure seu redditure prout dominus Bertrandus de Guerclino, dux Trastamare, et quid alii ex capitaneis dictarum societatum nobis medio juramento promiserant et promiserunt', etc. (AM, Montpellier, armoire H, cassette 6, Louvet, no. 3,961). On 8 April the duke appointed Arnaud Roux receiver of the tax 'pro evacuando et expellendo societates quae nuper in dictis partibus erant' (AD, Hérault, reg. A. 1, fos. 106v–8r).

and power, in 1365 he had attempted to hold up the transfer of the barony of Montpellier, granted to Charles of Navarre under royal treaty, on the grounds that it had been promised to him, although he had been given other lands in its place. His recent negotiations with Enrique of Trastámara and his support of the companies making incursions into the principality of Aquitaine were symptomatic of his desire to see a renewal of the war with England, in which he intended to take a leading part, and from which he doubtless hoped to benefit territorially.

Meanwhile, the prevailing situation in the county of Provence invited his attentions. The countess was far away in Italy and her marriage to the Mallorcan Pretender, Jaume IV, had involved her in a quarrel with Aragon. Moreover, since his participation in the Black Prince's expedition to Castile, Jaume was a prisoner of du Guesclin in Montpellier.[13] With Urban V's return of the papacy to Rome the defensive efforts of recent years in the Comtat Venaissin and the neighbouring provinces east of the Rhône had lost their momentum. With acute political perception, Louis had convoked the assemblies at Nîmes and Beaucaire to secure the necessary finance to remove the companies from the vicinity, realizing the possibility of employing them in Provence. With this intent he had sought the assistance of the person most likely to command their support and to be able to exercise effective authority over them. By 7 February du Guesclin, accompanied by Audrehem, had arrived at Montpellier on their way to consult with the duke in Nîmes. During the course of that month Bertrand, who was appointed captain-general of the ducal army, put together a force of around 2,000 men, largely recruited from the companies, which included the *routes* commanded by the bastard Bernard des Isles, Perrin de Savoie, Petit Meschin, Noli Pavalhon, Amanieu d'Ortigue, Perrot le Béarnais, Bouzomet de Pau, Jacques de Bray and other captains of the companies.[14] In addition to these he may also have been accompanied by the Breton contingents of his brother, Olivier du Guesclin, the Maunys (Olivier, Hervé and Alain) and Alain and Tristan de la Houssaye.[15] On 4 March they crossed the Rhône to besiege Tarascon.

The invasion, mounted on the flimsy excuse of some frontier incident, began with the siege of Tarascon by the forces under du Guesclin's immediate command (4 March to 22 May 1368) and of Arles, initially by

---

13 During the expedition Jaume had fallen ill and remained behind in Valladolid, where he was taken prisoner by Enrique in September or October 1367, only to be transferred to du Guesclin in lieu of part payment of Enrique's debts to Bertrand (Lecoy de la Marche, ii, p. 192; Delachenal, v, p. 45 n. 4). He had initially been taken prisoner by Bernard, bastard of l'Isle-Jourdain, to whom the pope wrote requesting his release (Urban V, *Lettres secrètes*, no. 2658; cf. no. 2621). He was subsequently taken to Montpellier by du Guesclin (Lecoy de la Marche, ii, p. 192; cf. Froissart, *Chroniques*, viii, p. 276).
14 *Thalamus parvus*, 382; Denifle, ii, pp. 781–4, appendix ii, nos. 4, 5; Bourilly, p. 164.
15 Labande, 1904, p. 64 n. 3.

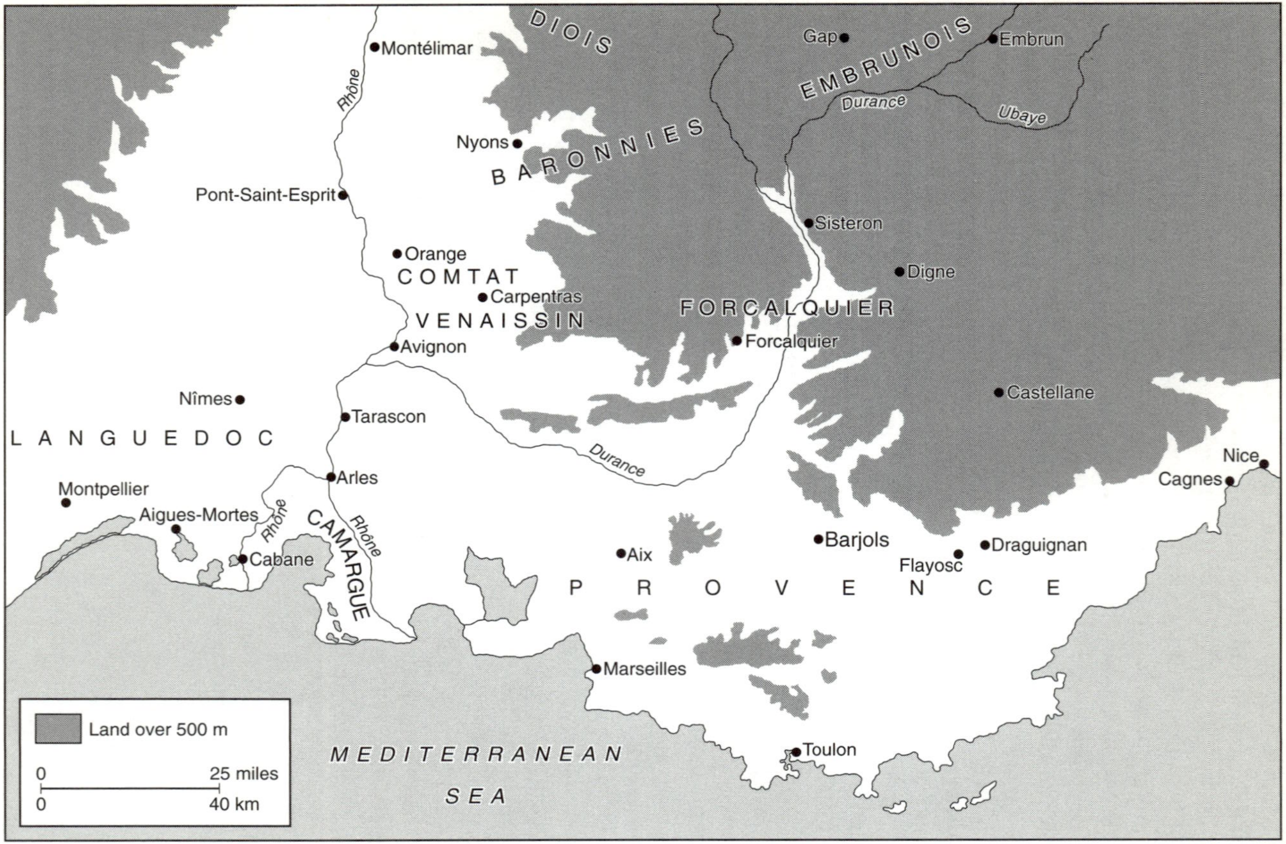

10 *The invasion of Provence, March–September 1368*

those under Louis of Anjou (11 April to 1 May), both towns situated on the east bank of the Rhône downstream from Avignon. The investment of Tarascon, carried out with siege towers and other equipment, on both the land and river side, evidently took longer than had been anticipated at the outset of the campaign,[16] and the siege of Arles was beyond the resources of the companies. After about a month an agreement was concluded with some of the inhabitants of Tarascon whereby the town would be handed over to the besieging army if no outside help was forthcoming within thirty days. Meanwhile, a number of hostages were handed over to the enemy and a messenger was sent to Queen Joanna, informing her of the situation. Du Guesclin then transferred his forces to Arles, which was blockaded for some three weeks.[17]

In the absence of the seneschal of Provence it fell to Louis de Trian, lord of Tallard, to organize the defensive measures made necessary by the invasion. This had been expected and already in January the consuls of Marseille had proceeded with the defence of their town, appointing six commissioners to see to its security and providing for the inspection and repair of the ramparts, towers and moat 'in view of the large number of armed men assembling near Provence'.[18] Tallard appointed four captains to defend Aix. François Baboyci, treasurer of the counties of Provence and Forcalquier, was sent to Avignon to raise funds from the vicar-general, Philippe de Cabassole, and several merchants of that town. The proctor-fiscal, Gautier d'Ulmet, was sent to Marseille to commission a number of armed galleys, which were to be sent up the Rhône and, following the arrangement concluded between du Guesclin and Tarascon, further assistance was sought from Marseille and Nice. The town was evidently sorely pressed, for during the course of April a galley sent by Rainier Grimaldi (the great war contractor of Monaco whose services Baboyci had engaged in Marseille), which was intended to pick up victuals in Avignon, was captured by the companies, although the inhabitants of Avignon had refused to load it. However, other supplies intended for the town were seized.[19] The seneschal then secured a further three armed galleys from Marseille, and these joined up with other forces which had already arrived in the Rhône from Nice and Toulon. With this assistance Arles was able to put up a successful defence. Although Tarascon derived some support from this action, the town finally surrendered on 22 May, some of the inhabitants being accused of treasonable conduct.[20]

16 Delachenal, iii, pp. 461–2, and see the letters published by Denifle, ii, pp. 781–5, appendix ii, nos. 4–6.
17 Bourilly, p. 165.
18 Ibid., p. 166.
19 Denifle, ii, p. 511; *Chron. premiers Valois*, p. 194; Bourilly, p. 168.
20 Bourilly, p. 170.

Another contributing factor to the surrender of Tarascon was the position taken by Grimaldi, who on 18 May had concluded an agreement with Louis of Anjou in Beaucaire. In return for his appointment as admiral of Languedoc and 10,000 florins annual rent, Rainier agreed to put the entire resources of himself, his family and friends at Anjou's disposal for the conquest of Provence, Forcalquier and their neighbouring territories. Several days later, on 3 June, Anjou effectively handed the conduct of the war over to him, authorizing in advance the expenditure he would incur in raising troops, arming galleys and securing other military necessities. He also empowered him to conclude terms with those willing to surrender to him, and promised to make good any damages which he and his associates might suffer because of the war.[21]

This allowed du Guesclin and the companies under his command to turn their attention to other parts of Provence, where galleys and elaborate siege equipment were not required. Augmented by further bands sent out from Languedoc by Anjou, some *routes* crossed the Durance and, without sparing the papal territories through which they passed, entered the county of Forcalquier. Here they planned to join forces with 500 lances which Olivier de Mauny had brought from Pont-Saint-Esprit by way of the Comtat Venaissin and the Baronnies. Still other *routes*, after menacing Aix, proceeded through the Arc valley to Barjols, attacked the fortified village and castle of Flayosc near Draguignan, and then appeared before that town, where they spent a night ransacking the *faubourgs*. They then proceeded to Castellane, from where they were believed to be intending to join forces with those of Grimaldi around Cagnes and Nice. However, the companies made little further headway in the maritime districts of Provence, and two galleys commanded by Rainier's captains, although recruited in Anjou's pay, were set on fire in the Menton roads. To prevent the companies penetrating further into the county of Forcalquier and Céreste the seneschal, Raimond d'Agout, alerted the governor of Dauphiné, requesting him to prevent any forces joining them from that province, and sent reinforcements to Sisteron.[22] He then concentrated the forces under his personal command in the lower Rhône valley, requisitioned all the galleys and barges he could muster there, and even conducted an offensive into Languedoc, where the defensive and piloting facilities at Cabane, which gave entry to the naval base at Aigues-Mortes, were destroyed and a number of prisoners carried off.[23]

Further damage was inflicted towards the end of June by some of the

21 Ibid., pp. 170–1.
22 Ibid., pp. 171–4. They included the company of sixty lances commanded by an Englishmen, 'Jenequin Anglici' (letter from the council of Aix to that of Marseille, AC, Marseille, BB 26, fos. 64v–5r, cited by Bourilly, p. 173 n. 1).
23 Bourilly, p. 174; *HGL*, ix, p. 795.

companies returning across the Rhône.[24] At the end of the month, on Anjou's orders, du Guesclin's companies fell back to the Rhône valley after appearing before Aix with a substantial artillery. Although it was rumoured that Bertrand intended to make a new attempt to take the town, no serious action followed. The main theatre of operations was further north, in the county of Forcalquier, where on 1 August a force of 160 men-at-arms and 300 infantry, which the seneschal had sent to resist the companies and which he subsequently joined, was cut to pieces by them. A large number of knights were killed and at least forty captured. The seneschal, with the help of an Englishman, succeeded in escaping to safety in Sisteron, where the fortifications of the town had recently been substantially improved.[25]

For her part, Queen Joanna, who had been kept informed of the situation in Provence and Forcalquier, had not been altogether inactive. She hired a force of 200 men and six galleys in Genoa, and these were followed by 500 lances under Roger of San Severino, count of Mileto in Calabria, whom she appointed her lieutenant-general. They disembarked at Nice on 11 August. In concert with the seneschal, Roger then summoned a meeting of the Estates to raise a further 200 lances and opened negotiations with Anjou and the governor of Dauphiné concerning the activities of the Dauphinois, who were suspected of collaborating with the companies. By way of reprisal the Provençals had taken to ambushing merchants and travellers entering their county from Dauphiné.[26] Then, with the assistance of English mercenaries who had been operating in Italy, they formed a company under the name of the Company of Saint-George, penetrated the Ubaye valley and ravaged the Embrunois.[27] In spite of the efforts of the archbishop of Embrun, Pierre Ameilh, to contain their activities and the passions they had aroused, this was only the beginning of a war between Provence and Dauphiné, involving a number of the companies, which was to continue for almost a year.[28]

From the outset of the invasion of Provence, Urban V had set in motion such measures as he could to contain the war. He had instructed the captain-general of Avignon and the Comtat Venaissin to conclude an agreement with du Guesclin, which he hoped would guarantee the security of the papal territories. This involved the payment of a ransom of 37,000

---

24 Notably around Chalencon in the Ardèche (AD, Hérault, reg. A 5, fos. 164r–v: letters of Louis of Anjou, dated 23 June 1368, giving instructions for the repair of fortifications and other defensive measures against the companies).
25 Bourilly, pp. 175–6. The Englishman, referred to as 'Richardi Anglici' in a letter of 2 August from the council of Aix to that of Marseille (AC, Marseille, BB 26, fo. 87, cited by Bourilly, p. 175 n. 4), may have been Richard Romsey.
26 Bourilly, p. 176.
27 Denifle, i, p. 519 and n. 2, ii, appendix iii, no. 16, pp. 801–2 and *passim*. See *La Correspondance de Pierre Ameilh*, nos. 401–3, 406, 410 and *passim*.
28 Bourilly, p. 176; see *La correspondance*, no. 401ff.

florins, of which 5,000 were to be handed over to Bertrand's proctor, the Englishman John Clerk, on 24 March. The arrangement involved a number of separate undertakings, given by du Guesclin, Noli Pavalhon, Bouzomet de Pau and Perrin de Savoie, to abide by the agreement and correct any infringements committed by their men or other troops; but they were not adhered to, either through default of payment or otherwise.[29] In addition, on 3 April Urban wrote to the king of France and the emperor, requesting them to bring pressure to bear on Anjou to stop the attacks against the lands and subjects of Queen Joanna.[30] But it was not until June that Charles V took any action, sending the abbot of Cluny first to the duke of Anjou and then to Italy to speak to both the pope and Joanna. Du Guesclin's recall to the Rhône valley at the end of the month may have resulted from the abbot's mission. If so, it did not contain the activities of the companies, which were by then probably no longer under the control of either Bertrand or Anjou.[31]

Urban had also taken other measures to defend Church lands. When the Comtat Venaissin was invaded at the end of May he had instructed the rector and captain-general to constrain those inhabitants who refused to resist them to take up arms under threat of censure.[32] But the worst attacks were still to come. Although walled towns were well enough defended, in July and August the open countryside was remorselessly pillaged and burned. The peasantry were so badly treated that they either appointed captains from among their number to resist the companies, or joined the companies against the local population. A conflict ensued which bore some resemblance to the Jacquerie which had occurred in northern France ten years earlier, and which had similar contributing factors.[33] On 8 August Urban wrote to the archbishop of Lyon, the bishop of Valence and the count of Valentinois, requesting them to assist the rector of the Comtat in the defence of Church lands, whilst at the same time insisting that the inhabitants should pay the taxes imposed on them for their defence.[34]

---

29 For the agreement and the separate undertakings, dated 20–4 March 1368, see Denifle, ii, pp. 778–87, appendix ii. For Clerk, see above, pp. 185n, 205n, and below, p. 295.
30 Urban V, *Lettres secrètes*, nos. 2733, 2741; Prou, pp. 157–8, PJ no. lxxviii. See Labande, 1904, p. 127ff., and Bourilly, p. 177.
31 *Mandements*, no. 454; Prou, p. 72. Cf. Delachenal, iii, p. 463. In an exchange of letters in which Louis d'Anduse, lord of la Voulte, had referred to du Guesclin and his men as *genz de compaigne*, and complained about their behaviour at Tarascon, Bertrand had expressed solidarity with his *petiz compaignons* and, in a letter of 5 July, written from Maillane, some five miles to the north-east of Tarascon, he accused the lord of attacking them and seeking to foment a rebellion (Delisle, 'Deux lettres', pp. 302–3).
32 Denifle, ii, pp. 511–13.
33 Labande, 1904, p. 31, citing AC, Carpentras, reg. CC 154, fo. 3. The peasants also appointed their own leaders to defend their property and interests on the frontiers of Forcalquier (Bourilly, p. 176 and n. 1, citing AD, Bouches-du-Rhône, B 1525).
34 Prou, pp. 72–3, 159–60, PJ nos. lxxx, lxxxi. See Denifle, ii, p. 517.

Then, on 1 September, his indignation could no longer be contained. In a bull of that date, which was not released until 14 September, after recalling the agreement reached before Tarascon in March, and the solemn oaths which du Guesclin and other captains of the companies had entered into, he went on to detail their worst excesses. He then ordered the papal official in Avignon to pronounce them excommunicate and to declare all of the places held by them, or which belonged to them, to be under interdict. They were to be ordered to surrender all goods which they had taken from the faithful around Avignon and in the Comtat, and a prohibition was placed upon receiving goods and trading or entering into any kind of relations with them.[35]

Nevertheless, the companies still had to be bought off. The proceeds of taxes levied on the three estates of the Comtat were applied to the cost of its defence and to the payment of the sums promised to du Guesclin before Tarascon, and advances had to be secured from a number of Avignon bankers in anticipation of the expected revenues. New negotiations then took place with the companies, which, early in the autumn, resulted in their departure from Church lands, to Languedoc and Dauphiné.[36] Some *routes* had already returned to Languedoc early in August, and during the second half of that month Perrin de Savoie, Petit Meschin and Amanieu d'Ortigue, who appear to have been operating in the county of Forcalquier, returned through the principality of Orange.[37] Du Guesclin followed a few weeks later, during the *vendange*.[38] Their presence was by then required in Languedoc, as the Provençals, with the assistance of forces recruited in Lombardy by Queen Joanna, took the war to the west of the Rhône, where their activities penetrated as far as Castres, between Albi and Carcassonne.[39]

It was not until the beginning of November that, under orders from Charles V, Louis of Anjou negotiated a truce to cover Provence with Roger de San Severino. Pending a general settlement this provided for the restitution of the places taken by Anjou's forces. However, although Tarascon was restored to the seneschal of Provence and placed under the command of a captain appointed by him, the truce was badly observed, and the Provençals were obliged to continue to take defensive measures against the possibility of further hostilities from across the Rhône, as well as against

---

35 Prou, pp. 73, 161–3, PJ no. lxxxiii; Labande, 1904, pp. 34–5.
36 Labande, 1904, pp. 35–6.
37 Ibid., pp. 34, 36–7; Bourilly, p. 177. According to Labande, p. 37 n. 1, Perrin de Savoie, Petit Meschin, Amanieu d'Ortigue, Bouzomet de Pau and Noli Pavalhon were enrolled by Anjou on their return to Languedoc in the autumn; but documentary evidence for other captains taken into royal service suggests that their recruitment is more likely to have been at the end of the year, or at the beginning of 1369 (see below, p. 284).
38 *Thalamus parvus*, p. 382.
39 *Douze comptes*, pp. 56–7.

marauding troops from a number of companies who had not returned to Languedoc. An agreement covering Dauphiné did not follow until 1369, and was not confirmed until May of the following year. A definitive settlement for both Provence and Dauphiné had to wait until 1371.[40] Long before that date the majority of the companies under du Guesclin's command had returned with him to the Iberian Peninsula.

After the Black Prince had returned from Castile to Aquitaine, only Sir Hugh Calveley and his men remained behind in Spain from among the prince's forces. The son of David and Joan Calveley of Lea in Cheshire, he had come a long way from the time of his first experiences of warfare in Brittany in the 1340s.[41] Whilst du Guesclin was engaged in Provence, he had been busy pursuing his own interests, as well as those of the prince, at the Aragonese court in Barcelona. He was now considerably more influential there as a result of the prince's victory at Nájera and the part which he had played in bringing about a rapprochement between Edward and the Aragonese king. While it was in Peter IV's interests to bind Calveley more closely in his service, it was equally in Sir Hugh's to make the most of the opportunities which were now presented to him. With his star in the ascendant and that of du Guesclin on the wane, he could consolidate his position at the Aragonese court and at the same time press for payment of certain sums outstanding to him by Bertrand, which he hoped to recoup from Aragonese Crown debts to the Breton captain. To this end, he filed proceedings in the Aragonese chancery court on 4 March 1368 through his proctor, Mark Foster.[42]

According to Foster the sums outstanding to Calveley for the wages of himself and his men from the time he had been in Bertrand's service in 1366 amounted to 55,000 florins.[43] In addition to a quarter of Borja and Magallón, which Calveley could claim under the terms of his indenture with du Guesclin, and which Foster estimated to have an annual rental value of 2,500 florins, making a total of 5,500 florins outstanding to date, he also had claims to a quarter of the revenues of Elda and Novelda in the kingdom of Valencia, which had initially been granted to du Guesclin. Nothing could be done about the latter, since in February 1367 Bertrand had surrendered all the financial claims which he had on Pere (save for the

---

40 Bourilly, pp. 178–80.
41 For his earlier career, see Fowler, 1991b, pp. 243–5, and my biography of him in the *New Dictionary of National Biography*.
42 For what follows, see Fowler, 1991b, pp. 249–51; 1992, pp. 232–5. The principal documentation here used is drawn from ACA, Cancilleria, regs. 734, fos. 129v–30v; 738, fos. 40v–6r; 1344, fos. 70v–1r, 109r–v; 1345, fos. 94v–5r, 128v, 132v, 137r–9r; 1346, fos. 18v, 102v; 1347, fos. 59r–v, 155r–6r; 1969, fo. 40r; Real Patrimonio, MR, reg. 353, fos. 125r, 161r, 176v; 356, fo. 81r; 645, fos. 154r–5r.
43 These were 'florins of Perpignan', minted from 1346 at Perpignan.

grants of Borja and Magallón and the services of two ships and a galley, which the king had also granted to him) for 40,000 florins, which were to have been paid by July of that year.[44] However, following Bertrand's capture at Nájera, 15,700 florins of the residue of the moneys outstanding to him had been made over to the Black Prince towards the payment of his ransom. To complicate Foster's calculations further, Calveley had himself secured a grant of the town of Elda as well as the castle and town of Mola, also in Valencia, in August of that year in realization of the 2,000 florins' annual rent granted to him in February 1366.

Nevertheless, he had endeavoured to recover some of the moneys outstanding to him, but without success, and had clearly written to du Guesclin about the matter. In a friendly reply, which Bertrand had written to him on 19 March, whilst besieging Tarascon, the Breton had himself proposed to Calveley that he could recover what he was due from the moneys outstanding to him by Pere. He also somewhat dubiously attributed Hugh's failure to secure his quarter part of Borja and Magallón to the actions of his cousin, Olivier de Mauny, whom he had appointed captain there under oath never to surrender them save to himself in person. The letter containing these details was delivered to Calveley by his cousin, Henry Bernard, who had previously been in the Black Prince's service in France, but who had subsequently been retained by du Guesclin. Bernard also brought Calveley another letter from Bertrand, authorizing payment of the residue of wages for military service still outstanding to him and his men, the total of which they were agreed upon, from Aragonese Crown debts which Bertrand claimed to be still outstanding to him. By way of conclusion, in words which are particularly revealing, he had urged Hugh to join him in Provence, 'where my lord of Anjou is making war, and where I think you will have more profit than in any other place. And if you are unable to come yourself, please send me Henry Bernard with your companions as soon as you can.'

Just over a fortnight before this letter was written, du Guesclin had been summoned to represent himself in court by 24 March, either in person or through a proctor, failing which judgement would be given in favour of the litigant, who would also be awarded full costs. Bertrand chose to be represented by the *viguier* of Toulouse, Gaston de la Parade, who appeared in court on the 24th to hear Foster present Calveley's case. The following Tuesday, the 28th, de la Parade presented the court with an instrument drawn up by French royal notaries and dated 1 March, which indicated that the Aragonese Crown debts still outstanding to du Guesclin totalled not 28,000 florins (as Calveley's proctor had been led to believe), but 42,000 florins, which were due to be paid to Bertrand in Montpellier in

---

44 See appendix A, no.4.

two instalments, 22,000 before 27 March and the remaining 20,000 by 20 November following. In addition, de la Parade pointed out that Bertrand still had claims to the services of the two armed ships and the galley, which had not been renounced in the settlement of February 1367. This was not contentious. More serious, the proctor indicated that he intended to demonstrate that Calveley's claims were not well founded, and that they did not constitute a valid reason for witholding the second instalment of what was due to Bertrand. In an allusion to other English claims on Pere's debts to du Guesclin – a reference, it would seem, to the attempts then being made to secure part of the Nájera ransom money – Bertrand had requested the Aragonese king to be generous to him. Having in mind the damage which du Guesclin's companies could do in Catalonia, on 1 April Pere ordered his officers in Roussillon to pay the first instalment as soon as possible; but in view of the difficulties in resolving Calveley's claims to a fourth part of the lands granted to Bertrand by the king, the case was adjourned until the beginning of June. In the event, it was not resumed until 27 July, and because du Guesclin then failed to represent himself in court, Calveley's proctor requested that judgement be given in his favour.[45]

It was at this critical juncture that Foster produced du Guesclin's letter to Sir Hugh of 19 March, in which Bertrand had quite clearly indicated that he accepted liability for the payment of the fourth part of the revenues of Borja and Magallón, and had suggested that Hugh recover them out of Aragonese Crown debts to him. The case was then referred to the royal council, who remitted it to the court, where, after much debate between the lawyers, who were initially divided on the matter, judgement was finally given in Calveley's favour on 4 August. Pere had, in fact, already anticipated the court's decision on 24 July, when he ordered the payment to Sir Hugh of 3,000 florins of the 20,000 outstanding to du Guesclin. However, this sum was only paid to Calveley by the king's treasurer at the beginning of August, and only then after he had received a sworn declaration from Hugh that he would reimburse the treasury if the judgement of the court went against him. In the following years, Calveley only appears to have secured a further 1,800 florins of the Aragonese debts to du Guesclin, and as late as 1395 Sir Hugh's heir, John Calveley, was still endeavouring to recover the remaining 15,200 of the 20,000 florins in question.

This did not mean that Sir Hugh's influence at court was less than he might have hoped. The Aragonese king could clearly not afford to antagonize du Guesclin, who crossed the frontier into Roussillon and threatened to invade Catalonia in August, and had to be pacified by more tempting

---

45 A new summons had been issued to du Guesclin on 4 June, instructing him to represent himself in the Aragonese court within twenty-six days of its receipt. This had been handed over to him at La Motte, in Provence, on 30 June.

offers.[46] On 2 October Pere wrote to Francesch de Perellós indicating that he had seen the agreements then concluded with Bertrand, and that he did not intend to get involved further in the dispute between the Breton captain and Calveley.[47] Nevertheless, the continued presence of the Cheshire knight and his troops remained highly desirable, and on more than one occasion Pere was to indicate his indebtedness to him. Sir Hugh's position had also been greatly strengthened through his friendly relations with Pere's queen, Elionor of Sicily, who exerted a powerful influence at court.[48] She had introduced him to one of the ladies of her household, Constança, the daughter of a Sicilian baron, Bonifacio d'Aragon.[49] The circumstances of their first meeting are not known, although it was evidently before July 1367, when Calveley sent four minstrels to serenade her.[50] He may have accompanied the queen's household when it travelled to Valencia in December 1367, and he continued to provide musical entertainment for the queen's ladies after he and Constança were married in June 1368.[51] Elionor made a substantial contribution to the cost of Constança's trousseau and to the dresses of the ladies in waiting who attended her at the ceremonies which took place in Barcelona to mark the occasion.[52] It was with the queen that Calveley had initially had to treat for Constança's hand, and doubtless Elionor had brought pressure to bear with her husband on the matter of Constança's dowry. Pere had amply provided for this in a charter of 24 May, by which date the marriage contract had evidently been concluded. Extensive rights and jurisdiction were settled on the couple in

---

46 See below, pp. 259–66.
47 ACA, Cancilleria, reg. 1347, fo. 59r–v.
48 For Elionor's influence see Pere, III, *Chronicle*, Introduction, p. 22ff; Tasis, p. 215ff.
49 ACA, Cancilleria, reg. 916, fo. 38r. Constança's residence in the queen's household is evident from the payments made to her and her lady-in-waiting for residence, meals, robes and shoes recorded in the accounts of Elionor's treasurer during the period from January 1366 to June 1368, but not thereafter (ACA, Real Patrimonio, MR, regs. 488, fos. 52v, 69r, 76v, 91r, 94v, 96r, 104v; 489, fos. 51v, 58r, 70r, 76v, 85r, 94r, 96r; 490, fos. 53v, 62r, 71v, 84r, 91r, 101r, 109r, 491, fos. 55v, 67r, 71r, 80v, 83v). I have not consulted the accounts for the years prior to 1366.
50 The queen rewarded them with twelve gold florins in July 1367 (ACA, Real Patrimonio, MR, reg. 490, fo. 53r).
51 The costs of the removal of the queen's household from Barcelona to Valencia are recorded in her treasurer's accounts (ACA, Real Patrimonio, MR, reg. 491, fo. 51r), as is the month of the marriage in the entries for July 1368 relating to the costs of materials purchased by Elionor for Constança's trousseau: 'a la noble na Constança d'Arago, donzella de casa sua, per les noçes que fo ab moss. Huch de Cavarloys en lo mes de juyn prop passat' (ibid., reg. 492, fo. 52v). In the following August the queen instructed her treasurer to pay twenty gold florins to 'Johanni Bearo, Anagera Mixaler et Johan Trompeta, ministrers de moss. Huch de Cavarlays' (ibid., fo. 63r).
52 Constança's annual allowance for robes in the queen's household was 360 *sueldos* of Barcelona (ACA, Real Patrimonio, reg. 489, fo. 94r; reg. 490, fo. 101r), but this was greatly exceeded by the cost of her trousseau, which amounted to over 597 Aragonese florins (i.e. 6,577 *sueldos* 8 *dineros* of Barcelona), recorded in two disbursements for July 1368 (ibid., reg. 492, fos. 52v–3r, 54v–5r).

the barony and castellany of Cervellón, a possession of the viscount of Bruni situated alongside the river Llobregat, just outside Barcelona. In addition Pere granted them the rights he had hitherto retained in Elda and Mola. The whole dowry had an annual value of 40,000 *libra* of Barcelona (some 3,636 florins), and was granted to them in perpetuity.[53] Other grants and transactions in which Calveley was the beneficiary and which were made around this time suggest that from 1368 he was planning to settle in Aragon. In the summer of that year, after acquiring the castle and place of Aspe, also in Valencia, and disposing of certain annuities which he held in Aquitaine, he purchased the castle and valley of Novelda from his comrade-in-arms, Sir Matthew Gournay.[54] His combined possessions in the kingdom of Valencia thus gave him considerable interests on the Castilian and Granadian frontiers.

No mention is made of Calveley's continuing service with the prince following Edward's return to the principality in September 1367, although he evidently continued to have interests there.[55] He was not involved in subsequent negotiations between the prince and Pere, although the king probably relied heavily on his judgement in these affairs. But in the spring of 1369, as Anglo-French relations deteriorated further and the clouds of war rolled in, he was recalled to Aquitaine and appears never again to have returned to Spain. His involvement north of the Pyrenees, which in the event proved permanent, was to send him on a different course from that which was in prospect in 1368.[56] Whether or not his return to the principality contributed to the estrangement of his wife, who appears not to have accompanied him, cannot now be determined.[57] There was no hint of open discord between them in a letter which Pere wrote to his eldest son, Joan, in December 1373, informing him that on the petition of

53   ACA, Cancilleria, reg. 916, fos. 38r–40v. On the same day Pere wrote to his eldest son, Joan, duke of Gerona, informing him of the grant and requesting his approval in letters under his seal (ibid., fos. 62v–3r). Novelda had been granted to Matthew Gournay on 9 June 1367 (ibid., reg. 914, fo. 69), but the king had retained certain rights there, as he had at Elda (ibid., reg. 1347, fo. 156v).
54   ACA, Cancilleria, reg. 915, fos. 167v–70r for Aspe; reg. 916 fos. 39r, 47v–8r for the purchase of Novelda and the annuities which Calveley enjoyed at Gardères (possibly dép. Landes, arr. and cant. Mont-de-Marsan) and Florencia (possibly dép. Gers, arr. Condom). See Fowler, 1992, pp. 237–8.
55   On 22 August 1368 Pere issued letters of safe-conduct for the bastard of la Tour and several others in his following from Calveley's household going to Aquitaine 'cum aliquibus alariis et aliis canibus et uno sturcio' (ACA, Cancilleria, reg. 916, fo. 36r).
56   For his subsequent career, see below, pp. 284, 288, 292–5, and my entry on him in the *New Dictionary of National Biography*.
57   However, a sign of trouble ahead may be indicated by an entry in the accounts of Queen Elionor's treasurer for April 1369, after Calveley's recall: 'Item, done a la nobla madonna Constança d'Arago, muller del noble moss. Huch de Calvilley, los quels la senyora reyna ab letra esser donats per algunas rahons o necessitats sues segons que apparer en la dita letra, laquel io cobre ensemps ab apoches – C florins d'or' (ACA, Real Patrimonio, MR, reg. 493, fo. 81r).

Thomas Bernard, who was acting as proctor for both Hugh and Constança, he had released them from all inquisitions in the valley of Elda.[58] Some three-and-a-half years later, when Pere wrote to Constança, who was then residing on their estates in Valencia, the story was a different one. Explaining that Sir Hugh had requested him to inform her that he had decided to sell all of his Aragonese possessions, he informed her that she could therefore no longer remain in Valencia, and that she was to leave peaceably and without contestation with Calveley's proctor, who would take her to her husband. She would also be accompanied, as honour required, by her cousin, Antoni de Vilaregut, one of Pere's councillors and a distinguished humanist.[59]

The possessions in question were in the castles and places of Elda and Aspe. These and 4,000 *sueldos* annual rent, which Pere had granted Calveley from rents due to the king in Murviedro, were to be sold to Pere for 40,000 Aragonese florins, the equivalent value of which was to be paid to Calveley or his proctor in Bruges, in either French francs or English nobles. However, in the agreement concluded on this matter between Pere and Hugh's proctor, Thomas Bernard, it was specifically stated that Constança was to give an undertaking not to oppose the sale on the grounds that it was part of her dowry, and Sir Matthew Gournay, who was believed to have rights in them, was also to give his approval.[60] Calveley had, in fact, disposed of the castle of Mola to Gournay and made a number of undertakings to him concerning certain rights in his other possessions in Valencia, in an indenture concluded between the two men at Bordeaux in November 1371.[61] Constança refused to comply with either her husband's or the king's wishes, and Pere was obliged to write to her again, this time in more conciliatory terms, informing her that he was sending one of his officers, the *battle-general* of the kingdom of Valencia, to explain certain matters touching her husband's affairs.[62]

Despite their pleadings, Constança held her ground, and in the spring of 1380, after Calveley had almost died in a storm in which most of the ships transporting an expeditionary force to Brittany had been destroyed, and was clearly envisaging retirement from active service, Pere was obliged to write to the governor of Valencia, informing him that Sir Hugh had requested that she should be forced to join him, 'since a wife should follow and stay with her husband'. Pere, considering his request entirely just and

58   ACA, Cancilleria, reg. 1240, fo. 23r–v.
59   Ibid., reg. 1260, fo. 98r (Barcelona, 20 July 1377). On Vilaregut, see Tasis, p. 337.
60   ACA, Cancilleria, reg. 1260, fo. 102r–v.
61   ACA, Cancilleria, reg. 922, fos. 118r–19v (notarial instrument, reciting the indenture, both dated Bordeaux, 7 November 1371, confirmed by Pere in letters dated Barcelona, 7 June 1372). See appendix A, no. 7.
62   Ibid., reg. 1260, fo. 189r (12 December 1377). Similar letters were sent to Vilaregut, Joan Ximènic de Salanova and the *battle-general*.

noting that Calveley had undertaken to meet the entire expenses of the journey, both of Constança and of those accompanying her, ordered the governor to force her to go and, if she refused, to shut her up in a Minorite convent, instruct the abbess and nuns to make sure that she could not escape, and sequestrate her belongings.[63] However, Constança had a protector and a lover, who was no less than the king's son and heir, Joan, who, although recently married to Yolande of Bar, took her into his household as his mistress. In a letter to Joan, written in Zaragoza on 31 May 1381, Pere expressed his displeasure at the relationship in no uncertain terms, pointing out that Constança was 'the wife of a notable and distinguished knight in feats of arms, who is our servant, who, thank God, was the first and principal cause of the recovery of our kingdom from King Don Pedro of Castile, for which reason his honour should the more so be maintained and defended by us and with our bodies, and we should in no way speak ill of him or shame him. For nobody should be rewarded for service or other things, if not he.' The king ordered his son that, 'the moment you have seen this letter, you cast out the said Constança, not only from your house, but also from your land, for a person as defamed as she should be supported by no man. And take care never to be in a public place with her, but put an end to the disgrace into which you have fallen, and put an end in the same way to the scandal that could follow.'[64]

It is not known whether Joan took any action following the receipt of this letter, which was clearly written following complaints from Calveley. On 17 April Pere had written to Sir Hugh's proctor, Thomas Bernard:

You have said to us that it has come to your knowledge that we have made certain provisions in favour of Dona Constança of Aragon which are prejudicial to Sir Hugh Calveley. And we wish Sir Hugh to know, and yourself also, that we would not hold him in such low esteem and so reward Constança, nor take so little to heart the great and wise service which the said Sir Hugh has rendered to us. Neither for her nor for any other person would we wish to prejudice him, but would regard our life as lost if we did not show all the honour and favour which we can to a person who is right worthy of them.[65]

Although Pere had been altogether opposed to his son's marriage to Yolande of Bar, and would have preferred to cement the English alliance through a union with John of Gaunt's daughter, Catalina, he had no regard

---

63   Ibid., reg. 1267, fos. 82v–3r (Barcelona, 18 April 1380). See appendix A, no. 8. For the shipwreck, see Walsingham, *Hist. Anglicana*, i, p. 426; *Chron. Angliae*, p. 254.
64   ACA, Cancilleria, reg. 1272, fos. 62v–3r (letter sent out under the king's signature); see appendix A, no. 9. Yolande (Violant in Catalonia) was Joan's third and last wife. They were married on 2 February 1380. His second wife, Marthe, daughter of Jean d'Armagnac, whom he had married in 1372, had died in 1378 (Pere III, *Chronicle*, ii, pp. 589 n. 14, 594 n. 28).
65   ACA, Cancilleria, reg. 1272, fo. 11v.

for Constança, whose affair with Joan further inflamed the deteriorating relationship between father and son.[66] In a letter to the authorities of Zaragoza, the king referred to her as 'that vile black woman, daughter of the devil', complaining of her disobedience, 'for which, if God wishes, you will punish her and similarily others who disobey us'.[67] However, it was not until December 1384, after the settlement of a difference over the castle and place of Aspe between Calveley and Sir Matthew Gournay, that the sale of the castles of Elda and Aspe to Pere, for 20,000 florins, finally took place. The king then believed himself to be in a position to write to Hugh that he shortly expected to be able to inform him of a satisfactory conclusion of his affairs in Aragon, in respect of both Constança and other matters.[68]

It is not known if, but it is unlikely that, Constança ever joined her husband in the ten years which elapsed between then and Sir Hugh's death; but the settlement of Calveley's affairs in Aragon was far from concluded. In 1392-5, with the support of Richard II and the duke of Lancaster, Calveley and Gournay, and after Sir Hugh's death in 1393 his nephew and heir, Sir John Calveley, were actively pursuing claims in the Aragonese court amounting to 300,000 francs. These included: the grant of galleys made in 1366; 15,200 florins, and rent and interest thereon for his part claims to Borja and Magallón; 10,000 florins promised by Pere on the sale of the barony of Cervellón; outstanding arrears of 4,000 florins annual rent which had been assigned in Valencia; 1,000 *doblas* given to Pere's *majordomo*; and a half of Aspe, which had been granted to Matthew Gournay.

Calveley's heir was clearly pushing his luck, and Joan, now king, seems to have been justified and reasonable in his responses. He was prepared to accept the 1,000 *doblas* given to Pere's *majordomo*, to admit Gournay's claim in respect of Aspe, and to sanction payment of the 10,000 florins for the sale of Cervellón, if the sale had actually taken place; but he could do nothing about it if this claim could not be admitted through Hugh's failure to enforce his rights. He was unable to accept the claims for the galleys, which we know to have been granted for a specific purpose and for a limited period, during which the grant had not been taken up. The 15,200 florins and 2,000 florins arrears of annual rent he rightly found not to be owing; but he was prepared to allow the claim concerning Borja and

---

66 Joan announced his intention to marry Yolande and not Catalina in a letter of 21 April 1379 to an Aragonese magnate, Pedro Boyl. Pere's efforts to prevent the union led to a serious estrangement between the two men (Russell, p. 278 n. 2).
67 Letter of Pere, quoted by Tasis, p. 363.
68 ACA, reg. 1289, fo. 63v (Perelada, 10 December 1384). See Fowler, 1992, p. 238 and n. 92, to which should be added, for the dispute over Aspe, ACA, Cancelleria, reg. 1274, fo. 19r.

Magallón, even though Hugh had never taken possession of the places. However, the case was still pending when Joan died, and his successor, Martin, committed it to two doctors of law in 1398. In addition to these claims on the Aragonese treasury, Gournay was also pursuing an alleged debt of 1,000 florins at the Castilian court in 1402. The lawyers, at least, were making money out of the activities of the mercenaries. As for Sir Hugh, the prospects of living the life of a wealthy and powerful Aragonese magnate, so clearly in his grasp in 1368, never materialized, and for all his undoubted abilities as a soldier, during the ensuing years he never achieved the power and eminence which were to be bestowed on his contemporary, Sir John Hawkwood, in Italy.[69]

---

69 For the details in this paragraph, see Fowler, 1992, pp. 238–9. Hawkwood's career will be dealt with in full in *Medieval Mercenaries II*. Pending publication, see Fowler, 1998, and my short biographies of both men in the *New Dictionary of National Biography*.

11

The Sardinian Proposals and the Drama of Montiel

The return of the companies from Provence posed immediate problems for Louis of Anjou in his capacity as Charles V's lieutenant-general in Languedoc. In the autumn of 1368, the southern seneschalsies were overrun with companies of Bretons, Gascons and Lombards, who threatened the stability of the province. Some units could be absorbed into the forces which Anjou was beginning to assemble for the renewal of the war with England, although active recruitment does not appear to have got under way before the end of the year and only increased significantly early in 1369. Another alternative was to send them across the Pyrenees, either to assist Enrique of Trastámara, whose return to Castile was now over a year old, or to harry the king of Aragon, who, thanks in large measure to the efforts of Calveley, had arrived at a rapprochement following the prince's victory at Nájera.[1] No immediate decision appears to have been taken at an official level on either of these possibilities, and in November Anjou was obliged to contract loans with a number of Toulouse merchants, among others, to pay the companies to depart.[2] It was at this juncture that du Guesclin was engaged by the duke to lead them out of Languedoc.[3]

Nevertheless, during the late summer and early autumn of 1368 rumours of an invasion by the companies were rife in Catalonia. Already in August a number of *routes* under du Guesclin were reported to have crossed the frontier into Roussillon.[4] In the following month Peter IV feared that they and other companies commanded by the count of l'Isle-Jourdain and other captains were about to penetrate Catalonia through Cerdagne, and he evidently believed that Bertrand's urgent need for money to pay the debts contracted for his ransom, as well as Aragonese Crown debts to him,

---
1 Russell, pp. 116–30.
2 *Thalamus parvus*, pp. 382–3; Delachenal, iv, pp. 107 n 2; 158 n. (letters obligatory and orders for payment of Louis of Anjou).
3 Delachenal, iii, p. 369 n. 4.
4 *Cortes de Cataluña*, iii, p. 12; Russell, p. 141.

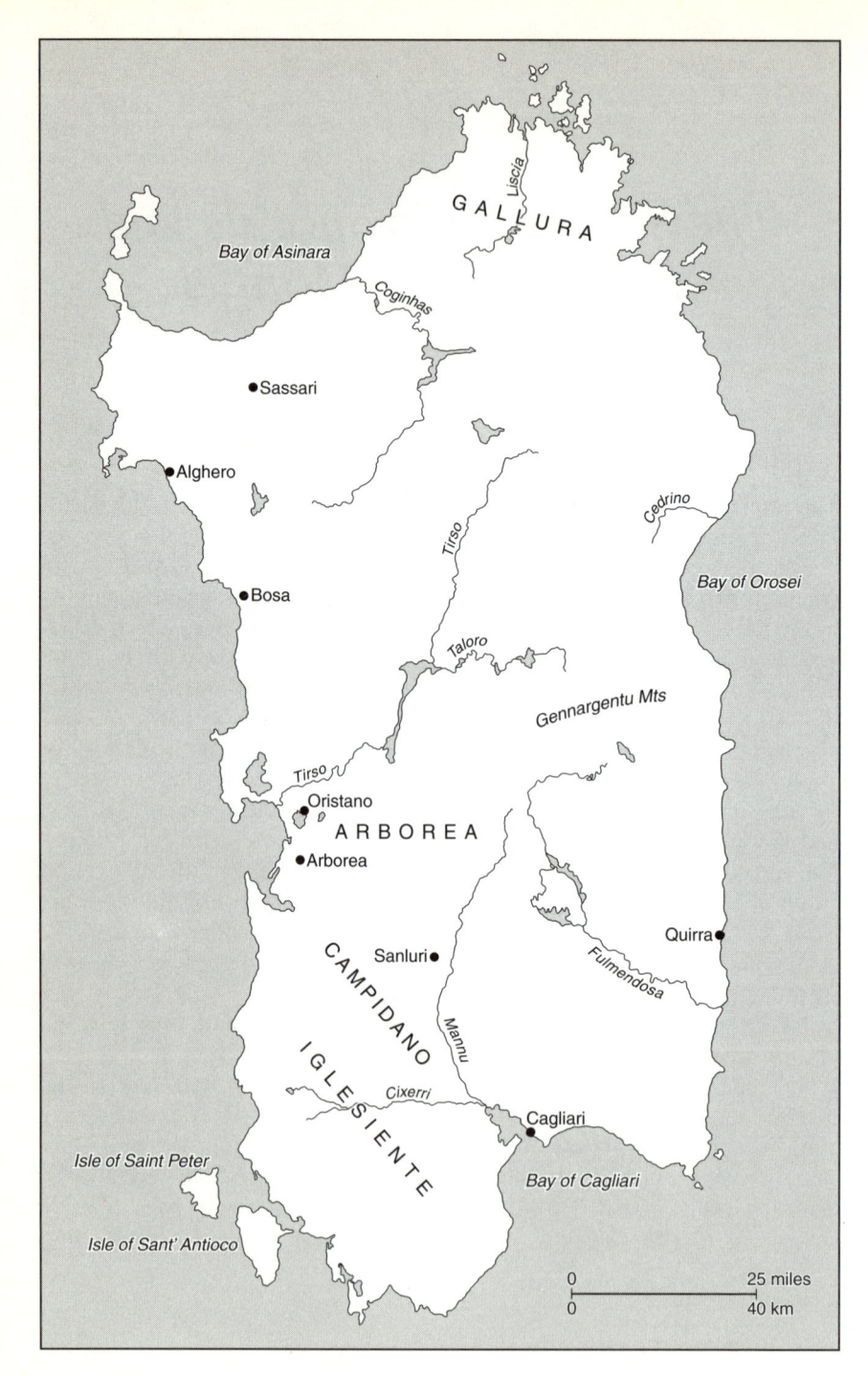

11 *Sardinia in the fourteenth century*

would provide the occasion and excuse for an incursion into his lands.[5] As it happened, Francesch de Perellós and Jean de Rye were at the time present in the Aragonese court in Barcelona as envoys of Charles V, seeking to bring about a rapprochement between Pere and Enrique. Not knowing the full extent of their remit, the king sent them on a mission to du Guesclin, to settle the matter of the moneys Bertrand claimed to be still outstanding to him, and to make certain other offers which were evidently intended to deflect the threatened invasion.[6]

The offers in question concerned a projected expedition to Sardinia, where a rebellion had broken out led by the *jutge* of Arborea. The Aragonese position had steadily deteriorated since the initial proposals for a campaign there had been put to du Guesclin in January and February 1367.[7] A force which had been sent to the island under Pere de Luna, who had been appointed the king's lieutenant there, and whose first task had been to relieve the town of Oristano, which was besieged by rebel forces, had suffered a succession of misfortunes before being defeated in May 1368 in a bloody battle in which de Luna, his brother, and a large part of his army had been killed. The *jutge*, Marià (or Mariano) d'Arborea, had then taken Sassari and, despite urgent appeals for help to be sent from Catalonia, Pere had to date only despatched a small force of two galleys under Francesch d'Averço. The Aragonese position had been further weakened by internal discords and their hold on the island reduced to two places, Cagliari and Alghero. Believing that victory would shortly be his, Marià had rallied all of the aggrieved parties against Aragonese rule. Conscious of the seriousness of the situation, Pere had determined to rally morale by proposing to lead an army to the island himself. He had begun to enlist troops under the royal standard when the latest threat from the companies, who had returned from Provence to Languedoc, emerged.

The proposals for du Guesclin to contribute substantially to the army destined to re-establish Aragonese power in Sardinia were actively pursued by Bertrand, who sent Arnaud de Lar, Charles V's secretary and his *rector* at Montpellier, together with Maurice de Tréséguidy, a Breton knight in Bertrand's entourage, as his nuncios and proctors to the Aragonese court. They were given full powers to treat on his behalf with Pere's deputies, namely Romeo Çescones, bishop of Lérida; Pere, count of Urgell; and

---

5 ACA, Cancilleria, reg. 1347, fos. 50v, 55r (letters from Pere to the governor of Roussillon, dated 12 and 21 September).
6 ACA, Cancilleria, reg. 1080, fo. 70r–v (letters of credence, dated Barcelona, 21 September 1368); see Delachenal, iii, pp. 471–2, 472 n. 1. On 19 July Perellós and Rye had been sent by Charles V on a double mission to Spain which also included the negotiation of an alliance with Enrique (Delachenal, iii, pp. 464–7; see below, pp. 269–70).
7 For the initial proposals, see above, p. 204, and for the situation in Sardinia, Tasis, pp. 288–9.

Francesch de Perellós.[8] Du Guesclin obviously took the new possibilities to renew his fortunes seriously. Excommunicated by the pope, heavily in debt to the Black Prince, and perhaps also still to Calveley and other captains who had fought with him in Spain, no other employ was as yet in prospect. However, the terms that Pere was prepared to offer him were dictated by the immediate threat which the companies posed in Aragon, and the king's prime concern was evidently to maintain the inviolability of his frontiers.

The Sardinian proposals, contained in twelve *capitulis* which were confirmed by Pere and du Guesclin's proctors in the queen's apartments of the royal palace in Barcelona on 17 October, and in a number of subsidiary letters dated there on the 17th, 19th and 22nd of that month, were based on two public instruments which had been drawn up by French notaries on 7 and 11 October.[9] The principal clauses (1–4 and 8–11) dealt with arrangements for the proposed expedition and the conditions of service of Bertrand and his men. They provided that, in the event of Pere or his son, Joan, duke of Gerona, leading an expedition to Sardinia against the *jutge*, du Guesclin, with Charles V's permission, would accompany either of them with a personal force of 1,200 lances and 400 archers. In the event of the king or the duke being unable to go, du Guesclin would take charge as captain-general and lieutenant, or find some other captain who would provide a further 500 lances and 200 archers. Perellós, the governor of Roussillon, Francesch Çagarriga, or two of them, were to verify that these forces were 'good and sufficient', as well as those of the king, who would send a minimum of 300–700 mounted men and 1,000 infantry, who were to include crossbow men and shield bearers (*ballistarios et empavesatos*). If Bertrand was able to take up the expedition he was to have a personal monthly allowance of 1,000 French francs for himself and his household, or their equivalent in Aragonese florins; but, if he was not, a captain going in his place would receive only 500 florins. The pay of the forces was to be at the rate of 100 florins a month for captains who commanded 500 or more lances; for each man-at-arms and archer an advance would be made of 25 florins a month. Pere was to provide, at his own expense, the necessary galleys, ships and other vessels required for shipment for

---

8 ACA, Cancilleria, reg. 1346, fo. 99r.
9 The main part of the agreement containing the *capitulis* is contained in a notarial instrument dated 17 October and headed: 'Conveno facto inter dominum regem et Bertrandum de Guercliono seu eis procuratores inter cetera promisit idem Bertrandus servire domino rege in insula Sardiniae' (ibid., fos. 99r–104r). The public instruments of 7 and 11 October upon which they are based were drawn up by Jean de Fontaines and Alain Petit, two French royal notaries. For the subsidiary letters, see ibid., fos. 104r–7v, 119r–2v, 124v.

both the outward and return journeys to Sardinia of the troops, horses, arms and other equipment; and the port envisaged for their embarkation was Collioure, to the south of Perpignan. The first month's pay was to be calculated from the day the forces left for that port, and the last was to end on the date of their return home, *ad domus proprias*, from the port of disembarkation in Aragonese territory. Accounting was to be on a three-monthly basis. The pay for the first three months was to be handed over at Collioure, or such other port of embarkation as the king might determine, but only after du Guesclin and his men had secured the permission of Charles V to undertake the expedition, and after they had sworn to serve Pere loyally. They were to continue in the king's service in Sardinia for as long as Pere, the duke of Gerona, or the king's captain-general determined (whether du Guesclin or some other person in his place), but were not to be paid in advance for any such extension. However, if the king or the duke decided not to undertake the expedition, the captains and their men were not obliged to go either.

Clauses 9–11 dealt with the arrangements once the army had arrived in Sardinia. Should the lands of the *jutge* be conquered, du Guesclin was to have half of them, to be held as a vassal of the king of Aragon. Prisoners and movable goods taken by him and his men in the *jutge's* lands could be disposed of as they saw fit, save in the event of Marià d'Arborea or his son being captured, in which case they could not be released without the express permission of the king. Any disputes over these matters were to be settled by the count of Urgell and du Guesclin. Castles and fortresses taken in the island by Bertrand's forces could be garrisoned by them in the king's name, but were to be handed over to the king's officers on request. However, an exception was made for the castle of Sanluri, a possession of Ponç de Senesterra, count of Quirra, which could only be garrisoned by Pere's men. In the event of du Guesclin's forces returning from Sardinia without any of the territories held by Marià d'Arborea being conquered, or of a peace or some other agreement having been concluded with the *jutge*, then the remuneration of his forces was to be determined by the counts of Urgell, Denia and Ampurias, or two of them.

The remaining clauses (5–7 and 12) reveal all of Pere's concern about the presence of the companies on the northern frontier of his kingdom. In addition to requiring Bertrand to renew his homage and fealty as a vassal of the Crown of Aragon, he was to undertake not to enter Pere's lands with his men, nor to instruct or permit them to enter without Pere's express licence. He was also to get the captains in his service and obedience to give a similar undertaking, especially those whom Pere's envoys (Perellós and Rye) had noted were with du Guesclin whilst on their mission to Bertrand in September. These included, among others, three captains of the companies – Perrin de Savoie, Noli Pavalhon (alias Papillon) and Amanieu d'Ortigue – and five other captains.[10] In particular, Bertrand was not to attempt to recover by force the lands and places which he had held by grant of the king of Aragon, to some of which he had surrendered his claims in February 1367, and those which had been the subject of the court ruling in favour of Sir Hugh Calveley.[11] Instead, he was to proceed through a proctor furnished with sufficient powers and, in the event of any fortress and lands being returned to him under court order, their release would be embodied in a public instrument which would provide that his military officers (*alcaides*) and other officers and vassals holding them would be obliged, in their oaths of fealty, to recognize their ultimate obedience to the king. This particular clause clearly reflected the intransigence which Pere's officers had encountered from Olivier de Mauny's deputy as du Guesclin's captain at Borja.[12] They may also have met with a similar lack of cooperation from the captains and other officers in Valencia to which Bertrand had surrendered his claims in the agreement concluded in February 1367, of which the financial undertaking made by Pere, modified in a further agreement concluded in March 1368, had still not been fulfilled.[13] Du Guesclin was to give an additional undertaking that neither he nor his men would enter or damage Aragonese lands within three months of the return of any of these lands or fortresses to him – a delay perhaps intended to cover Pere's possible absence in Sardinia – and the captains whom Perellós had noted in Bertrand's company during the initial overtures were to act as sureties of this undertaking. A final attempt to secure du Guesclin's compliance with all of these arrangements was made in a clause which would oblige him to support Pere 'against everyone in the world', with some notable exceptions, namely the king of France and his brothers, the duke of Orléans, the heirs of Charles of Blois and Enrique of Trastámara. In regard to the last, Pere's envoys clearly experienced some difficulties, given Pere's evident intention to secure the territories which Enrique had earlier surrendered to him in return for Aragonese support against Pedro of Castile in 1366. In the event of his deciding to make good these claims, he would first request Enrique for their return within a period of three months, of which du Guesclin would be informed, before proceeding to other means. The Black Prince's victory at Nájera, and the subsequent Anglo-Aragonese rapprochement, had clearly thrown the political situation in the Peninsula into complete disarray.

---

10   Robert de Guitté, Hervé de 'Iv', Pierre de 'Montibus', Guillaume de Montbouchier and Alain de la Houssaye.
11   See above, pp. 204, 250–2.
12   See above, p. 251. The situation had evidently deteriorated after October 1367 (Miret y Sans, 1905, p. 132).
13   ACA, Cancilleria, regs. 1345, fos. 137v–9r (1 March 1348), and 1347, fos. 155r–7r (27 February 1367). See above, p. 204, 204n.

The *capitulis* constituted a set of proposals which were to be ratified and confirmed in person by du Guesclin and his captains, who were all to do homage and swear fealty to the king of Aragon. The remainder of the agreement was concerned with the financial settlement. This provided that Bertrand was to receive 45,000 gold *doblas*, or their value in Aragonese florins (69,545 florins), which included outstanding debts to him of 22,555 florins, of which 20,000 were due on 20 November 1368 and the remainder the following Easter.[14] Of this sum 12,000 *doblas* (18,545 Aragonese florins) were to be paid to him for the remuneration of himself and his troops during the course of January1369, notwithstanding any judicial process to the contrary lodged by Calveley's proctors over the 22,555 florins' outstanding Crown debts. This advance was to be made through a Perpignan merchant, Pere Blau, in that town as soon as Bertrand's forces had assembled at Collioure or whatever other port of embarkation for Sardinia was decided upon. The remaining 33,000 *doblas* would be paid to du Guesclin's proctors as soon as Charles V's permission for his involvement in the expedition had been secured, the sureties given and the agreement confirmed by Bertrand and the captains. If his participation in the expedition failed to materialize, either because Charles V refused his permission, or for any other reason, he was to inform Pere or the duke of Gerona and return the initial payment of 12,000 *doblas* to Pere or his proctor and, pending repayment, surrender the castles and towns of Borja and Magallón as security. Blau was also to return any moneys remaining in his hands.

The letters subsidiary to the arrangement reveal even more about Pere's state of mind, as well as offering further insights into his diplomacy. In a letter written to du Guesclin on the same day, he recalled Bertrand's past service to him in his 'urgent war' with Pedro, his 'spontaneous' wish to serve in Sardinia to help pay off the ransom incurred by his capture at Nájera and, in the event of his being unable to take up the expedition or send a captain in his place, excused him of all obligation to return the 12,000 *doblas* which were to be advanced to him.[15] Only an advance on this sum of 3,000 Aragonese florins, which was made to Bertrand's proctors in Barcelona by Pere's special and verbal mandate to his treasurer, Ramon de Vilanova, and which was intended to expedite certain negotiations in which Bertrand was involved, appears to have been deducted from this sum.[16]

---

14 ACA, Cancilleria, reg. 1345, fos. 137v–9r. The exchange rate of 17 *sueldos* of Barcelona to each *dobla* is given in a letter of Pere to his treasurer dated 22 October 1368 (ibid., reg. 1346, fo. 124v), and of 11 *sueldos* of Barcelona to each Aragonese florin in the treasurer's accounts (ACA, Real Patrimonio, MR 351, fo. 110v).
15 ACA, Cancilleria, reg. 1346, fo. 104r–v.
16 Ibid., fo. 119r–v, and see fo. 124v. Du Guesclin may have been intending to recover the

Further *douceurs* were meted out to Bertrand's principal nuncio and proctor, Arnaud de Lar, who was to secure the moneys still outstanding from previous obligations to du Guesclin from a debt of 25,000 French florins assigned to Pere by Charles V on the moneys received by his treasurer, Pierre Scatisse, and on the proceeds of an *impôt* of 12 *deniers* per *livre* levied by Jean Perdiguier, receiver-general of Languedoc.[17] Arnaud was to retain 23,000 French florins for this purpose and pay 22,500 Aragonese florins to Bertrand. In a letter to his *maestro racional*, Berenguer de Codinachs, written in Barcelona on 19 October, Pere admitted that the envoy would make a profit out of the exchange rate, the French florin being worth more than the Aragonese florin, but explained that it was his wish that Arnaud should retain this and the 500 French florins difference 'to do what he wished with them'.[18] The Aragonese king's generosity was not disinterested. In the event of de Lar not being able to secure the repayment of Charles V's debts to Pere, the entire 23,000 French florins or its equivalent in Aragonese money, or whatever part of it was outstanding, was to be secured from the revenues raised in the kingdom of Valencia and, as a matter of urgency, transported to Perpignan for 28 November, for onward transmission to du Guesclin's proctor at Montpellier. This, Pere explained, was because any delay or difficulty over payment would result in Bertrand and his men invading Aragonese territory, 'from which innumerable damages will ensue in our lands'.[19]

Pere had no illusions about the men he was dealing with and he prepared for every eventuality. Whilst, on 13 October, he instructed his officers to give their protection to du Guesclin's envoys returning to France, on the same day he also informed them that Bertrand still threatened to invade his lands and ordered all victuals to be withdrawn into fortified places.[20] Six days later the story was very different. In a letter to the viscount of Castellbó he expressed relief that he had received a letter from du Guesclin bearing news that Bertrand had confirmed the treaty concluded by his proctors on his behalf, which they had taken to him.[21] Although reports of troop movements on the Aragonese frontier continued to come in to Barcelona during the rest of October and November, these were not of du Guesclin's forces, but rather of those of the count of Foix and other 'foreigners' who threatened incursions into his lands from Béarn through

---

3,000 gold florins awarded to Calveley in July, which were to have been deducted from the 20,000 florins royal debt to him (ibid., fo. 18v; Real Patrimonio, MR, reg. 356, fo. 81r. See above, p. 252).
17 ACA, Cancilleria, reg. 1346, fo. 104r–v (commission to Lar, dated 19 October).
18 Ibid., fos. 119v–20v.
19 Ibid.
20 Ibid., reg. 1347, fos. 64r, 66r.
21 Ibid., fo. 68v.

the mountains around Ansó and to the north of Jaca.[22] It was not until late November and early December that the threat spread further east to embrace the frontier counties of Ribagorza, Pallars and Urgell.[23] On 30 November and 3 December, Joan gave orders for the defence of the Pyrenean passes along the whole stretch of the mountain chain, from Ansó to the val d'Aran.[24] On 2 and 3 December, Pere sent further instructions to the countess of Urgell and the viscount of Castellbó about resisting the companies who had entered the realm, and he sent reinforcements to Pallars to guard the passes there, only to find that some enemy troops had already got through.[25] By 15 December it was known that du Guesclin was among them.[26]

In a letter of that date, written from Cervera to the viscount of Castellbó, Pere expressed astonishment that Bertrand and his companies could go against the agreement, concluded between them only two months earlier, whereby he had undertaken not to enter Aragon without licence, and Pere requested the viscount to do what he could to block their progress further pending the arrival of troops he was sending to resist them.[27] These were being concentrated at Cervera throughout the second half of December, whilst the companies continued to do a great deal of damage at Pallars. By 26 December they were reported to be a good four days into Aragonese territory, having taken Tremp on the Noguera Pallaresa, to the north of Lérida, and several other places in the plain.[28] From 16 December onwards Joan ordered a massive defensive effort to resist the 'Great Companies' which had entered Catalonia.[29] In a letter of 1 January to the viscount of Castellbó, Pere complained bitterly about the prisoners being taken and the looting carried out by the forces of du Guesclin and Olivier de Mauny.[30] Another letter, issued under his signet seal three days later, in reply to a communication from Bertrand offering his services to remove the 'wasters' from his lands, was couched in terse enough words. Thanking him for the offer, Pere pointed out that the only opportunities to serve him at that

---

22 Ibid, reg. 1390, fo. 1r–v (three letters from Joan, duke of Gerona, to Pere dated Zaragoza, 31 October 1368).
23 Ibid., fos. 2r–12v (further letters of Joan, dated 23 November, 3, 10 and 11 December 1368).
24 Notably *Crestine*, Ansó, *Tena*, *Loroco*, and in the val d'Aran (ibid., fos. 2v–3r, 4r–v).
25 ACA, Cancilleria, reg. 1347, fos. 86v–7r, and 1390, fo. 6v.
26 Ibid., reg. 1347, fo. 98r. See Delachenal, iii, p. 471 n. 5., citing ACA, Cancilleria, reg. 1222, fos. 96rff., 118v.
27 Ibid., reg. 1347, fo. 98r. The news was conveyed to Pere by the viscount, and to the queen by the count of Pallars (ibid., fo. 99r–v). On the 17th Pere wrote to both of them ordering them to have the passes situated in their lands well guarded, in order to stop further companies from entering (ibid., fo. 100r–v).
28 Ibid., fos. 107r–v, 152v–3r, 156r–v (Pere's letters, dated 18, 26 and 27 December).
29 Ibid., reg. 1390, fos. 16r–v, 22v and *passim*.
30 Ibid., fo. 120r.

moment lay outside his territories, but that he continued to look upon his as his 'special servant and friend'.[31] While it is possible that Pere had failed to raise the moneys due to be paid to du Guesclin at the end of November, it is more likely that other events outside Bertrand's control had determined his apparent lack of good faith. Almost certainly, Charles V had refused his permission for du Guesclin's participation in the proposed expedition to Sardinia.[32]

Well over a year had elapsed since the Black Prince had returned to Aquitaine in September 1367. No sooner had he arrived in the principality than Enrique of Trastámara had returned to Castile, despite the king of Aragon's endeavours to prevent him, and his clear instructions that he was not to cross Aragonese territory.[33] Picking his way through the Pyrenees with a small body of men, sometimes under cover of dark and sometimes in the full light of day, using paths through the mountains reputed unfit for horses, Enrique had returned into upper Aragon by the county of Foix and the val d'Aran unimpeded. From there he made his way south through the county of Ribagorza to Estradilla and Barbastro. A letter from Louis of Anjou, written in Montpellier on 18 September, in which the duke endeavoured to persuade Pere to reconsider his position, was a subterfuge intended to cover Enrique's passage.[34] By the time it reached its destination Enrique was known to be in Aragonese territory. As early as 24 September he was already near Huesca, from where, avoiding Zaragoza, he made for the Ebro valley through Navarrese territory, which he also violated, to arrive in Calahorra on the 28th. Once across the Ebro and on Castilian soil, he had made the sign of the cross in the sand of the river bed, kissed it, and swore never again to abandon Castile, perhaps recalling his reputed statement that the kingdom would be his by the following spring. Pere had conveyed this news to the Black Prince through an embassy which he had entrusted to Francesch de Sant Climent on 8 October, explaining how Enrique had put abroad false and contradictory reports, intended to disguise his true intentions.[35] These included information that he had intended to cross the Pyrenees into Catalonia by the col de Panissars; that

31 Ibid., reg. 1347, fo. 122v.
32 There is no record of payment of the moneys outstanding to du Guesclin in the accounts of Pere's treasurer for the period July to December 1368 (ACA, Real Patrimonio, MR, 356).
33 For what follows, see Delachenal, iii, pp. 429–30, 434–8; Russell, pp. 130–1.
34 ACA, Cartas Reales Diplomáticas, Pere III, caja 52, no. 6327. Pere's objections to Enrique's passage through his lands were made on the grounds that he was then 'en certain traittie avec le prince de Gales' and could not allow the passage of Enrique and 'les compagnes qu'il maine avecques lui' because of the damage they could cause in his kingdom. Louis attempted to assure him there was no danger: 'et les compagnes que il maine, treschier cousin, ne soiez en doubte. Car il ne sont pas si fortes ne si puissans que il vous puissent en riens grever ne faire desplaisir a vous ne a voz gens.'
35 ACA, Cancilleria, reg. 1218, fo. 24rff.

he was going to return to Spain by sea and reach Seville up the Guadalquivir; that he would return alone, dressed as a monk. Not knowing which of these and other stories to believe, Pere had been misled into sending a force under the duke of Gerona to the Catalonian frontier, and had ordered three Catalan galleys to pursue a number of ships which had entered Aragonese territorial waters from France. As a result, the bastard had eluded him.

However, Enrique had not achieved the success which had followed the invasion of March 1366. Accompanied by only a small body of mercenaries, but anticipating support for his cause when he arrived in Castile, it was not until the beginning of November that he had succeeded in taking Burgos, and then only by force. A number of towns in Old Castile had declared for him, as had Córdoba, but in general the kingdom appears to have remained loyal to Pedro, who had set up his headquarters in Seville. Not until the spring of 1368, after Enrique had taken Léon, did he proceed south, to appear on 30 April before Toledo, where he was to spend the best part of a year encamped before the massive defences of that city. Here he had received an embassy from Charles V, who, already planning a renewal of the war with England, was concerned to bring about a settlement of outstanding differences between Pere and Enrique, and to secure the bastard on his half-brother's throne in order to enlist Castilian military and naval support in the coming hostilities.[36] Just over a fortnight after the fateful council meeting at the end of June 1368, in which he had decided to accept the appeals of the Gascon lords, Charles had entrusted Francesch de Perellós and Jean de Rye with a mission 'to the kings of Aragon and Spain on certain weighty and secret matters with which we have charged them and which mightily concern the honour and profit of ourselves and our kingdom'.[37] After concluding their discussions with Pere they had proceeded to Castile, where they had joined Enrique before Toledo. Here, Charles's wishes were more than amply satisfied. In addition to persuading Enrique to accept the French king's arbitration of the differences between himself and Pere (who, however, also had to accept it), on 20 November the ambassadors had concluded the terms of an alliance by which Charles and Enrique undertook to support each other by land and sea in all wars, present and future. In return for French military support to defeat his enemies, Enrique was to guarantee Castilian support for Charles when the war was renewed with England and, at his own expense, to place the Castilian navy at Charles's disposal for as long as the war might last. In the event of the royal arsenal at Seville not having fallen into Enrique's hands by the time hostilities were opened

---

36 Russell, pp. 131–2, 138–40.
37 *Mandements*, nos. 457–8 (19 July 1378).

against England, Enrique nevertheless undertook to send into French waters whatever other naval support he was able to secure. Several clauses of the treaty make clear that what was envisaged was a renewal of the war against the English, both in their island fortress and in the principality of Aquitaine. The entire thrust of Charles V's diplomacy in Aragon and Castile was directed to this end.[38]

Certainly, some military support for Enrique would first be required if he was to consolidate his position in Castile and so allow Charles V to benefit from the support of the Castilian naval fleet when the war with England was renewed. According to Ayala, at the time of the conclusion of the treaty du Guesclin's services were promised with a company of 500 lances.[39] However, they were not immediately forthcoming. After entering Spain, Bertrand had first made for Borja with Olivier de Mauny and other Bretons, and during the course of January 1369 used it as a base to threaten Navarrese territories and then extract a ransom to desist from any further violations. At the time, Charles of Navarre was in the Ebro valley, consolidating his hold over some of the territories ceded to him by Pedro I before Nájera, and his queen was obliged to pawn her jewels to secure 26,000 Aragonese florins demanded by Bertrand and his companies.[40] But there was more. Charles's failure to honour the grants of land and rent made to du Guesclin and Mauny before Nájera were now made good by new agreements which the two Bretons ratified at Borja on 4 February. In Charles's lands in Normandy, in place of the castle of Gavray he now secured that of Tinchebrai. In addition, he was to have a lump sum of 15,000 florins and annual rent to the value of 2,000 *livres*. In return, he did homage to Charles, reserving only his obedience to the king of France, the duke of Orléans and Enrique of Trastámara. However, in the event of war breaking out between Enrique and Charles over the towns in Castile 'which had previously formed part of the kingdom of Navarre', he would desist from supporting either side. For his part, Mauny was also to have a castle in Normandy, together with 1,000 *livres* annual rent in neighbouring

---

38 The powers to Perellós and Rye, the treaty of alliance with Enrique, and the latter's acceptance of Charles V's arbitration have been published in *Foedera*, III, ii, p. 850ff. Among the clauses should be noted Enrique's undertaking: 'Item, Castra, Civitates, Villae, Fortalitia, sive Loca, quae et quas Nos aut gentes nostrae, in Regno et Terra Angliae, et Ducatu Aquitaniae, acquisiverimus, occupaverimus, acquiriverint, seu occupaverint, Nos, dicto Fratri nostro carissimo, Regi Franciae Primogenito, aut primo Haeredi, sive suo certo Nuncio aut Mandato, Nos et Gentes nostrae praedictae, et Filius Primogenitus noster liberè dare et restituere tenebimur, et etiam tenebuntur.' The treaty was ratified by Charles V in Paris on 6 April 1369 (Daumet, pp. 163–8). See Delachenal, iii, pp. 464–7; Russell, pp. 139–40.
39 Ayala, *Crónica*, i, p. 565.
40 AGN, Comptos, reg. 132; Brutails, *Documents*, p. 172, no. cxcviii; *AGN, Comptos*, vii, no. 879. See Delachenal, iii, pp. 472–3.

lands, for which he also did homage to Charles.[41] Shortly afterwards, accompanied by some 600 lances, du Guesclin joined Enrique at Orgaz, situated some twenty-one miles to the south of Toledo. At this point Enrique was in need of all the support he could muster, having heard that a relieving force was being brought up by Don Pedro.[42]

Leaving Seville, the Castilian king proceeded north as far as Alcántara on the Portuguese frontier, where he intended to join up with loyalist forces from Léon and Old Castile whom he had instructed to join him there.[43] After returning south to Puebla de Alcocer, he then made his way eastwards across Estramadura into La Mancha. Here, he set up camp in the villages around Montiel to the north of the Sierra Morena and to the east of Valdepeñas.[44] Informed of these movements, Enrique had left Orgaz around 10 March to move further south to Ciudad Real with an army of around 3,000 lances divided into two battles, of which the vanguard was commanded by du Guesclin and the masters of the Orders of Santiago and Calatrava. For his part, Pedro had about the same number of lances, but in addition some 1,500 horsemen supplied by his ally, Mohammed V of Granada. However, his army's intelligence was bad, and he seems to have been utterly unaware of Enrique's whereabouts. His scouts even mistook the torches of du Guesclin's companies, lit to guide them on their way through the southern darkness, for those of reinforcements of light cavalrymen, the famous *jinetes* whom he had summoned to join him from Andalusia.

With Pedro taken by surprise, the engagement which ensued the following morning, on Wednesday 14 March 1369, was brief but not bloody. A large part of his forces, who were billeted in the outlying villages, were nowhere near the scene of battle, and those who were involved in the engagement with Enrique's forces were quickly defeated. Unable to rally his men, who either could not reach him or fled the field, Pedro took refuge with a few of his more faithful servants in the castle of Montiel, which was then blockaded by Enrique's forces.[45] Had Pedro been prepared for a siege he could doubtless have held out for some time, but he lacked provisions and, most important, sufficient water. Meanwhile, Enrique had a wall

---

41 Brutails, *Documents*, pp. 165–71, nos. cxcvi–ii; *AGN, Comptos*, vii, no. 453. Among the witnesses to du Guesclin's homage we may note, in addition to Mauny, Alain de la Houssaye, Maurice de Tréséguidy, Renaud de Creleves, Gérard de Rayssa and Jean de Beaumont. Mauny's homage was witnessed by Boson de la Chèse, Jean d'Yrel and Eustache de Manin.
42 Ayala, *Crónica*, i, p. 589.
43 Ibid., pp. 585–6. See Delachenal, iii, pp. 467–8. Russell, p. 147, ignores these movements.
44 Ayala, *Crónica*, i, pp. 588–9. The name *Campo de Montiel* was given to a number of villages belonging to the military Order of Santiago which are today located in the provinces of Ciudad Real, Jaen and Albacete, of which the principal place was Villanueva de los Infantes, situated some twenty-two miles east of Valdepeñas (Delachenal, iii, p. 468 n. 3).
45 Ayala, *Crónica*, i, pp. 589–90; Delachenal, iii, pp. 474–5.

hastily erected around the fortress, enforcing a strict surveillance by day and night. Had Pedro tried to escape under cover of darkness, he would almost certainly have been taken prisoner and killed.[46] Instead, he chose to negotiate with some of the besieging forces, either to take him under safe-conduct to Enrique or to accept a large sum of money to get him safely through their lines.[47]

From the sordid events which ensued it is impossible to exculpate du Guesclin and some of the Bretons in his immediate entourage, although the precise role of different individuals is hidden in the brutal circumstances of Pedro's death. Some sort of assurance appears to have been given to Pedro by du Guesclin through the intermediary, it would seem, of the Asturian knight, Men Rodríguez de Sanabria, who was among those with Pedro in the castle of Montiel. Having initially supported Enrique, he had transferred his allegiance to Pedro after being taken prisoner at Nájera by Bernard de la Salle. On that occasion du Guesclin had secured his freedom by paying the Asturian's ransom, and consequently a certain rapport existed between them. According to Ayala, the two men had a secret meeting one night in which Men Rodriguez, on Pedro's behalf, offered Bertrand substantial rewards if he would assist the king to escape beyond Enrique's lines.[48] The proposal met with a firm rebuffal from du Guesclin, who is said to have protested his loyalty to Charles V and Enrique, and reported the incident to the latter. Enrique then devised a stratagem, offering the same rewards to Bertrand as well as an additional 200,000 *doblas*, if he would go ahead with Pedro's request, but bring the unfortunate king to his lodgings. Du Guesclin, Ayala continues, accepted these proposals, albeit with some misgivings, and, along with a number of Bretons in his entourage, gave the most solemn undertakings for Pedro's protection.

The Bretons included Bertrand's cousin, Olivier de Mauny, whose past conduct in France, his fraudulent capture of Charles of Navarre before the Nájera campaign, and his recent behaviour at Borja attested to a particularly noteworthy lack of scruple in an age in which the standards were not exactly high among many men of action. According to Chaucer, who had had first-hand experience of events in the Peninsula during the prince's expedition there three years earlier, and whose knowledge of them was subsequently maintained through the Iberian interests of his patron, John of Gaunt, it was Mauny who executed the plan for Pedro's downfall, in

---

46 According to Froissart, *Chroniques*, vii, pp. 78–80, he did make such an attempt; but the chronicler's evidence is not corroborated.
47 *Chron. Charles V*, ii, p. 69. For what follows, see Ayala, *Crónica*, i, pp. 590–3, and the account in Delachenal, iii, pp. 475–86.
48 The rewards in question included the towns of Soria, Almazán, Atienza, Monteagudo, Deza and Seron (Ayala, *Crónica*, i, p. 591).

which du Guesclin was principally involved, although the accusations against both men were embedded in an heraldic and linguistic riddle in the Monk's Tale in the *Canterbury Tales*:

> O noble, o worthy Petro, glorie of Spayne,
> Whom fortune heeld so hy in magestee,
> Wel oughten men thy pitous deeth complayne!
> Out of thy lond thy brother made thee flee;
> And after, at a sege, by subtiltee,
> Thou were bitrayed, and lad un-to his tente,
> Wher-as he with his owene hond slow thee,
> Succeding in thy regne and in thy rente.
>
> The feeld of snow, with th'egle of blak ther-inne,
> Caught with the lymrod, coloured as the glede,
> He brew this cursedness and al this sinne.
> The 'wikked nest' was werker of this nede;
> Noght Charles Oliver, that ay took hede
> Of trouthe and honour, but of Armorike
> Genilon Oliver, corrupt for mede,
> Broghte this worthy king in swich a brike.[49]

It was du Guesclin, referred to here through his armorial bearings, who brewed the treason, but Mauny (the 'Mau Nid', that is 'Wicked Nest'), not Oliver the brave and loyal companion of Charlemagne, but a Breton (of Armorike), Oliver Ganelon, who brought it to pass. Other writers, including Pere of Catalonia, in the *Chronicle* of his reign, insist that du Guesclin gave his word to Pedro that he had nothing to fear: Pedro had left the castle of Montiel under Bertrand's surety, but others rushed against him and took him prisoner.[50]

Ayala's account of Pedro's last hours is in all probability the most reliable. Leaving the castle of Montiel on the night of 23 March and wearing little armour, he was taken to du Guesclin's lodgings as a result of the prearranged plan. Lack of water and desertions from among those defending the castle would have made some move on his part inevitable if he was to surrender on some sort of terms, but Ayala makes plain that Pedro expected to secure his freedom in return for the offers already made to Men Rodríguez. There was no question of the Asturian having planned to betray Pedro. That suggestion was entirely rejected by the Castilian chronicler. It was Enrique himself who was at the centre of the piece. Froissart's story of the interception of Le Bègue de Villaines is perhaps not

---

49 Chaucer, *Complete Works*, iv, p. 256, and see Delachenal, iii, p. 481 and n. 1, for a summary of the explanations of the second verse offered by Furnivall and Skeat.
50 Pere III, *Chronicle*, ii, p. 581.

altogether at variance with Ayala's account, although he makes no mention of a prior arrangement with du Guesclin and has Pedro led off to Le Bègue's lodgings and, in particular, the rooms of Yvon de Lacoué – another Breton mercenary of unreliable habit and reputation, who had been enlisted into French royal service during the previous spring, Olivier de Mauny acting as a pledge for his good behaviour.[51] The details of what ensued given by these two writers are contradictory, although there was no difference in the outcome of the actions they described.

According to Ayala, on hearing the news of Pedro's arrival in his camp, Enrique proceeded to du Guesclin's lodgings fully armed and wearing his bassinet. The two brothers fell upon one another, rolling on the ground in locked combat until Enrique got the better of the struggle with several blows which finally killed his adversary.[52] According to Froissart, not only was the setting of these last moments different, but so also was the rôle of others present. The fighting between the two brothers occurred after a verbal shouting match. Pedro pinned Enrique down and would certainly have killed him had he been armed. The advantage was given to the bastard brother by Felip Dalmau, viscount of Rocaberti, a leading Catalan nobleman whom Peter IV had sent on a mission to du Guesclin.[53] Dalmau grabbed Pedro by the leg and brought him to the ground, thereby giving the advantage to Enrique, who finished him off with a long Castilian knife and the final bludgeonings of some of his men. Two of those present – an English knight called Ralph Helme or Elmham, formerly known as 'the Green Esquire', and Jacques Rollans – were also killed for attempting to intercept, but Fernando de Castro and others in Pedro's entourage were taken prisoner.[54] Some corroboration of this account is offered by Pere, who, in his *Chronicle*, simply says:

King Enrique, knowing that King *En* Pedro was in his hands and within a lodging where he found him, put hands on him to kill him. King Pedro tried to defend himself but, finally, those who were with Don Enrique killed him. And when he was dead they cut off his head, which King Don Enrique had sent to Seville. Thus ended the war between the two kings, leaving King Enrique lord and king of the kingdom of Castile.[55]

---

51   Froissart, *Chroniques*, vii, pp. 78–81; ibid., p. xxxii n. 2, for Lacoué's past service and Mauny's guarantee.
52   Ayala, *Crónica*, i, p. 592.
53   Delachenal, iii, p. 485 n. 6.
54   Froissart, *Chroniques*, vii, pp. 81–2. I have been unable to identify Ralph Helme, although he may have been related to William Elmham, whom Froissart frequently calls Helmen, or Richard Helmen, possibly another member of the same family (see Lettenhove in Froissart, *Oeuvres*, xxi, pp. 137–8, 539). It should be noted that the Iberian chroniclers referred to William Elmham as Allmante or Alemat (see Fernão Lopes, *Crónica*, p. 208 and n. 11).
55   Pere III, *Chronicle*, ii, p. 581.

For a second time Enrique owed his throne to du Guesclin and the companies under his command, and he was shortly to make good the promises made verbally at Montiel. By an act dated at Seville on 4 May following, in addition to the lordship of Molina and the title of duke, which had been promised to him on a previous occasion, he now granted him the towns of Soria, Atienza, Almazán, Moron, Monteagudo, Deza, Cihuela and Seron.[56] These were largely situated in the frontier territories which Enrique had promised to Peter IV by the conventions of Monzon and Binéfar in 1363, and Enrique doubtless calculated that Pere would not challenge du Guesclin's title to them, although the inhabitants of Molina immediately did homage to Pere and handed their town over to him. Enrique may have intended to deflect du Guesclin from entering Aragonese service by creating a source of friction between the Breton leader and the king of Aragon, and Bertrand was never successful in wresting Molina from Pere, although he did capture and reside in Soria in 1369-70.[57] However, Enrique was also assured of his support in that the grant was made on condition that du Guesclin remained in his service and, after his death, in the service of his son and heir, the Infante Don Juan.[58] It may well have been made to him as much to guarantee that continued involvement in face of tempting offers from Pere as in recognition of the services already rendered to him by the Breton captain.

Among the other mercenaries rewarded by Enrique during the ensuing months, Olivier Mauny was made lord of Agreda, Le Bègue de Villaines count of Ribadeo and lord of Salamanca, and Geoffroi Richon became lord of Aguilar de Campóo. In addition to these, one of the old captains of the Great Companies, Arnaud du Solier, better known as le Limousin, was made lord of Villalpando. Le Bègue and Limousin were among those who had returned to Castile with Enrique in 1367, along with Bernard de Béarn, who had already served with him during the *entrada* of 1366 and had been made count of Medicanelli in July of that year. All of them were present at the *Cortes* held at Toro in November, when some of them first secured their titles.[59] Like du Guesclin they had a continuing interest in the fortunes of the Trastámaran dynasty, and further service and profit were now within their grasp, not only in Castile, but also elsewhere in the Iberian kingdoms. For his part, Bertrand was now a military entrepreneur of considerable

---

56 Delachenal, iii, pp. 488–90. For Molina, see Morel-Fatio, pp. 145–77; Gutiérrez de Velasco, 1951b, pp. 75–128, and the map published at the end of that article.
57 For the capture of Soria, see Russell, p. 150.
58 Luce, in Froissart, *Chroniques*, vii, pp. xxxiii n. 2.
59 Ayala, *Crónica*, ii, p. 5; Froissart, *Oeuvres*, xxiii, pp. 80–3 (letters of du Guesclin and others, Toro, 18 November 1369); Russell, pp. 127–8, 128 n. 1, 160. For further details, see Fowler, 1988, pp. 34–5.

standing, and his services were most immediately sought after by the king of Aragon.

Neither Pere nor Bertrand seem to have put aside the Sardinian proposals of the previous autumn indefinitely, and at the beginning of March the Aragonese king had endeavoured to pursue them further by way of his envoy, Felip Dalmau, viscount of Rocaberti. Unaware of the Breton captain's movements, he first sent Dalmau to speak with Bertrand in the county of Pallars in Upper Aragon and then, when he failed to find him there, to Castile.[60] Following Rocaberti's mission, Bertrand sent Jacques de Pencoédic and Jean le Bouteiller as his proctors to the Aragonese court, and a new round of negotiations took place between them and three of Pere's councillors, Francesh Roma, Jaume Dezfar and Pere Dezvall. These took the arrangements arrived at in Barcelona during the previous October as their starting point. Du Guesclin had given his reactions to them, and a document containing the observations of Pere's councillors on his views was taken to both Bertrand and the viscount of Rocaberti by Roma, who was given detailed instructions about the way in which he was to proceed.[61]

He was first to hand over Pere's letters to the viscount and then explain to him how Pencoédic and Bouteiller had arrived in the Aragonese court as du Guesclin's proctors, had intimated that Bertrand was willing to go to Sardinia without the king or the duke of Gerona, and had concluded the necessary terms with himself and Dezfar, on Pere's behalf, as indicated in a number of *capítols* (chapters or items), of which he was to hand over a copy to the viscount. He was then to present Pere's letters to du Guesclin, Pencoédic and Bouteiller respectively – having first sought the viscount's advice on the best manner in which to proceed – and secure Bertrand's confirmation of the arrangements envisaged. In his discussions with the viscount, Bertrand and his proctors, Roma was to be particularly diligent and careful about this. He was to remind Pencoédic and Bouteiller of their undertaking to secure du Guesclin's confirmation of the *capítols*, at the

---

60 For the viscount's peregrinations, see Delachenal, iii, p. 485 n. 6. The instructions which were given to him are preserved in ACA, Cancilleria, reg. 1082, fos. 43v–5r: 'Parria que lo vezcomte de Rochaberti degues tractar ab moss. Bertran de Claqui sobre lo passatge faedor per lo dit moss. Bertran en la illa de Sardenya per manera seguent.'
61 The documentation in question is contained in ACA, Cancilleria, reg. 1347, fos. 150r–7r. It consists of four letters dated Lérida, 17 April 1369, which were sent to du Guesclin, Rocaberti, Dezfar and Bouteiller (fos. 150r–1r); a document containing du Guesclin's views on the proposals contained in the twelve *capitulles* of the previous autumn, together with the replies of Pere's ambassadors thereto (fos. 151r–2v; see appendix A, no. 5); the instructions given to Francesch Roma (fos. 153r–v; appendix A, no. 6); the form of the letters of obligation of du Guesclin's sureties for 6,000 florins advanced to his proctors (fos. 154r–5r); the details of an accord concluded between Pere and Bertrand at Lérida on 27 February 1367 (fos. 155r–6r; appendix A, no. 4); and the form of Bertrand's obligation to abide by the arrangement concluded with the proctors (fos. 156v–7r).

same time intimating Pere's indebtedness to them in this regard. In his letters on the subject Pere promised Pencoédic and Bouteiller appropriate financial incentives, which he believed would more than satisfy them for their pains. In his letter to Rocaberti the king pointed out the importance of the expedition proceeding, not only because of the turn of events in Sardinia, but also because of the number of companies – of nobles, knights and other men – he had raised to resist Marià of Arborea. At the same time, in view of the taxes currently being raised in Aragon and Valencia for a *royal* expedition to the island, he stressed the importance of maintaining secrecy over the terms of the agreement with du Guesclin.

The document containing the *capítols* is particularly revealing on specific points raised in the proposals of the previous October, giving, as it does, not only du Guesclin's views, but also the reactions to them of Pere's councillors. No objection was raised to Bertrand's wish to undertake the expedition without Pere or the duke of Gerona, but the councillors felt it appropriate to stipulate that the size of his forces should not be unrestricted, as du Guesclin wanted, but should be limited to 1,200 lances and 300 archers – 100 archers fewer than in the original proposals – and that, in addition, the king should provide a contingent of 200 mounted men and 1,000 crossbowmen *de sa nacio*. They also agreed that the rates of remuneration for himself and his men should be the same as those proposed in October, and that the remainder of the 45,000 *doblas* envisaged in the earlier proposals should be paid to him at the appropriate time. However, in the event of his taking full charge of the expedition (*comme cap, senz la persone du diz seignor Roy*) he wanted an additional 2,000 *doblas* a month personal allowance (*por l'estat de sa persone*). This was thought to be too much. Only 1,000 francs was envisaged in the original proposals, but the councillors were prepared to double this to 2,000 francs.[62] In view of du Guesclin's commitments to Enrique of Trastámara, they were rather less happy about his wish to postpone the expedition until the beginning of October. They thought this much too late and dangerous for the sea journey. They wanted Bertrand to be ready with his men by 10 August at a port of embarkation which would be indicated to him by the king a month beforehand. Du Guesclin's concern that other matters contained in the previous proposals should be confirmed by Pere, especially the clause guaranteeing shipping for the outward and return journeys to and from Sardinia for himself and his men, was fully comprehended by the councillors, who thought it entirely reasonable. A new element, about which they were rather more apprehensive, was du Guesclin's wish to undertake the expedition without Charles V's permission, unless the king of France could

---

62   The *dobla*, initially minted at 4.6 g of gold, remained heavier than the franc, at 3.82 g in 1369 (Spufford, pp. 159 and 191).

give a just and evident reason why he and the captains in his company should not undertake it. However, their main concern was not with diplomatic niceties, but rather to secure sufficient guarantees that du Guesclin and his men would not default on their obligations, once entered into.[63] Bertrand's reasons for the inclusion of this clause are rather more questionable.

Two further clauses concerned the position of du Guesclin's proctors, Pencoédic and Bouteiller, who were obliged to certain Lombards and other merchants in the sum of 5,000 to 6,000 florins, pending payment of which they could not leave Barcelona. Pere's councillors agreed that the sum in question should be advanced to them, but from the 45,000 *doblas* to be made over to du Guesclin, and then only after he and the majority of his captains had sworn to undertake the expedition, unless prevented from doing so by reason of death, grave illness or capture. In that event, ten of them were to oblige themselves individually for the whole to guarantee repayment. Roma was given specific instructions to draw Rocaberti's attention to the need for full compliance on this point, and du Guesclin's sureties were obliged to issue appropriate letters of obligation. To cover their own conduct, Pencoédic and Bouteiller requested that a 'sufficient person' be assigned to join them in returning to du Guesclin and the viscount with the Aragonese response to Bertrand's observations, as well as to secure the necessary confirmations and guarantee from Bertrand and his captains. The person in question was to report back to Pere on the great pains and diligence they would exercise on his behalf. Pere assigned Roma to the task.

Du Guesclin's confirmation of the revised agreement, which was to have been secured within the following three months, was evidently not forthcoming, as he and the companies under his command became daily more involved in Trastámaran service.[64] In April, Enrique ordered the imposition of *alcabalas* to pay for their services for a further twenty months, from 1 May 1369 to 31 December 1370, indicating the absolute necessity of raising the money if they were to be prevented from robbing and pillaging the country.[65] Among the different *routes* which made up Bertrand's forces the Bretons now predominated. In addition to those of Olivier de Mauny, they included contingents commanded by Jacques de Pencoédic, Maurice de Tréséguidy and Yvon de Lacoué, already noted, of Guillaume de Laval, lord of Pacy, Alain de Beaumont, Alain de la Houssaye, and Alain and

---

63 Pere took no chances. By letters dated Valencia, 27 June 1369, he wrote to Charles V requesting his authorization for du Guesclin to undertake the expedition (ACA, Cancilleria, reg. 1225, fo. 13v).
64 Nevertheless, as late as 27 June, Pere still appears to have hoped to secure his services (see previous note).
65 *Documentos de Enrique II*, pp. 3–4, no. iii.

Raoulet de Saint-Pol. But there were others, commanded by men like Le Bègue de Villaines from Beauce, Guillaume de Lannoy from Flanders and Olivier de Montauban from Aquitaine. These men were now given pre-eminence among Enrique's foreign mercenaries and rewarded for their services.[66] They gave cause for concern to Peter IV and the duke of Gerona, who throughout the summer of 1369 feared a renewal of war with Castile and the invasion of Aragon and Catalonia by du Guesclin's troops, and made all the necessary arrangements to resist them.[67] It was a false alarm. During the course of the summer Bertrand and his companies were in fact involved elsewhere, on the western frontiers of Castile, in Galicia and in Portugal.

Following the death of Pedro I of Castile, Fernando I, who had succeeded Dom Pedro of Portugal in 1367, had taken immediate advantage of loyalist support to lay claim to the Castilian throne and to incorporate Galicia and a number of loyalist centres along the western frontier of Castile into his kingdom.[68] To counteract this menace, Enrique, who had secured the surrender of Toledo in early June, first proceeded to besiege Zamora. Then, with the Breton and other companies under du Guesclin's command, he conducted a campaign to subdue the north-west of his kingdom. In a newsletter which he wrote to his wife on 18 August, Enrique was able to report their success in recovering Galicia and the invasion of Portugal, where he had proceeded to besiege Braga. He also indicated the central rôle being played by du Guesclin, not only in the conduct of the war, but also on the diplomatic front. Braga surrendered at the end of the month and Enrique then turned his attention to Guimarães, which put up a stout resistance and which he was unable to take. Meanwhile, the companies laid waste the entire Minho valley. By the middle of October Bragança, in Trás-os-Montes, had fallen to Enrique's forces; but a decisive victory eluded him and, by the end of that month, raids conducted into Andalusia by his erstwhile supporter Mohammed V of Granada, to whom Dom Fernando was allied, obliged him to abandon the campaign. An additional problem was his pressing need for money to pay du Guesclin and his men, as well as the need to secure additional troops for service against the king of Granada. These together obliged him to summon a meeting of the *Cortes* at Toro in November.

66 All of these men were with Enrique and du Guesclin at Toro on 18 November 1369, when they undertook not to make war on the count of Flanders because of his imprisonment of Jean de Saint-Pol (Froissart, *Oeuvres*, xxiii, pp. 80–3).
67 ACA, Cancilleria, reg. 1390, fos. 40v–2r, 45r (Pere's letters of 21 June and 19 August).
68 For what follows, see Ayala, *Crónica*, ii, pp. 3–4; Fernão Lopes, *Crónica*, chs xxv, xxvii–viii, xxx–xxxv; and a letter of Enrique to his wife (*Documentos de Enrique II*, pp. 34–6, no. xx); Russell, pp. 151–3.

Du Guesclin's return to Castile caused new alarms in the Aragonese court. By 22 November rumours were rife in Zaragoza that he was assembling his troops on the frontier, and that the invasion of Aragon and Catalonia was imminent. The duke of Gerona consequently began to concentrate forces to resist them.[69] Unconfirmed reports that Bertrand had taken Molina, which were circulating in December, were finally shown not to be true and on 18 December, when he was reported to be in Soria, the duke ordered troops to be sent to that frontier.[70] It then transpired that this was a show of force and that du Guesclin hoped to secure concessions from Pere through negotiation. The following day the duke ordered the governor-general of Aragon to provide a safe-conduct for Bertrand and up to a hundred riders in his company for the whole of January.[71] However, it is unlikely that any negotiations ensued, and du Guesclin's true intentions remained equivocal up to at least the end of March 1370, when Joan wrote to the viscount of Rocaberti that he had contradictory reports. Olivier de Mauny assured him that Bertrand intended to serve Pere, but only a few days earlier he had heard from another reliable source in Tortosa that he intended to make war in Aragon.[72] Having helped restore Enrique to the Castilian throne, du Guesclin's main aim appears to have been to neutralize Aragon whilst the war was renewed with England.

The Sardinian expedition passed into other hands, and by the summer of 1370 du Guesclin, if somewhat reluctantly, had returned to France.[73] According to Cuvelier, Charles V had requested him to return on no fewer than five occasions, the first over a year earlier, in June 1369, and it seems certain that he had refused Pere's request to permit him to serve in Sardinia, which was made on the 27th of that month. Du Guesclin was doubtless loath to forgo the possibilities of profit and personal advancement which service in the Peninsula held out, and even more to relinquish his title to Molina and other frontier towns, the continued possession of which was conditional upon his remaining in Trastámaran service. It was not until June 1370 that Enrique gave his permission for Bertrand and his companies to return to France, and although the royal licence then granted to him allowed him to retain his possessions in Spain, he disposed of them by sale to Enrique in 1373. To meet part of the considerable sums he had to find

---

69 ACA, Cancilleria, reg. 1390, fo. 61r.
70 Reports of the threatened invasion from Castile and of the capture of Molina were discounted by Pere in Zaragoza on 7 December (ibid., fo. 68r). Joan was more cautious and, having been informed of Bertrand's movements, ordered troops to the Soria frontier (ibid., fos. 73v–4r).
71 Ibid., fos. 74v–5r (Zaragoza, 19 December 1369).
72 Ibid., fos. 95r–v (Daroca, 25 March 1370).
73 He was at Soria on 26 April, Atienza on 11 May, Borja on 26 June, but back in France, at Moissac, on 26 July. For these details and what follows in this paragraph, see Fowler, 1988, p. 252; 1992, pp. 236–7.

for these, Enrique surrendered the earl of Pembroke, his prisoner since a naval battle off La Rochelle in the previous year, to Bertrand for 130,000 francs. But Pembroke died before any of the money had been handed over to him, and after a complicated history of claims and counter-claims, in 1377 Charles V, bearing in mind that du Guesclin had disposed of his Castilian possessions only to remain in his service, granted him a sum of 50,000 francs in compensation.[74] The remaining moneys outstanding for the sales were assigned on the *alcabalas*, and were still being paid to Bertrand's brother and heir, Olivier du Guesclin, as late as 1388. The wages for himself and his companies, on the other hand, appear to have been met in full. A meeting of the *Cortes* at Medina del Campo in April 1370 had approved the arrangements concluded with du Guesclin before Pedro's death at Montiel, and the assembly agreed to furnish the necessary 120,000 *doblas* outstanding to him and his companies. When they left for France in June they had been paid in full, although the money was subsequently devalued. Nevertheless, it was with some reluctance that du Guesclin left the Iberian Peninsula, which he was never to see again, even if the office of constable of France had already been offered to him, which seems probable. Some ten years later, in the last months of his life, embittered by accusations made against him and perhaps too readily accepted by Charles V, he threatened to give up the constable's sword and return to Spain, where, he was said to have commented, he could live 'a very honourable life, for there I am a duke'. It was no longer true, but there was perhaps something in the sentiment. Enrique's permission for him to return to France was doubtless issued under pressure from Charles V, and was more of an order than a licence. The Castilian king was too committed to the French alliance, and still too dependent on it, to risk a breach with Paris.

Pere made one further attempt to recruit the companies for service in Sardinia in 1371, when an English mercenary, Sir Walter Benedict or Bennet, agreed to take 1,000 men-at-arms, 500 archers and 1,000 infantry to the island.[75] Little is known about this adventurer, who may have first come to the Peninsula with Calveley's forces in 1366 and subsequently settled there. During the course of that year he was permitted to travel through Navarre with a retinue of twelve mounted men to recover his wife,

---

74 For the details, see Froissart, *Oeuvres*, xviii, pp. 511–43, PJ no. cxxii, and Luce, in Froissart, *Chronique*s, viii, pp. xcvi–xcviii, xcvi n. 3, 164–5. In a similar fashion, for the sale of Agreda, Olivier de Mauny was granted Guichard d'Angle, also taken at La Rochelle, but Guichard and his brother were exchanged for the lord of Roye, held hostage since the treaty of Brétigny (Froissart, *Chroniques* viii, pp. xcviii, 165–6). Froissart states, apparently erroneously, that Mauny thereby secured the marriage of the lord of Roye's daughter and heiress, which brought him a considerable dowry. The true nature and extent of his compensation are not known.

75 Tasis, p. 293.

who had taken the veil in the convent of Santa Clara in Seville.[76] Charles of Navarre then seems to have availed himself of his services as a tax-collector, an occupation he continued into the following year.[77] He was subsequently involved in various missions between the Aragonese king and John of Gaunt during the 1370s, possibly because he had knowledge of Catalan, and he again offered his services as a recruiting agent to Pere in 1377.[78] The troops Benedict assembled for service in Sardinia in 1371 were primarily recruited in Languedoc and Provence, and they were to have embarked for the island from Toulon. The count of Quirra was appointed captain-general of the expeditionary forces, and a Sicilian nobleman, Olfó Pròxida, was made admiral of the fleet.[79] Other companies were drawn from Italy, where they had occupied Livorno, from where they were to have embarked for Sardinia. Their presence there caused concern to the governing council, the *Anziani*, of Pisa.[80] For his part, Benedict was made count of Arborea, somewhat prematurely as things turned out. Whilst passing through Genoese territory on the way to the port of embarkation, a large part of his forces were killed or imprisoned. The latter included Benedict and the Catalan nobleman, Pere Çagarriga.

This incident provoked Pere's fury, since technically a peace existed between Aragon and the Genoese republic. The count of Quirra was sent to Genoa to demand an explanation and, from the confused account of the Genoese and the comfortable style in which Benedict was housed, he concluded that there had been collusion with Marià d'Arborea.[81] However, it is not easy to see why Benedict and his masters should have wished to compromise Aragonese interests at this juncture, and the Englishman certainly enjoyed Pere's full confidence in the following years. In January 1374, Gaunt despatched him to Barcelona with Sir William Elmham, to offer the services of 1,000 men-at-arms and 1,000 archers in Sardinia, providing that a similar number of Pere's troops first assisted Lancaster to conquer Castile.[82] It was the last that was to be heard of using the companies to re-establish Aragonese control in the island. Perhaps it had always been a bargaining counter. As for Benedict, by 1380 he had transferred his services to the Venetian republic, then at war with Genoa, and which had engaged a number of English companies, some of them apparently through his agency.[83]

76 Russell, p. 167 n. 2.
77 AGN, *Comptos*, vi, no. 869. See index, under 'Beneit'.
78 Russell, pp. 169 n. 2, 207, 209, 210 n. 1, 216, 251 n. 1, 253 n. 2, 563.
79 Tasis, p. 293.
80 AS, Pisa, Comune A, reg. 66, fos. 25v–29r, 33v (October and November 1371).
81 Tasis, p. 293.
82 Russell, p. 209.
83 AS, Mantua, Archivio Gonzaga, busta 1140; Verci, xv, p. 34; see *Cal. State Papers Venetian*, pp. 28–9, nos. 90–1.

12

Pontvallain

The war renewed between England and France gathered momentum slowly. Although Charles V had agreed to hear the count of Armagnac's appeal against the Black Prince as early as June 1368, the letters citing Edward to appear in Paris were not prepared until the end of that year and only delivered to the prince at the beginning of January 1369. Even then Charles kept up at least a semblance of diplomacy, dispatching an embassy to Edward III with a document listing all the French grievances, past and present, and the definitive rupture did not occur until the early summer, after the prince had failed to appear in Paris. During the second week in May, Charles summoned a great council to meet in *parlement*, which approved his action in accepting the appeals. Although no formal declaration of war was then made, nor any formal act of defiance passed, Charles's position was thereafter irreversible. On 21 May he ordered the appellants and their adherents to take up arms against the prince under the direction of Louis of Anjou, who, on 8 June, specifically instructed the inhabitants of Guyenne to conduct full-scale war on Edward III, the prince, their lands, men and subjects. Meanwhile, Edward had summoned parliament, which met at Westminster on 3 June, when he resumed the French royal title.[1]

In fact, military events had moved ahead of these formal declarations. The activities of the companies after their return from Castile in 1368 were already regarded by Charles V and Louis of Anjou as constituting an act of open hostility directed against them by the prince.[2] Towards the end of

---

1 The events leading up to the formal breakdown of relations between Edward III and Charles V are dealt with by Delachenal, iv, ch. v.
2 One of the specific accusations made against Edward and the prince in the council meeting held in *parlement* in May was that 'il estoient venuz contre les diz traictiez et alliances en soubstenent les compaignes ou souffrent ou royaume de France contre le dit traictié et alliance' (*Chron. Charles V*, iii, Appendix xix, p. 144; cf. Delachenal, iv, p. 140 n. 1). For Anjou's attitude, see above, pp. 235–6.

283

that year, in anticipation of the prince's likely response to the delivery of Charles's summons, Louis of Anjou was actively engaged in retaining forces for service in Aquitaine.³ These included, from among the Great Companies, the *routes* of Petit Meschin, Bouzomet de Pau, Amanieu d'Ortigue, Perrin de Savoie, Noli Pavalhon and Jacques de Bray, who had earlier served with du Guesclin in the war in Provence, as well as those of the *bourc* de Breteuil, Arnauton du Pin, and possibly also Bérard d'Albret. Some had been brought into French service earlier: Munde Bataillier, who in return for his homage and fealty had been retained as an esquire of the king's equerry and granted a life annuity of 300 *livres* by Charles V in January 1366; the *bourc* de Breteuil, Garciot du Castel and Frank Hennequin, who were recruited by Jean d'Armagnac and were serving under Louis of Anjou as part of his company.⁴ According to Froissart they together constituted the greater part of the Great Companies, amounting to some 3,000 combatants in all.⁵ Others who may be noted included the bastard of Terride, retained on 4 March, and Benedetto Chipperel, whose forces were mustered on 1 June and again on 24 October.⁶ In addition, the duke had recruited some of the leading Breton companies – those of Silvestre Budes, the Kerlouets (Hervé and Jean), and probably also those of Auffroy de Guébriant and Julliel Rollant, who were certainly in his service at a later date.⁷

Some of the English *routes* of the Great Companies remained in northern France, where, following the evacuation of Château-Gontier, they joined the English garrison forces at Saint-Sauveur or took up position in a number of fortresses which they had occupied in Anjou and the Loire valley. Sir John Cresswell, Sir Robert Cheyney and other *routes* of the companies who had served in Spain – most notably those of Naudon de Bageran, the *bourc* de Lesparre, Gaillard de la Motte and Aimery de Rochechouart – together with the *route* commanded by Lamit, were placed under the command of Sir Hugh Calveley, who was recalled from Aragon to conduct a destructive raid into the lands of the two chief appellants, the count of Armagnac and the lord of Albret, in the early spring.⁸

By the beginning of 1369, most of the companies had thus been recruited into the royal and princely armies of England or France, twice as many, if we may believe Froissart, onto the French side.⁹ Charles V had finally

3 'pour lui renforcier et en afoiblir le prince et les Engles' (BN, PO 3052. doss. Wissant); see Delachenal, iv, pp. 159–60.
4 See appendix D (1).
5 Froissart, *Chroniques*, vii, p. 336.
6 Contamine, 1975, pp. 392–3, PJ no. ii, for Terride; BN, nouv. acq. franç., 8603, nos. 67, 73, for Chipperel.
7 See appendix D (2).
8 Froissart, *Chroniques*, vii, pp. li–lii, lxiii, 117–18, 135, 337. See Breuils, p. 91.
9 Froissart, *Chroniques*, vii, p. 336.

succeeded in his plan to divide the loyalties of their captains,[10] and thereafter the fortunes of many of them either came to an abrupt end or rapidly declined. Already before this date a number of captains had either been killed in action or taken prisoner and executed. In 1364, John Amory had been mortally wounded in an engagement outside Sancerre and, although taken prisoner, died of his wounds.[11] In the summer of that year Jean de Chauffour was decapitated at Langres, probably together with his brother, Thibaud.[12] Guiot du Pin, Gilles Troussevache and Guillampot were all taken prisoner and handed over to the duke of Burgundy's officers, who had them executed in the autumn.[13] The following year Louis Roubaud was beheaded and quartered at Villeneuve-les-Avignon by order of the lord of la Voulte in Vivarais, two English captains, Thomas Morville and John Vieleston, were drowned in Lower Normandy, and in 1368 Munde Bataillier was decapitated in Paris.[14] In early March 1369, the *bourc* Camus, Jehannot le Nègre and the *bourc* de Caupène were taken prisoner in an engagement with the French at Lesterps, to the north-west of Limoges, and were transported to Paris, where they were executed as traitors by order of the king.[15] Then, on 11 May, after the discovery of a plot to have the duke of Anjou taken prisoner, handed over to the English or killed, Perrin de Savoie and Elías Machin were drowned in the Garonne at Toulouse, and Amanieu d'Ortigue, Noli Pavalhon and Bouzomet de Pau were decapitated and quartered in the same city and for the same offence.[16] Bernard de la Salle, on the other hand, escaped capture at Lesterps and was to continue his activities for many years to come. In the following August, in an exploit which astounded contemporaries, he and his brother Hortingo took the castle of Belleperche near Moulins by assault, and imprisoned the dowager duchess of Bourbon – the mother of the queen of France – who

10 The comments of Froissart, *Oeuvres*, vii, p. 279, on Anjou's recruitment of the companies are apposite: 'Si avoit atrais et atraioit encorres tous les jours touttes mannières de gens d'armes, espéciaument cappitainnes des compaignes, pour lui renforchier et afoiblir le prinche et les Englès. Si avoit ratrait Petit Mescin, Jake de Bray, Perrot de Savoie, Aimmenion de Lortighe et pluisseurs autres bons guerriuers, dont il peuist estre bien servis et aidiés, et qui estoient souverain des routtes, et leur donnoit et prommetoit grans dons et proufis à faire, et leur faisoit tous les jours. D'autre part, li roys de Franche se maintenoit en cas pareil, et avoit ossi retrais devers lui et fès de ses amis pluisseurs par dons et par larguèces, car il supposoit bien qu'il en aroit à faire.'
11 Froissart, *Chroniques*, xii, pp. xxxiii, 104.
12 Ibid., vi, p. xx, n. 4; *Oeuvres*, vii, p. 4.
13 Chérest, pp. 285–6, 291.
14 *Chron. normande*, pp. 165–7, and, for Munde Bataillier, Noyal, 'Chronique', p. 266. Vieleston came from Kent, and had been outlawed by the Court of Husting of London for a debt of £100 in 1357 (*CPR, 1354–8*, p. 654). He was dead by July 1365 (*CPR, 1364–7*, p. 157).
15 Lesterps, Charente, arr. and cant. Confolens (*Chron. normande*, pp. 75, 77–8, 92, 192–3, 347–8). According to Noyal, 'Chronique', p. 267, the *bourc* Camus was tormented with hot tongs before being executed. Cf. Froissart, *Oeuvres*, vii, p. 422.
16 *Thalamus parvus*, p. 384.

was in residence there. An expedition to recapture the place, organized by the duchess's son Louis and Marshal Sancerre, resulted in a siege of several months. It was not until the following March that Belleperche was finally evacuated by an arrangement whereby the companies were allowed to leave freely and with their prisoners, including the dowager duchess, who was removed to the tower of Broue in Saintonge, which was not recovered by the French until August 1372.[17]

Shortly after the arrival of Charles of Navarre in Cherbourg on 13 August 1369 Charles V made a concerted effort to recover the castle of Saint-Sauveur-le-Vicomte in Normandy, which was used as a refuge and base of operations by the companies following their evacuation of Château-Gontier.[18] The precise intentions of the Navarrese king were by no means evident, and once again he was simultaneously negotiating with both the French and the English, although initially the depredations carried out by the companies against his possessions in Normandy, and in particular in the Cotentin, did not incline him to be favourably disposed towards Edward III.[19] The French pursuit of the companies who made their way to Saint-Sauveur was conducted by the two marshals of France (Louis de Sancerre and Mouton de Blainville), the *vicomte* of Sancerre and a number of lords of the *basses-marches*, notably Amaury de Craon, Gui de Laval, Olivier de Clisson and the sire de Rays, whose lands had suffered attack from the companies based at Château-Gontier.[20] The latter were besieged in Saint-Sauveur, but the operation was soon abandoned, following the departure of Clisson's forces. Although Charles V gave instructions to Craon and the other captains that they should return to the scene of action,

17 For this episode, see Delachenal, iv, pp. 217–19.
18 'Et l'an LXIX vint le roy de Navarre en Costentin, eu moys d'aoust, et vint par Bretaigne, et parla au duc et à la duchesse, et l'amena mons. de Clison jusquez à Avrenches. Tantost les compaignons qui estoient au Chastel Gautier vindrent après en Costentin à Saint Sauveur le Viconte. Et tantost tous les grans seigneurs des basses marches vindrent après et les assidrent à Saint Sauveur' (Delisle, *Fragments*, p. 9). In a letter dated Saint-Georges-de-Boscherville, 27 August 1369, Charles V wrote to the *bailli* of Caen 'Nous avons entendu de certain que les Engloiz, gens de compaingne, qui sont yssus de Chastiau Gontier et estoient nagairez entrés en Bretaingne, s'en sont retournez et sont a present à Saint Sauveur le Viconte et environ, et ailleurs ou pais de Costentin, et ne savons à quel tiltre ou instance il y sont venus, ne quelle entencion ou vollenté il ont, ne quel aide ou confort il pevent avoir sur le dit pais.' He therefore ordered the *bailli* to instruct captains, castellans and others to be on their guard, to maintain watch by night and day, not to allow anyone other than well-known persons into their castles and fortresses, and in particular to look out for men-at-arms who might, as in the past, be dressed as women and labourers (Delisle, *Saint-Sauveur*, preuves, p. 170, no. 114, and *Mandements*, no. 570). According to *Chron. Charles V*, ii, p. 134, up to 1,000 *gens de compaigne* retreated to Saint-Sauveur. For the date and other details of Charles of Navarre's arrival in Cherbourg, see Delachenal, iv, p. 220, n. 3, and for this entire episode, ibid., pp. 219–22.
19 For Charles's diplomacy at this juncture, see Delachenal, iv, pp. 221–2.
20 Delisle, *Fragments*, p. 9.

the strength of the the investing army had been seriously depleted.[21] Apart from Cherbourg, most of the Cotentin was abandoned to the companies, who occupied lands and castles, financing themselves from the proceeds of protection money from strongholds like Eroudeville, just outside Montebourg, and Garnetot.[22]

The French offensive in 1369 was largely conditioned by geographical and political factors, and it was mainly concentrated on the frontiers of Aquitaine.[23] By the end of that year the whole of Rouergue and Quercy were in their obedience and the Agenais and Périgord penetrated by their forces and shortly to be lost to them. Rouergue had always been an outpost of the principality, an enclave in France, largely controlled by the count of Armagnac, whose territories elsewhere in Gascony were also taken into the French orbit. By the early summer the county of Ponthieu in northern France had also been secured. On the other hand, English military policy during this year lacked clear direction. After an offensive against the lands of the count of Périgord, the earls of Cambridge and Pembroke turned their efforts against La Roche-sur-Yonne in the Vendée, which was important in the line of communications with Brittany, but which had never been handed over to Edward III in conformity with the treaty of Brétigny. Invested by their forces at the beginning of July, it was finally secured after about a month's siege, although for their part the French retaliated by securing La Roche-Posay, which was situated on the north-eastern frontiers of Poitou, on the river Creuse, to the south-west of Châtellerault, and which, under the terms of the treaty, should have been returned to them. An expeditionary force sent out under John of Gaunt in August was primarily intended to destroy the naval armaments being assembled on the Normandy coast for an invasion of England, and its destination was Harfleur, the principal naval port at the mouth of the Seine. After disembarking at Calais and crossing Ponthieu, Gaunt's forces penetrated the *pays de Caux* and Upper Normandy before being repulsed and making a hasty retreat to Calais. It is unlikely that any link-up was intended with the English forces based at Saint-Sauveur, or at Cherbourg with Charles of Navarre, whose political position at this juncture remained unclear.

In none of these offensives did the companies play any significant part, and their activities appear to have been limited to a war of skirmishes and ambushes which characterized much of the military activity in Aquitaine. Most of their employ seems to have been under Sir John Chandos, who sent the *routes* commanded by Sir Robert Cheyney, John Chase and Hodgkin Russell to besiege Compeyre in Rouergue in June 1369.[24] Rather

21 Ibid., and *Chron. Charles V*, ii, p. 134.
22 Delisle, *Fragments*, p. 9.
23 For the details of what follows, see Delachenal, iv, pp. 163–94, 209–15.
24 *Docs. Millau*, no. 332.

more important was a *chevauchée* which the earl of Pembroke made into Anjou in early September, which included some 500 men from the companies under Calveley's command. While the army was unable to secure a bridgehead across the Loire at Saumur, which they unsuccessfully besieged, Calveley and his men proceeded further downstream, where they secured, fortified and garrisoned les Ponts-de-Cé, Beaufort-en-Vallée and the Benedictine abbey of Saint-Maur, maintaining themselves from ransoms levied on the surrounding countryside.[25] Situated just over three miles to the immediate south of Angers, in the fourteenth century Les Ponts-de-Cé was in many ways a suburb of that town.[26] Located in the middle of the Loire on three islands, joined together by a series of bridges, it commanded a stretch of road almost two miles long, across the territory which now includes the canal of Authion as well as the three large arms of the river. The northern bank was dominated by a castle, built on a mound, and controlling entry and exit from the first bridge. This castle, which had been constructed in 1206 by Guillaume des Roches on the ruins of an older fortress razed by Philip Augustus, was secured and fortified by Calveley. Along with the bridge it gave the companies control of the Loire, as the occupation of Lion d'Angers by Hodgkin Russell and John Chase in 1368 had made them masters of the Mayenne. Control of both places allowed the companies to hem in the capital of Anjou from the north and the south, and helped to keep open the lines of communication between the English garrisons in Aquitaine and those in Brittany and Normandy. The abbey of Saint-Maur, situated on the south bank of the river, was equidistant from Angers and Saumur, and had been occupied by Sir John Cresswell and Sir Hugh Calveley once before, in 1355, and again by the companies in 1361.[27] In 1369 Calveley put Cresswell in charge of the garrison there.[28]

A further offensive against the French was then mounted from Poitou, where the enemy had made little progress and where Sir John Chandos was seneschal. From his headquarters in Poitiers he moved into Louis of Anjou's lands in the Loire valley in October, and in particular into the Loudunois, which Charles V had ceded to his brother Louis in 1367. Proceeding along the Touraine frontier and by way of the Creuse valley, he then made an unsuccessful attempt to take the castle of Rochechouart, which was defended by the Breton captain Thibaud du Pont, before returning to base at Poitiers. Within a matter of months of the campaign Chandos was

---

25 'et le païs environ vivoit en pactis dessoubz luy': see Froissart, *Chroniques*, vii, pp. 189–90; Joubert, p. 59.
26 For the following details, see Luce in Froissart, *Chroniques*, vii, p. lxxxii n. 1.
27 Ibid., vii, p. lxxxii, n. 2; Venette, *Chronicle*, p. 107.
28 It was with Cresswell that the negotiations for its evacuation took place in December of the following year (AN, P 1334[i], fo. 38; see Luce in Froissart, *Chroniques*, vii, p. lxxxii n. 2).

mortally wounded at Lussac, after a night attack on the abbey of Saint-Savin, which had been taken by the Breton captain Jean de Kerlouet. His death was a serious blow to the English and allowed the French to make continued progress in 1370, their position being further reinforced with the return of du Guesclin from Castile in the summer of that year.

A new offensive from England, which was initially scheduled for the spring of 1370, but which had to be put off until the early summer of that year, involved liaison with the companies stationed in Normandy and the Loire valley. This was placed under the command of Sir Robert Knowles, who was recalled from Aquitaine in March of that year and who, by the terms of an indenture dated 20 June, was authorized to prosecute war in France on Edward III's behalf for a period of two years with an army of 2,000 men-at-arms and 2,000 archers.[29] The terms of this agreement were evidently concluded somewhat earlier, since on 13 June Knowles had sealed a document indicating that, although he had been appointed captain of the army, he had decided, with the king's consent, to share the command with Sir Alan Buxhill, Sir Thomas Grandson and Sir John Bourchier, and had agreed that they should share with him the profits of the campaign in proportion to the size of their retinues.[30] On 1 July all four were appointed the king's lieutenants in France.[31] From the outset the king or some of his councillors were evidently uneasy about giving this command to men of a lower social standing than those normally appointed to the office, and Knowles's past career suggested that they had cause for their anxiety.[32] They were evidently required to give some guarantee of their good behaviour, and four days later they put their seals to a document undertaking to serve the king faithfully and vigorously, to see that the army kept together throughout the expedition, that the different companies of which it was composed did not go their separate ways or allow divisions to arise between them over prisoners, castles, fortresses, towns, or on any other account, and to ensure that any discords were speedily amended.[33] The eventualities envisaged in this document proved prophetic of what was in fact to happen.

The total strength of the army under the command of the four lieutenants was at least 2,500 troops, made up in equal proportions of men-at-arms and archers, of which the largest personal retinues were provided by Knowles, with 299 men-at-arms and 300 archers, Sir John Minstreworth with 199 men-at-arms and 200 archers, Matthew Redman with 149 men-at-arms and 150 archers, and the lord of Grandson with 99 men-at-arms

---

29 PRO, E 101/68/4, no. 90; see Sherborne, p. 723.
30 *Foedera*, III, ii, p. 897. Sherborne, p. 723, wrongly says *Thomas* Bourchier.
31 *Foedera*, III, ii, pp. 894–5; see Delachenal, iv, p. 304, n. 5.
32 See the long list of disobediences referred to in the pardon granted to Knowles in November 1374 (*CPR, 1374–7*, pp. 20–1).
33 BM, Cotton Caligula D III, no. 44.

and 100 archers.[34] The financial arrangements made for the expedition were somewhat unusual in that the Crown only undertook to pay wages for a period of thirteen weeks, or for the length of time elapsing between the departure of the troops from their homes and their arrival in France, should that prove longer. Thereafter, the army was clearly intended to finance itself from the proceeds of ransoms to be levied during the campaign. The arrangements did not augur well for the undertakings which the lieutenants had made.

The intended point of disembarkation of this ill-fated expedition appears to have been La Hougue, where the forces sent out from England were to have joined up with their compatriots occupying Saint-Sauveur and other fortresses in the Cotentin; but owing to the opposition of Charles of Navarre, who feared for the security of his own possessions there, the planned disembarkation was shifted to the *pays de Caux*.[35] Contrary winds obliged Knowles to assemble his army at Rye and Winchelsea and to head for Calais. It was from there that he conducted a *chevauchée* which, beginning at the end of July, took his army across northern France via Arras, Bapaume, Roye and Ham to Noyon, and thence into the Laonnais, the county of Soissons and, after a show of force before Reims, the plains of Champagne. Crossing the Marne at Dormans, they pushed south by way of Troyes to arrive on the frontiers of Burgundy at Saint-Florentin. Finding the duchy too well defended, they then turned west, crossed the Yonne near Joigny, and proceeded through the Gâtinais in the direction of Paris, by way of Château-Landon, Nemours, Corbeil and Essonnes, 'burning all the country which refused to pay ransom money'. By 22 September they were in the vicinity of Longjumeau, where they took up position at Mons and Ablan. Two days later they assembled between Villejuif and Paris, conducting skirmishes to the barriers of the *bourg* Saint-Marcel and burning numerous villages in the suburbs – at Villejuif, Cachan, Arcueil and Bicêtre – of which the smoke and flames were visible from within the city. The show was pure bravado. Paris was well protected by its ramparts and a substantial garrison force. Nor was Charles V to be provoked into an engagement outside the city walls. The same evening Knowles's troops withdrew to Antony, from where they first made for Normandy, but finding it too well defended, four days later they returned to Étampes, where they first appear to have split up, some companies proceeding by

---

34 PRO, E 101/30/25. Documentary evidence of the strength of the army is limited to this incomplete retinue list, from which I calculate a total of 1,233 men-at-arms and 1,258 archers. Using the same source, Sherborne, p. 724, arrives at a figure of 1,416 men-at-arms and 1,512 archers, whilst Delachenal, iv, p. 303, calculates 1,411 men-at-arms and 1,536 archers. Both of these authors conclude that the total strength of the army was evidently somewhat greater, perhaps considerably greater.
35 The best account of the expedition is to be found in Delachenal, iv, ch. ix, pp. 301–42.

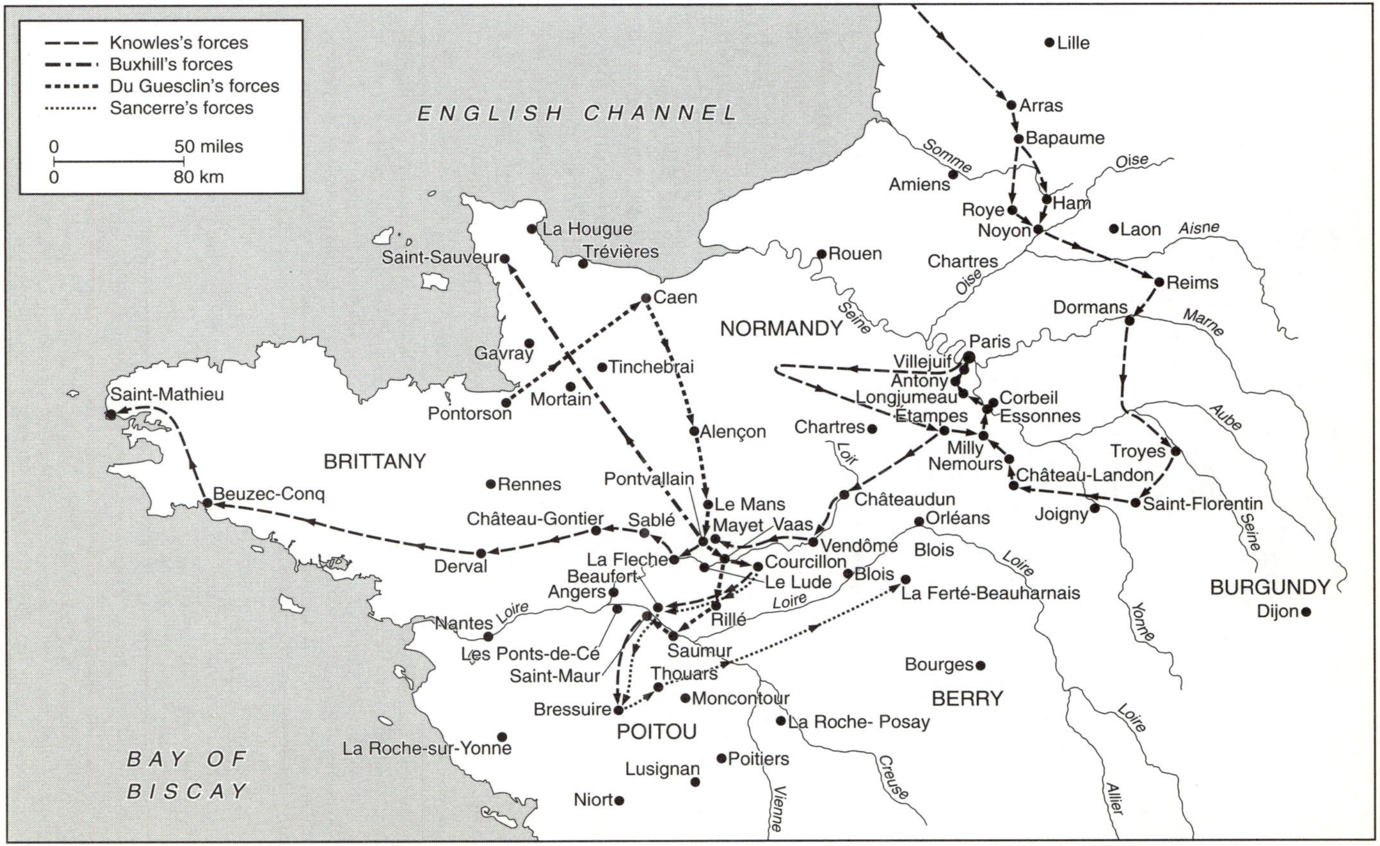

12 *The chevauchée of Sir Robert Knowles and the battle of Pontvallain, July–December 1370*

way of Milly into Gâtinais whilst others, under Knowles, made for Beauce, ransoming the town and castellany of Châteaudun for 500 francs on 5 October, before proceeding into the Vendômois and then making for the confines of Anjou and Maine.[36]

What exactly were the objectives of the expedition? Clearly it was intended to be a destructive raid, and throughout the campaign the army ruthlessly proceeded to devastate and ransom the countryside. It is possible that Knowles did not have any pre-conceived plan of action – other than to make the maximum profit in ransoms and booty for himself and his men – before heading for his lands at Derval in Brittany by way of the lower Loire.[37] On the other hand, the ultimate outcome of the campaign, of division between the leaders and the defeat of part of the army, has obscured what appears to have been a concerted strategy, to draw du Guesclin – and perhaps also Louis of Anjou – off from Aquitaine whilst the Black Prince, with reinforcements sent out from England under the duke of Lancaster, conducted a new offensive in Aquitaine.[38] Such a strategy had been employed in both 1346 and 1356,[39] and if on the latter occasion the plan had very nearly been compromised by the first duke of Lancaster's failure to get across the Loire, all the bridges being closely guarded, in 1370 Les Ponts-de-Cé and other river crossings were in the control of the companies under Calveley's command.

In the autumn of 1370 the plan did go badly wrong. In Aquitaine the prince and John of Gaunt got bogged down in besieging Limoges and Cognac, whilst in Anjou and Maine, Knowles's forces preoccupied themselves with capturing fortresses from which they could levy ransoms in enemy territory, in much the same way they had done in Brittany in the 1340s and 1350s, and subsequently in the Cotentin.[40] These included a string of places in the Loire valley between Vendôme and La Flèche,

---

36 'Le samedi apres le Saint Remi . . . Les habitantz de la ville de Chasteaudun, genz d'eglise, nobles, bourgois, marchans et autres, appellez par cri et voiz solempnel . . . est d'un commun assentement de tous ensemble . . . pour obliger la ville de Chasteaudun envers mons. Robert de Connoles, anglais, en la somme de cinq cenz frans d'or pour la rancon de la chastellenie et paroisses d'icelle, et en la somme de cent frans envers ceuls que ont preste yceuls cens frans pour le frai dessus dit' (Notarial register of Jean Chaillou, 1370: AD, Eure et Loir, E 2691, fo. 24r).
37 Delachenal, iv, p. 315.
38 Cuvelier, *Chronique*, ii, lines 17,745–6, believed that the English plan of action was to cross the Loire into Aquitaine.
39 Fowler, 1969, pp. 154–6.
40 According to the *Anonimalle Chronicle*, p. 64, the division of the expeditionary forces was occasioned 'pur grosour de coer et envye'. The chief occupation of the captains appears to have been the occupation of fortresses and the organization of reventions or ransom districts, particularly in Anjou and Maine. This occurred before Knowles made for Brittany. A grant of fortresses by Charles V to Olivier de Clisson of 24 March 1371 (Bibl. mun., Nantes, Fonds Bizeul, MS 1696 [français 1540]) demonstrates that the French were similarly levying ransoms in territories controlled by England and its allies.

including the fortified abbey of Notre-Dame-de-Vaas and the town of Le Lude.[41] To the south of that river they took Courcillon and, between Le Lude and Saumur, the fortified abbey of Notre-Dame de Loroux and Rillé, which, along with the garrison at Beaufort-en-Vallée, put them in direct communication with Cresswell's forces garrisoning the abbey of Saint-Maur on the Loire.[42]

It was at this juncture – sometime in November – that the differences which had been latent within the English army throughout the campaign came to the surface. Knowles incurred the envy of his fellow captains and some of the rank and file by retaining for himself an unwarranted proportion of the ransoms levied by the army. It was in his interests to call a halt to the campaign and head for his lordship of Derval in Brittany with the ransoms and booty which he had accumulated to date. The other leaders, on the contrary, preferred to remain in the fortresses which they had taken in Anjou and Maine, increasing their profits from the proceeds of the ransom districts. Sir John Minstreworth fomented the discord, calling Knowles an 'old brigand', and he was perhaps the first to part company, together with the *routes* under his command.[43] Grandson and Walter, Lord Fitzwalter, followed suit, with the result that the army divided into four parts, Knowles apparently making for Brittany by way of La Flèche, Sablé and Château-Gontier.[44]

In the event, the division of the army proved fatal. Following his return from Castile to Aquitaine in July, du Guesclin had been recalled to Paris by Charles V, who, on 2 October, elevated him to the high office of constable of France. The appointment of a man of his relatively modest background was, to say the least, somewhat unusual, but justified by his long experience of military affairs. However, it was also made in response to the immediate problems posed by Knowles's campaign, and intended to give him command of forces being assembled in Normandy to resist them.[45] On 24 October the new constable was at Pontorson, where he concluded a

---

41 Delachenal, iv, p. 334.
42 Ibid. The identification of Rillé (Indre-et-Loir, cant. Château-la-Vallière) and not Ruillé-sur-le-Loir (Sarthe, arr. Saint-Calais, cant. la Chartre-sur-le-Loir) is indicated by the proximity to Mouliherne (Maine-et-Loire, cant. Longué) in an account of these events related in a later part of Froissart's *Chronicle* (xiv, pp. ix–x, 5–7), not published until 1966, which consequently escaped the attention of Simeon Luce (see ibid., viii, p. iv n. 1).
43 'En quel tenps le dite sire Robert prist toutez les raunsones de diverses countres devers luy et pur ceo graunt envye et graunt rancore de coer sourdist parentre les seignours et communes et le dit sire Robert de Knolles' (*Anonimalle Chronicle*, p. 64). See Walsingham, *Hist. Anglicana*, i, p. 310, and Delachenal, iv, pp. 335–6.
44 'Et avaunt le fest de Nowelle departirent les chevetaynes del hoste pour grosour de coer et envye, en quatre parties a graunt confusione Dengleterre et graunt comfort des enmys, cest assavoir le seignour de Grauncoun od ses gentz en une partie, le seignour fitz Waltre en une autre et monsire Johan Misterworth en le tierce partie, et le dit sire Robert Knolles en la quarte partie' (*Anonimalle Chronicle*, p. 64). See Delachenal, iv, pp. 334–5.
45 Delachenal, iv, pp. 321–3.

pact of brotherhood-in-arms with Olivier, lord of Clisson.[46] By 6 November he was at Caen, where he assembled his forces, and it was from that town that he began his pursuit of the English army on 1 December.[47]

The most striking feature of du Guesclin's campaign was the speed of his military operations. Passing by Alençon on 2 December, he arrived at Le Mans the following afternoon after a brief halt at Juillé around midday.[48] At Le Mans he was informed that the rearguard of the English army under Grandson was at Mayet, some eight leagues further south, from where it was proceeding at a quick pace to rejoin Knowles's forces. According to Froissart, having had news from his scouts of du Guesclin's movements, Knowles had requested Grandson, Gilbert Giffard and Geoffrey Worsley to reassemble with their companies at a prearranged place, where he intended to engage the constable. He had also sent word to Calveley, who was at Saint-Maur, and to Cresswell, Cheyney and other captains of the companies who were in the vicinity, to join up with them there.[49] As things turned out, they were outmanoeuvred by du Guesclin, who, after arriving at Le Mans on the evening of 3 December, heard that Calveley, Grandson and about 600 combatants were lodged near Pontvallain, from where they were hoping to join Knowles's forces, which had already passed to the south of that town on their way to Brittany.[50] Despite the weariness of his men-at-arms and the exhaustion of their mounts, the constable immediately set out after them with a part of his army, proceeding at a brisk pace throughout the night, to fall on the English near the castle of Faigne, situated in a little valley on the left bank of the river Aune near its junction with the Bruant, around one and a half miles north-north-east of Pontvallain. Taken completely by surprise, the English attempted to escape across the wooded countryside of *la lande de Rigalet*, in the direction of Le Lude, and a large part of their forces were run to ground at La Croix Brette, just over half-way between Pontvallain and Le Lude. Grandson himself was taken prisoner, along with Giffard, Phillip de Courtenay, Hugh le Despenser, Sir William de Neville, Sir John Clanvowe, Sir Edmund Daumarle, Matthew Redman, Richard and David Green, and, from among the captains of the companies, Geoffrey Worsley, David Holgrave and Thomas Folifait.[51]

---

46 Ibid., iv, p. 332. The text has been published by Berville, ii, pp. 525–8.
47 Delachenal, iv, p. 333. According to Cuvelier, *Chronique*, ii, lines 17,943–4, Caen was the point of concentration and du Guesclin summoned the French forces to join him there.
48 For du Guesclin's itinerary and other details of his campaign, see Delachenal, iv, pp. 336–41.
49 Froissart, *Chroniques*, viii, p. 2.
50 *Chron. normande*, pp. 196–7.
51 The list of prisoners may be established from the names given by Luce in Froissart, *Chroniques*, viii, p. vii, n. 2; *Chron. normande*, p. 197; *Anonimalle Chronicle*, p. 64; Cuvelier, *Chronique*, ii, lines 18,484–6. See *RP*, ii, p. 343, for the imprisonment of some of these men,

Calveley and some of the other contingents under his command appear to have made for Saint-Maur before the engagement, but others who had not taken part or who had fled from the battlefield were systematically pursued by du Guesclin's forces. Some made for Vaas, where a further 300 Englishmen were killed or captured, including Lord Fitzwalter, who was taken by Jean d'Azay, seneschal of Toulouse, and whose ransom was subsequently disputed between one of the marshals of France, Louis of Sancerre, who was in charge of this operation, and du Guesclin, who appears to have arrived on the scene around three hours later.[52] Other contingents made for the castle of Courcillon, across the Loir from Château-du-Loir, but subsequently decamped and, crossing the Loire at Saint-Maur, made for Bressuire in Poitou, with the marshal in hot pursuit. As these contingents were unable to secure entry into the town, an engagement took place in the *faubourgs*, the English retreating into the *parquet* before the main gate, where several hundred of them were killed.[53] Still others, a significant proportion of them badly armed men and pillagers, who had made for Rillé and had planned to follow them to Bressuire, were preparing to depart at sunrise when they were ambushed and defeated by the *corps d'élite* of du Guesclin's forces, under his personal command.[54] Both sides dismounted, but the constable's troops met with stiff opposition until the arrival of sixty lances under Maurice de Tréséguidy, Geoffroi Richon, Geoffroi de Kerimel and Guillaume Picard, alias Morfouace, who together broke the English lines with a mounted charge. The English losses were substantial, but some contingents escaped – including Robert Cheyney, Richard Holm, Richard Gilles and one of Calveley's closest associates, John Clerk – who got across the Loire at Saint-Maur in a small boat.[55] Du

and PRO, E 101/30/38, for the release of Neville, Clanvowe and Daumarle (whose name is also rendered as Domer and Dunmier) in March. Sir John Bourchier may also have been taken prisoner on this campaign (see *RP*, iii, p. 256, and BL, Additional Charter, 7909). Thomas Folifait or *Fillefort* may have been related to Walter *Ferrefort*, who was taken prisoner on the 1374–5 expedition (Northumberland Record Office, Capheaton Collection, Swinburne MSS 4/60; I am grateful to my colleague, Prof. A. E. Goodman, for bringing this document to my attention).
52 *Chron. normande*, p. 198; Cabaret d'Orville, *Chronique*, pp. 25–6.
53 Cabaret d'Orville, *Chronique*, pp. 26–8.
54 According to a Breton knight, Guillaume d'Ancenis, who went over the battlefield with Froissart in 1387 and recounted the engagement to him, du Guesclin had 500 lances with him, whilst the English forces consisted of 900 combatants, but, d'Ancenis added, 'au voir dire, nous estiemes tous gens d'armes d'eslite; mais entre eulx en y avoit-il de mal armez grant plenté et de pillars' (Froissart, *Chroniques*, xiv, pp. 4–8).
55 Ibid. Cheyney continued in the Black Prince's service in Aquitaine; on 24 July 1373 he was a witness to an act whereby the inhabitants of Figeac swore allegiance to Edward III and the prince (BN, Doat, vol. 125, fo. 96v). Walsingham, *Hist. Anglicana*, i, pp. 401–2, later described Clerk as a 'vir armipotens et bellicosus, prudens et strenuus . . . socius et collega strenuissimi militis Domini Hugonis de Calverlee', and devoted a separately headed paragraph of his chronicle to him. For his previous service in Spain with both Calveley and du Guesclin, see above, pp. 185n, 205n, 248, and below, p. 330.

Guesclin attempted to prevent their escape, but was obliged to cross the river further upstream, at Saumur.[56] His engagement at Rillé may have caused him to miss the action at Bressuire.[57] Whatever the case, the town itself was taken by assault, although no attempt was made to occupy it on a permanent basis. The fortresses taken by Knowles's forces in Anjou and Maine were thus recovered in a matter of days.

Immediately following the action at Bressuire, Sancerre set out for La Ferté-Beauharnais, situated in Sologne, some fifteen miles above Romorantin, which had probably been taken by the companies which had earlier proceeded through Gâtinais. Following an engagement with the forces established there, it too appears to have been taken by his men.[58] Du Guesclin, meanwhile, had proceeded to Saint-Maur, where he negotiated the evacuation of the abbey with Sir John Cresswell for an unknown sum, before returning to Le Mans, where he was housed in the residence of Louis of Anjou, which had been specially prepared for his return.[59]

There can be no gainsaying du Guesclin's achievement. From Le Mans, Grandson, Fitzwalter and Matthew Redman were transported ignobly to Paris in carts and held there in strict imprisonment.[60] Some of the prisoners may have been released after their ransoms had been agreed at Le Mans, but others did not secure their liberty until towards the end of March.[61] However, the constable had failed to engage the greater part of the army under the command of Knowles, Buxhill and Minstreworth, whose companies eluded him, making for Normandy and Brittany. Already on 1 December – three days before the battle at Pontvallain – Buxhill, whose commission as captain and lieutenant of Saint-Sauveur is dated 26 November 1370, arrived in that fortress with a contingent of two knights, forty-six men-at-arms and twenty-eight archers to take up his command.[62] These probably constituted only a fraction of the forces originally placed under

---

56   *Chron. normande*, pp. 198–9, 352. The constable reviewed the troops of the other marshal of France, Mouton de Blainville, at Saumur on 6 December 1370 (ibid., p. 351, n. l; see Delachenal, iv, p. 340).
57   Cabaret d'Orville, *Chronique*, p. 28, says that he arrived too late for the main action, although the *Chron. normande*, p. 199, and the *Chron. Charles V*, ii, p. 148, suggests otherwise. See Delachenal, iv, pp. 339–40.
58   Cabaret d'Orville, *Chronique*, pp. 28–9.
59   Luce in Froissart, *Chroniques*, vii, p. lxxxii, n. 2, and viii, p. vii n. 1; *Regs. Tours*, ii, nos. 486, 489. See Delachenal. iv, p. 341.
60   The author of the *Anonimalle Chronicle*, p. 64, records that they were thus conducted *vilaynsement*. His account contrasts sharply with that of Froissart, *Chroniques*, viii, pp. 1–5, who says that they were treated honourably and subjected to moderate ransoms. The petitions made in parliament on their behalf bear out the former testimony (*RP*, ii, p. 343).
61   Notably Neville, Clanvowe and Daumarle (PRO, E 101/30/38, ms. 2–3).
62   Buxhill's retinue included three men evidently from the Low Countries: Hans Cokerych, knight, Hans Panewych, knight, and Chrispian van Wyberk, with ten, thirteen and eight men-at-arms respectively. Among the remaining fourteen men-at-arms we may note John de Wanton, who was subsequently on Knowles's payroll (PRO, E 101/30/25, 38).

him. Throughout the campaign he had cooperated closely with Knowles, who headed for his lands at Derval, doubtless with considerable booty, before continuing his retreat to his castle at Beuzec-Conq, just outside Concarneau. Both men appear to have lost a considerable number of troops in their precipitate retreat, and Knowles arrived at Derval too late to make use of the reinforcements – perhaps as many as 1,100 men – sent out from England with Robert Neville. There was nothing for them to do but to return to their port of disembarkation at Saint-Mathieu in Finistère. Here they were joined by other troops who were unable to find sufficient ships to facilitate their passage to England from Concarneau, men whom Knowles either could not or would not accommodate at Conq, possibly because some of them were from Minstreworth's companies. At Saint-Mathieu they were trapped by a force under Olivier de Clisson and a large part of them, perhaps as many as 500, were killed.[63] Other contingents of the broken army made for a number of Navarrese towns and castles in the marches of the Cotentin, notably Trévières, Tinchebrai, Gavray and Mortain, but were subsequently expelled and forced to take refuge at Saint-Sauveur, together with some of the prisoners later released by the French. By the end of March the latter fortress was positively bursting at the seams, so great was the influx of troops from the defeated army.[64]

Following the battle of Pontvallain the companies ceased to operate under the name of the *Great Companies*, which, with their numbers depleted and many of the founder captains no longer alive, had largely been absorbed into the royal armies of England and France.[65] Some of the English *routes* which had not been taken prisoner regrouped for a while under Walter Huet, John Cresswell and David Holgrave,[66] but both Cresswell and

---

63 *Anonimalle Chronicle*, pp. 65, 176.
64 Buxhill's expenses were greatly expanded as a result of the *magne multitudinis* of men-at-arms, armed men and archers, and diverse other English expelled from the Navarrese castles and towns, and also *propter refugium multorum aliorum prisonariorum* from diverse places in France and Brittany, who arrived in Saint-Sauveur on 15 February and 25 March. The total arrivals by the latter date amounted to 6 knights, 127 men-at-arms and 87 archers (PRO, E 101/30/38). Another account for the period from 26 November 1370 (the date of Buxhill's appointment as captain of Saint-Sauveur) to 15 February 1371 includes 3,034 francs for 'diversis solucionibus per ipsum factis pro redemcionibus diversorum prisonarium impotencium qui in servicio Regis per inimicos Franciae per diuers vices capit fuerunt' (PRO, E 101/30/39).
65 In the Navarrese accounts for December 1369 to May 1370 those of them in the garrison of Saint-Sauveur are still referred to as *gens de compaigne* and *gens des compaignes*, but these are among the last documents to describe them as such (Izarn, *Compte*, pp. 36, 303; see above, p. 235, n. 37).
66 'et y ordonnèrent à demourer monsigneur Gautier Huet, Carsuelle et David Holegrave et touttes les compaignes, qui là estoient de leur costé, et qui s'estoient remis enssamble depuis le desconfiture de Pont Volain' (Froissart, *Chroniques*, viii, p. 278). For Huet, whose career was largely made in Brittany, see Jones, 1970, pp. 48–51 and *passim*.

Holgrave were retained by the Black Prince,[67] and they operated in an official capacity in the attempt to prevent the French from recovering Poitou and Saintonge in the early 1370s. In August 1371 they joined the English army which laid siege to Moncontour, situated some twenty-eight miles to the north-west of Poitiers, which for the best part of a year they used as a base for raiding into Anjou and Maine.[68] In turn besieged there in the following summer by an army commanded by du Guesclin, they abandoned the place under treaty and were appointed by Jean de Grailly, captal de Buch (who had succeeded Chandos as constable of Aquitaine), to take up command at Niort along with Sir Thomas Percy.[69] In August 1372, when the captal and Percy were taken prisoner in an attempt to relieve the castle of Soubise near Rochefort, Cresswell and Huet were among those who escaped into the fortress with the help of the garrison, and when the castle was surrendered they were allowed to return under safe-conduct, to Niort and Lusignan respectively.[70] All three were subsequently involved in an attempt by the seneschal of Aquitaine, Sir Thomas Felton, to relieve Thouars, after which Huet returned to England,[71] and Cresswell succeeded him as one of the two captains of Lusignan.[72]

As the English hold in Saintonge and Poitou progressively crumbled, so too the luck of the former captains of the companies began to run out. In an attempt to relieve the garrison of Chizé, commanded by Sir Robert Mitton and Martin Scott, the English once again came up against an army commanded by du Guesclin, which included the contingents of some of his most experienced Breton captains, many of whom had served with him in Spain, notably the Beaumanoirs (Robert, Alain and Jean), Arnaud du Solier, alias Limousin, Geoffroi Richon, Yvon de Lacoué, Geoffroi Kerimel, Thibaud du Pont, Silvestre Budes and Alain de Saint-Pol.[73] In an engagement which ensued, on 21 March 1373, not only were Mitton and Scott taken prisoner, but so too were Cresswell, Holgrave and Richard Holm.[74]

---

67 Cresswell with a life annuity of 40 *livres guiennois* (*CPR, 1385–9*, p. 287) and Holgrave with a life annuity of £40 from the prince's revenues in Cheshire (*CPR, 1377–81*, p. 492; cf. *CCR, 1377–81*, p. 312).
68 Froissart, *Chroniques*, viii, pp. xv, 20–1, 278.
69 Ibid., pp. xxxi–xxxii, 51, 53, 304.
70 Ibid., pp. xxxvii–xxxix, 67–71. Cf. *Chron. premiers Valois*, pp. 238–41.
71 Froissart, *Chroniques*, viii, pp. liv–lv, 97.
72 He was in charge there, along with Geoffroi de Saint-Quentin, during the siege conducted by the French during Easter of 1373, and their custody was continued by an indenture concluded with John of Gaunt at Bordeaux on 4 April 1374 (*JGR*, I, i, no. 42, which also shows that Cresswell had appointed Thomas of Brancastre his lieutenant there). See Luce in Froissart, *Chroniques*, viii, p. lxiii n. l.
73 For this episode, see Froissart, *Chroniques*, viii, pp. lix–, xi, 107–14.
74 The other prisoners included John Devereux, Gregory Sais (Degory Seys), Geoffroi d'Argentan and Aimery de Rochechouart. Richard Neville and *William* Worsley were killed, and James Willoughby seriously wounded (Froissart, *Oeuvres*, viii, p. 234). Mitton and Holm,

The defeat resulted in the surrender of Chizé, which was shortly followed by that of Niort.[75]

The English position in Poitou now depended upon Lusignan. Cresswell was able to hold out there until the following summer, but was again taken prisoner in June 1374 and subjected to a ransom of 6,000 gold francs by Louis of Sancerre.[76] His capture was a matter for comment. Indeed, so great was his reputation that messengers who took the news to the duke of Berry and Charles V were both rewarded,[77] and his period in command at Lusignan (which fell to the French before the end of September 1374) even figured in a romance written at the request of the duke of Berry, for his sister Marie, duchess of Bar, by the *trouvère* Jean d'Arras.[78] Thereafter, there is no trace of him. Although, as one of the conditions negotiated for the surrender of Lusignan to the French, he may have recovered his liberty along with other English prisoners taken during the siege, he was certainly dead by the early summer of 1376.[79]

Slowly, but surely, the old captains of the companies were slipping away or finding employ elsewhere. Huet had been killed on John of Gaunt's expedition to France in 1373–4,[80] but Holgrave, who was retained as one of Richard II's esquires after the death of the Black Prince, like his compatriot Robert Knowles lived on to a ripe old age in the next century. Sometime before the summer of 1377 he married Elena, the daughter of Sir Robert Bertram, who not only was heiress to the castle and manor of Bothal near Morpeth in Northumberland, but also, through her previous

---

like Cresswell and Holgrave, had been among the captains of the English *routes* of the Great Companies in 1368–9 (Arch. dép. Loire-Atlantique, E 119/12, 13).
75   Froissart, *Chroniques*, viii, pp. lxi–lxiv, 114–15.
76   Lehoux, i, p. 345 n. 4.
77   On 24 June 1374 the duke of Berry, who was then at Issoudun, ordered the payment of 40s to the messenger Araby 'qui estoit venu de Poitou ... dire les novelles de la prise de Cressoelle' (Luce in Froissart, *Chroniques*, viii, p. lxiii n. 1; cf. Lehoux i, p. 334, n. 5), and on 16 August following Charles V ordered the payment of 50 gold francs to 'nostre amé sergent d'armes Pierre Groussaut, qui nous apporta pieça de par nostre très chier frere le duc de Berri et d'Auvergne les premieres nouvelles de la prise de Cresoelle' (*Mandements*, p. 552, no. 1060).
78   *Mélusine*, ed. Brunet, pp. 421–2, in which the legendary fairy who was supposed to have defended the house of Lusignan and founded the castle appeared to him in a vision, at first in the form of a serpent whilst he was in bed with a concubine from Sancerre called Alixandre. The story was probably written between 1392 and 1393, although in some of the manuscripts of the prose version the date of commencement is given as 1387 (see *Le roman de Mélusine*, ed. E. Roach, p. 13 n. 1).
79   See Lehoux, i, pp. 343–4, and Walsingham, *Hist. Anglicana*, p. 317, concerning the arrangements for the release of the prisoners. The duke of Berry undertook to reimburse Louis de Sancerre, who reduced the ransom demanded for Cresswell to 5,000 francs (Lehoux, i, p. 343 n. 4). Cresswell died during the Black Prince's lifetime, i.e. before 6 June 1376 (*CPR, 1385–9*, p. 287). The Bascot de Mauléon's account of his death at the hands of du Guesclin at the battle of La Rochelle in 1372 (Froissart, *Chroniques*, xii, pp. 106, 349) is evidently pure fiction.
80   Froissart, *Oeuvres*, viii, pp. 293–5.

marriage to a London pepperer, John of Hatfield, had secured considerable properties in London and Calais, although Holgrave was unable to get his hands on the Calais properties until December 1386.[81] He took part in the earl of Buckingham's expedition to France in 1380, represented Northumberland in parliament in 1382 and 1383, defended Carlisle against the French army sent to Scotland under Jean de Vienne in 1385, and accompanied John of Gaunt to Portugal in the following year.[82] Thereafter, he seems to have lived in semi-retirement at Bothal, with which he was chiefly connected after 1380;[83] but he continued to have interests in other counties, in particular in Shropshire.[84] On the accession of Henry IV he secured a confirmation of the life annuity which he had enjoyed under Richard II,[85] but appears to have died shortly thereafter.

Geoffrey Worsley, who was one of the two marshals of the English army in 1370, was once again taken prisoner in 1375, when he accompanied John IV of Brittany on the expedition intended to recover his duchy.[86] Subjected to a heavy ransom, two years later he was sub-warden of the Channel Islands for Sir Hugh Calveley, and in 1379 was among the forces sent to Cherbourg with the new captain, Sir John Harleston, and contributed substantially to the achievement of a victory over the French.[87] The following year he joined the earl of Buckingham's expedition to France, before being retained for life by John of Gaunt in 1381.[88] He disappears from the records in 1383, and possibly died shortly afterwards. Other captains of the English *routes* found employ in more distant parts. After their retreat to Saint-Sauveur, nothing is heard of Thomelin Bell and John Chase until the summer of 1383, when they were serving with Richard Romsey, who, as captain of a company of English, Italians and others, concluded a non-agression pact for two years with the town of Perugia.[89]

---

81 *CPR, 1377–81*, pp. 1–2; *CCR, 1385–9*, p. 293; cf. *Calendar of Wills*, ii, pp. 121–2. It is also clear from these sources that Holgrave's marriage to Elena is to be dated between 1368 and 1377.
82 *CCR, 1381–5*, pp. 133, 414; Froissart, *Chroniques*, ix, p. 239; xi, pp. lxix, 271; xii, pp. lxxiii, 298.
83 *CPR, 1381–5*, p. 287; *1385–8*, p. 148; *CCR, 1381–5*, 133, 414; *1381–5*, pp. pp. 133, 414; *1389–92*, pp. 144–5, 409.
84 *CPR, 1381–5*, pp. 228, 261, 324; *CCR, 1371–81*, p. 322; *1381–5*, p. 287; *1389–92*, p. 95.
85 *CPR, 1399–1401*, p. 144; *CCR, 1399–1402*, p. 347.
86 Froissart, *Chroniques*, vii, p. 234; *Foedera*, III, ii, p. 1009; *RP*, ii, p. 343.
87 Le Patourel, p. 130; Froissart, *Oeuvres*, ix, p. 137; Walsingham, *Hist. Anglicana*, i, p. 398, and *Chron. Angliae*, pp. 229–30.
88 Froissart, *Chroniques*, ix, p. 239. He was retained with an annuity of £20 and was still one of the duke's bachelors in January 1383 (*JGR*, II, nos. 38, 799).
89 AS, Perugia, Diplomatico, cass. 36, no. 260 (Perugia, 31 July 1383). Romsey's career in Italy will be covered in *Medieval Mercenaries II*. Robert Ramsey, possibly Richard's brother, was among the men-at-arms who arrived in Saint-Sauveur with Buxhill on 1 December 1370 (PRO, E 101/30/38, m. 2).

Among those who remained in France, it was the Gascons who continued to operate more or less independently, under captains like Bernard de la Salle and Bertucat d'Albret, who took the important town of Figeac in Quercy in October 1371 and were subsequently to play a significant part in the wars in Italy and Navarre respectively. During the 1370s and 1380s some of their lieutenants and subordinate officers came to control a large number of fortresses in the Massif-Central, in Rouergue, Auvergne and Limousin, using them as bases from which they were to conduct raids into the neighbouring provinces, in particular into Languedoc. They were then bought out by the count of Armagnac and the king's officers. A large number accompanied the count to Italy in 1391, where most of them were to perish, as well as de la Salle.[90] But whilst the descendants of the captains who had held most of France to ransom in the 1360s continued to trouble the central and eastern parts of the kingdom until the early 1390s, after 1370 the period of the Great Companies was over.

90   Bernard de la Salle's career in Italy, the activities of the companies occupying fortresses in France in the 1370s and 1380s, and their fateful expedition across the Alps will be covered in *Medieval Mercenaries II*.

Glossary

Adelantado mayor	Regional governor with military powers and some administrative functions.
Aides	Term used for all the taxes levied by the king of France.
Alcabala	Royal tax on commercial transactions in Castile.
Arrière-ban	Rear-vassals convoked for military service in the royal army.
Bailli	Local administrative officer in northern France.
Bailliage	Local administrative district in northern France.
Ban	Vassals convoked for military service in the royal army.
Banneret	A military rank, above that of a knight. Bannerets were distinguished by their square banners, as opposed to triangular pennons.
Barbuta	The name given by Italians to a mounted man-at-arms with a page or retainer, later known as a lance.
Batle, battle	Local administrative official.
Battle	A main division of an army; there were usually three and sometimes four battles in an army.
Bourg	Small town, or the more recent parts of a larger town which grew up around the *cité*, but within the walls.
Chevauchée	Mounted raid into hostile territory.
Cité	The oldest part of a town, usually around the castle.

GLOSSARY

Cortes, Corts	Representative assembly of the estates of society; 'parliament'.
Faubourg	The part of a town or city which lay outside the walls; suburbs.
Fief-rent	Annuity paid in return for homage and specified services, usually but not solely military.
Fouage	A tax assessed on a household or hearth.
Gabelle	Indirect tax.
Glaive	A lance.
Impôt	A tax, direct or indirect.
Indenture	A contract drawn up in two parts, one to be kept by each contracting party. The two were written on a single piece of paper or parchment, which was then divided by an irregular or indented cut.
Infanta	Princess.
Infante	Prince.
Jinetes	Light cavalry.
Maestro racional	An official of the Aragonese treasury responsible for financial disbursements.
Masnadiere	Pillager, brigand.
Merindad	Navarrese province in which the chief royal officer was known as the *merino*.
Meseta	Tableland, plateau.
Parlement	Sovereign court of justice in France.
Patis	Financial levy made by a garrison in the country surrounding a town or castle which they controlled.
Pennon	Triangular banner carried by an ordinary knight as opposed to a knight banneret. The word was also used for a group of men-at-arms fighting under such a banner.
Plat pays	The open countryside, outside the fortresses and towns.
Porte-oriflamme	The bearer of the ancient banner (*oriflamme*) of the kings of France, which was kept in the abbey of Saint-Denis and carried immediately before them in war. The banner was so called because it was a red standard sprinkled with gold flames.
Prest	An advance, usually against wages.
Prévôté	An administrative district under a *prévôt*.

GLOSSARY

Procuradors, pocuradores	Town representatives attending the *Corts* or *Cortes*.
Rachat	Ransom paid to troops evacuating a place; hence *racheter*.
Regard	A bonus, paid quarterly, the normal rate being 100 marks for the service of thirty men-at-arms.
Route	A company of men-at-arms.
Routier	A freelance soldier, fighting on his own account.
Seneschal	Local administrative officer in the south of France.
Seneschalsy	Local administrative circumscription in the south of France.
Sueffra, Sufferte, Suffrensa	Immunity from hostilities, usually purchased.
Syndic	In the Midi, the name given to a representative of the inhabitants of a town.
Taille	A tax.
Viguier	Local official in the south of France, with functions analagous to those of a *prévôt* in the north. The territory in which he exercised his jurisdiction was known as a *viguerie*.
Vuidement	Evacuation of a castle, fortress or town, usually against payment.

Note on Money

The different monetary systems in operation in western Europe during the 1360s, and the relative value of coins referred to in this volume, require some explanation.[1] In most countries transactions were conducted in money of account as well as actual coinage. Exchange rates between the different currencies and units of account fluctuated according to where and when the money was changed, and the prevailing level of monetary stability. England and Aragon had relatively stable currencies. France went through a period of extreme monetary instability before 1360, and in Castile the money was devalued in 1369. The nearest thing to an international standard of value was the florin of Florence, first minted in 1252, which circulated widely outside Italy. It contained 3·54 g of gold and was as near to 24 carats fine as was then technically practicable. The value of the monetary transactions in which the mercenary companies were involved is thus best conveyed by reference to the florin of Florence or the gold content of the other currencies referred to.

In England, the unit of account was the pound sterling (£), which was divided into 20 shillings (s), each of 12 pence (d). The pound was worth one and a half marks of silver (i.e. 13s 4d to the mark). The principal gold coin, the noble, minted from 1344, was worth 6s 8d (i.e. half a mark or one third of £1). It was kept at a fixed value by altering the amount of gold it contained from time to time. During the 1360s, the relationship of the pound sterling to the Florentine florin was fairly stable, at 3s to the florin.

In France, the units of account were the pound of Tours (*livre tournois*, *l.t.*) and the pound of Paris (*livre parisis*, *l.p.*); in the principality of Aquitaine the pound of Bordeaux (*livre bordelais*, *l.b.*). Like the pound sterling, the *livre* was divided into 20 shillings (*sous*), each of 12 pence

---

[1] In the ensuing note I have made use of the invaluable study by p. Spufford, *Handbook of Medieval Exchange* (London, 1986), and J. Lafaurie, *Les monnaies des rois de France* (2 vols, Paris and Basle, 1951).

(*deniers*). The monetary instability prevailing in France makes it difficult to arrive at comparative values. In the 1360s the exchange rate of the *livre tournois* against the Florentine florin varied by more than 100 per cent, but averaged around 22 *l.t.* over the decade. As a rough guide the pound sterling was worth five *l.t.*, four *l.p.* and five *l.b.* There were several gold coins in use in France during the 1360s. The *écu*, or *florin à l'écu* or *à la chaise*, was first minted between 1337 and 1355, and initially had a gold content of 4·532 g, but its value fell by more than a quarter with subsequent issues, from around 4s 0d to about 2s 10d sterling. The *mouton* or *florin au mouton* which replaced it was more prized and had a higher value at 4·706 g of gold. It was worth half as much again as the last issue of *écus* to be minted. The *royal*, first minted in 1358, contained 3·547 g of gold on first issue, but thereafter rather less. As a result of these fluctuations in value it became common to specify 'old' or 'new' *écus* and *royaux*. The *franc* was a more stable coinage. First issued as the *franc à cheval* in 1360 with a gold content of 3·89 g, it had a value of 20 *sous tournois* or 16 *sous parisis*. It was replaced by the slightly lighter *franc à pied* in 1365, which contained 3·82 g of gold. It was worth about 4s 0d sterling. In addition to these gold coins, from 1266 a large silver coin, the *gros tournois*, was also struck in France. Initially valued at 12d (one *sou*) *tournois*, in the 1360s it was worth 15d *tournois*.

Of the moneys used in the different kingdoms of the Crown of Aragon, only those of Catalonia and of Aragon are referred to in this study: the shillings (*sueldos*) and pence (*dineros*) of Barcelona; the *sueldos* and *dineros iacccensis* or *jaquesa* of Aragon, so called from the town of Jaca, where they were first minted; and the 'florin of Perpignan', first issued at Perpignan in imitation of the Florentine florin in 1346 and referred to as the 'florin of Aragon' in the 1360s. From 1369 onwards it was minted at Barcelona and Tortosa in Catalonia, at Zaragoza in Aragon, and at Valencia, as well as in Perpignan, and was intended to be used throughout the different Aragonese principalities. Although its gold content was slightly less than that of the Florentine florin (3·48 as opposed to 3·54 g), it was only 18 carats fine and consequently about three quarters of the value of the florin of Florence. It was worth 11 *sueldos* of Barcelona and 11 *sueldos iaccensis* in 1365–6.[2]

In Castile, the reckoning of money in *libras*, *sueldos* and *dineros* had been abandoned in the thirteenth century for a unit of account known as the *maravedi*, which was made up of 10 *dineros*. There were 25 *maravedis* to the Florentine florin before the devaluation of 1369, but 45 thereafter. The gold coin in use in Castile was the *dobla*, based on the double dinar of the Almoravid rulers of Andalusia and Morocco, which initially weighed

---

2 ACA, Real Patrimonio, MR, reg. 351, fo. 110v; 352, fo. 65r, 353, fo. 125r.

4·6 g. Struck in considerable quantities from the reign of Alfonso XI (1312–50), it had a value of around 36 *maravedis* before the devaluation of 1369. It was worth 1·545 Aragonese florins (17 *sueldos* of Barcelona) in 1368.[3]

In Navarre, after 1355, the units of account were the *sueldos carlines* (*s.c.*) and *dineros carlines (d.c.)*. There were 12 *s.c.* to the Florentine florin in 1361 and thirteen in 1364–7, but by 1373 the florin was worth 16*s* 6*d* carlines and by the end of the fourteenth century had reached three times its 1361 value.[4] In 1364 the *vieux écu* was worth 18*s carlines*, and in 1365 the *franc* was worth 16*s carlines*. At the time of the Black Prince's intervention in Castile in 1367, the value of the *franc* had risen to 16*s* 6*d* and the Castilian *dobla* was worth 20*s* 6*d carlines*.[5]

Modern equivalents of fourteenth-century monetary values are notoriously difficult to arrive at and frequently misleading. In the English royal armies of the period the standard daily rate of pay for a mounted knight was 2s 0d sterling, for a mounted esquire 1s 0d, and for a mounted archer 6d (i.e. 20, 10 and 5 Florentine florins a month respectively). In addition they usually received a bonus payment known as a *regard* and, in exceptional circumstances, double pay was not unknown.[6] In the French royal armies the rates of pay were expressed in money of account after 1360, and their real value was subject to fluctuations. From 1364 they were considerably greater than they had been at the beginning of the Hundred Years War: the equivalent of 32 Florentine florins for a mounted knight, 16 florins for a mounted esquire and just under 13 florins for a mounted archer or crossbowman.[7] The mean price for a war-horse, which for most soldiers was their most valuable movable property, was around nine pounds sterling.[8]

---

3 ACA, Cancilleria, reg. 1346, fo. 124v. For the devaluation and its immediate consequences, see Ayala, *Crónica*, ii, p. 3, and Fowler (1992), pp. 236–7.
4 For the values in 1361 and in 1390–1406, see Spufford, p. 163; for the values in the intervening years, see AGN, Comptos, regs. 111, fo. 64r; 113, fo. 45r; 118, fo. 124r; 121, fo. 103v; 148, fo. 55r.
5 AGN, Comptos, reg. 111, fo. 35r; 113, fo. 57r; 121, fos. 89r, 111v.
6 Prestwich, pp. 84–6, 93.
7 Contamine (1972), pp. 97–8.
8 Prestwich, p. 35.

Appendix A

Documents

1. *Agreement concluded between the lord of Terride, Raymond Arnaud de Preissac and Menon de Castelpers, on behalf of Jean d'Armagnac, on the one part, and Sir John Amory, John Cresswell and their companions, on the other. February/March 1363.*[1]
Bibliothèque Nationale, collection Doat, vol. 194, fos. 269r–71r (seventeenth-century copy).

Ce sont les convenances acordees entre noble et puissant seigneur monseigneur Jehan d'Armagnac, ou le sire de Tarride, messire Raymond Arnaud de Preyssac, et messire Menon de Castelpers par nom de luy, d'une part, et messire Jehan Emeric, chevalier, et Jehan Cressoel et leurs compagnons et autres gens de leur compagnie et rote d'autre part.

Premierement, que lesdits messire Jean Emeric et Jean Cressoel et leurs compagnons et gens de leur compagnie et rote ont promis et promettent servir bien et loyaument ledit monseigneur Jehan d'Armagnac en ses guerres contre ses ennemis la ou il les voudra mener ou capitaines de par ly de cy iusque a la feste de Pasques prochain venant, et obeir a luy et a ses deputtez sur le fait des dites guerres.

Item, est acordé que au cas que les dessusdits messire Jehan Emeric et Jehan Cressoel et autres gens de leur compagnie et de leur rote durant la terme dessusdit fussent en autre service, ou ledit messire Jean d'Armagnac ne les eusse mis en oeuvre de guerre, que apres ledit terme de Pasques il luy soient tenus de tant servir et restituer tant de temps comme ils auroient este en autruy service.

Item, que si durant ledit terme q'ils feront guerre pour ledit monseigneur Jehan d'Armagnac il auoient pris aucune forteresse qu'il la doient tenir

---

[1] The agreement is not dated, but it was evidently concluded either during the course of, or shortly after the conclusion of, a fifteen-day truce negotiated at Cassagnes-Royaux in Rouergue on 27 February 1363 between Jean d'Armagnac and Cresswell, acting as Amory's lieutenant (*HGL*, x, cols. 1302–3, no. 496).

pour luy et en son nom, et recueillir en icelles luy et ses gens toutes fois que n'auroit besoin, et au cas qu'il les voulussent vendre ou laisser par raenson que ledit messire Jehan d'Armagnac les peust avoir et retenir par telle finance ou plus petite comme il t[r]óuveroient[2] a autre part.

Item, est acorde que au cas que ledit monseigneur Jehan d'Armagnac aurie entreprise chevauchee contre ses ennemis, et durant icelle le terme que les dessusdits le doivent servir fust passe, ils le soient tenus de suir et accompagner six ou huit iours outre ledit terme en retournant en son pais par deca la Garonne.

Item, parmi les choses dessus dites ledit messire Jehan d'Armagnac a promis et promet donner aux dessus nommez et leurs gens [de] compaignie et rote, cinq mille florins d'or a payer aux termes qui s'ensuit; c'est assavoir, tantost en comencent trois mille et cinq cens florins, et les mil et cinq cens restans au mi temps du terme que sera du commencement dudit service iusques a Pasques.

Item, que des prisons de la terre de monseigneur le comte d'Armagnac, pere dudit monseigneur Jehan, qui ont este pris en la bataille dudit monseigneur d'Armagnac et du comte de Foix, lesquels n'ont tenu leur foy aux dessusdits ou a leur compagnie, ledit monseigneur Jehan d'Armagnac leur en fera raison selon droit d'armes.

Item, des autres prisons de la comte de Comenges de la terre du seigneur de Lebret, il leur en fera faire raison selon droit d'armes, a son pouvoir.

Item, quand a ce que lesdits messire Jehan Emeric et Jehan Cressoel et autres gens de leur rote demandent par la remson du lieu d'Espelien, lesdites parties ont promis a faire tenir et complir ce que quattre bons hommes, c'est assavoir deux de chacune partie, en ordonneront.

Item, est acorde que au cas que la volunte de Dieu fust que le comte de Foix fust pris et aprisonne en bataille, ou en autre maniere par les dessus nommez ou leurs compagnons ou gens de leur rote durant ledit service, que ledit messire Jehan d'Armagnac le puisse avoir, et il luy soit rendu par les dessusdits, payant a eux la somme dite.

Item, est acorde que les dessus nommez messire Jehan Emeric et Jehan Cressoel avec leurs compagnons et gens de leur rote depuis le jourd'huy puissent servir en quelque part et quel que leur plaise, sortant seulement les ennemis dudit monseigneur Jehan d'Armagnac, par huit ou dix iours, et passez les dits huits ou dix iours qu'ils soient tenus de venir servir ledit monseigneur d'Armagnac, layssie tout autre service quelconque en la maniere que dessus est dit.

---

[2] Letters or words in brackets here and elsewhere in this document are omitted in the seventeenth-century copy.

2. *Acquittance given to Jean d'Armagnac by Sir John Amory and John Cresswell for 3,500 florins, in part payment of 5,000 florins which he undertook to pay them. February/March 1363.*
Bibliothèque Nationale, collection Doat, vol. 194, fo. 317r–v (seventeenth-century copy).

Sachent tuit que nous, Jehan Emeri, chevalier, capitaine de la rote des anglois, et Jehan Cressuel, escuier, pour nous et nos compagnons et autres gens de nostre compagnie et rote, reconoissons avoir eu et receu de noble et puissant seigneur monseigneur Jehan d'Armignac, par les mains de monsieur Menon de Castelperte, chevalier, trois mille et cinq cens florins d'or bons, et de bon pois, de la somme de cinq mille florins d'or, lesquiels il nous devoit donner pour certain service que nous avec nosdits compaignons et autres gens d'armes de nostre rote li devons faire en ses guerres, ainsi comme est plus a plain contenu en les conventions sur ce faites entre li et nous et scellees de nos sceaux, desquiels trois mille et cinq cens florins sommes bien contens, et ledit monsieur Jehan en absoillons et quitons par ces presentes. Et en tesmoing des ces choses avons scellees ces letres de nos propres sceaux. Donnees a . . .[3]

3. *Letter from Berthelot Guillaume of Estella to the Charles II, king of Navarre. Angoulême, 13 February [1365].*
Archives départementales, Pyrénées-Atlantiques, E 520 (original).

A tres yllustre et noble prince, et mon tresredoubte et treshonorable seigneur le roy de Navarre.

Tresyllustre et noble princep, et mon treshonore seigneur. Plaise vous savoir que ycelle jeudy, xiiie jour de fevrier, vint en la ville d'Engolesme le gouverneur de Monpesler, messager envoye pour le roy de France envers mons' le prince. Et apporta lettres patentes empetreez a l'instance du dit roy et a la priere du Saint Pere, dressanz a mons' le prince de la partie du roy d'Angleterre son pere, les quels il presenta au dit mons' le prince, et aussi semblanz patentez qui se dressoyent a Chandoz. Et mons', quant il eu ycelles receuez, tant pour obeir le commandement de son pere, come a la priere du dit Saint Pere, il les ha obeyes. Et sur ce en a ordene et envoye a touz les cappitainez de la grant compaignie, qui sont yci de par deins escripz, ses lettres patentes en les quelles sont encorporrez les dites lettres patentes du dit roy d'Angleterre son pere, selon la forme et teneur que la vostre nobleze vostre noble conseil venez contenir en la copie d'icelles que ge vous envoye ci dedenz ces presentes clouse et scellee de mon seel. Et plus, mon tres redobte seigneur, vous plaise savoir que apres ce il bailla au

---

3 The transcript concludes here, without date.

dit mons' le prince un article contenu entre les autres de sa supplicacion et requeste que cy apres s'ensuit:

Item, ay entendu que le seigneur de Lebret s'apperelle d'aler encontre le roy de France pour le roy de Navarre. Pour ce vous plaise de metre remede qu'il ne le face.[4]

Sur le quel article mons' le prince a envoye une de ses dites lettres patentes. Et,[5] mon tresredoubte seigneur, ainssi sachez, quar vrayment ces lettres ne sont mie agreables en guerre a mons' et a son conseil, quar a ce que dit ou commancement du mandement que mons' envoye a chacun des [cappitainez][6] de la dite compaignie, sachez 'nous avons receu de par nostre trescher seigneur et pere le roy d'Engleterre ses lettres patentes empetreez a l'instance de nostre trescher oncle le roy de France', vous plaise savoir que ce dit mot de empetreez a l'instance de nostre trescher oncle le roy de France es mis com certaine cabtelle, et a fin que les genz de la grant compaignie s'apercevent que ce vient de la notice du roy de France. Et que pour despit de luy en facent plus mal en lur pays, quar bien pouvez entendre que se mons' le prince ne son conseil ne amassent a vous et avez amiz, il ne metissent mie ce mot 'senon' nous avons receu lettres patentes de nostre trescher seigneur et pere contenant la forme, &c. tant seulement.

Sy vous plaise sur ce ordenner einssy et par telle manere que vostre honneur et de voz subgiz et bien veuillanz en soit gardee. Et aussi bien vous supplie qu'il vous plaise voulloir ceste chouse en quant touche a moy faire tenir en secret. Car en verite ge ne le faiz pour autre chouse se ne pour ce que ge suis vostre subgiz et vourroye de bon cuer vostre accroissement de honeur. Car si les seigneurs du conseilh de par deca seussent de ceste chouse, je seroie dissepe de corps et de biens. Quar en verite, seigneur, je vourroye plus avoir perdu V^c nobles que avoir l'indignacion des seigneurs du conseill, c'est assavoir le chancellier et autres, quar dont je demourane en la chancellerie, maintenant me ont ordene demourer ou prive seel et me l'amene de touz. Nostre seigneur soie lo[is] de sa puissance et vous tiengne touz jours en sa garde. Et ne v[eu]lh [...][7] se vous aviez recevez ces lettres plus vous envoyas escript de plusieurs autres chouses que vous touchent, se ne pour ce que ge ne suis certain se vous recevrez ces presentes.

Ce sont les noms des capitaines de la grant compaignie les quels le dit gouverneur a escriptz:[8]

---

4 These words are entered in brackets between the two paragraphs.
5 The word *come* crossed out here.
6 This word omitted.
7 About six words illegible here.
8 These words are written in the margin.

Premier, mons' Seguin de Badefol
    mons' Jehan de Castelnou et de Berbeguenes
    mons' Berducat de Lebret
    mons' Bernard de Lebret
    Billos la Roche
    Loys Robaus
    le bort de Brutailh
    le bort Camus
    le Cozi
    Lamie   Vostre humble subgit
    Espiota   et servitour, clerc de
    Berrardeco   voz genz, Berthelot
    Sentszorgues[9]   Guillaume d'Estelle.
    Petit[10]
    Petit Meschin   Escript a
    Ferragut   grant haste.

4. *Memorandum of matters outstanding between Peter IV of Aragon and Bertrand du Guesclin. Lérida, 27 February 1367.*
    Archivo de la Corona de Aragón, Cancilleria, reg. 1347, fos. 155r–6r (contemporary copy).

En nom de Deu, sapien tuyt que sobre alscunas debats et questions que eren entr'el molt alt e molt excellent princep e senyor, lo senyor En Pere, per la grace de Deu rey d'Aragon, de Valence, de Mallorchas, de Sardenya e de Corcega, comte de Barchelona, de Rosseylo e de Cerdanya, d'una part, e lo molt noble baro mossen Bertran de Clequi, duch de Trestamara e comte de Longavila e de Borga de la altra part, per raho d'alscunas coses qu'el dit mossen Bertran entenia qu'el dit senyor rey li hagues a complir finalment tractants alscunas bonas personas qui amanen la honor del dit senyor rey d'una part, e lo dit mossen Bertran foren fets e concordats entr'el dit senyor rey d'una part e lo dit mossen Bertran de la altra los capitols seguents.

Tot primerament que lo senyor rey sia tengut per letra e prometa per sa fe de donar a mossen Bertran de Clequi, o aqui ell volra, quaranta mille florins d'or bons et sufficients d'Arago de la ley que son huy, ço es saber cinch mille tantost en sta vila o a Ceragoça, et vint mille d'aqui a la quinzena de Pascha de la resurectio a Barchelona, e los romanents onze mille per tot lo mes de juliol en la dita civitat de Barchelona.

Item, que lo senyor rey li sia tengut de livrar dues grande naus e una galea noljegadas e pagadas a sis meses a messio del senyor rey per anar en ultra

---

9 Johann Hazenorgue.
10 Evidently written twice, in error.

APPENDIX A

mar sobre los enamichs de la Sancta Crestiandat per tot lo mes de maig primera vinent. E si pervenia que lo dit mossen Bertran dians aquest temps no podie ferir lo dit viatge, qu'el senyor rey li sie tengut de delivrar los dits naus e galea del dit mes de maig a .i. an apres seguent, empero qu'el dit mossen Bertran sie tengut de fer ho saber al senyor rey tres meses abans que dege partir, axi qu'el senyor rey apres que sera request hara tres mese despay. E passat lo dit any lo senyor rey d'aquest capitol noli sie tengut.

Item, que lo senyor rey sian tengut de haver al dit mossen Bertran dues grans naus e una galea a despeses del dit moss' Bertran de vegni si es ha in [. . . ,][11]anc dessus dit.

E per totas las coses dessus ditas mossen Bertran de Clequi quita le senyor rey de totas cartas, covinences que fossen fetes en lo temps passat entro lo iour d'huy entre ells, axi del matrimoni de son frare e dels dampnatges que ell ha sofferts en Castella, e messions e d'injures e del fet de Bretanya e de les valls de Etla e de Novella, e de tota la terra qu'el senyor rey li haura dada e promesa, exceptats los lochs de Borja e de Magallo, los quals romanguen al dit mossen Bertran en titol de comtat e ab totas ses aldeas e ab los rendas e sdeveniments e emoluments, e ab les condicions que lo senyor rey los li dona l'altra vegada. E totes les altres coses que foren empreses enfre lo senyor rey e lo dit mossen Bertran, axi per sint com de peraula e la menys valença de ço que mossen Bertran demanava de la renda del dit comdat de Borja sien remeses al senyor rey.

E encara, si lo dit mossen Bertran fa lo viatge d'ultra mar, promet al senyor rey d'anar en Sardenya e aqui atardar a ses despeses .xv. jorns, e si mes hi demora a la requesta del senyor rey o de son lochtinent ab despeses del seynor rey. E tota la conquesta que mossen Bertran pora fer de la terra del jutge d'Arborea e dels altres enemichs del senyor rey sia del dit mossen Bertran, exceptada la terra que ja ere del senyor rey o de sos servidors, la qual lo jutge se hagues occuppada e exceptats Oristory e Bosa.

E totas les coses dessus ditas, las quals lo senyor rey es tengut de fer a mossen Bertran prometra en lur bona fe lo senyor rey e la senyora reyna, e semblant promissio fara lo dit mossen Bertran de Clequi de ço que haia a fer [. . .] [c]apitols totas [. . .] coses contengudas en aquellas los dit senyor rey [e la senyora] reyna e lo dit mossen Bertran de Clequi en presencia e poder di [. . .] de [. . .]gida, secretari del dit senyor rey e notari de eius sint e de mi Johan la Paya, clerch, secretari del dit mossen Bertran de Clequi, fermaren, loaren e approvaren. E prometera sur lur bona fe e jurare pe Deu e per los Sants iiii[e] Evvangelis de lurs mans corporalment tochats que los dits capitols e cascuna d'eles coses contengudas en aquellas tendran, compliran e observaran, e tenir, complir e observar faran, e contra no hi

11 Some of the folios are damaged by woodworm. In this, and documents 5 and 6, the missing words are shown in brackets, as are the letters which can be deduced.

314

vendran per alcuna causa o raho. En testimoni de les quels coses manaren queu fossen feres dues publiques cartes semblants closes per nos dits secretaris e segelladas en pendent ab lo segell secret del dit seynor rey, con altre segell ab si no hageues a present, e ab lo segell del dit mossen Bertran, les quals coses foren fetes fermadas e juradas en la ciutat de Leryda dissabte a xxvii dies de febrer en l'an de la Nativitat de nostre senyor MCCCLXVII. Visa Ro.

E foren hi testimonis lo noble mossen Huc, vezcomte de Cardona, mossen Ramon de Paguera, consellers del dit senyor rey, e mossen Guillem de Montanay de companya del dit mossen Bertran.

Fuit clausum per Bernardum de Bonastre, domini regis secretarium.

Por mon sengner lo duc, present le sire de Montonay. Le Pauge.

Ay pose a ces lettres le senu de mon dit segner.

5. *Articles of an agreement proposed to Peter IV of Aragon by Jacques de Pencoédic and Jean le Bouteiller, proctors of Bertrand du Guesclin, for an expedition to Sardinia, together with the king's responses thereto. April 1369.*

Archivo de la Corona de Aragón, Cancilleria, reg. 1347, fos. 151v–3r (contemporary copy, registered in chancery).

Trautament comaincie entre mos' Fraunçoys Roma, mos' Jacme dez Far et Pere dez Valls pour part du tresorer du seignor roy, d'une part, et moss' Jacques de Penehoedic et Johan lo Boteller pour part de mos' Bertran du Guerclin, d'autre part, lo quel trautament a doit firmer e camplir par le dit mos' Bertran en cas que il plaira que ainsi soit fait.

Primerament, est traute que celui mos' Bertran passera personalment au reyaume de Sardaine al [. . .] grand compaignie de genz d'armes et archiers qu'il poura bonnemient finer pour guerierer le juge d'Arboree et guarngner le reyaume si il pout. Et fera le dit mos' Bertran celui passage senz la persoenne du dit seignor roy ou en sa compaigne celui que au dit seignor plaura.

Par als dits mossen Francesch Roma et mossen Jacme dez Far e Pere dez Vall, tractadors desy dits, qu'el dit mossen Bertram vara si al senyor rey plaura senz lo dit senyor e sens lo senyor duch en la dita conquesta. Pero, per tal qu'el senyor rey pourrait complidament puxa bastar par quel nombre de les gents d'armes qu'el dit mossen Bertran menara en lo dit viatge deia esser e bast mil do [c]ents lances e tre cents arxers. E lo nombre de les gents qu'el dit senyor si trametra de sa nacio sien do [c]ents hommes a cavall et mil ballesters.

Item, que ou cas que lo dit mons' Bertran passera ou dit voyage sens la

persone du dit seignor roy, le dit seignor li sera tenu doner a luy et a touz les gents de su compaignie les soulz et gaiges en la manera que est contenu es capitulles faiz entre le dit mons' Bertran et le dit seignor roy.
Par als dits tractadors est rasonable.

Item, li sera tenu le dit seignor roy que au temps qu'est devise es ditz capitulles delli acumplir entierement le paiement de la reste des xlv^m doubles contenuz es ditz capitulles et selonc la forme qui y est contenu en yceulx capitulles.
Par als dits tractadors est rasonable que aço sara lo dit mossen Bertran passan meyns dels dits senyors e en la manera que era avengut en cas que si passas ab ells e al temps, empero que sera ara concordat que ell deia ara passar, del qual desus sera fa mencio.

Item, que ou cas que le dit mons' Bertran passera au diz voyage comme cap, senz la persone du diz seignor roy, il li covendra faire manere despens que si le seignor roy est present le dit seignor le donnria por chascun moys por l'estat de sa persone ii^m dobles.
Par als dits tractadors [b]ast que en lo d[it] cas haia lo dit mossen Bertran dos mylia francs per ca[s]u[ides] cor anat lo [d]it [s]eynor li bastaven mil francs seg[o]ns capitols concordit.

Item, que pour ce que le dit mons' Bertran a present affere grandement devers le roy Henri en Espaigne pour la batalle qui a present y a este, coment le dit voyage soit alongie pour tout le moys de septembre prouchain senz que le dit mons' Bertran soit tenu a plus tost fer le dit voyage.
Par als dits tractadors qu'el dit temps sia massa loncs per tal, com lo octubre serra fort perillos al reculler e al navegar, mas par que mossen Bertran ab ses gents deia esser al locs qu'el senyor rey li haura assignat, lo qual li haia assignar .i. mois abans a .x. jours a la fin d'agost apparellat encontinent de recuyler, e que lo dit senyor li hia apparellat lo nauili que per raso del dit viatge li sera mestier.

Item, que le dit seignor roy soit tenu au dit mons' Bertran de li acomplir toutes les couvenances faites et contenues es ditz capitulles, e par especial la covanence que fut fait sur le fait des navies que li doit bailler le dit seignor roy pour son passament se remouverint et retornament pour le dit mons' Bertran et pour tots les gentz de sa compaignie, senz que le dit seygnor roy li en puisse faire occupament en autre manera.
Par rasonable als dits tractadors segons la forma contenguda en los capitols concordats que foren fets aba[n]t que aquests.

Item, que comme les ditz mons' Jacques et Boteller soient tenuz et obligez a certains lombarts et marchenz de non partir de la la ville de Bassolone senz leur paier la summa de cinch ou six mille florins, que il plaise au dit seignor roy faire seurs ceuhs a qui est deu celle chevance d'estre paier de celle some si tost que le dit mons' Bertran haura ferme et jure ces presenz capitulles.

Par als dit tractadors que la dita de taula demanada per part del dit mossen Bertran sia feta sots aquestes condicions, es asaber que la dita quantitat li entre en sort e per rata de ço que li reste a pagar de les dessus dits .xlv.^{m} dobles, e que la dita no sia solta nes puxe espacxar fins qu'el dita mossen Bertran e tots sos capitans, o la major partida d'aquelles, hagen firmat e votat lo viatge e passatge dessus dit segons la forma dessus contenguda. E per fer e complir aquell haien donada la fe de lur cors e aço aparra als cambradors qui faran la dita ab carta publica. E [par]t aço lo deto mossen Bertran haia dono des fermaco al dit senyor, es assaber .x. [dels suis] capitans a[nci]s es asaber que per part del dit senyor seran demanats, e lo vezcomte de Rochaberti los [nom]s et cascun d'ells per lo tot se obliguen et donen la fe de lur cors que ense[mp] ab lo dit mossen Bertran et sens elle tornaran et resituiran al dit senyor la quantitat des dessus dits .vi.^{m} florins sens tota escusacio exceptio per longamint dampnatge et messions, declaran que e no complir et no fer lo dit viatge raso o ex[cu]s[e] alcuna per lo dit mossen Bertran no puxe dita ne allegada ne a ell reebuda sino de mort, de grev malaltia o prison que fessen enamichs, ço que Deus no vulla. E los presents capitols et les coses contengudas en aquelles haien esser fermados dins iii meses primers ugnidors en altra manera que la dita fos nulla. E que lo dit mossen Bertran haia açi tramesa proctario bastant a fermar apocha d'aquesta quantitat e tramesa la carta debitoria e dels capitols de les dits xlv^m dobles per tal que en aquella puxa esser escripta per deduida la dita quantitat per indempnitat del dit senyor.

Item, qu'el dit monss' Bertran yra ou dit voyage senz la licence du roy de France en cas qu'il n'auret juste excusacion evidente par la quel il li covendroyt dem[ora] sinz faire le dit voyage. Et auxi seront tenuz touz les cappitaines de la compaigne du dit mons' Bertran de servir le dit voyage senz la licence du dit roy de France.

Par rasonable als dits tractadors que sens alcuna retencio lo dit mossen Bertran e los dits seus capitayns faren lo dit passatge, pero parria que deguessen especifitar tals seguretats esser fasedores per lo dit mossen Bertran, per les quals lo dit senyor fos segur del dit passatge per lo dit mossen Bertran fasedor sens los dits senyors en tal manera que no pogues romanir, car gran perill si va.

Item, demandent los ditz mons' Jacques et Boteiller que le dit seignor roy envoye un home suffisant en leur companyie devers le dit mons' Bertran et devers lo vezcomte de Roquiberti pour estre present a veor faire au dit mons' Bertran et aux cappitaines de su companyie les fiermances et covenances dessusdits. Et pour repporter au dit seignor roy la bonne paine et diligence que los dits mons' Jacques et Bouteiller [...] voyage se puisse acomplir a honore et proufit du dit sei[gnor roy].

[Par a]ls dits tractadors que lo senyor rey enviara al dit mossen Bertran [...] per [un]a que dara bon recapte en aço escriva als vezcomte de Rochaberti [...] trametra los dits capitols.

Rochaberti.

6. *Matters to be raised by Francesch Roma with Bertrand du Guesclin and the viscount of Rocaberti. April 1369.*
Archivo de la Corona d'Aragón, Cancilleria, reg. 1347, fo. 153r–v (contemporary copy).

Capitols de ço que En Francesch ferer escriva de la escrivania del senyor rey ha a fer per lo dit senyor en Castella ab mossen Bertran du Guerclin e ab lo vezcomte de Rochaberti.

Primerament, que com lo dit Francesch sera el loch ou seran los dessus dits ans de tots coses se present al dit vezcomte e li don la letre que per ell li tramet lo dit senyor. E apres li diga com son estats en la cort del dit senyor mossen Jacques de Penehoedic e Johan lo Boteller, procuradors del dit mossen Bertran, es son offerts al dit senyor de part del dit mossen Bertran que si al dit senyor plau ell ira en Sardenya sens lo dit senyor e sens lo senyor duch de Gerona, e sobre aço han capitolejat e finat ab mossen Francesch Roma e mossen Jacme dez Far, los quals lo dit senyor [los] [a]ssigna per tractadors en certa forma acordada entre ells, la quel es contenguda en uns capitols que lo di Francesch s'en porta, los quals capitols dara al dit vezcomte.

Item, apres se informara ab lo dit vezcomte de la manera que tendra en presentar e donar les letres que lo dit senyor tramet per ell al dit mossen Bertran et als dits mossen Jacques de Penehoedic e Johan lo Boteller, e segons que per ell sera asmestrat e informat si presentara si mateix et les dites letres als dessus dites. E presentades les dites letres los explicara com ell es aqui trames per lo dit senyor per instar e tenir apper per que lo dit mossen Bertran ferm los capitols dessus dits e complesta les coses en aquelles contengudes. E en fer aço es mestier que lo dit Francesch hara gran diligencia e cura, axi devers lo dit vezcomte de Rochaberti com devers lo dit mossen Bertran e los altres dessus dits.

Item, diga de part del dit senyor als dits mossen Jacques de Penedoedic e Johan lo Boteller com ells se offeriren e promeseren al dit senyor que farien e procurarien per tal manera que per lo dit mossen Bertran serien fermats e complits los dessus dits capitols concordats e totas les coses contengudes en aquelles. E axi que lo dit senyor los prega que meten en obra la lur bona prometénça per manera [. . .]ço haia bon acabament. E que saren aço per tal manera qu'el dit senyor los haia que grahir e lo sia obligats per [. . .]ona [of]ra que f[er]an en [. . .].[12]

Item, com entre los altres coses contengudes e expressadet en los dits capitols [si]a lo[s] .vi.^{m} florins que lo dit senyor ha feta per part del dit mossen Bertran a certs Lombarts aquelles los dits mossen Jacques e Johan lo Boteller los devien per afers del dit mossen Bertran, e aquella dita nos deja solre fins que los dessus dits capitols [sera] f[ir]mats per lo dit mossen Bertran e per sos capitans. E lo dit mossen Bertran hara donadas fermances de restituir los dits .vi.^{m} florins en cas que ell no fes ne complis lo dit viatge per quals[evol] excusa, necessitat o raso, les quals fermançes deven esser .x. de sos capitans aq[uelles] que per part del dit senyor seran nomenats, e lo vezcomte de Rochaberti, los quals .x. capitans et lo dit vezcomte se deven obligar a restituir los dits .vi.^{m} florins en lo dessus dit cas que lo dit mossen no fes lo dit viatge, es assaber cascun per lo tot. Per ço lo dit Francesch abans que los dits capitols e la dita obligacio se ferm haia cura de demanar e saber quals dels capitans del dit mossen Bertran son m[. . .] lors in por abonats e a feats, e aquelles que sabra esser aytals elegesta e no[mbra] a la dita fermanceria e faça que aquelles aytals façen la dita fermanceria e cascun dells se oblich per lo tot en la forma contenguda en una nota que sobre aço s'en porta ia dictada. E tenga ement que aquesta obligacio sia fermada e fer[mad] en la forma dessus dita, car una es de lespus principals coses per qui hi va. Rex. P.

7. *Indenture between Sir Hugh Calveley and Sir Matthew Gournay concerning the disposal of the castle of Mola to Gournay and certain rights in Calveley's other possessions in the kingdom of Valencia. Bordeaux, 7 November 1371.*

Archivo de la Corona d'Aragón, Cancilleria, reg. 922, fos. 118r–9v (contemporary copy).

Ceste endenture faite entre mons' [Hues] de Calviley d'une part et mons' Matheu de Gornay d'autre, en presence et par amiable traicte des nobles et puissantz seignours le captal de Buch, conestable, et Thomas de Feltoun, seneschal d'Aquitaine, moss' Berard de Lebrit, seigneur de Rions, mestre Raymond Guilhem de Puy, jutge de Gascoigne, et autres, tesmoigns que les dessus diz mons' [Hues] et mons' Matheu sur aucunes demandes qui ont este mehnez entr'eux sur aucuns dons et guerredons faitz a chascun dez diz monss' Hues et mons' Matheu par le tresexcellent seigneur le rey d'Aragon, il sont finablement acourdez par la maniere que s'ensuyt. Premieyrament, le dit mons' Hues, par le grant honour et ben qu'il a trouve en le dit mons' Matheu

---

12 Possibly as much as one line missing here.

APPENDIX A

du temps passe et entant a trouver du temps a venir, il y a ottreye de son bon gre et de sa certaine science, et promis de donner pour li et par ses hoirs audit mons' Matheu et a ses hoirs en heretatge le castel de Mola en le reaulme de Valence, aveques ses appertenances. Et li promet de bailler la vraya possession du dit chastel dedens quinze jours empres que le dit mons' Matheu aura requis ou fait requerre ledit mons' Hues de li baillier la possession dudit chastel. Et apres ce que le dit monss' Matheu aura empatre et obtenu licence dudit roy d'Arragon, sur ledit alienacion et donacion du chastel dessus dit et la dicte licence monstre audit mons' Hues et notifiee ou acely que pardela sera son lieutenant, a la quelle licence empatrer et obtenir ledit mons' Hues a promis en bonne foy et come loyol chevalier audit mons' Matheu de li ayder devers le dit roy, pour lettres et pour prieres, a bonne foy, sans mal engin, et no fere le contraire autressi, le dit mons' Matheu pour le grant bien et honneur que il a trouve avec ledit mons' Hues du temps passe, et entent a trouver du temps avenir, li a octroie et promis que quant il aura obtenu la vraya possession dudit chastel par la maniere que dessus es dit, il ne metra james Johan de Vrayton,[13] officer illeques. Et plus que il fara jurer tous ses officiers qu'il metra en ledit chastel qu'il ne feront tort ni force aus vassals dudit mons' Hues durant la vie des avant dits mons' Hues et mons' Matheu. Et par mesme maniere ledit mons' Hues fera jurer ses officers qu'il a en ses chastels es lieux pardela. Et plus a promis ledit mons' Matheu audit mons' Hues, pour li et pour ses hoirs, que en cas qu'il ou ses hoirs vendroient ledit chastel de la Mola en la ville de Novella, qu'il le notifiera audit mons' Hues et li vendra davant tout autre et li lessera, s'il le veult acheptee mil florins menis que il en trouveront d'aucun autre personne autressi pour cause d'une demande que le dit mons' Matheu ha fait audit mons' Hues sur le lieu d'Aspe, a cause d'un don ou promission que le dit roy d'Aragon fist audit mons' Hues quant nostre tresredoubte et tressouverain seigneur le prince d'Aquitaine et de Galles estoit en Espaigne de deux mille florins de terre en heretatge. Est acorde que le dit mons' Hues disent et prometent en loiaute de chevalerie et reportant le plus tost qu'il poira bonnement lettre tesmoinable dudit roy d'Aragon seele du dit seel de la chancellerie du dit roy, qu'il n'a pas heu ledit lieu d'Aspe a cause dudit promesse que li fut fait par le dit roy quant le dit monss' le prince estoit en Espaigne, mais a causa de son mariatge le dit mons' Matheu cessera de la dita demanda a tots jorns mes. Et en cas que le dit mons' Hues n'auroit la dicta letre testimonial du dit roy, que le dit moss' Matheu aye la moyne en le dit lieu d'Aspe. Et autressi le dit mons' Hues a promis audit mons' Matheu que en cas que en temps a venir il puisse avoir ou aquerra aucune terre ou profit dudit roy d'Aragon a cause dudit promisse que le dit roy fit audit mons' Hues quant le dit mons' le prince estoit en Espaigne, sur quoy il fera son loial poueir que le dit mons' Matheu aura en

---

13   i.e. Drayton.

320

cela auxi bonne part come ledit mons' Hues, en paiant sa part des costatges et mises raisonables que ont este ou seront fait pour cela cause. Les quelles chouses tenir acomplir loialment de point en point pour la maniere que dessus est dit, sans null[14] engin, en presence des seigneurs surdiz, les avantdiz mons' Hues et mons' Matheu ont jure la foy qu'il doyvent a Dieu et chavalerie. En tesmoignance de verite des choses sus dites les avantdits mons' Hues de Calviley et monss' Matheu de Gornay as cestes presentes endentures entrechangeablement ont mis lours propres seelx. Donne a Bourdeaux, le vii[e] jour de novembre l'an de grace mil ccclxxi.

8. *Letter of Peter IV of Aragon to the Governor of Valencia, requesting him to oblige Constança of Aragon, wife of Sir Hugh Calveley, to join her husband. Barcelona, 18 April 1380.*
Archivo de la Corona d'Aragón, Cancilleria, reg. 1267, fos 82v–3r (contemporary copy).

Lo Rey.
Governador, sapiats que a nos es estat supplicat per parit de mossen Huc de Calviley que deguessem forcar la nobla na Constancia d'Arego a estare habitar ab lo dit mossen Huc, que es son marie, com la muler deia seguir la habitacio de son marie. E nos, considerant la dita supplicacio esser justa a nos denn a mariatge expressament e de certa sciencia per primera e segona jussions e encarie sots encourrment de la nostra ira e indignacio, que encontinent nos assegurets con pero secretament e sania porets de la persona de la dita madona Constancia e de ses bens. E si ella vol mar al dit mossen Huc, que es apperellat de pagar la messio della e d'aquello que la acompanyara lexats la anar gentas empero que ve essets que ella noy vol mar meteto la en lo monastir de les Menoretes, e tenits sos bens sequestrats e emperats. E quant le hauvets mesa en lo dit monastir, fets manament a la abbadessa a los monges que la tenguen en comanda e la guariden en tel manera que del monastir exir no puga. Dada en Barchilona sots nostre segell secret, a xviii dies de abril del any Mcccxxx. Rex Petrus.

9. *Letter of Peter IV, king of Aragon, to his son En Joan, requesting him to expel Constança of Aragon, wife of Sir Hugh Calveley, from his house and from his lands. Zaragoza, 31 May 1381.*
Archivo de la Corona d'Aragón, Cancilleria, reg. 1272, fos. 62v–63r (contemporary copy).

Lo Rey.
Molt car fill. Sabut havem con vos agran vostra difamacio d'entrara

---

14 *Sic*. The word should evidently be 'mal'.

confusio sin conexiets tenits ab la comtessa, vostra muller, na Constança d'Arago, muller de mossen Huc de Calviley, de la qual cosa som molt mervellats ens desplait tant per moltes raons que no paria pus la primera, per co com nos ne romanits fort mal perlat e difamat, car qu'es vulla haia entre nos – ella fama es publica que vos jahets ab ella – los gents ho creen fermament – vos qu'ils ho confermats ara que leve havets mesa en casa la segona que podets pensar ab quin plaer ne fets vivre la dita comtessa vostra muller, la qual es bona, saina e honesta, e per la qual vos possehits gran heretat en tant que ab ço d'ella, e ab ço que nos vos havem dat, lo nuls heretat hom sots d'Espanya, axi que si cone exeuta haura en vos nous en diriets axi comportar ne cap tenir la terra per que la dita Constança, en mala hora, pus tel es ha dente de sanch ab vos pays, que es muller d'un notable e assenyalat cavaller en fets d'armes, e qui es servidor nostre e loqual, imiatant Deu, primerament son causa principal per que nos recobram nostre regna del rey don Pedro de Castiella, per la qual rao merexessa honrat mantengut e de fes per nos e per nostres coses, e no en res vituperat ne en vergonyit, car nul hauria guardo el servey e com altre e oro rey haguns, sino aquesta vos si devriets aquest fet esquar co averii e mandament que podets prinsar que sa ell ha sentiment daco es hom y asprar s'en de venjar e de fer e enpendrea tal cosa que provetura vos no haursets daco pensado, eas ayrar vos hauriets fet gran salt per que dolents nos e no sens rao del dit fet vos manera sots pena de perdie la nostra gracia e amor que de continent vista aquesta lettra vos gitets la dita Constança no solament de casa vostra, mas encare de tota vostra terra, car persona tan difamada com ella no den cer mantenguda per null hom que be. E guardats vos de esser james en .i. loch civiliter ab ella, eas mitat cessara la difamacio en que vos ne sots, e cessaran axi mateix los escandols que son porren seguir. En altera manera siats cert que nos veni acordats de fer tal cosa vers vos que puys no sera en nos de esmenar ne reversar, ho es a co harats por feran. E tantost hora vostra e esposta a fer reverenz ho e a co haiats fet. Dada en Saragoça sots nostre sigilli secret, a xxxi dies de mays del an mccclxxxi.
Rex Petrus.   Fuit missa signata. R.

Appendix B

Tables of Captains

Table 1 Captains of the Great Companies

Key (see below)	1	2	3	4	5	6	7	8	9	10	11	12	13†
Alain, John	E								*	67			
Albret, Bérard d'	G	*	*			*	*Kn					F	
—, Bertucat d'	G					*	*Kn	*	*	78–9		EFE	1383
Amory, John	EC	*	*Kn	*									1364 ba
Anger, Étienne, alias Ferragut	Pr					*							
Badefol, Seguin de	Pé	*				*	*			65			1366 po
—, Tonnet	Pé											F	1370 ba
Bageran, Naudon de	G	*						*				E	
Bardolf, William	E										*		
Bataillier, Munde	?T	*											1368 ex
Bell, Thomelin	E										*		
Bertuquin	G	*	*	*						64			1364
Birkhead, Robert	E	*						*	66		*		1368 ba
Botiller, William	EL							*	66		*		
Bourdeille	Pé	*											
Bouvetault (Boias), Perrin, alias Savoie, Perrot de	Sa	*										F	1369 ex
Bras de Fer	G												
Bray, Jacques de	N	*										F	
Breteuil, Bertrand, the *bourc* de	G	*	*			*		*				F	1369 ex
Brown, Henry	E										*		
—, John	E										*		
Camus, le *bourc*	G	*				*		*	*			E	1369 ex
Castel, Garciot du	Py		*Kn	*	*			*				F	
Castelnau, Jean de	Q					*Kn							
Chabot, Gérard, lord of Rays♦	B							*				F	
Cheyney, Robert	EK	*						*			*	E	
Chiselden, John	E										*		
Cozi, le					*								
Cresswell, John	EN	*						*			*	E	1374/6
—, Edmund	EN										*	E	
Darrier, Frère	?G				*								
Devereux, John♦	E						*	66				E	
Eglisale, Henry	E									*			
Felton, William♦	E							*				E	1367 ba

323

APPENDIX B

Table 1 (*Cont.*)

Key (see below)	1	2	3	4	5	6	7	8	9	10	11	12	13†
Fischenich, Winrich von, alias Ourri l'Alemant	Ge	*								62/6			
Folifait, Thomas	E										*		
Hawkwood, John	EE	*											1394
Hawley, Robert	E							*		66/7			
Hazenorgue, Johann	Ge	*	*	*		*			*	65–6			
Hennequin, Frank	Ge	*									F		
Hilton, Roger	E										*		
Holgrave, David	EC										*	E	
Holm, Richard	EY										*	E	
Hormeston, Adam	E										*		
Jouel, John	E	*											1364 ba
Lamit	G	*					*		*	66			
Le Maitre des Vaisseaux; le Maitre des Nefs													
Lesparre, *bourc* de	G	*									EFE		
Machin, Heliés or Elías, alias Petit Meschin	G	*	*	*	*	*				64		F	1369 ex
Mauléon, Bascot de	Bé	*						*				E	
Mitton, Robert	E							*			*	E	
Montaut, Pierre de	G		*							78		F	
Motte, Gaillard de la	G	*						*		78		E	
Norbury, John	EC										*	E	
Oleron, Richard d'	G									*			
Ortigue, Amanieu d'	G	*										F	1369 ex
Pau, Guyonnet de	Bé	*											
Périgord, *bourc* de	Pé	*											
Peritant, Geoffrey	E										*		
Peverell, Thomas or John	E							*					
Pin, Arnauton du	Bé	*										F	
—, Guiot du	Po	*											1364 ex
Plantin, James	E	*											1364 ba
Raymont, Gourderon de, lord of Aubeterre♦	G						*						
Rocamadour	Q					*							
Roche, Billos la						*							
Rochechouart, Aimery de		*						*				E	
Roque, Raymond Bernard de la, alias Sandos													
Roubaud, Louis	Pr	*				*							1365 ex
Russell, Hodgkin	E										*	E	
Saint-Julien, Lopez de	G									75/8	*		
Saint Pierre, Berradeco de	G			*	*					66			
Salle, Bernard de la	G	*							*				1391 ba
—, Hortingo de la	G	*											
Sandes, John	E								*	67			
Scot, Hagre le	Sc	*											
Shakell, John	E							*					
Shelton, William	E										*		

324

APPENDIX B

Table 1 (*Cont.*)

Key (see below)	1	2	3	4	5	6	7	8	9	10	11	12	13†
Sobrossa, or Fabrossa	?G												
Solier, Arnaud de, alias 'le Limousin'	Li	*								63			
Spincta													
Sterz, Albert	Ge	*											1366 ba
Tallebard, Arnaud de, alias Tallebardon	Bé	*	*										
Taunton, Richard	E							*				E	
Tiriel, Jacques		*											
Vaire de Cap													
Villers, Menaud de, alias Espiote	Bé	*	*	*	*	*		*		64–5			1369 ex
Volemer, Folekin, alias Folcquin l'Alemant	Ge										*		
Waldeboef, John	E												
Walton, Geoffrey	E										*		
Worsley, Geoffrey	EL											*	E

Key (where no source is listed, the details are in the text)
- ♦ Led a contingent of the companies.
- 1 = Country or region of origin: Bé = Béarn, E = England (+ C Cheshire, + D Devon, + E Essex, + K Kent, + L Lancashire, + N Northumberland, + Y Yorkshire), G = Gascony (including Labourd), Ge = Germany (i.e. imperial territory), La = Languedoc, Li = Limousin, N = Normandy, Pé = Périgord, Po = Poitou, Pr = Provence, Py = Pyrenees, Q = Quercy, Sa = Savoy, Sc = Scotland, T = Toulousain.
- 2 = Named by Froissart, *Chroniques*, vi, pp. 62, 257; vii, pp. 115, 336; xii, pp. 99–100.
- 3 = Party to treaty of Clermont, 23-vii-62 (Hay du Châtelet, preuves, pp. 313–15). Kn = knight.
- 4 = Present at battle of Launac (5-xii-62).
- 5 = Referred to in instructions on what the duke of Anjou was to say to the pope concerning the companies being maintained by Charles of Navarre to make war in France (Secousse, *Recueil*, p. 206, art. 21).
- 6 = Party to the treaty for the evacuation of Brioude, 4-iv-64 (Chassaing, 'Traité, pp. 163–73; *Spicilegium*, pp. 361–8, no. 134).
- 7 = Listed in a Navarrese spy letter of 13-ii-65 (AD Pyrénées-Atlantiques, E 520; Appendix A, Document 3). Kn = knight.
- 8 = Indicated in a letter of 10-x-66 from Edward III to the Black Prince (*Foedera*, III, ii, p. 808).
- 9 = Present on the Nájera campaign (Chandos Herald, *Vie*, lines 1975–95, 2265–7, 2371–7).
- 10 = In Navarrese pay in the years indicated [AGN Comptos, regs. 111, 113, 118–19, 121, 161 (references in text) *AGN, Comptos*, v, vi, ix–xii (see indices)].
- 11 = Named as *cappitaines et chevetaennes des genz des routes des englaes des granz compaignes* in acquittances given to the receiver-general of Brittany on 30-xii-68 and 22-ii-69 (AD Loire-Atlantique, E 119/12, 13). See also BN, nouv. acq. franç., 5216, nos. 10–12. From these acquittances it is clear that William Bardolf, William Fisher and Hugh Felton, who are described as Birkhead's *compaignons*, were members of his *route*. Other members of the English companies included Jannekin Nowell, Robert Stoberiche, William Hulthet or Hughelot, Gerard Salveyn, Wuilket or Willicot Tee, William Danton, Robert Worsley and Richard Skyror.
- 12 = Side taken on renewal of war. E = English, F = French, EFE = English, then French, then English again.
- 13 = Date of death, where known (ba = died in battle or as a result of wounds sustained in battle; ex = executed; po = poisoned).

APPENDIX B

Table 2 Captains of other companies operating in the 1360s♦

Key (see below)	1	2 3 4 5 6 7 8 9	10	11	12	13†
Armagnac, Arnaud Guillaume, bastard of	G		78–9			
Aussain, *bourc* d'	G					
Campagne, *bourc* de						1369 ex
Chase, John	E					
Chauffour, Jean de	?Lo					1364 ex
——, Thibaud de	?Lo		59			1364 ex
Chipperel, Benedetto	L					
Dagworth, Nicholas	E					
Escalat, Pierre d', alias le Basquin de Lingot	G					
Espée, Raymonet de l', alias Ramonet d'Aspet	C					
Guillampot						1364 ex
Lawgoch, Owain, alias Owen of Wales	W			F		
Monsac, bastard de	Pé					
Montprivat, Bertrand de						
Morville, Thomas	E					1365 ex
Nègre, Jehannot le						1369 ex
Neufchâtel, Jean de	Bu		63			1369
Oignel, Pierre d'						
Pau, Bouzomet de	Bé			F		1369 ex
Pavalhon, Noli, alias Papillon				F		1369 ex
Roque, *bourc* de la	?G					
Roussillon, Bardot de	R					
Scot, Walter le (possibly Walter Leslie)	Sc					
Scott, Robert	E					1368 ex
Seys, Gregory or Desgarry	W	*				
Tamworth, Nicholas	E					
Troussevache, Gilles						1364 ex
Vieleston, John	E					1365 ex
Vigneulles, Renaud de	?E					
Wyn, Ieuan, alias 'le poursuivant d'amours'	W			F		

Key (as in table 1), other than:

- ♦ Some of these captains were closely associated with the Great Companies, but are not stated as being of their number.

1 = Country or region of origin: Bé = Béarn, Bu = Burgundy (county of), C = Comminges, E = England, G = Gascony, L = Lombardy, Lo = Lorraine, P = Périgord, R = Roussillon, Sc = Scotland, W = Wales.

APPENDIX B

Table 3   Captains of the Breton companies

	1	2	3	4	5	6
Agnay, G. d'			*			
Beaumont, Alain de			*	70		
Boistel, Guillaume	*		*			
Budes, Silvestre				68		*
—, Yvon			*			
Cornouaille, Jean de		i65				
Dinan, Hervé de			*			
Duant, Yvon			*			
Groeslort, Yvon de			*			
Guébriant, Auffroy de			*			
Guesclin, Olivier du			*			
Houssaye, Alain de la			*			
—, Tristan de la			*			
Isles, Bernard des, bastard de l'Île						
Isles, Jean des					*	
Kerimel, Geoffroi de			?*	72		
Kerlouet, Hervé de			*	68		
—, Jean de			*	71		
Lacoué, Yvon de		d63–5	*			
Lannion, Briand de		*[a]				
Laval, Brémond de			?*			
—, Guillaume de			*			
Malestroit, Jean de			*		*	*
Mauny, Alain de			*	71		
—, Henri de			*			
—, Hervé de			*			
—, Jean de			*			
—, Olivier de	*		*			
Pansard, Jean					*	*
Pedran, Narri de			?*			
Pencoédic, Jacques de		d63–7	*	71		
Poncet, le Basquin de						
Pont, Thibaud du			*	70		
Quélen, Guillaume de		*[a]			*	
Richon, Geoffroi			*	72	*	
Rollant, Julliel, or Juhel				74		
Saint-Pol, Alain de		d63–4	*			*
—, Ernauton		d63–4				
—, Jean de		d63–4	*	73		
—, Raoulet de		d63–4	*			
Saint-Ryot, Jean de		d64				
Spic, Henri		id62				
Tallay, Alyot de			*			
Tréséguidy, Maurice de		*				
Vaulx, Lyon de		i62				
Others						*[b]

327

APPENDIX B

Key (where no source is given the details are in the text)
1 = Served with du Guesclin at Cocherel (Cuvelier, *Chronique*, i, pp. 160, 178).
2 = Served in Burgundy, operating either independently (i) or in ducal service (d), in the years indicated between 1362 and 1367.
3 = Served with du Guesclin in Spain, 1366–70.
4 = Retained in French royal service on renewal of war with England (date given is first documentary record).
5 = Served on Jaume 'IV's expedition in 1374–5 (see *Medieval Mercenaries II*).
6 = In papal service in Italy after 1376 (see *Medieval Mercenaries II*; see note b).

Notes:
a   In the early summer of 1364 du Guesclin instructed them to bring the Breton companies, then in Burgundy (in particular those garrisoning Pontaillier), to join him in Normandy.
b   Others (not all Bretons) serving in Italy with Malestroit and Budes in 1376–7 included, in addition to Guillaume Pansard with fifty lances, Jean de Blary with eighty, Guillaume Trogorant and Aimon Treffily, each with sixty, Florimond Daviz, Roger de Bricqueville and Geoffroy le Vizier with forty lances (Mirot, lviii, p. 595, lix, pp. 273–4, 276–7, 294 and notes). For the identification of others whose names appear in Guillaume de la Penne, *Gesta Britonum*, see du Bois de la Villarebel, *Gestes*. The whole matter will be treated in *Medieval Mercenaries II*.

Appendix C

The Numerical Strength of the Great Companies

The numerical strength of the Great Companies depended on the number of *routes* brought together for a particular operation and on the size of each contingent. There is substantial evidence to suggest that an individual company frequently consisted of around 120 men-at-arms. A few examples will suffice. In September 1364, the strength of the company of the mercenary captain Guillampot was estimated by the *bailli* of Chalon to be 120 'bonnes lances' (Petit, x, p. 121). In a letter written by Peter IV of Aragon to the governor of Roussillon in January 1367, the king announced that he had been informed that the Mallorcan Pretender had recruited 13 captains of the companies then with the Black Prince, totalling 1,600 lances (Miret y Sans, 1905, p. 106). In 1372 Garciot du Castel was retained by Louis of Anjou with 120 men-at-arms at the rate of 15 francs per man-at-arms per month (BN, PO 612, doss. 14,399, du Castel, no. 5).

The Invasion of Castile in 1366

For the invasion of Castile in 1366 the chronicle evidence suggests that the total contingents brought from France amounted to some 10,000–12,000 combatants (Ayala, *Crónica*, i, p. 536; *Chron. Jean II et Charles V*, ii, p. 15). Perhaps as many as 3,000 were drawn from the companies, of which around 1,000 were under Calveley's immediate command. These estimates are based on the payments due to be made by Peter IV to du Guesclin and those in which du Guesclin was obliged to Calveley. However, interpretation of this evidence is complex. In a series of proposals for the recruitment of the Great Companies put to Pere by Enrique of Trastámara during the course of 1365, Enrique had envisaged two payments amounting to 100,000 florins for the cost of 3,000 lances (*glavis*) and 40,000 florins for other troops under his command. Pere's council thought this too much and suggested 60,000 florins per month (on the basis of 20 florins per lance) as a more realistic figure (ACA, Cartas reales diplomaticás, caja 50, no. 6178, fos. 1r, 2v). This was in fact the rate at which Pere was paying Enrique for each of the mounted men-at-arms in his service in November 1365 (viz. 20,000 florins per month for 1,000 men-at-arms), and it is clear that Enrique expected to continue on this basis during the first quarter of 1366 (Delachenal, iii, p. 278 n. 1, and p. 324 n. 5). It is unlikely that the wages paid to the forces under du Guesclin's command fell below this rate, although in December 1365 Pere offered only 15 florins per mounted man-at-arms for the 600 troops he invited Charles of Navarre to contribute to du Guesclin's forces for a quarter (Miret y Sans, p. 78). It is evident from the payments made to Enrique and those offered to Charles of Navarre that wages were computed quarterly, and this was the case with the wages paid by Enrique to the lord of Aubeterre (Molinier, PJ xciv, p. 320; see Delachenal, iii, p. 329 n. 2), as well as by du Guesclin to Calveley (ACA, Cancilleria, reg. 738, fo. 41r; published in Fowler, 1991b, 1992, Document iii). The payment due to du Guesclin of 120,000 florins in two instalments (Delachenal, iii, p. 318) therefore suggests 6,000 lances (around 50 companies), 3,000 lances (25 companies) or 2,000 lances (17 companies), depending on whether this sum represented pay for one month, two months or an entire quarter. According to Cuvelier (*Chronique*, i, p. 267, line 7363), du Guesclin had 25 captains of the companies under his command, which suggests a figure of 3,000 combatants.

The calculation of the likely strength of the companies under Calveley's command is rather less complex. According to the indenture which he concluded with du Guesclin on 16 February 1366 (ibid., fos. 41v–2r; Fowler, 1991b, 1992, Document i), Bertrand undertook *d'acompter oveque luy* [i.e. moss' Hues] *tant pour son estat come pour les gages de sez genz touz les foiy que le dit moss' Hues luy en requerra*. It is not clear if the two surviving letters obligatory made out by du Guesclin to Sir Hugh which have so far come to light (ACA, Cancilleria, reg. 738, fos. 40v–41r; published in Fowler, 1991b, 1992, Documents ii, iii), represent the entire sums due to Calveley for his services and those of his men. The first, dated Toledo, 5 May 1366, is for a sum of 63,008 florins. If this was the total outstanding for an entire quarter then, at a rate of 20 florins per man-at-arms per month, the total number of combatants would have been 1,050. If it was for the period dating from the general muster in Zaragoza and the conclusion of the contract between the two men, then the number of combatants under Calveley's command would have been slightly in excess of 1,200. Since the second letter obligatory, dated Seville, 3 July 1366, specifically states that the sum of 26,257 florins then outstanding for the wages of Calveley and Janequin Clerk and their men was for *le premier quartier qu'ils entrarent oveque nos* [i.e. du Guesclin] *en Castelle*, it is likely that the first interpretation is the correct one. It is possible, but unlikely, that the first letter obligatory was drawn up after an earlier payment (i.e. after Calveley had made an initial settlement of accounts), and it should be noted that the calculations do not take into account any moneys which may have been due to Hugh for his *estat* (however, the letters obligatory only refer to wages, *gages*). According to Ayala (*Crónica*, i, pp. 545–6), when Enrique disbanded the greater part of his forces in the summer of 1366, he retained only the Bretons under du Guesclin and the English under Calveley, amounting in all to 1,500 lances (1,000 lances in the abbreviated version of the chronicle: ibid., i, p. 546 n. 2). A figure of around 1,000 for the total number of men-at-arms under Calveley's command thus seems a reasonable estimate.

The Black Prince's Intervention in Castile in 1367

The figures of 10,000 cavalry for the vanguard and 20,000 for the main battle of the prince's army advanced by Chandos Herald (*Vie*, lines 2309, 2350) must be rejected as a gross exaggeration. Ayala's figure of 10,000 men-at-arms and as many archers (*Crónica*, i, p. 553) is doubtless nearer the mark, but still greatly inflated. According to the agreements concluded at Libourne on 23 September 1366 (*Foedera*, III, i, pp. 800–2, 805), the prince was to pay Charles of Navarre 36,000 florins for the first month's pay of 1,000 mounted men (*infanzones*) and 1,000 foot soldiers (*infanzones de abarca, villanos*) on the basis of 30 florins a month for a mounted man and 6 florins a month for each infantryman. The estimated cost of the forces to be provided by the prince to Pedro was 150,000 florins for the first three months, which, if they were all cavalry, would have amounted to 1,666 men, at the rate of remuneration offered to Charles's *infanzones*. The estimated costs of the forces to be provided by the Gascon lords for the first three months was 180,000 florins, which, on the same basis, would have financed 2,000 men-at-arms. However, these sums were evidently intended to cover the costs of archers and infantrymen as well as men-at-arms and, since the former were paid less than the latter, this would have resulted in a higher figure of combatants. In addition, it should be noted that the estimated costs for the prince's forces and those of the Gascon lords were to fall to 100,000 and 120,000 florins respectively for the second quarter. A figure of 3,500 combatants for the forces to be raised in Aquitaine might be taken as a rough estimate. If we add to these figures the 400 men-at-arms and 800 archers brought from England by John of Gaunt, the remaining 800 archers whose recruitment had also been ordered in Westminster (*Foedera*, III, i, 797, 799; Russell, 79 nn. 2 and 3; Barber, p. 194) and the handful of supporters who joined Pedro I of Castile during his exile in Gascony, a total of 8,500 combatants seems not unreasonable.

Russell, p. 80, arrives at a maximum of 10,000 men, but believes that the total may well have been less. Barber, p. 194, suggests 8,000, but believes 'there is good reason to put the total as low as 6,000 men'.

The total of 3,000 men drawn from the companies is based on the 23 pennons referred to by Chandos Herald (*Vie*, lines 1975–95, 2265–7, 2281, 2371–7; see Fowler, 1988, pp. 36–7, and above p. 198), and a further two routes (of Hazenorgue and Espiote) added by Ayala (*Crónica*, i, p. 553).

Appendix D

Forces Recruited by the Duke of Anjou in 1369

1 Forces recruited from among the Great Companies

According to Froissart, *Chroniques*, vii, pp. 115–6, 336, the forces recruited by the duke included those of Petit Meschin, the *bourc* de Breteuil, Amanieu d'Ortigue, Perrin de Savoie, Jacques de Bray and Arnauton du Pin. Bérard d'Albret was recruited on 5 January 1369 (BN, coll. Languedoc, 97, fo. 51). By letters dated Toulouse, 25 April 1369, the duke ordered his treasurer-of-wars, Etienne de Montmejean, to pay the *bourc* de Breteuil 620 francs remaining of a much greater sum 'en laquelle nous li summez tenuz pour aucunes certaines besoignes es quelles il avoit vaque, froie et grandement travaille, lui et les gens de sa compaigne, en ces presentes guerres du duche de Guienne touchans l'onneur et prouffit de monseigneur et de nous'. This was paid the following day 'pour debte que monseigneur le duc li devoit pour le fait de la guerre' (BN, PO, vol. 503, doss. 11,404, de Breteuil, nos. 2–3). Noli Pavalhon, as captain of 88 men-at-arms, was enrolled by Anjou in January 1369 (*HGL*, ix, p. 803; for his muster on 15 February following, see Contamine, 1975, pp. 390–2, PJ no. i). Perrin de Savoie was retained on 12 February with 126 men-at-arms and 9 mounted archers, and mustered at Buzet (BN, Ms. franç. 22,479, nos. 40–3). By letters dated Toulouse, 16 February 1369, the duke ordered Montmejean to pay 100 gold francs to 'Bousomet de Pau, escuier . . . lesquieux nous lui avons donnez oultre ses gaiges et donnons par ces presentes a prendre une foiz sur vostre recepte pour aucuns despens et fraiz les qeux il a faiz et soustenuz en nostre compaignie et en ces presentes guerres du duche de Guienne', and on 8 March 1369, 700 francs 'sus ses gages' (BN, PO, vol. 2213, doss. 50,007, Pau, nos. 2–3; see Contamine, 1975, pp. 393–4, PJ no. iii, for his muster). By other letters dated Toulouse, 16 February 1369, he ordered Montmejean to pay Jacques de Bray, esquire, 100 gold francs 'pour cause de certains despens et fraiz qu'il avoit fait et soustenuz en nostre compaignie' (ibid., vol. 495, doss. 11,155, de Bray, no. 2). On 20

May 1369, he retained him to serve in the present wars with 50 men-at-arms, and on 11 December following he once again retained him and Jacquemart Claret, with 110 men-at-arms in their company (ibid., nos. 4–5). On 22 February 1370/1371, when Bray is referred to as 'capitaine de lxx hommes d'armes', Anjou granted him 100 gold francs 'pour son estat soustenir' (ibid., no. 6). Bray gave acquittances for wages of 200 and 800 francs at Toulouse on 27 October and 20 November 1371 respectively (ibid., nos. 7–8), and on 20 May 1377, by which time he was an esquire in Louis' equerry, he was granted 100 gold francs 'pour consideracion des bons et agreables services qu'il a faiz a monseigneur et a nous en ces guerres du duchie de Guienne, et esperons qu'il face ou temps avenir' (ibid., no. 9, and no. 14 for the acquittance, dated Nîmes, 22 May 1377).

Some captains of the Great Companies had been brought into French service earlier. By letters dated Paris, 14 January 1365/6, the king 'consideratis gratis et laudebilibus serviciis que dilectus noster Mondonis Batailler, scutifer, in guerris nostris nobis impendis et que ab ipso in futurum impendirum speramus', granted him a fief-rent of 300 *livres* in the receipt of Toulouse (BN Clairambault, vol. 214, no. 83; vidimus under the seal of the *prévôt* of Paris, dated 5 October 1366). An instruction to see that this was paid, dated 13 October 1366, refers to him as an 'escuier de son escuierie' (ibid., no. 84; letter from the treasurers of the king in Paris to the receiver of Toulouse). The *bourc* de Breteuil and his company had already been recruited by Jean d'Armagnac by 21 May 1368 (BN, PO, 93, doss. Armagnac, no. 59). Hennequin (Hanequin l'aleman, chevalier) was among the 14 knights and 186 esquires serving under Armagnac who came into Anjou's service at Toulouse on 8 December 1368 (BN, Nouv. acq. franç., 8603, nos. 49–53). On 21 May 1369, Garciot du Castel acquitted Nicholas Odde, treasurer-of-wars, for the wages of himself and 29 esquires, also serving with Armagnac (Froissart, *Chroniques*, viii, p. xv, n. 9).

2 Forces recruited from among the Breton Companies

On 21 December 1368, Jeaufroy Vieux was paid to go to several places in Languedoc to retain and muster Breton and other men-at-arms (BN, coll. Languedoc, vol. 97, fo. 52), and again on 10 February 1369 Anjou charged Richard de Chemin and the bastard of la Roche to muster troops then ravaging the seneschalsy of Toulouse, and recruit and muster them at Buzet to make war in Guyenne (BN, PO, doss. 16,670, Chemin). Silvestre Budes was already in Anjou's service on 16 December 1368 when, by letters dated at Toulouse, the duke ordered Etienne de Montmejean, treasurer-of-wars, to pay 'Siluestre Budes, escuier, hun dez capitaines d'una rota de bretons', 200 gold francs 'pour cause dez despens et freys qu'il a faiz environ nous en parfenir lez paiemenz de si et de ces compaingnons de leurs gaitges deservis et a deservir en nostre compaingnie et soz nostre gouvernement, et ainsi afin qu'il serva monseigneur et nous de plus grant et melhour vouloir ez guerres' (BN, PO, vol. 548, doss. 12,354, no. 2). On 26 January following, the duke ordered Montmejean to pay a further 200 francs to him 'pour cause de pluseurs bons et agreables services qu'il a fais et fait chascun jour a monseigneur et a nous en ces presentes guerres' (ibid., no. 3). Hervé de Kerlouet and 13 esquires in his company were mustered, reviewed and taken onto Anjou's payroll at Gimont on 21 December 1368 (ibid., vol. 1603, doss. 36,916, de Karaleu, nos. 2–3). On 20 May following, he was once again retained at Toulouse, together with 55 men-at-arms, also for service with Anjou in Gascony, and on 24th of that month, when his forces were mustered at Cahors, the number of esquires had been augmented to 66 (ibid., nos. 6–7). For Jean de Kerlouet, see Froissart, *Chroniques*, vii, pp. xlix n. 1 and lxxiii n. 2. Budes and Guébriant, captains of a *route* of 46 men-at-arms and a trumpeter, were reviewed by Anjou at Agen on 29 August 1372 (BN, PO, vol. 548, doss. 12,354, no. 4), and by letters dated at Montpellier on 20 June 1374, Budes, Rollant and Hervé de Kerlouet, esquires, captains of 400 men-at-arms in the duke's service, acknowledged receipt of 3,000 gold florins for themselves and their men for fifteen days, commencing 20 June (ibid., no. 10).

Appendix E

The Death of Sir Robert Birkhead in 1368 and the Supposed Death of Sir Robert Cheyney at Olivet

Both the author of the *Chron. premiers Valois*, p. 197, and the Bascot de Mauléon in Froissart (*Chroniques*, xii, p. 106; *Oeuvres*, xi, p. 119) refer to the death in battle of Sir Robert Birkhead, which the first authority rightly places in 1368, indicating that the engagement was with a force sent by the marshals of France. The Bascot says that the encounter took place 'in the Orléanais, between the country of Blois and the domains of the duke of Orléans at a place called Olivet', with an esquire from Hainault called Alart de Donstienne, then governor of Blois. The place in question can probably be identified with Olivet (Loiret), now in the southern suburbs of Orléans. But in the account of what appears to be the same engagement (*Chron. normande*, pp. 167, 333) the action is said to have taken place with a force commanded by Louis de Sancerre (one of the marshals of France), Gui de Baveux and the governor of Blois, at Olivet 'on the river Cher', evidently the fortified abbey of Olivet, on the south bank of that river between Romorantin and Vierzon (cant. Mennetou-sur-Cher, comm. Saint-Julien-sur-Cher). According to this account, at the time Cresswell was captain of Olivet, and the English were defeated and 'nearly all killed, taken and drowned in the river. And those who were taken were afterwards killed for the evil war they conducted' (*presque tous mors, pris et noiz en la riviere. Et ceulz qui furent prins furent aprés tuez pour la mal[1] guerre*

---

[1] I have translated *mal* as 'evil', although it might more appropriately be translated as 'illegal' in the sense that the war they engaged in was conducted without just title, as that pursued around Bayeux by two other *routiers*, Morville and Vieleston, who were rounded up about the same time, together with their men, and drowned, the same author tells us, *pour cause que ilz faisoient guerre de compaignie et n'avoient point de tiltre de seigneur, et aussi estoient ilz escomeniez du saint pere pour la male guerre que ilz faisoient* (*Chron. normande*, pp. 165–7).

que ilz faisoient). But neither the author of this account nor the Bascot assign a date to the engagement. In his list of fortresses occupied in France by the Anglo-Navarrese companies between 1356 and 1364, Luce (*Du Guesclin*, p. 477) attributes the action to 1364, and the editor of the *Chron. normande* to 1365. Confusion is added by Luce's footnote in Froissart, *Chronique*, vi, p. xcii n. 3, published the same year, in which he says (citing BN, Ms franç., 4987) that Sir Robert Cheyney was taken prisoner at Olivet and all the garrison, including Cheyney, were decapitated. No mention is made of this in the printed edition of the manuscript in question (namely, the *Chron. normande*!), and it is evidently inaccurate. We know from a number of letters of acquittance that Birkhead was dead by 30 December 1368 (AD Loire-Atlantique, E 119/12; BN, nouv. acq. franç., 5216, nos. 11, 12), but from the same documentation (E 119/12, 13) Cheyney must have been alive at that time and on 22 February following, when his seal was applied to the letters of acquittance given by the English *routes* of the Great Companies. He continued to make war in France until at least 1373.

Sources and Bibliography

A Manuscript sources

England

Public Record Office (London)

Chancery:
  Gascon Rolls: C 61 (assorted)
  Treaty Rolls: C 76 (assorted)
  Warrants for the Great Seal: C 81/471, 472
Exchequer:
  Diplomatic Documents: E 30/102, 104, 123, 182, 184, 186, 1277, 1346, 1364, 1425, 1496
  Accounts Various: 101/28/29 and E 101/30/25, 38, 39 (army, navy and ordnance); E 101/68/4, 9 (indentures of war); E 101/174/4, 175/5, 180/9, 181/1 (English affairs in France); E 101/316/1 (nuncii); E 101/393/11 (Wardrobe account, William Farley)
  Ancient Deeds: E 43/361, 598
  Issue Rolls: E 403/304
  Writs and Warrants for Issue: E 404/6/37, nos. 14, 41, 86; E 404/6/40, no. 64; E 404/509/61

British Library

Cotton Manuscripts: Caligula D III
Harleian Manuscripts: 2111

Lambeth Palace

Archbishop Arundel's Register

SOURCES AND BIBLIOGRAPHY

Norfolk Record Office
MR 314 242 x 5

Scotland

Edinburgh University Library
MS 183

France

Archives nationales

Series J. Trésor des Chartes, Layettes: 362 (ransoms of prisoners), 381 (Bertrand du Guesclin), 641–42 and 654–5 (relations with England)
Series K. Monuments historiques: 48–50 (Cartons des Rois)
Series P. Chambre des Comptes: 1334, 2294
Series X. Parlement de Paris: XIa 20, 27

Bibliothèque nationale (Paris)

Collection de Bourgogne: 24, 26 (copies of letters and mandates to and from ducal officers)
Collection Clairambault: 26, 62, 72, 80, 92, 214–5 (Titres Scellés)
Collection Doat (Languedoc):
    117 (Aquitaine), 119 (Cahors), 125–7 (Figeac, Capdenac, Moissac), 142 (Abbey of Bonneval), 145 (Millau), 146 (Najac, Saint-Antonin), 147 (Villefranche-de-Rouergue), 149 (Saint-Affrique), 192–7 (Houses of Foix, Armagnac and Albret), 243–5 (Counts of Périgord)
Collection de Languedoc (Bénédictins): 96–7, 159
Manuscrits français: 26006, 26008 (acquittances and diverse other pieces), 22479 (musters)
Manuscrits latin: 9175
Nouvelles acquisitions: 5216, 8603
Pièces originales: selected files, including 24, 93, 108, 495, 503, 548, 604, 612, 669, 702, 1034, 1603, 1839, 2213, 2239, 2429, 2809, 2957, 3046, 3052

Archives départmentales

Aveyron (Rodez): C 1332, 1886 (accounts of treasurers and receivers in Rouergue)
Côte-d'Or (Dijon): B 11922–5 (treaty of Guillon), 11935, 1412–17 (accounts of the receiver-general of Burgundy)
Eure et Loir (Chartres): E 2691 (notarial register)
Hérault (Montpellier), A 1, 5 and 6 (administrative orders)
Jura (Lons-le-Saunier): E 533 (military affairs, mandates and treaties)

Loire-Atlantique (Nantes): E 119 (relations of dukes of Brittany with England)
Lot (Cahors): F 23, 28, 37–9, 53, 74 (Fonds Lacabane)
Pyrenées-Atlantiques (Pau): E 38, 40, 201, 213 (Albret), E 243 (Armagnac), E 410 (Foix), E 520 (Navarre)
Tarn-et-Garonne (Montauban): A 26, 217, 256 (Fonds Armagnac)
[For inventories, see *Inventaires-sommaires* in Published Sources below.]

Archives communales/municipales

Aurillac: EE 4 (military affairs; correspondence)
Conques (in AD, Aveyron): E 67/22 (consular accounts)
Gourdon: EE 1 (military affairs; correspondence)
Marseille: BB 26 (consular deliberations)
Martel: CC 5 (consular accounts, 1371–8); EE 1 (military affairs; correspondence)
Millau: CC 516 (acquittances); EE 15
Montpellier: BB 4 (notarial register; consular acts)
    Fonds du Grand Chartier, Armoire D XIX, E VII (Louvet, no. 2482); Armoire H VI (Louvet, no. 3961)
Najac (in AD, Aveyron): E 178/8 (consular accounts), E 178/12–13 (diverse acts)
Rodez, Cité: CC 224, 361 (documents subsidiary to the consular accounts)
    Bourg: CC 126–7 (consular accounts, 1359–68)
Saint-Pourçain-sur-Sioule (in AD, Allier, Moulins): 4 E 258/CC 1 (accounts, 1355–65)
Toulouse: CC 687, 1847, 1848 (accounts)
[For inventories, see *Inventaires-sommaires* in Published Sources below.]

Bibliothèque municipale (Nantes)

Fonds Bizeul

Spain

Archivo de la Corona de Aragón (Barcelona)

Cancilleria:
    Regs. 734, 738 and 760 (Comune); 914–6 and 922 (Gratiarum); 976 (Officialium); 1077, 1080–2 (Curiae); 1159, 1194, 1214, 1217–8, 1220–2, 1225, 1240, 1260, 1267, 1272, 1274, 1289 (Sigilli Secreti); 1293 (Secretorum); 1341–8 (Pecuniae); 1386–8 and 1390 (Guerrae); 1819, 1951, 1968–9, 2242
Cartas reales diplomáticas:
    Pere III, Cajas 50–3, cartas 6115–563; Juan I, Cajas 6–7, nos 839 and 1069
Real Patrimonio (Maestro Racional):
    Regs. 351–5 (Tesorería del Rey; Libros Ordinarios); 488–93 (Tesorería de la Reina; Libros Ordinarios); 645 (Libros de Albalaes); 688 (Registros de letras, citatorias, certificaciones, órdenes, etc.)

Archivo General de Navarra (Pamplona)

Sección de Comptos:
Cajones, 20, 25 (1365)
Registros, 111, 113-4, 118, 120-1, 123, 148, 151-3, 156, 161 (1364-78)

Italy

Archivio di Stato

Mantua: Archivio Gonzaga, busta 1140
Perugia: Diplomatico, cass. 36 [260 (VII, p. 1)]

B Published sources

Actas de las Cortes de Castilla (58 vols, Madrid, 1871-1964).
Alauzier, L., 'Comptes consulaires de Cajarc (Lot) au XIVe siècle', *BPH*, 1957 (Paris, 1958), pp. 89-103.
Albe, E., 'Inventaire raisonné et analytique des archives municipales de Cahors', *Bulletin de la Société des Études littéraires, scientifiques et artistiques du Lot*, xli (1920), pp. 1-48; xliii (1922), pp. 1-28; xlv (1924), pp. 29-99.
Anonimalle Chronicle, 1333 to 1381, The, ed. V. H. Galbraith (2nd edn, Manchester, 1927).
Archives de la ville de Montpellier: Inventaires et Documents, i, *Fonds dit des 'Grandes Archives' ou du 'Grand Chartrier', Inventaire rédigé par Louvet en 1662-1663*, eds F. Castets and J. Berthelé (Montpellier, 1895); ii, *Documents omis dans l'inventaire du Grand Chartier*, ed. M. Oudot de Dainville (Montpellier, 1955); xiii, *Inventaire analytique, Série BB*, eds M. de Dainville, M. Gouron and L. Valls (Montpellier, 1984).
Archives de la ville de Pézenas. Inventaires et documents: Inventaire de F. Ressequier (Montpellier, 1907).
Ayala, Pero López de, *Crónica*, ed. C. Rossell, in *Crónicas de los reyes de Castilla* (2 vols, Biblioteca de autores españoles, Madrid, 1953).
Bardonnet, A. (ed.), *Procès-verbal de délivrance à Jean Chandos, commissaire du roi d'Angleterre, des places françaises abandonnés par le traité de Brétigny* (Mémoires de la Société de Statistique, science et arts de Deux-Sévres, Niort 1867).
Bel, Jean le, *Chronique*, eds J. Viard and E. Déprez (2 vols, SHF, Paris, 1904-5).
Berthelé, J. (ed.), *Repertoire numérique des archives départmentales de l'Hérault. Archives civiles, série A: actes du pouvoir souverain* (Montpellier, 1918).
Brutails, J.-A. (ed.), *Documents des archives de la Chambre de Comptes de Navarre, 1196-1384* (Paris,1890).
Cabaret d'Orville, J., *La Chronique du bon duc Loys de Bourbon*, ed. A.-M. Chazaud (SHF, Paris, 1876).

SOURCES AND BIBLIOGRAPHY

Calendar of Close Rolls, Edward III, Richard II, Henry IV (25 vols, HMSO, London, 1896–1938).
Calendar of Patent Rolls, Edward III, Richard II, Henry IV (26 vols, HMSO, London, 1891–1916).
Calendar of State Papers and Manuscripts Relating to English Affairs Existing in the Archives and Collections of Venice, i (1202–1509), ed. R. Brown (London, 1864).
Calendar of Wills Proved and Enrolled in the Court of Husting, London, ed. R. R. Sharpe (2 vols, London, 1889–90).
Carte, T., *Catalogue des Rolles gascons, normans et françois conservés dans les archives de la Tour de Londres* (London and Paris, 1743).
Cartulaire du prieuré de Saint-Flour, ed. M. Boudet (Collection de documents historiques, Monaco, 1910).
Catálogo de Documentos inéditos del Archivo Municipal de Burgos, Sección Historica, eds J. A. Bonachia Hernando and J. A. Pardos Martínez.
Catálogo del Archivo General de Navarra. Sección de Comptos, vols I-LII: *Documentos,* eds J. R. Castro and F. Idoate (52 vols, Diputación Foral de Navarra, Pamplona, 1952–74).
Catálogo del Archivo General de Navarra. Sección de Guerra, Años 1259–1800: Documentos, ed. F. Idoate (Diputación Foral de Navarra, Pamplona, 1978).
Catalogue des archives historiques de la ville de La Roche-sur-Yon, eds E. Louis and A. Bitton (La Roche-sur-Yon, 1908).
Chandos Herald, *La vie du Prince Noir,* ed. D. B. Tyson (Tübingen, 1975). Earlier editions also referred to in the footnotes: *Le Prince Noir. Poéme du héraut d'armes Chandos,* ed. Francisque-Michel (London and Paris, 1883); *Life of Edward, the Black Prince,* eds M. K. Pope and E. C. Lodge (Oxford, 1910).
Chaplais, P. (ed.), 'Some Documents Regarding the Fulfilment and Interpretation of the Treaty of Brétigny (1361–1369)', *Camden Miscellany,* xix; *Camden Third Series,* lxxx (RHS, London, 1952), pp. 1–50.
Chaucer, G., *The Complete Works of Geoffrey Chaucer,* ed. W. W. Skeat (7 vols, Oxford, 1894–7).
Chronica Johannis de Reading et Anonymi Cantuariensis, 1346–1367, ed. J. Tait (Manchester, 1914).
Chronique catalane de Pierre IV d'Aragon, III de Catalogne, dit le cérémonieux ou 'del Punyalet', ed. A. Pagès (Toulouse and Paris, 1941).
Chronique des quatre premiers Valois (1327–1393), ed. S. Luce (SHF, Paris, 1862).
Chronique de Richard Lescot, ed. J. Lemoine (SHF, Paris, 1896).
Chronique des règnes de Jean II et de Charles V (Les Grandes Chroniques de France), ed. R. Delachenal (4 vols, SHF, Paris, 1910–20).
Chronique du bon duc Loys de Bourbon, ed. A. M. Chazaud (SHF, Paris, 1876).
Chronique du Religieux de Saint-Denis, ed. L. Bellaguet (6 vols, CDI, Paris, 1839–52).
Chronique normande du XIVe siècle, eds A. and E. Molinier (SHF, Paris, 1882).
Chroniques romanes des comtes de Foix composées au XVe siècle par Arnaud Esquerrier et Miégeville, eds H. Courteault and F. Pasquier (Foix and Paris, 1893).

Chronographia regum Francorum, 1270–1405, ed. H. Moranvillé (3 vols, SHF, Paris, 1891–1907).
Colección de documentos inéditos del Archivo General de la Corona de Aragón, eds L Benaiges et al. (46 vols, Barcelona, 1847–1974).
'Compte de Raoul de Louppy, gouverneur du Dauphiné, de 1361 à 1369', ed. U. Chevalier, *Bulletin d'histoire ecclésiastique et d'archéologie religeuse des diocèses de Valence, Gap, Grenoble et Viviers*, vii (Romans, 1886), pp. i–viii, 1–74.
Comptes consulaires de la cité et du bourg de Rodez, ed. H. Bousquet (2 vols, AHR, Rodez, 1926–43).
Comptes consulaires de Saint-Antonin du XIVme siècle, ed. R. Latouche (Nice, 1923).
Controversy between Sir Richard Scrope and Sir Robert Grosvenor in the Court of Chivalry, ed. N. H. Nicolas (2 vols, London, 1832).
Cortes de los antiguos reinos de Aragón y de Valencia y principiado de Cataluña: Cortes de Cataluña (26 vols, Real Academia de la Historia, Madrid, 1896–1922).
Cortes de los antiguos reinos de Léon y de Castilla (Real Academia de la Historia, Madrid, 1861–4).
Cortes del reino de Aragon, 1357–1451, eds Sesma Muñoz and E. Sarasa Sánchez (Valencia, 1976).
Crónica de Garcia Lopez de Roncesvalles, ed. C. Orcastegui Gros (Pamplona, 1977).
Cuvelier, J., *Chronique de Bertrand du Guesclin*, ed. E. Charrière (2 vols, CDI, Paris, 1839).
Delisle, L, 'Deux lettres de Bertrand du Guesclin et de Jean le Bon, comte d'Angoulême, 1368 et 1344', *BEC*, xlv (1884), pp. 300–4.
—— *Fragments d'une chronique inédite relatifs aux événements militaires arrivés en Basse-Normandie* (Saint-Lô, 1895).
Delpit, J., *Collection générale des documents français qui se trouvent en Angleterre* (Paris, 1847).
Documentos de Enrique II, ed. L. Pascual Martínez, *CDM*, viii (Murcia, 1983).
Documentos de Pedro I, ed. A.-L. Molina Molina, *CDM*, vii (Murcia, 1978).
Documentos del Siglo XIV, ed. F. Veas Artesoros, *CDM*, x (Murcia, 1985).
Documentos escogidos del archivo de la casa de Alba, pub. por la duquesa de Berwick y de Alba (Madrid, 1891).
Documents historiques relatifs à la vicomté de Carlat, eds G. Saige and the count of Dienne (2 vols, Monaco, 1900).
Documents historiques sur la maison de Galard, ed. J. Noulens (2 vols, Paris, 1871–3).
'Documents relatifs à la ville de Mâcon (1362–1367)', ed. L. Michon, *Rev. soc. savantes*, 5th ser., i (1870), pp. 161–83.
Documents sur la ville de Millau, ed. J. Artières (*AHR*, vii, Millau, 1930).
Douze comptes consulaires d'Albi du XIVe siècle, ed. A. Vidal (2 vols, Arch. hist. de l'Albigeois, Albi, 1906 and 1911).
Epistolari de Pere III, ed. R. Gubern (Barcelona, 1955).
Foedera, conventiones, litterae et cuiuscunque generis acta publica, ed. T. Rymer (Record Commission edn, eds A. Clarke et al., 4 vols, in 7 parts, London,

1816–69; original edn, 20 vols, London, 1704–35). References are to the Record Commission edition unless otherwise stated.

Froissart, Jean, *Chroniques*, eds S. Luce, G. Raynaud and L. and A. Mirot (15 vols, SHF, Paris, 1869–1975).

—— *Oeuvres*, ed. Kervyn de Lettenhove (25 vols in 26, Brussels, 1867–77).

—— *Voyage en Béarn*, ed. A. H. Diverres (Manchester, 1953).

Grandes Chroniques de France, ed. Paulin Paris (6 vols, Paris, 1836–8).

'Inventaire qui contient les titres et privilèges de la maison consulaire de la ville du Puy', ed. A. Aymard, *Annales de la Société d'agriculture, sciences, arts et commerce du Puy*, xv (1850), pp. 601–778.

Inventaires-sommaires des archives communales antérieures à 1790:
  Ville d'Angoulême, ed. M. Biais (Angoulême, 1889).
  Ville d'Aurillac, ed. G. Esquier (2 vols, Aurillac, 1906–11).
  Ville de Clermont-Ferrand. Fonds de Montferrand, ed. E. Teilhard de Chardin (2 vols, Clermont-Ferrand, 1922).
  Ville de Dax, ed. R. Teulet (Dax, 1934).
  Ville de Périgueux, ed. M. Hardy (Périgueux, 1897).
  Ville de Riom, ed. F. Boyer (Riom, 1892).
  Ville de Rodez, ed. H. Affre (Rodez, 1877).
  Ville de Saint-Jean-d'Angély, ed. L. C. Saudau (La Rochelle, 1895).
  Ville de Toulouse, serie AA, ed. E. Roschach (Toulouse, 1891).
  See above, under: Alauzier for Cajarc; Albe for Cahors; *Archives* for Montpellier and Pezenas; 'Inventaire' for Le Puy; below, *Inventaires-sommaires: Gironde, Landes*, for towns in those departments.

Inventaires-sommaires des archives départmentales antérieures à 1790:
  Aveyron, ed. H. Affre (2 vols, Paris, 1866–7).
  Charente, eds G. Babinet de Rencogue and Pierre de Fleury (Angoulême, 1880).
  Côte d'Or; *Archives civiles, série B*, ed. C. Rossignol and J. Garnier (6 vols., Paris and Dijon, 1863–94).
  Deux-Sèvres; *séries C–H*, eds M. Gouget and M. Dacier (Melle, 1896); *série E (supplément)*, eds A. Dupond, S. Canal and G. Loirette (Niort, 1920).
  Doubs; *Archives civiles, série B: Chambre des Comptes de Franche Comté*, ed. J. Gauthier (3 vols, Besançon, 1883–95).
  Eure-et-Loir; *Registres et minutes des notaires du comté de Dunois, 1369 à 1376*, ed. L. Merlet (Chartres, 1886).
  Gironde; *série E (supplément)*, ed. G. Ducaunnes-Duval (2 vols, Bordeaux, 1898–1901). Vol. 2 covers the archives communales of Blaye, Bourg-sur-Gironde, La Réole, Saint-Macaire, Monsegur and Libourne.
  Landes; *Archives civiles, séries A–F* (including E supplement), ed. M. H. Tartière Paris, 1868).
  Pyrénées-Atlantiques (formerly Basses-Pyrénées), ed. P. Raymond (6 vols, Paris, 1863–73). The important *série E* is inventoried in vols 4 and 5.
  Pyrénées-Orientales, ed. B. Alart (2 vols, Paris, 1868–77).
  Tarn-et-Garonne, *Archives civiles, série A: Fonds d'Armagnac*, eds M. Maisonobe, C. Samaran and M. Imbert (Montauban, 1910); *série E supplément*, eds G. Tholin and R. Bonnet (Agen, 1885–1932).
  See above, under: Berthelé for Hérault.

Itinéraires de Philippe le Hardi et de Jean Sans Peur, ducs de Bourgogne (1363–1419), ed. E. Petit (Paris, 1888).
Izarn, E., ed., *Compte des recettes et dépenses du roi de Navarre en France et en Normandie de 1367 à 1370* (Paris, 1885).
John of Gaunt's Register, ed. S. Armitage-Smith, Camden Third Series, xx–xxi (2 vols, RHS, London, 1911), cited as *JGR*, I, i and ii; *John of Gaunt's Register, 1372–1383*, eds E. C. Lodge and R. Somerville, Camden Third Series, lxvi–ii (RHS, London, 1937), cited as *JGR*, II, i and ii.
Knighton, H., *Chronicon*, ed. J. R. Lumby (2 vols, *RS*, London, 1889–95).
Königshofen, Jacob Twinger of, *Cronik*, ed. C. von Hegel, in *Die Chroniken der deutschen Städte*, vol. 8, pp. 153–498, vol. 9, pp. 409–917 (Leipzig, 1870–1).
'La bataille de Trente', ed. H. R. Brush, *Modern Philology*, ix (1911–12), pp. 511–44; x (1912–13), pp. 82–136.
La correspondance de Pierre Ameilh, archevêque de Naples puis d'Embrun (1363–1369), ed. H. Bresc (Paris, 1972).
Le roman de Mélusine, ou histoire de Lusignan par Coudret, ed. E. Roach (Paris, 1982).
Les Quatre Grans Cròniques, ed. F. Soldevila (Barcelona, 1971).
Leymarie, A., *Le Limousin historique. Recueil de toutes les pièces manuscrits pouvant servir à l'histoire de l'ancienne province de Limousin* (Limoges, 1837).
Lopes, Fernão, *Crónica do rei D. Pedro I*, ed. G. Macchi, trans. J. Steunou, Sources d'histoire médiévale publiées par l'Institut de recherche et d'histoire des textes (Paris, 1985).
Mandements et Actes divers de Charles V, 1364–1380, ed. L. Delisle (*CDI*, Paris, 1874).
Mascaro, Jacme, 'Le *Libre de Memorias* de Jacme Mascaro', ed. C. Barbier, *Revue des langues romanes*, ser. iv, xxxiv (1890), pp. 36–100.
Mélusine, ed. J. Stouff (Dijon, 1932).
Mélusine, par Jean d'Arras, ed. C. Brunet (Paris, 1854).
Mézières, Philippe de, *Le Songe du Vieil Pelerin*, ed. G. W. Coopland (2 vols, Cambridge, 1969).
Miguel del Verms, *Cronique dels comtes de Foix et senhors de Béarn*, in *Choix de Chroniques et mémoires sur l'histoire de France*, ed. J. A. C. Buchon (Paris, 1839), pp. 575–600.
Moranvillé, H., 'Procès-verbal de visite des places fortifiées du bailliage de Melun en 1367', *Annales de la Société historique et archéologique du Gâtinais*, xxi (1903), pp. 304–19.
Morice, P. H., *Mémoires pour servir de preuves à l'histoire ecclésiastique et civile de Bretagne* (3 vols, Paris, 1742–6).
Noyal, Jean de, 'Fragments inédits de la Chronique de Jean de Noyal', *Annuaire-Bulletin de la Société de l'histoire de France*, xx (1883), pp. 246–75.
Ordonnances des roys de France de la troisième race (23 vols, Paris, 1723–1849).
Pere III de Catalonia, *Chronicle*, ed. J. N. Hillgarth (2 vols, Toronto, 1980).
Philippe de Vigneulles, *Chronique*, ed. C. Bruneau (4 vols, Société d'histoire et d'archéologie de la Lorraine, Metz, 1927–33).
Political Poems and Songs Relating to English History, ed. T. Wright (2 vols, *RS*, London, 1859–61).

Preuves de la maison de Polignac. Recueil de documents pour servir à l'histoire des anciennes provinces de Velay, Auvergne, Gévaudan, Vivarais, Forez, etc., ed. A. Jacotin (5 vols, Paris, 1898–1906).

Recueil des documents concernant le Poitou contenus dans les registres de la Chancellerie de France, eds P. Guerin and L. Célier, 14 vols, *AHP*, xi, xiii, xvii, xix, xxi, xxiv, xxvi, xxix, xxxii, xxxv, xxxviii, xli, l, lvi (Poitiers, 1881–1958).

Registres consulaires de Saint-Flour (1376–1405), ed. M. Boudet (Paris and Riom, 1898).

Registres des comptes municipaux de la ville de Tours, ed. J. Delaville Le Roux (2 vols, Société archéologique de Touraine, Tours and Paris, 1878–91).

Rotuli Parliamentorum ut et Petitones et Placita in Parliamento, eds J. Strachey et al. (7 vols, London, 1767–1832).

Scalacronica. The Reigns of Edward I, Edward II and Edward III, as recorded by Sir Thomas Gray, ed. H. Maxwell (Glasgow, 1907).

Secousse, D., *Recueil de pièces servant de preuves au mémoires sur les troubles excités en France par Charles II, dit le Mauvais, roi de Navarre et comte d'Evreux* (Paris, 1755).

Spicilegium Brivatense. Recueil de documents historiques relatifs au Brivadois et à l'Auvergne, ed. A. Chassaing (Paris, 1886).

Thalamus parvus. Le petit Thalamus de Montpellier (Société archéologique de Montpellier, Montpellier, 1840), part iv, 313–475: *La chronique romane*, ed. MM. Pegat, Thomas and Desmazes.

Theiner, A. (ed.), *Codex diplomaticus Domini Temporalis S. Sedis: Recueil de documents, &c., extraits des archives du Vatican* (3 vols, Rome, 1861–2).

Thesaurus novus anecdotorum, eds E. Martène and U. Durand (5 vols, Paris, 1717).

Timbal, P.-C., *La guerre de Cent ans vue à travers les régistres du Parlement, 1337–1369* (Paris, 1961).

'Traité passé pour l'évacuation des montagnes de l'Auvergne, le 4 avril 1364', ed. A. Chassaing, *Revue des sociétés savantes des départements*, 6th. ser., iv (1876), pp. 163–73.

Urban V, *Lettres secrètes et curiales du pape Urbain V (1362–1370) se rapportant à la France*, eds P. Lecacheux and G. Mollat (Bibliothèque des Écoles françaises d'Athènes et de Rome, Paris, 1902–55).

Urkundenbuch der Stadt Strassburg. Politische Urkunden von 1332 bis 1380, 5 vols, eds H. Witte and Georg Wolfram (Strasbourg, 1896).

Venette, Jean de, *The Chronicle of Jean de Venette*, ed. R. A. Newhall, trans. J. Birdsall (Columbia University, Records of Civilization, Sources and Studies, no. 50, New York, 1953).

Veterum scriptorum et monumentorum, eds E. Martène and U. Durand (9 vols, Paris, 1724–33).

Villani, Matteo, *Istorie*, ed. L. A. Muratori, *Rerum Italicarum Scriptores*, xiv (Milan, 1729).

Walsingham, T., *Historia Anglicana*, ed. H. T. Riley (2 vols, *RS*, London, 1863–4).

—— *Chronicon Angliae*, ed. E. M. Thompson (*RS*, London, 1874).

Westminster Chronicle, 1381–1394, The, eds and trans. L. C. Hector and B. A. Harvey (Oxford, 1982).

C Secondary authorities

Abdal i Vinyals, Ramón de, 'Pedro el Ceremonioso y los comienzos de la decadencia politica de Cataluña', *Historia de España*, vol. 14, ed. Ramón Menéndez Pidal (Madrid, 1966), pp. ix–cciii, published separately as *Pere el Cerimoniós i els Inicis de la decadéncia politica de Catalunya* (Barcelona, 1962).

Allmand, 'War and the Non-combatant', in *The Hundred Years War*, ed. K. Fowler (London, 1971), pp. 163–83.

—— *The Hundred Years War. England and France at War, c.1300–c.1450* (Cambridge, 1988).

Allut, P., *Les routiers au XIVe siècle. Les Tard-Venus et la bataille de Brignais* (Lyon, 1859).

André, F., 'L'invasion anglaise en Gévaudan. Notice historique', *Bulletin de la Société d'agriculture, sciences, arts et commerce du département de la Lozère*, xxxiii (1882).

André-Michel, R., 'La construction des remparts d'Avignon au XIVe siècle', *Société française d'archéologie, Congrès archéologique de France, LXXXVIe session tenu à Avignon en 1909* (1910), ii, pp. 341–60.

—— 'La défense d'Avignon sous Urban V et Grégoire XI', *Mélanges d'archéologie et d'histoire de l'école française de Rome*, xxx (1910), pp. 128–54.

—— ' "Anglais", bretons et routiers à Carpentras sous Jean le Bon et Charles V', *Mélanges d'histoire offerts à M. Charles Bémont* (1913), pp. 341–52.

—— 'Les défenseurs des chateaux et des villes fortes dans le Comtat Venaissin au XIVe siècle', *BEC*, lxxvi (1915), pp. 315–30.

Armitage-Smith, S., *John of Gaunt* (London, 1964).

Atiya, A. S., *The Crusade in the Later Middle Ages* (London, 1938).

Barber, M., 'John Norbury (c.1350–1414): An Esquire of Henry IV', *EHR*, lxviii (1953), pp. 66–76.

Barber, R., *Edward, Prince of Wales and Aquitaine* (London, 1978).

Bardon, A., *Histoire de la ville d'Alais de 1341 à 1461* (Nîmes, 1896).

Bardy, H., *Enguerrand de Coucy et les grands bretons. Épisode de l'histoire d'Alsace, 1368–1376* (Paris and Saint-Dié, 1860).

Bennett, M. J., *Community, Class and Careerism. Cheshire and Lancashire Society in the Age of Sir Gawain and the Green Knight* (Cambridge, 1983).

Berville, G. de, *Histoire de Bertrand du Guesclin, comte de Longueville, connétable de France* (2 vols., Paris, 1772).

Bisson, T. N., *The Medieval Crown of Aragon* (Oxford, 1986).

Blanchard, R., *Le pays de Rays et ses seigneurs pendant la guerre de Cent ans, 1341–1372* (Vannes, 1898).

Bonal, A., *Comté et comtes de Rodez* (Société des Lettres, sciences et arts de l'Aveyron, Rodez, 1885).

Bossuat, A., *Perrinet Gressart et François de Surienne, agents de l'Angleterre* (Paris, 1936).
Bouchard, E., 'Les anglais à Saint-Pourçain', *Bulletin de la Société d'émulation et des beaux-arts du Bourbonnais* (1900), pp. 244–59.
Boudet, M., 'Assauts, sièges et blocus de Saint-Flour par les anglais pendant la guerre de Cent ans (1356–1391)', *Revue d'Auvergne* (1893), pp. 337–67.
—— *La Jacquerie des Tuchins, 1363–1384. Documents inédits du XIVe siècle* (Riom and Paris, 1895).
—— *Thomas de la Marche, bâtard de France, et ses aventures, 1318–1361* (Riom, 1900).
—— 'L'histoire d'un bandit meconnu: Bernard de Garlan, dit le Méchant Bossu, capitaine d'Alleuze', *Revue de la Haute-Auvergne*, xiv (1912), pp. 93–122, 230–64, 339–67.
Bourgeois, A., *Le Rouergue sous l'occupation anglaise, 1361–1370* (thèse complimentaire, DES, Paris; typescript deposited in the Archives départémentales de l'Aveyron, Rodez).
Bourilly, V.-L., 'Du Guesclin et le duc d'Anjou en Provence (1368)', *RH*, clii (1926), pp. 161–80.
Boutruche, R., *La crise d'une société. Seigneurs et paysans du Bordelais pendant la Guerre de Cent ans* (Paris, 1947).
Breuils, A., 'Jean Ier, comte d'Armagnac, et le mouvement national dans le Midi au temps du Prince Noir', *Revue des questions historiques*, lix (1896), pp. 44–102.
Bridge, J. C., 'Two Cheshire Soldiers of Fortune of the XIV Century: Sir Hugh Calveley and Sir Robert Knolles', *Journal of the Architectural, Archaeological and Historic Society for the County and City of Chester and North Wales*, n.s., xiv (1908), pp. 112–231.
Bruguier-Roure, L., 'La guerre autour du Pont-Saint-Esprit', *Mémoires de l'Académie de Vaucluse*, ix (1890), pp. 96–122, 233–52.
Cabié, E., 'Évenements relatifs à l'Albigeois pendant la querelle du comte de Foix et du duc de Berry, de 1380 à 1382', *Revue historique de la Société des sciences, arts et belles-lettres du département du Tarn* (1879), pp. 5–40.
Cabrol, É., *Annales de Villefranche de Rouergue* (2 vols, Villefranche, 1860).
Carr, A. D., 'Welshmen and the Hundred Years War', *Welsh History Review*, iv (1968), pp. 21–46.
Cazelles, R., *La société politique et la crise de la royauté sous Philippe de Valois* (Paris, 1958).
—— 'Le parti navarrais jusqu'à la mort d'Étienne Marcel', *BPH* (1960), pp. 839–69.
—— 'Les mouvements révolutionnaires du milieu du XIVe siècle et le cycle de l'action politique', *RH*, ccxxviii (1962), pp. 279–312.
—— 'La stabilisation de la monnaie par la création du franc (décembre 1360) – blocage d'une société', *Traditio*, xxxii (1976), pp. 293–311.
—— *Société politique, noblesse et couronne sous Jean le Bon et Charles V* (Geneva, 1982).
Chanson, M., *Les Grandes Compagnies en Auvergne au XIVe siècle: Seguin de Badefol à Brioude et à Lyon* (Brioude, 1887).
Charmasse, A. de., 'Note sur le passage et le séjour des Grandes Compagnies dans

la prevôté de Baigneux-les-Juifs en 1364 et 1365', *Mémoires de la Société Éduenne*, n.s., ix (Paris and Autun, 1881), pp. 497–507.
—— 'L'église d'Autun pendant la guerre de Cent ans, 1358–1373', *Mémoires de la Société Éduenne*, n.s., xxvi (Autun, 1898), pp. 1–135.
Chérest, A., *L'Archiprêtre. Épisodes de la guerre de Cent ans aux XIVe siècle* (Paris, 1879).
Cognasso, F., 'Note e documenti sulla formazione dello stato Visconteo', *Bolletino della Società pavese di storia patria*, xxiii (1923–4), pp. 23–169.
Contamine, P., *Guerre, état et société à la fin du moyen âge* (Paris and the Hague, 1972).
—— 'Les compagnies d'aventure en France pendant la guerre de Cent ans', *Mélanges de l'école française de Rome*, 87 (1975), pp. 365–96.
—— *La guerre au moyen âge* (Paris, 1980); English trans., *War in the Middle Ages*, trans. M. Jones (Oxford, 1984).
Cordey, J., *Les comtes de Savoie et les rois de France pendant la guerre de Cent ans, 1329–1391* (Paris, 1911).
Courteault, H., 'Un archiviste des comtes de Foix au XIVe siecle, le chroniquer Michel du Bernis', *AM* (1894), pp. 272–300.
Coville, A., *Les premiers Valois et la guerre de Cent ans (1328–1422)*, in *Histoire de France*, ed. E. Lavisse, iv (Paris, 1902).
Cox, E. L., *The Green Count of Savoy. Amadeus VI and Transalpine Savoy in the Fourteenth Century* (Princeton, 1967).
Daumet, G., *Étude sur l'alliance de la France et de la Castille au XIVe et au XVe siècles* (Paris, 1898).
Delachenal, R., *Histoire de Charles V* (5 vols, Paris, 1909–31).
Delisle, L., *Histoire du château et des sires de Saint-Sauveur-le-Vicomte* (Valognes, 1867).
Denifle, H., *La désolation des églises, monastères et hôpitaux en France pendant la guerre de Cent ans* (2 vols, Paris, 1897–9), vol. 2: *La guerre de Cent ans jusqu'à la mort de Charles V.*
Déprez, E., 'La bataille de Najera', *RH*, cxxxvi (1921), pp. 37–59.
Desplat, C., 'Figures de routiers pyrénéens de la première moitié de la guerre de Cent ans', *Bulletin de la société des sciences et lettres de Pau*, 4th ser., ii (1967), pp. 27–49.
Devic, C. and Vaissete, J., *Histoire générale de Languedoc avec des notes et les pièces justificatives* (new edn, 16 vols, Toulouse, 1872–1904).
Díaz Martín, L. V., *Itinerario de Pedro I de Castilla* (Valladolid, 1975).
—— *Los officiales de Pedro I de Castilla* (Valladolid, 1975).
—— *Pedro I y los primeros Trastamara* (Madrid, 1982).
Dognon, P., *Les institutions politiques et administratives du pays de Languedoc du XIIIe siècle aux guerres de Religion* (Toulouse and Paris, 1895).
Dumay, G., 'Guy de Pontailler, sire de Talmay, maréchal de Bourgogne, 1364–1392', *Mémoires de la Société bourguignonne d'histoire et de géographie*, xxiii (1907), pp. 1–222.
Durrieu, P., *Les Gascons en Italie. Études historiques* (Auch, 1885).
Entwistle, W. J., 'The *Romancero del Rey Don Pedro*, in Ayala and the *Cuarta Crónica General*', *Modern Languages Review*, 25 (1930), pp. 306–26.

—— *European Balladry* (Oxford, 1951).
Fernández de Larrea Rojas, J. A., *Guerra y sociedad en Navarra durante la edad media* (Bilbao, 1992).
Fillon, B., *Jean Chandos, connétable d'Aquitaine et sénéchal de Poitou* (London and Fontenay-le-Comte,1856).
Finot, J., *Recherches sur les incursions des Anglais et des Grandes Compagnies dans le duché de Bourgogne à la fin du XIVe siècle* (Vesoul, 1874).
Fournier, M. G., 'La défense des populations rurales pendant la guerre de Cent ans en Basse-Auvergne', *Actes du quatre-vingt-dixième congrès national des sociétés savantes, Nice, 1965; section d'archéologie* (Paris, 1966), pp. 157–99.
Fowler, K., 'Les finances et la discipline dans les armées anglaises en France au XIVe siècle', *Actes du colloque international de Cocherel, Les Cahiers Vernonnais*, 4 (1964), pp. 55–84.
—— *The Age of Plantagenet and Valois* (London and Toronto, 1967).
—— *The King's Lieutenant. Henry of Grosmont, First Duke of Lancaster, 1310–1361* (London and Toronto, 1969).
—— 'War and Social Change in Late Medieval France and England', in *The Hundred Years War*, ed. K. Fowler (London, 1971a), pp. 1–27.
—— 'Truces', in *The Hundred Years War*, ed. K. Fowler (London, 1971b), pp. 184–215.
—— 'L'emploi des mercenaires par les pouvoirs ibériques et l'intervention militaire anglaise en Espagne (vers 1361–vers 1379)', *Réalidad e imagines del poder: España a fines de la edad media*, ed. A. Rucquoi (Valladolid, 1988), pp. 23–55.
—— 'News from the Front: Letters and Despatches of the Fourteenth Century', *Guerre et société en France, en Angleterre et en Bourgogne, XIVe–XVe siècle* (Lille, 1991a), pp. 63–92.
—— 'Deux entrepreneurs militaires au XIVe siècle: Bertrand du Guesclin et Sir Hugh Calveley', *Le combatant au moyen âge. Actes xu XVIIIe congrès de la SHMESP*, Montpellier, 1987 (Saint-Herblain, 1991b; 2nd edn, Paris, 1995), pp. 243–56.
—— 'The Wages of War: The Mercenaries of the Great Companies', *Viajeros, peregrinos, mercaderes en el Occidente medieval: Actas de la XVIII Semana de Estudios Medievales de Estella, 22–26 de julio de 1991* (Pamplona, 1992), pp. 217–44.
—— 'Sir John Hawkwood and the English Condottieri in Trecento Italy', *Renaissance Studies*, xii (1998), pp. 131–48.
—— 'Les lieutenants du roi d'Angleterre en France à la fin du moyen âge', *Les serviteurs de l'État au Moyen Âge. Actes du XXIXe congrès de la SHMESP, Pau, 1998* (Paris, 1999), pp. 193–205.
Fréville, E. de, 'Des grandes compagnies au quatorzième siècle', *BEC*, iii (1841–2), pp. 258–81; v (1843–4), pp. 232–53.
Gabotto, F., 'La Guerra del Conte Verde contro i marchesi di Saluzzo e di Monferrato nel 1363', *Piccolo archivo dell'antico marchesato di Saluzzo*, i (1901).
Galabert, F., 'Désastres causés par la guerre de Cent ans au pays de Verdun-sur-Garonne à la fin du XIVe siècle', *BPH* (1893) pp. 166–74.

Galland, B., *Les papes d'Avignon et la maison de Savoie (1309–1409)*, Collection de l'École française de Rome, no. 247 (Rome, 1998).
Garcia y Lopez, J. C., *Castilla y León durante los reinados de Pedro I, Enrique II, Juan I e Enrique III* (2 vols, Madrid, 1891–2).
Gaujal, M. A. F. de, *Études historiques sur le Rouergue* (4 vols, Paris, 1858–9).
Gimeno Casalduero, J., *La imagen del monarca en la Castilla del siglo XIV* (Madrid, 1972).
Goyheneche, M. E., 'Bayonne, port d'embarquement des Navarrais vers la Normandie', *Actes du colloque international de Cocherel, Les Cahiers Vernonnais*, 4 (1964), pp. 107–17.
Guigue, G., *Les Tard-Venus en Lyonnais, Forez et Beaujolais, 1356–1369* (Lyon, 1886).
Gutiérrez de Velasco, A., 'Los Ingleses en España', *Estudios de Edad Media de la Corona de Aragón*, iv (1951a), pp. 215–319.
—— 'Molina en la Corona de Aragón (1369–1375)', *Teruel*, vi (1951b), pp. 75–128.
—— 'Incidencias de un desafio caballeresco en la Valencia del siglo XIV', published under the auspices of the Consejo superior de investigaciones científicas by the Instituto Jerónimo Zurita, from *Hispania*, lx (1955).
—— 'La financiación Aragónesa de la *Guerra de los Dos Pedros*', published under the auspices of the Consejo superior de investigaciones científicas by the Instituto Jerónimo Zurita, from *Hispania*, lxxiv (1959).
Hay du Châtelet, P., *Histoire de Bertrand du Guesclin* (Paris, 1666).
Henneman, J. B., *Royal Taxation in Fourteenth Century France* (2 vols, Princeton and Philadelphia, 1971 and 1976), ii: *The Captivity and Ransom of John II, 1356–1370*.
Hewitt, H. J., *The Black Prince's Expedition of 1355–1357* (Manchester, 1958).
Hillgarth, J. N., *The Spanish Kingdoms, 1250–1516* (2 vols, Oxford, 1976–8).
Honoré-Duvergé, S., 'Chaucer en Espagne? (1366)', *Recueil de travaux offerts à M. Clovis Brunel* (Paris, 1955), pp. 9–13.
—— 'Participation navarraise à la bataille de Cocherel', *Actes du colloque international de Cocherel, Les Cahiers Vernonnais*, 4 (1964), pp. 99–106.
Housley, N., 'The Mercenary Companies, the Papacy and the Crusades, 1356–1378', *Traditio*, xxxviii (1982), pp. 253–80.
—— 'King Louis the Great of Hungary and the Crusades, 1342–1382', *Slavonic and East European Review*, 62 (1984), pp. 192–208.
—— *The Avignon Papacy and the Crusades, 1305–1378* (Oxford, 1986).
Jarry, E., *La vie politique de Louis de France, duc d'Orléans, 1372–1407* (Paris and Orléans, 1889).
Jones, M., *Ducal Brittany, 1364–1399* (Oxford, 1970).
Jones, T., *Chaucer's Knight: The Portrait of a Medieval Mercenary* (London, 1980).
Jorga, N., *Philippe de Mézières, 1327–1405, et la Croisade au XIVe siècle* (Paris, 1896).
Joubert, A., *Les invasions anglaises en Anjou au XIVe et XVe siècle* (Angers, 1872).
Keen, M., 'Brotherhood in Arms', *History*, 47 (1962), pp. 1–17.
—— *The Laws of War in the Late Middle Ages* (London and Toronto, 1965).

— 'Chivalry, Nobility and the Man-at-Arms', in *War, Literature and Politics in the Late Middle Ages*, ed. C. T. Allmand (Liverpool, 1976), pp. 32–45.
— *Chivalry* (New Haven and London (1984).
Labande, E. -R., 'Louis Ier d'Anjou, la Provence et Marseille', *MA*, liv (1948), pp. 297–325.
Labande, L. H., 'L'occupation du Pont-Saint-Esprit par les Grandes Compagnies (1360–1361)', *Revue historique de Provence*, i (1901), pp. 79–95, 146–64.
— 'Bertrand du Guesclin et les États pontificaux de France. Passage des routiers en Languedoc (1365–1367). Guerre de Provence (1368)', *Mémoires de l'Académie de Vaucluse*, n.s., iv (1904), pp. 43–80.
Labroue, É., *Le livre de vie. Les seigneurs et les capitaines du Périgord Blanc au XIVe siècle* (Bordeaux and Paris, 1891).
— *Bergerac sous les anglais. Essai historique sur le consulat et la communauté de Bergerac au moyen âge* (Bordeaux and Paris, 1893).
La Chauvelays, 'Les armées des trois premiers ducs de Bourgogne', *Mémoires de l'Académie des sciences, arts et belles-lettres de Dijon*, 3rd ser., vi (1880), pp. 19–335.
Lacoste, G., *Histoire générale de la province de Quercy* (2nd edn, with supplementary notes, 4 vols, Cahors, 1883).
Lafaurie, J., *Les monnaies des rois de France* (2 vols, Paris and Basle, 1951).
Larrea Rojas, J. A. F. de, *Guerra y sociedad en Navarra durante la Edad Media* (Bilbao, 1992).
Larroyoz-Zarranz, 'Reacción de Carlos el Malo, rey de Navarra, a la noticia de la Derota De Cocherel', *Actes du colloque international de Cocherel, Les Cahiers Vernonnais*, 4 (1964), pp. 107–40.
Lebeuf, J., *Mémoires concernant l'histoire ecclésiastique et civile d'Auxerre* (4 vols, Paris, 1851–5).
Lecoy de la Marche, A., *Les relations politiques de la France avec le royaume de Majorque* (2 vols, Paris, 1892).
Ledos, E.-G., 'Deux documents relatifs aux compagnies en Auvergne après 1360', *Revue de l'Auvergne*, vii (1890), pp. 41–58.
Lefranc, A., *Olivier de Clisson connétable de France* (Paris, 1898).
Lehoux, F., *Jean de France, duc de Berri. Sa vie, son action politique, 1340–1416* (4 vols, Paris, 1966–8).
Léonard, E. G., *Histoire de Jeanne Ire, reine de Naples, comtesse de Provence, 1343–1382* (3 vols, Monaco and Paris, 1932–6).
— *Les Angevins de Naples* (Paris, 1934).
Le Patourel, J., *The Medieval Administration of the Channel Islands, 1199–1399* (Oxford, 1937).
Leroy, B., *La Navarre au moyen âge* (Paris, 1984).
Lewis, A. R., 'North European Sea Power and the Straits of Gibraltar, 1031–1350 A.D.', *Order and Innovation in the Middle Ages. Essays in Honor of Joseph R. Strayer* (Princeton, 1976), pp. 139–65.
Loirette, G., 'Le traité d'alliance de 1365 entre Charles le Mauvais et Arnaud Amanieu, sire d'Albret', *Bulletin de la Société des sciences, lettres et arts de Pau*, 2nd ser., 38 (Pau, 1910), pp. 237–45.

—— 'Arnaud Amanieu, sire d'Albret, et l'appel des seigneurs Gascons en 1368', *Mélanges d'histoire offerts à M. Charles Bémont* (Paris, 1913), pp. 317–40.
—— 'Arnaud-Amanieu, sire d'Albret, et ses rapports avec la monarchie française pendant la règne de Charles V (1364–80)', *AM*, xliii (1931), pp. 5–39.
Lowe, A., *The Catalan Vengeance* (London and Boston, 1972).
Luce, S., *Histoire de Bertrand du Guesclin et de son époque* (Paris, 1876).
Masson d'Autume, M., *Cherbourg pendant la guerre de Cent ans* (Cherbourg, 1948).
Maubourguet, J., *Le Périgord méridional des origines à l'an 1370. Étude d'histoire politique et religieuse* (Cahors, 1926).
—— *Sarlat et le Périgord méridional, 1370–1453* (Paris, 1930).
—— 'Seguin de Badefol, le roi des Grandes Compagnies', *Bulletin de la Société historique et archéologique du Périgord*, lxv (1938), pp. 139–57, 215–29, 293–315.
Ménard, M., *Histoire civile, ecclésiastique et littéraire de la ville de Nismes, avec des notes et les preuves* (7 vols, Paris, 1744–58).
Mérimée, P., *Histoire de don Pèdre Ier, roi de Castile* (Paris, 1865).
Miret y Sans, *Investigacion historica sobre el vizcondado de Castellbo* (Barcelona, 1900).
—— 'Négociations de Pierre IV d'Aragon avec la cour de France (1366–1367)', *Revue Hispanique*, xiii (1905), pp. 76–135.
—— 'Lettres closes de Louis d'Anjou, roi de Sicile, à Pierre, roi d'Aragon', *MA*, 2nd ser., xviii (1914), pp. 295–302.
Mirot, L., 'Sylvestre Budes (13??-1380) et les Bretons en Italie', *BEC*, lviii (1897), pp. 579–614; lix (1898), pp. 262–324.
Mirot, L., and Déprez, E., 'Les ambassades anglaises pendant la guerre de Cent ans. Catalogue chronologique, 1327–1450', *BEC*, lx (1898), pp. 177–214.
Moisant, J., *Le prince noir en Aquitaine* (Paris, 1894).
Molinier, É., *Étude sur la vie d'Arnoul d'Audrehem, maréchal de France, 1302–1370* (Mémoires présentés par divers savants à l'Académie des Inscriptions et Belles Lettres, ser. ii, vi, Paris, 1883), pp. 1–359.
Mollière, H., *Guy de Chauliac et la bataille de Brignais* (Lyon, 1894).
Monicat, J., *Les grandes Compagnies en Velay, 1358–1392* (Paris, 1928).
Morel-Fatio, A., 'La donation du duché de Molina à Bertrand du Guesclin', *BEC*, lx (1899), pp. 145–77.
Pagès, A., ed., 'Recherches sur la chronique attribuée à Pierre IV d'Aragon', *Romania*, xviii (1889), pp. 233–80.
Paravicini, W., *Die Preussenreisen des Europäischen Adels* (2 vols, Sigmaringen, 1989–95).
Partner, P., *The Lands of St Peter. The Papal State in the Middle Ages and the Renaissance* (Berkeley and Los Angeles, 1972).
Perroud, C., 'Les Grandes Compagnies en Bresse et en Dombes', *Annales de la Société d'émulation de l'Ain* (1874), pp. 261–84.
Perroy, E., 'Edouard III d'Angleterre et les seigneurs Gascons en 1368', *AM*, lxi (1948–9), pp. 91–6.
Petit, E., *Histoire des ducs de Bourgogne* (10 vols, Paris, 1885–1909), vol. x: *Ducs de Bourgogne de la maison Valois*, i, *Philippe de Hardi*, i, *1363–1380*.

Plancher, U., *Histoire générale et particulière de Bourgogne* (4 vols, Dijon, 1739–81).
Portal, C., *Histoire de la ville de Cordes* (Albi and Cordes, 1902).
Prestwich, M., *Armies and Warfare in the Middle Ages. The English Experience* (New Haven and London, 1996).
Prince, A. E., 'A Letter of Edward the Black Prince', *EHR*, xli (1926), pp. 415–18.
Prou, M., *Étude sur les relations politiques de pape Urbain V avec les rois de France Jean II et Charles V* (Paris, 1888).
Reuss, R., 'La première invasion des "anglais" en Alsace. Épisode de l'histoire du quatorzième siècle', *Mélanges d'histoire offerts à M. Charles Bémont* (Paris, 1913), pp. 281–303.
Rouquette, J., *Le Rouergue sous les anglais* (Millau, 1887).
Russell, P. E., *The English Intervention in Spain and Portugal in the time of Edward III and Richard II* (Oxford, 1955). Cited as 'Russell', without title or date.
—— 'The *Memorias* of Fernán Alvárez de Albornoz, Archbishop of Seville, 1371–1380', *Hispanic Studies in Honour of I. González Llubera* (Oxford, 1959).
Salch, C.-L., *Dictionnaire des châteaux et des fortifications du moyen âge en France* (Strasbourg, 1979).
Samaran, C., 'Pour l'histoire des Grandes Compagnies: Le "vuidement" de Château-Gontier par les anglais (1369)', *Mélanges d'histoire du moyen âge dédiés à la mémoire de Louis Halphen* (Paris, 1951), pp. 641–4.
—— *La maison d'Armagnac au XVe siècle et les dernières luttes de la féodalité dans le Midi de la France* (Paris, 1907).
Schäfer, K. H., *Deutsche Ritter und Edelknechte in Italien während des XIV Jahrhunderts* (Quellen und Forschungen aus dem Gebiet der Geschichte, vols 15, 16 and 25; Paderborn, 1911, 1914, 1940).
Servais, V., *Annales historiques du Barrois de 1352 à 1411* (2 vols, Bar-le-Duc, 1865).
Sherborne, J. W., 'Indentured Retinues and English Expeditions to France, 1369–1380', *EHR*, lxxix (1964), pp. 718–46.
Simonnet, J., 'Joyaux de l'abbaye Saint-Germain d'Auxerre soustraits par deux gentilshommes de Franche-Comté (1359–62)', *Revue des sociétés savantes*, 5 ser., ii (1870), pp. 64–8.
Sitges, J. B., *Las mujeres del Rey Don Pedro I de Castilla* (Madrid, 1910).
—— *La muerte de D. Bernardo de Cabrera, consejero del Rey D. Pedro IV de Aragón, 1364* (Madrid, 1911).
Soldevila Zubiburu, Ferran, *Historia de Catalunya* (2nd edn in 1 vol., Barcelona, 1963).
Spufford, P., *Handbook of Medieval Exchange* (RHS, London, 1986).
Suárez Fernández, L., *El canciller Pedro López de Ayala y su tiempo, 1332–1407* (Vittoria, 1962).
—— 'Castilla, 1350–1406', in *Historia de España*, ed. R. Menéndez Pidal, vol. 14 (Madrid, 1966), pp. 3–378 .
Sumption, J., *The Hundred Years War* (2 vols, London, 1990–9, in progress).
Tasis, R., *La vida del rei En Pere III* (Barcelona, 1954).

Temple-Leader, J., and Marcotti, G., *Sir John Hawkwood (L'Acuto). Story of a Condottiere*, trans. L. Scott (London, 1889).
Trease, G., *The Condottieri. Soldiers of Fortune* (London, 1970).
Tucoo-Chala, P., *Gaston Fébus et la vicomté de Béarn, 1342–1391* (Bordeaux, 1960).
—— *La vicomté de Béarn et le problème de sa souveraineté, des origines à 1620* (Bordeaux, 1961).
—— *Gaston Fébus: Un grand prince d'Occident au XIVe siècle* (Pau, 1976).
Vaughan, R., *Philip the Bold. The Formation of the Burgundian State* (London, 1962).
Verci, G. B., *Storia della Marca Trivigiana e Veronese* (20 vols, Venice, 1786–91).
Vernier, J., 'Le duché de Bourgogne et les compagnies dans la seconde moitié du XIVe siècle', *Mémoires de l'Académie des sciences, arts et belles lettres de Dijon*, 4th ser., viii (1901–2), pp. 219–320.
Viard, J., 'Philippe VI de Valois. Début du règne (février–juillet 1328)', *BEC*, xcv (1934), pp. 259–83.
Walckenaer, A., *Louis Ier, duc d'Anjou, lieutenant-général en Languedoc, 1364–1380* (École des Chartes thesis, now deposited in the Archives Nationales, Paris, no. AB XXVIII[1]).
Walker, S. K., *The Lancastrian Affinity, 1361–1399* (Oxford, 1990).
Werunsky, E., *Geschichte Kaiser Karls IV und seiner Zeit* (3 vols in 4, Innsbrück, 1880–92).
Wright, N. A. R., 'The Tree of Battles of Honoré Bouvet and the Laws of War', in *War, Literature and Politics in the Late Middle Ages*, ed. C. T. Allmand (Liverpool, 1976).
—— *Knights and Peasants. The Hundred Years War in the French Countryside* (Woodbridge, 1998).
Yangas y Miranda, J., *Diccionario de antigüedades del reino de Navarra* (3 vols, Diputación Foral de Navarra, Institución Principe de Viana, Pamplona, 1964).
Zabalo Zabalegui, J., *La administración del reino de Navarra en el siglo XIV* (Pamplona, 1973).
Zurita y Castro, Géronimo, *Anales de la Corona de Aragón*, ed. Angel Canellas López (9 vols, Institución 'Fernando el Católica', Zaragoza, 1967–86).

Index

Where a reference to the same person/place/subject appears in the text and footnotes on the same page only the page number is given and the footnote reference is omitted. Bibliographical references are not indexed.

Abbotsbury   11
Ablan   290
Acigné, Guillaume de   152
Acquigny   100
Acrivant   41
Acy   230
Adour, river   12
Adrianople   124
Agde   37, 188
Agen   16, 19, 99, 335
Agenais   24, 27n, 40n, 287; seneschal of   199n
Agnay, G. d'   327
Agout, Raimond d', seneschal of Forcalquier and Céreste   246–7
Agreda   177, 280n
Aguilar   175
Aigle, L'   87
Aigremont, Guillaume d'   53
Aigues-Mortes   240, 246; treaty of   240n
Aimé, Pierre, bishop of Auxerre   124
Aix-en-Provence   245–7
Alain, John   198, 323
Álava   194, 206, 208, 210
Albacete   271n
Albania, kingdom of   117, 144
Albarano Montreal d', alias Fra Moriale   2

Albi   249; bishop of   39, 71
Albigeois   16, 38, 62, 69, 71, 73, 76
Albon, Humbert d'   51
Albornoz, Gil   123
Albret, Amanieu d', lord of Langoiran   26n, 27n; Arnaud-Amanieu, lord of   10, 12–13, 63, 66, 71, 76, 80–2, 84, 110–11, 113, 115, 141, 173, 179, 199, 214, 232–3, 284, 312; Bérard d'   12–13, 27n, 38, 44, 49n, 56, 58, 64, 66, 68n, 76, 80, 111, 226, 319, 323, 333; Bernard d'   113, 227, 313; Bernard-Ezii II, lord of   12; Bertucat d'   5, 9n, 10, 12–13, 15, 18, 23, 39, 42, 64, 66, 68n, 73, 76–7, 80, 82, 84, 96, 113, 142, 150, 188–9, 198–9, 214, 301, 313, 323; *bourc* d'   10; family of   13, 15, 76; Géraud d'   66, 68n, 111; Moni d'   66; Raymond d'   68n
Albuquerque, Juan Alfonso de   161–2
Alemant, Ourri l' *see* Fischenich, Winrich von
Alemant, Raudekin l'   41
Alençon   294
Alès   31
Alesón   213
Alfaro   179, 194
Alfonso XI, king of Castile   54, 161–2

Alghero 261
Allier, river 82, 84, 93, 102, 227
Almazán 221, 272n
Almodóvar, castle of 182
Almudevar 171
Alsace 91, 121, 130–5, 142, 146
Álvarez de Albornoz, Fernan 215
Álvárez de Toledo, Garcia, Master of the Order of Santiago 181
Ameilh, Pierre, archbishop of Embrun 247
Amory, John 5, 16, 22, 39, 49n, 56, 64, 66, 69–71, 73, 77n, 309–11, 323; Roger 16
Amosco 219
Añastro 208
Ancenis, Guillaume d' 295n
Andalusia 162, 271, 279
Andorra 62
Anduse, Louis d', lord of la Voulte 248n, 285
Anet 100
Anger, Étienne, alias Ferragut 113, 323
Angers 238–9, 288
Angle, Guichard d', marshal of Aquitaine 99, 199, 214, 281n
Angoulême 25, 112; county of 87
Angoumois 24–5, 41; seneschal of 199n
Aniane 37
Anjou 17, 19, 24–5, 40–1, 145, 234–5, 284, 288, 292–3, 296, 298
Anjou, Louis I, duke of 109, 115, 122, 140, 288, 292, 296; and Anse 135, 138; appointed lieutenant in Languedoc 84, 108, 126n; and Aragon 114, 126–8, 200–1, 220; and Charles of Navarre 115; and companies 154, 187–90, 235–6, 259, 285; and Enrique of Trastámara 217, 223, 235, 240, 268; forces recruited by 15, 249n, 283–5, 329, 333–5; and Montpellier 116; and Provence 241–51
Anse 33, 85, 107–10, 112, 129, 131, 135–44, 150

Ansó 267
Apremont 95
Apulia 117
Aquitaine, principality of 16, 40, 62, 69, 137, 189, 200, 235, 279; companies recruited in 7–8, 150; constable of see Chandos, John, Grailly; English garrisons in 39; forces arrayed in 193, 197, 331; frontiers of menaced 217, 221, 223, 243; passage of companies through 100–1, 150, 226–7; prince's return to 17, 219, 223–4, 250, 268; prince's rule in 232; and renewal of war 238–9, 254, 270, 284, 287–9, 292; seneschal of 199n, 298 and see Felton, Thomas; see also Gascony, Guyenne
Aragon 126, 171, 174, 201, 217, 220, 239, 282; Bonifacio of 253; Castilian garrisons in 180; companies in 150, 153–4, 163–70, 172–3, 179, 181, 262, 267; Constança of, daughter of Bonifacio and wife of Hugh Calveley 253–7, 321–2; forces entering and passing through 38–9, 186–8, 268; governor-general of 280; kings of see Peter IV, Joan, Martin I; passes into see Pyrenean passes; queen see Sicily, Elionor of; war with Castile see under Castile
Aran, val d' 267–8
Arborea, Marià or Mariano d', *jutge* of 203–4, 261–3, 277, 282, 315
Archaic, Foucaut d' 164
archers: at Launac 65; at Nájera 214–15; see also 114, 130, 197, 200, 206, 218, 224, 239, 262, 277, 289–90, 296, 331
Archevêque, Guillaume, lord of Parthenay 199
Arcueil 290
Arcy-sur-Cure 94
Ardeche, river 30
Ares or Ades, Robin d' 149, 176
Argentan 100; Geoffroi d' 298n

358

Argenton, sire d'   199n
Argilly, castle of   105
Ariñez   208, 211
Ariza   221
Arles   121, 128, 245; kingdom of 122, 242
Armagnac, Arnaud-Guillaume, bastard of   9n, 326; Géraud V, count of 61; Jean I, count of   15, 56–7, 62–6, 68–71, 73, 80, 199, 214, 232; Jean d', son of Jean I   62, 69–70, 77, 95–6, 102, 105, 225–7, 284, 287, 309–11, 334: Quarelles, esquire of   225; Jean III, count of   301; Jean d', *vicomte* of Fezensaguet   63, 66, 68n; Jeanne d'   62n; Marguerite de Bourbon, wife of Jean I   232n
Arras   290; Jean d'   299
Artois, county of   90
Aspe   254–5, 257, 320
Aspet, lord of   66
Aspremont, Gaillard d', bastard of Orta   9n
Asturias   162, 180
Ateca   221
Atienza   221, 272n, 280n
Aube, river   230
Auberchicourt, Eustache d'   4, 22, 104, 149, 173, 175–6, 179, 187, 192, 198–9
Aubeterre-sur-Dronne, lord of *see* Raymont, Gourderon de
Aude, valley of   38
Audley, Peter   92
Audrehem, Arnoul d', marshal of France   34–7, 39, 52, 54–9, 71–2, 74, 78, 82–4, 101, 108, 110, 124–5, 151, 164, 167–8, 187, 204–5, 210–11, 213, 216, 231, 240–3; appointed lieutenant in Languedoc 45–6
Augentonville, Raoul d'   237
Augsburg   132
Aune, river   294
Auray, battle of   14, 104, 129, 146, 148–9
Aure, lord of *see* Barthe, Jean de la

Aurillac   101
Aussain, *bourc* d'   10n, 130, 142, 326
Autun   46, 105, 140; *bailli* of   227
Autunois   105, 109
Auvergne   4–7, 10, 18n, 24–5, 27n, 33, 44–6, 48, 55, 56n, 73–85, 93, 101–2 140–2, 224, 227, 301; Béraud II, dauphin of   130–2; governor of 77–9
Auvillar, *vicomté* of   62
Auxerre   94, 106, 145–6, 150, 231
Auxerrois   3, 25, 26n, 46, 54, 94, 228
Auxois   91, 94, 105, 109–10, 114; *bailli* of   54, 102n, 104, 106
Auxonne   103, 114
Avallon   94
Avallonais   94, 106
Averço, Francesch d'   261
Aveyron, river   69
Avignon   147, 192, 245, 249; bishop of *see* Grimouard; defence of   74, 118, 152; menaced by companies 3–5, 16, 27n, 31–4, 48, 76, 107, 119, 142, 150–1: paid off   247–8; negotiations in   73n, 112, 115, 121–9 131, 135–6, 163, 242; papal official in   249; plague in   242
Avila   181
Ay   230
Ayala, Pedro López de   55, 66, 160, 169–70, 180–2, 185, 210, 213, 219, 241, 270, 272–4, 331
Azay, Guy d', seneschal of Toulouse 189; Jean d', seneschal of Toulouse 295
Azay-sur-Indre   238
Azergue valley   108

Baboyci, François, treasurer of Provence and Forcalquier   245
Badefol, castle of   124; Gaston, alias Tonnet de   76, 82, 111n, 112, 131, 323; Seguin de   5–6, 9–10, 12, 22, 30n, 37–8, 44, 49, 71–85, 107–13, 119, 135–9, 141, 150, 313, 323
Baden, margrave of   132

INDEX

Bâgé-le-Châtel   143
Bageran, Naudon de   44, 49, 129–30, 142, 149, 198–9, 227, 284, 323
Bagnères   224
Bagnols-sur-Cèze   31, 35
Baigneux, Gontier   127
Baigneux-les-Juifs   114
Bâle   121, 130–1, 133; bishop of   130
Balearic Isles   155; *see also* Majorca
Balsièges, castle of   76
Bañares   206, 208, 210
Banaster, Thomas   199n
Bapaume   290
Bar, duchy of   129, 135; Henri de, governor of Burgundy   53; Marie, duchess of   299; Pierre de   130; Yolande of   256, 257n
Barbastro   169, 268
Barbazan, lord of   63, 66
Barbe Noli   10
Barcelona   159–60, 163–5, 167–9, 171, 197, 202, 204, 250, 253–4, 261–2, 265–6, 276, 278, 282, 313, 317, 321
Bardolf, William   19, 26n, 323
Barfleur   105
Barjols   246
Baronnies   246
Barrière, La, lord of   66
Bar-sur-Seine   105
Barthe, Jean de la, lord of Aure   63, 66, 68n
Basset, John   41
Bataillier, Munde   30, 44, 49, 95–6, 102, 105, 149, 284–5, 324, 334
battles *see* Auray, Brignais, Champgeneteux, Cocherel, Crécy, Launac, Montech, Nájera
Baux, Amelin des   52n
Baveux, Gui de   238, 336
Bayeux   40n, 234
Bayonne   13, 61, 101, 184, 192–4, 197, 200–1, 208, 218, 222
Béarn, *vicomté* de   7–8, 61–4, 99, 203, 266; Bernard of, count of

Medicanelli   180, 189, 275; Gaston VII, *vicomte* of   61
Béarnais, Perrot le   243
Beatriz, eldest daughter of Pedro I of Castile and Maria de Padilla   182–3, 196, 218
Beaucaire   243, 246; estates of   35, 39; seneschal of   56n, 73, 112, 189; seneschalsy of   36, 38–9, 46, 54–5, 59, 72, 80, 83–4, 98, 137, 152–3, 242
Beauce   292
Beauchamp, William   199, 214
Beaufort, castle of   92
Beaufort-en-Vallée   287, 293
Beaugency   232, 238
Beaujeu   150; Antoine, lord of   33, 47, 135; barony of   45
Beaujolais   33, 46, 79, 109, 135, 151
Beaumanoir, Alain de   298; Jean de   298; Robert de   298
Beaumont   84; Alain de   149, 278, 327; Jean de   271n
Beaumont-le-Roger   87, 100
Beaune   53, 94, 106
Beausamblant, Guillaume de   51
Beauvais, bishop of   144
Beauvaisis   3, 87
Bel, Jean le   11
Belfort Gap   133, 135
Bell, Thomelin   17, 19, 233, 237, 300, 323
Bellegarde, fortress of   152
Belleperche   285–6
Belleville   33
Belmont, Andrew   4n, 45n
Benamarin   146–7, 170
Benedict, Walter   281–2
Benfeld   133
Bergerac   75
Berland, William   241
Bermeo   195
Bernard, Henry   251; Thomas   255–6
Bernay   100
Berne   121, 131, 133
Berry   7, 19, 24–5, 26n, 27n, 45, 94,

224, 227; duchess of   85; governor of   6; John, count of Poitiers, duke of Berry and Auvergne   62–3, 80–2, 111, 128, 137, 140, 227, 231, 299
Bertram, Robert, and Elena, daughter and heiress of   21, 299
Bertuquin   6, 14, 49n, 56, 59, 64, 66, 72–4, 77, 79, 99, 101n, 323
Besançon   135, 140
Beuil, Jean de   127
Beuzec-Conq, castle of   297
Beverley   19; Robert de   239
Beziers   58, 73
Biard, Le   41n
Bicêtre   290
Bigorre, county of   14, 24, 40n, 61, 64, 100, 224; seneschal of   199n
Bilbao   195
Bilsera, lord of   66
Binéfar, convention of   275
Birkhead, Robert   5, 9, 16–17, 22, 30n, 44–5, 49, 93, 149, 152, 176, 198, 214, 233–4, 238, 323, 336–7
Blainville, Jean de Mauquenchy, alias Mouton de Blainville, marshal of France   103, 231, 233–4, 237, 286, 296n
Blary, Jean de   328
Blau, Pere   265
Blois   336; Charles of   34, 104, 264; governor of   238, 336 *and see* Baveux, Gui de; Marie de Châtillon, daughter of Charles of   242n
Blot, castle of   84, 142
Bloville, Guillaume   236
Boccanegra, Egidio, admiral of Castile   183, 185
Boistel, Guillaume   183, 188, 327
Bolandoz, Jean de, alias Brisbarre   53–4
Bonny-sur-Loire   103
booty   21, 79, 94, 109, 235, 292; *see also* military depradations, ransoms
Borde-au-Château, La   53
Bordeaux   62, 184, 186, 192–4, 197, 200, 216, 222, 255; financial officers in   20n, 242; indenture concluded in   319–20; prince's chancery in   7–8; prince's council in   151; prisoners in   240–2; spies in   7–8, 197; truce of   24, 76, 91
Bordelais   10n, 13, 62
Borja   168, 177, 204, 207, 250–2, 257, 264–5, 270, 272, 280n, 314
Bosa   204
Bothal   299–300
Botiller, John   20; William   19, 149, 176, 198, 234, 323
Boucicaut, Jean I le Meingre, alias Boucicaut, marshal of France   103, 231
Boulogne, Guy de   52, 54, 84, 137; Jean de, count of Boulogne and Auvergne   56n, 80–1, 88; Joan, countess of, queen of France   88
Bourbon, Blanche of, queen of Castile   147, 151, 161–2; duchess of   285–6; Jacques de, count of La Marche   46–52, 51–2, 151: Jean de, son of   151, 168: Louis de, son of   286: Pierre de, son of   49
Bourbonnais   25, 27n, 48, 78–9, 93, 224, 227
Bourchier, John   199n, 289, 295n
Bourdeille, mercenary captain   323
Bourg-en-Bresse   79
Bourges   94
Bourguignon, Gerard le   41
Bournac   39, 69
Bourrouilhan, lord of   63
Bouteiller, Jean le   276–8, 315–19
Bouvetault or Boias, Perrin, alias Perrin or Perrot de Savoie, alias the bastard of Savoy   10, 44, 55, 73, 149, 224n, 243, 248–9, 263, 284–5, 323, 333
Boves, Jeannin de   51
Braga   279
Bragança   279
Brancastre, Thomas of   298n
Bras de Fer, mercenary captain   149, 152, 323
Bray, Jacques de   243, 284, 285n, 323, 333–4

Bresse 79, 91, 107–9; *bailli* of 108: *see* Corgenon, Humbert de
Bressuire 295–6
Brest 20
Breteuil 87; *bourc* de 10, 44, 49, 55–6, 58–9, 64, 83, 113, 129, 142, 149, 198–9, 284, 313, 323, 333–4
Brétigny, peace of (ratified at Calais) 6, 24–8, 33, 40, 45n, 62–3, 75–6, 78, 88, 130, 137, 189, 200, 287
Bricquebec 100–1, 105n
Bricqueville, Roger de 328
Brie 2, 4, 25, 26n, 28, 44, 90, 110
Brignais 46–51; battle of 6, 16, 30n, 45n, 46, 49–53, 55, 69–70, 76, 146, 151
Briones 194, 212
Brion-sur-Ource 92
Brioude 77, 108, 141; artillery at 83; capture of 6, 74n, 77; evacuation of 80–3, 110, 135; raids from 78–80, 93
Brittany 3, 11–12, 14, 18, 20, 22, 24, 27n, 41n, 91, 104–5, 125, 129, 148–52, 235–6, 250, 255, 286n, 287–8, 292–4, 296; duke of *see* John de Montfort; receiver-general of 5n
Briviesca 179
Broue 285
Brouillamenon 26n
Brown, Henry 10n, 19, 235n, 323; John 323
Bruant river 294
Bruges 255
Brulhois, the 68
Bruni, viscount of 254
Bruniquel 69
Buch, captal of *see* Grailly
Buckingham, Thomas of Woodstock, earl of 300
Budes, Yvon 149, 153, 327; Silvestre 224, 284, 298, 327, 334–5
Burghersh, Bartholomew 25
Burgos 148, 179–81, 195, 201–2, 206, 213, 216–18, 269; bishop of 179
Burgundy 2, 8, 24–5, 26n, 27, 30, 32n, 45–6, 48, 53, 55, 74, 77–80, 86, 88–98, 101–6, 108–11, 114, 122–3, 125, 130–5, 139–40, 142–3, 146, 151, 154, 176, 224, 227, 230–1, 290; ducal council in 84; dukes of *see* Eudes IV, Philip de Rouvres, Philip, duke of Touraine (Philip the Bold); estates of 27n; governor of 54 *and see* Bar, Henri de, Sombernon, lord of; Margaret, countess of 94, 102–3; marshal of *see* Pontailler
Burley, Richard 208
Buxhill, Alan 289, 296–7
Buzet 334
Byzantium 124–5; John V Palaeologus, emperor of 124

Cabaret d'Orville 21
Cabasole, Philippe de, vicar-general of Avignon 245
Cabrera, Bernat de 126, 158; Bernat de, son of, count of Osono 203, 205
Cachan 290
Cadillac 99; Guillaume Raimon de, lord of Rauzan 95
Cadiz 155
Cadreita 174
Caen 234, 237, 294
Çagarriga, Francesch 262; Pere 282
Cagliari 261
Cagnes 246
Cahors 41, 335
Calahorra 174, 179, 194, 268
Calais 21, 24–5, 287, 290, 300; Pas de 11, 19, 36n
Calatayud 55, 61, 217
Calatrava, Grand Master of the Order of 215, 271
Calmette, La 31
Calveley, Hugh 3, 7, 10, 11n, 21–2, 104, 145, 164, 175, 250, 281, 300; and Aragonese court 220, 250–3, 259; and Constança of Aragon 253–8, 321–2; count of Carrion 180; and 'crusade' in Spain 125,

147–8, 167, 177–9, 185; and du Guesclin 147–8, 170, 181, 185, 204, 250–3, 262, 264–5; forces under his command 149–50, 154, 169, 176, 191, 211, 214, 284, 288, 329–31; grants to 170–1; at Nájera 214; in Navarre 176–7, 202, 206; properties of 253–8, 319–21; recalled from Aragon, and campaign north of Loire 239, 284, 288, 292, 294–5
Camarès 223
Cambrai, bishop of 68
Cambridge, Edmund Langley, earl of 123, 239, 287
Campagne, *bourc* de 10n, 326
Camus, the *bourc* 10, 44, 49, 113, 130, 142, 149, 188, 198–9, 227, 285, 313, 323
Canfranc 217
Caparroso 174
Capbreton 184
Captieux 68
Caraman, viscount of 189, 199n
Carcassès, the 38
Carcassonne 14, 38, 63, 74, 249; seneschal of 56n, 59; seneschalsy of 32, 38–9, 54, 72, 98, 137; treasurer of 38n
Cardona, Hugh, viscount of 315
Carentan 234
Carhaix 41n
Carladais 76
Carman, lord of 38n
Carmona, castle of 162
Carpentras 35, 76, 152
Carrillo, Pero 162
Cartagena, bishopric of 219
Cascante 177
Cáseda 174
Cassagnes-Royaux 70
Castel, Garciot du 14–15, 38–9, 44, 49, 56, 58–9, 63–4, 66, 68n, 69, 188, 198, 284, 323, 329, 334
Castelbajac, lord of 66
Castellane 246

Castellbó, viscount of *see* Foix, Roger Bernard of
Castelnau 152; lord of 38
Castelnau de Berbeguenes, Jean de 113, 313, 323
Castelnaudry 38
Castelón 174
Castelpars, Menou de 70, 309, 311
Castelsarrasin 71, 189
Castile 155, 162, 170, 174, 279, 282, 314, 318; admiral of *see* Boccanegra; Bretons rewarded in 275; companies campaign in (1366) 6, 8, 14, 16, 147, 163–72, 176–81, 191, 329–30: return from 203, 226, 283, 289, 293; Enrique of Trastámara's departures from and return to 55n, 57, 163, 219, 259, 268–71; Pedro I of Castile's departure from 182–4; prince's intervention in (1367) 6, 20, 186, 190–200, 205–22, 236, 240–1, 243: return from 223, 250; war with Aragon 36, 54–5, 61n, 114, 126, 167
Castres 249
Castro Urdiales 195, 222
Castro, Fernando de, *adelantando mayor* of Galicia and Asturias 183, 200–1, 274
Catalonia 155, 261; companies' entry into 165, 167, 203, 252, 259, 267–8, 279–80; damages in 252; defence of frontiers of 186–7, 198
Caterington, Thomas 235n
Caumont, lord of 42
Caupène, *bourc* de 149, 152, 223, 285
Caupenne, lord of 41
Caux, *pays de* 287, 290
Caylus 76
Cazères-sur-Garonne 64
Cerdagne 127, 155, 167, 259
Cervellón, barony and castellany of 254, 257
Cervera 267
Cervole, Arnaud de, alias the

INDEX

Archpriest of Velines 2, 21–2; assassinated 143; companies of 4, 54, 57, 79, 95, 139; 'crusade' against Turks 125, 128–36, 142–3, 151; and evacuation of fortresses 136, 139, 142–3; in French service 46–7, 50, 93–5, 102; invasions of Provence 3, 33; ransomed 52; taken prisoner 51
Chabot, Gérard, lord of Rays 13–14, 323
Chalançon, lord of 51
Challonais 95
Chalon, Louis de, 'the Green Knight' 167
Chalon-Arlay, Hugues de 95; Jean de 91
Châlons-sur-Marne 2, 4, 230
Chalon-sur-Saône 6, 45, 53, 84, 93–5, 105–6, 108n, 109, 140; *bailli* of 77, 93, 114, 139, 227, 329; Jean and Louis de 51
Chambéry 121
Champagne 7, 17, 45–6, 92, 135, 224, 231, 290; companies assembled in 2, 4, 27, 30, 33, 110, 150; evacuation of 24–5, 26n; Navarrese claims to 86, 90, 129, 146
Champgeneteux, battle of 19
Chanceaux 42
Chandos, John, lord of Saint-Sauveur-le-Vicomte and constable of Aquitaine 99, 113, 195n, 234–6, 298; and 'crusade' in Spain (1365–6) 113, 125, 151, 154, 311; du Guesclin taken prisoner by 148; and execution of treaty of Brétigny 40–2, 69; the herald of 198, 202, 207–8, 331–2; on prince's Spanish campaign (1367) 170, 211: recruits companies for 198–9, 214, 236; and renewal of war 287–9
Chandos, Thomas 41
Channel Islands 300
Chapelles, Master Thomas de 115
Chardoigne, Jean de 53

Charité-sur-Loire, La 15, 93–4, 96, 98, 102–5, 107–8, 150
Charles IV, Emperor 34, 248; visits Avignon 112, 121–5, 128–9, 131, 242; and Archpriest's 'crusade' 132–3
Charles of Spain (de la Cerda) 86–7
Charles V, king of France 8, 141, 288, 293; and Anse 135–6, 139; and Aragonese alliance 126–7; and Archpriest's 'crusade' 128–9; and Charles of Navarre 87, 100, 115–16, 123, 176, 200; and companies 103, 114, 124, 189, 223–6, 231, 284–6, 290, 299; and du Guesclin 272, 280–1: his expedition to Spain 146–8, 151, 163–4, 191: his proposed expedition to Sardinia 262, 265–6, 268, 277, 317; and Enrique of Trastámara 200–1, 210, 261; and Gascon lords 13, 231–3; and Provence 248–9; and renewal of war 236, 238, 269–70, 283
Charlieu 45; *bailliage* of 135
Charolais, county of 62, 227
Chartrain 25, 26n, 125, 148
Chartres 103, 224; bishop of 145
Chase, John 237, 287–8, 300, 326
Château-Chinon 105
Château-du-Loir 295
Châteaudun 292
Château-Gontier 17–18, 234–5, 237–8, 284, 286, 293
Château-Landon 290
Châteauneuf-de-Randon, lord of 80
Château-Thierry 4, 230
Châtellerault 287
Châtellier, Le 42
Châtillon, *bailliage* of 92
Châtillon-sur-Loing 231
Chaucer, Geoffrey 146, 175, 243
Chauffour, Jean and Thibaut de 92, 285, 326
Chaumes 96
Chaumont 92
Chaves 183

INDEX

Chemin, Richard de 334
Cher, river 238, 336
Cherbourg 18, 100, 105n, 233, 235–6, 286–7, 300; abbot of 235
Cheshire 3, 7, 16, 20–2
Cheyne, Thomas 241
Cheyney, Robert 10, 18, 189n, 284, 287, 294–5, 323, 336–7; Thomas 20n
Chinon 232, 238
Chipperel, Benedetto 284, 326
Chiselden, John 323
Chizé 18–19, 298–9
Choiseul, Guillaume de 115
Chusclan 30
Cihuela 275
Ciudad-Real 181, 271
Clanvowe, John 294
Clarendon, treaty of 87
Claret, Jacquemart 334
Clerk, John or Janequin 185n, 205n, 248, 295, 330
Clermont 56n, 78–9, 81, 84; Béraud II, count of, and dauphin of Auvergne 78; bishop of 56n; treaty of 17, 49, 56–8, 64, 69, 72–3, 75–6, 80–3, 144
Clermont l'Hérault 72
Clermont-en-Beauvaisis 15
Clisson, Olivier de 199n, 214, 286, 292n, 294, 297
Clitheroe 20
Cluny, abbot of 248
Cocherel, battle of 8n, 12n, 16, 100–1, 105, 110, 114, 141
Cockayn, John 235
Codelet 31
Codinachs, Berenguier de, treasurer of Peter IV of Aragon 266
Cognac 292
Coincy-l'Abbaye 230
Coligny, Jacques 112
Collioure 263, 265
Colmar 130, 133
Colombier, Pierre Bertrand de, cardinal archbishop of Ostia 34–5
Combret 69, 71

Comminges, county of 8, 61, 63, 71; Pierre Raymond, count of 63, 66, 68, 199n
companies: Anglo-Gascon 14, 20, 93n, 114, 154, 185, 191, 200, 231; Anglo-Navarrese 3, 4, 6, 8, 18, 22, 27, 87n, 92, 114, 337; Aragonese 169; Breton 4, 6, 8, 22, 26, 53, 94–6, 135, 152, 185–6, 188–90, 259, 284; Castilian (of Enrique of Trastámara) 38, 46, 48, 55, 72; Catalan 2, 117, 121; of Fortune 3; Gascon 4, 5, 7–9, 15n, 36, 39, 41, 94–6, 135, 142, 150, 152, 154, 173, 189, 225, 231–2, 238, 259; German 36, 154, 186; Lombard 259; Navarrese 117; of Saint George 247; White Company 3–4, 32n, 144, 196; see Great Companies
Compeyre 18, 287
Compiègne 224
Comtat Venaissin 15, 34, 36, 74, 118–19, 123, 128, 152–3, 164, 243, 246–8; captain-general of 248; estates of 39, 248–9
Concarneau 297
Conches 87
Condom, lord of 199n
Confluent 202
Constanza, daughter of Pedro I of Castile 182–3, 196, 218
Coq, Robert le, bishop of Laon 116
Corbeil 290
Corbeilles 103
Cordes-Tolosanes 69
Córdoba 182, 185, 269; Martín Lopéz de 153
Corella 174
Corgenon, Humbert de, *bailli* of Bresse 224
Cornouaille, Jean de 327
Coruche 183
Cosington, Stephen, marshal of Aquitaine 25, 40n, 149, 176, 192, 199, 214
Cosne-sur-Loire 102n, 103

365

Costeroste 42
Cotentin 18, 87, 99–100, 105, 234–6, 238, 286–7, 290, 292, 297
Courcillon, castle of 293, 295
Courtenay, Phillip de 294
Cousant, lord of 80
Coventry 19
Cozi, le, mercenary captain 113, 313, 323
Craon, Amaury, lord of 41n, 238, 286
Cravant 228
Crécy, battle of 49–50
Creleves, Renaud de 271n
Cresswell 16, 70n; Edmund 16, 323; John, jnr 16, 70n; John, snr 5, 10n, 16, 18–21, 30n, 44–5, 69–71, 93, 129n, 149–50, 176, 198, 233–4, 238, 284, 288, 293–4, 296–8
Creswey, John, of Burnham 70n
Creuse, river 287–8
Croix Brette, La 294
Croix-Saint-Leufroy, La 103
Cromary, Hughues de, alias Brisbarre 53
Cuenca 181; *concejo* of 219
Curton, Petiton de, lord of 82, 199n
Cussac, lordship of 13
Cuvelier, Jean 144, 147, 280
Cyprus, Peter I, king of 121, 124

Dagworth, Nicholas 84, 154, 326
Dalmau, Felip, viscount of Rocaberti 274, 276–8, 280, 317–19
Dambach 133
Dampierre, castle of 95
Darcy 96
Darrier, Frère 130, 142, 150, 188
Daumarle, Edmund 294
Dauphiné 46, 49, 109, 122, 247, 249; governor of *see* Louppy, Raoul de; treasurer of 2
Dautre, Thomas 40
Daviz, Florimund 328
Dax 10n, 184, 193, 199, 203, 205

Déaux, Gaucelin de, bishop of Nîmes 122
defence measures: in Aragon 164–6, 187–8, 267, 277; at Avignon, in the Comtat Venaissin and the Rhône valley 35, 152; in Burgundy 228; in Bresse 143; in France 224–6; at Montpellier 152–3; in Navarre 174–5, 187, 206; *see also* Urban V
Denia, count of *see* Villena, Alfonso de
Derval 292–3, 297
Despenser, Hugh 294
Devereux, John 19, 149, 173, 176, 179n, 198, 214, 298n, 323
Deza 275, 272n; peace of 54n
Dezfar, Jaume 276, 315, 318
Dezvall, Pere 276, 315
Dijon 53–4, 96, 102, 106, 114, 131
Dijonnais 95
Dinan, Henri de 152; Hervé de 327
Doat, Bernard 10
Dôle 103, 140
Dombes 78–9, 108–9
Donat, Bernard 142
Donnezan 62
Donzy, barony of 45
Dordogne, river 42, 75, 101
Dormans 290; Guillaume de, chancellor of Viennois 123, 136
Dourdain, Guillaume 234
Daguenel, Philippe 235
Draguignan 246
Drayton, John de 320
Dreux 103
Drouais 25, 26n
Duant, Yvon 149, 327
Duoro, river 162
Durance, river 246
Duthel, Ayme 42

Ebro, river 174, 177–9, 194, 201, 207–8, 211–12, 268, 270
Echarri-Arañez 175
Edward III, king of England: and principality of Aquitaine 13, 62; and Burgundy 91–2; campaigns in France 2, 18, 92, 210; and

366

companies 7, 104, 114, 189; and du Guesclin's 'crusade' 113, 117, 144, 154, 170, 191, 311–12; and Flemish succession 90; and Navarrese 87, 200, 286; and Pedro I of Castile 153, 186, 192, 196; and renewal of war with France 231, 283, 289; territories in France, ceded to 24, 287, and evacuated by 24–8, 40–3

Edward of Woodstock, prince of Wales, the Black Prince: his 1355 campaign in France 62–3; captains in his service 16, 21–2, 25, 51, 69, 70n, 75, 95: retained by Charles of Navarre 176, 191–2; character and reputation 197; and Charles of Navarre 98, 184, 193–6, 222; and companies 7, 138, 185, 187–90, 226, 283, 329, 332; and du Guesclin's 'crusade' 149, 151, 154, 191–2; and Gascon lords 13–14, 76, 164, 231–3; his intervention in Castile 177, 187–8, 191–200, 205–22, 236, 320, 331–2: return from 223, 240n, 250, 268; and Pedro I of Castile 147, 162, 183–6, 189–96, 217–18; and Peter IV of Aragon 173, 220–1, 259, 264, 268; summoned before Paris *parlement* 238, 283; his victory at Najera 212–17: letter to his wife recounting 216: prisoners from in Bordeaux 240–2, 251, 262; and Urban V's crusading plans 112–14, 117, 124–5, 136–7, 144

Eglisale, Henry 323

Elda 168, 204n, 250–1, 254–5, 257, 314

Elmham, Ralph, 'the Green Esquire' 274; Richard 18n; William 154, 171n, 192, 202, 220, 282

Embrun 34n; archbishop of *see* Ameilh

Embrunois 247

Enrique II, of Trastámara, natural son of Alfonso XI of Castile: attacks Aquitaine 223–4, 243; on campaigns in Castile (1366) 164–5, 169–73, 177–87, 329–31, and in Portugal (1368) 279; character 162–3; and Charles of Navarre 193–4, 201–2; claims to Castilian throne 147, 157, 196; and companies 5, 48; and du Guesclin 277–8, 280–1, 316: crowns him king of Granada 148, 170; engages to recruit companies, but fails to deliver 56–60, 76; exiled in France 5, 160, 217; and prince's intervention 195, 198, 200–1, 206–17, 222; rewards mercenaries 275; return to Castile (1367) and battle of Montiel (1368) 240, 268–74; serves in Languedoc 46, 54–5: depradations there 58, 72, after prior threatened entry into 38; wife of *see* Villena, Juana de; *see also under* Anjou, Louis I, Peter IV, Trastámara

Enríques de la Carra, Martín, *alférez* of Navarre 214

Épernay 230

Eroudeville 287

Escalat, Pierre d', alias le Basquin de Lingot 326

Espagne, Arnaud d' 189

Espalion 39, 42, 69, 310

Espée, Raymonet de l', alias Ramonet d'Aspet 326

Espiote *see* Villers, Menaud de

Esquerrier, Arnaud 64–5

Essonnes 290

Estella 174–5, 187, 206–7; Berthelot Guillaume of 112–14, 311–13

Estibeaux, les landes de 199

Estivarelles 33, 44

Estrabonne 135, 140

Estradilla 268

Estramadura 271

Étampes 231, 233, 290

Étrechy 231

Eudes IV, duke of Burgundy 88–91

Eure, river 100

evacuations 42, 52, 82, 106; of Anse

112, 135–41; of Brioude 78; of Château-Gontier 238n, 239; of Lignan 74; of Vire 237
evacuation treaties 58–9, 71; for Anse 135–7; for Brioude and the mountains of Auvergne 80–3
Évreux 87, 100, 103, 235
Ewes, Robin de 40n

Faigne, castle of 294
Falga, Le, lord of 66
Felton, Thomas, seneschal of Aquitaine 206–8, 211–12, 214, 319; William 40n, 43n, 199n, 211, 323
Fenelon 42
Fenouillèdes 54
Ferragut *see* Anger, Étienne
Ferrefort, Walter 295n
Ferté-Beauharnais, La 296
Ferté-sur-Grosne, La 53
Fiennes, Robert de, constable of France 30n, 34–8
Figeac 10, 15, 18, 295n, 301
Finistère 297
Fischenich, Winrich von, alias Ourri l'Alemant 5, 45n, 324
Fitzwalter, Walter, lord 292, 295–6
Flanders, countess of 64n; Louis de Male, count of 88: Margaret, daughter of 27n, 88; Louis de Nevers, count of 88: Margaret, wife of 88–90
Flavigny 27
Flayosc 246
Flèche, La 41, 292–3
Flor, Roger of 2
Florac 73, 76
Florence 15
Florensac 37
Fogg, Thomas 18, 26n
Foix 13, 59, 61–2, 64, 68, 167, 268; Gaston Fébus, count of 14, 57, 59–69, 71, 73, 99, 111, 159, 180, 198, 202–3, 217, 266; Roger Bernard of, viscount of Castellbó 167n, 187–8, 266–7
Folifait (alias Filefort, Folifet), Thomas 9n, 19, 129, 135, 234, 294, 324; William 9n
Fontaine 53
Fontaines, Jean de 262n
Forcalquier, county of 74, 246–7, 248n, 249; seneschal of *see* Agout, Raimond d'; treasurer of *see* Baboyci
Forez 31, 33, 44–5, 48, 53, 78–9, 83–4, 109, 141; Louis, count of 47, 49, 51–2; Renaud de 51, 52n
Fossat, Amaury de 27n
Foster, Mark 250–2, 265
Froissart, Jean 6, 11–14, 30–2, 46, 48–9, 70, 109, 124, 146–7, 151, 154, 159, 198, 240, 273–4, 284, 294
Frontignan 37

Gabriel, Paul 192
Galard, Pierre de 9n
Galicia 183–5, 192, 200, 279
Ganges 37
Garlanx, *bourc* de 10
Garnetot 287
Garonne, river 13, 310; captains drowned in 285
Gascony 5, 7, 10, 12, 17, 20, 24, 61–2, 66, 88, 98, 114, 175, 184, 187–8, 192–3, 195, 200, 207, 214, 218, 287, 331, 335; *see* Aquitaine, Guyenne
Gâtinais 25, 26n, 230–1, 290, 292, 296
Gaunt, John of, duke of Lancaster 184, 197–8, 200, 203, 214–15, 217–18, 220, 256, 272, 282, 287, 290, 298n, 299–300, 331; Catalina, daughter of 256, 257n
Gaure 24
Gavardan, *vicomté* of 62, 68
Gavaston, Peyron de 99n
Gavray 234, 270, 297
Geneva 121, 131
Genoa, doge of 74; republic of 127, 142, 247, 282
Génolhac 31
Gerona (Girona), duke of *see* Joan

INDEX

Gévaudan 10, 35, 62, 76, 80, 84
Gibraltar, Straits of 148, 170
Gien-sur-Loire 103
Giffard, Gilbert 294
Gignac 37
Gilles, Jean 32; Richard 295
Givrey (Gevrey-Chambertin)106
Glaris 133
Gleizé 143
Gleteins, castle of 108
Gontaut, family and lordship of 15; Seguin de 12, 75
Gos, Gerard 41
Gourdon 41
Gournay, Matthew 10, 11n, 149, 170-1, 186, 192, 220n, 254-5, 257-8, 319-21
Graffart 41
Grailly, Jean de, captal of Buch 27n, 98, 100, 116, 125, 199, 214, 234-5, 298
Granada 119, 123, 125, 128, 146-8, 151n, 155, 170, 176, 196; Mohammed V, king of 147, 148n, 180, 182, 185, 271, 279; *see* Guesclin, Bertrand du
Grancey, Eudes de 124
Grandson, Thomas 289, 293-4, 296; William, lord of Saint-Croix 26n, 27, 92
Granollers 168
Gray 95, 103
Gray, Thomas 2
Great Companies: formation of 2-5, 24, 27; name 2-5; organization of 8-10; numerical strength of 6, 132, 169, 185, 197-8, 329-32; personnel of 323-5; *see also* companies
Green, Richard 294; David 294
Gregory XI, pope 15
Grenoble 119, 122, 131
Grimaldi, Rainier 245-6
Grimouard, Anglic, bishop of Avignon 122
Groeslort, Yvon de 327
Grôlée, Jean de, *bailli* of Mâcon and seneschal of Lyon 51, 113n; lord of 49
Grosmont, Henry of, duke of Lancaster 87, 92
Guébriant, Auffroy de 149, 152, 284, 327, 335
Guesclin, Bertrand du 8, 11n, 21-2, 96, 292, 299n; appointed constable 293; and Black Prince's 1367 campaign 210, 213-16, 218; Breton companies of 149, 190, 224, 236, 243, 272, 278-9, 298; and Calveley 125, 147-8, 170-1, 181, 185, 204, 250-3, 264, 295, 330-1; and Charles of Navarre 207; at Cocherel 100, 193; and companies in Spain (1366) 6, 15-16, 20, 128, 142-3, 146-53, 164, 167-72, 176-80, 184-5, 187-8, 191-2, 196-7, 200, 329-31; and Enrique's 1368 campaigns 270-81; excommunicated 249; and Granada 147-8, 170, 176, 180, 185; grants to 168, 170, 180, 280-1; Jaume 'IV', prisoner of 243; at Montiel 272-5; and Peter IV of Aragon 203-4, 266-7; and Pontvallain campaign (1370) 293-8; proctors of *see* Bouteiller, Clerk, Pencoédic; and Provence (1368) 242-50; ransomed 148, 205n, 220n, 241-2; returns to Spain (1368) 259, and to France (1370) 280-1, 289; and Sardinia 204, 261-6, 276-8, 313-19; taken prisoner 104, 148, 176n, 216, 240-2
Guesclin, Olivier du 204n, 243, 281, 284, 327
Guibert Bertrand 38
Guillampot *see* Pot
Guillon 27, 54; treaty of 92
Guimerà, Guillem de 166, 186
Guimarães 279
Guines 24
Guipúzcoa 194, 208
Gunat, lord of 66
Guyenne 24, 57, 62, 80, 126, 189,

215, 283, 333–4; *see* Aquitaine, Gascony
Guzmán, Leonor de, mistress of Alfonso XI   161–2

Ham   290
Hammes   19, 36n
Hapsburg, Albert of, duke of Austria   122
Harcourt, Jean V, count of   4; Louis de, viscount of Châtellerault   199
Harfleur   287
Harleston, John   124, 300
Haro   194, 202
Hastings, Hugh   20, 199, 214
Hatfield, John of   300
Hawkwood, John   9n, 11n, 15, 22, 30–1, 32n, 36, 44, 45n, 49, 69, 145, 324
Hawley, Robert   198, 324
Hay, Henry   99
Hazenorgue, Johann   5–6, 49n, 56, 64–6, 72, 77, 79, 93, 99, 100n, 113, 173, 176, 313, 324, 332
Helme, Ralph *see* Elmham
Hennequin, Frank   5, 11, 41n, 45n, 284, 324, 334
Heredia, Juan Fernández de   34, 36, 74, 84, 127n, 128, 142, 164, 166,
Hestonne, Dakin de   40n
Heuse, Jean ('Le Baudrain') de la   231
Hilton, Roger, alias Hochequin   19, 235n, 324; William   19, 235n
Hoderington, Jannekin   9n
Holgrave, David   19, 21, 70n, 294, 297–300, 324
Holland, Thomas, earl of Kent   26, 27n, 39, 42
Holm, Richard   19, 295, 298, 324
Hoo, Walter   36n
Hôpital, Jean de l', treasurer of France   127n
Hormeston, Adam   324
Houghton, Adam   40n
Hougue, La   40, 290
Houssaye, Alain de la   149, 243, 278,
  264n, 271n, 327; Eustache de la   236; Tristan de la   243, 327
Huesca   150, 165, 167, 173, 187, 240n, 268
Huet, Walter   18, 149, 214, 297–9
Hugate (Hulthet, Hughelot), William   12
Huillé   41n
Hungary   124–5, 130, 132, 139; Elizabeth of   122; Louis the Great, king of   122, 124–5

Île-de-France   7, 25, 26n, 87
Illueca   217
Innocent VI, pope   2, 32n, 33–6, 52, 59, 64, 68, 118–20
Irurzún   208
Isabel, daughter of Pedro I of Castile   182–3, 196, 218
Isle-Jourdain, count of   259; Bernard, bastard of   408n
Isles, Bernard des   389, bastard de l'Île   243, 327; Jean des   327
Italy   15, 37, 39, 44–5, 49, 70
Iv, Hervé de   264n

Jaca   187, 267
Jacquerie   248
Jaen   271n
Joan, En, duke of Gerona or Girona (afterwards Joan I of Aragon)   205, 254, 256–8, 262–3, 265, 267, 269, 276–7, 279–80, 318–19, 321–2
Joanna, queen of Naples and countess of Provence   242–5, 247–9
John de Montfort (afterwards John IV, duke of Brittany)   25, 27n, 41n, 104, 149, 235n, 236, 300
John II, king of France   3–4, 25, 32–3, 40n, 41, 48, 52, 57, 86–92, 98, 121, 196–7, 224
Joigny   290
Jouel, John   11, 12n, 324
Juan, Don (subsequently Juan I), Infante of Castile   275
Juillé   294

Kent 18
Kerimel, Geoffroi de 168n, 295, 298, 327
Kerlouet, Hervé de 9n, 10n, 284, 327; Jean de 10n, 284, 289, 327
Knighton, Henry 3–4
Knowles, Robert 3, 9, 7, 11n, 21–2, 84, 92–3, 145, 176n, 199n, 206, 289–97, 299

La Coruña 184
La Mancha 271
Labarde, lord of 199n; lordship of 13
Labastida 194
Labastide-Clairence 193
Labourd 17
Labraza 175
Lacoué, Yvon de 95–6, 149, 224, 274, 278, 298, 327
Laguépie 69
Laizé 143
Lamit 13, 30, 49, 113, 129, 135, 142, 149, 198–9, 284, 313, 324
Lamothe 42
Lancashire 7, 18, 20
Lancaster, duke of *see* Gaunt, John of; Grosmont, Henry of
Landes, Les 10n, 12
Landiras, Pierre de 41, 101
Lanes, Raymond, lord of 64
Langres 284
Languedoc 5, 10, 37–9, 44–6, 54–5, 56n, 57–8, 72–5, 79, 82–4, 109, 116, 119, 137, 154, 167, 168n, 203, 217, 227, 242, 246, 249–50, 259, 261, 282, 301, 334; admiral of 246; estates of 55, 84, 242n; lieutenancy of 61–3, 126n, 86, 168, 108, 137, 259; Jean Perdiguier, receiver-general of 242, 266
Languedoil 224
Lannion, Briard de 8n, 327
Lannoy, Guillaume de 279
Lanta, lord of 66
Lantar, Poco de 9n
Lanzo 3n, 45

Laonnais 290
Lar, Arnaud de 261, 266
Laroque 165
Lárraga 175
Larrasoaña 99
Las Huelgas, monastery of 180, 217–18
Launac, battle of 15, 64–6, 76, 99, 172, 310; ransoms of prisoners taken at 66–8, 71, 111
Lausanne 131
Lautrec, *vicomté* of 62
Laval, Brémond de 168n, 327; Gui, sire de 241, 286; Guillaume de, lord of Pacy 149, 278, 327
Lawgoch, Owen, alias Owen of Wales 198, 326
Lega, 'lo Baroat de la' 66n, 68n
Lemos, county of 184
Léon 155, 269, 271
Lequeito 195
Lérida 167–8, 186, 204, 267; Romeo Çescones, bishop of 261; captain of 204
Lerin 141
Lescure, lord of 71
Leslie, Walter 36, 73; *see also* Scot, Hagre the
Lesparre, *bourc* de 10n, 13, 44, 49, 149, 284, 324; Florimund, lord of 13, 199n
Lesterps 285
Lestrade, Soudich de 199n
Leulinghen, truce of 17
Libournais 62
Libourne 20; treaties of 194, 197, 200–1, 205, 217–19, 331
Lichtenberg, lord of 130
Lignan 73–4
Limoges 285, 292; *vicomté* of 34
Limousin 7, 18n, 24, 41, 46, 227, 301; seneschal of 199n
Limousin, le, mercenary captain *see* Solier
Lincolnshire 19
Lingèvres 40n
Lion d'Angers, Le 237, 288

Lisbon 186
Lisieux 234
Listrac, lordship of 13
Livorno 282
Lizy 230
Llobregat, river 254
Loches 238
Lodève 72
Logroño 179, 183–4, 194–5, 201, 206–7, 211–12
Loire, river 3–4, 14, 45, 53, 84, 93, 103–4, 107, 149–50, 227, 232, 238, 284, 288–9, 292–3, 295; provinces 87
Lomagne, Jean de 9n; *vicomte* of 153; *vicomté* of 62
Lombardy 36, 39, 44n, 74, 249
London 21, 192, 300; Tower of 18
Longeville, county of 116, 148
Longie, Philibert 106
Longvy, Henry of, lord of Rahon 92
Longwy-sur-le-Doubs 135, 140
López de Córdoba, Martin 184
López de Uriz, Sancho 192n, 193
Loring, Nigel 26n, 40n, 199n
Lorraine, duchy of 129, 132; duke of 130; marches of 91
Lorris, Robert de 56n
Lot, river 76
Loudunois 288
Louis X, king of France and I of Navarre 86
Louppy, Raoul de, governor of Dauphiné 34, 47, 74, 110, 112, 122, 139, 246
Lourdes 14
Louviers 17, 100, 233–4
Lucaro, Dominico de 138
Lucerne 133
Lude, Le 293–4
Ludlow, William 149, 176
Lugo 200
Lumbier 174
Luna, Pere de 261
Lunel 83, 109; Jean de 32
Lusault 42
Lusignan 16, 298–9

Lussac 289
Luxembourg 135
Lyon 4, 31, 33, 44–7, 50–3, 55, 79, 84–5, 107–10, 131, 135, 138–40, 150; archbishop of 34–5; dean and chapter of 136; diocese of 122, 138
Lyonnais 25, 27n, 30, 33, 78–9, 85, 109, 137, 141; *bailli* of 85

Machin, Hélie or Elías, alias Petit Meschin 6, 11, 14, 30, 44, 48–50, 56, 64, 65n, 66, 72, 76–7, 99,100n, 113, 149, 243, 249, 284–5, 313, 324, 333
Mâcon 33, 45, 93, 95, 108–9, 122, 129, 143; *bailli* of 47; *bailliage* of 135; captain of 107n
Mâconnais 25, 27n, 33, 46, 56n, 109, 135, 137, 227
Madaillan 13
Madrid 181
Madrigal de las Atlas Torres 219, 221
Magallón 168, 177, 204, 250–2, 258, 265, 324
Magneville 101
Maine, county of 17, 19, 24–5, 27n, 40–1, 145, 252, 292–3, 296, 298
Mainz 132
Mairey, Girard de, marshal of Navarre 92
Majorca (Mallorca) 155
Maldière, Barthélemy de la 51; Jean de la 51
Malestroit, Jean de 327
Mallorca, Jaume III of 158, 160; Jaume 'IV', Pretender to the kingdom of 8, 158, 199, 202–3, 214, 220, 242n, 243, 329
Mans, Le 294, 296
Mantes 100, 116
Marche, La 104
Marchès, Aimerigot 23
Marcigny-les-Nonnains 45, 93, 227
Marcillac 69n
Marck 11

Mareuil, Raymond de   199n
Marigny   231
Marmande   13
Marne, river   290
Marsan, *vicomté* of   62, 68
Marsat   84
Marseille   245
Martial   102n
Martiel   102n
Martin I, king of Aragon   258
Masclat   42
Massilargues   35
Mauléon, Bascot de   2n, 6, 14, 16, 18, 69, 75n, 109, 146, 299n, 324, 336–7
Mauny, Alain de   149, 243, 327; Henri de   149, 327; Hervé de   243, 327; Jean de   327; Olivier de   149, 188–90, 207, 236, 243, 246, 251, 264, 267, 270, 272–4, 278, 281n, 327
Mayenne, river   288
Mayet   294
Maynard, John   192n
Mazères   59, 67
Meaux   63, 66, 230
Medina del Campo   219, 281
Medina Sidonia   162
Médoc   13
Mélhac   39n
Melun, Guillaume de   51; Jean de, count of Tancarville   43n, 45–8, 51–3, 58, 92–3, 110
Mende   76
Menton   246
Merle, Guillaume de, lord of Messei   237
Merval, Louis de   199n
Méry   230
Metz   129–30
Meulan   100, 116
Meung-sur-Loire   238
Meuse, river   130, 135
Middleton or Milton, Hugh   238n
Milagro   174
Milan   3, 15, 36
military atrocities   1, 133, 167n, 169
military depradations   1–3, 32, 38,   45, 71, 73, 75, 77–9, 83, 85, 129, 131–5, 138, 145–6, 151–2, 166, 168, 177, 181, 187, 196, 205–6, 219, 224, 230–1, 235–7, 248–9, 267, 286, 290, 292; *see also* booty, *patis*, protection money, ransoms, rape
Millau   38, 69, 73, 151, 223; militia of   69n
Milly   292
Minho valley   279
Minstreworth, John   289, 293, 296–7
Miranda de Arga   202
Miranda de Ebro   206, 208, 210
Mirepoix   64n
Mitton, Robert   18, 211, 235n, 298, 324
Moissac   19, 280n
Mola   221, 251, 254–5, 319–20
Molina, lordship of   255, 280
Monaco   245
Monastier-Saint-Chaffre   39, 73; abbey of   84
Moncaut, lord of   66
Moncontour   298
Mondragon   35
Monjardin, castle of   175
Monlezun, count of   66
Monnay, castle of   106
Monreal   175
Mons   290
Monsac, *bourc* or bastard of   10n, 51, 326
Montagu, county of   130; Jean de, lord of Sombernon, governor of Burgundy   102–3; sire de   56n
Montargis   103–4, 231
Montauban   69, 71, 72n, 189; Olivier de   279
Montaut, Giraud de   95; lord of   63; Pierre de   9n, 49n, 68n, 56, 64, 66, 324; Raymond de *see* Mussidan, lord of
Montbéliard, Henri de Montfaucon, count of   91, 101–3, 114, 133
Montbourchier, Guillaume de   264n
Montbrison   44, 79, 141

Montbrun, castle of   76
Montcenis   140
Montclar, *vicomte* of   71
Monteagudo   272n, 275
Montebourg   287
Montech, battle of   189–90
Montélimar, lord of   49
Monterrey   183
Montesquieu, lord of   63, 66
Montesquiou, lord of   66n, 68n
Montferrand   77–8, 80–1, 84; consuls of   84; lord of   27n
Montferrat, John, marquis of   3–5, 9n, 36, 44, 45n, 69, 73, 111n, 142, 224
Montfort, county of   25
Montibus, Pierre de   264n
Montiel   271–3, 275, 281
Montignac, lordship of   13
Montluçon   227
Montméjan, Étienne de   72n, 333–5
Montmorillon, lord of   51, 52n
Montolieu   38
Montot, castle of   95
Montpellier, town and barony of   30n, 35, 37–8, 55, 58, 72–4, 83, 109, 116–17, 126, 137, 151–3, 186, 188, 190, 240n, 243, 251, 266, 268, 335; chronicle of   146, 152; consuls of   63; governor of see Pruniers; *rector* of   261
Montpensier   55
Montprivat, Bertrand de   142, 326
Montréal   54
Montréal-en-Auxois   28
Montreuil   24
Montsaugeon, castle of   92
Monzón, convention of   275; *Corts* of   157; treaty of   61n
Morat   122
Morea   117
Morilhon, mercenary captain   26n
Moron   275
Morpeth   16, 299
Mortagne-sur-Gironde   20
Mortain   17n, 297
Morvan   227

Morville, Thomas   22, 285n, 326
Motte, Gaillard de la   9n, 16, 130, 142, 198, 284, 324
Moulineaux   101, 103
Moulins   93, 285
Multien   230
Murat, *vicomte* of   76
Murbach, abbot-prince of   130
Murillo   174
Murviedro   255; siege of   163–4
Musard, Richard, 'the Black Squire'   36
Mussidan, lord of   80, 82, 111, 199; Seguin de   111

Nájera   194, 206, 212–13, 215; battle of   212–17, 220, 222, 224, 231, 240–2, 250–2, 259, 264–5, 270, 272: prisoners taken at   215–17, 220
Najerilla, river   212–13, 215
Nant   223
Naples   117
Narbonnais   38
Narbonne, viscount of   189
Nassi, Garciot du   58
Navarette   179, 212–13, 215–16
Navarre, Charles II, king of   4, 63, 104, 126–7, 159, 177, 183–4, 188, 221, 243, 282; and the Black Prince's intervention in Spain   191–8, 200–2, 205–8, 330–1; and Burgundy   45, 88–92, 96, 98–102, 114, 123; captains recruited by   17, 74, 110, 172–3, 175–6, 179, 187; defence measures of   174–5, 187, 206; and du Guesclin   207; fraudulent capture of   207–8, 272; grievances against French monarchy   86–7; peace with king of France   88, 91, 115–16, 121; retainers and clients of   7–8, 13–14, 16, 20; and Seguin de Badefol   110, 141; spy of see Estella, Berthelot Guillaume of; and Urban V   144; and war in Normandy   100–1, 103, 114, 234–6, 286–7, 290; see also Peter IV

INDEX

Navarre, kingdom of 20, 86, 98, 100, 110, 114, 126–7, 141, 155, 171–7, 179, 184, 187, 193–4, 196, 199, 201–8, 210, 222, 268, 270, 281, 301
Navarre, Louis of 16, 93n, 98–9, 100n, 101–3, 105, 108, 117, 176n; 'Navarre', *roi des heraults* of 235; Philip of 12n, 87, 144
Nébian 72
Nébouzan 62
Nègre, Jehannot le 130, 142, 285, 326
Nemours 290
Neubourg, Le 18n
Neufchâtel, Jean de 91, 95, 98, 102–3, 114–15, 326; Louis, count of 91
Neuville, Jean de 216
Neuville-sur-Saône 107
Nevers 150; bishop of 123, 136; count of 94; county of 45
Neville, John, lord of Raby 16n, 20, 199; Richard 298n; Robert 297; William 294
Nice 245–7
Nîmes 31–3, 35, 55, 57–9, 73, 83, 109, 334; seneschalsy of 32, 137
Niort 298–9
Nivernais 3, 25, 46, 91, 94, 227
Nogent-sur-Seine 230–1
Norbury, John 20–1, 324
Normandy 7–8, 17–18, 20, 24–5, 27n, 40–1, 86–7, 96, 98, 100, 103–4, 110, 114, 117, 148, 150, 176, 233–7, 239, 270
Northumberland 7, 299–300
Notre-Dame-de-Loroux, fortified abbey of 293
Notre-Dame-de-Vaas, fortified abey of 293
Nouans 42
Novelda 168, 204n, 250, 254, 314, 320
Nowell, Jannekin 20, 325; Laurence 20
Noyon 290

Nuits-Saint-Georges 94
Nuremberg 121, 132

Ochsenstein, lord of 130
Oignel, Pierre d' 96, 130, 142, 326
Oleron, Richard d' 324
Olite 141, 174–5, 179, 207
Olivet 17–18, 238, 336–7
Orange 122; principality of 249
Orbec 100, 234
Orense 183
Orgaz 271
Oristano 204, 261
Orléanais 17, 25, 26n, 94, 232, 336
Orléans 336; Louis, duke of 264, 270, 336
Orthez 6, 14, 61–2, 67, 99, 199, 217, 193n
Ortigue, Amanieu d' 45n, 149, 243, 249, 263–4, 284–5, 324, 333
Osono, count of *see* Cabrera
Ostia, cardinal archbishop of *see* Colombier
Oussoy-en-Gâtinais 103
Oye, castle of 19, 36n

Pacy 100
Padilla, Maria de, mistress of Pedro I of Castile 162
Paesnel, Guillaume, lord of Hambaye 237
Pallars, county of 267, 276
Pamiers 59, 64n, 67, 76
Pamplona 17, 101n, 111, 175–6, 202, 206–8, 312; monastery of San Francisco in 141
Panewych, Hans 296n
Pansard, Jean 327
Parade, Gaston de la, *viguier* of Toulouse 251
Pardailhan, lord of 63
Pardiac, lord of 66, 68n; Arnaud-Guillaume, count of 63
Paris 25–6, 32, 40, 63, 87–8, 100, 104, 126–7, 133, 140, 150–1, 225, 231–2, 235, 281; bishop of 144; *parlement* of 27n, 138, 238

patis 21, 78, 80, 83, 116, 203; *see also* protection money, ransoms
Pau, Bouzomet de 243, 248, 249n, 284–5, 326, 333; Guyonnet de 14, 45n, 324
Pavalhon, Noli 243, 248, 249n, 263, 284–5, 326, 333
Pedran, Narri de 168n, 327
Pedro I, king of Castile 46, 54, 98, 155, 159, 171–3, 189, 240–1, 256, 264–5; and the Anglo-Castilian alliance 153–4; and the Aragonese war 54–5, 61, 126–7, 157; and the Black Prince's intervention in Castile (1367) 191–201, 205–7, 210, 212, 214–22, 331; character of 160–2; and Enrique of Trastámara's return to Spain (1368) 269–71; flight of, to Portugal and Gascony 183–6; and the invasion of Castile by the companies (1366) 163, 167–9, 179–82, 322; mistress of *see* Padilla; at Montiel 271–4; queen of *see* Bourbon, Blanche of; *see also* Trastámaran propaganda
Pembroke, John Hastings, earl of 239, 281, 287–8
Pencoédic, Jacques de 95, 149, 276, 278, 315–19, 327
Penthièvre, Jeanne de 241
Peralta 174, 207
Perche 25, 26n; count of 233
Percy, Thomas 151, 214, 298
Pere III of Catalonia *see* Peter IV
Pere, En, count of Ribagorza and Prades 128
Perellós, Francesch de, *vescomte* of Roda 126–7, 155, 164, 220n, 231, 253, 261–2, 264, 269, 270n
Pérez Durries, Jordan, governor of Aragon 186–7
Périgord 5, 7, 12, 14, 24, 27n, 76, 141, 287; *bourc* de 10n, 324; count of 199n, 222–3, 287; seneschal of 199n; Cardinal Talleyrand of 121, 212, 233
Peritant, Geoffrey 324

Perpignan 37, 150–1, 154, 164, 167, 169n, 263, 266; consuls of 164; merchant of *see* Blau
Perugia 300
Pesmes 135, 140
Peter IV, king of Aragon (Pere III of Catalonia) 197, 273–4; and the Black Prince 184, 186, 202–3, 220–1; and Calveley 170–1, 220, 250–9, 319–22; character of 157–61; and Charles of Navarre 96, 98, 127, 171–3, 177, 193; his defence measures 164–6, 187–8, 198, 267, 277; and du Guesclin 147, 168, 170, 203–4, 261–8, 275–80; and employ of Great Companies 61, 72, 154, 163–71, 181, 329–30; and Enrique of Trastámara 54–6, 181, 185, 200; and the Franco-Aragonese alliance 126–8, 200–1, 269; and Innocent VI's 'crusade' 34–5; and Jaume 'IV' 202–3, 220; *maestro racional* of 266; queen of *see* Sicily, Elionor of; and Sardinia 281–2 *and see* Guesclin, Bertrand du; treasurer of 265–6
Peterborough, Walter of 208, 211–12
Petit, Alain 262n; Guillemin 141
Petrarch, Francesca 118
Peverell, Thomas or John 198, 324
Peyrehorade 205
Peyrelade, castle of 223
Peyriac 74
Philip de Rouvres, duke of Burgundy 27, 33–4, 45, 86, 88, 90–2
Philip, duke of Touraine, subsequently Philip 'the Bold', duke of Burgundy 77, 93–6, 102–4, 106, 110, 112, 115, 124–5, 128, 131, 133, 139–40, 151, 227, 230–1, 285
Phines (Prohins) *see* Pruniers
Picard, Guillaume, alias Morfouace 295
Picardy 7, 24, 87
Piedmont 122
Pierre-Buffière, sire de 199n

Pierrepertuse, castle of 217
Pigache, Pierre 41
pillagers 9, 41, 53–4, 83n, 106, 295
Pin, Arnauton du 284, 324; Guiot du 30, 45n, 49, 78, 105–6, 324
Pino de Ebro 169
Pirmil 41
Pisa 123; *anziani* of 282
Pithiviers 103
plague 21, 35, 38–9, 59, 115
Plantin, James 41, 324
Plassan or Plassac, Monnot de 9n
Plessis-Buret 41
Poitiers 288–9; battle of 49–51, 75, 87, 91, 95, 146, 176, 196–7, 212, 214, 241
Poitou 7, 16, 19, 24, 40–1, 125, 148, 232, 287–8, 298–9; seneschal of 199n
Polignac 83, *vicomte* of 73, 76
Pomerols 37
Pommiers, Amanieu de 26n, 27n, 78–9, 95–6, 102, 199n; Élie or Élias de 27n, 199n; Jean de 95, 105, 199n
Poncet, le Basquin de 26, 42, 327
Pons, sire de 199n
Pont-sur-Yonne 230
Pont, Thibaud du 149, 153, 168n, 288, 298, 327
Pontailler, Gui de, marshal of Burgundy 106, 146
Pontailler-sur-Saône 8n, 54, 95–6, 102, 115, 140
Pont-Audemer 87, 100
Pont-de-l'Arche 12n, 234
Pont-de-Sorgues 33, 122
Pont-de-Vaux 143
Pont-de-Veyle 143
Pont-du-Château 84
Pont-du-Gard 170
Pontenas, lord of 66
Ponthieu, county of 24, 287
Pontoise, peace of 88, 91
Pontorson 150, 293
Pont-Saint-Esprit 4, 27n, 28, 30–3, 35–7, 44, 45n, 69, 73, 75–7, 107–8, 120, 144, 149, 152, 235, 246
Ponts-de-Cé, Les 287, 292
Pontvallain 294, 296–7
Port-Joulain 41
Portugal 155, 181–3, 185, 271, 279, 300; Pedro I of 16, 177, 182–3, 185–6, 221, 279; Fernando, son of (afterwards Fernando I) 182–3, 279
Pot, Guillaume (alias Guillemin Pot, Guillampot) 92, 96, 106, 285, 326
Pouilly 103, 230, 329
Prague 121–2
Preissac, Raymond Arnaud of, alias the Soudich of Préchac and La Trau 70, 78–9, 95–6, 309
prisoners 81, 263, 298–300; at Auray 104; at Brignais 51; at Launac 66–8, 310; at Montiel 274; at Nájera 215–17; at Pontvallain 294, 296; *see also* ransoms
protection money 21, 28, 228, 235–6 *see also patis*, ransoms
Provence 3–4, 7, 35n, 36, 46, 54, 74, 55n, 152–3, 241–7, 249–51, 259, 261, 282, 284; estates of 247; seneschal of 74, 245, 249; treasurer of *see* Baboyci
Provins 4, 230
Pròxida, Olfó 282
Pruniers, Guy de, governor of Montpellier 112–14, 125, 139, 140
Prussia, crusade to 63
Puebla de Alcocar 271
Puente la Reina 202, 206
Punchardon, Richard 199n
Puy, Le 44, 73, 78, 80, 83, 110, 227; Raymond Guilhem de 319
Puycornet, lord of 199n
Pyrenean passes 163, 173, 187, 192, 198, 201, 203, 205, 267; col de Panissars 165, 268; col de la Perche 167; col de Soulor 288; Puigcerda 167; Roncesvalles 174, 187, 200, 202, 205, 225; Somport 186, 217

Quatreten, William   9n
Quélen, Guillaume de   8n, 327
Quercy   7, 10, 15, 18, 24, 27n, 38, 42, 287, 301; seneschal of   199n
Quigney, Jean de   98
Quirra, count of see Senesterra

rachats   25–7, 237; *see also patis*, ransoms
Rada   174
Railly, Guillaume de   106
Ramsey, Robert   300n
ransoms   21, 32, 40n, 42, 76–8, 95, 105–6, 108, 228, 272, 292–3; of merchants and travellers   32, 95; of places and territories   26n, 27, 38–9, 57, 72–4, 105, 153, 230, 247–8, 270, 288, 290, 292–3, 296; of prisoners   32–3, 52, 59, 66–8, 70–1, 116, 120, 148, 153, 238, 240–2, 243n, 251, 259, 272, 296, 299, 300, 310; *see also* booty, evacuations, evacuation treaties, *patis*, protection money
rape, incidences of   20, 32, 131, 133, 230
Rauzan, lord of   199n
Raymont, Gourderon, lord of Aubeterre-sur-Dronne   14, 149–50, 153, 198, 324, 330
Rays, lord of   198, 216
Rayssa, Gérard de   271n
Redman, Matthew   19, 289, 294, 296
Regennes   92, 146
Reims   24, 92, 230
Remiréz de Arellano, Juan   171–2, 216
Réole, La   15
Reulée   53
Reyal   173
Rhine, river   131, 133, 135
Rhineland   132
Rhône, river   3–4, 10, 16, 28–37, 45, 47, 55, 58, 74, 76, 80, 84, 107–9, 121, 125, 131, 135, 150, 152–3, 243, 245–7, 249
Ribagorza, county of   267–8

Ribeaupierre, lord of   130
Ribera, La   174–5, 187
Richard II, king of England   17, 19, 70n, 257, 299, 300
Richelieu   232
Richon, Geoffroi   224, 295, 298, 327; made lord of Aguilar de Campóo   275
Ricodano mountains   31
Rigalet, la land de   294
Rigney, lord of   95, 98
Rillé   293, 295–6
Riom   55, 78, 84, 140
Risle, river   100
Rive-de-Gier   44
Rivière, lord of   66
Rivière-Basse   68
Roanne   79, 150, 227
Rocaberti, viscount of see Dalmau
Rocamadour, mercenary captain   188, 198, 324
Roche, Billos la   113, 313, 324
Roche, Jean de la   153
Roche, La, bastard of   334
Rochechouart   288; Aimery de   16, 198, 284, 298n, 324
Rochefort   298
Rochelle, La   281, 299n; seneschal of   199n
Roche-Posay, La   26, 42, 287
Roches, Guillaume des   288
Roche-sur-Yonne, La   287
Roche-Tesson, La   148
Rodez   136–7; county of   62
Rodríguez de Sanabria, Men   162, 179, 272–3
Rollans, Jacques   274
Rollant, Julliel   284, 327, 335
Rolleboise   12n
Roma, Francesch de   127, 276, 278, 315, 318
Romans   128, 131
Rome   118, 121, 145, 243; English hospital in   146; pilgrimage to   146
Romenay   96
Romont, castle of   131

INDEX

Romorantin 238, 296, 336
Romsey, Richard 247, 300
Roncesvalles 101, 187, 206; *see also* Pyrenean passes
Roque, *bourc* de la 326; Raymond Bernard de la, alias Sandos 10n, 76, 130, 142, 324
Roquemare 30–1
Rosny 100
Roubaud, Louis 7, 10, 11n, 72–3, 74n, 78–9, 83, 109, 113, 285, 313, 324
Rouen 87, 101
Rouergue 7, 10n, 16, 18, 24, 39, 42, 69–70, 80, 152, 223, 287, 301; communes of 137; seneschal of 70n, 199n
Rouffach 133
Roussillon 8, 38, 101n, 127, 150, 164–5, 167, 168n, 181, 188, 202–3, 217, 240n, 252, 259; Bardot de 326; governor of 202, 329; lord of 49, 51, 155
Rouvres 106; castle of 210
Roye 290
Rue, Jacquet de 141
Ruffin, *routier* 4
Russell, Hodgkin 17, 19, 20n, 233, 237, 287–8, 324
Rye 290
Rye, Jean de 261–2, 263, 269, 270n

Sablé 293
Sagy, castle of 105
Saint-Affrique 39n, 69, 223
Saint-Amour, Simon de 79
Saint-Antoine-de-Viennois, abbey of 131
Saint-Antonin 69
Saint-Aubin 140
Saint-Bazeille 41
Saint-Bernard 108–9
Saint-Chaffre *see* Monastier-Saint-Chaffre
Saint-Cirques, castle of 82
Saint-Denis 91
Saint-Emilion 196

Saintes 25
Saint-Etienne 109
Saint-Farjou 64
Saint-Florentin 290
Saint-Flour 76, 119, 150
Saint-Gengoux 96; *bailliage* of 135
Saint-Genis-Laval 110
Saint-Germain-au-Mont-d'Or 108, 110, 112
Saint-Jean-de-Losne 45, 95
Saint-Jean-Pied-de-Port 101n, 193, 205–6, 222, 240n; castellan of 175; provisioning of 174
Saint John, prior of Order of 215–16
Saint-Julián, Juan de 102
Saint-Julien, Lopez de 17, 324
Saint-Léons 39n
Saint-Lô 237
Saint-Malo 239
Saint-Mathieu 297
Saint-Maur, Benedictine abbey of 293–6, 298
Saintonge 16, 24–5, 40n, 41, 149, 164, 298; seneschal of 199n
Saint-Palais 100–1
Saint-Papoul 38
Saint-Paulien 83
Saint-Pierre, Berradeco of 13–14, 72, 100n, 113, 193n, 313, 324
Saint-Pierre-le-Moutier 93
Saint-Pol, Alain de 149, 224, 278, 298, 327; Ernauton de 95–6, 327; Jean de 95–6, 102, 105, 149, 168n, 327; Raoulet de 149, 279, 327
Saint-Pourçain-sur-Sioule 79, 93
Saint-Quentin, Geoffroi de 298n
Saint-Rome-de-Tarn 39n
Saint-Ryot, Jean de 95, 327
Saint-Sauveur-le-Vicomte 99, 234–5, 237; garrison of 20n, 100, 233, 239, 284, 287, 290; John Buxhill, captain and lieutenant of 296; John Chandos, lord of 40, 99, 198, 236; John Stokes, captain of 12; siege of 286; used as a refuge 297, 300
Saint-Savin, abbey of 289

379

Saint-Sever 17
Saint-Sévère 19
Saint-Sulpice 230
Saint-Symphorien-le-Châtel 141
Saint-Symphorien-sur-Coisne 33
Saint-Thorette 19, 26n
Saint-Urcisse 77n; lord of 71
Saint-Urcize 77n
Saint-Vidal 83; lord of 83
Salle, Bernard de la 10, 15, 18, 45n, 93, 149, 179, 198–9, 272, 301, 324; Hortingo de la 10, 45n, 93, 199n, 285, 324
Salle, Robert 11
Salm, count of 130
Salses 165–6
Salvatierra 173, 208
San Adrian 174, 187
San Cugat del Vallés 168
San Sebastian 184, 194, 200
San Severino, Roger of, count of Mileto 247, 249
San Vincente de la Sonsierra 212
Sancerre 285, 299n; count of 105; Louis de, marshal of France 231, 238, 286, 295–6, 299n, 336
Sánchez de Tovar, Fernán, governor of Castile 179
Sancho, Don, brother of Enrique of Trastámara 54, 55n, 56–7, 180, 195, 213, 216
Sandes, John 198, 324
Sangüesa 174, 187
Sanluri, castle of 263
Santa Cruz de Campezo 201–2, 207
Santa Eulalia 173
Santarem 183
Sant Climent, Francesch de 268
Santiago 145, 215; archbishop of 161; dean of the chapter of 161; Grand Master of the Order of 215–16, 271
Santo Domingo de la Calzada 206, 212
Saône, river 45, 47, 53, 74, 79, 84, 93, 95–6, 102–3, 107–8, 121, 131, 135, 140, 142–3, 150, 154

Sardinia 127, 155; proposed expedition to 204, 259–68, 276–82, 314–15, 318; rebellion in 203
Sarlat, diocese of 138
Sarrebrück, Jean, count of 51
Sarriá, county of 184
Sassari 261
Saugues 44, 46–7, 50, 55
Sault, Pierre or Peyran de 41, 101
Saumur 41, 115, 288, 293, 296
Sauveterre-en-Béarn 14
Savignac 39n
Savigny, abbey of 79, 107
Savoie, Perrin or Perrot de see Bouvetault
Savoy, Amadeus VI, count of, 'The Green Count' 34, 44, 74, 107, 112, 122, 131: crusade of 142–3; county of 8, 44–6, 122
Scatisse, Pierre, treasurer of France 30, 58–9, 127n, 240n, 266
Schwitz 133
Scot, Hagre the 7, 45n, 324; Walter the 73n, 326
Scott, Martin 298; Robert 22, 104, 149, 153, 175, 326
Segovia 181
Segrié 41n
Seine, river 4, 100–1, 105, 107, 116, 149, 230, 233, 237, 287
Sélestat 130, 133
Seltz 131–2
Semur-en-Auxois 94, 106, 114
Senesterra, Ponç de, count of Quirra 263, 282
Senlis 230
Sénonais, the 46
Sens 45, 224–5; archbishop of 123, 136; *bailli* of 103
Sensacq, lord of 66
Sermur 76
Seron 272n, 275
Severac, Gui, lord of 214, 222n, 223n
Sévérgais, the 39n
Seville 161–2, 179, 181–6, 192, 194,

200, 217, 269, 271, 274, 330; convent of Santa Clara in 282
Seys, Gregory or Desgarry 199n, 211, 298n, 326
Shakell, John 19, 198, 324
Shelton, William 19, 234, 324
Ships, the Master of the 73, 324
Shropshire 300
Sicily, Elionor of, queen of Peter IV of Aragon 158, 163, 253; Joanna of, duchess of Durazzo 117
Simon, Thomas 235
Sisteron 246–7; Jean de 138
Sivrey, Jean de 227
Sobrosso (alias Fabrossa, Fabrousse), lieutenant of Bertucat d'Albret 10n, 73, 325
Soissons, county of 290
Soleure 122–3
Solier, Arnaud de, alias 'le Limousin' 11, 83, 109, 149–50, 153, 224, 298, 325; made lord of Villalpando 275
Solière, lord of 51
Sologne 232, 296
Sombernon, lord of, governor of Burgundy 139–40, 151
Sorgues 31; Bernard de 30–1
Soria 159, 177, 183, 217, 221, 272n, 275, 280
Sort, Ramonet du 10, 23
Soubise, castle of 298
Southampton 239
Souvain, Jean *see* Beaucaire, seneschal of
Spic, Henri 53
spies 105, 112–14, 197, 311–13
Spincta, mercenary captain 74n, 188, 325
Spire 132–3
Stafford, Richard de 26n, 40n
Stanley, John 20
Stapleton, Miles 26n
Starkey, William 92
Sterz, Albert 3, 5, 22, 44–5, 325
Stokes, Hugh 12n; John 12, 192n; Robert 12n

Strasbourg 121, 130–2, 139; bishop of 130
Swinford, Norman 149, 176
Swiss cantons 130, 132, 133

Tafala 175
Taillebourg 41
Talaru, Jean de 112
Talavara 181
Tallay, Alyot de 224, 327
Tallebard, Arnaud de, alias Tallebardon 45n, 49, 56, 59, 64, 78, 96, 105, 325
Tamarite de Litera 169
Tamworth, Nicholas 26n, 27, 146, 326
Tancarville, count of *see* Melun, Jean de
Taranto, Louis of 242n
Tarascon 248n, 249; siege of 243, 245, 251
Tarazona 177
Tards-Venus 2
Tarn, river 189; Gorges du 223
Tarragona 165, 169, 187, 204
Tartas, Gérard de, lord of Poyanne 184, 199n
Tastes, Aimeri de 199n
Taunton, Richard 129, 135, 142, 198, 211, 325
Tavira 182
taxation 242–3, 248, 266, 278, 281; for the Black Prince's intervention in Castile 218–19, 232–3; crusading tenth 143; for defence 36, 71, 201, 225, 249; to employ the companies 163, 281; for evacuations 36, 59, 61, 71, 135, 137, 142, 153, 249; exemptions from 71–2, 84, 206; inability to collect 110, 206; for the invasion of Provence 242; for King John's ransom 225; objections to 137–8; for the war between Aragon and Castile 186
Tee, Willicot or Wuilket 19, 234
Tello, Don, brother of Enrique of

Trastámara 54, 55n, 56, 179–80, 195, 210, 213, 215
Terrer, peace of 36, 37n
Terretá, Penni 223
Terride, Bernard II, lord of 66, 69–70, 309; Bertrand, bastard of 69n, 199n, 284
Testador, Juan 172, 175–6
Teutonic Knights 146
Thouars 41, 298
Thouars-sur-Gironde 13
Thurey, Gérard de, marshal of Burgundy 51
Tinchebrai 267, 297
Tiriel, Jacques 235
Toledo 180–1, 185, 218–19, 269, 271, 279, 330
Tonnay-Bouton, sire de 199n
Tonnay-Charente 41
Tonnere 94
Tordesillas 162
Toro, *Cortes* of 275, 279
Tortosa 280
Totesham, Richard 40n, 41
Toulon 245, 282
Toulousain 7, 38–9, 72, 76
Toulouse 61, 63–4, 285, 333–5; bishop of 64; Franco-Aragonese negotiations in 114, 126–7; merchants of 259; ransomed by Great Companies 72; seneschal of 56n *and see* Azay, Guy and Jean d'; seneschalsy of 32, 38, 137, 334
Touques, river 100
Tour, La, bastard of 254n; Bertrand II of 80; sire de 56n
Touraine 24–5, 27n, 40, 232, 288
Tournon, lord of 51
Tournus 45, 93, 96, 139, 142; abbot of 93
Tours 26, 238
Trás-os-Montes 279
Trastámara, county then duchy of 161, 180, 184; house of *see* Enrique II, Sancho, Tello; Trastámaran propaganda 147, 153, 160, 191
Trau, Soudich de la *see* Preissac

Trémouille, Gui de la 115; Guillaume de la 115
Tremp 267
Trefilly, Aimon 328
Tréséguidy, Maurice de 149, 261, 271n, 278, 295, 327
Trèves 41, 132
Trévières 297
Trevino 194
Trian, Louis de, lord of Tallard 245
Trogorant, Guillaume 328
Troussevache, Giles 94, 106, 285, 326
Troyes 4, 95, 105, 150, 230–1, 290; bishop of 227
Tuchins 79
Tudela 172, 174, 177, 198, 207

Uchizy 93
Ufford, Thomas 199, 214
Uhart-Cize 206
Ulmet, Gautier d', proctor-fiscal of Avignon 245
Ultrapuertos 17, 193, 206
Uncastillo, treaty of 96–7, 101n, 171
Unterwalden 133
Urban V, pope: action against the companies 118–21, 144–5, 226, 248–9, 262, 311; attitude to Pedro I of Castile 162; character of 118; and the defence of Avignon and the Comtat Venaissin 74, 118, 153, 243, 247–8; efforts to make peace 68, 115–16; and the emperor Charles IV 122–5; and the employment of the companies on 'crusades' 118, 121, 123–9, 148, 151, 163–4; and the evacuation of Anse 112, 114, 135–8
Urgell, county of 267; countess of 267; Jaume, count of 158; Pere, count of 203, 261, 263
Uri 133
Uriz, Rodrigo de 101
Urslingen, Werner of 2

INDEX

Vaas 295
Vabres 223
Vaire de Cap, mercenary captain 77, 325
Valcarlos 174
Valdepeñas 271
Valence 122; bishop of 34, 74, 139, 248
Valencia 155, 160, 186, 253, 266, 277, 319–20; *battle-general* of 255; governor of 255, 321; properties of Calveley and du Guesclin in 168, 171, 221, 250–1, 255, 257, 264; *Unión* of 157–8
Valentinois 109; count of 34, 74, 248
Valladolid 162, 218
Valognes 100–1, 105; *vicomté* of 19
Valtierra 174
Varennes 80–1
Varzy 94
Vaud, pays de 131
Vaudemont, Henri de Joinville, lord of 95n, 130
Vaulx, Lyon de 53, 327
Velay, *bailli* of 78, 82; nobles of 35; planned evacuation of 80; operations of companies in 7, 73, 75, 78–9, 109: road through used by them 31: taxes to pay them off 82–4
Vendée 287
Vendôme 52, 292
Vendômois 292
Venette, Jean de 2–3
Venice 143; republic of 283
Verdet, Pierre 51
Verdun 129
Verduzan, lord of 63
Véretz 26
Vergonhat, lord of 66
Vermenton 228
Verms, Miguel del 64
Vernon 100
Verteuil 41
Vertheuil 100

Vésigneux 94
Vesoul 95
Vèvre, La, castle of 106
Viana 211
Vichy 79
Vieleston, John 22, 285, 326
Vienne, archbishop of 34
Vienne, Jacques de, lord of Longwy, captain-general of Burgundy 85, 114; Jean de 300
Vierzon 19, 336
Vieux, Geoffroi or Jeaufroy 334
Vigan, Le 37
Vigneulles, Renaud de 153, 326
Vilanova, Ramon de, treasurer of Peter IV, king of Aragon 265
Vilaregut, Antoni de 255
Villaines, Pierre de, alias Le Bègue de 151, 213, 216, 273, 279; made count of Ribadeo and lord of Salamanca 275
Villaines-les-Prévôtés 114
Villani, Matteo 31–2, 36, 46–50
Villanueva de los Infantes 271n
Villars, lord of 49
Villedieu 189
Villefranche 112
Villemur, lord of 38n; *vicomté* of 80
Villena, Alfonso de, count of Denia and Ampurias 172, 180, 214–16, 263; Juana de, wife of Enrique of Trastámara 58, 162, 180n, 220, 279
Villeneuve, Ayard de 112
Villeneuve-les-Avignon 32, 58, 109, 144, 152, 285
Villepinte 38
Villers, Menaud de, alias Espiote 6, 14, 49, 56, 64, 66, 72, 77, 99, 113, 130, 142, 149, 176n, 313, 325, 332
Villers-Farlay 103
Villiers, Adam de, alias le Bègue de 150; Pierre de 150, 237
Vire 17, 20, 233–4, 237–8
Visconti, Bernabò, duke of Milan 4, 123

INDEX

Vitoria 194, 206–8, 210–11
Vitry-en-Perthois 230
Vivarais 35, 53, 109
Viverols 44
Viviers, bishop of 34
Vizcaya 195, 222
Vizier, Geoffroy le 328
Voissins, Pierre de, lord of Rennes-les-Bains 54
Volemer, Folekin, alias Folcquin l'Alemant 5, 17, 20, 233, 325
Vosges mountains 130
Voulte, La, lord of *see* Anduse

Waldboef, John 92, 325
Walton, Geoffrey 19, 234, 235n, 325
Wanton, John de 296n
Warre, Roger de la 199n
Warwick, Thomas Beauchamp, earl of 25
Westminster 20, 192, 197
Wetenhale, Thomas 20n, 199n
Weymouth 11
Willoughby, James 298
Winchelsea 290
Wissant, Pierre de 187
Wolde, Jannekin 40n
Worms 132
Worsley, family 10n; Geoffrey 18, 129n, 235, 294, 300, 325; John 18; Robert 18; William 298n
Wurtemberg, count of 132
Wyberk, Chrispian van 296n
Wyn, Ieuan, alias 'le poursuivant d'amours' 326

Xaintrailles, lord of 66

Yañez, Martin 182–3, 185
Yonne, river 230–1, 290
York 12
Yorkshire 7

Zadorra, river 210
Zaldiarán, castle of 210
Zamora 183–4, 279
Zaragoza 160, 164, 186, 203, 256–7, 268, 440; archbishop of 171, 201; archepiscopal palace in 172; concentration of companies around 167–9, 176; invasion of Castile launched from 177; payments to companies in 164, 204
Zug 113
Zuñiga 175
Zurich 113
Zurita, Géronima 159